OPINIONS
Throughout
HISTORY

Presidential Authority

OPINIONS
Throughout
HISTORY

Presidential Authority

By
Micah L. Issitt

GREY HOUSE PUBLISHING

PRESIDENT: Richard Gottlieb

PUBLISHER: Leslie Mackenzie

EDITORIAL DIRECTOR: Laura Mars

PROJECT EDITOR: Annette Calzone

MARKETING DIRECTOR: Jessica Moody

PRODUCTION MANAGER: Kristen Hayes

Grey House Publishing, Inc.

4919 Route 22

Amenia, NY 12501

518.789.8700

Fax 518.789.0545

www.greyhouse.com

e-mail: books@greyhouse.com

Publisher's Cataloging-In-Publication Data
(Prepared by The Donohue Group, Inc.)

Names: Issitt, Micah L., author.

Title: Presidential authority / Micah L. Issitt.

Other Titles: Opinions throughout history.

Description: Amenia, NY : Grey House Publishing, [2020] | Includes bibliographical references and index.

Identifiers: ISBN 9781642654509

Subjects: LCSH: Executive power--United States--History. | Executive power--United States--Public opinion. | United States. Executive Office of the President--History. | United States. Executive Office of the President--Public opinion. | Presidents--United States--History.

Classification: LCC JK516 .I87 2020 | DDC 352.23/50973--dc23

Table of Contents

1. Defining the Presidency
George Washington (1789–1797)

2. The Natural Aristocracy
John Adams (1797–1801)

3. Aristocratic Progressivism
Thomas Jefferson (1801–1809)

4. Father of the Constitution
James Madison (1809–1817)

5. Controlling the Americas
James Monroe (1817–1825)

6. A Populist Revolution
John Quincy Adams and Andrew Jackson (1825–1837)

7. A Conservative Division
Martin Van Buren, William Henry Harrison, and John Tyler (1837–1845)

8. Manifest Destiny
James K. Polk (1845–1849)

9. The Last of the Whigs
Zachary Taylor and Millard Fillmore (1849–1853)

Appendixes

Publisher's Note

Opinions Throughout History: Presidential Authority is the ninth volume in Grey House Publishing's *Opinions Throughout History* series. Designed to trace public opinion on current, controversial topics from our nation's early history to the present, each volume includes a range of primary and secondary source documents, including newspaper and magazine articles, speeches, court decisions, and other legislation. These sources are accompanied by expert commentary and analysis explaining their historical significance and placing them in the context of how they contributed to, or are a reflection of, the changing attitudes of the American public on important issues.

Content

A detailed Introduction begins this volume, explaining the unique characteristics of the U.S. presidency as defined by the Framers of the Constitution and briefly outlining the development and expansion of the executive office. A comprehensive Historical Timeline comes next, highlighting significant events related to presidential authority from the election of George Washington in 1789 to the impeachment of Donald Trump in 2019.

Following the Timeline are 29 chapters covering every president who has served in the chief executive position of the United States. From the purposely vague parameters for the presidency written into the Constitution, the power wielded by the executive branch has grown significantly. The scope of presidential authority has been redefined by each president, largely based on personality and management style. This book examines the waxing and waning of the influence of the presidency by exploring how each president approached his term in office. The checks and balances of the legislative and judicial branches are examined, as is the ability of individual presidents to gain the support of the American people.

Public opinion, which this series chronicles, plays a distinctive role with regard to presidential authority, often determining the success or failure of a president's agenda, particularly against an opposition Congress. A fundamental tenet of our government system is that the president represents the people—all the people—and the Framers hoped that the president would serve as the embodiment of the popular will. Few presidents achieve this, and the most successful are those who are able to galvanize the public and to build coalitions with members of all parties in Congress. The balance sought by the Framers between a figurehead president and one with significant authority, between possible anarchy and tyranny, is still in play today. The current impeachment proceedings against Donald Trump provide a rare and highly visible window into the system of checks and balances in action.

Arrangement

Each chapter starts with a brief Introduction, List of Topics Covered, and the source document or documents discussed in the chapter. The text of the chapter relates the source documents to their historical context, and details contemporary public opinion. Most source documents are reprinted in their entirety and are clearly distinguished by a shaded title bar. Photos and other images enhance the text, and sidebars provide a lighter, often humorous, perspective on the time period being discussed. Pull quotes and other visual elements increase accessibility.

Each chapter ends with a brief Conclusion, thoughtful Discussion Questions, and a list of Works Used. Footnotes referenced in the text begin on page 807.

The final chapter, 30, is a detailed conclusion, and is followed by the Historical Snapshots section—a broad, bulleted overview of political, social, and cultural developments from 1880 to 2019 that help provide context and understanding of the political and social climate of the time.

This volume also includes a complete list of Primary and Secondary Sources that are reprinted in the text, a Glossary of frequently used terms related to presidential authority, a comprehensive Bibliography and a detailed Index.

The *Opinions Throughout History* Series

Presidential Authority is the first title published in 2020.

The next *Opinions Throughout History* volume will be *Guns in America*, followed by *Globalization* and *Robotics & Artificial Intelligence*.

Introduction

Unpresidented Governance

The U.S. President is part legislator, part executive, part general, and part celebrity. Presidents have run the gamut from mild-mannered bureaucrats to radical activists, and the office has been at the center of some of the world's most transformative events. The evolution of the presidency can be traced to how the executive office was designed, with an intentional degree of malleability, from George Washington's regal generalship, to a more bureaucratic office, increasing with the addition of executive divisions. This growth has allowed presidents to take a greater role in shaping legislative priorities. The presidency is approached in different ways by different leaders, enabling the nation's Commander in Chief to adapt his or her power to the needs of the nation.

What is the Presidential System?

The presidential system of government in the United States is original, dreamed up by America's patriot rebels, called "Founding Fathers" or "Framers," and formally written into the Constitution of 1787. James Madison, one of America's most intelligent presidents, was most directly responsible for designing the Constitution. The roles and duties of the presidency were the product of much debate—and a few fistfights—resulting in a blend of new ideas and ancient archetypes of leadership.

When naming this new office, the Framers used a term known in global governance and derived from the Latin *praesidens*, meaning "governor," which was first used in 1532 in Scotland. England later adopted the term, when John Bradshaw become Lord President of the Council of State of England in 1649. As most of the initial American colonists were English, it is no surprise that they used English governmental terms. The term "president" was also used for leaders in the state of Virginia and elsewhere, and so was conveniently folded into the new constitutional system. The Founding Fathers borrowed this term, dropped the "Lord" honorific, which smacked of English aristocracy, and wrote the office into Article II, Section I of the Constitution: "Power shall be vested in a President of the United States of America who shall hold his Office during the term of four years."[1]

It is a testament to the influence of Britain and, to a lesser extent, the United States that most countries that are not monarchies in 2019 have a presidential office, typically to serve as head of state. The American system, in which the president serves as both head of state and head of government, was adopted in several Central and South American, African, and Asian countries.

A head of state represents his or her country in the international sphere. They serve in a more or less ceremonial capacity, or, may be vested with substantial power. In France, the president is a head of state empowered by the French Constitution to create treaties and agreements with foreign governments and also to direct the armed forces, serving as a commander in chief. A number of former monarchies that have transitioned to democracies have retained vestiges of their monarchy in the form of a head of state. This occurs in England, for instance, where the leading regent has no direct political powers, but symbolically represents the nation.

A head of government is a chief executive of a nation's executive division, and typically presides over a legislature or cabinet. In parliamentary governments, like that of England, the head of state is usually known as the chief councilor or the prime minister. In many nations, it is the head of government, rather than the head of state, who occupies the most powerful office. Heads of government act directly to establish, support, and oppose legislation and are expected to use their office to establish a national agenda. A prime minister might, for instance, make the economy a primary goal and then campaign legislators to create economic policy. In some countries, the head of government is elected directly by the people, but more commonly the head of government is elected by members of the parliament or appointed by the political party holding majority power in the legislature.

In America, the president serves as both head of state *and* head of government, giving him or her wide-ranging and sometimes conflicting powers. The U.S. president can influence both domestic affairs and foreign policy, and so is directly linked to the character and evolution of American government and culture. Also, because the president is not part of the legislature, but heads an independent branch of government, he or she can assume a more independent course than can a leader elected by legislators in his or her party.

A fundamental tenet of the U.S. presidency is that the president represents and serves the people.

Alexander Hamilton wrote of the office (in *The Federalist* no 70):

> *"Energy in the executive is a leading character in the definition of good government. It is essential to the protection of the community against foreign attacks: it is not less essential to the steady administration of the laws; to the protection of property . . . and to the security of liberty against the enterprises and assaults of ambition, of faction, and of anarchy."*[2]

By protecting the nation from "faction," Hamilton refers to the influence of political parties. Because the powers of the presidency are vested in a single individual, the Framers hoped that this individual would represent all people, whatever their party affiliation or ideology. They imagined a person with sufficient vision to serve as a single embodiment of the popular will. Few presidents manage to achieve this. Most enter office with the support of members of their political faction and act to further the fortunes of that faction. In *The Soul of America*, Pulitzer Prize-winning historian Jon Meacham argues that the greatest presidents were able to embrace their role as mediator and diplomat, campaigning for policies and reforms that would benefit the greatest number of citizens and would address the moral and ethical evils of their time.[3] Presidents who are unable to find a conciliatory voice are remembered as failures or not remembered at all.

A System of Checks and Balances

Alexander Hamilton and other Founding Fathers created the Federalist political party, and were not willing to give up the idea of strong, central leadership as they had known under the English monarchy. Their solution was to create a powerful and semi-independent executive office that would, through indirect election, serve as a representation of the popular will and also provide strong, independent central leadership to guide legislative factions. Hamilton's opponents included Thomas Jefferson and Benjamin Franklin, who wanted a more symbolic executive office, fearing that unchecked executive ambition would lead to despotic leadership. The Federalists won and the presidency was established as a more powerful office. However, a compromise resulted in a series of "checks and balances," granting each branch certain independent powers that are "checked" by the powers of other branches. The system works as follows:

Executive

The president, as head of government and head of state, is empowered to set a national agenda, which includes proposing legislative priorities and using executive power to address issues not covered in existing law. At the most basic level, the power of the executive branch is to "enforce the laws," though this is a poorly defined duty. Most generally, the president should see laws carried out as they are created by the legislature and interpreted by the judicial branch.

The basic powers of the presidency are as follows:

1. The president is commander-in-chief of the armed forces, with the power to call the National Guard into action and to manage national security issues in times of emergency. Presidential military powers are subject to congressional review, and only Congress can declare war.

2. The president is the nation's "chief diplomat." He or she can receive foreign dignitaries and, with congressional approval, establish treaties and international agreements.

3. The president can nominate individuals to lead and serve within the executive branches of government, i.e. the Departments of Labor, Defense, Education, etc., and can also nominate federal justices, which are subject to congressional approval.

4. The president can issue executive orders, which are temporary laws that are meant to address a situation in which a new law is needed but legislation is not forthcoming.

5. The president can pardon individuals convicted of federal crimes, but has no pardon powers over individuals convicted under state law.

6. The president can convene Congress for a special session to ask for permission to use emergency powers, to declare war, or to propose legislative actions.

7. The president can veto any bill passed by both houses of Congress, but only the entire bill, not part of it. Congress can override a presidential veto with two-thirds majority.

Legislative

The legislative branch makes and alters the laws. The legislature is composed of the two houses of Congress—the Senate and the House of Representatives. Members of both houses are elected directly by individuals in their states, and thus represent the interests of their states and their constituents in the national arena. The basic powers of the legislature are:

1. The legislature makes laws by creating bills, debating those bills, and then voting to make the bill into law.

2. The legislature can override a presidential veto, and reject a presidential treaty by at least two thirds votes.

3. The legislature has the sole power to declare war and fund military actions. This gives Congress the ability to limit a president's use of the military by withholding funding or not approving presidential use of the military.

4. The legislature can create amendments to the Constitution, which are used to limit the powers of the judiciary by overriding judicial rulings on the constitutionality of certain laws or bills.

5. Congress can reject presidential appointments for federal offices or to the judiciary.

6. Congress approves the budget of the executive branch.

7. Congress is empowered to remove, or "impeach," a sitting president. The House of Representatives determines the validity of such action; the law states that a president may be impeached

for treason, bribery, or other "high crimes and misdemeanors." If the House votes to impeach, the Senate holds a trial to consider the evidence and then determines whether or not to acquit (resulting in no action) or convict (resulting in removal from office).

Judicial

The judicial branch is empowered to "interpret the law," which means that the courts determine if a law applies in a certain case and may also rule on whether or not a law violates the Constitution. Members of the judiciary review laws passed by Congress or executive orders created by a president, and determine if these laws or orders violate the Constitution. The judicial branch is also empowered to punish individuals who violate the law.[4]

Beyond the Constitution

The Constitution holds that all power comes from the people and that all elected officials are only representatives of the people. The Framers of the Constitution created the office of the presidency as both powerful and limited, but most importantly, empowered through its relation to the people and to the other two branches of government. When a president enters office, he or she immediately has powers as established by the Constitution, but these powers are limited unless a president can work with Congress and lead the American people. A president who fails to create the perception of leadership will find his or her powers very weak indeed.

Richard E. Neustadt, one of the most respected scholars on the presidency, was presidential advisor to both parties at different times, and wrote a number of influential books on the nature of leadership and the presidency. Through his teaching at Harvard and Columbia Universities, his reasoned approach influenced many who became president. Neustadt wrote his doctoral dissertation on Harry S. Truman's legislative efforts, and came to believe that the constitutional powers of the presidency were only part of what made a president powerful. His magnum opus was *Presidential Power*, a best-selling study of the presidency published in 1960. Neustadt's take explains why characteristics traditionally seen as powerful—uncompromising dedication, strong personality, or faith in one's convictions—do not alone make a president great.

Neustadt wrote that a president's power comes through persuasion. The most powerful presidents are those who make bargains with both the people and fellow politicians. The most powerful presidents energize the populace and the legislature, negotiate through deadlock, and command not through fear but through inspiration and admiration. An important takeaway from Neustadt, and other scholars who have built on his work, is that the presidency is powerful only in cooperation, both with the public and with the legislature. Those who find ways to fruitfully cooperate can achieve much, and those who fail in this regard achieve comparatively little.[5]

Power, Privilege, and Justice

The Constitution says that all power originates from the people, but this depends on how one approaches the American political system. While Americans choose their political leaders, they do not have direct control over the passage of laws or policies. A politician elected by 51 percent of the people might pursue policies that are opposed by 49 percent of the people. The two-party system in America means that a large portion of Americans often feel that their needs are underrepresented. In addition, the wealthy and powerful exert more political power than the average American and so manage to dominate policy.

In 2014, scholars Martin Gilens and Benjamin Page, from Princeton and Northwestern Universities, respectively, studied the concentration of power in the American political system:

"When the preferences of economic elites and the stands of organized interest groups are controlled for, the preferences of the average American appear to have only a miniscule, near-zero, statistically non-significant impact upon public policy."[6]

This does not mean that the average American might not see his or her views come to fruition, but rather that this primarily occurs when that person's views align with more powerful interests or with the preferences of the economic elite. The authors reason that America is an oligarchy, rather than a democracy, but analyses of their findings indicate this is not true. What is true, however, is that money has an outsized influence on American politics, that many politicians pursue policies and agendas based on economic concerns rather than public welfare, and that America's corporate elite and the military-industrial complex command influence far beyond the popular will of average middle-class Americans.

Many of the Framers, especially John Adams and Alexander Hamilton, believed that only certain people should be allowed to govern. The American political system therefore developed not as a pure democracy— in which the people create and vote to adopt laws directly—but as a representative democracy—in which the people elect representatives who create and vote on policies. This representative system was thought to be necessary by the Framers because, at the time, the average American lacked education. The problem with this system is that politicians often fail to serve the welfare of their constituents but use their office for personal gain.

Over time, Americans became more educated, with increased access to information, and less trusting of their government. As the people's perceptions of their government changed, so did the presidency. During periods of great turmoil, presidents became champions for radical social change. Presidents were elected because of the promise that they would fight for the interests of the people instead of for the power of big business or other special interests. Since the late 1800s, few presidents have made good on this promise.

Nevertheless, one of the greatest expressions of presidential power comes when a president challenges American traditions and the status-quo. These presidents may face resistance and controversy, but often leave a lasting impact and are remembered for their pioneering efforts. Abraham Lincoln, for example, whose effort to end slavery was so controversial that it caused many states to leave the Union, is now frequently ranked as America's best president. Lincoln's enduring legacy is the result of the fact that, while he challenged the power structure of American society, he was also highly skilled in persuasion. He elevated the goal of preserving the Union and ending slavery into one of the nation's most cherished victories. Presidential power can also be expressed through the willingness to challenge and confront American society. To be successful at this, a president must demonstrate uncommon leadership and character.

The Changing Face of America

For many Americans, the presidency represents the entire American government. This is reflected by how prevailing presidential administrations are called a period of time, like "Nixon Era," or "Obama Years." In reality, the president is one of many factors that contribute to the political state of the nation, and there are many aspects of American culture over which a president has little influence. Nevertheless, because presidents are representatives of an era, they are typically blamed or credited for conditions during their presidency.

One reason why the office of the president is associated with the state of the nation is because the presidency is a single-person office. Success or failure is more easily attributed to an individual than to a collective law-making body, like Congress. Further, presidents regularly state their intention to accomplish unrealistic goals and failure to do so leads to disappointment among voters. In reality, a president's power is limited by the legislature, and collaboration is necessary to achieve serious results.

The presidency was so nebulously crafted at its inception that it was George Washington, a military man with no governmental experience, who defined the role. Washington's personality—formal, stoic, soft-spoken, distrustful of faction—drove the personality of the presidency in its early years. Each president that came after Washington changed the office in ways subtle or dramatic. The evolution of the presidency, and its power, depended on the personalities of the men who held the office. It is those personalities, and each president's unique history and experience, that shape each president's vision of America and its possible future. Understanding their lives and histories illuminates how each president approached the office and the use of presidential power and authority. This work, therefore, provides a window into the personal lives of our American presidents and, from there, into how each approached the power of the office. On a broader scale, *Opinions Throughout History: Presidential Authority*, shows the evolution of America, as the presidents and legislators struggle to adjust to changing values, needs, and hopes of the American people.

Works Used

"Federalist No 70 (1788)." *Bill of Rights Institute*. 2019. https://billofrightsinstitute.org/founding-documents/primary-source-documents/the-federalist-papers/federalist-papers-no-70/.

Gilens, Martin, and Benjamin L. Page. "Testing Theories of American Politics: Elites, Interest Groups, and Average Citizens." *Perspectives on Politics*. 2014. https://scholar.princeton.edu/sites/default/files/mgilens/files/gilens_and_page_2014_-testing_theories_of_american_politics.doc.pdf.

"How Popular/Unpopular Is Donald Trump?" *FiveThirtyEight*. 21 Oct. 2019. https://projects.fivethirtyeight.com/trump-approval-ratings/.

Longley, Robert. "Separation of Powers: A System of Checks and Balances." *Thought Co.* 25 May 25. https://www.thoughtco.com/separation-of-powers-3322394.

Meacham, Jon. *The Soul of America*. New York: Random House, 2018.

Neustadt, Richard. *Presidential Power: The Politics of Leadership*. New York: John Wiley & Sons, 1960.

"Presidential Approval Ratings—Gallup Historical Statistics and Trends." *Gallup*. 2019. https://news.gallup.com/poll/116677/presidential-approval-ratings-gallup-historical-statistics-trends.aspx.

Rattner, Steven. "Trump Can't Beat Obama on the Economy." *New York Times*. 27 Aug. 2019. Retrieved from https://www.nytimes.com/2019/08/27/opinion/trump-obama-economy.html.

Tan, Kevin YL. "Presidential Systems." *Oxford University Constitutional Law*. Feb. 2017. https://oxcon.ouplaw.com/view/10.1093/law-mpeccol/law-mpeccol-e430.

Historical Timeline

1732: George Washington is born in Westmoreland, Virginia.

1735: John Adams is born in the Massachusetts Bay Colony.

1743: Thomas Jefferson is born in Western Virginia.

1751: James Madison is born in Port Conway, Virginia.

1758: James Monroe is born in Westmoreland, Virginia

1767: John Quincy Adams is born in Braintree, Massachusetts.

1773: William Henry Harrison is born in Virginia.

1774: First Continental Congress is held in Philadelphia.

1775: Second Continental Congress is held; George Washington is asked to lead the patriot armies.

1776: The Declaration of Independence is issued.

1780: Battle of Yorktown results in a patriot victory.

1782: Washington voluntarily surrenders military power to the Continental Congress, affirming Congressional authority over declaring a state of war.

Martin Van Buren is born in Kinderhook, New York.

1784: Zachary Taylor born in Barboursville, Virginia.

1787: Second Continental Congress is held.

James Madison, Alexander Hamilton, and John Jay begin writing the Federalist Papers.

1789: First U.S. presidential election leads to the election of General George Washington.

U.S. Constitution establishes the basis of presidential authority.

1790: Naturalization Act established rules for how immigrants can gain citizenship.

Congress passes the Residence Act, which leads to the creation of Washington, D.C., and the White House.

John Tyler is born in Charles City County, Virginia.

1791: James Buchanan is born in Pennsylvania.

1794: Washington dispatches troops to quell the Whiskey Rebellion.

The Jay Treaty between the U.S. and Britain leads to the nation's first foreign policy controversy.

1795: James K. Polk born in Pineville, North Carolina.

1796: Washington delivers the first presidential farewell address.

John Adams is elected America's 2nd president.

1798: First partisan election between Thomas Jefferson and John Adams.

The Alien and Sedition Acts mark the first partisan use of legislation to gain a national electoral advantage.

1799: The Logan Act prohibits citizen diplomacy and establishes that all foreign negotiations are under presidential authority.

1800: Thomas Jefferson is elected America's 3rd President.

John Adams becomes the first president to live in the White House.

Millard Fillmore is born in Locke Township, New York.

1803: The Supreme Court case of *Marbury v. Madison* establishes that the courts may strike down laws and statutes that violate the Constitution.

The Louisiana Purchase expands the American frontier and becomes controversial in terms of presidential authority to gain economic control of new territory.

1804: Franklin Pierce is born in Hillsboro, New Hampshire.

1807: The Embargo Act marks the first use of economic sanctions to address a foreign policy issue.

1808: James Madison is elected America's 4th president.

Andrew Johnson is born in Raleigh, North Carolina.

1809: Abraham Lincoln is born in 1809 in Kentucky.

1810: Eldridge Gerry uses corrupt redistricting to disenfranchise Federalist voters, a practice called gerrymandering.

1812: The War of 1812 begins.

1814: The British invade Washington, D.C.

1816: James Monroe is elected America's 5th president.

1819: The Panic of 1819 is America's first period of major economic turmoil.

Invasion of Florida by rogue troops led by Andrew Jackson adds Florida to the United States.

1822: Ulysses S. Grant born in Point Pleasant, Ohio.

Rutherford B. Hayes born in Delaware, Ohio.

1823: The Monroe Doctrine establishes that the United States will oppose foreign or European intervention in the Americas and states that the United States will support Latin America.

1824: John Quincy Adams is elected America's 6th president, winning the Electoral College vote while Andrew Jackson wins the popular vote.

First presidential straw poll is published by the *Harrisburg Pennsylvanian*.

1828: Andrew Jackson is elected America's 7th president.

First election year in which more than 50 percent of eligible voters participated in the election.

1830: Indian Removal Act is passed under the Jackson administration; the first time the U.S. government took part in an ethnic cleansing campaign.

1831: James A. Garfield born in Moreland Hills, Ohio.

1833: Benjamin Harrison born in North Bend, Ohio.

1836: Martin Van Buren is elected America's 8th president.

1837: Grover Cleveland is born in Caldwell, New Jersey.

1840: William Henry Harrison is elected America's 9th president.

1841:	John Tyler is appointed America's 10th president after the death of William Henry Harrison in office.
1843:	William McKinley born in Niles, Ohio.
1844:	James K. Polk is elected America's 11th president.
1846:	The Mexican-American War leads to the U.S. annexation of California and the New Mexico territory.
1847:	The Spot Resolutions mark the first time Congress challenged presidential authority to declare war based on misleading claims.
1848:	The Seneca Falls Convention marks the beginning of the national women's suffrage movement.
	Zachary Taylor is elected America's 12th president
1850:	Compromise of 1850 leads to the expansion of slavery and deepens sectarian tensions that led to the Civil War.
	Millard Fillmore becomes America's 13th president after the death of Zachary Taylor.
1851:	The Christiana Riot demonstrates the growth of the abolition movement and limitation of presidential power to enforce laws against majority opposition.
1852:	Franklin Pierce is elected America's 14th president.
1854:	The Kansas-Nebraska Act results in another failed attempt to address sectarian tensions surrounding the legality and expansion of slavery.
1856:	James Buchanan is elected America's 15th president.
	Woodrow Wilson born in Staunton, Virginia
1857:	*Dred Scott* case is decided, with the Supreme Court ruling that slavery is constitutional. Buchanan conspires to direct the verdict.
	William Howard Taft born in Cincinnati, Ohio.
1858:	Lincoln delivers his famous "House Divided" speech during his presidential campaign.
	Theodore Roosevelt is born in New York City, New York.
1860:	Abraham Lincoln is elected America's 16th president.

1861:	The Civil War begins.
1863:	Congress authorizes the suspension of the habeas corpus during war time.
	Lincoln issues the now famous "Emancipation Proclamation."
1865:	Civil War ends with the surrender of Robert E. Lee on April 9.
	Abraham Lincoln is assassinated in a confederate plot.
	Ku Klux Klan is formed.
	Andrew Johnson is appointed the nation's 17th president.
	Thirteenth Amendment abolishes slavery within U.S. territories.
	Warren G. Harding is born in Blooming Grove, Ohio.
1866:	National Labor Union becomes America's first industrial workers' rights organization.
1868:	Fourteenth Amendment guarantees voting rights under the law.
	Andrew Johnson becomes the first president to be impeached.
	Ulysses S. Grant is elected America's 18th president.
1869:	Fifteenth Amendment grants African Americans the right to vote.
	Black Friday scandal raises widespread fear of government corruption.
1871:	Victoria Woodhull becomes the first woman to run for president.
	The Enforcement Acts represent a short-lived effort to protect civil rights with federal authority.
1872:	Grant makes history in establishing America's first national park, Yellowstone.
	Calvin Coolidge is born in Plymouth Notch, Vermont.
1876:	Controversial 1876 election sees the highest level of voter participation in history at nearly 82 percent.
	Rutherford B. Hayes is elected America's 19th president.
1880:	James A. Garfield is elected America's 20th president.

1881:	James A. Garfield becomes the second president to be assassinated while in office.
	Chester A. Arthur becomes America's 21st president.
1882:	Franklin Delano Roosevelt born in Hyde Park, New York.
1884:	Grover Cleveland is elected America's 22nd president.
	Harry S. Truman is born in Lamar, Missouri.
1888:	Benjamin Harrison is elected America's 23rd president, winning the Electoral College but losing the popular vote to Grover Cleveland.
	The Chinese Exclusion Act prohibits immigration from China and is later expanded to exclude all individuals of Asian origin.
	The Dawes Act begins forced Native American acculturation.
1889:	Harrison helps organize the Pan-American Conference, the first international, inter-governmental experiment in national governance.
1890:	Dwight D. Eisenhower born in Denison, Texas.
1892:	Grover Cleveland is reelected as America's 24th president, becoming the first and only to serve non-consecutive terms.
1893:	The Panic of 1893 becomes the nation's most severe economic disaster.
	Cleveland secretly has an operation for oral cancer, hiding his condition from Congress, the public, and the vice president.
1897:	William McKinley is elected America's 25th president.
1898:	The United States invades and occupies Cuba in the Spanish-American War.
	The Paris Peace Treaty gives the U.S. control of Puerto Rico, Guam, and the Philippine Islands.
	The Philippine revolt begins.
	Mark Twain becomes a leader in the anti-imperialist opposition to McKinley's presidency.
1901:	William McKinley is assassinated.
	Teddy Roosevelt becomes America's 26th president.

1902: Roosevelt becomes the first president to use presidential authority to negotiate during a domestic workers' strike and the first president to strongly support labor unions.

1904: Roosevelt issues the Roosevelt Corollary to the Monroe Doctrine, which states that America reserves the right to intervene in Latin American countries in order to protect regional peace.

1905: Roosevelt founds the U.S. Forest Service under the Department of Interior.

1906: Roosevelt establishes the first of America's national monuments under the Antiquities Act.

1908: William Howard Taft becomes America's 27th president.

Lyndon Baines Johnson is born in Stonewall, Texas.

1909: The Sixteenth Amendment allows the federal government to charge an income tax.

1911: Ronald Reagan is born in Tampico, Illinois.

1912: Woodrow Wilson is elected the nation's 28th president.

Theodore Roosevelt forms one of the nation's first prominent third parties with his Bull Moose Party.

1913: Women's rights activists stage the first protest in front of the White House.

The Seventeenth Amendment establishes the right to direct election of Senators to the U.S. Congress.

Richard Milhouse Nixon is born in Yorba Linda, California.

Gerald Ford, born Leslie Lynch King, Jr., is born in Omaha, Nebraska.

1917: The United States enters World War I.

Wilson authorizes the creation of America's first propaganda division.

John F. Kennedy is born in Brookline, Massachusetts.

1918: Wilson delivers his famous "Fourteen Points" speech calling for a stronger international government and leading to the attempted establishment of the League of Nations.

1919: The Nineteenth Amendment grants women the right to vote.

Wilson suffers a stroke while in office and is confined to his bed for the rest of his presidency. Congress and other governmental officers are not informed of Wilson's condition.

1920: Warren G. Harding is elected the nation's 29th president and becomes the first president whose campaign was funded by fossil-fuel companies.

1923: Calvin Coolidge becomes the nation's 30th president after the death of Warren G. Harding in office.

1924: Indian Citizenship Act grants Native Americans U.S. citizenship.

James Earl Carter, Jr. is born in Plains, Georgia.

George Herbert Walker Bush is born in Milton, Massachusetts.

1928: Herbert Hoover is elected the nation's 31st president.

1929: The Great Depression begins.

1932: Roosevelt is elected America's 32nd president.

Roosevelt introduces the New Deal social welfare reforms.

1933: Roosevelt delivers the first of his radio addresses to the nation, which became known as his fireside chats.

1935: First Gallup Poll is published, introducing representative polling.

1936: Roosevelt's Committee on Administrative Management begins a comprehensive reorganization of the executive branch, dramatically increasing the scope of presidential authority.

1939: The Reorganization Act of 1939 creates permanent changes to the administration and created the Executive Office of the President (EOP).

1941: The National Opinion Research Center introduces non-commercial representative polling.

The Japanese military attacks Pearl Harbor.

Congress declares war on the Axis Powers.

1942: Roosevelt signs the Japanese removal act that calls for Japanese Americans to be interned without due process.

1943:	The Magnusson Act gives Chinese Americans the right to citizenship and voting rights.
1945:	Roosevelt wins a historic fourth term in office, but dies shortly before it begins.
	Harry S. Truman becomes America's 33rd president.
	The United States uses atomic bombs on the Japanese cities of Nagasaki and Hiroshima.
	The United Nations is created.
1946:	William Jefferson Clinton is born in Hope, Arkansas.
	George W. Bush is born in New Haven, Connecticut.
1947:	The National Security Act of 1947 unites Army, Navy, and Air Force, creates the Department of Defense, and the position of Secretary of Defense.
1948:	Famous incorrect "Dewey Defeats Truman" projection printed in *Daily Tribune*.
1950:	The Korean War begins.
1952:	Dwight D. Eisenhower is elected the nation's 34th president.
1954:	Vietnam Conflict begins.
	Eisenhower secretly commits CIA agents to Vietnam to undermine the North Vietnamese military organization.
	Eisenhower uses the CIA to depose the legitimate government of Iran and to install Reza Shah Pahlavi.
	In the case of *Brown v. Board of Education*, the Supreme Court rules that segregation is unconstitutional.
1955:	First U.S.-Russian summit of the Cold War.
1957:	Martin Luther King, Jr. is elected head of the Southern Christian Leadership Conference.
	The Civil Rights Act creates the Civil Rights Division of the Justice Department.
1960:	A U.S. U-2 spy plane is shot down over Russia, leading to a major international incident.

	John F. Kennedy is elected the nation's 35th president.
1961:	The Bay of Pigs controversy results from a failed U.S. invasion of Cuba.
	Barack Hussein Obama is born in Honolulu, Hawaii.
1962:	The Cuban missile crisis begins when intelligence suggests the Soviet Union will station ballistic missiles in Cuba.
1963:	John F. Kennedy is assassinated in Dallas, Texas.
	Lyndon Baines Johnson takes office as America's 36th president.
1964:	Congress passes the Civil Rights Act.
	Vietnamese ships attack American vessels in the Gulf of Tonkin incident.
1965:	Voting Rights Act is passed.
	Lyndon Johnson introduces his Great Society system of social reforms.
1968:	Richard Nixon is elected America's 37th president.
1969:	Nixon administration authorizes the secret bombing of Cambodia and Laos.
1971:	The Twenty-Sixth Amendment lowers the national voting age from 21 to 18.
	A federal employee leaks the Pentagon Papers to the press showing that Presidents Eisenhower through Nixon misled Congress and the American people about the Vietnam conflict.
1972:	A group of individuals working for the Nixon administration are apprehended trying to break into the Watergate Hotel in Washington D.C.
1973:	Congress passes the War Powers Resolution, placing limits on presidential war-time authority.
	The U.S. energy crisis begins.
1974:	Richard Nixon becomes the first president to resign from office.

	Gerald Ford takes office as America's 38th president.
	Ford pardons Nixon.
1976:	Jimmy Carter is elected the nation's 39th president.
	OPEC oil crisis results in a loss of support for Carter.
1978:	Carter's leadership in the Camp David Accords results in a tentative peace agreement between Egypt and Israel after years of warfare.
1979:	Revolution in Iran leads to the Iran Hostage Crisis after the U.S.-installed Reza Shah Pahlavi is overthrown in a coup led by radical right-wing militants.
	Carter delivers his "Crisis of Confidence" speech.
1980:	Ronald Reagan is elected America's 40th president.
1985:	Reagan Administration conducts illegal arms deals with Iran and uses the funds to secretly fund a right-wing regime in Nicaragua; leaked information about this effort leads to a major controversy.
1986:	Reagan has a historic meeting with Russian leader Mikhail Gorbachev.
1988:	George H.W. Bush is elected America's 41st president.
1991:	The Persian Gulf War begins with a U.S. invasion of Iraq.
1994:	William Clinton is elected America's 42nd president.
	The North American Free Trade Agreement (NAFTA) is established.
	The Clinton administration's "Don't Ask, Don't Tell" policy is established.
1998:	Clinton's relationship with intern Monica Lewinsky leads to charges of obstruction of justice and lying under oath.
1999:	Clinton becomes the second president in history to be impeached on the charges of obstructing justice and lying to congress.
2000:	George W. Bush loses the popular vote but wins the Electoral College vote to become America's 43nd president.
2001:	Radical militants attack the United States.

The United States invades Afghanistan at the beginning of the War on Terror.

2003: The United States invades Iraq as part of the global War on Terror.

2008: Barack Obama is elected America's 43rd president.

Obama is awarded the Nobel Peace Prize for his achievements in promoting diversity and equality.

The Great Recession begins.

2016: Hillary Clinton becomes the first woman nominated to run for president by one of America's dominant political parties.

The government of Russia interferes in the U.S. election system to support the election of Donald Trump.

Donald Trump loses the popular vote to Clinton but wins the Electoral College vote.

2019: A federal employee anonymously reports that Trump attempted to utilize presidential authority to gain an advantage over Democratic rival and former vice president Joe Biden.

The U.S. House of Representatives begins an investigation of charges against Trump.

Trump becomes the third president in history to be impeached for obstruction of justice and abuse of presidential power.

Introduction

When the Constitution of the United States was being drafted, there was considerable debate as to the role of the president. Anti-Federalists wanted the president to function as head of state, a largely ceremonial office for foreign policy and diplomacy. The Federalists wanted the president to serve as head of government and head of state, a more powerful executive office with numerous powers. George Washington, who was enormously popular due, in large part, to his heroic role in the American Revolution, was elected to preside over the Constitutional Convention and had considerable say in how the Constitution was written. He approved of the Federalist proposal for a strong central government, seeing this as the way to protect public welfare and secure America's diplomatic and military security.

As the first president, Washington's use of executive power became the model. He organized his cabinet like his military command, and he alone had executive authority. His cabinet secretaries were like military subordinates, reporting directly to him and taking action only once they received his approval. His secretaries then supervised lower-level officials. Washington was a military general, not a bureaucrat, who ran the country like he would a large plantation. He was also the first and only president not to take part in partisan politics. He chose his cabinet from men he called "first characters"—those with strong qualifications who had already held positions of importance, rather than those with unified political views. He valued diversity of opinion and emphasized that the president is intended to represent all the people of the United States, and not just those who shared his political opinions.

George Washington established the link between the presidency and the military, and approached presidential decisions with a military mindset. This unique style of executive governance was copied by every president who followed.

Topics covered in this chapter include:
- Early life of George Washington
- How presidential power was first established
- Military approach to presidential power
- George Washington's chance to become king
- Washington's first inaugural address
- Washington's farewell address

This Chapter Discusses the Following Source Documents:
To George Washington from Lewis Nicola, May 22, 1782
Letter from George Washington to Lewis Nicola, May 22, 1782
Letter of the President of the Federal Convention, to the President of Congress, September 17, 1787
Washington's Inaugural Address, April 30, 1789
Washington's Farewell Address, 1796

Defining the Presidency
George Washington (1789–1797)

A U.S. president has many roles. He or she is expected to serve as both head of government and head of state. As such, the president is intimately involved in crafting legislative priorities, and in promoting and collaborating on the creation of foreign policies. As commander in chief of the nation's army, a president must also be prepared to respond to international and domestic military threats. At the time that the nation was founded, the Constitution was somewhat vague about the powers and responsibilities afforded to the presidency. The style of the presidential office was established to a great extent by George Washington, the first man to hold the office and a larger-than-life figure both at the time of and in the centuries since his historic presidency.

Over the years, presidents have come to the office with diverse experience. The Constitution only requires that an individual be a natural-born citizen, a resident for 14 years, and over the age of 35. Some presidents have been experienced in governance, having served as state governors or mayors. Others have been legislators, either in the House of Representatives or the Senate. Some have direct experience of the executive offices, as heads of federal departments in a presidential cabinet. In other cases, those seeking the presidency come through the nation's military. In total, 29 presidents—more than half—served in the military before seeking election.[1] General George Washington, the greatest hero of the American Revolution, became the nation's first president after being the nation's first commander in chief, establishing early on the link between the military and the presidency.

We the People

George Washington's Legendary Life

George Washington was born into a moderately wealthy family of Virginia's "plantation gentry." Because of his father Augustine's death in 1743, Washington received little formal education. Despite being self-taught, he was literate and well informed and had the benefit of being inculcated into the aristocracy through his half-brother Lawrence.[2] Thanks to his family's connections, Washington found another mentor in the wealthy and influential Fairfax family, descended from Yorkshire nobility. George William Fairfax recommended Washington for a position in the lucrative trade of surveying, and he got his first job as an official surveyor for the Virginia territory in 1748, at only 17 years old.[3] By 1750, Washington had completed nearly 200 surveys, covering some 60,000 acres of previously unexplored Virginia wilderness. He resigned from his position in 1750 after his brother Lawrence fell ill; and after Lawrence's death in 1752, he joined the Virginia military.

By 1753, the 21-year-old Washington was a major in the local militia, which was then an offshoot of the British Army. One of Washington's first big assignments became one of his most famous adventures. Governor Robert Dinwiddie dispatched Washington and a small contingent to the region around Lake Erie, where it was reported that French soldiers from Canada had established a military base in British territory. According to Dinwiddie, Washington almost lost his life on the return journey after falling into the nearly frozen Allegheny River, which helped him acquire an international reputation that he built on through successful skirmishes with French soldiers during the French and Indian War. He rose to supreme commander of the Virginia Militia after a heroic defeat in which he had two horses shot out from under him and four holes shot into his coat.

After returning to his plantation, in 1759 Washington married wealthy heiress Martha Dandridge Custis, a widow with two young children. For the next 20 years, he grew his family business into one of the

George Washington, first president of the United States. By Gilbert Stuart, via Wikimedia.

most successful in the country. In the years approaching the American Revolution, Washington was firmly aligned with the patriots. His letters indicate he felt exploited by British merchants, shipping regulations, and unfair tax schemes, and he spoke out against the new spate of taxes levied by Britain in the 1770s.[4]

At the Second Continental Congress in Philadelphia in May of 1775, Washington was one of the Virginia delegates and, thanks to his fame in the French and Indian Wars, was chosen to serve as commander in chief of the Continental Army. Washington was ill-prepared for what was to come, with no direct knowledge of how to manage cavalry or artillery, how to field supply lines, or how to command such a large contingent. Inexperience contributed to early losses, but Washington reasoned it was best to avoid large-scale engagements, settling instead for a slow retreat punctuated by small-scale assaults. The British lost Boston, but returned with a massive force to lay siege to New York. Washington's forces suffered defeats at Long Island and Kip's Bay and they lost the city, retreating north as the British pursued. The British were on course to win the war easily, but William Howe, commander in chief of the British army, decided to postpone further attacks during the winter. Washington made a daring calculation, crossing the Delaware River to attack the British garrison in Trenton, New Jersey. He then defeated a much larger contingent in Princeton. An alliance with the French, and the arrival of a French army contingent led by comte de Rochambeau in 1780, proved a turning point. Together, Washington and Rochambeau, with an army of some 9,000, won a major victory at Yorktown, Virginia. After a long and deadly siege, British General Charles Cornwallis surrendered to Washington's forces on October 19, 1781, marking the end of the war, though two further years would pass until an official peace treaty was signed.[5]

The Ginger House

Washington is often portrayed with white hair that looks very much like the formal wigs that British aristocrats once wore as part of their general costume. Many Americans have, therefore, come to believe that Washington also wore a wig, but historians have found that Washington grew his natural hair long and wore it tied into a tail or queue. Washington's hair is typically depicted as grey or white in paintings because he powdered his hair, with either starch or Cyprus powder. Powdering one's hair white was in fashion at the time, a practice imported from France and Britain intended to make men look older and more learned and distinguished. A perfume was typically added to cover up any foul odors. Without his powder, George Washington had, in fact, red hair, making him the first ginger to occupy the highest office, though he would not be the last. Washington is not considered the first ginger president in the White House; because the White House did not yet exist, and Washington, DC, had not yet been designated the nation's capital. During his two terms as president, Washington and his family instead resided in the Samuel Osgood house in New York City, a stately manor just at the edge of the city overlooking the New York countryside. It wasn't very long before another redhead occupied the White House, however, as the famously ginger-haired Thomas Jefferson became the nation's third president after John Adams had established Washington DC as the capital and the White House as the residence of the nation's chief executive.[a]

Works Used

a. Fessenden, Marissa. "How George Washington Did His Hair." *Smithsonian*. June 9, 2015. www.smithsonianmag.com/smart-news/how-george-washington-did-his-hair-180955547/.

The Man Who Wouldn't Have Been King

Historians and lay history buffs alike for years held that Washington was offered the chance to be king just as the revolution came to a close. This myth is born out of a misinterpretation of an exchange between Washington and one of his colonels, Lewis Nicola, a veteran whose expertise had been indispensable to Washington during the war. In the letter Nicola recounts the hardships of the soldiers serving under him, the result of a poorly managed war effort. At the time the Articles of Confederation were the unifying law tying the states together, and they left the states as more or less autonomous entities under a weak central authority. As a result, the union was fragile, and the states had been slow to dispense payment and supplies to the soldiers on the field. As the war neared its end, some factions were near mutiny.

On May 22, 1872, Lewis Nicola wrote to Washington:

TO GEORGE WASHINGTON FROM LEWIS NICOLA
May 22, 1782
Source Document Excerpt

The injuries the troops have received in their pecuniary rights have been, & still continue to be too obvious to require a particular detail, or to have escaped your Excellencies notice, tho your exalted station must have deprived you of opportunity of information relative to the severe distresses occasioned thereby. Tho doubtless the particular circumstances of the times have occasioned many of these injuries, yet we have great reason to believe they are not all owing to that cause, but often occasioned by schemes of economy in the legislatures of some States, & publick ministers, founded on unjust & iniquitous principles; and tho, as the prospect of publick affairs cleared up, the means of fulfilling engagements encreased, yet the injuries, instead of being lessened, have kept pace with them. This gives us a dismal prospect for the time to come, & much reason to fear the future provision promised to officers, and the setling & satisfying their & the men's just demands will be

continued

little attended to, when our services are no longer wanted, and that the recompence of all our toils, hardships, expence of private fortune &c. during several of the best years of our lives will be, to those who cannot earn a livelyhood by manual labour, beggary, & that we who have born the heat & labour of the day will be forgot and neglected by such as reap the benefits without suffering any of the hardships.

It may be said that depreciations have been made up, but how has this been done? By depreciated paper money & certificates of such a nature as to be of little benefit to the original possessors, whose necessities have compelled them to part with those obligations to speculators for a small part of their value, never more, as far as I can learn, than one tenth, but often less.

From several conversations I have had with officers, & some I have overheard among soldiers, I believe it is [sincerely] intended not to seperate after the peace 'till all [grievances] are redressed, engagements & promises fulfilled, but how this is to be done I am at a loss, as neither officers or soldiers can have any confidence in promises. We have no doubt of Congresses intention to act uprightly, but greatly fear that, by the interested views of others, their abilities will not be equal to the task.

God forbid we should ever think of involving that country we have, under your conduct & auspices, rescued from oppression, into a new scene of blood & confusion; but it cannot be expected we should forego claims on which our future subsistance & that of our families depend.

Another difference there is between our fellow citizens and us is, that we must live under governments in the framing of which we had no hand, nor were consulted either personally or representatively, being engaged in preventing the enemy from disturbing those bodies which were entrusted with that business, the members of which would have found little mercy had they been captured.

Dangers foreseen may be removed, alleviated, or, in some cases, turned to benefits, [bossibly] what I apprehend may be susceptible, of even the latter, by means I beg leave to propose, but must request your Excellencies patience if I digress a little before I open my project.

I own I am not that violent admirer of a republican form of government that numbers in this country are; this is not owing to caprice, but reason & experience. Let us consider the fate of all the modern republicks of any note, without running into antiquity, which I think would also serve to establish my system.

To George Washington from Lewis Nicola
continued

The republicks of later days, worth our notice, may be reduced to three, Venice, Genoa & Holland, tho the two former are rather aristocratical than republican governments, yet they resemble those more than monarchical.

These have, each in their turns, shone with great brightness, but their lustre has been of short duration, and as it were only a blaze. What figure has Holland, that, in her infancy, successfully opposed the most formidable power of Europe, made for more than half of the present century, or actually makes at present? Mistress of nearly half the commerce of the earth, has she occasioned any considerable diversion of the naval power of Britain? Six or eight ships of the line have been able to oppose her, & unable to protect herself and her extensive commerce, has she not been obliged to apply for assistance to a neighbouring monarch? Does not the great similarity there is between her form of government & ours give us room to fear our fate will be like hers. His it not evidently appeared that during the course of this war we have never been able to draw forth all the internal resources we are possessed of, and oppose or attack the enemy with our real vigour?

In contrast to this scene let us consider the principal monarchies of Europe, they have suffered great internal commotions, have worried each other, have had periods of vigour & weakness, yet they still subsist & shine with lustre. It must not be concluded from this that I am a partisan for absolute monarchy, very far from it, I am sensible of its defects, the only conclusion I would draw from the comparison is, that the energy of the latter is more beneficial to the existence of a nation than the wisdom of the former. A monarch may often be governed by wise & moderate councels, but it is hardly possible for large bodies to plan or execute vigorous ones.

The inference I would deduce from what I have premised is, that each form of government has its defective & valuable parts, therefore that form which partakes of all, or most of the latter & is purged of the former, must be the most eligible.

In the brittish Government we have a sketch of this, [far,] it is true from perfect, but no despicable basis of a good one. The english constitution has been the result of repeated strugles between prince & people, but never received anything of a regular or stable form 'till the revolution, & yet is still short of perfection. The principal defects are pointed out by the experience of almost a century, & I believe may be reduced to two, one in the legislative the other in the executive authorities. Were elections annual, & confined to representatives

continued

for counties a & few large trading cities only, & all contributing to the support of government priviledged to elect, and had the king no command of money beyond what is requisite to the support of his family & court, suitable to the dignity of his station, I believe the constitution would approach much nearer to that degree of perfection to which sublunary things are limited. In a well regulated legislative body I conceive a third branch necessary— Montesquieu observes that a hereditary nobility is requisite in a monarchy but incompatible with a republick, taking this for granted, some degree of nobility may be proper in a mixed government, but limited, suppose not hereditary.

I shall now proceed to my scheme.

Congress has promised all those that continue in the service certain tracts of land, agreable to their grades, [some] States have done the same, others have not, probably owing to their not having lands to give, but as all the military have equal merits so have they equal claims to such rewards, therefore they ought all to be put on a footing by the united States.

Besides those who may be actually in the service at the peace, I conceive all those dismissed, or put on half pay, through schemes of economy, have [equal] rights, as their being out of the service was not volontary.

These things premised, I think Congress should take on itself the discharging all such engagements, made or that ought to be made, for lands & discharge them by procuring a sufficient tract in some of the best of those fruitful & extensive countries to the west of our frontiers, so that each individual should have his due, all unprofitable mountains & swamps, also lakes & rivers within the limits of this tract not to be reckoned as any part of the lots, but thrown in for the benefit of the whole community. This tract to be formed into a distinct State under such mode of government as those military who choose to remove to it may agree on.

Debts due to the army should be adjusted with dispatch & liquidated in the following manner. One third to be paid immediately, to enable the setlers to buy tools for trades & husbandry, & some stock, the other two thirds by four notes payable, with interest, in three months, & the others on the same terms at three months interval between each payment. In order to give such notes a due value, good funds should be appropriated for the discharge of principal & interest, but previous to such first payment & notes given, a sum should be deducted from each non commissioned & private mans debt, sufficient to victual him & family for one year from the first harvest succeeding the arrival of the

To George Washington from Lewis Nicola
continued

colony to be granted lands; during the intermediate time those persons to be victualled at the expence of the continent, & also to receive pay & clothing to the time the accounts are all adjusted & the troops ready to march.

Officers being entitled to half pay, such as choose to emigrate, should have provisions &c. allowed them as above & quarterly notes with interest for three years full pay to commence & be computed from the time they begin their march, in full discharge of all such half pay.

As I have already observed that it may be objected depreciations & other payments have been made good; but can a just debt be equitably discharged by certificates of very small comparative value, or depreciated paper money? certainly no, consequently the States are still bound to make good the deficiency. To this it will probably be answered that those certificates have generally passed into other hands, who have paid consideration for them; but what consideration? A tenth or a twentieth of the principal value expressed therein, independent of interest; and is it not generally understood in some States, if not in all, that when those certificates are to be paid off they will be estimated at no more than what was given for them? I therefore conceive the following rules

should be observed in discharge of these obligations.

Every person in whose favour a certificate has been, or shall be given, & who will keep it to the conclusion of the war, to be paid its full value.

To every person paid in depreciated money the depreciation thereof to be made good.

To the original possessers of certificates sold two thirds of the value expressed, the other third to be considered as received when the certificate was sold. This is certainly much beyond what, on an average, has been received for all certificates sold, but as it will be difficult, if at all possible, to ascertain in a reasonable time the money paid, it is requisite to fix some rule.

This war must have shewn to all, but to military men in particular the weakness of republicks, & the exertions the army has been able to make by being under a proper head, therefore I little doubt, when the benefits of a mixed government are pointed out & duly considered, but such will be readily adopted; in this case it will, I believe, be uncontroverted that the same abilities which have lead us, through difficulties apparently unsurmountable by human power, to

continued

victory & glory, those qualities that have merited & obtained the universal esteem & veneration of an army, would be most likely to conduct & direct us in the smoother paths of peace.

Some people have so connected the ideas of tyranny & monarchy as to find it very difficult to seperate them, it may therefore be requisite to give the head of such a constitution as I propose, some title apparently more moderate, but if all other things were once adjusted I believe strong arguments might be produced for admitting the title of king, which I conceive would be attended with some material advantages.

I have hinted that I believed the United States would be benefited by my scheme, this I conceive would be done, by having a savage & cruel enemy seperated from their borders, by a body of veterans, that would be as an advanced guard, securing the main body from danger. There is no doubt but Canada will some time or other be a seperate State, and from the genious & habits of the people, that its government will be monarchical. May not casualties produce enmity between this new State & our Union, & may not its force under the direction of an active prince prove too powerful for the efforts of republicks? It may be answered that in a few years we shall acquire such vigour as to baffle all inimical attempts. I grant that our numbers & riches will encrease, but will our governments have energy enough to draw them forth? Will those States remote from the danger be zealously anxious to assist those most exposed? Individuals in Holland abound in wealth, yet the government is poor & weak.

Republican bigots will certainly consider my opinions as heterodox, and the maintainer thereof as meriting fire & faggots, I have therefore hitherto kept them within my own breast. By freely communicating them to your Excellency, I am persuaded I run no risk, & that, tho disapproved of, I need not apprehend their ever being disclosed to my prejudice.[6]

We the People

A superficial reading of the letter, coupled with modern interpretation of terms like "scheme," might lead to the misapprehension that it was Nicola's intention to initiate a mutiny that would have made Washington king. Washington's strongly worded rejection seems to indicate that he was not pleased with this suggestion.

LETTER FROM GEORGE WASHINGTON TO LEWIS NICOLA
May 22, 1782
Source Document Excerpt

Newburgh May 22nd 82

Sir,

With a mixture of great surprise & astonishment I have read with attention the Sentiments you have submitted to my perusal. Be assured, Sir, no occurrence in the course of the War, has given me more painful sensations than your information of there being such ideas existing in the Army as you have expressed, & I must view with abhorrence, and reprehend with severity—For the present, the communicatn of them will rest in my own bosom, unless some further agitation of the matter, shall make a disclosure necessary.

I am much at a loss to conceive what part of my conduct could have given encouragement to an address which to me seems big with the greatest mischiefs that can befall my Country. If I am not deceived in the knowledge of myself, you could not have found a person to whom your schemes are more disagreeable—at the same time in justice to my own feeling I must add, that no man possesses a more sincere wish to see ample Justice done to the Army than I do, and as far as my powers & influence, in a constitution[al] way extend, they shall be employed to the utmost of my abilities to effect it, should there be any occasion—Let me [conj]ure you then, if you have any regard for your Country, concern for your self or posterity—or respect for me, to banish these thoughts from your Mind, & never communicate, as from yourself, or any one else, a sentiment of the like nature. With esteem I am Sir Yr Most Obedt Servt

Go: Washington

The foregoing is an exact copy of a Letter which we sealed & sent off to Colonel Nichola at the request of the writer of it.

D. Humphrys Aid de Camp
Jona. Trumbull Jun. Secty[7]

This exchange has been called the "Nicola Affair." A more detailed reading of Nicola's further correspondence with Washington shows that he was not suggesting a military coup but rather wanted to establish a new state on the western border of the United States. Further, though he suggested Washington might serve as a kind of "king," he intended this to be a constitutional office rather than a hereditary kingship. Nicola had lost faith in the Senate and believed that Washington could be the leader of a new country, one with a strong central government with constitutional protections and the cohesive centralized authority similar to that of a monarchy. In no way was Nicola's "scheme" part of a broader movement, and at no time was Washington offered the "crown" of America. Thus, while the idea that Washington rejected the American crown has been the fuel for much fan fiction, there is little basis in reality to the idea that Washington could have become an American king.[8]

On December 23, 1783, Washington appeared before Congress to resign his commission as commander in chief. Washington could certainly have secured a central position in Congress when the war was over, yet he chose not to seek political office. His letters indicate that he wanted nothing more than to return to his comfortable, familiar life in Mount Vernon. Historians found that he was relatively soft-spoken, forthright, reserved, and had little interest in the world of politics. He'd served in the war out of a sense of duty and justice and, at its conclusion, hoped that his involvement in the business of politics would be ended.

The fact that Washington did not try to seek power under the creation of a military junta—as many other generals did after leading the military branch of a revolution (like Oliver Cromwell of England and Napoleon Bonaparte in France)—established an important precedent for the American presidency. The issue of military authority was one of the major debates of the Constitutional Convention, and one of the complaints levied against King George was that he had made the military so powerful that it

This painting by John Trumbull, who had served under Washington in the Continental Army, depicts Washington resigning his commission to Congress, an act that established a civilian, rather than a military, precedent for the presidency. Via Wikimedia.

had eclipsed civil power in Britain. In 1776, the patriot legislature of Virginia met to discuss the nation's first constitution and a state declaration of rights. Washington was one of the delegates, where it was decided that the military in America's republican form of democracy would remain permanently subordinate to the civilian government. Further, it was decided that no president should ever be a member of the military at the time of his or her appointment, but would be a civilian who would serve as commander in chief, thereby establishing a clear system of civilian authority over the military.

However, critics worried that vesting such power in a single individual might ultimately lead to despotism. Elbridge Gerry, a prominent progressive member of the Constitutional Convention, worried that a president might order the military to crush dissent among the populace. It was Alexander Hamilton who suggested the solution that was eventually adopted: in wartime, the president would act as commander in chief, but the power to raise armies, fund the military, and declare war would belong to Congress. By splitting authority over the military between two branches of government, the presidency and Congress, the Founding Fathers hoped that civilian control of the military would be preserved and presidential tyranny prevented.

Four times during his two terms in office, Washington dispatched troops to deal with issues impacting national security. The first three occasions all involved conflicts in territories north of the Ohio River, where the Wabash and Miami people once resided and where members of those tribes had been in conflict with colonists. In these engagements, Washington conferred with military leaders, personally selected generals to lead the effort, and consulted with Congress on his plans, but he took personal responsibility for directing his generals and for their conduct.

In 1794, Washington faced an insurrection in Pennsylvania, where whiskey distillers were refusing to pay newly established federal taxes, even going so far as to tar and feather federal tax collectors. Washington consulted with Congress, and then utilized his constitutional authority to call out a militia of more than 12,000 to put down the insurrection. Donning his military uniform, Washington visited the battlefield himself to confer with the soldiers and to direct the effort firsthand. He reported to Congress that he'd delegated authority to his generals and was returning to his post, leaving Virginia native Harry "Light Horse" Lee in command. The "Whiskey Rebellion," as it has since been known, was over within a matter of weeks. Again, Washington helped establish a traditional relationship between the state and the military that would continue under future

presidents. He took an intimate role, but typically delegated direct management, though Washington remains the only president to actively lead troops while in the presidency.

None of these conflicts required a declaration of war by Congress, and in dispatching troops without an official declaration of war, Washington established another important precedent. While Congress would manage military funding, raise armies and declare war, Washington established that the president had the power to dispatch troops to "defend and protect" the nation or national interests. Congress could, of course, interrupt such an action by refusing funding, and so there remained an interplay, with the president ultimately in charge, but Congress able to curtail presidential authority.[9]

King by Another Name

Though Nicola has been vilified in history as a man who would have undone the hard work of the Revolution and returned America to monarchic tyranny, his central premise—that there should be a strong central government with powers similar to a monarchy—was a sentiment shared by many. In particular, John Adams, Alexander Hamilton, and the other members of what gradually became America's first political party, the Federalists, were advocates of strong, centralized authority. Political factions in the early years of the union were different than the familiar division of conservative and progressive ideology that would be established in the twentieth century. The Federalists were like modern conservatives in that they wanted to preserve tradition, were aggressively pro-business, and placed strong emphasis on the rule of law. However, they were also like modern progressives in that they favored a larger central bureaucracy. Critics, typically called "anti-Federalists" in Washington's era, were not organized into a distinct faction at this time, but they emphasized state's rights and decentralized power, like modern conservatives, while also focusing on personal liberties and elevating the popular will, which is similar to modern progressivism.

The debate between these two factions defined the Founding Era, and the final form of the Constitution represents the victory of those who became the Federalists. As the Constitution came into being, structures were designed to limit the power of each branch to prevent the concentration of power and the potential for tyranny, but the Constitution was also designed to limit the power of the people and to ensure that only those seen as having greater "value" would be capable of achieving leadership. A new aristocracy was created, consisting of wealthy landowners and various territorial "gentlemen," and these individuals held a dominant role in the nation's politics.

When designing the Constitution, there was considerable debate over how to define the duties of the executive branch. The anti-Federalists wanted the president to function as head of state, a largely ceremonial office for foreign policy and diplomacy. The Federalists wanted the president to serve as head of government *and* head of state, a more powerful executive office with numerous powers. That this approach won out was largely due to Washington's campaigning, as well as that of the nation's first vice president, John Adams.

Many critics were concerned that the presidency would lead to tyranny. Specifically, many in the South felt that the northern states, which had higher populations, would dominate the executive if the president was elected by popular vote. Much of the South's population consisted of slaves, who were not citizens under the law and could not vote. Southern delegates, therefore, argued that they would be at a permanent disadvantage. The presidency became a focus of this debate, and two methods were established to balance political power between the South and North. The Electoral College was created, designating a certain number of electors to each state based in part on population. Southern states were given a number of electors based on the population of eligible voting white males plus one fifth of the population of non-voting slaves. Further,

it was determined that the House of Representatives would be constituted according to population, but that each state, regardless of size,
would get the same number of senators. These two methods were used
to prevent the secession of the southern states by providing a way for the
southern states to gain more political influence and were accompanied
by promises that the newly formed legislature would not interfere with the
slavery industry.

Despite not wanting to play a role in the convention, Washington was
frustrated by the mismanagement of state legislatures and the inability of
the Confederation Congress to manage the alliance between them; and
so, in 1787, Washington again left Mount Vernon to attend a convention
intended to rewrite the Articles of Confederation. Due to his widespread
popularity, he was unanimously chosen to preside over the Constitutional Convention, and championed a radical reinvention of the Articles of
Confederation rather than a minor reform. Delegates voted to discard the
articles entirely and replace them with a new constitution. Washington approved of the basic Federalist proposal for a strong central government,
as he saw such an organ as a necessary evil to protect public welfare and
to secure the nation's diplomatic and military security. He was less sanguine, however, about the increasing factionalization he saw among the
delegates. He himself signed the introductory "cover letter" of the constitution that accompanied the document as it was delivered to the president of Congress following the convention.

LETTER OF THE PRESIDENT OF THE FEDERAL CONVENTION, TO THE PRESIDENT OF CONGRESS, TRANSMITTING THE CONSTITUTION

September 17, 1787
Source Document Excerpt

In Convention, September 17, 1787.

Sir,

We have now the honor to submit to the consideration of the United States in Congress assembled, that Constitution which has appeared to us the most adviseable.

The friends of our country have long seen and desired, that the power of making war, peace, and treaties, that of levying money and regulating commerce, and the correspondent executive and judicial authorities should be fully and effectually vested in the general government of the Union: But the impropriety of delegating such extensive trust to one body of men is evident-Hence results the necessity of a different organization.

It is obviously impracticable in the federal government of these states, to secure all rights of independent sovereignty to each, and yet provide for the interest and safety of all: Individuals entering into society, must give up a share of liberty to preserve the rest. The magnitude of the sacrifice must depend as well on situation and circumstance, as on the object to be obtained. It is at all times difficult to draw with precision the line between those rights which must be surrendered, and those which may be reserved; and on the present occasion this difficulty was encreased by a difference among the several states as to their situation, extent, habits, and particular interests.

In all our deliberations on this subject we kept steadily in our view, that which appears to us the greatest interest of every true American, the consolidation of our Union, in which is involved our prosperity, felicity, safety, perhaps our national existence. This important consideration, seriously and deeply impressed on our minds, led each state in the Convention to be less rigid on points of inferior magnitude, than might have been otherwise expected; and thus the Constitution, which we now present, is the result of a spirit of amity, and of that mutual deference and concession which the

Letter of the President of the Federal Convention, to the President of Congress, Transmitting the Constitution continued

peculiarity of our political situation rendered indispensible.

That it will meet the full and entire approbation of every state is not perhaps to be expected; but each will doubtless consider, that had her interest been alone consulted, the consequences might have been particularly disagreeable or injurious to others; that it is liable to as few exceptions as could reasonably have been expected, we hope and believe; that it may promote the lasting welfare of that country so dear to us all, and secure her freedom and happiness, is our most ardent wish.

With great respect, We have the honor to be, Sir,

Your Excellency's most obedient and humble servants,

GEORGE WASHINGTON,
President.

By unanimous Order of the Convention.

His Excellency the PRESIDENT of CONGRESS.[10]

Washington hoped to retire to Mount Vernon at the conclusion of the constitutional debate, but each of the electors of the Electoral College cast their vote for him for president, and he became the first and only president to be elected by a unanimous vote of the College.

Washington expressed his reservations about taking on the job to friends and colleagues, reportedly telling his long-time friend and future Secretary of War Henry Knox that his "movements to the chair of government will be accompanied with feelings not unlike those of a culprit who is going to the place of his execution." Washington's journey to New York deepened his anxieties. Before he departed Virginia, his friend and former aide James McHenry had told him, "You are now a king under a different name;" and as he crossed through Delaware and into Pennsylvania, he was greeted by hundreds of receptions very much the way a populace might celebrate the passage of a monarch. His image had been painted in historic custom astride white horses. Bridges and roads were decorated in flowers and thronged with well-wishers. At the Schuylkill River, a boy dressed as a cherub was hoisted in the air to lay a laurel wreath on Washington's head. In Philadelphia, he was greeted by a parade 20,000 strong and accompanied with music and speeches from local leaders. The *Federal Gazette* reported, "His Excellency rode in front of the procession, on horseback, politely bowing to the spectators who filled the doors and windows by which he passed. What a pleasing reflection to every patriotic mind, thus to see our citizens again united in their reliance on this great man who is, a second time, called upon to be the savior of his country!"[11]

Once in New York, Washington struggled with his inaugural address, the first draft of which was vetoed by James Madison as being politically confusing and overly long. His second draft drew upon his fears and anxieties at his fitness for the office and was one of the most humble and simple inaugural speeches in history:

WASHINGTON'S INAUGURAL ADDRESS
A Transcription
April 30, 1789
Source Document Excerpt

Fellow Citizens of the Senate and the House of Representatives.

Among the vicissitudes incident to life, no event could have filled me with greater anxieties than that of which the notification was transmitted by your order, and received on the fourteenth day of the present month. On the one hand, I was summoned by my Country, whose voice I can never hear but with veneration and love, from a retreat which I had chosen with the fondest predilection, and, in my flattering hopes, with an immutable decision, as the asylum of my declining years: a retreat

Washington's Inaugural Address
continued

which was rendered every day more necessary as well as more dear to me, by the addition of habit to inclination, and of frequent interruptions in my health to the gradual waste committed on it by time. On the other hand, the magnitude and difficulty of the trust to which the voice of my Country called me, being sufficient to awaken in the wisest and most experienced of her citizens, a distrustful scrutiny into his qualifications, could not but overwhelm with dispondence, one, who, inheriting inferior endowments from nature and unpractised in the duties of civil administration, ought to be peculiarly conscious of his own deficiencies. In this conflict of emotions, all I dare aver, is, that it has been my faithful study to collect my duty from a just appreciation of eve ry circumstance, by which it might be affected. All I dare hope, is, that, if in executing this task I have been too much swayed by a grateful remembrance of former instances, or by an affectionate sensibility to this transcendent proof, of the confidence of my fellow-citizens; and have thence too little consulted my incapacity as well as disinclination for the weighty and untried cares before me; my error will be palliated by the motives which misled me, and its consequences be judged by my Country, with some share of the partiality in which they originated.

Such being the impressions under which I have, in obedience to the public summons, repaired to the present station; it would be peculiarly improper to omit in this first official Act, my fervent supplications to that Almighty Being who rules over the Universe, who presides in the Councils of Nations, and whose providential aids can supply every human defect, that his benediction may consecrate to the liberties and happiness of the People of the United States, a Government instituted by themselves for these essential purposes: and may enable every instrument employed in its administration to execute with success, the functions allotted to his charge. In tendering this homage to the Great Author of every public and private good I assure myself that it expresses your sentiments not less than my own; nor those of my fellow-citizens at large, less than either. No People can be bound to acknowledge and adore the invisible hand, which conducts the Affairs of men more than the People of the United States. Every step, by which they have advanced to the character of an independent nation, seems to have been distinguished by some token of providential agency. And in the important revolution just accomplished in the system of their United Government, the tranquil deliberations and voluntary consent

continued

of so many distinct communities, from which the event has resulted, cannot be compared with the means by which most Governments have been established, without some return of pious gratitude along with an humble anticipation of the future blessings which the past seem to presage. These reflections, arising out of the present crisis, have forced themselves too strongly on my mind to be suppressed. You will join with me I trust in thinking, that there are none under the influence of which, the proceedings of a new and free Government can more auspiciously commence.

By the article establishing the Executive Department, it is made the duty of the President "to recommend to your consideration, such measures as he shall judge necessary and expedient." The circumstances under which I now meet you, will acquit me from entering into that subject, farther than to refer to the Great Constitutional Charter under which you are assembled; and which, in defining your powers, designates the objects to which your attention is to be given. It will be more consistent with those circumstances, and far more congenial with the feelings which actuate me, to substitute, in place of a recommendation of particular measures, the tribute that is due to the talents, the rectitude, and the patriotism which adorn the characters selected to devise and adopt them. In

these honorable qualifications, I behold the surest pledges, that as on one side, no local prejudices, or attachments; no seperate views, nor party animosities, will misdirect the comprehensive and equal eye which ought to watch over this great assemblage of communities and interests: so, on another, that the foundations of our National policy will be laid in the pure and immutable principles of private morality; and the pre-eminence of a free Government, be exemplified by all the attributes which can win the affections of its Citizens, and command the respect of the world.

I dwell on this prospect with every satisfaction which an ardent love for my Country can inspire: since there is no truth more thoroughly established, than that there exists in the economy and course of nature, an indissoluble union between virtue and happiness, between duty and advantage, between the genuine maxims of an honest and magnanimous policy, and the solid rewards of public prosperity and felicity: Since we ought to be no less persuaded that the propitious smiles of Heaven, can never be expected on a nation that disregards the eternal rules of order and right, which Heaven itself has ordained: And since the preservation of the sacred fire of liberty, and the destiny of the Republican model of Government, are justly considered as deeply, perhaps as finally staked, on the experiment entrusted to the hands of the American people.

Washington's Inaugural Address
continued

Besides the ordinary objects submitted to your care, it will remain with your judgment to decide, how far an exercise of the occasional power delegated by the Fifth article of the Constitution is rendered expedient at the present juncture by the nature of objections which have been urged against the System, or by the degree of inquietude which has given birth to them. Instead of undertaking particular recommendations on this subject, in which I could be guided by no lights derived from official opportunities, I shall again give way to my entire confidence in your discernment and pursuit of the public good: For I assure myself that whilst you carefully avoid every alteration which might endanger the benefits of an United and effective Government, or which ought to await the future lessons of experience; a reverence for the characteristic rights of freemen, and a regard for the public harmony, will sufficiently influence your deliberations on the question how far the former can be more impregnably fortified, or the latter be safely and advantageously promoted.

To the preceeding observations I have one to add, which will be most properly addressed to the House of Representatives. It concerns myself, and will therefore be as brief as possible. When I was first honoured with a call into the Service of my Country, then on the eve of an arduous struggle for its liberties, the light in which I contemplated my duty required that I should renounce every pecuniary compensation. From this resolution I have in no instance departed. And being still under the impressions which produced it, I must decline as inapplicable to myself, any share in the personal emoluments, which may be indispensably included in a permanent provision for the Executive Department; and must accordingly pray that the pecuniary estimates for the Station in which I am placed, may, during my continuance in it, be limited to such actual expenditures as the public good may be thought to require.

Having thus imparted to you my sentiments, as they have been awakened by the occasion which brings us together, I shall take my present leave; but not without resorting once more to the benign parent of the human race, in humble supplication that since he has been pleased to favour the American people, with opportunities for deliberating in perfect tranquility, and dispositions for deciding with unparellelled unanimity on a form of Government, for the security of their Union, and the advancement of their happiness; so his divine blessing may be equally *conspicuous* in the enlarged views, the temperate consultations, and the wise measures on which the success of this Government must depend.[12]

Exercising Authority

As the first president, Washington's use of executive powers became the model for expression of the office as well. Some in the legislature hoped that the president would be led by Congress. Others, like Hamilton, hoped that the members of the executive cabinet would perform similarly to ministers in Britain, with independent discretion coordinated with Congress. Washington, whose experience was not in governance but in the military, chose to organize his cabinet like his military command. He alone had executive authority, and his cabinet secretaries were like military subordinates, reporting to him alone and acting only once they'd received his approval. These secretaries then supervised lower-level officials. Washington was a military general and the operator of a large plantation, not a bureaucrat, and he approached the presidency with this frame of mind, shaping a unique style of executive governance copied by every successive president.

Washington also established the dominance of the federal government over the states when national needs arose or conflicted with the desires of the states. The first major congressional controversy regarding presidential authority concerned how members of the president's cabinet would be appointed to and removed from office. Out of several options—the power might have been granted to Congress; Congress and the president might have cooperated in this regard; cabinet members might have been subject to impeachment; or decisions might fall to the president alone—Washington established a system in which the president has the sole power to nominate, appoint, and remove members from the cabinet and other federal posts, while Congress has the right to approve or disprove of the president's nominations.

Washington's first appointment, to a position in the customs department, was rejected by Congress, who issued a statement that future appointments would require face-to-face meetings. Washington rejected this and was able to get his way. By claiming sole right of dismissal, Washington established that the officers of the federal government under the executive branch are not independent and are not under the authority of Congress but serve at the will of the president alone.

Finally, Washington was the first and only president who did not take part in what was then called "factionalism," now generally known as "partisanship" or "party politics." He was not a member of a political party, as America had none, and he was, therefore, not limited by allegiance to a specific faction or by the goal of trying to advance other members of that faction. He refused to appoint any member who was openly against the establishment of the federal government, then known as "anti-Federalists," but, beyond this, he was open minded and unafraid of opposing views. His choices for the nation's first Supreme Court came from six different states and represented a spectrum of political views, which is far different than the highly partisan nominations characteristic of most presidents in the modern era. For his cabinet, he chose men he called "first Characters," meaning those already holding positions of importance who had strong qualifications, but he did not seek to create a cabinet of unified political views. This was a bold strategy more in keeping with parliamentary politics than the now familiar American system, and held both advantages and disadvantages. One advantage was that Washington's cabinet was able to provide him with diverse views and opinions. A disadvantage was that his cabinet was quarrelsome and given to internal division. Washington's Secretary of the Treasury, Alexander Hamilton, so bitterly disagreed with and disliked Washington's Secretary of State, Thomas Jefferson, that the cabinet rarely met together to avoid angry clashes between the two.[13]

Washington valued this diversity of opinion and was perhaps one of the only U.S. presidents to emphasize the idea that the president is intended to represent all the people of the United States, not only those who

agreed with him politically. When Washington's second term ended, he willingly relinquished the presidency and, in his farewell address, he spoke out against the dangers he perceived in the "factionalization" of the nation's political environment.

WASHINGTON'S FAREWELL ADDRESS
1796
Source Document Excerpt

Friends and Citizens:

The period for a new election of a citizen to administer the executive government of the United States being not far distant, and the time actually arrived when your thoughts must be employed in designating the person who is to be clothed with that important trust, it appears to me proper, especially as it may conduce to a more distinct expression of the public voice, that I should now apprise you of the resolution I have formed, to decline being considered among the number of those out of whom a choice is to be made.

I beg you, at the same time, to do me the justice to be assured that this resolution has not been taken without a strict regard to all the considerations appertaining to the relation which binds a dutiful citizen to his country; and that in withdrawing the tender of service, which silence in my situation might imply, I am influenced by no diminution of zeal for your future interest, no deficiency of grateful respect for your past kindness, but am supported by a full conviction that the step is compatible with both.

The acceptance of, and continuance hitherto in, the office to which your suffrages have twice called me have been a uniform sacrifice of inclination to the opinion of duty and to a deference for what appeared to be your desire. I constantly hoped that it would have been much earlier in my power, consistently with motives which I was not at liberty to disregard, to return to that retirement from which I had been reluctantly drawn. The strength of my inclination to do this, previous to the last election, had even led to the preparation of an address to declare it to you; but mature reflection on the then perplexed and critical posture of our affairs with foreign nations, and the unanimous advice of persons entitled to my confidence, impelled me to abandon the idea.

We The People

Washington's Farewell Address
continued

I rejoice that the state of your concerns, external as well as internal, no longer renders the pursuit of inclination incompatible with the sentiment of duty or propriety, and am persuaded, whatever partiality may be retained for my services, that, in the present circumstances of our country, you will not disapprove my determination to retire.

. . .

Here, perhaps, I ought to stop. But a solicitude for your welfare, which cannot end but with my life, and the apprehension of danger, natural to that solicitude, urge me, on an occasion like the present, to offer to your solemn contemplation, and to recommend to your frequent review, some sentiments which are the result of much reflection, of no inconsiderable observation, and which appear to me all-important to the permanency of your felicity as a people. These will be offered to you with the more freedom, as you can only see in them the disinterested warnings of a parting friend, who can possibly have no personal motive to bias his counsel. Nor can I forget, as an encouragement to it, your indulgent reception of my sentiments on a former and not dissimilar occasion.

Interwoven as is the love of liberty with every ligament of your hearts, no recommendation of mine is necessary to fortify or confirm the attachment.

The unity of government which constitutes you one people is also now dear to you. It is justly so, for it is a main pillar in the edifice of your real independence, the support of your tranquility at home, your peace abroad; of your safety; of your prosperity; of that very liberty which you so highly prize. But as it is easy to foresee that, from different causes and from different quarters, much pains will be taken, many artifices employed to weaken in your minds the conviction of this truth; as this is the point in your political fortress against which the batteries of internal and external enemies will be most constantly and actively (though often covertly and insidiously) directed, it is of infinite moment that you should properly estimate the immense value of your national union to your collective and individual happiness; that you should cherish a cordial, habitual, and immovable attachment to it; accustoming yourselves to think and speak of it as of the palladium of your political safety and prosperity; watching for its preservation with jealous anxiety; discountenancing whatever may suggest even a suspicion that it can in any event be abandoned; and indignantly frowning upon the first dawning of every attempt to alienate

We the People

continued

any portion of our country from the rest, or to enfeeble the sacred ties which now link together the various parts.

For this you have every inducement of sympathy and interest. Citizens, by birth or choice, of a common country, that country has a right to concentrate your affections. The name of American, which belongs to you in your national capacity, must always exalt the just pride of patriotism more than any appellation derived from local discriminations. With slight shades of difference, you have the same religion, manners, habits, and political principles. You have in a common cause fought and triumphed together; the independence and liberty you possess are the work of joint counsels, and joint efforts of common dangers, sufferings, and successes.

But these considerations, however powerfully they address themselves to your sensibility, are greatly outweighed by those which apply more immediately to your interest. Here every portion of our country finds the most commanding motives for carefully guarding and preserving the union of the whole.

. . .

In contemplating the causes which may disturb our Union, it occurs as matter of serious concern that any ground should have been furnished for characterizing parties by geographical discriminations, Northern and Southern, Atlantic and Western; whence designing men may endeavor to excite a belief that there is a real difference of local interests and views. One of the expedients of party to acquire influence within particular districts is to misrepresent the opinions and aims of other districts. You cannot shield yourselves too much against the jealousies and heartburnings which spring from these misrepresentations; they tend to render alien to each other those who ought to be bound together by fraternal affection. The inhabitants of our Western country have lately had a useful lesson on this head; they have seen, in the negotiation by the Executive, and in the unanimous ratification by the Senate, of the treaty with Spain, and in the universal satisfaction at that event, throughout the United States, a decisive proof how unfounded were the suspicions propagated among them of a policy in the General Government and in the Atlantic States unfriendly to their interests in regard to the Mississippi; they have been witnesses to the formation of two treaties, that with Great Britain, and that with Spain, which secure to them everything they could desire, in respect to our foreign relations, towards confirming their prosperity. Will it not be their wisdom

Washington's Farewell Address
continued

to rely for the preservation of these advantages on the Union by which they were procured? Will they not henceforth be deaf to those advisers, if such there are, who would sever them from their brethren and connect them with aliens?

To the efficacy and permanency of your Union, a government for the whole is indispensable. No alliance, however strict, between the parts can be an adequate substitute; they must inevitably experience the infractions and interruptions which all alliances in all times have experienced. Sensible of this momentous truth, you have improved upon your first essay, by the adoption of a constitution of government better calculated than your former for an intimate union, and for the efficacious management of your common concerns. This government, the offspring of our own choice, uninfluenced and unawed, adopted upon full investigation and mature deliberation, completely free in its principles, in the distribution of its powers, uniting security with energy, and containing within itself a provision for its own amendment, has a just claim to your confidence and your support. Respect for its authority, compliance with its laws, acquiescence in its measures, are duties enjoined by the fundamental maxims of true liberty. The basis of our political systems is the right of the people to make and to alter their constitutions of government. But the Constitution which at any time exists, till changed by an explicit and authentic act of the whole people, is sacredly obligatory upon all. The very idea of the power and the right of the people to establish government presupposes the duty of every individual to obey the established government.

All obstructions to the execution of the laws, all combinations and associations, under whatever plausible character, with the real design to direct, control, counteract, or awe the regular deliberation and action of the constituted authorities, are destructive of this fundamental principle, and of fatal tendency. They serve to organize faction, to give it an artificial and extraordinary force; to put, in the place of the delegated will of the nation the will of a party, often a small but artful and enterprising minority of the community; and, according to the alternate triumphs of different parties, to make the public administration the mirror of the ill-concerted and incongruous projects of faction, rather than the organ of consistent and wholesome plans digested by common counsels and modified by mutual interests.

continued

However combinations or associations of the above description may now and then answer popular ends, they are likely, in the course of time and things, to become potent engines, by which cunning, ambitious, and unprincipled men will be enabled to subvert the power of the people and to usurp for themselves the reins of government, destroying afterwards the very engines which have lifted them to unjust dominion.

Towards the preservation of your government, and the permanency of your present happy state, it is requisite, not only that you steadily discountenance irregular oppositions to its acknowledged authority, but also that you resist with care the spirit of innovation upon its principles, however specious the pretexts. One method of assault may be to effect, in the forms of the Constitution, alterations which will impair the energy of the system, and thus to undermine what cannot be directly overthrown. In all the changes to which you may be invited, remember that time and habit are at least as necessary to fix the true character of governments as of other human institutions; that experience is the surest standard by which to test the real tendency of the existing constitution of a country; that facility in changes, upon the credit of mere hypothesis and opinion, exposes to perpetual change, from the endless variety of hypothesis and opinion; and remember, especially, that for the efficient management of your common interests, in a country so extensive as ours, a government of as much vigor as is consistent with the perfect security of liberty is indispensable. Liberty itself will find in such a government, with powers properly distributed and adjusted, its surest guardian. It is, indeed, little else than a name, where the government is too feeble to withstand the enterprises of faction, to confine each member of the society within the limits prescribed by the laws, and to maintain all in the secure and tranquil enjoyment of the rights of person and property.

I have already intimated to you the danger of parties in the State, with particular reference to the founding of them on geographical discriminations. Let me now take a more comprehensive view, and warn you in the most solemn manner against the baneful effects of the spirit of party generally.

This spirit, unfortunately, is inseparable from our nature, having its root in the strongest passions of the human mind. It exists under different shapes in all governments, more or less stifled, controlled, or repressed; but, in those of the popular form, it is seen in its greatest rankness, and is truly their worst enemy.

Washington's Farewell Address
continued

The alternate domination of one faction over another, sharpened by the spirit of revenge, natural to party dissension, which in different ages and countries has perpetrated the most horrid enormities, is itself a frightful despotism. But this leads at length to a more formal and permanent despotism. The disorders and miseries which result gradually incline the minds of men to seek security and repose in the absolute power of an individual; and sooner or later the chief of some prevailing faction, more able or more fortunate than his competitors, turns this disposition to the purposes of his own elevation, on the ruins of public liberty.

Without looking forward to an extremity of this kind (which nevertheless ought not to be entirely out of sight), the common and continual mischiefs of the spirit of party are sufficient to make it the interest and duty of a wise people to discourage and restrain it.

It serves always to distract the public councils and enfeeble the public administration. It agitates the community with ill-founded jealousies and false alarms, kindles the animosity of one part against another, foments occasionally riot and insurrection. It opens the door to foreign influence and corruption, which finds a facilitated access to the government itself through the channels of party passions. Thus the policy and the will of one country are subjected to the policy and will of another.

There is an opinion that parties in free countries are useful checks upon the administration of the government and serve to keep alive the spirit of liberty. This within certain limits is probably true; and in governments of a monarchical cast, patriotism may look with indulgence, if not with favor, upon the spirit of party. But in those of the popular character, in governments purely elective, it is a spirit not to be encouraged. From their natural tendency, it is certain there will always be enough of that spirit for every salutary purpose. And there being constant danger of excess, the effort ought to be by force of public opinion, to mitigate and assuage it. A fire not to be quenched, it demands a uniform vigilance to prevent its bursting into a flame, lest, instead of warming, it should consume.

It is important, likewise, that the habits of thinking in a free country should inspire caution in those entrusted with its administration, to confine themselves within their respective constitutional spheres, avoiding in the exercise of the powers of one department to encroach upon

continued

another. The spirit of encroachment tends to consolidate the powers of all the departments in one, and thus to create, whatever the form of government, a real despotism. A just estimate of that love of power, and proneness to abuse it, which predominates in the human heart, is sufficient to satisfy us of the truth of this position. The necessity of reciprocal checks in the exercise of political power, by dividing and distributing it into different depositaries, and constituting each the guardian of the public weal against invasions by the others, has been evinced by experiments ancient and modern; some of them in our country and under our own eyes. To preserve them must be as necessary as to institute them. If, in the opinion of the people, the distribution or modification of the constitutional powers be in any particular wrong, let it be corrected by an amendment in the way which the Constitution designates. But let there be no change by usurpation; for though this, in one instance, may be the instrument of good, it is the customary weapon by which free governments are destroyed. The precedent must always greatly overbalance in permanent evil any partial or transient benefit, which the use can at any time yield.

. . .

Observe good faith and justice towards all nations; cultivate peace and harmony with all. Religion and morality enjoin this conduct; and can it be, that good policy does not equally enjoin it—It will be worthy of a free, enlightened, and at no distant period, a great nation, to give to mankind the magnanimous and too novel example of a people always guided by an exalted justice and benevolence. Who can doubt that, in the course of time and things, the fruits of such a plan would richly repay any temporary advantages which might be lost by a steady adherence to it? Can it be that Providence has not connected the permanent felicity of a nation with its virtue? The experiment, at least, is recommended by every sentiment which ennobles human nature. Alas! is it rendered impossible by its vices?

. . .

Against the insidious wiles of foreign influence (I conjure you to believe me, fellow-citizens) the jealousy of a free people ought to be constantly awake, since history and experience prove that foreign influence is one of the most baneful foes of republican government. But that jealousy to be useful must be impartial; else it becomes the instrument of the very influence to be avoided, instead of a defense against it. Excessive partiality for one foreign nation and excessive dislike of another cause those whom they actuate to see danger only on one side, and serve

Washington's Farewell Address
continued

to veil and even second the arts of influence on the other. Real patriots who may resist the intrigues of the favorite are liable to become suspected and odious, while its tools and dupes usurp the applause and confidence of the people, to surrender their interests.

The great rule of conduct for us in regard to foreign nations is in extending our commercial relations, to have with them as little political connection as possible. So far as we have already formed engagements, let them be fulfilled with perfect good faith. Here let us stop. Europe has a set of primary interests which to us have none; or a very remote relation. Hence she must be engaged in frequent controversies, the causes of which are essentially foreign to our concerns. Hence, therefore, it must be unwise in us to implicate ourselves by artificial ties in the ordinary vicissitudes of her politics, or the ordinary combinations and collisions of her friendships or enmities.

Our detached and distant situation invites and enables us to pursue a different course. If we remain one people under an efficient government, the period is not far off when we may defy material injury from external annoyance; when we may take such an attitude as will cause the neutrality we may at any time resolve upon to be scrupulously respected; when belligerent nations, under the impossibility of making acquisitions upon us, will not lightly hazard the giving us provocation; when we may choose peace or war, as our interest, guided by justice, shall counsel.

Why forego the advantages of so peculiar a situation? Why quit our own to stand upon foreign ground? Why, by interweaving our destiny with that of any part of Europe, entangle our peace and prosperity in the toils of European ambition, rivalship, interest, humor or caprice?

It is our true policy to steer clear of permanent alliances with any portion of the foreign world; so far, I mean, as we are now at liberty to do it; for let me not be understood as capable of patronizing infidelity to existing engagements. I hold the maxim no less applicable to public than to private affairs, that honesty is always the best policy. I repeat it, therefore, let those engagements be observed in their genuine sense. But, in my opinion, it is unnecessary and would be unwise to extend them.

Taking care always to keep ourselves by suitable establishments on a respectable defensive posture, we may safely trust to temporary alliances for extraordinary emergencies.

continued

Harmony, liberal intercourse with all nations, are recommended by policy, humanity, and interest. But even our commercial policy should hold an equal and impartial hand; neither seeking nor granting exclusive favors or preferences; consulting the natural course of things; diffusing and diversifying by gentle means the streams of commerce, but forcing nothing; establishing (with powers so disposed, in order to give trade a stable course, to define the rights of our merchants, and to enable the government to support them) conventional rules of intercourse, the best that present circumstances and mutual opinion will permit, but temporary, and liable to be from time to time abandoned or varied, as experience and circumstances shall dictate; constantly keeping in view that it is folly in one nation to look for disinterested favors from another; that it must pay with a portion of its independence for whatever it may accept under that character; that, by such acceptance, it may place itself in the condition of having given equivalents for nominal favors, and yet of being reproached with ingratitude for not giving more. There can be no greater error than to expect or calculate upon real favors from nation to nation. It is an illusion, which experience must cure, which a just pride ought to discard.

. . .

With me a predominant motive has been to endeavor to gain time to our country to settle and mature its yet recent institutions, and to progress without interruption to that degree of strength and consistency which is necessary to give it, humanly speaking, the command of its own fortunes.

Though, in reviewing the incidents of my administration, I am unconscious of intentional error, I am nevertheless too sensible of my defects not to think it probable that I may have committed many errors. Whatever they may be, I fervently beseech the Almighty to avert or mitigate the evils to which they may tend. I shall also carry with me the hope that my country will never cease to view them with indulgence; and that, after forty five years of my life dedicated to its service with an upright zeal, the faults of incompetent abilities will be consigned to oblivion, as myself must soon be to the mansions of rest.

Relying on its kindness in this as in other things, and actuated by that fervent love towards it, which is so natural to a man who views in it the native soil of himself and his progenitors for several generations, I anticipate with pleasing expectation that retreat in which I promise myself to realize, without alloy, the sweet

We The People

Washington's Farewell Address
continued

enjoyment of partaking, in the midst of my fellow-citizens, the benign influence of good laws under a free government, the ever-favorite object of my heart, and the happy reward, as I trust, of our mutual cares, labors, and dangers.[14]

Washington's warning was not heeded and the evils of factionalization intensified into the twenty-first century, when the ideological gulf between the parties has become the most extreme in history.

Man of Myth and Legend

Washington has become perhaps the most widely mythologized figure in American history. There has been a persistent desire among Americans to claim the legacy of Washington as their own, and so politicians have reinvented the man and reinterpreted his actions to service their view of American culture and society. Conservatives have argued that Washington was one of them, justifying this with references to Washington's support for military authority and state's rights, while progressives have likewise attributed liberal motives to many of Washington's behaviors. Among the many myths are a whole host of urban legends, some designed to vilify Washington and others designed to elevate his memory. It has been falsely claimed that Washington smoked marijuana, that he had children out of wedlock, that he was a heavy drinker, that he and his wife had an open marriage. Most of these myths receive little attention, but there are some persistent myths that have been repeated again and again by historians, beginning with Washington's first biographers.

It has been widely believed, for instance, that Washington was so conspicuously honest that he confessed to chopping down his father's apple tree, stating, "I cannot tell a lie . . .I did cut it with my hatchet." It is then typically said that Washington's father embraced him and stated that his honesty was worth a thousand trees. This myth was invented by Mason Locke Weems, a minister and bookseller who became the first to publish a biography of Washington and thus the first American presidential biographer.[a] Weems, a charlatan interested only in profiting off of the hunger for Washington lore, filled his book with many half-truths and entirely fabricated stories meant to portray Washington as a towering, mythological figure. The story of Washington's compulsive honesty became the most enduring myth of his legacy.[b]

Other myths about Washington are less impactful, and it is uncertain how some of them originated. For instance, the myth that Washington had wooden dentures has become widespread, though historians note that his false teeth, though they may have had a wooden complexion, were made of human and possibly animal teeth, ivory, lead-tin, copper, and silver. Another famous legend says that young Washington once skipped a silver dollar across the Potomac River, an impossible feat as the river is over a mile wide at Mount Vernon, and there were no silver dollars in existence in Washington's youth. This myth is typically used, like the cherry tree myth, to demonstrate Washington's heroic perfection, but is a transformation of a story told by Washington's step-son, George Washington Parke Custis, in which his step-father hurled a piece of slate across the much narrower Rappahannock River.[c]

Another enduring myth of Washington was that he was from a working-class family and pulled himself up from proverbial rags to literal riches. Although it is true that Washington's family suffered hardship, the Washingtons were not truly a working-class family. Washington was born into a family of "gentlemen planters," a sort of farming aristocracy comparable with the upper class of the modern world. The Washington family owned slaves, a luxury not available to most in the lower classes. Washington inherited eleven slaves after his father's death, and then inherited an additional twenty-four slaves from his half-brother Lawrence in 1754. Another twelve slaves came to Washington when he married Martha Dandridge Custis in 1759, as well as part interest in the estate of Daniel Park Custis, Martha Custis's former husband, which included 300 slaves and plantations in six counties. By 1786, Washington owned some 216 slaves.[d]

Works Used

a. "Biography of George Washington." *Mount Vernon.* 2019. www.mountvernon.org/george-washington/biography/.

b. Richardson, Jay. "Cherry Tree Myth." *Mount Vernon.* 2019. www.mountvernon.org/library/digitalhistory/digital-encyclopedia/article/cherry-tree-myth/.

c. "Ten Common Misconceptions About George Washington." *Mount Vernon.* 2019. www.mountvernon.org/george-washington/facts/ten-misconceptions-about-washington/.

d. "Slavery and George Washington." *Mount Vernon.* 2019. www.mountvernon.org/george-washington/biography/.

Despite his faults, however, Washington holds a unique place among American presidents. A 2012 poll found that a full 89 percent of Americans viewed George Washington as America's best president, followed by Abraham Lincoln, Thomas Jefferson, Teddy Roosevelt, John Adams, Harry Truman, Dwight Eisenhower, John F. Kennedy, John Quincy Adams, and Franklin D. Roosevelt. Of the other presidents, only John F. Kennedy, Jefferson and Lincoln have popularity ratings over 70 percent, and only Lincoln comes close to knocking Washington from the No. 1 spot.[15] In other polls, Lincoln has proven slightly more popular, but Washington and Lincoln are nearly always tied in the first and second positions.

As the nation's first president, first commander in chief, first head of state, and first head of government, Washington paved the way for all presidents who have come since. His legacy is outsized and often misinterpreted, but he holds a place of unique honor and importance to all who value the underlying ideals that continue to fuel the American experiment.

CONCLUSION

George Washington holds a unique place in American history as our first president. His approach to the office, and the power it holds, paved the way for all presidents who followed. He led the country as president much like he led his troops as general in the American Revolution. Washington's role in developing the U.S. Constitution showed that he was in favor of the president being less a figurehead and more a powerful leader. He was neither a bureaucrat, nor a partisan player, but believed in a diverse cabinet of men with experience that would be of value to his administration—a good example for those to follow. However, as the following chapter reveals, Washington's vice president, John Adams, as America's second president, was a bureaucrat who favored running the country like the British monarchy he was used to—including being president for life. While that didn't happen, partisan politics did.

DISCUSSION QUESTIONS

- How did George Washington's role in the American Revolution influence his role as president?
- Do you think military experience is valuable for a president? Why or why not?
- Does the Constitution give too much power to the president? Why or why not?
- Were any foreign leaders used as a model for presidential power? Who?
- How much influence did Washington's style have over the presidents who came after him?

Works Used

Cain, Áine. "29 American Presidents Who Served in the Military." *Business Insider*. 19 Feb. 2018. www.businessinsider.com/american-presidents-who-served-in-the-military-2016-6.

Chapman, Ben. "Americans Have Forgotten the Story of Cincinnatus." *Medium*. 25 June 2018. medium.com/@Ben_Chapman/americans-have-forgotten-the-story-of-cincinnatus-b49728164ce1.

Chernow, Ron. *Washington: A Life*. New York: Penguin, 2010.

From George Washington to Lewis Nicola,22 May 1782, *Founders Online*. National Archives. founders.archives.gov/documents/Washington/99-01-02-08501.

Geist, Christopher. "George Washington and the Evolution of the American Commander in Chief." *CW Journal*. Colonial Williamsburg. Summer 2012. www.history.org/foundation/journal/summer12/george.cfm.

"George Washington." *White House*. 2006. www.whitehouse.gov/about-the-white-house/presidents/george-washington/.

Haggard, Robert F. "The Nicola Affair: Lewis Nicola, George Washington, and American Military Discontent during the Revolutionary War." *Proceedings of the American Philosophical Society*, vol. 146, no 2, (June 2002), pp. 139–69. *JSTOR*, www.jstor.org/stable/1558199.

Hoock, Holger. *Scars of Independence: America's Violent Birth*. New York: Crown, 2017.

McDonald, Forrest. "Washington, George." *American National Biography*. Feb. 2000. www.anb.org/view/10.1093/anb/9780198606697.001.0001/anb-9780198606697-e-0200332.

"Surveying Career." *Mount Vernon*. 2019. /www.mountvernon.org/george-washington/washingtons-youth/surveying/.

"To George Washington from Lewis Nicola, 22 May 1782." *Founders Online*. National Archives. founders.archives.gov/?q=nicola%2C%20lewis&s=1111311111&sa=&r=51&sr=.

Washington, George. "Letter of the President of the Federal Convention, Dated September 17, 1787, to the President of Congress, Transmitting the Constitution." *Avalon Project*. Yale Law School. 2008. avalon.law.yale.edu/18th_century/translet.asp.

Washington, George. "Washington's Farewell Address 1796." *Avalon*. Yale Law School. 2008. avalon.law.yale.edu/18th_century/washing.asp.

"Washington's Inaugural Address of 1789." *Archives*. National Archives and Records Administration. 2019. www.archives.gov/exhibits/american_originals/inaugtxt.html.

Weinger, Mackenzie. "Poll: George Washington Still Tops." *Politico*. 17 Feb. 2012. www.politico.com/story/2012/02/poll-george-washington-still-tops-073032.

Yoo, John. "George Washington and the Executive Power." *University of St. Thomas Journal of Law and Public Policy*, vol 5, no 1, 2010–2011. scholarship.law.berkeley.edu/cgi/viewcontent.cgi?article=2272&context=facpubs.

John Adams (1797–1801)

Introduction

John Adams was the nation's first vice president and the nation's second president. A respected statesman and chief architect of the move toward independence, he thought himself the natural choice to follow in George Washington's footprints. Adams felt that wealth and birth determined privilege, and that privilege led to greater experience and exposure, which in turn led to more capable leaders. He was sympathetic to the kind of government that ruled England, and wanted to continue, to a large degree, that tradition. He advocated for both a hereditary Senate, in which members would inherit office from their forebears, and for a president-for-life system. Adams's ties to the tradition of English royalty included the use of titles for the president, and the support of a new national capital.

Regarding his use of presidential power, he was less forceful than Washington, who ran the government like the military. Adams was a bureaucratic leader, unable to capture popular support. He signed into law the Alien and Sedition Acts, which, although lasting for only a short period, granted the president power to deport any alien deemed a threat to national security, and the power to restrict freedom of aliens from an enemy country. The acts also made it illegal to oppose laws passed by the federal government or to publish criticism of the government. These arguably despotic powers did not have popular support, and were used by the Adams administration to censure and interfere with Democratic-Republican efforts to gain public support. Journalists sympathetic to the Democratic-Republicans and critical of the Federalists were arrested and their publications confiscated and censured.

Topics covered in this chapter include:

- John Adams transition from America's first vice president to second president
- Influence of the British monarchy
- Adams as a leader of the Federalist Party
- Thomas Jefferson and the Democratic-Republican Party
- XYZ Affair
- Alien and Sedition Acts
- Abigail Adams
- Alexander Hamilton's opinion of John Adams

This Chapter Discusses the Following Source Documents:
Instructions Adopted by the Braintree Town Meeting, September 24, 1765
From Thomas Jefferson to James Sullivan, February 9, 1797
Letter from Alexander Hamilton, Concerning the Public Conduct and Character of President John Adams, October 24, 1800

We the People

The Natural Aristocracy
John Adams (1797–1801)

John Adams was the nation's first vice president, serving under George Washington for two terms. He was among the most respected statesmen in the country, one of the chief architects of the independence movement, and considered himself the natural choice to lead the country after Washington. When the time came for the election, however, Adams found himself facing stiff competition in the form of rival candidate Thomas Jefferson and his newly formed political party, the Democratic-Republicans. This was the first contested election in American history and began the era of party politics that continues to the present day. Along the way, the actions of Adams stretched the limits of presidential authority and brought about new controversies regarding how a president may use executive powers.

Patriot Philosopher

Adams was born in the Massachusetts Bay Colony in 1735, the fifth generation of his American-born family who was wealthy by modern standards, but not members of the most powerful elite. They were Puritans and socially conservative. As was their tradition, the eldest son was sent to the best college that his family could afford, and John was sent to Harvard College and then pursued a career in law. Adams married Abigail Smith in 1764, and the following year they had their first child, Abigail "Nabby" Adams, followed shortly by a son, John Quincy, who would go on to follow in his father's political footsteps.[1]

Adams was a student of political philosophy and became a fervent supporter of independence from the very first stirrings of the movement. He penned strong criticisms of British policies, especially with regard to law and taxation. Among his most famous was "The Braintree Instructions," a document written for a town meeting in Braintree, Massachusetts, for the Massachusetts General Court. In this letter, Adams describes the new taxes levied by Britain as unconstitutional under the American charter:

Federalist president John Adams, by Gilbert Stuart, via Wikimedia.

INSTRUCTIONS ADOPTED BY THE BRAINTREE TOWN MEETING
September 24, 1765
Source Document Excerpt

We further apprehend this Tax to be unconstitutional, By the great Charter no americament shall be assessed but by the oath of Honest and Lawfull men of the Vicinage. And by the Same Charter no Freeman shall be taken or imprisoned or be disseised of his Freehold or Liberties or Free Customs nor passed upon nor Condemned but by Lawfull Judgment of his Peers or by the Law of the Land: And we have Always understood it to be a grand and fundamental principal of the British Constitution that no Freeman should be Subjected to any Tax to which he has not given his own Consent in person or by proxy. And the maxims of the Law as we have Constantly Received them are to the Same Effect that no Freeman can be Seperated from his property but by his own act or Fault. We take it clearly therefore to be inconsistant with the Spirit of the Common Law and of the Essential Fundamentall principles of the British Constitution that we should be Subjected to any Tax imposed by the British Parliament because we are not Represented in that assembly in any sense unless it be by a Fiction of Law as insensible in Theory as it would be Injurious in Fact if so heavy a Taxation should be grounded on it.[2]

This document laid out one of the fundamental claims of American revolutionaries, that they had been subject to "taxation without representation," and this became a rallying cry of the revolutionary movement.

In 1774, Adams was chosen as a representative from Massachusetts to the First Continental Congress, held in Philadelphia's Carpenter's Hall from September 5 to October 26 of that year. This meeting of revolutionary leaders was a response to the "Intolerable Acts," a new set of oppressive regulations handed down by the British monarchy. Approximately one-third of the representatives were lawyers, and the rest were mostly plantation gentry like George Washington. The delegates were, in general, divided into those who wanted to work out the colonies' issues with England and those who sought the more radical path of Independence.

By 1775, it was clear that the conflict with England would not be resolved through negotiation alone. The Continental Congress voted to defy English orders, and Washington was selected to lead the continental armies. Adams, and his close friend Thomas Jefferson, wrote and promoted the Declaration of Independence, signed on July 4th of 1776. Adams meanwhile began sketching ideas for the new independent government, and it was he who first conceived of the three-branch system with duties shared between the executive, judicial, and legislative branches and a system of "checks and balances" to prevent any one of the three branches from overstepping its authority. Following Washington's defeat of the British at Yorktown, Adams also wrote the Massachusetts Constitution of 1780, which became an important model for the U.S. Constitution and contained his three-branch government system. Adams also played a major role in helping to negotiate the U.S. Constitution at the September 1787 Constitutional Convention in Philadelphia, where George Washington, the hero of the American Revolution, presided over 55 delegates in an attempt to reform the 1777 Articles of Confederation.[3] It was eventually decided that the articles were unsalvageable, and they were discarded entirely and replaced with the U.S. Constitution which was based on Adams's design and written largely by James Madison and Thomas Jefferson.

Constitutional Powers

Friends (and rivals) John Adams and Thomas Jefferson ultimately became the leaders of America's first two political parties, the Federalists and Democratic-Republicans, respectively. This helped to define the powers and traditions of the presidency after George Washington's historic first two terms. With Adams serving as the nation's second president, and Jefferson as the third, both men, and their respective ideologies, left an impact on the nation and the presidential office.

Both Jefferson and Adams believed that there were individuals of high talents and virtues who were better suited to lead. Both men referred to

this as a "natural aristocracy," but they defined it differently. Jefferson saw a natural division in skill and intelligence among humanity and that it was the job of government to identify and reward talent. He wanted America to become a "meritocracy," a government in which leadership is afforded to those who demonstrate merit. Adams surmised that the structure of society and the nature of humanity made it near impossible to select individuals for their virtue and talent because starting conditions gave some individuals a better chance to succeed, to achieve education, and become members of the elite. Wealth and birth determined privilege, and privilege led to greater experience and exposure.[4] Adams was, therefore, more sympathetic to the kind of aristocracy that existed in England, one in which familial status and wealth governed one's access to leadership, because he believed that that same privilege would lead to more capable leaders. Both Adams and Jefferson were members of the elite educated class. Adams believed that what Jefferson called "artificial aristocracy," the aristocracy of wealth and class, was nothing more than a reflection of an underlying "natural aristocracy." Adams wanted to continue the English aristocratic system, though under a different guise.[5]

In a February 1797 letter written by Thomas Jefferson to James Sullivan, Jefferson explains how the U.S. Republican system is a democracy with monarchic characteristics:

FROM THOMAS JEFFERSON TO JAMES SULLIVAN
February 9, 1797
Source Document Excerpt

To James Sullivan

"Where a constitution, like ours, wears a mixed aspect of monarchy and republicanism, it's citizens will naturally divide into two classes of sentiment, according as their tone of body or mind, their habits, connections, and callings induce them to wish to strengthen either the monarchical or the republican features of the constitution. Some will consider it as an elective monarchy which had better be made hereditary, and therefore endeavor to lead towards that all the forms and principles of it's administration. Others will [view it] as an energetic republic, turning in all it's points on the pivot of free and frequent elect[ions].[6]

Adams was decidedly more "monarchist" in his tendencies and advocated for a hereditary senate, in which members would inherit office from their forbearers. He also advocated for a "president for life" system that would have made the presidency very much closer to the English monarchy. For Adams and like-minded founders, the House of Representatives would have been the only branch of government actually formed by popular will. He viewed the Senate as the balance to this, with one house representing the masses and the other the natural aristocracy.

Professor of Law at the University of Virginia Saikrishna Bangalore Prakash, a prominent conservative ideologue, wrote in a 2015 article for the *Washington Post*, "Stop fighting it. America is a monarchy, and that's probably for the best," arguing that the founding fathers knew full well that they were creating a more or less regal office in the presidency, and that they did so intentionally so as to create a more powerful central government. This was why critics like Jefferson, Luther Martin of Maryland, and Virginian Patrick Henry objected so forcefully to the Constitution, seeing within it the seeds of permanent, institutionalized inequality. They were correct, and this inequality has remained, but it was not an accident or manipulation of the American ideal so much as an intentional design based on the belief of those like Adams that there were benefits in the hereditary transmission of wealth and privilege.[7]

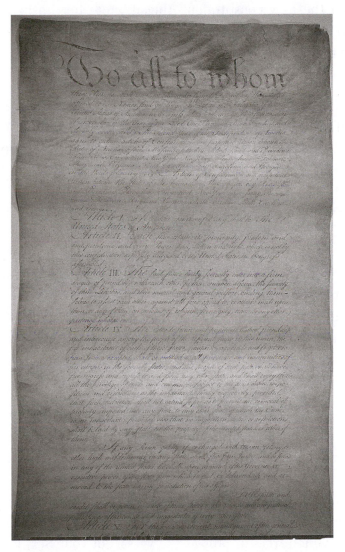

The Constitution was modeled after the Articles of Confederation. Via Wikimedia.

John Adams and his wife Abigail Adams had a close, loving relationship. Historians have learned a great deal about both from the lengthy correspondence between them whenever Adams's duties carried him away from their Massachusetts home. A remarkable and intelligent woman, Abigail's letters reveal a remarkably forward-thinking mind. While her husband was convening with the delegates of the states and working on the new constitution, Abigail wrote her husband a remarkable letter in which she raised the issue of women's rights decades before the topic would become mainstream:

March 31, 1776

> "Tho we felicitate ourselves, we sympathize with those who are trembling least the Lot of Boston should be theirs. But they cannot be in similar circumstances unless pusilanimity and cowardise should take possession of them. They have time and warning given them to see the Evil and shun it. —I long to hear that you have declared an independency—and by the way in the new Code of Laws which I suppose it will be necessary for you to make I desire you would Remember the Ladies, and be more generous and favourable to them than your ancestors. Do not put such unlimited power into the hands of the Husbands. Remember all Men would be tyrants if they could. If perticuliar care and attention is not paid to the Ladies we are determined to foment a Rebelion, and will not hold ourselves bound by any Laws in which we have no voice, or Representation.

> That your Sex are Naturally Tyrannical is a Truth so thoroughly established as to admit of no dispute, but such of you as wish to be happy willingly give up the harsh title of Master for the more tender and endearing one of Friend. Why then, not put it out of the power of the vicious and the Lawless to use us with cruelty and indignity with impunity. Men of Sense in all Ages abhor those customs which treat us only as the vassals of your Sex. Regard us

then as Beings placed by providence under your protection and in immitation of the Supreem Being make use of that power only for our happiness."

Adams was too much of a traditionalist to challenge the established hierarchy between the sexes, and there is no record that he ever raised the issue of women's rights during his political career. Abigail Adams was correct in her warning that women would ultimately "foment a rebellion" to win their legal agency and political rights. By the early 1900s, women organized the first picket of the White House and campaigned against the traditionalist legislators who'd long prevented the cause of women's rights. Though perhaps not a rebellion, the Women's Rights movement was one of the most transformative in history, a phenomenon that Abigail Adams predicted more than a century before women achieved equal rights.[a]

Works Used

a. "Letter from Abigail Adams to John Adams, 31 March—5 April 1776." *Massachusetts Historical Society*. Adams Family Papers. 2019. www.masshist.org/digitaladams/archive/doc?id=L17760331aa.

Abigail Adams, the surprisingly progressive wife of John Adams, by Benjamin Blyth, via Wikimedia.

To the Winner, the Spoils

Approaching America's first presidential election, in 1888, it was widely believed that it would be impossible to beat George Washington, whose universal acclaim made him the clear candidate both of the masses and the elite. The structure of presidential elections at this time was different than today. A host of candidates were nominated and each federal elector cast two votes. The person receiving the most votes became president, while the person receiving the second-highest number became vice president. Adams enjoyed broad support of the New Englanders who favored a strong aristocratic central government, while Alexander Hamilton stood as Adams's chief rival. In the lead-up to the election, Hamilton convinced several electors to withhold votes from Adams, and only to cast votes for Washington, arguing that this would ensure that Washington received a unanimous victory and would further cement the legitimacy of his leadership. When Adams received only 34 electoral votes to Washington's 69, he was disappointed and suspected foul play. He believed that the election system, as it was, would lead to civil war and "sedition," and over much of his career he continued to advocate for a "president-for-life" system.

Though he hadn't come close to beating Washington, Adams's 34 electoral votes made him vice president, and America's first "second in command." While Washington defined the role of the presidency, John Adams defined the vice-presidential office and, in many ways, his subordination to Washington established the traditional presidential authority over the vice president's office. Adams had a good relationship with Washington, but was rarely active in helping to steer policy. He did his best to fill the constitutional role proscribed to the vice president as "President of the Senate" and his fondness for monarchic tradition was evident in senate debates over how to address the new president. Most members of the House of Representatives felt that the title "George Washington: President of the United States" was sufficient, but Adams argued that an honorific title, such as "Your Excellency," was necessary to convey

to international dignitaries the importance of the office. Adams' frequent debates over Senate and House matters led to his being a controversial and much-despised figure, earning censure in the Senate for his habit of lecturing legislators.

The French Revolution, and the 1793 French declaration of war against Britain, changed the nature of politics and helped to create the seeds of America's first political parties, the Federalists represented by Adams and the Democratic-Republicans led largely by Jefferson. The emerging Democratic-Republican camp was sympathetic to revolutionary France, and celebrated their victories over former rival Britain, while Adams and the Federalists wished to remain loyal to Britain. Adams wrote a series of articles arguing that the French Revolution was destined to fail because they had abandoned the aristocratic institutions needed to preserve order and social stability and again warned that the United States needed to rely on its own "natural aristocracy" to avoid this same fate.[8] Washington despised the formation of political parties, but was aligned with the Federalist position of neutrality and so was supported by the Federalists through his second term.

The Federalists pushed to strengthen the alliance with Great Britain, and this resulted in the 1794 Jay Treaty, which settled some existing trade disputes. The treaty, however, failed to resolve more controversial diplomatic issues, such as the Canadian-Maine boundary dispute, unpaid debts owed to the United States by Britain, and controversial seizures of American ships by the British navy. Washington signed the treaty—though he knew that it was immensely unpopular among the American people—considering it necessary to secure peace with Britain and to give the United States time to prepare for a possible war.[9] The controversy over the Jay Treaty was the final straw in Washington's decision to retire at the end of his second term. Adams was the natural choice for succession, but a Federalist cadre led by Alexander Hamilton preferred Thomas

Pinckney, a former minister to Great Britain who'd proved easier for the Federalist hierarchy to control than Adams.

As he had in the 1788 election, Hamilton schemed against Adams in 1796, privately meeting with southern electors and convincing them to withhold votes from Adams so that Pinckney, the Federalist vice-presidential candidate, would become president by default. Hamilton had underestimated the appeal of rival Democratic-Republican candidates Thomas Jefferson and Aaron Burr, however, and had miscalculated the backlash from New England Federalists who still supported Adams. When New England electors realized that Hamilton had been scheming to influence the southern vote, they withheld their votes from Pinckney so that Adams would become president. The result was that the Federalists lost the vice-presidency altogether and nearly lost the presidency as well, with Adams winning the election by a margin of 71 electoral votes to Jefferson's 68. Adams would be president, but with his increasingly bitter rival Thomas Jefferson as his vice president rather than his fellow Federalist Pinckney, marking the first time that the nation would have a president and vice president from different parties.

In many ways, the 1798 election was the first partisan, and bitterly contested election in America, presaging the power struggles that have become characteristic of the nation's political environment. It was also the first election to see partisan mudslinging. Under the law of the era, candidates were prohibited from political campaigning, but Aaron Burr, Jefferson's running mate, ignored this directive. More egregious were the actions of Alexander Hamilton, whose use of false claims presaged modern partisan attacks. In 1796 Hamilton, using the pseudonym "Phocion," published an article claiming that Jefferson had run from British soldiers, making him less honorable than his "brave friend" Alexander Hamilton. More damaging, Hamilton claimed that Jefferson, if elected, had promised to free all the slaves, thereby inciting fear from wealthy Americans whose livelihoods depended on the industry. While Jefferson's allies frequently argued that Adams was a "monarchist" and an "elitist," claims not untrue, Hamilton's use of false claims was the start of a new, patently unethical dimension of American politics, one that has remained part of the American political system.[10]

A Brief Time in the Spotlight

As America's second president, Adams was unlikely to achieve the level of support and admiration that had been given his predecessor, whose mere status as the warrior of America's independence granted him unimagined status. Washington had won the presidency on the basis of his achievements, sacrifices for his country, and his personality; and he established a fundamental tradition in American politics, wherein the presidency is associated with a person and not the office, making it a position of personality rather than political capability. John Adams, the first bureaucrat and intellectual to occupy the office, did not enjoy the same level of support either from the public or within the aristocracy. Nevertheless, Adams' Federalists were certainly better connected than the rival Democratic-Republicans and were able to control not only the White House, but both houses of Congress as well, and the judiciary, which gave Adams the power to pass legislation at will.

Adams immediately faced a crisis in U.S. relations with France. The French Directorate (revolutionary government) had suspended relations and trade and had refused envoys from America. Adams was still committed to the cause of neutrality and so sent three commissioners, Charles Pinckney, Elbridge Gerry, and John Marshall, to negotiate with the French government. Meanwhile, Adams received authorization from Congress to raise and fund a militia for a potential war with France. When his envoys arrived in France, however, they were openly disrespected and were refused access to the French Foreign Minister Marquis de Talleyrand. The envoys were then approached by four representatives, Nicholas Hubbard (W), Jean Hottinguer (X), Pierre Bellamy (Y), and Lucien

Hauteval (Z), who presented themselves as intermediaries of Talleyrand's and offered to arrange a meeting with Talleyrand in return for a bribe and a substantial loan from America. When word of the incident reached Adams, he began preparations for war in earnest. The Democratic-Republicans demanded transparency, and Adams, therefore, released the correspondences from his envoys, but replaced the names of the French intermediaries with the letters X, Y, and Z. Later releases added Nicholas Hubbard's "W" to the story.

This incident, known as the "XYZ affair," led to an explosion of public outrage and panic. Jefferson and the Democratic-Republicans, who'd advocated protecting the American alliance with France, were painted by the Federalists as possible traitors, while the Federalists saw their fortunes rise significantly. Though Adams never asked Congress to officially declare war, the Federalist Congress approved of substantial expenditures to prepare for war, including a fleet of new frigate ships and a state-wide recruitment drive. Adams went so far as to call for George Washington to come out of retirement to once again lead the nation's forces into battle.[11] Though Talleyrand attempted to walk back his behavior, the Federalists wouldn't be easily satisfied. United States warships and armed merchant vessels began clearing French ships from the shipping lanes and engaged the French Naval fleet in the Caribbean.

Former Quaker minister and Philadelphia-based physician George Logan—a friend of Jefferson's, member of the Democratic-Republicans, and a future senator—was so opposed to what historians now call the "Quasi War" that he travelled to France to negotiate directly with the French government. Arriving in Paris in 1798, Logan was successful in meeting with Talleyrand and managed to convince the French government to lift its embargo against the United States and to release captive American ships and sailors. Logan returned with news of his success, but his actions inspired a partisan feud. Connecticut Federalist Roger Griswold proposed a law to "guard by law against the interference of

individuals in the negotiation of our Executive with the Government of foreign countries," informally known as the Logan Act, which made it illegal for an independent citizen to enter into negotiations with a foreign government. No one has been convicted on the basis of the law since, but it remains in effect and became controversial during the transition of Donald Trump to the presidency, when his administration officials may have violated the law in negotiations with Russia, when they were still considered private citizens.[12]

With the growing fear of war, many Federalists believed, or at least claimed to believe, that there were dangerous individuals in America who were loyal to France and, therefore, might act as spies. The hawks in the Federalist camp passed four separate laws, collectively known as the "Alien and Sedition Acts," which increased the period of residency for naturalization to fourteen years; authorized the president to deport any "alien" deemed dangerous to national security; granted the president the power to deport or restrict the freedom of any aliens from an enemy country; and made it illegal to oppose the laws passed by the federal government or to publish criticisms of the government.[13]

The Alien and Sedition acts lasted only for a brief period, but during its enactment granted the presidency nearly unfettered and arguably despotic powers. Adams and the Federalists used the acts for purely political purposes, by arresting, censuring, or in other ways interfering in Democratic-Republican efforts to gain popular support or to protest the policies of the Federalists. Journalists and publishers sympathetic to the Democratic-Republicans were arrested or had their publications confiscated and censored. Democratic-Republican politicians were threatened and, in some cases, arrested. Benjamin Franklin's grandson, Benjamin Franklin Bache, editor and publisher of the *Philadelphia Aurora*, was perhaps the most famous target of the Sedition Act. Bache had been one of the earliest and strongest critics of the Federalists and George Washington's

administration. He was arrested in June of 1798 for "libel" after publishing articles critical of Adams's government, but died of yellow fever that September before he was scheduled to appear in court.[14]

In the years that followed, legislative debate over the Alien and Sedition Acts helped inspire some of the earliest debates about speech and the free press, issues still controversial and relevant in the modern world. For Adams, the passage of the Alien and Sedition Acts was a mistake and a blow to his presidency. Hundreds of citizens wrote letters accusing him of "monarchism" and of assaulting free speech and the free press. Adams was reluctant to sign the acts into law, fearing such a backlash, and his concerns proved prescient. The Alien and Sedition Acts largely erased the boost in approval Adams had enjoyed after aggressively announcing the nation's preparation for war.

Ultimately, it was internal conflict that damaged Adams's career more than anything else. Though the war, or the threat of war, had been good for the Federalists, seemingly providing justification for the kind of semi-authoritarian government they favored, Adams knew that a war with France would provide little legitimate benefit, and so he decided to place his country before his political party, something that the more hawkish and ambitious Federalists, like Hamilton, were unwilling to do. A month after the United States scored its first major victory against France, capturing the French ship *L'Insurgente* off the coast of St. Kitts Island, Adams took the diplomatic route and on March 30, dispatched new envoys to Paris seeking a new peace agreement, which was completed by July, though minor skirmishes at sea continued for several years. Hamilton and other Federalists were furious with Adams, and Hamilton campaigned against him in the 1800 election. In his most aggressive attack, Hamilton published a long letter criticizing Adams's personal character and performance:

LETTER FROM ALEXANDER HAMILTON, CONCERNING THE PUBLIC CONDUCT AND CHARACTER OF PRESIDENT JOHN ADAMS

October 24, 1800
Source Document Excerpt

It is time to conclude—The statement, which has been made, shews that Mr. ADAMS has committed some positive and serious errors of Administration; that in addition to these, he has certain fixed points of character which tend naturally to the detriment of any cause of which he is the chief, of any Administration of which he is the head; that by his ill humors and jealousies he has already divided and distracted the supporters of the Government; that he has furnished deadly weapons to its enemies by unfounded accusations, and has weakened the force of its friends by decrying some of the most influential of them to the utmost of his power; and let it be added, as the necessary effect of such conduct, that he has made great progress in undermining the ground which was gained for the government by his predecessor, and that there is real cause to apprehend, it might totter, if not fall, under his future auspices. A new government, constructed on free principles, is always weak, and must stand in need of the props of a firm and good administration; till time shall have rendered its authority venerable, and fortified it by habits of obedience.

Yet with this opinion of Mr. ADAMS, I have finally resolved not to advise the withholding from him a single vote. The body of Federalists, for want of sufficient knowledge of facts, are not convinced of the expediency of relinquishing him. It is even apparent, that a large proportion still retain the attachment which was once a common sentiment. Those of them, therefore, who are dissatisfied, as far as my information goes, are, generally speaking, willing to forbear opposition, and to acquiesce in the equal support of Mr. ADAMS with Mr. PINCKNEY, whom they prefer. Have they not a claim to equal deference from those who continue attached to the former? Ought not these, in candor, to admit the possibility that the friends who differ from them, act not only from pure motives, but from cogent reasons? Ought they not, by a co-operation in General PINCKNEY, to give a chance for what will be a *safe* issue, supposing that they are right in their preference, and the best issue, should they happen to

continued

be mistaken? Especially, since by doing this, they will increase the probability of excluding a third candidate, of whose unfitness all sincere federalists are convinced. If they do not pursue this course, they will certainly incur an immense responsibility to their friends and to the Government.

To promote this co-operation, to defend my own character, to vindicate those friends, who with myself have been unkindly aspersed, are the inducements for writing this letter. Accordingly, it will be my endeavor to regulate the communication of it in such a manner as will not be likely to deprive Mr. ADAMS of a single vote. Indeed, it is much my wish that its circulation could forever be confined within narrow limits. I am sensible of the inconveniences of giving publicity to a similar developement of the character of the Chief Magistrate of our country; and I lament the necessity of taking a step which will involve that result. Yet to suppress truths, the disclosure of which is so interesting to the public welfare as well as to the vindication of my friends and myself, did not appear to me justifiable.

The restraints, to which I submit, are a proof of my disposition to sacrifice to the prepossessions of those, with whom I have heretofore thought and acted, and from whom in the present question I am compelled to differ. To refrain from a decided opposition to Mr. ADAMS's re-election has been reluctantly sanctioned by my judgment; which has been not a little perplexed between the unqualified conviction of his unfitness for the station contemplated, and a sense of the great importance of cultivating harmony among the supporters of the Government; on whose firm union hereafter will probably depend the preservation of order, tranquility, liberty, property; the security of every social and domestic blessing.[15]

The division within the party looked bad to the public, and left the Federalists unable to mount an effective campaign. In the end, Thomas Jefferson won by a small margin—something that, given the Federalist control over all three branches of the government, would not have been possible if not for the infighting in the Federalist camp.

The exercise of power in Adams's administration was less forceful than under Washington, who ran his cabinet and, in fact, the entire government, in a military tradition. Adams, as the first bureaucrat to hold the office, was unable to capture public support. This meant that he needed to consolidate power through coalition and party politics, setting America on a path from which the nation has never recovered. Even more than most of the other Federalists, Adams was tied to the tradition of English royalty that he'd known and admired in his youth. He, therefore, came to believe that the trappings and traditions of the royal court were important to establishing the importance of office, political power, and national identity. This is why Adams passionately argued for the use of titles to address the American president and why he supported the effort, underway during his term in the presidency, to create a new national capital.

The effort for a new nation capital began in 1790, under the Washington Administration, with the passage of "An Act for Establishing the Temporary and Permanent Seat of the Government of the United States," otherwise known as the "Residence Act." Under this act, Philadelphia was to remain the capital for ten years, during which time French engineer Pierre Charles L'Enfant worked to design a new capital, located near Virginia, in a city that would come to be called "Washington DC," after the nation's first president. The official transfer of power from Philadelphia to Washington, DC, was scheduled for November of 1800, just before Adams faced reelection. At this time, only one wing of the U.S. Capitol Building had been finished and the town had less than 400 houses and a population of only 3,000, with few roads and little in the way of entertainment or commercial viability. Adams nonetheless moved into the still incomplete presidential mansion, now known as the White House, where he spent the final months of his presidency.[16]

CONCLUSION

After two terms, Americans saw John Adams stretch the powers of the presidency, which began the debate about how a president should use the power of the office. While Adams and others, like Alexander Hamilton, wanted America to be run in the spirit of a monarchy, as evidenced by the passage of the powerful Alien and Sedition Acts during Adams's presidency, Thomas Jefferson, our third president and the father of modern progressivism, championed a nation run by individuals from all backgrounds. This major difference in opinion led to the nation's first partisan political contest, and the next chapter shows President Jefferson leading the nation based on the philosophy that all individuals are entitled to certain unalienable rights.

DISCUSSION QUESTIONS

♦ Describe the difference in style between Presidents Washington and Adams.
♦ Which do you think is a more effective approach? Why?
♦ What is the difference between the Federalists and the Democratic-Republican Parties?
♦ What are the differences between the political parties of Adams's day and the Democratic and Republican parties of today? What are the similarities?
♦ How does executive power of the Alien and Sedition Acts compare to executive actions of modern presidents?

Works Used

Adams, John. "Instructions Adopted by the Braintree Town Meeting." *Massachusetts Historical Society*. Papers of John Adams, vol 1. 2019. Adams Paper Digital Edition. www.masshist.org/publications/adams-papers/index.php/view/PJA01d073.

"Alien and Sedition Acts (1798)." *Our Documents*. 2019www.ourdocuments.gov/doc.php?flash=false&doc=16&page=transcript.

"Articles of Confederation, 1777–1781." *U.S. Department of State*. Office of the Historian. 2016. history.state.gov/milestones/1776-1783/articles.

"Benjamin Franklin Bache." *Mount Vernon*. 2019. www.mountvernon.org/library/digitalhistory/digital-encyclopedia/article/benjamin-franklin-bache/.

Carson, John. *The Measure of Merit: Talents, Intelligence, and Inequality in the French and American Republics, 1750–1940*. Princeton, NJ: Princeton U P, 2007.

Ellenbogen, Paul D. "Another Explanation for the Senate: The Anti-Federalists, John Adams, and the Natural Aristocracy." *Polity*. vol. 29, no 2, Winter 1996. pp. 247–71. jstor.org/stable/3235302?seq=1#page_scan_tab_contentsck.

Hamilton, Alexander. "Letter from Alexander Hamilton, Concerning the Public Conduct and Character of John Adams, Esq. President of the United States, [24 October 1800]." *Founders Online*. National Archives. 2019. founders.archives.gov/documents/Hamilton/01-25-02-0110-0002.

Hemel, Daniel J., and Eric A. Posner. "The Logan Act and its Limits." *Lawfare*. 7 Dec. 2017. www.lawfareblog.com/logan-act-and-its-limits.

Illing, Sean. "How Meritocracy Harms Everyone—Even the Winners." *Vox*. 21 Oct. 2019. www.vox.com/identities/2019/10/21/20897021/meritocracy-economic-mobility-daniel-markovits.

Jefferson, Thomas. "From Thomas Jefferson to James Sullivan, 9 February 1797." *Founders Online*. National Archives. 2016. founders.archives.gov/documents/Jefferson/01-29-02-0231.

"John Adams Biography." *National Park Service*. National Historic Park Massachusetts. 31 Mar. 2012. www.nps.gov/adam/john-adams-biography.htm.

"John Jay's Treaty, 1794–95." *U.S. Department of State*. 2016. history.state.gov/milestones/1784-1800/jay-treaty.

"On This Day: The First Bitter, Contested Presidential Election Takes Place." *National Constitution Center*. Constitutional Daily, Nov. 4, 2018. constitutioncenter.org/blog/on-this-day-the-first-bitter-contested-presidential-election-takes-place.

Prakash, Saikrishna Bangalore. "Stop Fighting It. America Is a Monarchy, and That's Probably for the Best." *Washington Post*. 23 June 2015. www.washingtonpost.com/posteverything/wp/2015/06/23/stop-fighting-it-america-is-a-monarchy-and-thats-probably-for-the-best/.

"Residence Act." *LOC*. Library of Congress. 2016. www.loc.gov/rr/program/bib/ourdocs/residence.html.

"Summation of John Adams in The Soldiers Trial." *Crispus Attucks Museum*. 17 Sept. 2012. www.crispusattucksmuseum.org/summation-john-adams-boston-massacre-trials/.

"The XYZ Affair and the Quasi-War with France, 1798–1800." *U.S. Department of State*. 2016. history.state.gov/milestones/1784-1800/xyz.

Introduction

Thomas Jefferson was one of the most influential men in American history. Jefferson was the author of the Declaration of Independence, the advocate for the Bill of Rights, and a key architect of the U.S. Constitution, as well as becoming one of the most prominent enlightenment philosophers of his age. Jefferson laid down the foundations for American progressivism, and future generations of liberals and progressives often look to Jefferson's writings and his activism on behalf of a more egalitarian democratic process. Jefferson's friendship-turned-rivalry with John Adams created the first partisan election contest and paved the way for the partisan feuding that still dominates U.S. politics. Historians widely view the campaign of 1800 as the first negative political campaign in the history of the presidency. Despite political divisiveness limiting his ability to accomplish some of his agenda, Jefferson was a strong president with considerable skill in capturing public support and an admirable capacity for negotiation. During his tumultuous eight years, Jefferson confronted the thorny issue of international trade and attempted to balance American relations in Europe, a difficult task due to increasing tensions and violence between France and England.

Topics covered in this chapter include:

- Jefferson and Adams contentious 1800 election
- Jefferson alliance with France and tensions with England
- The formation of the Jeffersonian Republicans
- XYZ Affair
- The Barbary Wars
- Alexander Hamilton

This Chapter Discusses the Following Source Documents:

Declaration of Independence, July 4, 1776

To James Madison from Thomas Jefferson, December 20, 1787

From Thomas Jefferson to Abigail Smith Adams, June 13, 1804

First Annual Message to Congress, December 8, 1801

From Thomas Jefferson to United States Congress, January 13, 1806

Aristocratic Progressivism
Thomas Jefferson (1801–1809)

Thomas Jefferson was the father of modern progressivism. He believed that it was possible to create a society that would allow individuals (Jefferson would have restricted this to men) from any sphere to achieve greatness and that there was a natural social evolution toward egalitarianism. Jefferson promoted religious freedom, championed the creation of the Bill of Rights, and was the principal architect of the Declaration of Independence. He championed the cause of democracy against the opposition of men like Alexander Hamilton and John Adams, who wanted the nation to retain the spirit of a monarchy within a constitutional framework they called "republican government." The competition between these views created the nation's first partisan political contests and continues to underlie the division of political parties and ideologies in the twenty-first century. As president, Jefferson was hampered by a hostile House and Senate, but he used his authority to effectively address a threat to America's naval trade and broke new ground when he became the first president to authorize the purchase of new territory for the nation.

From Aristocrat Planter to Revolutionary Philosopher

Thomas Jefferson was born on the Shadwell Plantation in western Virginia in 1743. His father was a well-known gentleman planter and his mother a Randolph, one of the most distinguished families of Virginia's aristocracy. Jefferson inherited his family's plantation, some 5,000 acres, at fourteen years old, upon the death of his father. He attended the College of William and Mary, where he was introduced to Enlightenment Philosophy under the tutelage of Professor William Small, a Scottish academic who'd immigrated to Williamsburg. Jefferson then studied law under George Wythe and was admitted to the Virginia Bar Association in 1767.

Traveling as a lawyer throughout Virginia, Jefferson met and married Martha Wayles Skelton, a 23-year-old widow, with whom he had six children, two—daughters Martha and Mary—surviving to adulthood. The Jeffersons initially lived in the family's Shadwell plantation, but, in 1769, Jefferson built a new house located atop an 868-foot mountain just behind Shadwell. Beginning as a simple brick one-room house, it gradually grew to become a sprawling manor known as Monticello, one of the most famous historic houses in America.[1]

In 1769, Jefferson became a member of the Virginia House of Burgesses, a quasi-governmental body meant to represent the interests of the various plantation communities to the colonial British government. As Britain's taxes became more onerous, fueling a growing independence movement, the house of Burgesses became a source of revolutionary agitation. In 1774, Jefferson wrote an article entitled "Summary View of the Rights of British America," which quickly spread through independence circles. He was, along with fellow Virginian Patrick Henry, one of the first Americans to claim that Britain no longer had the right to pass laws for the colonists. Jefferson was a member of the Second Continental Congress in 1776 and became the principle author of the Declaration of Independence, working alongside John Adams, Benjamin Franklin, Roger Sherman, and Roger Livingston.

Thomas Jefferson, by Rembrandt Peale, via Wikimedia.

In studying Enlightenment philosophy, Jefferson had come to believe that political independence was not a privilege granted through hereditary membership in an aristocratic oligarchy, but was an outgrowth of "natural rights," a philosophical concept stating that all living humans are entitled to certain rights. Jefferson's belief in the natural rights of mankind is clear from the opening paragraph of the Declaration of Independence:

DECLARATION OF INDEPENDENCE: A TRANSCRIPTION
July 4, 1776
Source Document Excerpt

In Congress, July 4, 1776.

The unanimous Declaration of the thirteen united States of America, When in the Course of human events, it becomes necessary for one people to dissolve the political bands which have connected them with another, and to assume among the powers of the earth, the separate and equal station to which the Laws of Nature and of Nature's God entitle them, a decent respect to the opinions of mankind requires that they should declare the causes which impel them to the separation.

We hold these truths to be self-evident, that all men are created equal, that they are endowed by their Creator with certain unalienable Rights, that among these are Life, Liberty and the pursuit of Happiness.—That to secure these rights, Governments are instituted among Men, deriving their just powers from the consent of the governed,—That whenever any Form of Government becomes destructive of these ends, it is the Right of the People to alter or to abolish it, and to institute new Government, laying its foundation on such principles and organizing its powers in such form, as to them shall seem most likely to effect their Safety and Happiness.[2]

Though born into high society, Jefferson had come to believe that the monarchic system, in which both wealth and privilege were equated with value and political power, was unequal and immoral. While Adams and Hamilton still prized some of the vestiges of the monarchy, Jefferson believed that America should be a country governed by popular rule in which the government functioned to elevate those with particular skills and talents to leadership positions. His opposition to the idea of hereditary transmission of power is clear from his actions in the Virginia House of Delegates, where he worked successfully to abolish "entail and primogeniture," legal traditions that dictated that a person's land and property would automatically pass to his eldest son.

Jefferson's next major contribution to the revolutionary cause was his now famous Virginia Bill for Establishing Religious Freedom, which became law thanks to Jefferson's campaigning with his friend and protégé James Madison. Jefferson, like some of the other Founding Fathers, was a deist, believing that the universe had been set in motion by a divine being that was thereafter no longer needed. He, therefore, rejected the "personal god" approach dominant at the time and saw no value in embracing a state cult. He believed further that the nation's future leaders might well come from different religious backgrounds and felt that the establishment of a national religion, or laws meant to force religious conformity, would threaten this natural evolutionary progression. Fighting for religious freedom was one of Jefferson's proudest accomplishments, and he requested that the Virginia Bill for Establishing Religious Freedom should be one of the three accomplishments carved into his tombstone.

After the Revolutionary War ended with a surprising American victory, Jefferson returned to Monticello to be near his wife and children. When Martha died in childbirth in November of 1782, Jefferson was severely depressed. It was during this time that he wrote his only known book, *Notes on the State of Virginia*, wherein he argued his position on freedom of religion and also explored another of his most radical ideas: free public education. Jefferson, like his friend and rival John Adams, believed that society was best-led by an aristocracy, representing the brightest that the nation had to offer. However, while Adams believed that the aristocracy should be composed of wealthy citizens and their offspring, Jefferson believed that education was the key. By providing citizens with a free education, Jefferson believed that teachers could help to cultivate the talents of the most intellectually gifted, those who would hopefully become the leaders of American society.[3]

Jefferson's famous home, Monticello, by YF12s, via Wikimedia.

In 1785, Jefferson was named Minister to France, a position that he used to negotiate America's first treaties of mutual military protection. He was in France while the U.S. Constitution was being written, but helped council his friend Madison, who became the chief author. In one of these letters, written in December of 1787, Jefferson advocated for the inclusion of a Bill of Rights that would guarantee basic rights and freedoms to all citizens:

TO JAMES MADISON FROM THOMAS JEFFERSON
December 20, 1787

Dear Sir,

My last to you was of Oct. 8. by the Count de Moustier. Yours of July 18, Sep. 6, & Oct. 24, have been successively received, yesterday, the day before & three or four days before that. I have only had time to read the letters, the printed papers communicated with them, however interesting, being obliged to lie over till I finish my dispatches for the packet, which dispatches must go from hence the day after tomorrow. I have much to thank you for. First and most for the cyphered paragraph respecting myself. These little informations are very material towards forming my own decisions. I would be glad even to know when any individual member thinks I have gone wrong in any instance. If I know myself it would not excite ill blood in me, while it would assist to guide my conduct, perhaps to justify it, and to keep me to my duty, alert. I must thank you too for the information in Thos. Burke's case, tho' you will have found by a subsequent letter that I have asked of you a further investigation of that matter. It is to gratify the lady who is at the head of the Convent wherein my daughters are, & who, by her attachment & attention to them, lays me under great obligations. I shall hope therefore still to receive from you the result of the further enquiries my second letter had asked. The parcel of rice which you informed me had miscarried accompanied my letter to the Delegates of S. Carolina. Mr. Bourgoin was to be the bearer of both and both were delivered together into the hands of his relation here who introduced him to me, and who at a subsequent moment undertook to convey them to Mr. Bourgoin. This person was an engraver particularly recommended to

We the People

To James Madison from Thomas Jefferson
continued

Dr. Franklin & mr. Hopkinson. Perhaps he may have mislaid the little parcel of rice among his baggage. I am much pleased that the sale of Western lands is so succesful. I hope they will absorb all the Certificates of our Domestic debt speedily in the first place, and that then offered for cash they will do the same by our foreign one.

The season admitting only of operations in the Cabinet, and these being in a great measure secret, I have little to fill a letter. I will therefore make up the deficiency by adding a few words on the Constitution proposed by our Convention. I like much the general idea of framing a government which should go on of itself peaceably, without needing continual recurrence to the state legislatures. I like the organization of the government into Legislative, Judiciary & Executive. I like the power given the Legislature to levy taxes, and for that reason solely approve of the greater house being chosen by the people directly. For tho' I think a house chosen by them will be very illy qualified to legislate for the Union, for foreign nations &c. yet this evil does not weigh against the good of preserving inviolate the fundamental principle that the people are not to be taxed but by representatives chosen immediately by themselves. I am captivated by the compromise of the opposite claims of the great & little states, of the latter to equal, and the former to proportional influence. I am much pleased too with the substitution of the method of voting by persons, instead of that of voting by states: and I like the negative given to the Executive with a third of either house, though I should have liked it better had the Judiciary been associated for that purpose, or invested with a similar and separate power. There are other good things of less moment. I will now add what I do not like. First the omission of a bill of rights providing clearly & without the aid of sophisms for freedom of religion, freedom of the press, protection against standing armies, restriction against monopolies, the eternal & unremitting force of the habeas corpus laws, and trials by jury in all matters of fact triable by the laws of the land & not by the law of Nations. To say, as mr. Wilson does, that a bill of rights was not necessary because all is reserved in the case of the general government which is not given, while in the particular ones all is given which is not reserved, might do for the Audience to whom it was addressed, but is surely a gratis dictum, opposed by strong inferences from the body of the instrument, as well as from the omission of the clause of our present confederation which had declared that in express terms. It was a hard conclusion to say because there has

continued

been no uniformity among the states as to the cases triable by jury, because some have been so incautious as to abandon this mode of trial, therefore the more prudent states shall be reduced to the same level of calamity. It would have been much more just & wise to have concluded the other way that as most of the states had judiciously preserved this palladium, those who had wandered should be brought back to it, and to have established general right instead of general wrong. Let me add that a bill of rights is what the people are entitled to against every government on earth, general or particular, & what no just government should refuse or rest on inference. The second feature I dislike, and greatly dislike, is the abandonment in every instance of the necessity of rotation in office, and most particularly in the case of the President. Experience concurs with reason in concluding that the first magistrate will always be re-elected if the constitution permits it. He is then an officer for life. This once observed it becomes of so much consequence to certain nations to have a friend or a foe at the head of our affairs that they will interfere with money & with arms. A Galloman or an Angloman will be supported by the nation he befriends. If once elected, and at a second or third election outvoted by one or two votes, he will pretend false votes, foul play, hold

possession of the reins of government, be supported by the states voting for him, especially if they are the central ones lying in a compact body themselves & separating their opponents: and they will be aided by one nation of Europe, while the majority are aided by another. The election of a President of America some years hence will be much more interesting to certain nations of Europe than ever the election of a king of Poland was. Reflect on all the instances in history antient & modern, of elective monarchies, and say if they do not give foundation for my fears. The Roman emperors, the popes, while they were of any importance, the German emperors till they became hereditary in practice, the kings of Poland, the Deys of the Ottoman dependancies. It may be said that if elections are to be attended with these disorders, the seldomer they are renewed the better. But experience shews that the only way to prevent disorder is to render them uninteresting by frequent changes. An incapacity to be elected a second time would have been the only effectual preventative. The power of removing him every fourth year by the vote of the people is a power which will not be exercised. The king of Poland is removeable every day by the Diet, yet he is never removed. Smaller objections are the Appeal in fact as well as law, and the binding all persons Legislative Executive & Judiciary by oath to

To James Madison from Thomas Jefferson
continued

maintain that constitution. I do not pretend to decide what would be the best method of procuring the establishment of the manifold good things in this constitution, and of getting rid of the bad. Whether by adopting it in hopes of future amendment, or, after it has been duly weighed & canvassed by the people, after seeing the parts they generally dislike, & those they generally approve, to say to them 'We see now what you wish. Send together your deputies again, let them frame a constitution for you omitting what you have condemned, & establishing the powers you approve. Even these will be a great addition to the energy of your government.' At all events I hope you will not be discouraged from other trials, if the present one should fail of it's full effect. I have thus told you freely what I like & dislike: merely as a matter of curiosity, for I know your own judgment has been formed on all these points after having heard every thing which could be urged on them. I own I am not a friend to a very energetic government. It is always oppressive. The late rebellion in Massachusets has given more alarm than I think it should have done. Calculate that one rebellion in 13 states in the course of 11 years, is but one for each state in a century & a half. No country should be so long without

one. Nor will any degree of power in the hands of government prevent insurrections. France, with all it's despotism, and two or three hundred thousand men always in arms has had three insurrections in the three years I have been here in every one of which greater numbers were engaged than in Massachusets & a great deal more blood was spilt. In Turkey, which Montesquieu supposes more despotic, insurrections are the events of every day. In England, where the hand of power is lighter than here, but heavier than with us they happen every half dozen years. Compare again the ferocious depredations of their insurgents with the order, the moderation & the almost self extinguishment of ours. After all, it is my principle that the will of the Majority should always prevail. If they approve the proposed Convention in all it's parts, I shall concur in it chearfully, in hopes that they will amend it whenever they shall find it work wrong. I think our governments will remain virtuous for many centuries; as long as they are chiefly agricultural; and this will be as long as there shall be vacant lands in any part of America. When they get piled upon one another in large cities, as in Europe, they will become corrupt as in Europe. Above all things I hope the education of the

continued

common people will be attended to; convinced that on their good sense we may rely with the most security for the preservation of a due degree of liberty. I have tired you by this time with my disquisitions & will therefore only add assurances of the sincerety of those sentiments of esteem & attachment with which I am Dear Sir your affectionate friend & servant

Th: Jefferson

P.S. The instability of our laws is really an immense evil. I think it would be well to provide in our constitutions that there shall always be a twelve-month between the ingrossing a bill & passing it: that it should then be offered to it's passage without changing a word: and that if circumstances should be thought to require a speedier passage, it should take two thirds of both houses instead of a bare majority.[4]

Jefferson's correspondence with Madison reveals much about his attitudes. His focus on the benefits of education is evident as is his feeling that the preservation of agriculturalism and pastoralism held the key to preserving America's virtues. Jefferson seems to have equated urbanization and the subsequent concentration of population as one of the keys to societal decline. During the debates over the Constitution, the delegates generally split into two camps: Federalists wanted a strong central government, and anti-federalists wanted small government with emphasis on civil liberties. Jefferson was, philosophically, between these two camps. He saw that the central government had an important purpose, but he did not trust too powerful a government, which he saw as an inevitable source of corruption and potentially authoritarianism. His focus on the Bill of Rights was an outgrowth of this skepticism, reflecting his belief that fundamental constitutional law was needed to preserve and protect civil rights and to prevent the government from becoming tyrannical.

Serving a New Master

George Washington called Jefferson out of retirement to serve as his Secretary of State. During his tenure in this role, he strengthened relations

with France and advocated for lending military aid to France after the French Revolution led to war between France and Britain. This brought him into conflict with Hamilton, who had been one of Washington's aides in the war and now led the faction of British-sympathizers in Congress who sought to keep America neutral. Hamilton's clique won out, and Washington declared the nation's neutrality. Jefferson became increasingly disillusioned with Hamilton and Adams's vision of America, and when Washington announced his retirement in 1796, Jefferson decided to run for president.

At the time, politicians were prohibited from campaigning. Friends at lower levels of the state and highly partisan newspapers campaigned for Jefferson and Adams. Despite Washington's warnings against factionalism, partisanship became more widespread, and the public became increasingly ideologically xenophobic and intolerant. The 1796 campaign was the first partisan political contest for the presidency and quickly devolved into mudslinging, with journalists and ideologues not only elevating their own candidate, but spreading misinformation and publishing insulting and often false claims about rivals. Jefferson carried most of the South, while Adams dominated the more powerful northern states and; in the end, Adams won a close electoral victory, by a margin of 71 to 68 electoral votes. As the winner of the second highest number of votes, Jefferson automatically became Adams's vice president, a role that he found lacking in substance, but tried to fulfill to the best of his abilities.

The issue of American allegiance in the Anglo-French war remained among the most controversial issues of the day. The French Revolution was, like the American Revolution, an effort to instate popular rule after centuries of monarchic autocracy. However, the French Revolution involved the complete destruction of the aristocratic class. While Jefferson sympathized with the goal of the movement and sought to retain France as an ally, Hamilton and Adams feared popular uprising against the aristocratic class, of which they were both members. Many aspects of constitutional law and American public policy were designed to elevate the status of the wealthy and to reduce the power of the popular will, and both Adams and Hamilton feared what might happen if the lower classes of America ever decided to mount their own revolution, removing America's elites from power. The Federalists could not advocate for a full alliance with Britain, as many Americans were still hostile toward Britain, so they settled for neutrality, which preserved their lucrative trade deals with both sides.

Relations between France and the United States deteriorated after the French revolutionary government attempted to extort diplomatic envoys sent to France by Adams. This controversy led to America preparing for war, providing a major boon to the Federalists. However, worried that their rivals, the Democratic-Republicans, were gaining support, the Federalists enacted increasingly controversial and oppressive policies to target their political rivals, so much so that public opinion began to turn against them. Jefferson competed with John Adams again in the 1800 election, which is perhaps among the most hostile and "dirtiest" electoral contests in American history. Journalists and ideologues in both camps hurled insults at members of the other. Hamilton spread fake news stories about Jefferson, and undermined Adams at the same time, leading to a split in the Federalists. Jefferson's allies published harsh criticisms of Adams and the Federalists as well. Federalist critics attacked Jefferson's "deist" views, accusing him of being anti-Christian and perhaps in league with the devil, while Adams's critics alleged that he would return America to the British monarchy. Claims made by rival factions were extreme, even by modern standards.

One article from a Connecticut Federalist claimed that if Jefferson were elected, "There is scarcely a possibility that we shall escape a *Civil War*.

Murder, robbery, rape, adultery, and incest will all be openly taught and practiced, the air will be rent with the cries of distress, the soil will be soaked with blood, and the nation black with crimes."

Meanwhile, Democratic-Republican John Preston wrote that Adams's reelection would mean that, "chains, dungeons, transportation (import/export of criminal laborers), and perhaps the gibbet (gallows)," would be the fate for Democratic-Republicans.[5]

The election of 1800 was a bizarre moment in history and demonstrates how easily human culture can devolve under the influence of fear and political manipulation. Citizens on both sides truly believed that the election of the candidate from their rival faction would lead to catastrophe of epic proportions, giving rise to violent factionalism.

The election resulted in Democratic-Republicans Jefferson and Aaron Burr each receiving 73 votes, while Federalists Adams and Charles C. Pinckney received 65 and 64 votes, respectively. The Democratic-Republicans beat the Federalists, but the Jefferson and Burr tie presented a new problem, with no provision in constitutional law to address it. The Tenth Amendment later called for electors to cast separate votes for president and vice president, but at the time it was decided that a runoff election among state legislators was the best way to proceed. Hamilton, one of Jefferson's fiercest critics, settled the election in Jefferson's favor because he hated Burr more vehemently than he did Jefferson. Hamilton visited federal electors and convinced several to change their votes or to rescind their vote for Burr. Jefferson won the election, and Burr was furious with Hamilton's interference. Four years later, with the enmity between the men deepening, Burr and Hamilton met in a fatal duel that claimed Hamilton's life but also ended Burr's political career, leaving both men casualties of America's first political party rivalry.

Minority Leader

The intense discord between the Federalists and Democratic-Republicans spilled over into Jefferson's first term in the White House. A lame-duck session of Congress—when Congress meets before a successor's term begins—and the outgoing Adams conspired to fill as many federal posts as possible with ardent Federalists. In its final days, Congress also passed the Judiciary Act of 1801, reducing the number of Supreme Court justices from 6 to 5 and, therefore, denying Jefferson the opportunity to make an impression on the court, which was at the time completely dominated by Federalists. After 12 years in complete control of Congress, the presidency, and the courts, the Federalists had created a government hostile to progressivism and loyal to the partisan line. Entering this atmosphere, Jefferson's first years as president tested his authority to challenge the actions and appointments of the previous administration.

The Democratic-Republicans tried to impeach two of the federal justices appointed by Adams, marking the first test of the impeachment powers granted to Congress with regard to federal justices. In the first of these cases, Jefferson and his allies were successful in impeaching Justice John Pickering because a number of people, including his own son, came forward to testify that Pickering had lost control of his mental faculties and was unfit to serve. The second test of judicial impeachment involved Samuel Chase, who was an outspoken critic of Jefferson's but not guilty of any obvious failure in his duties. Moderate Democratic-Republicans intervened, and the impeachment process failed.[6]

Jefferson felt that the outgoing Federalist administration's strategy, using what were called "midnight appointments" and other tactics to hinder his presidency, were unethical, and he was personally wounded by the behavior of his long-time friend John Adams. This he revealed later in an 1804 letter to Abigail Adams, at the close of his first term in office:

FROM THOMAS JEFFERSON TO ABIGAIL SMITH ADAMS
June 13, 1804

"Mr. Adams's friendship & mine began at an earlier date. it accompanied us thro' long & important scenes. the different conclusions we had drawn from our political reading & reflections were not permitted to lessen mutual esteem, each party being conscious they were the result of an honest conviction in the other. like differences of opinion existing among our fellow citizens attached them to the one or the other of us, and produced a rivalship in their minds which did not exist in ours. we never stood in one another's way: for if either had been withdrawn at any time, his favorers would not have gone over to the other, but would have sought for some one of homogeneous opinions. this consideration was sufficient to keep down all jealousy between us, & to guard our friendship from any disturbance by sentiments of rivalship: and I can say with truth that one act of mr Adams's life, and one only, ever gave me a moment's personal displeasure. I did consider his last appointments to office as personally unkind. they were from among my most ardent political enemies, from whom no faithful cooperation could ever be expected, and laid me under the embarrasment of acting thro' men whose views were to defeat mine; or to encounter the odium of putting others in their places. it seemed but common justice to leave a successor free to act by instruments of his own choice."[7]

It was also during Jefferson's time in office that the Supreme Court delivered a landmark decision in *Marbury v. Madison*. James Madison, who had been appointed as Jefferson's secretary of state, refused to deliver a justice of the peace commission to William Marbury, a wealthy real-estate mogul in Washington, DC, and one of Adams's midnight appointees. Marbury claimed that Madison had no right to deny him his commission and asked the Supreme Court to intervene based on the Judiciary Act of 1789, which gave the Court the power to issue a "writ of mandamus"—a judicial order compelling an inferior government official to perform an appointed function. Though the justices agreed that Marbury and other commissioned officers were due their commissions, they also found that, under the constitutional guidelines regarding separation of powers, the Court did not have the power to issue a writ of mandamus. This invalidated the Judiciary Act of 1789 and gave Jefferson the power to deny Marbury's appointment. More important for the future of executive and congressional authority, the ruling established the precedent that the Supreme Court could invalidate both an executive order or an act of Congress if either were deemed to violate constitutional law. *Marbury v. Madison* was, therefore, a major step in defining the powers of the Supreme Court, as well as establishing limits to both presidential and congressional authority.[8]

A President at Sea

Jefferson also found his overall goals for the government thwarted due to external pressures. He had long opposed the Federalist policy, owing primarily to Hamilton, of maintaining a large standing army. A strict state's-rights advocate, Jefferson preferred to allow each state to create and train its own militia, thereby allowing soldiers to remain citizens rooted in their communities while awaiting active duty. This proved impossible, however, because the administration faced naval threats on two fronts. The brewing tension in Europe led to naval conflict with England as British ships began seizing American vessels suspected of delivering supplies to France. Jefferson's solution was to call for economic sanctions, and the Democratic-Republican Congress responded with the Embargo Act, which prohibited all trade with Europe. This ultimately proved disastrous for the economy, and Jefferson lost public support; he later called for a reform of the law, and Congress amended it to allow trade with Europe but restricted trade with both Britain and France.

Jefferson also faced a new naval conflict with the Barbary States, a collection of small countries around North Africa that included Morocco, Algiers, Tunis, and Tripolitania. All of these states practiced "state-sponsored piracy," allowing ships to patrol the coasts to capture supplies

and captives from passing merchant vessels. France and Britain paid the Barbary Pirates for protection and encouraged disruptive attacks on other nations. Both Washington and Adams paid the Barbary nations for protection and safe merchant passage, and Jefferson's inclination was to do the same. In 1801, Yusuf Qaramanli, the Pasha of Tripoli, accused the United States of failing to pay tribute and threatened to declare war. Jefferson was unable to get a timely message to Qaramanli that he would pay the tribute, and preemptively sent naval vessels to Tripoli describing the fleet as a "squadron of observation," and offered his hope that his ships would "give umbrage to no power."[9] Qaramanli, not waiting for Jefferson's response, ordered an attack on the American vessels, taking dozens hostage, and beginning a three-year conflict and leading America into what would now be considered nation building. United States ships responded by blocking Tripolitan ships, leading to the American *Enterprise* defeating the Tripolitan ship *Tripoli* off the coast of Malta Harbor.

Although both Washington and Adams had taken full advantage of their role as commander in chief, both men had conferred with Congress before taking military action, something Jefferson did not do before dispatching the first ships to Tripoli, hoping that a display of force would lead to negotiation. He informed Congress of what had occurred in his first address to the legislature, explaining that the situation had become violent before proper channels could be consulted.

FIRST ANNUAL MESSAGE TO CONGRESS
December 8, 1801
Source Document Excerpt

"To this state of general peace with which we have been blessed, one only exception exists. Tripoli, the least considerable of the Barbary states, had come forward with demands unfounded either in right or in compact, and had permitted itself to denounce war, on our failure to comply before a given day. The style of the demand admitted but one answer. I sent a small squadron of frigates into the Mediterranean, with assurances to that power of our sincere desire to remain in peace; but with orders to protect our commerce against the threatened attack. the measure was seasonable and salutary. The Bey had already declared war in form. His cruisers were out. Two had arrived at Gibralter. Our commerce in the Mediterranean was blockaded; and that of the Atlantic in peril. the arrival of our squadron dispelled the danger. One of the Tripolitan cruisers having fallen in with, and engaged the small schooner Enterprize, commanded by Lieut. Sterritt, which had gone out as a tender to our larger vessels, was captured, after a heavy slaughter of her men, without the loss of a single one on our part. The bravery exhibited by our citizens on that element will, I trust, be a testimony to the world, that it is not a want of that virtue which makes us seek their peace; but a conscientious desire to direct the energies of our nation to the multiplication of the human race, and not to its destruction. Unauthorised by the constitution, without the sanction of Congress, to go beyond the line of defence, the vessel being disabled from committing further hostilities, was liberated with it's crew. The legislature will doubtless consider whether, by authorising measures of offence also, they will place our force on an equal footing with that of it's adversaries. I communicate all material information on this subject, that in the exercise of the important function, confided by the constitution to the legislature exclusively, their judgment may form itself on a knolege and consideration of every circumstance of weight."[10]

Despite Jefferson's reluctance to confer with legislators, Congress agreed to fund an expanded naval force the purchase of privateer vessels. The situation worsened in 1803, when the frigate *Philadelphia* ran aground near Tripoli, and the Pasha forces captured the ship and took 307 men hostage. Though a major blow for Jefferson, Congress immediately rallied behind him, approving new wartime taxes and expenditures to send additional ships to Tripoli.[11]

Under the command of Commodore Samuel Barron, and with a new fleet of 11 vessels, the U.S. blockade became much more effective. Meanwhile, James Madison wrote a letter to Tobias Lear, Jefferson's envoy to Saint-Domingue, informing Lear that he was sanctioned to enlist the aid of Pasha Qaramanli's elder brother Hamet, if absolutely necessary, which in effect was covertly supporting a coup against a foreign government.[12]

Admiral Barron wrote a letter to Madison expressing doubt at the wisdom of returning Hamet to power. When word came to Jefferson from Tripoli that the Pasha was ready to negotiate, Jefferson immediately dispatched Lear, and by June of 1805 a peace agreement had been reached that freed the United States from any obligation to pay future tributes. In concession, the United States agreed to pay $60,000 for the return of captives and supplies.

With the announcement of the war's conclusion, Jefferson's popularity peaked. Paintings, patriotic songs, and books celebrated the victory; and Jefferson won significant praise from legislators impressed that his administration had finally freed the United States from an unfavorable financial bargain to which both Washington and Adams had submitted. Famed lawyer, amateur poet, and songwriter Francis Scott Key, remembered for writing America's national anthem, used the Barbary Wars as inspiration when he penned a stanza for what later became the official anthem of the Colonial Marines:

_____ From the halls of Montezuma

To the shores of Tripoli

We fight our country's battles

In the air, on land and sea.

William Eaton, a U. S. Army officer and the diplomatic officer Consul General to Tunis who had fought with Hamet to overthrow the Pasha, was angered by what he saw as his government's betrayal of Hamet, and felt that his plan would have granted the United States a more substantial victory in the region and a government indebted to the United States, which became a standard U.S. nation-building approach: stabilizing a U.S. –backed government in exchange for U.S. trade and security. Jefferson justified his actions in a letter to the Senate in 1806:

FROM THOMAS JEFFERSON TO UNITED STATES CONGRESS
January 13, 1806
Source Document Excerpt

In operations at such a distance, it becomes necessary to leave much to the discretion of the agents employed: but events may still turn up beyond the limits of that discretion. unable in such a case to consult his government, a zealous citizen will act, as he believes that would direct him, were it apprised of the circumstances, & will take on himself the responsibility. in all these cases, the purity & patriotism of the motives should shield the agent from blame, & even secure a sanction, where the error is not too injurious. should it be thought by any that the verbal instructions, said to have been given by Commodore Barron to Mr. Eaton, amount to a stipulation that the US should place Hamet Caramalli on the throne of Tripoli, a stipulation so entirely unauthorised, so far beyond our views, & so onerous, could not be sanctioned by our government.[13]

William Eaton felt that the United States had betrayed Hamet Qaramanli after accepting his help in getting his brother, Pasha Yusuf Qaramanli of Tripoli, to sign a peace treaty during the First Barbary War. By Rembrandt Peale, via Wikimedia.

Though the effort was later disowned and abandoned, Eaton's capture of Derne was the first U.S. attempt to overthrow a foreign power and to install a friendly government. Such an action would undoubtedly have been seen as beyond presidential authority had the coup succeeded.

America the Bountiful

By far the most momentous use of executive power under Jefferson was the Louisiana Purchase, an executive action that doubled the size of the nation and provided important access to shipping routes for inland communities. After the Revolutionary War, France surrendered its North American territory but Spain held control of a large portion, from New Orleans through the Rocky Mountains. In October of 1802, King Charles IV of Spain secretly transferred control of this territory to Napoleon's France. Jefferson initially preferred a diplomatic negotiation, but those who distrusted France were concerned by the prospect of France legally owning territory roughly the same size as the United States and containing important waterways to the Gulf of Mexico. As Federalist legislators called for war, Jefferson dispatched his friend and ally James Monroe to negotiate with France.

Although Jefferson had committed to reducing the size of the federal government, this presented an unprecedented opportunity for expansion. Napoleon's forces suffered losses in their attempt to recolonize their new world territories. Napoleon knew that another war with Britain was coming, so was willing to sell France's territory for $15 million, just four cents per acre. Though controversial, the Louisiana Purchase solved many of the problems with French ownership and provided direct benefits to the western states. Even Jefferson supporters who opposed the purchase saw it as the best option, and the Senate ratified the treaty 24 to 7.[14]

The Louisiana Purchase forced Jefferson to use executive authority in ways he most likely never thought would be necessary, and some saw it as an overreach of his office. Even before the treaty was complete, Jefferson requested and received funding for his secretary Meriwether Lewis and former army officer William Clark to lead an expedition through the territory. The two-year, 45-man expedition became one of the most famous and cherished stories of America's founding era, with historians still investigating and reporting on details from the expedition and its sociopolitical consequences. At the end of his career, Jefferson listed the Louisiana Purchase as one of his proudest achievement as chief executive.

Thomas Jefferson has a checkered legacy in terms of the fight for racial equality that existed during his time and eventually led to the Civil War and Civil Rights Movements. Jefferson and his family, like most white members of Virginia's planter gentry, owned slaves, and the fortunes of his family plantation were dependent on slave labor. On average, Jefferson owned around 200 slaves at any given time, and around half of those were children. Because he was a scrupulous bookkeeper, Jefferson kept detailed records of all his slaves. Over the course of his life, Jefferson owned some 600 slaves. Most were provided little in the way of education or training, which was common practice. Some select slaves were afforded educational advancements or training in a trade or artisan craft. The furniture in Jefferson's Monticello home, for instance, was primarily built by slaves who had learned advanced woodworking.

Jefferson's father-in-law, John Wayles, raped at least one of his female slaves. This was not uncommon practice, but was typically kept secret. Jefferson inherited a slave named Elizabeth Hemings, and it was well known that Wayles had fathered six of her children. The Hemings children, being of mixed race, were afforded special privileges. They were made into house slaves, working inside Monticello or as personal servants to Martha and Thomas. The most famous of Jefferson's slaves was Sally Hemings, born in 1773. Hemings was the daughter of John Wayles and so the half-sister of Martha. In her youth, she was nursemaid to Jefferson's daughter Maria. After the revolution, Jefferson was appointed an ambassador to France, along with Benjamin Franklin, and took Sally Hemings, then 14, along with him as domestic servant to his daughter. Two years earlier, Jefferson had sent Sally's brother James to France to study French cooking. In France, Sally lived along with Jefferson and his daughters Maria and Martha "Patsy" at the Hôtel de Langeac.

The French Revolution of 1789 meant the abolition of slavery, and so Sally Hemings and her brother were also legally free while living there. Historians have found records that Jefferson began paying Hemings a fee of $2 per month for her services. While in France, Jefferson paid for Hemings to be tutored in French, sewing, and clothes making. Though she was legally permitted to request her freedom and to remain in France, Hemings became pregnant with Jefferson's child at the age of 16 and agreed to return with Jefferson if he freed their child upon reaching the age of majority (then 21). Madison Hemings later claimed that his mother Sally had become Jefferson's concubine and returned after negotiating what he referred to as "extraordinary privileges" for herself and her future children. Their first child together, a daughter, died shortly after childbirth. There is evidence to suggest that Jefferson continued his relationship with Hemings for most of the remainder of his life, until his death in 1826. He fathered at least six children by Hemings, four of whom survived to adulthood. His sons Madison and Eston became carpenters, while Eston was also a prominent musician. Both later joined free black societies in the north. Daughters Beverly and Harriet were allowed to leave Monticello, being apparently so fair skinned that they were able to enter white society. After Jefferson's death, his daughter Martha freed Harriet for the remainder of her life. Hemings relocated to Charlottesville, where she was listed as a "free mulatto" in a census taken after the Nat Turner Rebellion of 1831. Eston relocated to Ohio and used the last name "Jefferson" until his death in 1856.[a]

For many years, rumors circulated about Jefferson's mixed-race children, and accounts directly from his son Madison and grandson Beverly Frederick Jefferson have added detail to the story. Jefferson's scandalous relationship with Sally Hemings was first made public to the press in September of 1802 by journalist James Callender, who was also famous for exposing Alexander Hamilton's affair with the married Maria Reynolds. In 1802, when Callender published the first article about Jefferson's alleged affair and illegitimate mixed-race children, Jefferson had been president for only two years.

[b]The Callender article sparked a major scandal, though not so major as to prevent Jefferson's second term. There were racist poems written about the affair, including one referring to the president's relationship with "Dusky Sally," and Federalist opponents used the incident to suggest that Jefferson was unfit for office. Jefferson's family denied the claims of Jefferson's sexual relationship with Hemings for years, and the official conservator of the Jefferson heritage, the Monticello organization, also refused to add information about the alleged

affair to Jefferson's official biography. A 1998 DNA test finally ended the long debate, proving a definite link between the Jefferson and Hemings line. In 2018, Monticello debuted a new exhibit describing Jefferson's relationship with Hemings and containing artifacts of Hemings existence at Monticello. Historians have been conflicted about how to present the relationship. As slaves had no legal rights, was the relationship rape? Depictions from individuals with inside knowledge typically used words like "concubine" or "mistress," but the nature of the emotional relationship between Jefferson and Hemings remains unclear. Jefferson's attempts to convince Hemings to return with him from France to Monticello indicate the possibility that he, at least, was attached to her in more than a passing way, as does the fact that their sexual relationship seems to have lasted as long as 40 years. However, as to Hemings, her complete lack of legal and social agency makes it difficult to characterize her perspective on the relationship in the absence of personal statements. Even if Hemings did have a romantic attachment to Jefferson, the imbalance of power means that the relationship must, at least on some level, be characterized as exploitative.[c]

Interestingly, historians have found evidence suggesting that Jefferson's oldest friend and professional rival, John Adams, knew about Jefferson's affair with Hemings before it became public and that it might have been his gossip that unintentionally spread the rumor. After Jefferson resigned as George Washington's Secretary of State in 1793, he announced he was going to retire from public life to Monticello. Adams, then serving as vice president, clearly did not believe that Jefferson would permanently retire. In a letter to his son Charles Adams he wrote,

"Mr Jefferson is going to Montecello to Spend his Days in Retirement, in Rural Amusements and Philosophical Meditations—Untill the President dies or resigns, when I suppose he is to be inviced from his Conversations with Egeria in the Groves, to take the Reins of the State…"

To his son John Quincy, he made a similar reference:

"Numa was called from the Forrests to be King of Rome. And if Jefferson, after the Death or Resignation of the President should be summoned from the familiar Society of Egeria, to govern the Country forty Years in Peace and Piety, So be it."

Adams is referring in his letters to Roman mythology figures: Numa, a king of the Sabine people, claimed that he had been meeting the goddess Egeria, a nymph-like figure, in a secret grove, where they made love and she instructed him on religion and the philosophy of the state. As Numa's reign was known as a golden age of peace and prosperity in Rome, the comparison to Jefferson seems complimentary, but some historians have taken the allusion to conversation—a term that was regularly used as an indirect way to refer to sexual intercourse—with Egeria as code for his affair with Hemings.

Adams was, among the Founding Fathers, perhaps the only powerful one who opposed slavery. In an 1810 letter to Joseph Ward, he referred to the scandal surrounding Jefferson again,

"Callender and Sally will be remembered as long as Jefferson as Blotts in his Character. The story of the latter, is a natural and almost unavoidable Consequence of that foul contagion (pox) in the human Character Negro Slavery. In the West Indies and the Southern States it has the Same Effect. A great Lady has Said She did not believe there was a Planter in Virginia who could not reckon among his Slaves a Number of his Children. But is it Sound Policy will it promote Morality, to keep up the Cry of such disgracefull Stories, now the Man is voluntarily retired from the World. The more the Subject is canvassed will not the horror of the Infamy be diminished? and this black Licentiousness be encouraged?"[d]

Jefferson's offspring with Hemings got a 50-year head start on emancipation. Some lived as white people, thanks to their light complexion, and others lived as African Americans, finding their way to free black communities. Jefferson's writings make it clear that he was racist, believing strongly in the inferiority of the African race. Sally Hemings, who was described as both lovely and so fair as to almost look white, might have seemed to him more worthy of differential treatment on behalf of her European blood. It is also possible that Jefferson's attitudes about the value of race changed over time, though is writings leave no clear evidence of this. The story of Jefferson and Hemings, though it did not provide his political opponents as pointed a weapon as they might have hoped, has been useful to historians, helping to dispel the mythological depictions of the Founding Fathers as morally unimpeachable while, in reality, their behavior might classify them as something other than heroes by modern sensibilities.

Works Used

a. "The Life of Sally Hemings." *Monticello*. 2019. www.monticello.org/sallyhemings/.

b. Callender, James. "The President Again. " Originally appeared in the *Richmond Recorder, 1802, on Thomas Jefferson and Sally Hemings. Digital History*. Digital History ID 1378, www.digitalhistory. uh.edu/disp_textbook.cfm?smtID=3&psid=1378.

c. Stockman, Farah. "Monticello Is Done Avoiding Jefferson's Relationship with Sally Hemings." *New York Times*. June 16, 2018. www.nytimes.com/2018/06/16/us/sally-hemings-exhibit-monticello.html.

d. Silk, Mark. "Did John Adams Out Thomas Jefferson and Sally Hemings?" *Smithsonian*. Nov. 2016. www. smithsonianmag.com/history/john-adams-out-thomas-jefferson-sally-hemings-180960789/.

CONCLUSION

Jefferson entered the presidency with egalitarian ideas about democratic reform, but found himself coping with more practical concerns for most of his time in office. His use of military power further helped to establish traditions of executive military leadership, and his role in the Louisiana Purchase resulted in a dramatic expansion of U.S. territory. Jefferson's two terms were also impacted by the controversy regarding whether the United States would seek to take a side in the deepening military conflict between France and Britain, but this was an issue that would largely fall upon Jefferson's successor, the great American statesman and intellectual James Madison, whose leadership style and use of presidential power is discussed in the next chapter.

DISCUSSION QUESTIONS

♦ How did Jefferson's concept of a "natural aristocracy" differ from Adams's? Which makes more sense to you and why?

♦ How do the Democratic-Republicans compare with modern political parties?

♦ In what way was Jefferson's use of power in the Louisiana Purchase controversial? Would a modern president have the power to expand American territory in this same way? Why or why not?

♦ How did Jefferson alter the interpretation of executive military leadership in the Barbary Wars? Do you agree with his style of leadership in this case? Why or why not?

Works Used

"Barbary Wars, 1801–1805 and 1815–1816." *U.S. Department of State*. Office of the Historian. Milestones. history.state.gov/milestones/1801-1829/barbary-wars.

"Declaration of Independence: A Transcription." *National Archives*. July 26, 2019. www.archives.gov/founding-docs/declaration-transcript.

Dunn, Susan. *Jefferson's Second Revolution: The Election Crisis of 1800 and the Triumph of Republicanism*. New York: Houghton Mifflin Company, 2004.

Jefferson, Thomas. "First Annual Message to Congress, 8 December 1801." *Founders Online*. National Archives. founders.archives.gov/documents/Jefferson/01-36-02-0034-0003.

_____. "From Thomas Jefferson to Yusuf Qaramanli, Pasha and Bey of Tripoli, 21 May 1801." *Founders Online*. National Archives. 2019. founders.archives.gov/documents/Jefferson/01-34-02-0122.

_____. "From Thomas Jefferson to Abigail Smith Adams, 13 June 1804." *Founders Online*. National Archives. founders.archives.gov/documents/Adams/99-03-02-1280.

_____. "From Thomas Jefferson to United States Congress, 13 January 1806." *Founders Online*. National Archives, 2019. founders.archives.gov/documents/Jefferson/99-01-02-3010.

Madison, James. "From James Madison to Tobias Lear, 6 June 1804." *Founders Online*. National Archives. founders.archives.gov/documents/Madison/02-07-02-0300.

"Marbury v. Madison. 5 U.S. 137 (1803)" *Justia*. 2019. supreme.justia.com/cases/federal/us/5/137/.

Meacham, Jon. *Thomas Jefferson: The Art of Power*. New York: Random House, 2012.

Onuf, Peter. "Thomas Jefferson: Life Before the Presidency." *Miller Center*. 2019. millercenter.org/president/jefferson/life-before-the-presidency.

"The Louisiana Purchase." *Monticello*. 2019. www.monticello.org/thomas-jefferson/louisiana-lewis-clark/the-louisiana-purchase/.

Thompson, Frank Jr., and Daniel H. Pollitt. "Impeachment of Federal Judges: An Historical Overview." *North Carolina Law Review*, vol. 49, no 1, Article 9, Dec. 1, 1970. scholarship.law.unc.edu/cgi/viewcontent.cgi?article=2416&context=nclr.

"To James Madison from Thomas Jefferson, 20 December 1787." *Founders Online*. National Archives. 2019. founders.archives.gov/documents/Madison/01-10-02-0210.

"To Thomas Jefferson from John Barnes, 31 August 1802." *Founders Online*. National Archives. 2019. founders.archives.gov/documents/Jefferson/01-38-02-0286.

Introduction

James Madison was a protégé of Thomas Jefferson and, as such, continued Jefferson's focus on limited government and states' rights. Madison continued the legacy of the Virginia aristocracy, but was a wise and considerate executive, engaging in debate and negotiation with his Federalist opponents to achieve key goals of his administration. Madison was the first president to face a major military conflict while in office, and his performance during the War of 1812 helped to establish executive war-time tradition. However, his and Jefferson's efforts to reduce the size of the military resulted in heavy losses during the war. Madison was also tasked with administrating the expansion of the United States following the Louisiana Purchase, and questions of federal investment in state infrastructure that emerged during his presidency continue to be a familiar part of American politics. One of the most lasting contributions of the Madison administration was in defining the role of First Lady. Madison's wife, Dolley, was extremely popular in Washington and around the world, inspiring new fashion and cultural trends, and aiding her husband with her penchant for casual diplomacy.

Topics covered in this chapter include:

- The War of 1812
- Settlement after the Louisiana Purchase
- Presidential veto power
- The First Lady of the United States
- The Bill of Rights
- The Anglo-French Wars
- Embargo Act of 1807

This Chapter Discusses the Following Source Documents:
Federalist Papers: No. 51, 1788
Veto Message on the Internal Improvements Bill, March 3, 1817

Father of the Constitution
James Madison (1809–1817)

James Madison was the successor to Jefferson's states-rights and civil liberties-oriented presidency and is seen as one of the most influential of the Founding Fathers. Known as the "Father of the Constitution," Madison fought for religious tolerance and egalitarianism as a revolutionary patriot, but, like Jefferson, he struggled with partisan politics as the Democratic-Republican Party faced off against the New England Federalists. Famed journalist Washington Irving said of Madison, who was sickly, short, and with a wizened appearance, that he gave the impression of a "withered little apple john" (an apple left in cold storage too long). Robert A. Rutland, editor of Madison's papers, said of Madison's legacy in an interview with the Washington Post, "The trouble is, we're so accustomed to show people, that when we get an honest-to-God intellect, we don't know what to do with them. We want a few spangles and they don't have spangles."[1]

Wisdom and the Republic

James Madison was born in 1751 in Port Conway, Virginia, into an aristocratic, slave-owning plantation family. His family home, built in the 1760s became known as Montpelier, and is a landmark of the nation's founding era. The oldest of 12 children, Madison was sickly in his youth and suffered throughout his life from medical problems, including "bilious fever," which may have been related to liver disease. He complained of sudden attacks, possibly epileptic seizures. He was America's shortest president, at 5'4", and his voice was so weak that people often complained they could not hear him when he spoke.

As a child, Madison studied mathematics, geography, philosophy, and languages. Though most children of the Virginia aristocracy, like Madison's friend and mentor Thomas Jefferson, attended the College of

James Madison, fourth president of the United States and "father of the Constitution." By John Vanderlyn, via Wikimedia.

William and Mary, it was believed that its coastal climate might be detrimental to his health; and Madison was sent to Princeton University, then called the University of New Jersey. Beginning his studies in 1769, he finished a four-year degree in two years, remained at the college after graduation, taking courses in Hebrew and political philosophy. Princeton University has since commemorated Madison as its first graduate student.

As a keen reader of Enlightenment and political philosophy, Madison was naturally drawn to the Patriots' cause as the relationship between the colonies and the British crown began to deteriorate. Madison was appointed to the Orange County Committee of Safety in 1774 and became one of the delegates to the Virginia Revolutionary Convention of 1776[2], at which Virginia aristocrats got together to discuss their relationship with Britain and the independence movement. It was here that Madison and Jefferson became friends and colleagues, a relationship that would last until the end of their careers. During this time Madison began his rivalry with Patrick Henry, the Virginia farmer and statesman whose famous "Give me liberty, or give me death," speech became a rallying cry of the revolution. Henry led the most radical faction of the Virginia delegates, men who'd been calling for independence before 1775, while more moderate and intellectual patriots were still weighing the options between independence and seeking a more favorable accord with Britain. Madison earned a reputation for forming political coalitions, and was instrumental in helping to break growing political tensions between members of the revolutionary legislatures of the states.

Ode to Bumbo

In the 1770s, politicians in the United States engaged in a potentially illegal, though widespread, campaign practice known as "swilling the planters with bumbo," essentially plying potential voters with food and drink to gain their support. The practice predates the United States, and was common in Britain and before that in imperial Rome and ancient Greece, where politicians used gifts of food and liquor to mollify the masses. When George Washington, then 24, first attempted to win election to the Virginia House of Burgesses, he lost and later attributed this to not providing enough alcohol to voters. Two years later, Washington tried for office again, this time using his considerable fortune to enhance his appeal. In that election, his campaign officers dispersed 144 gallons of rum, punch, hard cider, and beer, amounting to approximately half a gallon for every voter who ended up casting their ballot for him. James Madison encountered similar difficulties when he attempted to run for office in 1777, but refused to, as he saw it, "bribe" the masses with liquor and food. His far less-qualified and less-able opponent was not above passing out the bumbo and easily beat Madison at the polls. The tradition of plying voters with booze was accompanied by another tradition, getting drunk on election day. Even as the practice of directly bribing voters with liquor faded, local polling places still frequently provided beer and spirits to voters. This continued until prohibition, when the practice was banned, along with liquor consumption in general. Prohibition, a disastrous federal policy, was abandoned, but the age of bumbo never returned.[a]

Work Used

a. Bramen, Lisa. "Swilling the Planters with Bumbo: When Booze Bought Elections." Smithsonian.com. 20 Oct. 2010. www.smithsonianmag.com/arts-culture/swilling-the-planters-with-bumbo-when-booze-bought-elections-102758236/.

Madison served in the Continental Congress in 1780, where he became increasingly critical of the Articles of Confederation, the precursor to America's constitution. The articles were poorly designed, providing too much freedom to the states and insufficient authority to the central government. The lack of central leadership nearly derailed the revolution, as state legislatures failed to respond to the needs of the troops, which nearly led to mutiny and disbandment. Though the war was won, the new union was fragile. The Articles of Confederation provided too little structure, and the laws passed by the state legislatures were inconsistent and often contradictory. The nation struggled to pay its debts, and the Continental Congress had little power to compel the states to join together for mutual benefit.

Though solutions were contentious, delegates across the nation were in agreement that the Articles of Confederation had failed to achieve the strong unity they sought. In 1787, another Constitutional Convention was planned; and, in preparation, Madison composed the "Virginia Plan,"— the basic framework for what became the U.S. Constitution. His plan included a three-branch form of government with interlinked powers, so as to enable each branch to serve as a check on the powers of the other two. A similar plan had been devised by scholar John Adams but was not as robust and developed in its execution. Madison formed a coalition with Adams and together they promoted the new constitution to the delegates. After considerable debate and compromise, a final form of the document was drafted by Madison. To build public support, Madison, Alexander Hamilton, and John Jay wrote a series of 85 newspaper articles, collectively called the *Federalist Papers* published in the New York press and disseminated across the country, which explained how this new proposed government would function to protect civil liberties while retaining a strong central structure to coordinate collective action.

One of the biggest debates concerned the power granted to the executive branch. Some preferred a parliamentary system, giving the executive little direct power except in foreign relations. This group felt that unfettered power in a single individual encouraged tyranny. Federalists believed that a powerful executive, tempered by checks and balances, was necessary to creating a functional government. This group felt that without a powerful executive, government would function by committee and fail to reach agreement.

FEDERALIST PAPERS: NO. 51
1788
Source Document Excerpt

The Structure of the Government Must Furnish the Proper

Checks and Balances Between the Different Departments

To the People of the State of New York:

TO WHAT expedient, then, shall we finally resort, for maintaining in practice the necessary partition of power among the several departments, as laid down in the Constitution? The only answer that can be given is, that as all these exterior provisions are found to be inadequate, the defect must be supplied, by so contriving the interior structure of the government as that its several constituent parts may, by their mutual relations, be the means of keeping each other in their proper places. Without presuming to undertake a full development of this important idea, I will hazard a few general observations, which may perhaps place it in a clearer light, and enable us to form a more correct judgment of the principles and structure of the government planned by the convention.

In order to lay a due foundation for that separate and distinct exercise of the different powers of government, which to a certain extent is admitted on all hands to be essential to the preservation of liberty, it is evident that each department should have a will of its own; and consequently should be so constituted that the members of each should have as little agency as possible in the appointment of the members of the others. Were this principle rigorously adhered to, it would require that all the appointments for the supreme executive, legislative, and judiciary magistracies should be drawn

continued

from the same fountain of authority, the people, through channels having no communication whatever with one another. Perhaps such a plan of constructing the several departments would be less difficult in practice than it may in contemplation appear. Some difficulties, however, and some additional expense would attend the execution of it. Some deviations, therefore, from the principle must be admitted. In the constitution of the judiciary department in particular, it might be inexpedient to insist rigorously on the principle: first, because peculiar qualifications being essential in the members, the primary consideration ought to be to select that mode of choice which best secures these qualifications; secondly, because the permanent tenure by which the appointments are held in that department, must soon destroy all sense of dependence on the authority conferring them.

It is equally evident, that the members of each department should be as little dependent as possible on those of the others, for the emoluments annexed to their offices. Were the executive magistrate, or the judges, not independent of the legislature in this particular, their independence in every other would be merely nominal. But the great security against a gradual concentration of the several powers in the same department, consists in giving to those who administer each department the necessary constitutional means and personal motives to resist encroachments of the others. The provision for defense must in this, as in all other cases, be made commensurate to the danger of attack. Ambition must be made to counteract ambition. The interest of the man must be connected with the constitutional rights of the place. It may be a reflection on human nature, that such devices should be necessary to control the abuses of government. But what is government itself, but the greatest of all reflections on human nature? If men were angels, no government would be necessary. If angels were to govern men, neither external nor internal controls on government would be necessary. In framing a government which is to be administered by men over men, the great difficulty lies in this: you must first enable the government to control the governed; and in the next place oblige it to control itself.

A dependence on the people is, no doubt, the primary control on the government; but experience has taught mankind the necessity of auxiliary precautions. This policy of supplying, by opposite and rival interests, the defect of better motives, might be traced through the whole system of human affairs, private as well as public. We see it particularly displayed in all the subordinate distributions of power, where the constant aim is to

Federalist Papers: No. 51
continued

divide and arrange the several offices in such a manner as that each may be a check on the other that the private interest of every individual may be a sentinel over the public rights. These inventions of prudence cannot be less requisite in the distribution of the supreme powers of the State. But it is not possible to give to each department an equal power of self-defense. In republican government, the legislative authority necessarily predominates. The remedy for this inconveniency is to divide the legislature into different branches; and to render them, by different modes of election and different principles of action, as little connected with each other as the nature of their common functions and their common dependence on the society will admit. It may even be necessary to guard against dangerous encroachments by still further precautions. As the weight of the legislative authority requires that it should be thus divided, the weakness of the executive may require, on the other hand, that it should be fortified.

An absolute negative on the legislature appears, at first view, to be the natural defense with which the executive magistrate should be armed. But perhaps it would be neither altogether safe nor alone sufficient. On ordinary occasions it might not be exerted with the requisite firmness, and on extraordinary occasions it might be perfidiously abused. May not this defect of an absolute negative be supplied by some qualified connection between this weaker department and the weaker branch of the stronger department, by which the latter may be led to support the constitutional rights of the former, without being too much detached from the rights of its own department? If the principles on which these observations are founded be just, as I persuade myself they are, and they be applied as a criterion to the several State constitutions, and to the federal Constitution it will be found that if the latter does not perfectly correspond with them, the former are infinitely less able to bear such a test.

There are, moreover, two considerations particularly applicable to the federal system of America, which place that system in a very interesting point of view. First. In a single republic, all the power surrendered by the people is submitted to the administration of a single government; and the usurpations are guarded against by a division of the government into distinct and separate departments. In the compound republic of America, the power surrendered by the people is first divided between two distinct governments, and then the portion allotted to each subdivided among distinct and separate departments. Hence a double security

continued

arises to the rights of the people. The different governments will control each other, at the same time that each will be controlled by itself. Second. It is of great importance in a republic not only to guard the society against the oppression of its rulers, but to guard one part of the society against the injustice of the other part. Different interests necessarily exist in different classes of citizens. If a majority be united by a common interest, the rights of the minority will be insecure.

There are but two methods of providing against this evil: the one by creating a will in the community independent of the majority that is, of the society itself; the other, by comprehending in the society so many separate descriptions of citizens as will render an unjust combination of a majority of the whole very improbable, if not impracticable. The first method prevails in all governments possessing an hereditary or self-appointed authority. This, at best, is but a precarious security; because a power independent of the society may as well espouse the unjust views of the major, as the rightful interests of the minor party, and may possibly be turned against both parties. The second method will be exemplified in the federal republic of the United States. Whilst all authority in it will be derived from and dependent on the society, the society itself will be broken into so many parts, interests, and classes of citizens, that the rights of individuals, or of the minority, will be in little danger from interested combinations of the majority.

In a free government the security for civil rights must be the same as that for religious rights. It consists in the one case in the multiplicity of interests, and in the other in the multiplicity of sects. The degree of security in both cases will depend on the number of interests and sects; and this may be presumed to depend on the extent of country and number of people comprehended under the same government. This view of the subject must particularly recommend a proper federal system to all the sincere and considerate friends of republican government, since it shows that in exact proportion as the territory of the Union may be formed into more circumscribed Confederacies, or States oppressive combinations of a majority will be facilitated: the best security, under the republican forms, for the rights of every class of citizens, will be diminished: and consequently the stability and independence of some member of the government, the only other security, must be proportionately increased. Justice is the end of government. It is the end of civil society. It ever has been and ever will be pursued until it be obtained, or until liberty be lost in the pursuit. In a society under the forms of which the

Federalist Papers: No. 51
continued

stronger faction can readily unite and oppress the weaker, anarchy may as truly be said to reign as in a state of nature, where the weaker individual is not secured against the violence of the stronger; and as, in the latter state, even the stronger individuals are prompted, by the uncertainty of their condition, to submit to a government which may protect the weak as well as themselves; so, in the former state, will the more powerful factions or parties be gradnally[sic] induced, by a like motive, to wish for a government which will protect all parties, the weaker as well as the more powerful.

It can be little doubted that if the State of Rhode Island was separated from the Confederacy and left to itself, the insecurity of rights under the popular form of government within such narrow limits would be displayed by such reiterated oppressions of factious majorities that some power altogether independent of the people would soon be called for by the voice of the very factions whose misrule had proved the necessity of it. In the extended republic of the United States, and among the great variety of interests, parties, and sects which it embraces, a coalition of a majority of the whole society could seldom take place on any other principles than those of justice and the general good; whilst there being thus less danger to a minor from the will of a major party, there must be less pretext, also, to provide for the security of the former, by introducing into the government a will not dependent on the latter, or, in other words, a will independent of the society itself. It is no less certain than it is important, notwithstanding the contrary opinions which have been entertained, that the larger the society, provided it lie within a practical sphere, the more duly capable it will be of self-government. And happily for the REPUBLICAN CAUSE, the practicable sphere may be carried to a very great extent, by a judicious modification and mixture of the FEDERAL PRINCIPLE.

PUBLIUS.[3]

Madison's belief in a strong executive authority put him at odds with Jefferson and other more radical patriots, who saw the Constitution as providing too much power to the central government. Madison engaged in a famous series of debates with anti-Federalist Patrick Henry in Virginia, and both men presented strong, reasoned arguments. The more powerful and populated northern states won out over the objections of radicals like Henry, who wanted a more parliamentary government, with decentralized power and more freedom for the states. Jefferson, too, had reservations, and he wrote to Madison in an effort to convince him that the Constitution alone was not sufficient to protect personal liberties and that it was important to develop a "Bill of Rights," that would protect the freedoms and liberties of the people. Madison was skeptical, thinking that the framework of the Constitution should be all that was needed. He worried, too, that the inclusion of a Bill of Rights might be seen as meaning that any rights not enumerated specifically within the document would not be protected. Jefferson ultimately convinced Madison that the Bill of Rights was necessary to secure ratification, and Madison enumerated a list of 19 basic rights, of which only 12 were selected in committee, and only 10 were ratified by the states. Another of Madison's proposed amendments was later adopted in the form of the Fourteenth Amendment's due process clause.[4]

After the ratification of the Constitution, Madison sought to serve on the U.S. Senate, which was by appointment rather than election. After rival Patrick Henry successfully blocked Madison's appointment, Madison sought a seat on the House of Representatives representing Virginia, which was decided by popular vote. Again Henry tried to prevent Madison from achieving office, by what some historians believe is the first example of political gerrymandering.[5]

Though he fought for the Federalist cause, Madison split with the Federalists during the Washington administration over the issue of whether or not the United States should have a central bank. Hamilton said yes; Madison

and Jefferson said no. Madison further disagreed with Federalist views on Great Britain and its war with France, leading him, and Jefferson, to found a new political party that came to be known as the Democratic-Republicans.

The European Wars

The careers of Washington, Adams, Jefferson, and Madison were shaped by the Anglo-French Wars in Europe. Madison was one of the strongest critics of Federalist policy toward Great Britain during the Anglo-French wars and, along with Jefferson, became one of the strongest critics of the Alien and Sedition Acts passed under Adams, which were a transparent effort to stifle opposition from the Democratic-Republicans. After Jefferson was elected in 1800, marking the beginning of a shift toward Democratic-Republican leadership, Madison became Jefferson's head of state. He helped Jefferson reduce military spending, dismantle the standing army, and abandon plans for a national bank. Collectively these actions helped reduce national debt, but the war in Europe threatened American prosperity.

At the end of Jefferson's second term, the situation with Britain worsened. British ships became more aggressive in their harassment of American merchant vessels, and British ships began to forcibly conscript captured American sailors into service, known as "impressment," under which the British crown claimed the right to forcibly "press" any Englishman into service. Legally, citizens of foreign nations could not be impressed, but this law was ignored. British ships frequently stopped American vessels under the pretense of searching for English deserters. English Americans who could not prove their citizenship were frequently pressed into service and the U.S. government did nothing to stop this practice.

In 1807, British ships fired on the USS Chesapeake off the coast of Virginia due to a complicated situation involving impressed American merchant sailors, and a London sailor who deserted his country. [6] The attack on the

Chesapeake was an escalation in the conflict with Britain and press coverage led to widespread anger among Americans. Calls for military action briefly united the more hawkish members of the nation's rival political parties, but there was little that Jefferson could do; he had reduced military spending and the size of the navy and was also dealing with Barbary pirates off the coast of Africa. Jefferson diplomatically bided his time, allowing the furor and calls for war to subside, while he attempted to devise an economic strategy. For their part, the British remained publicly smugly defiant of American demands, but quietly acceded to some. According to the Naval Chronicle of 1812, the three American sailors who'd been pressed were sentenced to 500 lashes each; but this sentence was commuted, and they were returned to America.[7] The only true deserter, London native Jenkin Ratford, was sentenced to death and hung. Back in the United States, the government tried to defray some of the public outrage by blaming the incident, in part, on Admiral James Barron, who was court-martialed for failing to prepare his ship, the USS Chesapeake, for a possible attack.

With open war out of the question, Madison and Jefferson settled on an aggressive economic attack. They convinced Congress to pass the Embargo Act of 1807, which essentially prohibited all trade with Europe. Madison reported on the ongoing impressment of Americans, telling Congress in early 1808 that it appeared that as many as 4,228 American seamen had been impressed into British service, with 936 subsequently released. Britain issued a statement indicating that the government had no intention of stopping impressments, while France also issued a proclamation threatening American ships. The Embargo Act, though negatively impacting France and Britain, hurt American business most of all. Without this revenue, America entered a depression. Just before leaving office, Jefferson signed an update of the law that imposed more targeted economic sanctions on Britain and France, but eased restrictions in other areas.[8]

In the 1808 presidential election, the Federalists nominated Charles C. Pinckney of South Carolina and New Yorker Rufus King to run against Madison and Jefferson's second vice president, George Clinton. Federalist press blamed the Democratic-Republicans for the economic depression linked to the Embargo Act and hoped that this and Jefferson's failure to address British hostility would be sufficient to secure victory. Jefferson, still influential despite the Embargo Act, campaigned on Madison's behalf. Madison won 122 electoral votes to Pinckney's 44, while Clinton managed only 6 votes, all from his home state. Madison entered office in 1809 with a definite public mandate, having received more than 120,000 public votes to Pinckney's 60,000, but he faced difficult choices in the realm of national security.[9]

Over the course of his first term, Madison tried to maintain America's neutrality, striking back at the British through economic actions, but this policy was insufficient and did not satisfy the public sentiment. In 1812, after years of failed negotiations, Congress voted (in a contentious and split vote) to declare war on Britain. Both Madison and members of the legislature referred to this conflict, now known as the War of 1812, as a "Second War of Independence" from Britain. By the fall of 1812, American forces had suffered major defeats. In 1813, American forces managed to turn the tide temporarily.[10] In 1814, British forces aggressively pressed their war on the United States. British forces launched successful attacks against American ports across the East coast, occupying about half of Maine and parts of Georgia in the process. Then, in September of 1814, British forces marched on Washington, DC. It was the first and only time that the U.S. capital saw an invasion, and Madison himself, armed with dueling pistols, went to the front lines to rally his troops, becoming one of only two presidents ever to be directly involved in a military engagement (the other was Abraham Lincoln). Unfortunately, the British forces were too strong and the U.S. militia was routed. Madison and the troops fled the city, leaving British forces to sack and set fire to the White House and the U.S. Capitol. Madison's wife, First Lady Dolley Madison, returned to the burning White House to ensure that the famous portrait of George Washington was saved from fire or vandalism.[11] The British offensive was halted in Baltimore, as British soldiers tried unsuccessfully to lay siege to Fort McHenry, a battle that inspired Francis Scott Key to write "The Star-Spangled Banner."

Thwarted in their path from the northeast, the British sent an army of some 6,000 soldiers to lay siege to New Orleans. It was here that General Andrew Jackson and 4,000 soldiers met the British forces in a field outside the city on January 8. The battle was a disaster for the British, with more than 2,000 British soldiers killed in less than an hour, while the Americans suffered only 70 losses. Even before victory was declared in New Orleans, British and U.S. envoys reached a peace agreement, resulting in the Treaty of Ghent signed in Ghent, Belgium. [12]

Madison's public approval ranged from incredible highs to near-disastrous lows over the course of his first and second terms in office, reflecting the tremendous anxiety and uncertainty that surrounded the War of 1812. The Federalists, seeking to retain their earlier dominance, used the failures of the war to portray Madison and his Democratic-Republicans as weak on foreign policy and to paint the war with Britain as a mistaken struggle against an important ally. The attitude about the war in New England, where the Federalists still held power, was far different than in the south or southeast. Many among the Federalists still objected to the war and America's de facto alliance with France, considering Napoleon Bonaparte to be a tyrant and an alliance with France immoral. This attitude was fueled in part by a vestigial sense of "Britishness" that still formed a strong undercurrent in New England, as well as ethnic prejudice against the French, as well as legitimate concerns regarding Napoleon's imperial ambitions. Further, the northeast had been especially hard hit by the Embargo Act, as much of the trade in the region was with Britain.

In December of 1814, a group of Federalists called a meeting of delegates in Hartford, Connecticut. This meeting, known as the Hartford Convention, was intended to formalize complaints against the administration. Rumors spread that the Federalists wanted to secede from the union, though such a strategy appealed only to a few of the most extreme members of the party. The Hartford Convention concluded with a resolution calling for the federal government to provide financial assistance to New England and proposing a constitutional amendment increasing the majority needed to declare war from a simple majority to a super, or two-thirds, majority. The Hartford Convention's declaration reached Congress on January 5, 1815, but was poorly timed. News of the Treaty of Ghent arrived shortly thereafter, and the Federalists appeared unpatriotic, and to some, traitorous. The already compromised Federalist Party was unable to recover and ultimately disbanded.[13]

Madison, the Man and the Leader

It is safe to describe James Madison as a divisive president. In the wake of the War of 1812, his popularity surged in a wave of patriotic nationalism and, for a time, Madison was hailed as one of the great heroes and patriots. Over the course of his eight years in office, however, Madison also saw grim drops in public approval that brought the federal government to its lowest level of public opinion since the founding of the nation. Nevertheless, Madison ended his second term with high public approval and with the respect of many if not most in the government.

The unfinished U.S. Capitol building was set on fire by the British during the War of 1812. By George Munger, Library of Congress Prints and Photographs division, via Wikimedia.

The War of 1812 was the most significant event of his presidency and, in this capacity, Madison attempted to find a balance between those in Washington calling for war and those who wanted to remain neutral in the conflict. He has been criticized for waiting too long to act, and the nation's losses in the War of 1812 (over 2000 deaths) were, in part, the result of his and Jefferson's efforts to shrink military spending and broader opposition to a standing federal military force. Military historians have come to the general consensus that the War of 1812 was in no way a major U.S. victory. Given that the White House was burned and the capital sacked, at best the war can be described as a draw, with little significant territory gained or advanced for either side. Nevertheless, the dramatic victory in New Orleans led to a surge of patriotic pride that benefitted Madison and the Democratic-Republicans. The war also became a source of political advancement, with two presidents, Andrew Jackson and William Henry Harrison, as well as congressmen and state representatives getting their political start based on their reputation from the war. As Commander-in-Chief, Madison was no warrior, and demonstrated his tendency toward building coalitions and alliances by delegating authority. However, when Washington, DC, was attacked, Madison willingly joined the troops on the front line.

As the man most often credited as the "Father of the Constitution," and the man most directly responsible for creating and defending the "checks and balances" between the three branches of government, it is perhaps unsurprising that Madison's use of presidential powers was intelligent and measured. Perhaps the prime example of this came at the very end of his presidency, when Madison vetoed the so-called "Bonus Bill" on March 3, 1817, a bill that would have provided federal funding for the construction of roads and canals to increase domestic transportation and business. What is unique about Madison's veto is that he had a long history of supporting the idea that the federal government might take an active role in promoting infrastructure projects like the ones proposed in the Bonus Bill. At the Constitutional Convention, James Madison was one of several delegates who strongly favored the idea that Congress should be given the power to create "charters of incorporation" that would have allowed for the construction of transportation corridors to promote trade between the states. Anti-Federalists managed to defeat this proposal at the convention, feeling that federal authority to build canals and roads would give the federal government too much authority to interfere in state commerce and economics. The proposal failed, and the Constitution did not contain a clause granting Congress the power to fund incorporation projects.

During his presidency, it was clear that the rapid growth of the nation, stimulated in part by the Louisiana Purchase, was creating a whole host of problems. There were few roads and few safe shipping routes that could be used either to facilitate public transportation or to increase interstate trade. Madison proposed that Congress work on a Constitutional amendment granting the legislature the power to authorize the federal government to build national roads and canals. Legislators proposed the Bonus Bill to divert profits from the National Bank toward the building of roads and canals. One of Madison's last acts as president was to veto this bill, not because he opposed the federal funding of infrastructure projects, but because he felt the action was beyond the constitutional powers afforded to Congress; and he believed that it was his duty to use executive power, in the form of the veto, to check the powers of the legislature. Madison explained this in a speech given to Congress on March 3, 1817:

VETO MESSAGE ON THE INTERNAL IMPROVEMENTS BILL
Transcript
March 3, 1817
Source Document Excerpt

To the House of Representatives of the United States:

Having considered the bill this day presented to me entitled "An act to set apart and pledge certain funds for internal improvements," and which sets apart and pledges funds "for constructing roads and canals, and improving the navigation of water courses, in order to facilitate, promote, and give security to internal commerce among the several States, and to render more easy and less expensive the means and provisions for the common defense,"

I am constrained by the insuperable difficulty I feel in reconciling the bill with the Constitution of the United States to return it with that objection to the House of Representatives, in which it originated.

The legislative powers vested in Congress are specified and enumerated in the eighth section of the first article of the Constitution, and it does not appear that the power proposed to be exercised by the bill is among the enumerated powers, or that it falls by any just interpretation within the

Veto Message on the Internal Improvements Bill
continued

power to make laws necessary and proper for carrying into execution those or other powers vested by the Constitution in the Government of the United States.

"The power to regulate commerce among the several States" can not include a power to construct roads and canals, and to improve the navigation of water courses in order to facilitate, promote, and secure such a commerce without a latitude of construction departing from the ordinary import of the terms strengthened by the known inconveniences which doubtless led to the grant of this remedial power to Congress.

To refer the power in question to the clause "to provide for the common defense and general welfare" would be contrary to the established and consistent rules of interpretation, as rendering the special and careful enumeration of powers which follow the clause nugatory and improper. Such a view of the Constitution would have the effect of giving to Congress a general power of legislation instead of the defined and limited one hitherto understood to belong to them, the terms "common defense and general welfare" embracing every object and act within the purview of a legislative trust. It would have the effect of subjecting both the Constitution and laws of the several States in all cases not specifically exempted to be superseded by laws of Congress, it being expressly declared "that the Constitution of the United States and laws made in pursuance thereof shall be the supreme law of the land, and the judges of every State shall be bound thereby, anything in the constitution or laws of any State to the contrary notwithstanding." Such a view of the Constitution, finally, would have the effect of excluding the judicial authority of the United States from its participation in guarding the boundary between the legislative powers of the General and the State Governments, inasmuch as questions relating to the general welfare, being questions of policy and expediency, are unsusceptible of judicial cognizance and decision.

A restriction of the power "to provide for the common defense and general welfare" to cases which are to be provided for by the expenditure of money would still leave within the legislative power of Congress all the great and most important measures of Government, money being the ordinary and necessary means of carrying them into execution.

If a general power to construct roads and canals, and to improve the navigation of water courses, with the train of powers incident thereto, be not

continued

possessed by Congress, the assent of the States in the mode provided in the bill can not confer the power. The only cases in which the consent and cession of particular States can extend the power of Congress are those specified and provided for in the Constitution.

I am not unaware of the great importance of roads and canals and the improved navigation of water courses, and that a power in the National Legislature to provide for them might be exercised with signal advantage to the general prosperity. But seeing that such a power is not expressly given by the Constitution, and believing that it can not be deduced from any part of it without an inadmissible latitude of construction and a reliance on insufficient precedents; believing also that the permanent success of the Constitution depends on a definite partition of powers between the General and the State Governments, and that no adequate landmarks would be left by the constructive extension of the powers of Congress as proposed in the bill, I have no option but to withhold my signature from it, and to cherishing the hope that its beneficial objects may be attained by a resort for the necessary powers to the same wisdom and virtue in the nation which established the Constitution in its actual form and providently marked out in the instrument itself a safe and practicable mode of improving it as experience might suggest.

JAMES MADISON.[14]

America's First Family

Beyond his use of presidential powers and authority, Madison also left an indelible mark on the presidency by becoming the first president whose wife played an important public and political role. Madison met the woman who was to become his wife, Dolley Payne Todd, in 1794, at a meeting arranged by mutual acquaintance Aaron Burr. Todd was 26 at the time and a widow, having lost her husband and younger son in the famous yellow fever epidemic of Philadelphia in 1793. Born into a Quaker family, the young widow enchanted Madison, who was nearly 20 years her senior at 46 and never had children of his own. Madison set about courting her; and, later that year, they were married.

Dolley Madison, the first "First Lady" of the United States, played an important public and political role during her husband's presidency. By Gilbert Stuart, via Wikimedia.

They seemed an odd pair, both in appearance and in temperament. She was taller, buxom, and had an outgoing, vivacious personality whereas James was described as a short, somewhat stern-looking man whose demeanor was frequently chilly. However, friends who knew the couple described James as a romantic who loved to indulge in high quality wine and told risqué jokes. Though Madison's lasting image has been of a lonely intellectual, fuming over difficult political questions, it seems that he had a reputation for good wit and thoroughly enjoyed the social sphere. At the couple's home in Montpelier, children of relations, nieces and nephews were frequently present (they had some 50 between them), as well as cousins, aunts, uncles, and friends. Those who knew them well have said that the couple, even while living at the Executive Mansion (now called the White House), would "sometimes romp and tease each other like two children," with the larger, heavier Dolley even occasionally lifting and carrying her presidential husband on her back. Their letters to one another, even after decades of marriage, demonstrate passion and an immense friendship and tenderness, making them one of the great romantic stories of the White House.[15]

As Madison grew in importance, Dolley's charm and penchant for hospitality made her popular among the inner circles of the Washington elite, even across partisan lines. When Madison became president, his wife not only accompanied him to the Executive Mansion but became a key part of his administration. Dolley Madison was, in many ways, the first "First Lady" of America, though this term would not come into fashion until after her time in office. Even before her husband was elected president, Dolley Madison was the most popular woman in the capital. She became something of a fashion icon with her signature turban, an exotic accessory she used to compliment her more conformist dresses. She sometimes violated the feminine customs of the day, in her conversations and personality, but did so with such charm that she was never criticized. On a number of

occasions, Dolley made strategic social advances to those whose political favor her husband required. She also used her influence to secure many individuals federal positions through her husband or her many other acquaintances. At a time when women enjoyed little in the way of political agency, Dolley Madison's role in her husband's presidency was far from trivial. She helped to define a new style of American womanhood at a time when the country was still grappling with creating a sense of identity separate from its European ancestry.

Washington and Adams had used official social gatherings only for formal business, and attendees described these as relatively austere functions. Jefferson, having occupied the office during a period of intense partisan competition and divisiveness, either met with members of either party separately, or tended to throw gatherings that were all-male and booze-filled, sometimes leading to actual fights. With Dolley's casual, welcoming demeanor, Madison was able to transform the White House into something quite different. Political allies and enemies alike were invited and encouraged to socialize, drink, and to put aside politics for the sake of pleasant conversation at the couple's Wednesday Night parties, events so popular they came to be called "squeezes" because of how the guests needed to "squeeze in" to attend. Politicians' spouses were invited to attend as well, and sometimes even their children, and the White House became, for the first time, a home as much as a symbol of the presidency. James and Dolley Madison were the first "first family," and their warm hospitality and diplomatic demeanor changed the nature of the White House and invented the role of the First Lady. From Dolley Madison on, First Ladies of America took on a new role, a blend of hostess and diplomat and symbol for American family values. Though many historians have sometimes reduced Dolley Madison's importance to that of "hostess," a more intimate depiction of the Madison's social sphere reveals a deeper role for the nation's First Lady.

While James Madison could sometimes appear unapproachable, Dolley Madison became one of the most famous and popular women in America, as attendance at her funeral suggests. On July 16, 1849, thousands lined the DC sidewalks and 48 horse-drawn carriages accompanied her body to the Congressional Cemetery. Dolley Madison's funeral was the largest in the history of Washington, DC—a testament to her lasting influence and her role in creating the American presidency and culture.[16]

CONCLUSION

James Madison is one of the most widely respected and admired of the founding generation. Though marginalized by partisan disputes, Madison demonstrated the role of the president as negotiator and mediator and proved an able coalition builder. The War of 1812, and the controversy over U.S. relations with France and Britain, dominated much of his presidency, and led to Madison, though not a military man, being one of only two presidents to accompany troops into battle. Though the Federalists were gaining power in the Northeast, Madison maintained sufficient popularity, at least among the elite class, to continue Jeffersonian dominance. Fellow Jefferson protégé James Monroe, the last of the Virginia dynasty, took over the presidency after Madison's second term, and is discussed in the next chapter.

DISCUSSION QUESTIONS

♦ How did Madison violate presidential authority in the War of 1812?

♦ How did the Madison family change the social environment in Washington?

♦ Does Dolley Madison's role represent an overreach of presidential authority, and how does it compare to modern First Ladies?

♦ Why didn't Madison believe that the Bill of Rights was necessary? In your opinion, was he correct?

♦ How did Madison's vision of presidential power differ from Jefferson's?

Works Used

"Becoming America's First Lady." *Montpelier*. 2019. www.montpelier.org/learn/dolley-madison-becoming-americas-first-lady.

Buel, Richard Jr. *America on the Brink: How the Political Struggle Over the War of 1812 Almost Destroyed the Young Republic*. Palgrave MacMillan, 2005.

Dunaway, W. F. "The Virginia Conventions of the Revolution." *Virginia Law Register*, vol. 10, no.7, Nov. 1904, p. 567–86. www.jstor.org/stable/pdf/1100650.pdf.

"Embargo of 1807." *Monticello*. 2019. www.monticello.org/site/research-and-collections/embargo-1807.

"Five Items Congress Deleted from Madison's Original Bill of Rights." *Constitution Daily*. National Constitution Center. 15 Dec. 2018. constitutioncenter.org/blog/five-items-congress-deleted-from-madisons-original-bill-of-rights.

"Flight of the Madisons." *White House History*. White House Historical Association. 2019.www.whitehousehistory.org/flight-of-the-madisons.

Grove, Lloyd. "The Man Who Was the Madison." *The Washington Post*. 7 May 1982. www.washingtonpost.com/archive/lifestyle/1982/05/07/the-man-who-was-the-madison-by-lloyd-grove/4f67af5b-a4d8-4542-aa43-9433c67d4694/.

Hickey, Donald R. *The War of 1812: A Forgotten Conflict*. Chicago, IL: University of Illinois, 2012.

Hunter, Thomas Rogers. "The First Gerrymander? Patrick Henry, James Madison, James Monroe, and Virginia's 1788 Congressional Districting." *Early American Studies*. vol. 9, no. 3, Fall 2011, pp. 781–820. *JSTOR*, www.jstor.org/stable/23546676.

Madison, James. "Federalist No. 51." *Bill of Rights Institute*. billofrightsinstitute.org/founding-documents/primary-source-documents/the-federalist-papers/federalist-papers-no-51/.

_____. "March 3, 1817: Veto Message on the Internal Improvements Bill." *Miller Center*. 2019.millercenter.org/the-presidency/presidential-speeches/march-3-1817-veto-message-internal-improvements-bill.

"Naval Chronicle Vol XXVII," USS Constitution Museum Collection.

Stagg, J.C.A. "James Madison: Campaigns and Elections." *Miller Center*. 2019. millercenter.org/president/madison/campaigns-and-elections.

Stewart, David O. "The Surprising Raucous Home Life of the Madisons." *Smithsonian*. 10 Feb. 2015. www.smithsonianmag.com/history/surprising-raucous-home-life-madisons-180954205/.

"The Chesapeake Affair of 1807." *The Mariners Museum*. 2000. www.marinersmuseum.org/sites/micro/usnavy/08/08b.htm.

"War of 1812–1815." *U.S. Department of State*. Office of the Historian. history.state.gov/milestones/1801-1829/war-of-1812.

Introduction

James Monroe was the last of the "framers" to serve as president and the last of the Virginia dynasty. A strong and independent man, Monroe resisted partisan politics and cultivated relationships with politicians in both parties. Presiding over what historians call the "era of good feelings," Monroe was the only president, other than Washington, who was elected unopposed during his second term. During his presidency, Monroe confronted the controversy over federal investment in infrastructure and accomplished a great deal in the field of international diplomacy. Monroe's most notable use of executive authority came with the establishment of the Monroe Doctrine, a broad guideline to shape the American approach to foreign policy in the Americas that guided future presidents in addressing foreign encroachment and Latin American independence movements, and fueled the rise of American imperialism in the nineteenth century.

Topics covered in this chapter include:
- The Monroe Doctrine
- John Quincy Adams
- Andrew Jackson and the annexation of Florida
- The U.S.-Canadian border
- U.S.-British relations
- Federal infrastructure investment
- Partisan politics

This Chapter Discusses the Following Source Document:
The Monroe Doctrine, December 2, 1823

Controlling the Americas
James Monroe (1817–1825)

James Monroe was the last of the Virginia Dynasty, a powerful group of patriots hailing from the aristocracy of Virginia gentleman planters that included George Washington, Thomas Jefferson, and James Madison. Monroe presided over an America created by the Federalist Party and represented the powerful families and businesses of the northeast. He won two terms in office with little competition and was also one of the most qualified men ever to become president. Before his first election, Monroe had been a commanding soldier in the Revolutionary War, an appointee to the Continental Congress and to the U.S. Senate, and he had served as secretary of state and secretary of war. He was respected across partisan lines and admired for his intellect and diplomatic skill, and his presidency coincided with and helped to bring about a period of uncommon stability. In terms of the exercise of presidential authority, Monroe was the first president to use the prestige of his office to establish America's place in the broader political spectrum of the Western Hemisphere, and the product of his foreign policy efforts, the so-called "Monroe Doctrine," shaped the fate of North America.

The Last of the Founding Fathers

Monroe was born in Westmoreland County, Virginia, in 1758, the son of a wealthy slave-owning plantation family. Both parents died when he was in his teenage years, and he and his siblings shared an inheritance of land and slaves that saw them through to adulthood. Monroe attended the College of William and Mary, alma mater of Jefferson and many other Virginia aristocrats. As a young man he joined the Virginia Militia, and then the Infantry, serving under George Washington in New York, Trenton, Monmouth, Brandywine, and Germantown. He was nearly killed after being wounded in the shoulder by canon fire in the battle of Trenton and was thereafter promoted to Colonel in the Virginia Service.

James Monroe, whose Monroe Doctrine set an important precedent for the foreign policy of the United States. By Samuel Morse, via Wikimedia.

After the war, Monroe pursued studies in law, with Thomas Jefferson as his friend and mentor. He was elected to the Virginia Assembly in 1782 and was chosen as a delegate to the Continental Congress in 1783. Monroe was an opponent of the U.S. Constitution and joined Thomas Jefferson in calling for a Bill of Rights and direct election of Senators (who were at the time appointed to office by state legislators). Though he was a rival of James Madison and lost a contest for election to the U.S. House of Representatives, he was later appointed to the U.S. Senate by the state legislature. Later, when Madison shifted away from the Federalists, Monroe, Madison, and Jefferson became the leaders in the emerging Democratic-Republican opposition to what they saw as Federalist monarchism.[1]

Under Washington, Madison was a minister to France, where he struggled to maintain Washington's policy of neutrality and to keep the French Revolutionary government satisfied that the United States was not planning to side with the British. Following this appointment, he returned to Virginia and successfully ran for the Governor's seat in 1799, a position he used to support Thomas Jefferson's aims in the presidency over his two terms. After Jefferson's elections, Monroe was selected as one of the envoys to negotiate the Louisiana Purchase, then served as minister to Britain. Appointed an envoy to Spain in 1805, Monroe attempted to negotiate a new treaty with Spain that would have given the United States additional territory along the Gulf of Mexico. Though his effort at this time was unsuccessful, controlling Spanish territory was a subject he would address again as president. There were some among the Democratic-Republicans who wished to see Monroe become president instead of Madison, but Monroe did not seriously challenge Madison's candidacy in 1808. He returned to Virginia and won election to the governor's seat again in 1811, though he would not remain in the position as Madison selected Monroe to serve as his secretary of state.[2]

The Second War for Independence

Monroe rose to national prominence as secretary of state and secretary of war under Madison during the War of 1812. Prior to the war, Monroe attempted to maintain neutrality with both France and Britain, as had been Jefferson's policy, but with British ships forcibly impressing American sailors and encroaching on American territory at sea, the situation became untenable. Upon Madison's insistence, Congress declared war on Britain in 1812, which caused great confusion and uncertainty in the nation. While the war was popular in the south and, to some degree, among the new western states, Madison's administration drew heavy criticism from the northeast, where shipping interests were more dependent on trade with Britain. Previous Democratic-Republican efforts to "get tough" on Britain using trade embargos and economic sanctions had proven disastrous for the New England economy, and the Federalists criticized both Madison and Monroe for their failure to prevent the war.

The United States was ill-equipped to win a war against Britain, and from the beginning, the situation was grim. United States forces engaged in an ill-advised and ultimately failed attempt to invade parts of Canada. Monroe was successful as Madison's secretary of war thanks to his previous military experience. In August of 1814, when British troops marched from the Potomac River to the capital, Monroe personally accompanied a scouting party to check on the British position. Returning to Washington, he remained in the city to aid in evacuation efforts, and fled only when British troops arrived and began burning government buildings. When the British left, after being routed at Fort McHenry, Monroe was placed in charge of defending Washington, DC, against further encroachment. Monroe's performance during the war brought him to the attention of the populace, and with nationalism surging after the end of the war—essentially a draw with Britain—both Madison and Monroe enjoyed status as heroes of the republic, helping to forestall another British challenge to American independence.[3]

Good Feelings All Around

Madison was a popular president; and with the war seemingly "won," he likely could have been successful in running for a third term. In the early 1800s, there were no presidential term limits, but a tradition had been set by Washington in which a president served two terms and then voluntarily retired. Any president might have been the first to break with this tradition, but the members of the Virginia Dynasty followed in the footsteps of Washington. Madison, therefore, declined to run for a third term in the lead-up to the 1816 election; and he personally advocated Monroe as his successor. While there was some limited opposition to the idea of yet another president from Virginia, Monroe had more support both within the public and the political elite thanks to his visibility as a member of the Constitutional Convention and as secretary of war under Madison. Supporters promoted Monroe as "the last framer," the final member of the historic Revolutionary generation, and highlighted his fighting alongside Washington. His opponent, Rufus King, who'd had a long and impressive career in public service, lacked both the marketing appeal of Monroe and popular party backing. The Federalists had all but disbanded because they lost public support after their opposition to the War of 1812 had come to seem cowardly or even traitorous. With the Federalists having lost support, and the opposition lacking Monroe's patriotic appeal, Monroe won an easy victory, carrying 183 electoral votes to King's 34 and earning nearly twice the popular votes as his opponent.[4]

Monroe's first four years went well, though there was plenty of political controversy in the nation, and his style of leadership earned him some enemies in Congress. In many ways, he returned to the style of Washington in creating his cabinet. Unafraid of conflict and differences of opinion, Monroe chose John Quincy Adams, son of former President John Adams as his secretary of state. Though they differed on some major issues, Adams and Monroe developed a good working relationship and a friendship as well. This move—granting one of their most prominent Bostonian legislators a major role in his administration—earned Monroe respect in New England. Monroe also sought geographic diversity, and appointed Georgian William H. Crawford as secretary of the treasury and South Carolina's John C. Calhoun as secretary of war. The Washingtonian strategy, creating a cabinet of diverse political and geographic backgrounds, proved even more fruitful for Monroe than for Washington. Though his first term included the Panic of 1819, a four-year recession that saw a huge rise in unemployment, Monroe ended his first term with high public approval and with the respect and admiration of the political and economic elite. The relative peace between the parties led to many historians referring to the period from 1816 to 1825 as the "Era of Good Feelings."[5]

Monroe was so popular as he ended his first term that the Democratic-Republicans did not even hold a caucus to re-nominate him. The Federalists also perceived little utility in trying to oppose him and did not field a candidate. Monroe thus became the first president since Washington, and the last, to run unopposed in an election. He, therefore, won all the nation's electoral votes except for one, which elector Governor William Plumer of New Hampshire had cast for John Quincy Adams, who was not running.[6]

Like Washington, Monroe was an opponent of partisan politics; and he openly promoted the idea that America should avoid the party system, allowing each candidate for office to instead run as an individual, competing solely on merit rather than banking on the support and funding of a political party. To accomplish goals, Monroe believed that presidents and congresspersons alike should be required to build coalitions, personally reaching out to individuals in different political cliques and factions to gain support for their legislative or broader governmental goals. Monroe himself did exactly this in his presidency and was the first and last president to function without a partisan support base. However, the absence of parties that existed during Monroe's eight years in office had created a power vacuum that could be exploited. Aspiring legislators and politicians recognized that they could beat their ideological opponents for office and in achieving political goals. New factions began to form within the legislature, both at the federal level and in the states, and as the Monroe era came to an end, a new party system emerged, with the Whigs rising to challenge the dominance of a new generation of Democratic-Republicans.

The Appropriate Way to Appropriate

Several of the major events of Monroe's presidency demonstrate how he viewed the use of presidential power and how he helped to shape the nature of the presidency going forward. Monroe, like his predecessor Madison, was faced with a nation in desperate need of infrastructural improvements. But the federal government lacked a system to fund such projects and leaving infrastructure development in the hands of the states risked uneven results when what the country actually needed was a system of canals, roads, and other improvements that would create opportunities to travel and trade *between* states.

Madison's response to this issue had been to advise Congress to pass a constitutional amendment granting the legislature the power to fund and build national infrastructure. Congress did not follow Madison's advice and, instead, passed legislation allowing the legislature to collect funds from the National Bank and to use them for the construction of roads and other improvements. One of Madison's last actions as president was to veto this bill, arguing that Congress did not have the constitutional power to take such action. When this issue arose again under Monroe, Monroe felt similarly to Madison, that a constitutional amendment was necessary granting Congress the power to fund, build, maintain, and operate a national transportation system. Many legislators did not believe that an amendment was needed and held that the Constitution implied that Congress already had such power. In 1822, Congress tried to bypass this

deadlock by passing a bill that would have allowed Congress to install a series of tolls on the Cumberland Road, or National Road, between Maryland and Virginia, in order to repair it. Monroe vetoed the bill, arguing that the power to construct infrastructure belonged to the states alone.

Over the next few months, Monroe considered his position on the issue and spoke with jurists (including at least two Supreme Court justices) and members of the legislature. He eventually wrote another memorandum to Congress that—although not altering his position that Congress had no authority to place federal tolls on roads—stated that Congress had the power, under the Constitution, to appropriate funds for national projects, so long as Congress avoided taking any action that would amount to assuming sovereignty in place of the states. A president's constitutional powers are to "enforce" the laws as created by Congress and the Constitution, and both Monroe and Madison had used the president's constitutional veto power to strike down legislation they saw as violating the separation of powers. By ruling that Congress had the right to appropriate, so long as doing so did not violate state sovereignty, Monroe created an approach to congressional appropriation that guided future congressional action. This not only impacted Congress's capability to collect funding for infrastructure, but guided future congressional efforts to appropriate funds for state programs involving social welfare, health care, commerce, agriculture, and education. Monroe's interpretation of the constitutional powers of Congress, therefore, established the system of Congressional investment in state-based programs that remains in place in the twenty-first century.

Congress passed a new appropriations bill on February 28, 1823, that Monroe signed, permitting Congress to appropriate $25,000 from the Treasury Department toward a new infrastructure program. Monroe then became the first president to appoint a superintendent to manage this new federal program, which was described as being in the "general welfare." The program was successful, unifying efforts to increase interstate trade and addressing a lack of funding within the states to do the same. On his last day in office, Monroe expanded the program, with a further appropriation of some $150,000, to extend the National Road through the Ohio River and into the Midwest.[7]

An International America

Having come out of the War of 1812, improving relations with Britain toward the goal of regulating trade was a major priority for Monroe. Monroe and John Quincy Adams worked together to establish several new treaties with Britain, one effectively ending the conflict over control of the Great Lakes and another that established what is essentially the modern border between the United States and Canada. More controversial were the administration's efforts to secure the northeast border with Florida, then controlled by the Spanish.

Within Florida lived the remainder of the Seminole people, a once wide-ranging race forced back into the swamplands of Florida by decades of European aggression. The Seminole were the only Native American society never to surrender and never to be fully defeated, though many American military units tried to eliminate them. In the 1810s, the Seminole occasionally raided white encampments near the Florida border, and they were considered a major threat. Even more infuriating to the slave-owning white families nearby was that the Seminole frequently gave refuge to escaped slaves, ultimately leading to populations of "Black Seminole" scattered throughout parts of Florida. Monroe considered the Seminole a threat and sent General Andrew Jackson, America's most famous military man, to secure the Florida border. Jackson did more than this, leading an invasion into Florida where he captured the city of Pensacola, deposing the sitting Spanish governor, and capturing a Spanish fort. Some in Congress and in the cabinet saw Jackson as having abused the authority given to him by Monroe, and Secretary of War John Calhoun called for Jackson to be reprimanded. Jackson claimed he'd had secret

instructions to invade Florida, though Monroe later discredited this claim. In any case, the ease with which Jackson managed to march through Florida made it clear that the Spanish were not invested in their colony. Adams and Monroe pressed the advantage, recognizing that Spain was consumed with rebellions in some of its other colonies, and approached Spain about purchasing the territory. They were successful, and Florida became part of the United States in 1819.

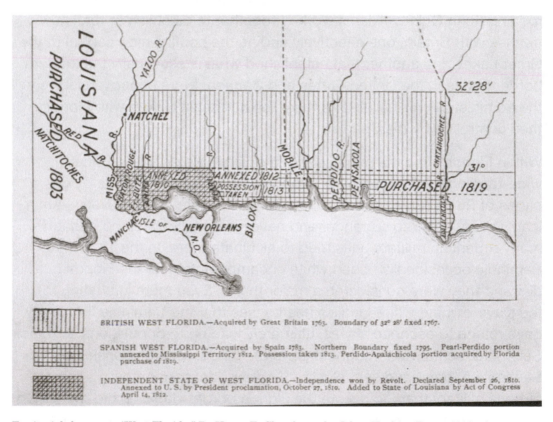

BRITISH WEST FLORIDA.—Acquired by Great Britain 1763. Boundary of 32° 28′ fixed 1767.

SPANISH WEST FLORIDA.—Acquired by Spain 1783. Northern Boundary fixed 1795. Pearl-Perdido portion annexed to Mississippi Territory 1812. Possession taken 1813. Perdido-Apalachicola portion acquired by Florida purchase of 1819.

INDEPENDENT STATE OF WEST FLORIDA.—Independence won by Revolt. Declared September 26, 1810. Annexed to U. S. by President proclamation, October 27, 1810. Added to State of Louisiana by Act of Congress April 14, 1812.

Territorial changes to "West Florida." By Henry E. Chambers, the Johns Hopkins Press, 1898, via Wikimedia.

Ownership of Florida was only part of Monroe's concerns about the colonial Spanish colonies surrounding the United States. The Spanish colonial government had been weakening since the late 1700s; and in the early 1800s, most of the former Spanish colonies in North America and the surrounding islands began breaking from Spanish control. Mexico announced its independence from Spain in 1810, as did Chile and Colombia, followed by Argentina and Peru in 1816 and 1821, respectively. Many U.S. legislators were sympathetic to the Latin American independence movements, some seeing them as mirrors of America's own independence struggle, and some called for formal U.S. recognition of independence in many of the former Spanish colonies. Monroe and some of the most conservative legislators were reluctant to risk angering Spain into conflict and so reserved official recognition. Monroe's administration only recognized the independence of Mexico and the other early countries to break free from Spain in 1822.

About this same time, there was a rumor spreading that Spain and its allies were going to attempt to retake their former colonies, and British envoys reached out to the Monroe administration suggesting a partnership to prevent this. British Foreign Minister George Canning proposed a joint declaration prohibiting any further intervention in the Americas from Europe. John Quincy Adams, then Monroe's secretary of state, opposed this proposal, feeling that it would leave the United States looking dependent on British foreign policy. Instead, he and his allies believed that the United States should stake its own claim with regard to European intervention. Monroe agreed; and in his 1823 annual message to Congress, Monroe issued a statement formulating what would become America's official stance on foreign interference in the Americas, a foreign policy that came to be called the "Monroe Doctrine."

THE MONROE DOCTRINE
December 2, 1823
Source Document Excerpt

The Monroe Doctrine was expressed during President Monroe's seventh annual message to Congress, December 2, 1823:

. . . At the proposal of the Russian Imperial Government, made through the minister of the Emperor residing here, a full power and instructions have been transmitted to the minister of the United States at St. Petersburg to arrange by amicable negotiation the respective rights and interests of the two nations on the northwest coast of this continent. A similar proposal has been made by His Imperial Majesty to the Government of Great Britain, which has likewise been acceded to. The Government of the United States has been desirous by this friendly proceeding of manifesting the great value which they have invariably attached to the friendship of the Emperor and their solicitude to cultivate the best understanding with his Government. In the discussions to which this interest has given rise and in the arrangements by which they may terminate the occasion has been judged proper for asserting, as a principle in which the rights and interests of the United States are involved, that the American continents, by the free and independent condition which they have assumed and maintain, are henceforth not to be considered as subjects for future colonization by any European powers.

It was stated at the commencement of the last session that a great effort was then making in Spain and Portugal to improve the condition of the people of those countries, and that it appeared to be conducted with extraordinary moderation. It need scarcely be remarked that the results have been so far very different from what was then anticipated. Of events in that quarter of the globe, with which we have so much intercourse and from which we derive our origin, we have always been anxious and interested spectators. The citizens of the United States cherish sentiments the most friendly in favor of the liberty and happiness of their fellow-men on that side of the Atlantic. In the wars of the European powers in matters relating to themselves we have never taken any part, nor does it comport with our policy to do so. It is only when our rights are invaded or seriously menaced that we resent injuries or make preparation for our defense. With the movements in this hemisphere we are of necessity more immediately connected, and by causes which must be obvious to all enlightened and impartial observers. The political system of the allied powers is essentially different in this respect from that of America. This difference

continued

proceeds from that which exists in their respective Governments; and to the defense of our own, which has been achieved by the loss of so much blood and treasure, and matured by the wisdom of their most enlightened citizens, and under which we have enjoyed unexampled felicity, this whole nation is devoted. We owe it, therefore, to candor and to the amicable relations existing between the United States and those powers to declare that we should consider any attempt on their part to extend their system to any portion of this hemisphere as dangerous to our peace and safety. With the existing colonies or dependencies of any European power we have not interfered and shall not interfere. But with the Governments who have declared their independence and maintain it, and whose independence we have, on great consideration and on just principles, acknowledged, we could not view any interposition for the purpose of oppressing them, or controlling in any other manner their destiny, by any European power in any other light than as the manifestation of an unfriendly disposition toward the United States. In the war between those new Governments and Spain we declared our neutrality at the time of their recognition, and to this we have adhered, and shall continue to adhere, provided no change shall occur which, in the judgement of the competent authorities of this Government, shall make a corresponding change on the part of the United States indispensable to their security.

The late events in Spain and Portugal show that Europe is still unsettled. Of this important fact no stronger proof can be adduced than that the allied powers should have thought it proper, on any principle satisfactory to themselves, to have interposed by force in the internal concerns of Spain. To what extent such interposition may be carried, on the same principle, is a question in which all independent powers whose governments differ from theirs are interested, even those most remote, and surely none of them more so than the United States. Our policy in regard to Europe, which was adopted at an early stage of the wars which have so long agitated that quarter of the globe, nevertheless remains the same, which is, not to interfere in the internal concerns of any of its powers; to consider the government de facto as the legitimate government for us; to cultivate friendly relations with it, and to preserve those relations by a frank, firm, and manly policy, meeting in all instances the just claims of every power, submitting to injuries from none. But in regard to those continents circumstances are eminently and conspicuously different.

It is impossible that the allied powers should extend their political system to

The Monroe Doctrine
continued

any portion of either continent without endangering our peace and happiness; nor can anyone believe that our southern brethren, if left to themselves, would adopt it of their own accord. It is equally impossible, therefore, that we should behold such interposition in any form with indifference. If we look to the comparative strength and resources of Spain and those new Governments, and their distance from each other, it must be obvious that she can never subdue them. It is still the true policy of the United States to leave the parties to themselves, in hope that other powers will pursue the same course. . . .[8]

The Monroe Doctrine is a groundbreaking step in foreign policy and demonstrates the use of executive authority to chart a course, both for immediate and future policy, with regard to foreign relations, diplomacy, and the proper use of military power. The doctrine establishes two important precedents. First, it established that the United States no longer recognized any European country as having the right to colonize the Americas. Second, the doctrine essentially states that the United States would use its military might to defend the right of the Latin American countries to remain independent and to chart their own governmental course.

Monroe was the first president to create an international "doctrine" while in office, demonstrating how influential the presidency could be with regard to America's foreign policy and position within the global community. While Latin American independence was part of the doctrine, more realistically the doctrine is a claim of ownership over the Americas. The doctrine was also an important statement to Europe, in specific, warning them that the United States stood as a global power, ready to defend against European power or encroachment. By taking this stance independently, Monroe's administration essentially stated that no alliance with any European country was necessary for the United States to claim a role as defender of democracy in the Western Hemisphere. This was, at the time, largely a bluff. Had any of the European powers wanted to challenge the United States, it is unlikely that the United States had the military might to defend the region on its own. The U.S. alliance with Britain was the only reason that the doctrine had any teeth at all, and yet, taking this independent, national stance was symbolically important. The Monroe Doctrine marks a turning point away from Britain and toward the creation of a unique, global identity for the United States. This shift was due, in large part, to Monroe and his use of presidential authority to chart a new and important course for the nation as a participant in global culture.

CONCLUSION

Monroe was the last president who attempted, in the Washingtonian mold, to call for political unity and to end the bitter partisanship that was beginning to dominate American politics. His role in shaping executive policy in Latin America was his most lasting contribution, but Monroe also made major advances in the field of national investment, working with legislators to determine how the federal government might invest in infrastructure for national benefit, without encroaching on states' rights or independence. One of the most independent and experienced men to ever hold the office, Monroe's two terms in office was the culmination of the Jefferson Democrats' influence, but also set the stage for an even more bitter partisan feud that arose in the wake of Monroe's presidency. The next chapter covers the contentious campaign of John Quincy Adams vs. Andrew Jackson.

DISCUSSION QUESTIONS

♦ How did the Monroe Doctrine impact American foreign policy in Latin America? How did it impact American foreign policy in Europe?

♦ How did Monroe differ from Madison and Jefferson in his approach to the Democratic-Republican agenda?

♦ In what key ways did Monroe attempt to address the increasing partisanship in American society? Was he successful?

♦ How did Monroe's stance on infrastructure differ from Madison's? Which do you agree with and why?

Works Used

McNamara, Robert. "The Era of Good Feelings." *Thought Co.* www.thoughtco. com/era-of-good-feelings-1773317.

Poston, Brook. *James Monroe: A Republican Champion.* U P of Florida, 2019.

Preston, Daniel. "James Monroe: Campaigns and Elections." *Miller Center.* U of Virginia. millercenter.org/president/monroe/campaigns-and-elections.

_____. "James Monroe: Life Before the Presidency." *Miller Center.* U of Virginia. millercenter.org/president/monroe/life-before-the-presidency.

Sky, Theodore. *The National Road and the Difficult Path to Sustainable National Investment.* Newark, U of Delaware P, 2011.

"The Monroe Doctrine." *Jamesmonroemuseum.* 2019. jamesmonroemuseum. umw.edu/about-james-monroe/research/articles/.

Unger, Harlow Giles. *The Last Founding Father: James Monroe and a Nation's Call to Greatness.* New York: Da Capo P, 2009; 2010.

Introduction

In the 1824 election, Federalist John Quincy Adams lost the popular vote, but won the Electoral College to beat out Andrew Jackson, one of the most popular men in America thanks to his fame from the War of 1812. Adams, the son of former President John Adams, was a capable and careful politician, but his contentious election left him with a limited popular mandate. Jackson became the first president to begin campaigning as soon as the previous president took office, and Jackson's allies spent four years maligning Adams and the Federalists in preparation for the 1828 election. After finally winning the seat in 1828, Jackson served two terms and became the first president to attract more than half of the nation's voting-age population to the polls. Jackson notably used his presidential power to prevent Congress from accomplishing much of anything. The one exception was a controversial bill that made it through the legislature while he was in office, directing federal agents to conduct what amounted to ethnic cleansing against Native Americans. Though popular among white men at the time of his election, Jackson is typically remembered in the modern world as a poor president.

Topics covered in this chapter include:

- Indian Removal Act
- Tariff of Abominations
- Election controversy of 1824
- Increasing popularity of voting
- Trump and Jackson comparisons
- The "spoils system" and political corruption

This Chapter Discusses the Following Source Documents:

Veto Message Regarding Funding of Infrastructure Development, May 27, 1830

Effect of the Protective System on the Staples of the South, August 3, 1830

Cherokee Nation v. Georgia, 1831

"On Indian Removal": President Jackson's Message to Congress, December 6, 1830

A Populist Revolution
John Quincy Adams and Andrew Jackson (1825–1837)

Andrew Jackson was a president widely despised by those who knew him but so deft at crafting his own public image that he became a much admired and beloved figure among the general public. His actions were calculated to elevate his own reputation and legacy, first and foremost, and he openly utilized the powers of the office to advance his own political power and economic fortunes. Andrew Jackson was the first populist president, the first "common president," and the first presidential hopeful who successfully challenged the dominance of Washington's elite class.

One of history's most divisive figures, some consider Jackson a hero based on his war record and maverick approach to leading the country, while others see him as one of America's greatest villains. Jackson's rise to the White House provides an interesting look at the struggle between popular and aristocratic power that continues to dominate politics, but also marks an important moment in the history of the presidency. Professor Daniel Feller, editor of the Papers of Andrew Jackson at the University of Tennessee, wrote of Jackson, "He expanded executive powers and transformed the President's role from chief administrator to popular tribune."[1]

Ending a Dynasty

John Quincy Adams, who preceded Jackson, was extremely qualified for the presidency. The son of former President John Adams and First Lady Abigail Adams, he was educated at Harvard College, where he studied law. He was appointed minister to the Netherlands at 26, then to Berlin, Germany. He served in the Senate during the Jefferson Administration, then was minister to Russia under Madison. Under Monroe, Adams became one of the great secretaries of state, which was at the time considered a direct stepping-stone to the White House.

John Quincy Adams, by Mathew Brady, National Archives and Records Administration, via Wikimedia.

Until Quincy Adams, the president was chosen largely by the aristocracy, and popular choice had only a subordinate role in the process. The election of 1824 was a turning point. The single-party system, the Democratic-Republicans, had split into factions, and each felt they had a better candidate for the presidency. James Monroe chose not to endorse any candidate; thus, the election developed into a bitter, four-way struggle. In addition to Adams, William Crawford of Georgia had support from some of the New England bigwigs, though he was considered temperamental and difficult to work with (and hated by Monroe, who nearly came to blows with Crawford in a cabinet meeting).[2] House Speaker Henry Clay of Kentucky was a viable candidate, with widespread respect and experience, and many New Englanders preferred him to Adams. The wild card of the 1824 election was General Andrew Jackson of Tennessee. In attempting to build support and patriotic pride over the War of 1812, politicians had celebrated the victory of the Battle of New Orleans, in which Jackson and a group of irregulars repelled a massive British invasion force. He was also famous for his ethnic cleansing campaigns to remove Native Americans from Florida and elsewhere. Jackson positioned himself as the candidate of the people, an everyman who rose from rags to riches and risked his life to defend the republic. Supporters called him a new "George Washington;", in fact, he was the most famous military general since Washington. Jackson's rallies in Pennsylvania, Illinois, and Indiana demonstrated that he carried at least as much popular support as any of the other candidates.

Even though Jackson could have been defeated if another candidate created a strong enough coalition to carry parts of the south and northeast, the number of candidates divided support among moderates and the elite, leaving Jackson as the most popular figure in the race. Adams was the next most popular, but his anti-slavery position reduced his support in the south, and there were some in the west who felt he was too moderate. Jackson won both the popular vote and the Electoral

College, receiving 152,901 votes to Adams's 114,023; Clay received 47,217 and Crawford 46,979. This divided the Electoral College votes into 99 for Jackson, 84 for Adams, 41 for Crawford, and 37 for Clay. Jackson was the winner but fell short of a majority. Under the Twelfth Amendment to the U.S. Constitution, this led to a vote in the House of Representatives. Clay urged his followers to give their votes to Adams, who beat out Jackson, by one electoral vote.[3]

Jackson and his followers called the 1824 election a "corrupt bargain," though the depiction is not entirely accurate. Jackson, though the "people's choice," had not commanded enough support to claim a true popular majority. The House election was within the confines of constitutional law, and Adams was thus the legitimate choice for the presidency. However, Jackson argued that the popular vote had been ignored. Jackson's strategy was to incite anger in his followers, urging them to feel they had been cheated and their views ignored, and he immediately began his campaign for the 1828 election. Over the next four years, Jackson held rallies, lambasted the administration as corrupt, and promoted himself as the popular president wrongly denied his term in office.[4]

Adams found his presidency hopelessly weakened by the 1824 election. He faced a higher level of popular opposition than any past president and was not skilled enough to consolidate support. He proposed a more aggressive system of national infrastructure, including a national university and an astronomical observatory, but met with too much resistance to see any of these programs through. Adams was also criticized for overstepping his authority with the Tariff of 1828, an economic bill designed to increase the cost of imported or exported goods to encourage domestic trade. The tariff had a particularly negative impact on the southern textile market, and this provided political ammunition for Jackson, whose followers named it the "Tariff of Abominations," and decried it as an unconstitutional overreach of the presidency.

Leading up to the 1828 election, Jackson depicted the election as "the people" against Adams. He issued what he called "memorandums," which were better described as informal letters, in which he complained that corrupt bureaucrats had ruined the economy, threatened the welfare of the people, and ignored popular will in favor of a dynastic political network. This was the first election to involve political swag, in the form of snuffboxes, medallions, buttons, posters, tokens, flasks, mugs, and wall hangings, mostly produced by Jackson's campaign. Because Jackson had the nickname "Old Hickory," followers placed hickory rods and poles all over the country and served barbeques with hickory-smoked meats. Adams's supporters attempted to depict Jackson as a savage, racist murderer of Indians, and proponent of slavery. They highlighted Jackson's penchant for dueling and brawling with his enemies, and further, Jackson's behavior during the War of 1812 became a major point. Jackson claimed he had been given permission from Monroe to invade Florida in order to take the state from the Spanish. Adams's camp argued that this was not true, and in fact Monroe gave a statement confirming that Jackson had acted without authorization.

Killer President

Jackson's violent past became one of the controversial issues in his 1828 election. Jackson's reputation for having a temper is borne out by his record. Arguments had a tendency to turn personal, devolving into brawls and fistfights, some deadly. Jackson and his rivals often engaged in duels to the death. Historians have uncovered more than 100 instances in which Jackson was either challenged to, or engaged in, a duel, reflecting his divisive personality and tendency to accrue enemies.[a] In one instance, while working as a lawyer in 1788, Jackson was defeated in a trial by Waightstill Avery, a veteran of the Revolution and a successful attorney. Avery turned one of Jackson's arguments around with such skill that Jackson was embarrassed to the point that he insulted Avery on a personal level, accusing him of taking illegal fees. The two men met for a duel, though neither was shot, and the duel ended as a draw.

In 1806, Jackson dueled fellow lawyer and rival horse breeder Charles Dickinson after Jackson reneged on a $2000 horse bet. The two met at the Red River in Logan, Kentucky. Dickinson shot first, putting a bullet in Jackson's chest that lodged near Jackson's heart and lung but didn't damage either organ. Jackson shot next, hitting and killing Dickinson with his own shot to the chest. Though Jackson survived, the bullet wound left him with medical problems for the remainder of his life and was a contributing factor in his painful death. The duel with Dickinson is the only time Jackson is said to have killed another duelist, but it was one of many duels in which the future president found himself. In addition to the bullet from Dickinson, Jackson carried another bullet lodged in his body for decades, and he'd been shot at least four times, though none were fatal wounds.[b]

Works Used

a. Drapkin, Jenny. "The Nine Lives of Andrew Jackson." *Mental Floss.* 16 Apr. 2008. www.mentalfloss.com/article/18445/nine-lives-andrew-jackson.

b. Brands, H. W. *Andrew Jackson: His Life and Times*. New York: Anchor Books, 2006.

None of the political attacks on Jackson made any difference. For members of the voting public, Jackson's departure from the image of the aristocratic bureaucrat was part of his appeal. His past adventures, brawling, and dueling his way to power and fortune were more relatable and exciting than Adams, who seemed to represent the old guard, a stodgy politician keeping with the aristocracy of the old Federalists and perhaps even the monarchic colonials. The 1828 election was a landslide victory for Jackson, with a wide margin of 647,276 popular votes and 178 electoral votes to Adams's 508,064 and 83. What's more, the number of voters quadrupled from 1824, and 1828 was likely the first election in which a slight majority (around 57 percent) of eligible voters participated in the election.[5]

The 1828 election was important for a number of reasons. This was the first election in which a majority of the American people felt they had a role in choosing their president. The explosion in voter turnout shows how this shift in perception energized the masses into civic action. It was also the first election in which the presidency shifted from a contest between qualified political rivals to a popularity contest in which political coalitions competed for a share of popular support. Further, it was one of the most unethical elections in history, with demonstrably false claims emanating from both camps. The campaign devolved into a contest to see whose lies the American people would believe, and Jackson's people proved the more believable liars. For his part, Adams, who was more principled than Jackson, refused to take any personal role in the mudslinging. Jackson took the other approach, personally directing newspapers how to attack his rival and actually creating some of the false claims that spread about Adams through the press. For better or worse, Jackson helped to create the modern popularity-based presidential contest and the tradition of bitter, often unethical political rivalry that has come to characterize America's presidential politics.

American Iconoclasts

Jackson historians have said that Donald Trump's election and his perceived and self-described similarities to Jackson invited renewed interest in America's controversial seventh president.

The similarities between the two men are largely in the realm of personality and public image. Both men have been called vain and have been known to brag about wealth. Jackson collected media articles about himself and angrily scribbled over the critical ones; Trump behaves similarly via social media. Both men marketed themselves as political outsiders who aimed to restore popular power and to "clean up" corruption in Washington.[6]

Despite similarities in style, the differences between Trump and Jackson are striking. Jackson served in the armed forces and became one of America's most famous generals; Trump avoided military service with a questionable draft deferment. Jackson served as both a Senator and Representative; Trump had no experience as a public servant. Though both men claimed to represent a populist revolution, Trump never commanded majority support among the people and has engendered the most widespread popular opposition movement in presidential history. Jackson had majority support when he took office and his power rested in popular appeal. Jackson was born a "common man," rising to wealth and the presidency from a disadvantaged background. Trump was born wealthy and inherited leadership of his father's real estate empire.

A substantive similarity between Jackson and Trump is that both men proved to be poor managers. Jackson demanded absolute loyalty from his advisers and essentially invented the concept of the "kitchen cabinet," where a leader surrounds himself or herself with personal advisers who are not always qualified for the role. In his two terms in office, Jackson went through four secretaries of state and five secretaries of the treasury. Those who worked in his administration complained about his fiery temperament and inability to take criticism. His absolute dominance of his cabinet and use of unofficial advisers remains one of Jackson's most lasting and controversial contributions in the realm of presidential authority. Opponents saw Jackson's style as authoritarian, and he received the nickname "King Andrew" to reflect his tyrannical approach to running his executive branch.[7]

Jackson also initiated a system of giving lucrative federal jobs to friends and supporters, persons who benefitted Jackson financially, either as president or personally. After taking office, Jackson claimed that a government "purge" was needed to eliminate corruption, although his use of power could be portrayed as corrupt. Jackson eliminated federal workers he perceived as political opponents and used lucrative federal contracts and jobs as rewards for loyalists. The "spoils system" added a new level of political intrigue to presidential politics and deepened the impact of economics on the political system by tying presidential support to economic opportunities typically spread among a president's close, wealthy supporters, or aspiring political followers.[8]

Jackson's invention of the spoils system undercuts any claim that he might have made about legitimately combating corruption. Jackson replaced successful and respected civil servants with untrained, inexperienced friends who performed horrendously in their positions: Postmaster General John McLean was replaced with Jackson's friend William Barry, who used the department for personal profit; Jackson appointed Samuel Swartwout as collector of the Port of New York, who embezzled more than $1 million from New York before fleeing the country.[9] Swartwout and Barry were only two such appointments that Jackson made during his presidency.

Jackson also made liberal use of his office to punish rivals, whether for political or personal insults. Jackson's vice president, John Calhoun, defended Jackson's controversial presidential style, but their relationship fell

into disrepair when Jackson learned that Calhoun had criticized him for invading Florida without President Monroe's direct permission. Further, in 1829 Jackson appointed John Eaton as his secretary of war whose wife, Margaret "Peggy" Eaton, was accused of cheating with Eaton, causing her former husband, a naval officer, to commit suicide. Many in Washington society refused to associate with Mrs. Eaton, including Calhoun's wife and Jackson's daughter. The "Eaton Affair," or the "Petticoat Affair," as it was called, divided the White House and the cabinet.

This personal rivalry developed into a political one that challenged presidential authority. When Jackson switched his position, supporting the Tariff of Abominations that he'd earlier depicted as the product of Adams's corruption, Calhoun and others in the South, where the impact of the tariff was more pronounced, accused Jackson of betraying them. This led to the Nullification Crisis of 1832, in which Calhoun and a southern coalition argued that the states had the right to refuse to obey federal laws to which they objected, to the point of leaving the Union. Jackson dissolved his cabinet and brought in a new cadre of loyalists who would join him in opposing Calhoun. Calhoun resigned as vice president, and was replaced by Martin Van Buren, Jackson's former campaign manager and heir apparent to Jackson's political clique.[10]

The Obstructionist

Jackson created the national Democratic Party, though the Jacksonian Democrats had little in common with the Democratic Party as it exists in the 2010s. Jackson's Democrats were strident opponents of big government, and he worked to reduce the role of the government as no president before had. Jackson opposed federal intervention in the economy, infrastructure, and legislation, and stands as one of the most committed opponents of "big government" in U.S. history. Jacksonian Democrats were also firm supporters of white supremacists and the pro-slavery movement, and he used his executive powers to further these interests as well.

The accomplishment that Jackson personally cherished was eliminating the national debt; he is the only president to do so. He did this by abandoning nearly every federally funded project that came before him. Jackson and colleagues dismantled the National Bank and ended the "American System," a series of economic development programs that were intended to stimulate industry, all to foster independence among the states and the citizens. Jackson's refusal to support investment programs and federal regulations only appeared successful, however, because the nation was in the midst of an economic boom period, a prosperity largely due to the policies and laws enacted under Madison and Monroe.

At the time, few politicians agreed with Jackson's policy about federal investment, which left poor populations in many parts of the country lacking transportation systems and industrial amenities, as well as funds to create them. Because Jackson did not have congressional support, he settled for blocking congressional action. Over the course of his two terms, Jackson vetoed 12 bills, more than all previous presidents combined. According to the constitutionally designated presidential veto power, a president has several options when it comes to passing legislation: Once a bill has passed through both houses of Congress, the president can sign that bill into law; alternatively, the president can return the bill to Congress for reconsideration within ten days. Congress must then either override the presidential veto, which requires a two-thirds majority vote, or change the bill and resubmit. However, a president can also circumvent Congress by waiting until Congress is no longer in session or has been out of session for more than 10 days, when he or she can then veto a bill. This is known as a "pocket veto," because the bill cannot be returned to Congress to be changed, making the veto final.

Regarding government spending, Jackson positioned himself as a follower of Jefferson, who was a strong proponent of states' rights and limited government. Jackson's address to Congress on vetoing the Maysville

Road proposal, part of the "American System" series of legislative efforts, demonstrates how Jackson viewed himself as allied with the former Founding Father:

VETO MESSAGE REGARDING FUNDING OF INFRASTRUCTURE DEVELOPMENT
May 27, 1830
Source Document Excerpt

The constitutional power of the Federal Government to construct or promote works of internal improvement presents itself in two points of view—the first as bearing upon the sovereignty of the States within whose limits their execution is contemplated, if jurisdiction of the territory which they may occupy be claimed as necessary to their preservation and use; the second as asserting the simple right to appropriate money from the National Treasury in aid of such works when undertaken by State authority, surrendering the claim of jurisdiction. In the first view the question of power is an open one, and can be decided without the embarrassments attending the other, arising from the practice of the Government. Although frequently and strenuously attempted, the power to this extent has never been exercised by the Government in a single instance. It does not, in my opinion, possess it; and no bill, therefore, which admits it can receive my official sanction.

But in the other view of the power the question is differently situated. The ground taken at an early period of the Government was "that whenever money has been raised by the general authority and is to be applied to a particular measure, a question arises whether the particular measure be within the enumerated authorities vested in Congress. If it be, the money requisite for it may be applied to it; if not, no such application can be made." The document in which this principle was first advanced· is of deservedly high authority, and should be held in grateful remembrance for its immediate agency in rescuing the country from much existing abuse and for its conservative effect upon some of the most valuable principles of the Constitution. The symmetry and purity of the Government would doubtless have been better preserved if this restriction of the power of appropriation could have been maintained without weakening its ability to fulfill the general objects of its institution, an

continued

effect so likely to attend its admission, notwithstanding its apparent fitness, that every subsequent Administration of the Government, embracing a period of thirty out of the forty-two years of its existence, has adopted a more enlarged construction of the power. It is not my purpose to detain you by a minute recital of the acts which sustain this assertion, but it is proper that I should notice some of the most prominent in order that the reflections which they suggest to my mind may be better understood.

In the Administration of Mr. Jefferson we have two examples of the exercise of the right of appropriation, which in the considerations that led to their adoption and in their effects upon the public mind have had a greater agency in marking the character of the power than any subsequent events. I allude to the payment of $15,000,000 for the purchase of Louisiana and to the original appropriation for the construction of the Cumberland road, the latter act deriving much weight from the acquiescence and approbation of three of the most powerful of the original members of the Confederacy, expressed through their respective legislatures. Although the circumstances of the latter case may be such as to deprive so much of it as relates to the actual construction of the road of the force of an obligatory exposition of the Constitution, it must, nevertheless, be admitted that so far as the mere appropriation of money is concerned they present the principle in its most imposing aspect. No less than twenty-three different laws have been passed, through all the forms of the Constitution, appropriating upward of $2,500,000 out of the National Treasury in support of that improvement, with the approbation of every President of the United States, including my predecessor, since its commencement.[11]

Representative Henry Clay of Kentucky, who was Jackson's opponent in the 1832 presidential election, spoke out against Jackson's veto. The following excerpts portray Clay's perception that Jackson abused the power of his office in vetoing the project.

EFFECT OF THE PROTECTIVE SYSTEM ON THE STAPLES OF THE SOUTH

Nullification and Other Topics
Cincinnati
August 3, 1830
Source Document Excerpt

"If any thing could be considered as settled, under the present Constitution of our Government, I had supposed that it was its authority to construct such internal improvements as may be deemed by Congress necessary and proper to carry into effect the power granted to it. For near twenty-five years, the power has been asserted and exercised by the Government. For the last fifteen years it has been often controverted in Congress, but it has been invariably maintained, in that body, by repeated decisions, pronounced after full and elaborate debate, and at intervals of time implying the greatest deliberation. Numerous laws attest the existence of the power; and no less than twenty-odd laws have been passed in relation to a single work. This power, necessary to all parts of the Union, is indispensable to the West. Without it, this section can never enjoy any part of the benefit of a regular disbursement of the vast revenues of the United States . . .

. . . Let us glance at a few only of the reasons, if reasons they can be called, of this piebald Message. The first is, that the exercise of the power has produced discord, and, to restore harmony to the National Councils, it should be abandoned, or, which is tantamount, the Constitution must be amended. The President is therefore advised to throw himself into the minority. Well—did that revive harmony? When the question was taken in the House of the people's Representatives, an obstinate majority still voted for the bill, the objections in the Message notwithstanding. And in the Senate, the Representatives of the States, a refractory majority stood unmoved. But does the Message mean to assert that no great measure, about which public sentiment is much divided, ought to be adopted in consequence of that division? Then none can ever be adopted. . . . The principle is nothing more or less than a declaration, that the right of the majority to govern, must yield to the perseverance, respectability, and numbers, of the minority. It is in keeping with the nullifying doctrines of South Carolina . . .

The Veto Message proceeds to insist, that the Maysville and Lexington Road is not a national but a local road, of sixty miles in length, and confined within

continued

the limits of a particular State. If, as that document also asserts, the power can, in no case, be exercised until it shall have been explained and defined by an amendment of the Constitution, the discrimination of national and local roads, would seem to be altogether unnecessary. What is or is not a national road, the message supposes may admit of controversy, and is not susceptible of precise definition. The difficulty which its authors imagine, grows out of their attempt to substitute a rule founded upon the extent and locality of the road, instead of the use and purposes to which it is applicable. If the road facilitates, in a considerable degree, the transportation of the mail to a considerable portion of the Union, and at the same time promotes internal commerce among the several States, and may tend to accelerate the movements of armies, and the distribution of the munitions of war, it is of national consideration. Tested by this, the true rule, the Maysville Road was undoubtedly national. It connects the largest body, perhaps, of fertile land in the Union, with the navigation of the Ohio and Mississippi rivers, and with the canals of the States of Ohio, Pennsylvania, and New York. It begins on the line which divides the States of Ohio and Kentucky, and, of course, quickens trade and intercourse between them. Tested by the character of other works, for which the President, as a Senator, voted, or which were approved by him only about a month before he rejected the Maysville Bill, the road was undoubtedly national."[12]

Utilizing the powers of one branch of the government to obstruct the process of government is a perennially controversial political strategy. It can be argued that Jackson received a public mandate in his two elections, 1828 and 1832, so Jackson's decision to unilaterally pursue his executive agenda was in keeping with the popular will and a just use of his powers. On the other hand, Jackson's percentage of the popular vote was only 57.6 percent in 1828, and 55.4 percent in 1832, showing that more than 40 percent of Americans were opposed to his approach and/or his presidency. Most of Congress was also opposed to many of Jackson's strategies. Members of Congress are also the elected representatives of the people, and their legislative efforts an expression of popular will. Jackson's use of his powers to obstruct the legislature (allowing only one bill to pass into law over eight years in the White House) could be described as a violation of the public trust. Similar questions might be raised about congressional obstruction of presidents, such as when a Republican-controlled Congress used their power to obstruct the executive agenda of Barack Obama.

American Ethnic Cleansing

While opinions differ on the value and virtues of Andrew Jackson, there are legitimate reasons for Native Americans and for opponents of slavery and racism to deny Jackson any credit as a national hero. An empirical argument can be made, in fact, to suggest that Jackson deserves to be ranked among history's most evil men, not only because Jackson consciously and willingly participated in strengthening and perpetuating the institution of slavery, and gave federal approval for more violent treatment of slaves in order to prohibit rebellion, but also for being personally responsible for a national program of ethnic cleansing that destroyed the cultures of Native Americans, resulted in tens of thousands of federally sanctioned deaths, and marginalized Native American societies in ways still relevant in the modern world.

Jackson's policies on Native Americans were largely based on the clash between the Cherokee and the white residents of Georgia; Cherokee occupied potential farmland that white settlers wanted to use and blocked access to rivers that Georgians deemed necessary for future prosperity. Georgia also hoped that increasing its population would grant more power to the southern slave block, but the Cherokee population blocked any such expansion. Jackson, a devout white supremacist, disagreed with federal policy regarding Native Americans, which was documented and expressed through treaties between sovereign Native American nations and the federal government. Jackson believed that Native Americans were not entitled to sovereignty and demanded that Native Americans submit to state law and domination of whites within those states or surrender their lands and move west of the Mississippi River. Jackson then declared that all previous federal treaties with Native American nations were invalid, the product of overly liberal northerners unconcerned about the rights of farmers.

Until Jackson, the official policy on Native Americans had been to recognize their own limited sovereignty. This had been official executive policy from Washington through John Quincy Adams and was reflected in federal treaties. The United States Supreme Court, under Chief Justice John Marshall, had provided legal precedent to support this position in three landmark cases. First, in the 1823 case of *Johnson v. M'Intosh*, the court ruled that Natives had the right of occupancy to the land, though not of absolute ownership. Second, in *Cherokee Nation v. Georgia*, the court ruled that the Cherokee were not foreign nations, but "domestic dependent nations" within the bounds of the United States not subject to state law. Justice Marshall's opinion in the case demonstrates that there were many in the United States sympathetic to how U.S. development had impacted the Native American people and shows that the court's rulings tried to strike a balance that would prevent the future exploitation of Native Americans:

CHEROKEE NATION V. GEORGIA
1831
Source Document Excerpt

Opinion

MARSHALL, C.J., Opinion of the Court

Mr Chief Justice MARSHALL delivered the opinion of the Court.

This bill is brought by the Cherokee Nation, praying an injunction to restrain the State of Georgia from the execution of certain laws of that State which, as is alleged, go directly to annihilate the Cherokees as a political society and to seize, for the use of Georgia, the lands of the Nation which have been assured to them by the United States in solemn treaties repeatedly made and still in force.

If Courts were permitted to indulge their sympathies, a case better calculated to excite them can scarcely be imagined. A people once numerous, powerful, and truly independent, found by our ancestors in the quiet and uncontrolled possession of an ample domain, gradually sinking beneath our superior policy, our arts and our arms, have yielded their lands by successive treaties, each of which contains a solemn guarantee of the residue, until they retain no more of their formerly extensive territory than is deemed necessary to their comfortable subsistence. To preserve this remnant, the present application is made.

. . .

A question of much more difficulty remains. Do the Cherokees constitute a foreign state in the sense of the Constitution?

The counsel have shown conclusively that they are not a State of the union, and have insisted that, individually, they are aliens, not owing allegiance to the United States. An aggregate of aliens composing a State must, they say, be a foreign state. Each individual being foreign, the whole must be foreign.

This argument is imposing, but we must examine it more closely before we yield to it. The condition of the Indians in relation to the United States is perhaps unlike that of any other two people in existence. In the general, nations not owing a common allegiance are foreign to each other. The term foreign nation is, with strict propriety, applicable by either to the other. But the relation of the Indians to the United States is marked by peculiar and cardinal distinctions which exist nowhere else.

We the People

continued

The Indian Territory is admitted to compose a part of the United States. In all our maps, geographical treatises, histories, and laws, it is so considered. In all our intercourse with foreign nations, in our commercial regulations, in any attempt at intercourse between Indians and foreign nations, they are considered as within the jurisdictional limits of the United States, subject to many of those restraints which are imposed upon our own citizens. They acknowledge themselves in their treaties to be under the protection of the United States; they admit that the United States shall have the sole and exclusive right of regulating the trade with them, and managing all their affairs as they think proper; and the Cherokees, in particular, were allowed by the treaty of Hopewell, which preceded the Constitution, "to send a deputy of their choice, whenever they think fit, to Congress." Treaties were made with some tribes by the State of New York, under a then unsettled construction of the confederation by which they ceded all their lands to that State, taking back a limited grant to themselves in which they admit their dependence.

Though the Indians are acknowledged to have an unquestionable, and heretofore unquestioned right to the lands they occupy, until that right shall be extinguished by a voluntary cession to our government, yet it may well be doubted whether those tribes which reside within the acknowledged boundaries of the United States can, with strict accuracy, be denominated foreign nations. They may, more correctly, perhaps, be denominated domestic dependent nations. They occupy a territory to which we assert a title independent of their will, which must take effect in point of possession when their right of possession ceases. Meanwhile they are in a state of pupilage. Their relation to the United States resembles that of a ward to his guardian.[13]

A third case, *Worchester v. Georgia*, resulted in the specific ruling that states did not have any constitutional authority over Native American nations. These three rulings together formed a pillar of constitutional law with regard to Native Americans with two major points. First, that Native Americans have "inherent" sovereignty, not sovereignty granted through the Constitution or by the states into which their territory was located.

Second, that Congress had ultimate authority over determining how America would negotiate with Native American nations.

Jackson's strategy, in the face of this opposition, was to ignore the Court and force Congress to pass the Indian Removal Act, which gave states and the federal government the power to force Native Americans to leave whatever lands the government dictated and to relocate to lands west of the Mississippi. Jackson based his decision on the idea that while it was up to the Supreme Court to interpret constitutional law, it was the executive's role to enforce it. He then challenged the Court, stating, "Well, John Marshall has made his decision, now let him enforce it." He reportedly said to a friend, "The decision of the Supreme Court has fell stillborn, and they find they cannot coerce Georgia to yield to its mandate."[14]

The Indian Removal Act was the only piece of legislation that Jackson allowed to pass through the legislature during his time in office. Jackson promoted the act by alleging that it was a victory for state sovereignty and against unconstitutional governmental interference in personal liberties. His speech to Congress (but directed to the American people) on the issue, demonstrates the depth of Jackson's racial prejudice and embrace of white supremacy.

"ON INDIAN REMOVAL" PRESIDENT JACKSON'S MESSAGE TO CONGRESS
December 6, 1830
Source Document Excerpt

"It gives me pleasure to announce to Congress that the benevolent policy of the Government, steadily pursued for nearly thirty years, in relation to the removal of the Indians beyond the white settlements is approaching to a happy consummation. Two important tribes have accepted the provision made for their removal at the last session of Congress, and it is believed that their example will induce the remaining tribes also to seek the same obvious advantages.

The consequences of a speedy removal will be important to the United States, to individual States, and to the Indians themselves. The pecuniary advantages which it promises to the Government are the least of its recommendations. It puts an end to all possible danger of collision between the authorities of the General and State Governments on account of the Indians. It will place a dense and civilized population in large tracts of country now occupied by a few savage hunters. By opening the whole territory between Tennessee on the north and Louisiana on the south to the settlement of the whites it will incalculably strengthen the southwestern frontier and render the adjacent States strong enough to repel future invasions without remote aid. It will relieve the whole State of Mississippi and the western part of Alabama of Indian occupancy, and enable those States to advance rapidly in population, wealth, and power. It will separate the Indians from immediate contact with settlements of whites; free them from the power of the States; enable them to pursue happiness in their own way and under their own rude institutions; will retard the progress of decay, which is lessening their numbers, and perhaps cause them gradually, under the protection of the Government and through the influence of good counsels, to cast off their savage habits and become an interesting, civilized, and Christian community.

What good man would prefer a country covered with forests and ranged by a few thousand savages to our extensive Republic, studded with cities, towns, and prosperous farms embellished with all the improvements which art can devise or industry execute, occupied by more than 12,000,000 happy people, and filled with all the blessings of liberty, civilization and religion?

"On Indian Removal"
President Jackson's Message to Congress
continued

The present policy of the Government is but a continuation of the same progressive change by a milder process. The tribes which occupied the countries now constituting the Eastern States were annihilated or have melted away to make room for the whites. The waves of population and civilization are rolling to the westward, and we now propose to acquire the countries occupied by the red men of the South and West by a fair exchange, and, at the expense of the United States, to send them to land where their existence may be prolonged and perhaps made perpetual. Doubtless it will be painful to leave the graves of their fathers; but what do they more than our ancestors did or than our children are now doing? To better their condition in an unknown land our forefathers left all that was dear in earthly objects. Our children by thousands yearly leave the land of their birth to seek new homes in distant regions. Does Humanity weep at these painful separations from everything, animate and inanimate, with which the young heart has become entwined? Far from it. It is rather a source of joy that our country affords scope where our young population may range unconstrained in body or in mind, developing the power and facilities of man in their highest perfection. These remove hundreds and almost thousands of miles at their own expense, purchase the lands they occupy, and support themselves at their new homes from the moment of their arrival. Can it be cruel in this Government when, by events which it cannot control, the Indian is made discontented in his ancient home to purchase his lands, to give him a new and extensive territory, to pay the expense of his removal, and support him a year in his new abode? How many thousands of our own people would gladly embrace the opportunity of removing to the West on such conditions! If the offers made to the Indians were extended to them, they would be hailed with gratitude and joy.

And is it supposed that the wandering savage has a stronger attachment to his home than the settled, civilized Christian? Is it more afflicting to him to leave the graves of his fathers than it is to our brothers and children? Rightly considered, the policy of the General Government toward the red man is not only liberal, but generous. He is unwilling to submit to the laws of the States and mingle with their population. To save him from this alternative, or perhaps utter annihilation, the General Government kindly offers him a new home, and proposes to pay the whole expense of his removal and settlement."[15]

The result of Jackson's policy of ethnic cleansing was that the Cherokee, Creek, Choctaw, and Chickasaw were forcibly removed from their lands and marched, under guard, to new reservation lands chosen for them past the Mississippi River. The relocation of Native Americans took 28 years, and cost the federal government $40 to $60 million, ten times what Jackson had estimated. Thousands of Native Americans were murdered by soldiers for refusing to comply, and thousands more died on the difficult trek across the country. The lands chosen for them were not productive or appropriate for farming. By relocating Native Americans to locations that were fundamentally lacking the resources, spiritual landmarks, and ecosystems of their native territories, the U.S. government decimated Native American culture in ways from which most Native American nations never recovered. Under Jackson's administration alone, more than 46,000 Native Americans were forcibly moved and more than 10,000 killed.[16]

The Indian Removal Act represents one of the most dramatic expansions of executive power in United States history. As with his behavior regarding the legislature, Jackson used obstruction to bypass the judicial branch and the constitutional system of checks and balances. By choosing to enforce a law that was deemed unconstitutional by the Supreme Court, Jackson openly defied constitutional law and demonstrated a fundamental failure in the checks and balances system—there was no method in place for the courts to enforce their interpretation of constitutional law if a president refused to recognize their rulings. Had Congress been willing to fight Jackson on the issue, he might have been impeached, but Jackson's relationship with the people paralyzed the legislature. He commanded such popular appeal that legislators who opposed him found themselves struggling to gain enough political support for their own efforts. Further, Jackson ingenuously presented himself to the American people, claiming that he was their representative in an environment filled with self-interested bureaucrats. This positioned those who agreed with

him as representatives of the people, while those who opposed him were viciously attacked as corrupt conspirators seeking to undermine the popular will.[17]

The Presidency for Personal Gain

Amazingly, Jackson had, in the past, demonstrated the capability to see Native Americans as equals. When Native American mercenaries supported his invasion of Florida, he wrote that they were to receive equal pay and treatment to his white soldiers and argued that those who fell in battle should be buried alongside white soldiers and shown equal respect. Though Jackson was undeniably a white supremacist, as evinced by his attitudes towards African Americans, he had respect for the Native American people and believed that some, at least, should be thought of as equals. When it came to the Indian Removal Act, Jackson's support was less a product of his racism than it was a product of his profiteering attitude.

The Indian Removal Act increased territory available for slave-owning colonists and thus increased the Electoral College power and representation of the southern states, which sat in Jackson's power base. Among those who benefitted directly from this were Jackson's strongest friends and allies, and Jackson himself, who was in the real estate business.

Long before becoming president, Jackson realized that the land on the banks of the Tennessee River, which was occupied by the Cherokee, was prime real estate. In 1814, Jackson was placed in charge of dealing with a rebellion of the Creek people. He successfully ended the rebellion and claimed 23 million acres formerly controlled by the Creeks. This was the land that became Alabama. Jackson was placed in charge of postwar military affairs in the wake of the Creek War, and he used this position to claim territory further north, under the control of the Cherokee, though this was not part of the territory claimed by the United States from the Creek. Jackson and his friends began allowing white settlers to move into this region, and when local Native Americans protested, Jackson hired bodyguards and gunmen to threaten them into submission. Jackson used these practices to claim an additional two million acres of land, illegitimately claimed as part of the former Creek territories.

Jackson's secret land grab hit a snag when a delegation of Cherokee came to Washington, DC, led by John Ross, an English-speaking Cherokee and a veteran who'd served under Jackson. Ross complained about Jackson's methods to the War Department, and the James Madison administration agreed, arguing that Jackson would have to purchase the territory legally. Jackson engaged in months of negotiations and told the Cherokee that they had no choice. Either they would sell, or white settlers would eventually remove them from their land. The Cherokee agreed to sell Jackson some of the land he most coveted but kept part of their territory, receiving $65,000, which was only a fraction of the amount that the land would command once Jackson had the territory divided into plots and sold.[18]

Andrew Jackson was the first president to successfully challenge the elite and win the populist vote. By Ralph Eleaser Whiteside Earl, via Wikimedia.

This corrupt land grab was the source of Jackson's wealth. By breaking up and selling off pieces of the Tennessee Valley, Jackson went from living a modest life with his wife to one of the wealthiest men in the region. Jackson was able to gain his fortune partly due to his government connections. He invested in several plots within the newly purchased territory; then, because of his position with the government, he was able to choose where roads would be constructed and where towns would be located. He thus turned his plots into the best available plots, increasing his own profits by exploiting his reputation and government connections.

The Indian Removal Act was another example of the self-serving dedication to his own fortune that Jackson demonstrated in his 1818 land grab. By forcing Indians off prime agricultural territories, Jackson increased the power of his Jacksonian Democratic Party by providing allies with key investment opportunities that he personally profited by. Following his second term, Jackson retired but remained intimately involved in politics. He used his economic influence in the South to influence the presidencies of Martin Van Buren, his immediate successor and protégé, and then of John Tyler, who was an opponent and yet concurred with Jackson on some principles. Jackson's greatest triumph was in supporting Tennessean James K. Polk, arguably his primary successor, for the presidency in 1844. Through Van Buren, Tyler, and Polk, Jackson's influence extended into the middle of the nineteenth century, making him one of the most influential and controversial presidents in U.S. history.

Notes on Popular Support

Historians, and fans of Jackson, highlight the fact that Jackson drew enormous popular support in comparison to past presidents. In the nation's first election, in 1789, approximately 10–11 percent of the voting age population turned out to vote. In 1792, for Washington's second term, only around 6 percent voted. The contentious 1796 election drew only around 20 percent, while the 1800 election that saw a major turnover, with Jefferson's Democratic-Republicans forcing the Federalists out of office,

attracted around 32 percent of voters. Jefferson's second election saw a drop back to around 24 percent, followed by the 1808 election in which Madison attracted nearly 37 percent of voters, and then the 1812 election, which drew a whopping 40 percent of eligible voters. The next three elections saw little in the way of popular interest, with 17 percent voting in 1816, 10 percent in 1820, and 27 percent in 1824, when Jackson lost his "corrupt bargain" election to John Quincy Adams.

A fundamental change occurred during the four years that Jackson and campaign manager Martin Van Buren, a cunning political strategist, spent campaigning against John Quincy Adams—the emerging Jacksonian Democratic Party took their campaign right to the people. The result was that, in 1828, a whopping 57.3 percent of the voting age population came to the polls. This was the first time in history that the popular vote mattered in the presidential election and decided the race, and it was also the first time in history that more than 50 percent of voters voted in the election. The Jacksonian Democrats' populist appeal continued, with Jackson garnering 57 percent of voters for his re-election bid, and his follower, Martin Van Buren, attracting 56.5 percent for his election in 1836.[19]

None of the elections, however, provides an actual measure of popular support. From the nation's beginning through the middle of the nineteenth century, only a small percentage of Americans were allowed to vote. Many states had laws that made it difficult or entirely prohibited voting among poor people, and women were barred from voting. African Americans were still slaves and thus not afforded any political agency. Native Americans, Latino Americans, Asian Americans, and every other non-white group was likewise excluded from the elective franchise. This means that between 70–80 percent of people living in America could not vote, so measurements of popular support are misleading. Jackson became the first president to attract more than 50 percent of eligible voters, but this does not mean he was truly a popular president. How might women voters have viewed Jackson, whose personal life was often controversial? African Americans and Native Americans almost certainly would have been opposed to Jackson, who was a slave owner and built his personal fortune by oppressing and exploiting Native Americans. In an egalitarian America, one in which the nation truly embodied the "natural law" that all persons are created equal, it is unlikely that Jackson would be depicted as a populist or a representative of the people. What Jackson had was majority support among the relatively small number of white male voters who could vote, and he commanded the support of just over half of them.

CONCLUSION

Jackson may be one of the nation's most overrated presidents. His obstructionist tactic, which he sustained due to his comparatively high level of public support, resulted in little in the way of accomplishment. Jackson dramatically increased corruption in U.S. politics by utilizing the spoils system in which political appointments were given to friends and allies rather than qualified professionals. Further, many of Jackson's actions and policy positions were designed to provide him with personal profit or political gain, a use of presidential authority that is considered a fundamental violation of constitutional law. The spectacle of Jackson's elections, however, drew Americans into the political process and marked a turning point in public perception of the presidency. Following the presidency of Andrew Jackson, public interest in presidential politics increased steadily, an interest that continued into the twentieth century.

DISCUSSION QUESTIONS

♦ Was Jackson's use of the veto power appropriate? Why or why not?

♦ How did Andrew Jackson change the political campaign process? Were these changes beneficial to the country or not? Explain your answer.

♦ Was the Indian Removal Act motivated by racism on Jackson's part? Why or why not?

♦ In your opinion, was Jackson a powerful president? Did he use presidential authority appropriately?

♦ How was Jackson's presidency a sign of the modern "fake news" era?

Works Used

Celano, Daniele. "The Indian Removal Act: Jackson, Sovereignty and Executive Will." *The Purdue Historian*, vol. 8, art. 6, 2017. docs.lib. purdue.edu/cgi/viewcontent.cgi?article=1025&context=puhistorian.

"Cherokee Nation v. Georgia." *LII*. Cornell Law School. 2019. www.law. cornell.edu/supremecourt/text/30/1#writing-USSC_CR_0030_0001_ZO.

Clay, Henry. *The Speeches of Henry Clay*, edited by Calvin Colton. New York: A.S. Barnes & Co, 1857.

Donovan, Thomas A. "'John Marshall Has Made His Decision, Now Let Him Enforce It.'—Attributed to President Andrew Jackson, 1832." *Federal Lawyer*. At Sidebar. Sept. 2012. www.fedbar.org/Resources_1/Federal-Lawyer-Magazine/2012/September/Columns/At-Sidebar.aspx?FT=.pdf.

Feller, Daniel. "Andrew Jackson." *Miller Center*. University of Virginia. 2019. millercenter.org/president/Jackson.

"Indian Removal, 1814–1858." *PBS*. 2016. www.pbs.org/wgbh/aia/part4/4p2959.html.

Inskeep, Steve. "How Jackson Made a Killing in Real Estate." *Politico*. 4 July 2015. www.politico.com/magazine/story/2015/07/andrew-jackson-made-a-killing-in-real-estate-119727_full.html.

Jackson, Andrew. "Andrew Jackson's Speech to Congress on Indian Removal." *National Park Service*. NPS. www.nps.gov/museum/tmc/MANZ/handouts/Andrew_Jackson_Annual_Message.pdf.

_____. "May 27, 1830: Veto Message Regarding Funding of Infrastructure Development." *Miller Center*. University of Virginia. 2019. millercenter.org/the-presidency/presidential-speeches/may-27-1830-veto-message-regarding-funding-infrastructure.

Jordan, Mary. "Andrew Jackson Was a Rich Populist Who Bragged and Invited Scorn. Trump Draws New Interest in the 7th President." *The Washington Post*. 31 Jan. 2017. www.washingtonpost.com/news/post-nation/wp/2017/01/31/andrew-jackson-was-a-rich-populist-who-bragged-and-invited-scorn-trump-is-drawing-new-interest-in-the-7th-president/.

Marszalek, John F. *The Petticoat Affair: Manners, Mutiny, and Sex in Andrew Jackson's White House*. Baton Rouge, LA: Louisiana State U P, 1997.

McNamara, Robert. "The Spoils System: Definition and Summary." *Thought Co*. 3 July 2019. www.thoughtco.com/the-spoils-system-1773347.

Meacham, Jon. *American Lion: Andrew Jackson in the White House*. New York: Random House, 2009.

"National General Election VEP Turnout Rates, 1789–Present," *Elect Project*. University of Florida. 2018. www.electproject.org/national-1789-present.

Parsons, Lynn H. *The Birth of Modern Politics: Andrew Jackson, John Quincy Adams, and the Election of 1828*. New York: Oxford U P, 2009.

Ratcliffe, Donald John. *The One-Party Presidential Contest: Adams, Jackson, and 1824's Five-Horse Race*. U P of Kansas, 2015.

Traub, James. "The Ugly Election That Birthed Modern American Politics." *National Geographic*. Nov./Dec. 2016. www.nationalgeographic.com/history/magazine/2016/11-12/america-presidential-elections-1824-corrupt-bargain/.

Unger, Harlow Giles. *The Last Founding Father: James Monroe and a Nation's Call to Greatness*. New York: Da Capo P, 2009.

Wilentz, Sean. *Andrew Jackson: The American Presidents Series: The 7th President, 1829–1837*. New York: Times Books, 2005.

Introduction

Eight years of Andrew Jackson transformed the Democratic-Republican Party. With Jackson as the party's primary figurehead, the Democratic-Republicans became more staunchly focused on states' rights and limiting the central bureaucracy, to such an extent that Jackson hardly allowed the government to do anything. He was succeeded by Martin Van Buren, a brilliant and skilled political schemer who did not have Jackson's charisma or pull with the public. Van Buren, however, had to contend with a severe financial crisis, the Panic of 1837, which was largely the result of Jackson's financial policies. The public lost faith in Van Buren and the Democratic-Republican vision and shifted briefly to the newly emerged Whig Party, a generalist political outfit that nominated war hero William Henry Harrison. Harrison's untimely death led to him being replaced by his vice president, John Tyler, a white supremacist southerner who became one of America's least-liked presidents, to the point that he nearly became the first president to face impeachment.

Topics covered in this chapter include:
- Panic of 1837
- U.S.-Canadian border disputes
- Texas Independence Movement
- Harrison's death in office after 30 days
- Tippecanoe and Tyler Too
- Presidential line of succession
- Presidential impeachment
- Annexation of Texas

This Chapter Discusses the Following Source Document:
Inaugural Address of William Henry Harrison, March 4, 1841

A Conservative Division
Martin Van Buren, William Henry Harrison, and John Tyler (1837–1845)

Martin Van Buren was the chief architect of the Jacksonian Democratic Party, a populist, states-rights-focused conservative party. Van Buren, like Jackson, was committed to small government, and as Jackson's campaign manager, was willing to use whatever tactics he deemed effective to promote this agenda. Van Buren and Jackson willfully used false claims to gather power, but saw themselves as doing this for righteous reasons, to fight against an entrenched aristocracy.

Over the course of Jackson's two terms in office, a new opposition emerged, the Whigs. The Whigs were the more progressive of the emerging two-party system, favoring federal investment in infrastructure and other internal improvements and a protective tariff system, though they would still be classified as social conservatives by modern standards. The name came from Scotland, where it was the nickname for anti-royalists in England and Scotland, and the Whigs in the United States presented themselves as defenders of democratic principles and the public welfare against Jackson's authoritarian approach to the presidency.

Jackson's Heir Apparent

Van Buren was the first American president born after the transition to independence, the first not born a British subject. His parents were from Holland; Van Buren's Dutch ancestry broke British dominance of the office. He hailed from Kinderhook, New York, a small town near the capital of Albany. Like Jackson, Van Buren came from a modest background, though his family were slaveowners and so his claims of going from "rags to riches," like Jackson's, were largely fabricated. Also like Jackson, Van Buren was uneducated and never attended college. He worked his way into the New York bar by working as a legal clerk for seven years.

Martin Van Buren, known as the "Little Magician" for his spin doctoring. By Mathew B. Brady, Metropolitan Museum of Art, via Wikimedia.

Van Buren entered politics in New York and was a Democratic Republican who strongly believed in the Jeffersonian focus on individual liberty. He became a key figure in New York State politics before being elected to the U.S. Senate in 1821, where he became a champion of limited government and an opponent of the American System of internal infrastructure investment. Van Buren was selected by Jackson to serve as his campaign manager after Jackson's 1824 loss, and it was his political savvy that created a political party built around Jackson's polarizing approach. After winning a landslide election, Jackson selected Van Buren as his secretary of state, then as his vice president during his second term, replacing John Calhoun. Van Buren was both respected and feared in political circles for his skill in creating political spectacle and spinning news. This skill, his intelligence, and diminutive (5'7") size earned him the nickname "Little Magician."[1]

Jackson left the White House retaining the support of a majority of white upper-class male voters; he began endorsing Van Buren as the inheritor of his legacy in 1834, nearly two years before he would leave office. This was one of the innovations that Van Buren brought to presidential politics—campaigning for many months, if not years, before an election. By the election of 1836, Jackson's opponents had combined forces to create a political coalition to oppose the Jacksonian Democrats. It drew support from former Democratic-Republicans and other factions and emerged as the Whigs. The Whigs were not well organized in 1836, and put forward a number of regional candidates rather than a single unifying one. These included Tennessee senator Hugh White, who carried support from the South; Massachusetts native Daniel Webster in the East; and the famed war hero William Henry Harrison, who drew his support from the western states. With the opposition divided, Van Buren did well, drawing 85,000 more votes than Jackson had in his second election, and more popular votes than all three of the opposing Whig candidates combined, 764,176

to 738,124.[2] Though a convincing win, the power of the Jacksonian Democrats was already waning. They'd lost Georgia and Tennessee in the election and won many states by narrow margins.

While Jackson undoubtedly gave the White House to Van Buren, their aggressive dismantling of the U.S. economic system proved Van Buren's downfall. Jackson entered office during a "boom period" in the U.S. economy, when British purchasing of U.S. products was fueling massive growth in the U.S. economy. Previous presidents had attempted to perpetuate this growth by establishing the National Bank, creating protective tariffs, and investing in infrastructure to promote interstate commerce. Just as Van Buren was coming into office, a downturn in the British economy reduced funds coming into the American economy. Local banks, unregulated thanks to the Jackson administration's opposition to federal regulation, had overextended credit during the boom period and had left themselves, and their customers, ill-prepared for financial fluctuations. Finally, widespread speculation of newly opened federal lands, created through the ethnic cleansing of Native Americans, created a credit crisis, which Jackson attempted to address by creating a policy whereby federal lands could only be purchased with "hard currency," meaning silver, gold, or precious metals, rather than paper money.

Historian Graham Sumner said of the situation:

"Van Buren was now at the height of his ambition; but the financial and commercial storm which had been gathering for two or three years, the accumulated result of rash ignorance and violent self-will acting on some of the most delicate social interests, was just ready to burst. High prices and high rents had already before the election produced strikes, trades-union conflicts, and labor riots, things that were almost unprecedented in the United States."[3]

Without the National Bank, the nation was ill-prepared for the financial crisis. Jackson's simplistic economic thinking precipitated the greatest economic crisis in American history to date, which dominated Van Buren's time in office. Many politicians urged Van Buren to break with Jackson and engage in more aggressive, centrist strategies, but Van Buren was reluctant. He knew that Jackson had a fragile ego and had a tendency to turn quickly from friend to enemy, and he did not want to offend his most important political patron. The Panic of 1837 grew worse, and critics began calling Van Buren "Martin Van Ruin." Van Buren promoted a new solution, an "Independent U.S. Treasury" that could be used to regulate currency and credit and to protect against crises and panics. Votes on the issue were split on party lines; the treasury was finally adopted in 1840, too late to give Van Buren a boost heading into his next election.[4]

A Great Inactivist

Van Buren has been perhaps wrongly maligned in history because public and political opinion turned against him so spectacularly in his first term. Jackson had left Van Buren a difficult situation to manage. His solution, the Independent Treasury, might have saved his public image if implemented sooner. Van Buren was unable to build a coalition of support, because he was living in the shadow of a president who made many more enemies than friends in his life.

Although Van Buren did little to expand or change the use of executive power, his use of executive authority provides an interesting lesson. Van Buren attempted to use his authority as a balancing force. In domestic affairs he attempted a conciliatory treasury solution; and in foreign policy, Van Buren championed neutrality. This became an issue in several ways during Van Buren's time in office. There were disputes along the U.S. –Canada border and the more hawkish Congressmen still pushed for U.S. annexation of Canada, something that failed in both the Revolutionary War and the War of 1812. The new crisis was the result of an emerging Canadian separatist movement, with rebels fleeing into the United States and sheltering near the Niagara River. American privateers began supplying weapons to this movement, and loyalists attacked the *U.S.S. Caroline*. Many in the United States were calling for a new war with England, but Van Buren rejected this path and, despite the political backlash, issued strong statements in favor of neutrality and encouraged Congress to pass a neutrality law discouraging American private intervention. Another crisis erupted in Maine in 1838, involving American settlers on British lands who were forcibly removed by British troops. Again, there were calls for war, but Van Buren opted for diplomacy. Meeting with the British minister, he established a stronger peace agreement and a promise to negotiate border disputes. He also dispatched military to Maine, not to defend against British hostilities, but to check the power of local military leaders exacerbating the problem. It was a subtle, diplomatic approach that sought to restrain American sentiments toward a national policy of neutrality and nonintervention—a non-activist use of presidential authority.[5]

One of Van Buren's most aggressive uses of political power was blocking the annexation of Texas. The sparsely populated region had been home to an English population for years. The influx of Anglo-Americans began in the 1820s, at the invitation of the local government, who were looking to settle the area for political and economic reasons. Roughly 20 percent of the population were slaves, most from the United States. Slavery became a key issue, as Mexico banned slavery after independence. For years, they ignored slavery continuing in Texas, and the government also ignored the rule that all settlers needed to be Catholic or to convert to Catholicism. A short-lived rebellion in 1826 was the first event of the Texas independence movement. The government passed new rules and restrictions and outlawed slavery. Mexican President Santa Anna sent forces into Texas to establish military governance in 1835, and a coalition of Anglo-Americans living in the state announced their independence on March 2, 1836. The Battle of San Jacinto followed, in which rebel forces defeated the forces of General Santa Anna. However, the Mexican legislature refused to acknowledge independence. Now nominally independent but without protection, the settlers of Texas feared a resurgence of hostilities and sought to become part of the United States, thus granting them protection.[6]

Jackson supported Texas independence, but did not want to formally recognize Texas as independent in 1836, for fear it would damage Van Buren's campaign. The issue was politically fraught because the admission of another slave state would increase the power of the slave lobby in Washington, which might have brought anti-slavery activists, most of whom gravitated toward the Whig Party, together. Further, as the Mexican government refused to recognize Texas independence, American intervention might lead to war. Van Buren recognized that the situation was volatile and treated it with care. When Texas Representative Memucan Hunt Jr. presented Van Buren with an annexation proposal, Van Buren rejected it; and Congress twice rejected similar bills.[7] Over the next two years, thanks to considerable diplomatic skill on the part of Van Buren and Secretary of State Georgian John Forsyth, Van Buren negotiated with the Mexican government, resulting in an agreement for arbitration of issues that would involve two U.S. representatives, two Mexican representatives, and arbitration by the King of Prussia. This was a path toward a potentially peaceful resolution of the Texas issue between the United States and Mexico and demonstrates how a president might use authority to search for diplomatic solutions.

Two Can Play That Game

The Whig Party learned from Jackson and the Jacksonian Democrats in time for the 1840 election. They chose a single candidate, military hero William Henry Harrison. The Whigs presented Harrison as a simple every-

man and a patriotic war hero opposing pampered bureaucrat Van Buren. Pamphlets and articles said he was a frontier "Indian fighter" who preferred to spend time in his log cabin drinking cider. In reality, Harrison had been born into a wealthy Virginia family, studied history and medicine in college before entering the military, and was involved in the Battle of Fallen Timbers, which resulted in the settlement of most of modern Ohio. He then became Army Secretary of the Northwest Territory and later a delegate to Congress for the newly established territories. In 1801, he was elected Governor of Indiana Territory, a position he held for 12 years. Over this time, he did forcibly remove many Native American communities from their land. His fame came from the battle of Tippecanoe, in which Harrison led an army regiment that repelled an attacking force of Native Americans under the Chieftain Tecumseh, though they suffered more than 190 dead in the process. Harrison is also known for the Battle of the Thames on Lake Erie, where he led a regiment that killed Tecumseh and defeated the coalition of Native Americans that opposed white colonial encroachment on their land.[8]

William Henry Harrison had the shortest tenure of any U.S. president, dying just days after his inauguration. By Albert Sands Southworth and Josiah Johnson Hawes, Metropolitan Museum of Art, via Wikimedia.

The 1840 election broke new ground for creative campaigning. Musical groups traveled from town to town playing the campaign's unofficial theme song, written by Alexander Coffman Ross, an Ohio jeweler, who introduced it at a New York Whig rally:

————————— O what has caused this great commotion (motion, motion)

Our country through,

It is the ball that's rolling on,

For Tippecanoe and Tyler too,

For Tippecanoe and Tyler too,

And with them we'll beat little Van, Van, Van,

Van, oh he's a used-up man,

And with them we'll beat little Van.[9]

Harrison campaign promoters hired local bands to play this song while they rolled a giant canvas ball. Historian Ronald Shafer has opined that the 1840 campaign forever changed American presidential campaigning, using more showmanship and pageantry than even the Jacksonian Democrats, and creating what Shafer describes as a "carnival atmosphere." Harrison proved an apt candidate for the Whigs. He traveled tirelessly from town to town and delivered speeches directly to the public. Harrison's 1840 campaign rallies were the first to include grassroots campaign donations and elaborate fanfare, and they succeeded in attracting more public attention than had ever been devoted to a presidential election.[10]

Though Van Buren suffered a major blow to his public approval due to the financial panic, and though the Whigs engineered the most spectacular campaign for public approval in presidential history, Van Buren's calm, measured leadership still won him supporters, more votes than he had in 1836, and a higher proportion of votes in many key states. However, demand for change in the wake of the depression, coupled with the success of the Whig campaign, were too much for a reserved politician like Van Buren to combat. The 1840 election attracted 80 percent of registered voters, one of the highest proportions in the history of presidential elections. Harrison and his running mate, southern conservative John Tyler, won 1,275,390 popular votes, which was enough to beat Van Buren's 1,128,854 votes, though still a close race. The difference was the Electoral College, with Harrison winning 234, and Van Buren receiving only 60 Electoral College votes.[11]

Van Buren, despite his loss, still cherished his chance to take on the role. He was a skilled administrator and strategist, but suffered from poor circumstance and the failings of his political patron Andrew Jackson. Van Buren was quoted as saying that the two happiest days of his life were "those of my entrance upon the office and my surrender of it."[12]

The President Who Never Was

Harrison might have been a good president, but the world would never know. Arriving in Washington in February of 1941, Harrison delivered an inaugural address edited by famed orator Daniel Webster. It was the longest inaugural address ever delivered at nearly two hours and more than 8,000 words. He delivered it outside on a wet, winter day, without a coat or gloves. Harrison concluded by promising not to be a partisan president, but to search for ways to serve the whole of the American people.

INAUGURAL ADDRESS OF WILLIAM HENRY HARRISON
March 4, 1841

If parties in a republic are necessary to secure a degree of vigilance sufficient to keep the public functionaries within the bounds of law and duty, at that point their usefulness ends. Beyond that they become destructive of public virtue, the parent of a spirit antagonist to that of liberty, and eventually its inevitable conqueror. We have examples of republics where the love of country and of liberty at one time were the dominant passions of the whole mass of citizens, and yet, with the continuance of the name and forms of free government, not a vestige of these qualities remaining in the bosoms of any one of its citizens. It was the beautiful remark of a distinguished English writer that "in the Roman senate Octavius had a party and Anthony a party, but the Commonwealth had none." Yet the senate continued to meet in the temple of liberty to talk of the sacredness and beauty of the Commonwealth and gaze at the statues of the elder Brutus and of the Curtii and Decii, and the people assembled in the forum, not, as in the days of Camillus and the Scipios, to cast their free votes for annual magistrates or pass upon the acts of the senate, but to receive from the hands of the leaders of the respective parties their share of the spoils and to shout for one or the other, as those collected in Gaul or Egypt and the lesser Asia would furnish the larger dividend. The spirit of liberty had fled, and, avoiding the abodes of civilized man, had sought protection in the wilds of Scythia or Scandinavia; and so under the operation of the same causes and influences it will fly from our Capitol and our forums. A calamity so awful, not only to our country, but to the world, must be deprecated by every patriot and every tendency to a state of things likely to produce it immediately checked. Such a tendency has existed—does exist. Always the friend of my countrymen, never their flatterer, it becomes my duty to say to them from this high place to which their partiality has exalted me that there exists in the land a spirit hostile to their best interests—hostile to liberty itself. It is a spirit contracted in its views, selfish in its objects. It looks to the aggrandizement of a few even to the destruction of the interests of the whole. The entire remedy is with the people. Something, however, may be effected by the means which they have placed in my hands. It is union that we want, not of a party for the sake of that party, but aunion of the whole country for the sake of the whole country, for the defense of its interests and its honor against foreign aggression, for the defense of those principles for which our ancestors so gloriously contended

continued

As far as it depends upon me it shall be accomplished. All the influence that I possess shall be exerted to prevent the formation at least of an Executive party in the halls of the legislative body. I wish for the support of no member of that body to any measure of mine that does not satisfy his judgment and his sense of duty to those from whom he holds his appointment, nor any confidence in advance from the people but that asked for by Mr. Jefferson, "to give firmness and effect to the legal administration of their affairs."

I deem the present occasion sufficiently important and solemn to justify me in expressing to my fellow-citizens a profound reverence for the Christian religion and a thorough conviction that sound morals, religious liberty, and a just sense of religious responsibility are essentially connected with all true and lasting happiness; and to that good Being who has blessed us by the gifts of civil and religious freedom, who watched over and prospered the labors of our fathers and has hitherto preserved to us institutions far exceeding in excellence those of any other people, let us unite in fervently commending every interest of our beloved country in all future time.

Fellow-citizens, being fully invested with that high office to which the partiality of my countrymen has called me, I now take an affectionate leave of you. You will bear with you to your homes the remembrance of the pledge I have this day given to discharge all the high duties of my exalted station according to the best of my ability, and I shall enter upon their performance with entire confidence in the support of a just and generous people.[13]

Despite his mightily impressive speech, Harrison became something of a national joke because he died just a month later, allegedly of pneumonia. Popular history held that Harrison's long speech, delivered with no coat while standing outside in the cold caused his death. It was more likely, however, that he likely died from a fever contracted from bacterially infected water. Records indicate that his primary complaint was intestinal difficulty. Nonetheless, Harrison died just days after his election and before he had any chance to make any mark on the office. His election, though, brought a new figure to power in John Tyler, a dedicated pro-slavery activist whose agenda was markedly different from Harrison's and diverged considerably from the Whig agenda, which was, in part, shaped by the New England abolitionist movement.

The Last Gasp of the Virginia Gentry

Tyler was born in 1790 into a wealthy family of the Virginia aristocracy. He has been described as the last president from the Virginia aristocracy established in the Founding Era. He graduated from the College of William and Mary, like Jefferson, and became a lawyer, working in a prestigious Richmond law firm. His father's economic influence saw him appointed to the Virginia House of Delegates, where he opposed the National Bank. He served in the military in 1812, receiving no accolades, but parlayed his patriotic military service to win election to the House of Representatives.

John Tyler was the first president to face impeachment, an effort led by his own party. By Edwards & Anthony, Library of Congress Prints and Photographs division, via Wikimedia.

As a southern planter, Tyler was a firm believer in the old system in which only landowners were afforded political power. He viewed efforts to expand the political franchise to the poor and laboring class as an affront to the traditionalist system. He was also committed to the South and to the institution of slavery, which he knew was responsible for all southern political and economic influence. He, therefore, opposed centralized control of the economy and tariffs, which were central to the Whig Party platform. Harrison's rise to the presidency provides a lesson on the importance of running mates. The Whigs chose Tyler not because they liked his politics, but because Tyler had been an outspoken critic of Jackson's and because he could appeal to the slave owners. Many of the Whigs were enmeshed in the growing abolitionist movement, though the party was not firmly committed to this. Rather, they sought a middle-ground, opposing the expansion of slavery, but not fighting its continued existence. Harrison was anti-slavery, and so could appease those in the Whigs more committed to abolitionism, while Tyler, who was sympathetic to slavery, was chosen to draw support from the slave owning southern elite. When Harrison died, however, the Whigs found that they were left with a chief executive who disagreed with their platform.[14]

Certainly, few politicians or members of the public who voted for Harrison expected Tyler to become president so rapidly. There were many in Congress and in the public who felt that Tyler was little more than an acting president. Questions circulated regarding the need for a new election, but Tyler firmly rejected any questions about his authority asserting that the U.S. Constitution gave him full and immediate presidential power, with no need for him to qualify through any further electoral process. In a conciliatory move, Tyler did not disband Harrison's cabinet, even though there were political enemies among the secretaries. This was a symbol of the continuation of power, or perhaps a token gesture to the public that he would strive to further the agenda that Harrison had been elected to realize.

Tyler's strong personal convictions facilitated an orderly transfer of power. This was the first time that a vice president had assumed power after the quick death of a president, and it tested the constitutional transfer of power that was supposed to occur in such an event. Despite calls for his removal, Tyler weathered political intemperance and was able to justify taking full presidential power by citing constitutional precedent. He asserted that he, too, had been duly elected by the people of the United States, and, though he was not their first choice for chief executive, his election as vice president carried the meaning that he had been chosen to replace the president should the need arise. Thus, Tyler insisted the he be treated not as an interim leader, but as the nation's empowered chief executive, with all the powers entrusted to that office. This was an important moment in the history of presidential authority, establishing precedent for future vice presidents who would assume office after the death of a chief executive. Tyler's surprising rise to power also demonstrates why the strategic political choice of a vice president is a dangerous tactic. Future presidents sometimes chose vice presidential running mates for political leverage, but rarely one so diametrically different as Tyler was to Harrison.

A President Without A Base

Tyler was, however, not skilled at building political coalitions and too committed to his own, largely antiquated view of political power. Tyler immediately vetoed a bill to resurrect the National Bank, a keystone of the Whig agenda. All Tyler's cabinet save one resigned in protest and, the following year, Henry Clay had Tyler expelled from the Whig Party. Whig supporters even protested near the White House and debates in Congress became quite heated. There was even a fistfight in Congress between Representative Edward Stanley of North Carolina and Tyler's friend, Virginia Representative Henry Wise.

On July 22, 1842, Virginia Representative John Minor Botts, from Tyler's own home state, proposed that the House should bring articles of

impeachment against Tyler. The notice read: "On the grounds of his ignorance of the interest and true policy of this government, and want of qualification for the discharge of the important duties of President of the United States." Botts clarified his charges later, arguing that Tyler was guilty of the "high crime and misdemeanor" of "endeavoring to excite a disorganizing and revolutionary spirit in the country, by inviting a disregard of, and disobedience to a law of Congress." He further charged the president with abusing his veto power.

Henry Clay, then the leader of the Whigs, was more cautious. He reportedly said of Tyler's proposed impeachment, "There is enough cause, God knows, but it is a novel proceeding, full of important consequences, present and future, and should not be commenced but upon full consideration." The House voted to table the issue, but called for an investigation, choosing John Quincy Adams, who had become a congressman in Massachusetts after losing his bid for a second term, to lead the investigation into Tyler's alleged wrongdoings. Meanwhile, Tyler continued to veto bills, including a tariff bill, drawing increasing scorn from the Whigs. Adams's committee found that Tyler was guilty of "gross abuse of constitutional power and bold assumptions of powers never vested in him by law," and accused him of having assumed legislative power beyond the president's constitutional role. He was further charged, in a portent of future impeachment inquiries, of withholding information important to the investigation and thus of obstruction of justice. However, Adams stopped short of recommending proceeding with impeachment. Given the highly divided state of internal affairs, Adams's report recommended that he be censured by Congress.[15]

Tyler went on to fight against the Whig agenda, vetoing a total of ten bills. Clay was content to leave Tyler in office, hoping to beat him in the 1844 election, and he had already left Congress to prepare for his presidential bid. Meanwhile, Botts's articles of impeachment reached a vote; but the

Whigs had lost control in the 1842 election, and the impeachment drive failed. This first attempt to impeach a sitting president tested the waters of congressional power with regard to impeachment. The movement failed, because it did not gain support and because of political posturing within Congress, but it proved a portent of future impeachment proceedings. Tyler was in many ways the successor to Jackson, though he lacked the popular support behind his agenda. Like Jackson, he used presidential power in an almost entirely obstructionist way; and while he had little power to set the national agenda, neither did Congress unless they could unite to oppose him. Factionalism prevented this, and the government was essentially in deadlock.

Tyler's presidency also marks another important exercise of the checks and balances system used to constrain presidential power. At the end of Tyler's time in office, he vetoed another Whig-supported bill that prohibited the president from authorizing military expenditures, such as the construction of Coast Guard ships. The bill was a legislative effort to limit presidential power over military spending, a power that the Constitution grants exclusively to Congress. Presented by Connecticut Senator Jabez Huntington, the bill sought to preserve the Constitutional relationship between the president and Congress by forcing the president to seek approved appropriations before committing to military funding projects. Tyler vetoed the bill on the grounds that he wished to protect existing ship-building contracts and that it was the president's prerogative to decide on minor military spending issues. The House voted to override Tyler's veto, marking the first time in history that Congress successfully overrode a presidential veto, with only one dissenting vote. Since then, though presidents have vetoed over 2,500 bills, overriding a presidential veto has remained rare, at less than five percent.[16]

American Expansionism

Lacking political support, Tyler pinned his hopes at a second term on his own vision of America's future that included slavery. He formed his own

political party, and sought support by promising to annex Texas and to make it a state. Mexico had threatened war if the United States chose to intervene in their national affairs, but Tyler saw an opportunity to build support. Politicians who were also singularly interested in the Texas annexation joined with him to form a new Democratic Republican Party, with the motto "Tyler and Texas" as their campaign slogan.

Tyler drafted a treaty proposal to annex Texas, but he mistakenly appointed John C. Calhoun as his new secretary of state in 1844, who delivered speeches before Congress, that clearly stated that the ultimate goal of Texas annexation was the key to increasing southern power and thus staving off the encroaching abolitionist movement. This hurt Tyler. There were those who wanted Texas annexed but were abolitionists, or, at least, were not pro slavery and didn't want a fight with the abolitionist faction. It was clear that Tyler, with Calhoun at his side, wanted Texas to increase the slave-owning lobby's power in Washington. Martin Van Buren utilized his skills as the "Little Magician" once again, speaking to representatives and senators, and ensured that Tyler's annexation treaty would fail. Even Andrew Jackson's support wasn't sufficient, and Van Buren's efforts to defeat the treaty drove a wedge between him and Jackson.

In the 1844 election, Tyler had no chance of success. Rival Henry Clay, representing the Whigs, was certain to beat him. The Jacksonian Democrats nominated James Polk, who was not widely known, but was a Tennessee man and protégé of Andrew Jackson. Tyler ran as an independent, which split the Jacksonian vote between Tyler and Polk. Jackson intervened, telling Tyler that it was in the best interest of the party for him to resign and allow Polk to stand in as the party's representative. If he wouldn't, Clay would win. Tyler agreed, withdrawing in late August, and supporting for Polk, who won a narrow election to carry on the Jacksonian legacy. [17] As a lame-duck president, Tyler finally saw Texas annexation realized in the form of a joint resolution that made Texas the newest state of the Union.[18]

CONCLUSION

Just as Van Buren's presidency was poisoned by Jackson's poor leadership, the fate of the Whig Party was darkened by their choice of Tyler as Harrison's vice president. Had they chosen a candidate with a similar view, or one who might have worked with the Whigs in Congress, rather than one to help the party carry the pro-slavery vote, the Whigs might have recovered from Harrison's unexpected death. As it was, Tyler's disastrous presidency gave the White House back to the Jacksonian Democrats under Jackson protégé James K. Polk. Van Buren and Tyler both demonstrated different interpretations of presidential authority. Van Buren used the powers of the office to try and balance the partisan friction in Congress, while Tyler followed a more Jacksonian approach, using presidential power to obstruct congressional action. The Texas independence movement and increasing sectional tensions were the primary issues that Van Buren and Tyler contended with, and neither president proved to have the leadership capability to address these issues, or the support to achieve much of their agendas while in office.

DISCUSSION QUESTIONS

♦ How did the Harrison/Tyler campaign change the nature of American political campaigning?

♦ Why did the Whig Party choose a war hero like Harrison for their candidate?

♦ How did Van Buren use presidential power in foreign affairs? How does this compare with modern presidents?

♦ Why was the annexation of Texas politically controversial?

Works Used

Freehling, William. "John Tyler: Campaigns and Elections." *Miller Center*. U of Virginia. 2019. millercenter.org/president/tyler/campaigns-and-elections.

Freehling, William. "John Tyler: Impact and Legacy." *Miller Center*. U of Virginia. millercenter.org/president/tyler/impact-and-legacy.

Harrison, William Henry. "Inaugural Address of William Henry Harrison." *Avalon Project*. Lillian Goldman Law Library. avalon.law.yale.edu/19th_century/harrison.asp.

"History-Essays." *Lehrman Institute*. 2018. lehrmaninstitute.org/history/Andrew-Jackson-1837.html.

Kelly, Martin. "Quotes from Martin Van Buren." *Thought Co*. 19 Oct. 2019. www.thoughtco.com/quotes-from-martin-van-buren-103962.

May, Gary. *John Tyler*. New York: Times Books, 2008.

Moore, Stephen. *Eighteen Minutes: The Battle of San Jacinto and the Texas Independence Campaign*. Dallas, TX: Republic of Texas P, 2004.

"Presidential Election of 1836: A Resource Guide." *LOC*. Library of Congress. 23 Oct. 2018. www.loc.gov/rr/program/bib/elections/election1836.html.

"Presidential Election of 1840: A Resource Guide." *LOC*. Library of Congress. 23 Oct. 2018. www.loc.gov/rr/program/bib/elections/election1840.html.

Schroeder, John H. "Annexation or Independence: The Texas Issue in American Politics, 1836–1845." *The Southwestern Historical Quarterly*. vol. 89, no. 2, 1985, pp. 137–64, *JSTOR*, www.jstor.org/stable/30239906.

Shafer, Ronald. *The Carnival Campaign*. Chicago, IL: Chicago Review P, 2016.

Shafer, Ronald G. "'He Lies Like a Dog': The First Effort to Impeach a President Was Led by his Own Party." *The Washington Post*. 23 Sept. 2019. www.washingtonpost.com/history/2019/09/23/he-lies-like-dog-first-effort-impeach-president-was-led-by-his-own-party/.

Sibley, Joel H. *Martin Van Buren and the Emergence of American Popular Politics*. Lanham, MD: Rowman & Littlefield Publishers, Inc. 2005.

Sumner, William Graham. *Andrew Jackson as a Public Man*. Cambridge, MA: The Riverside P, 1884.

"The First Congressional Override of a Presidential Veto." *History*. U.S. House of Representatives. 2017. history.house.gov/Historical-Highlights/1800-1850/The-first-congressional-override-of-a-presidential-veto/.

Watt, Paul, Patrick Spedding, and Derek B. Scott. *Cheap Print and Popular Song in the Nineteenth Century*. New York: Cambridge U P, 2017.

"William Henry Harrison." *White House*. 2019. www.whitehouse.gov/about-the-white-house/presidents/william-henry-harrison/.

Wilson, Major L. *The Presidency of Martin Van Buren*. U of Michigan P, 1984.

Introduction

James K. Polk was a protégé of Andrew Jackson and the first president from the original western frontier. He was known as a somber, hardworking man, and promised that he would only serve one term in office, a promise which he kept. While in office, Polk used every power available to him to pursue his agenda, and accomplished more of his campaign promises in a single term than most other presidents achieve in two terms. On the international front, Polk presided over, and was largely responsible for, the invasion of Mexico, and he helped settle the border dispute between the U.S. and Canada. Domestically, he helped to bring back a degree of federal banking oversight, something that even Jacksonians had come to see as necessary to avoid another financial recession like the Panic of 1837.

Topics covered in this chapter include:

- Mexican-American War
- Annexation of Oregon
- Annexation of Texas
- New Mexico Territory
- Manifest Destiny
- Alexander Hamilton

This Chapter Discusses the Following Source Documents:
Inaugural Address of James Knox Polk, March 4, 1845
War Message to Congress, May 11, 1846
Spot Resolutions in the House of Representatives, December 22, 1847

Manifest Destiny
James K. Polk (1845–1849)

The Jacksonian age continued under James K. Polk, one of the most disciplined and accomplished presidents in history. While Polk has since been celebrated for increasing the scope of America by pursuing an aggressive philosophy of Manifest Destiny, his presidency contributed significantly to the growing sectionalism that resulted in Civil War.

The Dark Horse from Tennessee

Polk was born in North Carolina and was Scots-Irish, Calvinist extraction. When Polk was ten, his family took a wagon convoy to Tennessee, where they established a plantation. According to biographers, the poverty and hardship Polk suffered during his youth, coupled with a series of illnesses, affected his health as an adult. Polk was home-schooled but attended the University of North Carolina for two years. Polk then read law with Nashville lawyer Felix Grundy, a future Attorney General under Martin Van Buren.

Polk's father, Samuel, did well in Tennessee, owning thousands of acres and 50 slaves. Wealth bought Samuel political influence, and he became a fervent supporter of Andrew Jackson during Jackson's failed 1824 presidential bid. Samuel's political connections enabled a young James Polk to win election to the Tennessee House of Representatives in 1823 and then, with Jackson's endorsement, to win a seat in the U.S. House in 1825. While there, Polk remained a Jackson loyalist in return for Jackson's patronage. His political star was on the rise as he left Congress to seek the governorship of Tennessee in 1839, winning a close election. However, a financial downturn turned the tide against the Jacksonians, and Polk was voted out of the governorship and retired from politics.[1] While it seemed his career was over, Polk was surprised to learn that Andrew Jackson had put his name on the ballot for the Democratic Presidential nomination.

As the 1844 election approached, Jacksonians got a boost as it became clear that John Tyler, kicked out of the Whig Party and now running as an independent, did not have popular or aristocratic support. The Whigs nominated Representative Henry Clay of Kentucky, who adopted an anti-slavery position but at the same time promised that the annexation of Texas, which he supported, would not alter the balance of power between slave and free states. Clay also promised to serve only a single term if elected. With Jackson's guidance, Polk also supported annexation, but without committing to any specific stance on the slavery question. Polk further promised that he would pursue other efforts to expand U.S. territory, including an ongoing dispute with Britain over what became the state of Oregon, and would seek to expand U.S. territory into California. Polk, like Clay, also promised that he would only seek a single term if elected. Though the annexation of Texas was a major campaign issue in 1844, none of the candidates would play a direct role in this decision. Rather, annexation was accomplished by the Lame Duck Congress in the final days of the Tyler administration, leaving the incoming president to determine the new state's diplomatic boundaries.

James K. Polk, most remembered for the Mexican-American war. By Mathew Brady, via Wikimedia.

Polk could not have won the election on his own; though well-known in Tennessee, he was a "dark horse"—virtually unknown elsewhere. Although his campaign platform was designed to give him widespread appeal, popular and political support was divided among a number of candidates. Jackson tipped the balance by convincing Tyler to drop out of the race and support Polk in order to avoid a victory by Clay. The election drew widespread interest, with 79 percent of the voting-age population showing up at the polls. It was also close, with Polk winning the popular vote by just over 39,000 votes, and 170 Electoral College votes to Clay's 105.[2] Polk's connection to Jackson was no secret, and he quickly became known as "Young Hickory," an allusion to Jackson's "Old Hickory" moniker.

The Polks Go to Washington

Polk was a hard-working and determined man, but was short on social graces. Described as "dour," "humorless," and "boring," Polk lacked the charisma of many of the nation's former chief executives and was not well-liked by those who knew him, though he was frequently written with some measure of political and professional respect. Despite this, Polk's White House and the social environment of the era was well managed thanks to his wife, Sarah Childress, who was perhaps the nation's second-most influential presidential wife after Dolley Madison.

Unlike many presidential wives, Sarah Polk was educated at the Salem Female Academy. There, she studied Greek and Roman literature, geography, music, drawing and sewing, and English composition and grammar. From the beginning, Sarah shared her husband's political ambitions, and she managed his political career from the time he first ran for the governorship of Tennessee. It was Sarah Polk who kept her husband's schedule, who kept track of media coverage, and who managed his political meetings, and often his subordinates. As Polk moved into the White House, Sarah took an even larger role. She handled his correspondence and helped write his speeches, and she privately met with politicians and their wives, acting as a behind-the-scenes political strategist. Polk's correspondence indicates that he did not hesitate to ask his wife's advice even on political matters, a realm to which most women of the era were denied access.

As a hostess, Sarah Polk offered warmth and welcome where her husband typically fell short. She is said to have consulted with Dolley Madison, arguably the nation's most popular First Lady, in learning how to comport herself in the role, and she adopted some of Madison's quirks, such as wearing a "turban" instead of a more traditional hat. However, unlike the Madisons, who were fun-loving and enjoyed a good party, the Polks were more serious and deeply religious. It is said that the Polk parties were relatively light on humor, though Sarah Polk was described as an able and warm hostess. Liquor was not served at their functions, except for wine with dinner, and music and dancing disappeared from the White House. Sarah's religious views also played into her embrace of white supremacism and misogyny. Records of her conversations and letters indicate that she believed that slavery had been preordained by God and that the atrocities committed against

The Polks Go to Washington
continued

African Americans and Native Americans were simply the result of their place in a spiritual hierarchy of value.[a]

Works Used

a. "First Lady Biography: Sarah Polk." *First Ladies*. National First Ladies Library. www.firstladies.org/biographies/firstladies.aspx?biography=12.

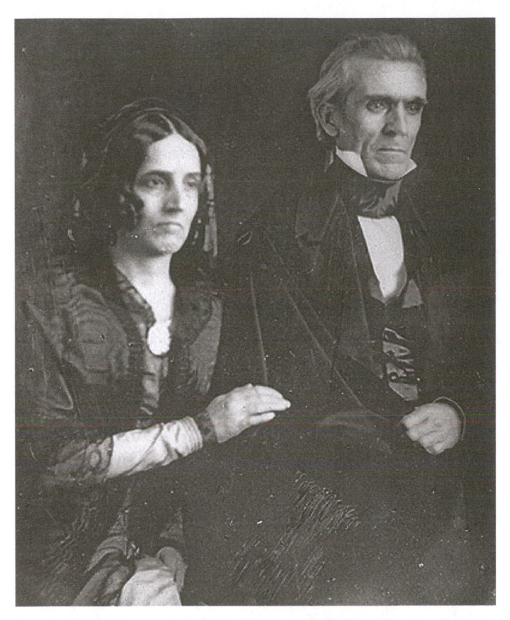

James and Sarah Polk, c 1949, James K. Polk Presidential Museum, via Wikimedia.

The Great Expansion

In his inaugural address, James Polk laid out his goals for his presidency: 1) to acquire the Oregon Territory, California, and the Territory of New Mexico, 2) to settle the Texas border issue, and 3) to establish a new federal depository system. He became the first president since George Washington to accomplish all his campaign promises while in office and proved surprisingly willing to work across partisan lines.

Polk's success came down to his shrewd use of executive powers. He acted like a diplomat in Congress, promoting a compromise in the form of a national deposit system that helped temporarily heal the rift between those promoting "soft currency" (paper money) and those who wanted the economy to continue operating on "hard currency" (gold and precious metals). Polk's deft navigation of this issue, using the threat of veto power to force a legislative compromise, provides one example of how presidential authority can be used effectively in periods of divisiveness. Polk is remembered most, of course, for his role in expanding the reach of the United States. In this, he demonstrated a firm commitment to the use of presidential authority as commander in chief.

The same year that Polk took office, a new perception of American identity was beginning to emerge, which came to be called "Manifest Destiny." The phrase came from an article written by journalist John O'Sullivan and published in *The Democratic Review,* a publication funded by Jacksonian Democrat contributors. O'Sullivan wrote:

> *Texas is now ours. . . . Her star and her stripe may already be said to have taken their place in the glorious blazon of our common nationality; and the sweep of our eagle's wing already includes within its circuit the wide extent of her fair and fertile land. She is no longer to us a mere geographical space—a certain combination of coast, plain, mountain, valley, forest and stream. She is no longer to us a mere country on the map. She comes*

within the dear and sacred designation of Our Country. . . other nations have undertaken to intrude themselves. . . in a spirit of hostile interference against us, for the avowed object of thwarting our policy and hampering our power, limiting our greatness and checking the fulfillment of our manifest destiny to overspread the continent allotted by Providence for the free development of our yearly multiplying millions. This we have seen done by England, our old rival and enemy; and by France, strangely coupled with her against us. . . . [3]

The idea of Manifest Destiny—that the United States had a special, God-given mission to spread the perceptive benefits of American-style democratic republicanism across North America—was an evolution of American identity common among the early colonists, who believed that the settlement of the United States was part of a spiritually ordained mission. O'Sullivan's grandiose depiction of expansionism provided a sense of fate and spirituality to this effort and helped to foster a sense of American exceptionalism still popular among some Americans today.

Texas, New Mexico, California, and Oregon were all disputed areas with Americans, as well as, foreign claims. There were also important political and practical reasons for acquiring these territories. Oregon and California, in particular, provided access to coastal territory useful both for economic expansion and military strategy. By seeing these efforts as the destiny of America, rather than to obtain political or economic advantages, Americans were able to emotionally connect to this effort, and Polk saw a huge swell in popular support. As Polk said in his inaugural address:

INAUGURAL ADDRESS OF JAMES KNOX POLK

March 4, 1845

Source Document Excerpt

In the earlier stages of our national existence the opinion prevailed with some that our system of confederated States could not operate successfully over an extended territory, and serious objections have at different times been made to the enlargement of our boundaries. These objections were earnestly urged when we acquired Louisiana. Experience has shown that they were not well founded. The title of numerous Indian tribes to vast tracts of country has been extinguished; new States have been admitted into the Union; new Territories have been created and our jurisdiction and laws extended over them. As our population has expanded, the Union has been cemented and strengthened. AS our boundaries have been enlarged and our agricultural population has been spread over a large surface, our federative system has acquired additional strength and security. It may well be doubted whether it would not be in greater danger of overthrow if our present population were confined to the comparatively narrow limits of the original thirteen States than it is now that they are sparsely settled over a more expanded territory. It is confidently believed that our system may be safely extended to the utmost bounds of our territorial limits, and that as it shall be extended the bonds of our Union, so far from being weakened, will become stronger.

None can fail to see the danger to our safety and future peace if Texas remains an independent state or becomes an ally or dependency of some foreign nation more powerful than herself. Is there one among our citizens who would not prefer perpetual peace with Texas to occasional wars, which so often occur between bordering independent nations? . . .

Nor will it become in a less degree my duty to assert and maintain by all Constitutional means the right of the United States to that portion of our territory which lies beyond the Rocky Mountains. Our title to the country of the Oregon is "clear and unquestionable," and already are our people preparing to perfect that title by occupying it with their wives and children. But eighty years ago our population was confined on the west by the ridge of the Alleghanies. Within that period—within the lifetime, I might say, of some of my hearers—our people, increasing to many millions, have filled the eastern valley of the Mississippi, adventurously ascended the Missouri to its headsprings, and are already

continued

engaged in establishing the blessings of self-government in valleys of which the rivers flow to the Pacific. The world beholds the peaceful triumphs of the industry of our emigrants. To us belongs the duty of protecting them adequately wherever they may be upon our soil. The jurisdiction of our laws and the benefits of our republican institutions should be extended over them in the distant regions which they have selected for their homes. The increasing facilities of intercourse will easily bring the States, of which the formation in that part of our territory can not be long delayed, within the sphere of our federative Union. In the meantime every obligation imposed by treaty or conventional stipulations should be sacredly respected.[4]

When it came to the border dispute over Oregon, Polk claimed that he would seek to control all territory below 40 minutes above the 54th parallel. The slogan "Fifty-four forty or fight" became common among Polk supporters with an interest in the Oregon territory dispute. Such a territorial claim would have left the United States in control of a portion of what is now Canada stretching up to Alaska, and there was little chance that Britain would be willing to surrender such an expansive part of their territory. However, Polk's campaign claims were part of a shrewd political strategy.

Polk had no legitimate desire to go to war with Britain, but he allowed his supporters and Britain to believe he would be willing to fight for the 54/40 designation. After winning the election, Polk shifted his attention to the Mexican border and did not directly address his Oregon claims, leaving to Britain the decision of how important the territory was. The strategy worked, and in the 1846 Treaty of Oregon, diplomats were able to set the boundary at the 49th parallel. Polk faced some political blowback from politicians and citizens who'd been committed to the 54th parallel plan, but the compromise granted Polk a political victory and prevented a war that the United States could not have won.

Pork Barrel Politics

Though a success for the Polk administration, the Treaty of Oregon left the administration of a series of small islands undecided, including San Juan, a small forested territory sitting in one of two navigable channels along the parallel. At the time, both sides felt that control of these islands was essential, and the sense of manifest destiny was still driving a widespread popular interest in expansion in America.

The British sent Charles Griffin to San Juan in 1853, where he set up a sheep and pig ranch. Griffin's posting was meant to increase Britain's claim to the island, but Americans soon began arriving, too, many joining in the push west. One of these men was Lyman Cutlar, an American potato farmer and failed businessman from Kentucky who left for the Oregon territory seeking a fresh start. In 1859, several black boars owned by Griffin infiltrated the potato patches on Cutlar's farm, where they began uprooting tubers. Cutlar arrived on the scene and shot one of Griffin's black boars. The two men fought over the issue, and Cutlar offered to replace the pig, but Griffin demanded an exorbitant fee of $100. When word of the incident spread, tensions escalated, leading to what historians have called the "Pig War." Both the United States and Britain ended up sending naval forces to the island, where they occupied opposite sides and remained in a standoff for nearly 12 years. The occupation continued even as America engaged in the Civil War. British and American soldiers lived on the island, farming and even socializing with one another, as they waited in limbo. Finally, in 1872, Germany's Kaiser Wilhelm was brought in to arbitrate, and he secured ownership of the islands for the United States in return for concessions to England. Amazingly, the 12-year occupation involved no bloodshed, largely because the experienced veterans in charge of the occupying forces from either side chose patience over rash action and simply instructed their soldiers to wait until something changed in the broader political world. Though a footnote in history, the Pig War provides a lesson on the benefits of inaction.[a]

Works Used

a. Franklin, Deborah. "Boar War." *Smithsonian Magazine*. June 2005. www.smithsonianmag.com/history/boar-war-75236932/.

American Imperialism or American Destiny?

While settling the Oregon territory was an essential part of Polk's presidency, he is known primarily for involving America in the Mexican-American War. Mexico, at the time, was in deep disarray. A political vacuum led to rival forces competing for power, and there was little agreement among Mexico's leaders regarding how to handle Texas or America's other designs on Mexican-controlled territories in California and New Mexico. Polk initially tried diplomacy, dispatching special envoy John Slidell with permission to purchase California from the Mexican government. The government in power at the time was willing to bargain, but others in the government were not, and Slidell's arrival triggered a revolt in the Mexican government. In an April 1846 diplomatic incident, Mexican troops crossed the Rio Grande River and killed 11 U.S. soldiers.

The attack was not sanctioned by the sitting Mexican government, but Polk declared war, claiming that Americans had been attacked on sovereign American soil. On May 11, 1846, he delivered the following message to Congress:

WAR MESSAGE TO CONGRESS
James K. Polk
May 11, 1846
Source Document Excerpt

The strong desire to establish peace with Mexico on liberal and honorable terms, and the readiness of this Government to regulate and adjust our boundary and other causes of difference with that power on such fair and equitable principles as would lead to permanent relations of the most friendly nature, induced me in September last to seek the reopening of diplomatic relations between the two countries. Every measure adopted on our part had for its object the furtherance of these desired results. . . . In communicating to Congress a succinct statement of the injuries which we had suffered from Mexico, and which have been accumulating during a period of more than twenty years, every expression that could tend to inflame the people

War Message to Congress
continued

of Mexico or defeat or delay a pacific result was carefully avoided. An envoy of the United States repaired to Mexico with full powers to adjust every existing difference. But though present on the Mexican soil by agreement between the two Governments, invested with full powers, and bearing evidence of the most friendly dispositions, his mission has been unavailing. The Mexican Government not only refused to receive him or listen to his propositions, but after a long-continued series of menaces have at last invaded our territory and shed the blood of our fellow-citizens on our own soil.

. . .

Mr. Slidell arrived at Vera Cruz on the 30th of November, and was courteously received by the authorities of that city. But the Government of General Herrera was then tottering to its fall. The revolutionary party had seized upon the Texas question to effect or hasten its overthrow. Its determination to restore friendly relations with the United States, and to receive our minister to negotiate for the settlement of this question, was violently assailed, and was made the great theme of denunciation against it. The Government of General Herrera, there is good reason to believe, was sincerely desirous to receive our minister; but it yielded to the storm

raised by its enemies, and on the 21st of December refused to accredit Mr. Slidell upon the most frivolous pretexts.

. . .

Five days after the date of Mr. Slidell's note, General Herrera yielded the Government to General Paredes without a struggle, and on the 30th of December resigned the Presidency. This revolution was accomplished solely by the army, the people having taken little part in the contest; and thus the supreme power in Mexico passed into the hands of a military leader.

Determined to leave no effort untried to effect an amicable adjustment with Mexico, I directed Mr. Slidell to present his credentials to the Government of General Paredes and ask to be officially received by him. . . . This minister in his reply, under date of the 12th of March, reiterated the arguments of his predecessor, and in terms that may be considered as giving just grounds of offense to the Government and people of the United States denied the application of Mr. Slidell. Nothing therefore remained for our envoy but to demand his passports and return to his own country.

Thus the Government of Mexico, though solemnly pledged by official acts in October last to receive and accredit

continued

an American envoy, violated their plighted faith and refused the offer of a peaceful adjustment of our difficulties. Not only was the offer rejected, but the indignity of its rejection was enhanced by the manifest breach of faith in refusing to admit the envoy who came because they had bound themselves to receive him. Nor can it be said that the offer was fruitless from the want of opportunity of discussing it; our envoy was present on their own soil. Nor can it be ascribed to a want of sufficient powers; our envoy had full powers to adjust every question of difference. Nor was there room for complaint that our propositions for settlement were unreasonable; permission was not even given our envoy to make any proposition whatever. Nor can it be objected that we, on our part, would not listen to any reasonable terms of their suggestion; the Mexican Government refused all negotiation, and have made no proposition of any kind.

In my message at the commencement of the present session I informed you that upon the earnest appeal both of the Congress and convention of Texas I had ordered an efficient military force to take a position "between the Nueces and the Del Norte." This had become necessary to meet a threatened invasion of Texas by the Mexican forces, for which extensive military preparations had been made. The invasion was threatened solely because Texas had determined, in accordance with a solemn resolution of the Congress of the United States, to annex herself to our Union, and under these circumstances it was plainly our duty to extend our protection over her citizens and soil.

This force was concentrated at Corpus Christi, and remained there until after I had received such information from Mexico as rendered it probable, if not certain, that the Mexican Government would refuse to receive our envoy.

Meantime Texas, by the final action of our Congress, had become an integral part of our Union. The Congress of Texas, by its act of December 19, 1836, had declared the Rio del Norte to be the boundary of that Republic. Its jurisdiction had been extended and exercised beyond the Nueces. The country between that river and the Del Norte had been represented in the Congress and in the convention of Texas, had thus taken part in the act of annexation itself, and is now included within one of our Congressional districts. Our own Congress had, moreover, with great unanimity, by the act approved December 31, 1845, recognized the country beyond the Nueces as a part of our territory. . . .

The movement of the troops to the Del Norte was made by the commanding

War Message to Congress
continued

general under positive instructions to abstain from all aggressive acts toward Mexico or Mexican citizens and to regard the relations between that Republic and the United States as peaceful unless she should declare war or commit acts of hostility indicative of a state of war. He was specially directed to protect private property and respect personal rights.

The Army moved from Corpus Christi on the 11th of March, and on the 28th of that month arrived on the left bank of the Del Norte opposite to Matamoras, where it encamped on a commanding position, which has since been strengthened by the erection of fieldworks. A depot has also been established at Point Isabel, near the Brazos Santiago, 30 miles in rear of the encampment. The selection of his position was necessarily confided to the judgment of the general in command.

The Mexican forces at Matamoras assumed a belligerent attitude, and on the 12th of April General Ampudia, then in command, notified General Taylor to break up his camp within twenty-four hours and to retire beyond the Nueces River, and in the event of his failure to comply with these demands announced that arms, and arms alone, must decide the question. But no open act of hostility was committed until the 24th of April. On that day

General Arista, who had succeeded to the command of the Mexican forces, communicated to General Taylor that "he considered hostilities commenced and should prosecute them." A party of dragoons of 63 men and officers were on the same day dispatched from the American camp up the Rio del Norte, on its left bank, to ascertain whether the Mexican troops had crossed or were preparing to cross the river, "became engaged with a large body of these troops, and after a short affair, in which some 16 were killed and wounded, appear to have been surrounded and compelled to surrender."

The grievous wrongs perpetrated by Mexico upon our citizens throughout a long period of years remain unredressed, and solemn treaties pledging her public faith for this redress have been disregarded. A government either unable or unwilling to enforce the execution of such treaties fails to perform one of its plainest duties. . . .

Had we acted with vigor in repelling the insults and redressing the injuries inflicted by Mexico at the commencement, we should doubtless have escaped all the difficulties in which we are now involved.

Instead of this, however, we have been exerting our best efforts to propitiate her good will. Upon

continued

the pretext that Texas, a nation as independent as herself, thought proper to unite its destinies with our own she has affected to believe that we have severed her rightful territory, and in official proclamations and manifestoes has repeatedly threatened to make war upon us for the purpose of reconquering Texas. In the meantime we have tried every effort at reconciliation. The cup of forbearance had been exhausted even before the recent information from the frontier of the Del Norte. But now, after reiterated menaces, Mexico has passed the boundary of the United States, has invaded our territory and shed American blood upon the American soil. She has proclaimed that hostilities have commenced, and that the two nations are now at war.

As war exists, and, notwithstanding all our efforts to avoid it, exists by the act of Mexico herself, we are called upon by every consideration of duty and patriotism to vindicate with decision the honor, the rights, and the interests of our country. . . .

In further vindication of our rights and defense of our territory, I invoke the prompt action of Congress to recognize the existence of the war, and to place at the disposition of the Executive the means of prosecuting the war with vigor, and thus hastening the restoration of peace. To this end I recommend that authority should be given to call into the public service a large body of volunteers to serve for not less than six or twelve months unless sooner discharged. A volunteer force is beyond question more efficient than any other description of citizen soldiers, and it is not to be doubted that a number far beyond that required would readily rush to the field upon the call of their country. I further recommend that a liberal provision be made for sustaining our entire military force and furnishing it with supplies and munitions of war. . .[5]

Polk did not have universal congressional support for military action. A majority of the Whigs, chief among them first-term Congressman Abraham Lincoln, accused Polk of violating his powers by illegitimately depicting his reasoning for declaring war. On December 22, 1847, Lincoln issued what came to be called the "Spot Resolutions," in which he asked Polk to provide proof that the violence had, in fact, occurred on legally recognized American soil.

SPOT RESOLUTIONS IN THE HOUSE OF REPRESENTATIVES

Abraham Lincoln
December 22, 1847
Source Document Excerpt

WHEREAS the President of the United States, in his message of May 11th. 1846, has declared that "The Mexican Government not only refused to receive him, [the envoy of the U.S.] or listen to his propositions, but, after a long continued series of menaces, HAS at last invaded *our teritory* and shed the blood of our fellow-citizens on *our own soil:*"

And again, in his message of December 8, 1846 that "We had ample cause of war against Mexico, long before the breaking out of hostilities. But even then we forbore to take redress into our own hands, until Mexico herself became the aggressor by invading *our soil* in hostile array, and shedding the blood of our citizens:"

And yet again, in his message of December 7, 1847, that "the Mexican Government refused even to hear the terms of adjustment which he [our minister of peace] was authorized to propose; and finally, under wholly unjustifiable pretexts, involved the two countries in war, by invading the territory of the State of Texas, striking the first blow, and shedding the blood of our citizens on *our own soil.*"

And whereas this House is desirous to obtain a full knowledge of all the facts which go to establish whether the particular spot of soil on which the blood of our citizens was so shed was or was not *our own soil*, at that time; Therefore,

Resolved by the House of Representatives, That the President of the United States be respectfully requested to inform this House—

1st. Whether the spot of soil on which the blood of our citizens was shed, as in his message declared, was or was not within the territory of Spain, at least from the treaty of 1819, until the Mexican revolution.

2d. Whether that spot is or is not within the territory which was wrested from Spain by the revolutionary Government of Mexico.

3d. Whether that spot is or is not within a settlement of people, which settlement had existed ever since long before the Texas revolution, and until its inhabitants fled before the approach of the United States Army.

continued

4th. Whether that settlement is or is not isolated from any and all other settlements by the Gulf and the Rio Grande on the south and west, and by wide uninhabited regions on the north and east.

5th. Whether the people of that settlement, or a majority of them, or any of them, have ever submitted themselves to the government or laws of Texas or of the United States, by consent or by compulsion, either by accepting office, or voting at elections, or paying tax, or serving on juries, or having process served upon them, or in any other way.

6th. Whether the People of that settlement did or did not flee from the approach of the United States Army, leaving unprotected their homes and their growing crops, *before* the blood was shed, as in the messages stated; and whether the first blood, so shed, was or was not shed within the *enclosure* of one of the people who had thus fled from it.

7th. Whether our *citizens*, whose blood was shed, as in his messages declared, were or were not at that time, armed officers, and soldiers, sent into that settlement by the military order of the President through the Secretary of War.

8th. Whether the military force of the United States was or was not so sent into that settlement after Genl. Taylor had more than once intimated to the War Department that, in his opinion, no such movement was necessary to the defence or protection of Texas.[6]

Though Polk claimed that the violence occurred on U.S. soil, the attack actually occurred in disputed territory then occupied by Mexicans. The attackers did not represent the official government of Mexico, and the attack was not intended as a military assault on the United States. The soldiers involved were reacting to what they believed was illegal American encroachment into their territory.

Abraham Lincoln was one of the few members of Congress to oppose the Mexican-American War. Photo attributed to Nicholas H. Shepherd, a law student of Lincoln's. Library of Congress, Prints and Photographs Division, via Wikimedia.

Lincoln's resolutions were ignored, and Jacksonians portrayed him as an unpatriotic traitor. Most of the other Whigs were unwilling to aggressively oppose the war, remembering the political fallout that occurred when the Federalists opposed the War of 1812. With manifest destiny fever spreading through the nation, there was a huge swell of nationalism and patriotic sentiment supporting Polk's war. Lincoln's aggressive opposition meant that he lost support from the Whigs in the west, and he resigned from Congress and retired to Illinois. In total, fourteen members of the House and two senators opposed the war, and with legislative support, Polk's declaration of war was official.

The Mexican-American War was resolved within seven months because Mexico was too divided, it lacked defense resources, and its leaders were inexperienced. Poverty was rampant, and army recruitment deepened the destitution of Mexico's poorest communities. The first phase of the war was led by General Zachary Taylor, nicknamed "Old Rough and Ready" for his aggressive and swift captures of Palo Alto and Resaca de la Palma. General Stephen Watts Kearny, meanwhile, occupied New Mexico, and then marched through Chihuahua to Monterrey, where he joined with Taylor's armies. Forces under U.S. Army Brevet Lieutenant Colonel John C. Fremont occupied California, where his battalion planted their regimental flag, containing the image of a grizzly bear. The operation became known as the "bear-flag revolt," and the grizzly bear became part of the state emblem. General Winfield Scott ended the war when he led an audacious five-month march over two hundred miles into central Mexico to occupy Mexico City, which his forces captured on September 14, 1847.

Polk's secretary of state, future president James Buchanan, recommended his chief clerk Nicholas Trist (married to Thomas Jefferson's granddaughter and a former private secretary to both Jefferson and Jackson) to negotiate a treaty with Mexico, and Polk agreed. Polk recalled Trist while he was traveling to Mexico, deciding that holding the negotiations in

Washington would be more visible, but the letter delivering this order took six weeks to arrive, during which time Trist had already begun negotiations and found the government willing to make major concessions. Boldly, Trist ignored Polk's recall and produced an agreement that allowed the United States to purchase California and New Mexico, essentially half of Mexico's territory, for $15 million, as well as establish a new border at the Rio Grande. On February 2, 1848, Trist signed the Treaty of Guadalupe Hidalgo and returned to Washington. Polk was furious, hoping for larger territorial gains, but accepted the treaty rather than extend negotiations. Trist was fired, denied payment for his role, and driven out of government service. He was later pardoned and granted back pay under the Grant Administration in 1871.[7]

Polk submitted the treaty to Congress, where it was approved by a margin of 34 to 14. Objections came not only from those who opposed the war, but from many Jacksonians who had hoped not only for larger gains, but for the United States to control the entirety of Mexico. Though Polk also wanted more territory, he wisely did not pursue the complete annexation of Mexico, believing that such a burden would ultimately provide little advantage to the United States. As a result of the war, the United States acquired the present-day states of Arizona, Utah, Nevada, California, New Mexico, Wyoming, and Colorado. It was a massive increase in both territory and resources and fulfilled the public expansionist fever, but at a significant cost. Around 2,000 Americans were killed in combat, while an additional 11,000 died of disease related to the war. The cost of the war, too, would impact economic growth for the next half century. In Mexico, between 25,000 and 50,000 died, and much of the already poverty-stricken country was left in ruins.[8]

A Disputed Legacy
Polk left office, as promised, at the conclusion of his first term. Long-term struggles with illness, and the stress of the presidency contributed to his death just three months after leaving office, at 53. Biographers have

often opined that he worked himself to death, often working 12-hour days nonstop. Polk was the first president since Washington to accomplish all of the goals he set out to achieve while in office. Although some describe his legacy as that of an effective, skilled leader, e others view him as the last of the individualistic and power-hungry Jacksonians.

Ulysses S. Grant, the famed Civil War general who would later serve as president, was a young lieutenant when the Mexican-American War was declared. He later said of the conflict, "I do not think there was ever a more wicked war than that waged by the United States on Mexico." The Mexican-American War organized the U.S. anti-war movement and saw protests in many cities around the country. The experiences of soldiers who fought against Mexicans, who were almost entirely poorly armed peasants, created a new narrative in the United States, explored beyond the patriotic trumpeting that heralded America's victory and God-given mission. Opposition to the Mexican-American War also produced unusual stories of lost loyalty, including the case of a group of Irish-Catholic American soldiers, who faced persecution in America, defected, and fought for Mexico as mercenaries. Some were motivated by promises of land and wealth offered by the Mexican government, but others reported feeling conflicted at participating in wantonly destroying Catholic churches and communities. John Riley, an Irish immigrant and a former West Point officer, was one of the Irish Americans who defected and the founder of what became known as the Battalion of Saint Patrick. In Mexico, where the Mexican-American War is known as the "American Invasion," the soldiers of Saint Patrick's Battalion are still celebrated as heroes, and the prime minister of Ireland still visits Mexico on the anniversary of the battalion's ill-fated resistance.[9]

Grant and Abraham Lincoln are perhaps the most famous figures who opposed Texas annexation and the war with Mexico. Grant felt that the entire Texas annexation movement was little more than a veiled attempt

to protect the slave trade from the growing influence of the abolition movement. He said in his memoir, "For myself, I was bitterly opposed to the measure, and to this day regard the war, which resulted, as one of the most unjust ever waged by a stronger against a weaker nation." Grant carried shame at his role in the war for the rest of his life, but while anti-war activists were typically labeled as unpatriotic or cowardly, none of these labels would ever be affixed to Grant, whose military performance during the Civil War rendered such criticisms invalid. Whereas anti-war activism was typically ignored, the questionable morality of America's invasion of Mexico, and the number of well-known figures who opposed it promoted the idea that the opposition to war might have been the morally upstanding and more patriotic stance.[10]

A deeper failing affixed to Polk is his inability to recognize how his actions as president would exacerbate sectional disputes. Polk has been described as the last "strong president" before the Civil War, and he certainly proved willing to fully utilize the authority of his office, but his failure to perceive the long-term implications of his actions as president led the nation down a dangerous path.

CONCLUSION

Polk was, in many ways, a very successful president who used presidential power in varied and effective ways. His use of misinformation to gain support for the invasion of Mexico, however, raises important questions about whether or not presidents have a responsibility to act in an honest manner and avoid misleading their constituents, regardless of the desired outcome. Nonetheless, careful public marketing coupled with shrewd Congressional negotiations was a winning combination for Polk, as evidenced by his record of accomplishments. On the down side, however, Polk's single-minded drive for American expansionism, and his belief in the philosophy of Manifest Destiny, took America further down the path toward the Civil War, as tensions over the expansion of slavery became key political controversies due to the opening up of new territories. The next chapter profiles President Zachary Taylor, an independent war hero who advocated for strong states rights.

DISCUSSION QUESTIONS

♦ Why did Abraham Lincoln oppose the Mexican-American War? Were his concerns valid?

♦ How did Polk utilize executive power in negotiating with Britain over the Oregon border?

♦ Is the idea of Manifest Destiny racially prejudiced? Explain your answer.

♦ How did Jackson intervene in Polk's political career?

♦ Is it ever appropriate for a president to purposefully mislead Congress and the American people in order to accomplish a political goal? In what circumstance?

Works Used

Bicknell, John. *America 1844*: Religious Fervor, Westward Expansion, and the Presidential Election That Transformed the Nation. Chicago, IL: Chicago Review P, 2015.

Bomboy, Scott. "The Man Who Delivered California to the U.S., and Was Fired for It." *National Constitution Center*. Constitution Daily. 10 Mar. 2019. constitutioncenter.org/blog/the-man-who-delivered-california-to-the-u-s-and-was-fired-for-it.

Greenberg, Amy S. *A Wicked War*: *Polk, Clay, Lincoln, and the 1846 U.S. Invasion of Mexico*. Vintage 2013; Penguin Random House 2019.

Guardino, Peter . *The Dead March: A History of the Mexican-American War*. Cambridge, MA: Harvard U P, 2017.

Lincoln, Abraham. "Spot Resolutions in the U.S. House of Representatives." *Teaching American History*. December 22, 1847. teachingamericanhistory. org/library/document/spot-resolutions-in-the-u-s-house-of-representatives/.

O'Sullivan, John. "Annexation." *The United States Magazine and Democratic Review*. vol. 17, no. 1, (July–August 1845), pp.5–10. pdcrodas.webs.ull.es/anglo/OSullivanAnnexation.pdf.

Polk, James Knox. "Inaugural Address of James Knox Polk." March 4, 1845. *Avalon*. Yale Law School. avalon.law.yale.edu/19th_century/polk.asp.

Polk, James Knox. "May 11, 1846: War Message to Congress." *Miller Center*. U of Virginia. 2019. millercenter.org/the-presidency/presidential-speeches/may-11-1846-war-message-congress.

Seigenthaler, John. *James K. Polk*, edited by Arthur M. Schlesinger. New York: Times Books, 2003.

Uenuma, Francine. "During the Mexican-American War, Irish-Americans Fought for Mexico in the 'Saint Patrick's Battalion.'" *Smithsonian*. 15 Mar. 2019. www.smithsonianmag.com/history/mexican-american-war-irish-immigrants-deserted-us-army-fight-against-america-180971713/.

Introduction

The Whig Party returned to power with another war hero, Zachary Taylor, who led one of the most famous missions of the Mexican-American War. Taylor was an independent executive who demonstrated from the outset that he would chart his own course. His initial proposals were strongly states'-rights-oriented and based on a different type of compromise from those suggested by other politicians of the era. Long before his policies could amount to anything that could be evaluated, history repeated itself, and Taylor became the second elected Whig to die suddenly in office, serving from March of 1849 to July of 1850. Taylor was replaced by Millard Fillmore, an ineffective bureaucrat who endeavored to reestablish a peace between the North and South but largely served to make the situation more acute. The passage of the Fugitive Slave Law, specifically, left abolitionists little choice but to defy federal law and the Fillmore administration proved unable to enforce the law, with state officials largely reluctant to prosecute or imprison individuals for violating what all abolitionists viewed as an immoral stance taken by the federal government.

Topics covered in this chapter include:
- California, New Mexico, and Arizona statehood
- The Compromise of 1850
- Anti-Freemasonry movement
- Fugitive Slave Law
- Christiana Riot
- Jerry Incident

This Chapter Discusses the Following Source Documents:
Clay's Resolutions, January 29, 1850
Speech at Syracuse, Daniel Webster, May 1851

The Last of the Whigs
Zachary Taylor and Millard Fillmore (1849–1853)

Between the polarizing presidency of James K. Polk and the Civil War, America's political system was transformed. The Jacksonian Democrats and the Whigs had long tried to ignore the growing sectionalism in the United States, focusing instead on issues like taxation, infrastructure, tariffs, and export revenues. With expansion exacerbating sectionalism, the Whigs launched a final play for power during the presidencies of Zachary Taylor, a centrist war hero whose presidential legacy was cut short, and Millard Fillmore, an ineffective bureaucrat whose mismanagement brought the Whig Party to its end and led to the rise of the Radical Republicans.

The White House War Chief

Zachary Taylor was perhaps the most popular man in America when he was chosen by the Whigs as their candidate for the 1848 election. Born in Virginia, Taylor owned a cotton plantation for most of his life, though he was more soldier than farmer. Taylor spent forty years in the army, rising to the rank of Major General, and earned the nickname "Old Rough and Ready" for his aggressive military leadership. He spent the War of 1812 fighting Native American mercenaries and also served in the Black Hawk War of 1832 and in the Second Seminole War in Florida. In his presidential campaign, Taylor was promoted as an "Indian fighter," though his private writings indicate that he admired the Native American contingents he met in battle and opposed the use of the military for what he saw as the theft of land from Native Americans.

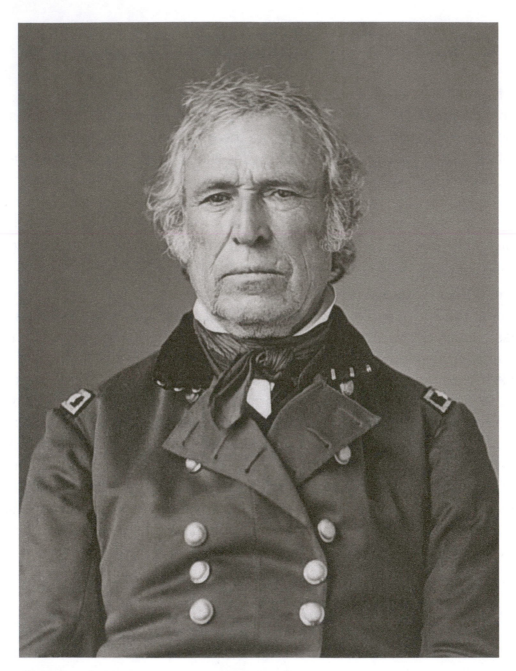

Military hero Zachary Taylor proved difficult for the Whig Party to control, via Wikimedia.

Taylor earned national fame during the Mexican-American War after his 1846 capture of Monterrey, a city widely considered too well-fortified to defeat. This victory made him a favorite in the popular press. Newspapers compared him to George Washington and Andrew Jackson, and journalists took great interest in his idiosyncratic behaviors, including fighting hand-to-hand alongside his troops on the front line, often dressed in a tattered uniform and a straw hat, and calmly sitting in the midst of battle astride his cherished horse, "Old Whitey," even as gunfire and artillery erupted around him.[1]

In the wake of Taylor's 1846 victory in Mexico, the general controversially declared a two-month armistice, allowing Mexican forces to retreat without the threat of pursuit. Taylor's gentlemanly armistice was great fodder for the popular press and an excellent talking point for Whig politicians, who suggested Taylor as a future presidential candidate. Taylor's action angered President Polk, who felt Taylor had overstepped his authority. Polk attempted to relieve Taylor of command, but Taylor ignored Polk's orders and engaged the armies led by Mexican General Santa Anna. This was the end of the Mexican-American War, resulting in Santa Anna's defeat, the capture of Mexico City, and the Treaty of Guadalupe Hidalgo.[2]

Taylor was surprised by his nomination for the presidency, but he was a prime candidate for the Whig Party, whose focus on widespread appeal often led them to select former military leaders as candidates. This strategy had worked well when the Whigs nominated William Henry Harrison, who won popular support thanks to his fame as an "Indian Fighter." With Taylor, they had another Indian Fighter and a bona fide war hero.

The Whigs also considered Taylor a good candidate because he could draw support from Americans on both sides of the slavery issue. He believed strongly in preserving the Union and voiced support for limiting the expansion of slavery, but he was also a plantation owner in Louisiana and a slave owner himself. Around 72 percent of eligible voters turned out for

the 1848 election, which pitted Taylor and running mate Millard Fillmore against Democrats Lewis Cass and William O. Butler. Despite Taylor's fame and popular appeal, the contest between the Whigs and Democrats would have been quite close if not for the entrance of a new third party, known as the "Free Soil Party," which based its platform on prohibiting the expansion of slavery. The Free Soilers, led by Martin Van Buren, drew support from the Jacksonian Democrats, giving the Whigs an advantage. In the final tally, the Whigs received 1,361,393 votes to 1,223,460 for the Democrats, and 291,501 for the Free Soil Party.[3]

Tensions were high as Taylor entered office. Southern slaveholders were pushing for the new territories captured from Mexico to be slave states, while abolitionists would only accept admission of free states. At the time, there were 30 states, 15 of which were slave states and 15 of which were free, so the addition of either would shift the balance of power. It soon became clear that Taylor was a critic of Whig party politics and, once in office, created a cabinet of knowledgeable men from across the country from both sides of the slavery issue.

Regarding admission of new states, Taylor favored allowing the residents of each state deciding for themselves whether or not to allow slavery; he also favored bypassing the "territorial stage" and moving directly to statehood for states that could agree on a new constitution. California succeeded in doing this, and in early 1850, applied for admission to the Union as a free state. The residents of New Mexico likewise began work on a new constitution, and it appeared that they too would enter as a free state.

Southern slave owners were concerned, seeing the potential of two more free states as a threat to southern power and the institution of slavery. In addition, Taylor faced resistance in Congress, as a significant number of Senators and Representatives felt that Taylor's stated policy violated norms of presidential authority and that he had usurped Congressional

power. A number of Southern Democrats threatened to secede from the Union over the issue, and in conference in February of 1850, Taylor told southern leaders that he would hang anyone who tried to foment a rebellion or secession "with less reluctance than he had hanged deserters and spies in Mexico."[4]

Taylor was subject to passionate criticism, especially from Henry Clay, who gave a long speech on the Senate floor accusing Taylor of undermining Congressional powers and killing any chance of compromise. There were five major issues at play in Congress, as described by Clay in his criticism of Taylor:

"Here are five wounds—one, two, three, four, five—bleeding and threatening the well-being, if not the existence of the body politic. What is the plan of the president? Is it to heal all these wounds? No such thing. It is only to heal one of the five, and to leave the other four to bleed more profusely than ever, by the sole admission of California, even if it should produce death itself. I have said that five wounds are open and bleeding. What are they? First, there is California: there are the Territories second; there is the question of the boundary of Texas the third; there is the fugitive slave bill the fourth; and there is the question of the slave-trade in the district of Columbia fifth. The president, instead of proposing a plan comprehending all the diseases of the country, looks only at one."[5]

Clay was the chief architect of a new bill known as the Compromise of 1850, which allowed for California to be admitted as a free state and for the abolition of slavery in Washington, DC, both elements that appealed to abolitionists. To appease the slave lobby, Congress passed a fugitive slave law prohibiting individuals in free states from abetting or aiding escaped slaves and required authorities, even in free states, to arrest and return any escaped slave. Clay also proposed that New Mexico and Utah should become territories open to settlement without deciding the issue

of slavery. This appealed to Southern Democrats, as they hoped to settle the new territories with slave owners and pro-slavery politicians.

Here are Clay's eight resolutions that constituted the framework of the 1850 compromise proposal:

CLAY'S RESOLUTIONS
January 29, 1850
Source Document Excerpt

It being desirable, for the peace, concord, and harmony of the Union of these States, to settle and adjust amicably all existing questions of controversy between them arising out of the institution of slavery upon a fair, equitable and just basis: therefore,

1. Resolved, That California, with suitable boundaries, ought, upon her application to be admitted as one of the States of this Union, without the imposition by Congress of any restriction in respect to the exclusion or introduction of slavery within those boundaries.

2. Resolved, That as slavery does not exist by law, and is not likely to be introduced into any of the territory acquired by the United States from the republic of Mexico, it is inexpedient for Congress to provide by law either for its introduction into, or exclusion from, any part of the said territory; and that appropriate territorial governments ought to be established by Congress in all of the said territory, not assigned as the boundaries of the proposed State of California, without the adoption of any restriction or condition on the subject of slavery.

3. Resolved, That the western boundary of the State of Texas ought to be fixed on the Rio del Norte, commencing one marine league from its mouth, and running up that river to the southern line of New Mexico; thence with that line eastwardly, and so continuing in the same direction to the line as established between the United States and Spain, excluding any portion of New Mexico, whether lying on the east or west of that river.

4. Resolved, That it be proposed to the State of Texas, that the United States will provide for the payment of all that portion of the legitimate and bona fide public debt of that State contracted prior to its annexation to the United States, and for which the duties on foreign imports were pledged by the said State to its creditors, not exceeding the sum of - dollars, in consideration of the said duties so pledged having been no longer applicable to that object

continued

after the said annexation, but having thenceforward become payable to the United States; and upon the condition, also, that the said State of Texas shall, by some solemn and authentic act of her legislature or of a convention, relinquish to the United States any claim which it has to any part of New Mexico.

5. Resolved, That it is inexpedient to abolish slavery in the District of Columbia whilst that institution continues to exist in the State of Maryland, without the consent of that State, without the consent of the people of the District, and without just compensation to the owners of slaves within the District.

6. But, resolved, That it is expedient to prohibit, within the District, the slave trade in slaves brought into it from States or places beyond the limits of the District, either to be sold therein as merchandise, or to be transported to other markets without the District of Columbia.

7. Resolved, That more effectual provision ought to be made by law, according to the requirement of the constitution, for the restitution and delivery of persons bound to service or labor in any State, who may escape into any other State or Territory in the Union. And,

8. Resolved, That Congress has no power to promote or obstruct the trade in slaves between the slaveholding States; but that the admission or exclusion of slaves brought from one into another of them, depends exclusively upon their own particular laws.[6]

Taylor had little chance to make his opinions known on the Compromise of 1850, though statements made to colleagues indicated he was prepared to veto the bill. In July, Taylor fell ill, and died unexpectedly at the White House on July 8, 1850. In the 1990s, Taylor's body was exhumed to see if he had been poisoned with arsenic, but it appears that he died from a form of gastroenteritis. Historians have noted that, had he survived, Taylor might have greatly altered the course of history. He was not an anti-slavery president, but his firm commitment to central authority and to states' rights might have prevented the Compromise of 1850, which deepened sectional tension.

The Poor-Man's Lawyer

In a repeat of history, the Whigs again found themselves represented by the candidate they had chosen as a Vice President. In 1841 they were left with John Tyler after the sudden death of William Henry Harrison days after his election. Tyler completely rejected the Whig platform and pursued policies so divisive that he became an enemy to both parties and was nearly the first president removed from office. This time, the Whigs had more carefully chosen Millard Fillmore, a moderate party bureaucrat. In many ways, the death of Taylor benefitted the Whigs, as Fillmore proved more amenable to party influence.

Fillmore was born into a poor Vermont farming family, the second of eight children, and the oldest son. Fillmore's father, Nathaniel Fillmore, committed young Millard to an apprenticeship as a cloth maker. At the time, poor parents would place their children with a professional who would compensate the family with a small monthly stipend. To escape the situation, an individual needed to buy freedom from their employer, but this was difficult as apprentices were not paid directly. Borrowing $30 from a friend, Millard Fillmore purchased his freedom and reportedly walked the more than 100 miles from the cloth maker's shop to his family farm.

Back home, Fillmore met young schoolteacher Abigail Powers, who encouraged his studies and loaned him books. Convinced that his son might have the aptitude for more intellectual work, Fillmore's father arranged a clerkship for him with a local judge, who also agreed to allow Millard to study law. Millard spent several years as a law clerk, while teaching classes to support himself. He also began courting Abigail Powers, who accepted his proposal of marriage in 1819.

From Secret Society to High Society

Fillmore's entrance into politics came during the scandal over the Freemason organization that erupted in the late 1820s and early 1830s. A surprising number of the political elite were members of the Freemasons, and artifacts of this association can be found across America today. The Masonic "all seeing eye" symbol even graces the U.S. one-dollar bill. Some historians believe that as many as 21 of the signers of the Declaration of Independence, including George Washington, were Masons, and the writings of the Founding Fathers seem to have been influenced by several well-known Masonic precepts, including free enterprise and individualism.

Millard Fillmore pushed through the ill-fated Compromise of 1850, via Wikimedia.

The Masonic society came to the United States from Britain, where Masonic organizations served as a cauldron for anti-Royalist plotting. Masons developed secret handshakes, pass phrases, and coded language. This secrecy was essential and allowed anti-Royalists to hide their revolutionary activities behind the veil of religious community. In Colonial America, the Masons served a similar purpose. Anti-monarchists used membership in Masonic temples to conceal their schemes and to organize.

However, Freemasonry is also part of a system of transmitted wealth and power that contributes to many of America's less-well-thought-of characteristics. In the early days of American Freemasonry, Masons who traveled to a new town were afforded significant advantages through the Masonic network. It was not uncommon for Masonic politicians to pass on opportunities and contracts to other Masons. Because Masons included many influential and wealthy white men, Freemasonry became one way that the wealth-based aristocracy of American political power functioned for much of the nation's history.[7]

In 1826, a former Mason named William Morgan resigned from the organization and threatened to publish an exposé of Masonic secrets. On the night of September 12, 1826, Morgan disappeared, and it was widely believed that he had been murdered for his threats. This coincided with Andrew Jackson's rise into politics. Jackson, a member of the Masons, aroused suspicion and fear over the group's potentially sinister political power and this, coupled with Morgan's disappearance, led to a political movement against Freemasonry.[8] Fillmore joined the Anti-Masonic Party in New York, and as one of the few qualified figures in the new party, was chosen to run for the New York State legislature, where he served three terms. During this time, Fillmore worked to limit the secret influence of Freemasonry in the state, which also meant that he worked to defeat the power of the state's wealthy aristocrats.

As a state legislator, Fillmore's poor upbringing was evident in his successful campaign to end debtor imprisonment, which won him great acclaim in the working-class district he represented. He was encouraged to run for the U.S. House of Representatives in 1832 and won a landslide victory.[9]

Fillmore had been one of the few Anti-Masonic Party politicians elected, and his party merged with the remnants of the Federalists and other politicians opposed to Jackson in the 1830s, which gave rise to the Whig Party. Though he was personally opposed to slavery and had supported the abolitionist movement, within the Whig Party Fillmore gravitated toward the centrists who preferred compromise. This aligned him with Henry Clay, the most powerful leader of the Whigs and the chief architect of the Compromise of 1850. Fillmore campaigned to become Henry Clay's running mate for the 1844 election, but Whig Party bosses wanted Fillmore to run for the governorship of New York instead. He lost this election, but won a subsequent election to become New York Comptroller. In the wake of Polk's divisive candidacy, Fillmore was one of the top contenders for the Whig nomination, but the party ended up choosing Taylor, whose fame and war record they felt gave him a better chance in the popular vote. Fillmore was, therefore, chosen as vice president in 1848.

Compromising Morality

Millard Fillmore might have made an interesting president in his own right, but he did not enter office under ideal conditions. Taylor's surprising death dropped Fillmore right in the middle of a sectional crisis, requiring him to make near-immediate decisions on key issues. It was widely known that Fillmore was more of a party loyalist than Taylor, whose entire cabinet resigned after Fillmore took office. Fillmore quickly appointed a cabinet of Whigs who favored compromise. At the same time an old and exhausted Clay retired, leaving the task of contentious debate to newcomer Stephen Douglas, a young politician from Illinois and heir apparent to the party. Douglas and Fillmore adopted a new strategy, splitting Clay's

Compromise of 1850 into five separate bills. This proved to be the key to the bills' passage, and Clay's compromise became law.

Fillmore considered the compromise bills a victory, but they did little to help heal the fractional divide. For the pro-slavery lobbyists, the compromise was a major victory. Over the previous decade, thousands of slaves had escaped bondage, many of whom made it to free states. The new law imposed a fine of $1,000 (roughly $33,000 in 2019) for anyone who failed to arrest a fugitive slave, or who abetted a runaway slave or provided food or water. The law further required all law enforcement officers to arrest anyone suspected or accused of being a runaway slave. Anyone so accused had no legal rights, including rights to a trial or arbitration.

Arguments against the Fugitive Slave Law came not only from abolitionists, who viewed slavery as immoral, but also from states' rights advocates. A number of free states, such as Pennsylvania, had laws in place prohibiting the removal of any African American from the state to be sold or placed into slavery. The Fugitive Slave Law required residents of the state to participate in, or at least allow, any effort to recover runaway slaves, invalidating state law and state sovereignty. Fillmore gave speeches declaring that federal law would be enforced, and he dispatched Secretary of State Daniel Webster to do the same. Webster visited Syracuse, New York, which had long been a keystone in the abolition movement, to warn residents that refusal to obey the law would not be tolerated:

SPEECH AT SYRACUSE
Daniel Webster
May 1851
Source Document Excerpt

"I am a lawyer, and I value my reputation as a lawyer more than anything else, and I tell you, if men get together and declare a law of Congress shall not be executed in any case and assemble in numbers to prevent the execution of such law, they are *traitors*, and are guilty of treason, and bring upon themselves the penalties of the law.

No! No! It is time to put an end to this imposition upon good citizens, good men and good women. It is treason, *treason*, TREASON and nothing else, (cheers) and if they do not incur the penalties of treason, it is owing to the clemency of the law's administration, and to no merit of their own.

Who and what are these men? I am assured some of them are clergymen, and some, I am sorry to say it, are lawyers, and who the rest are, God only knows.

They say that law will not be executed. Let them take care, for those are pretty bold assertions. The law must be executed, not only in carrying back the slave, but against those guilty of treasonable practices in resisting its execution.

Depend upon it, the law will be executed in its spirit, and to its letter. It will be executed in all the great cities; here in Syracuse; in the midst of the next Anti-Slavery Convention, if the occasion shall arise; then we shall see what becomes of their lives and their sacred honor.

Do not debauch your own understandings, your own judgements; do not render ridiculous your own sympathy, humanity, and philanthropy, by any such ideas.

The course of your duty towards all that are in bondage, within your power and influence, is plain. Happily the teaching of the sacred book , which is our guide, instructs us in that matter. What we can do, we will do, to let the oppressed go free, to succor the distressed, and to visit the prisoner in affliction. We must do our duty, and we must content ourselves with acting conscientiously in that sphere of life in which we are placed; politicians in their sphere; individuals in their sphere; and all of us under the deep, earnest sense of obligation that our Creator has impressed upon us.

It is not unfrequently said by a class of men who whom I have referred, that

Speech at Syracuse
continued

the Constitution is born of hell; that it was the work of the devil; and that Washington was a miserable blood-hound, set upon the track of the African slave. How far these words differ from words that have saluted your ears within yonder hall, you will judge.

Men who utter such sentiments are ready at any moment to destroy the charter of all your liberties, of all your happiness, and of all your hope. They are either insane, or fatally bent on mischief.

The question is, therefore, whether we will sustain the Government under which we life; whether we will do justice to the Southern States, that they may have no excuse for going out of the Union. If there is anybody that will not consent that the South shall have a fair hearing, a fair trial, a fair decision upon what it things the Constitution secures to it, I am not of that number."[10]

However, several high-profile events proved that the Fillmore administration could not enforce the Fugitive Slave Law.

The "Christiana Riot" involved a group of slaves from Maryland who had escaped to Pennsylvania and were hiding on a farm. The slave owner, Edward Gorsuch, found the four fugitive slaves and attempted to arrest them. There was an exchange of gunfire, in which someone, reportedly one of the escaped slaves, shot and killed Gorsuch. A manhunt followed, but the Underground Railroad—a nationwide network of abolitionists—and Frederick Douglass, intervened, and the slaves made it to freedom in Canada. Angry slave hunters arrested others accused of harboring or aiding in the slaves' escape, including Quaker abolitionist Castner Hanway.

Fillmore took a personal interest and announced that his administration supported charging some 40 people involved in the escape with treason against the United States. At the trial of Hanway, however, the federal position proved impossibly weak. Defense attorney Thaddeus Stevens

argued that the incident was clearly a local issue and not an attempt to overthrow the government. The jury agreed, Hanway was acquitted, and prosecutors dismissed the remaining cases as well. This proved a major embarrassment to federal authorities and to Fillmore, who became increasingly unpopular. [11]

In October of 1851, another incident in Fillmore's home state of New York further challenged the administration's promise to enforce the Fugitive Slave Law. Abolitionists had promised the Fillmore administration that they would thwart the law, and local chapters now needed to decide how to do this. On October 1, federal marshals from Rochester, along with local police, arrested a man calling himself "Jerry" who had been working as a barrel maker. He was told that he was being arrested under the Fugitive Slave Law.[12]

The New York State Convention of abolitionists armed themselves and reportedly used a battering ram to break into the building where Jerry was being charged, and officials surrendered the prisoner. Jerry was hidden within the town for several days and eventually shuttled through a series of friendly abolitionists to Ottawa, Canada, where his fate remained unknown.

Federal authorities filed 19 separate indictments against individuals involved in the armed rescue of Jerry, who were arrested and taken to jail in Auburn, New York. All the accused were bailed out by powerful abolitionists, including William H. Seward, former governor turned senator of New York. Over the next two years, each of the prosecutions failed to produce a conviction save one, and the target of that conviction died before his case was heard on appeal. The failure to secure convictions in this high-profile case further proved that the Fillmore administration had little power to enforce the law and that Fillmore and supporters of the compromise had dramatically underestimated the level of popular opposition to the Fugitive Slave Law.

There was little chance that Fillmore could win a second term, so the Whigs selected Mexican-American War hero Winfield Scott to run in 1850. However, because of the unpopular Compromise of 1850, Democratic nominee Franklin Pierce beat out Winfield Scott by nearly 200,000 votes and took the Electoral College by a landslide of 254 to 42.

The End of an Era

The Whig Party emerged as a reaction to Andrew Jackson's election, the dissolution of the Federalists, and the emergence of slavery as the nation's top political issue. The coalition that became the Whigs had no central platform. On the slavery issue, for instance, there were Whigs who were abolitionists and Whigs who were slave owners. Ultimately, many of the staunch abolitionists left to join issue-oriented third parties, like the Liberty Party or the more moderate Free Soil Party. The Jacksonian Democrats were firmly aligned with the pro-slavery lobby, so there was little room for a mainstream pro-slavery third party, but there were fringe extremist groups lobbying to legalize slavery across the entire Union.

The Whig Party's lack of central platform would lead to a coalition made up of northern Whigs, members of the Free Soil and Liberty Party, and disaffected Democrats, who would unite behind the new Republican Party, which was, at the time, somewhat progressive in comparison to the Democratic Party.[13] This coalition succeeded because they united behind opposition to slavery, giving the Republicans the cohesive vision that the Whigs lacked. This explains how the Republican Party rose to prominence, while the Whigs struggled for decades to achieve effective executive leadership.

Fillmore was a bureaucrat and a skilled and experienced politician, but his compromise approach to the slavery crisis proved untenable. Therefore, the Whigs disappeared and were replaced by a coalition of politicians willing to take a stronger stance on what became America's most important political battle.

CONCLUSION

The presidencies of Zachary Taylor and Millard Fillmore were the last gasps of the Whig Party—America's moderate, conciliatory conservative party. The Whigs were a counterpoint to the violent white supremacist conservatism that dominated the Democratic-Republican party, but their solutions to America's problems were impotent and ineffective. The Whigs succeeded by playing on superficial associations with patriotism and heroism, but lacked a substantial platform or a political voice. With the Democratic-Republican leadership veering to the far right, there was room for a political movement aimed at social welfare reform, but the Whigs were far too moderate to fill this void. Fillmore's uninspiring presidency, though not a complete failure, was enough to hand the presidency back to the Democratic-Republicans, which exacerbated the problem further and left the nation careening inexorably towards disunion, as the next chapter on Franklin Pierce and James Buchanan illustrates.

DISCUSSION QUESTIONS

♦ How did Zachary Taylor compare to the Whig Party's other winning candidate, William Henry Harrison?

♦ How did Taylor's proposal for handling California's statehood differ from other politicians of the era?

♦ What was the purpose of the Anti-Masonic Party?

♦ How was Freemasonry considered a threat to America's democracy?

♦ In your opinion, were the abolitionists in Syracuse, New York, justified in violating the Fugitive Slave Law? Why or why not?

Works Used

Bauer, K. Jack. *Zachary Taylor: Soldier, Planter, Statesman of the Old Southwest*. Baton Rouge, LA: LSU P, 1993.

Brooks, Corey. "What Can the Collapse of the Whig Party Tell Us About Today's Politics"? *Smithsonian.com.* 12 Apr. 2016. www.smithsonianmag.com/history/what-can-collapse-whig-party-tell-us-about-todays-politics-180958729/.

Clay, Henry. "Clay's Resolutions January 29, 1850." *Transcript of Compromise of 1850. Our Documents*. www.ourdocuments.gov/doc.php?flash=false&doc=27&page=transcript.

_____. *The Speeches of Henry Clay*, edited by Calvin Colton. New York: A.S. Barnes & Co, 1857.

Feuerherd, Peter. "The Strange History of Masons in America." *JSTOR Daily*. 3 Aug. 2017. daily.jstor.org/the-strange-history-of-masons-in-america/.

Han, Lori Cox, editor. *Hatred of America's Presidents: Personal Attacks on the White House from Washington to Trump*, ABC–CLIO, LLC, 2018.

Holt, Michael. "Millard Fillmore: Life Before the Presidency." *Miller Center*. U of Virginia. 2019. /millercenter.org/president/fillmore/life-before-the-presidency.

_____. "Zachary Taylor: Life Before the Presidency." *Miller Center*. University of Virginia. 2019. millercenter.org/president/taylor/life-before-the-presidency.

McNamara, Robert. "The Christiana Riot." *ThoughtCo*. Dotdash. 17 Mar. 2017. www.thoughtco.com/the-christiana-riot-1773557.

"Presidential Election of 1848: A Resource Guide." *LOC*. Library of Congress. 23 Oct. 2018.www.loc.gov/rr/program/bib/elections/election1848.html.

"The Jerry Rescue." *New York History Net*. New York History. www.nyhistory.com/gerritsmith/jerry.htm.

Vaughn, William Preston. *The Anti-Masonic Party in the United States: 1826–1843*. Lexington, KY: U P of Kentucky, 1983.

Webster, Daniel, and Edward Everett. *The Writings and Speeches of Daniel Webster*. (National Edition, vol. 13), pp. 419–20. Boston, MA: Little, Brown & Company, 1903.

We the People

Introduction

Franklin Pierce and James Buchanan are typically rated as among the worst presidents in history. Pierce was a chronically depressed alcoholic with little in the way of political ability outside of his considerable oratory skill, and Buchanan was a compromise candidate with insufficient sway in any region to achieve anything close to reconciliation. Pierce's administration saw the introduction of the Kansas-Nebraska Act during a period of intense controversy over whether slavery would be legal in the newly founded states of Kansas and Nebraska. Pierce also invested effort in the long-time pro-slavery goal of acquiring Cuba, which would have become a new slave state for the Union. Pierce was so unpopular that he became the first and only president not to be nominated for reelection by his own party. Following Pierce, Buchanan did not fare much better. He worked inappropriately to dictate the Supreme Court process, representing a serious violation of presidential power and constitutional checks and balances. His administration also saw the now infamous Dred Scott case, which gave constitutional validation to slavery.

Topics covered in this chapter include:

- Kansas-Nebraska Act, 1854
- Dred Scott case
- Imperialist designs on Cuba

This Chapter Discusses the Following Source Documents:

Inaugural Address of Franklin Pierce, March 4, 1853

Inaugural Address of James Buchanan, March 4, 1857

Dred Scott v. Sanford, Justice Benjamin Robbins Curtis dissenting, 1857

State of the Union, James Buchanan, December 3, 1860

An Inevitable Collapse
Franklin Pierce and James Buchanan (1853–1861)

Professor Jean H. Baker of Goucher College said that Franklin Pierce served as an example of why "difficult times require forceful leadership that is sensitive to issues both of change and continuity."[1] Presidents Franklin Pierce and James Buchanan have been criticized for their failure to substantially address slavery, the most divisive issue of both their presidencies. Whereas presidents before them might be criticized for abusing the power of their office, Pierce and Buchanan are typically seen as "weak" presidents, unable to utilize their power effectively. The political environment during their terms was violently contentious, and many sought to hedge their bets with moderate candidates, but the lack of strong leadership contributed to the onset of the Civil War.

A Poor Choice

Franklin Pierce was born into a politically connected New Hampshire family. He went to private schools and then Bowdoin College in Maine. A middling student, Pierce graduated trained in public speaking and law, and in 1826, after his father Benjamin was elected governor, Franklin Pierce easily won a seat on the state legislature. The Pierce family became ardent supporters of Andrew Jackson, who rewarded their loyalty by supporting Pierce's bid for a seat in the House of Representatives.

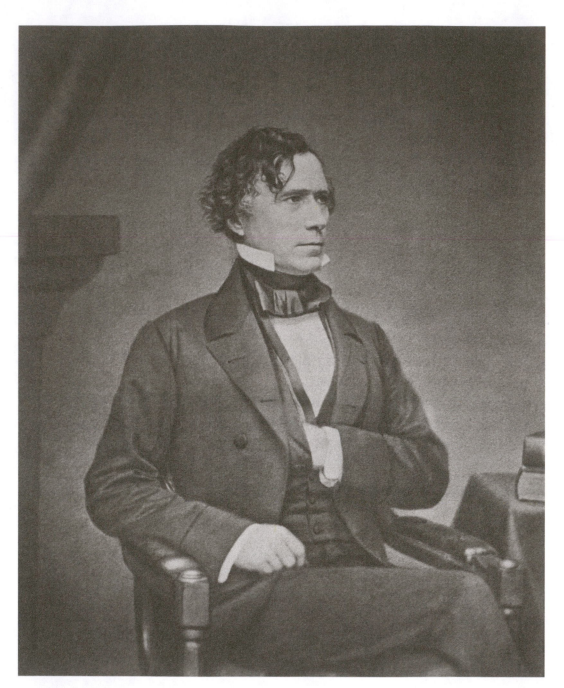

Franklin Pierce, by Mathew Brady Library of Congress Prints and Photographs Division, via Wikimedia.

In Washington, Pierce developed a reputation as a heavy drinker. He was often the subject of ridicule, and viewed as an ineffective politician. No major bills came from his office, and he voted along strict Jacksonian party lines. In 1841, Pierce resigned from the Senate and returned to New Hampshire, where he stopped drinking, joined the temperance movement, and successfully campaigned to outlaw liquor in his hometown of Concord. Pierce found new success as a lawyer. In a pre-television world, where public trials were considered a form of entertainment, Pierce's cases drew huge crowds. Handsome with a commanding presence, Pierce became a darling in the local press, re-entering politics by working on the campaign of Jackson protégé James K. Polk during Polk's presidential campaign, which left Polk in his debt.

When Polk declared war on Mexico, Pierce signed up for service and convinced Polk to give him a command position despite no previous training. He was named a brigadier general commanding two thousand men under General Winfield Scott. At the Battle of Contreras, Pierce fell from his horse and injured his leg, after which his company retreated. The nickname "Fainting Frank" followed him when he returned to politics.

In 1852, with Millard Fillmore at the end of an unpopular term in office, the Democrats and Whigs were searching for presidential candidates with broad, moderate appeal, fearing that an activist would exacerbate sectional tensions. Young, attractive Pierce was an ideal candidate for the Democrats who promoted him as a fresh new voice. His time in Congress, popularity in New England, and war record (although questionable) gave him the credentials to gain popular votes. Pierce was a compromise candidate on slavery; he came from the North and did not own slaves, but he was also opposed to abolition.

The Whigs chose Winfield Scott, Pierce's former commander, who'd gained national fame for his victories in the Mexican-American War.

General Scott, who was called "Old Fuss and Feathers" for his strict adherence to military code, is described by historians as one of the greatest American generals besides Washington and Ulysses Grant. Scott's historic march from the Mexican city of Veracruz to Mexico City in 1847 is seen as one of the most confidently executed military campaigns in global history.[2] Scott, at 6'5" and nearly 300 pounds, supported centralized power and opposed slavery, though he did not commit to abolition, making him a compromise candidate for the Whigs.

The contest of 1852 pitted Pierce, nicknamed "Handsome Frank" or "Young Hickory of the Granite Hills" against a traditional Whig candidate, a military war hero with a strong sense of unified authority. The election attracted a nearly 70 percent turnout. Pierce won 1,607,501 popular votes and 254 electoral votes; Scott won 1,386,942 popular votes and 42 electoral votes.[3] Overall, historians describe the 1852 campaign as "tame" and relatively uneventful. The *New York Herald* wrote of the contest on August 17, 1852:

> *"The acute observer of passing events has a fine field for study in the present aspect and bearing of the Presidential campaign. He can not fail to be struck with the absence of anything like popular enthusiasm, as respects the candidates themselves, the value of the prize in dispute, and the result of the contest. Violent efforts have been made by either (each) party to create a popular furor in favor of one or the other of the candidates; but they have been complete failures. . . . "*

> *"The fact is, there never has been such a ludicrous, ridiculous, and uninteresting Presidential campaign in his country since it ceased to be a British Province as the present one is, although the politicians have been straining every nerve to get up an excitement and enlist the popular feelings in the strife. They have been puffing and blowing in every direction, but all they can do*

they can not get up the steam; the people only laugh at them, and continue proof against all their attempts to bamboozle them. All the old experiments have been tried to arouse them from their indifference; but all to no purpose. . . ."[34]

The Saddest President

The Pierces had three children; their first died in infancy in 1836, a second child died as a toddler, and their remaining son, Benjamin "Bennie" Pierce, was thrown from a train when it derailed and died in 1853. Jane Pierce became deeply depressed, believing that her son's death had been preordained to help her husband focus on the presidency. She dressed in black mourning attire for the entirety of her time in the White House, never held social events, rarely accepted visitors, and it has been claimed that she wandered the upper levels of the house speaking to herself and uttering obscenities. Pierce began drinking again, which consumed him over his years in office. Visitors to the White House described the environment as cold and nearly haunting.

Pierce's inaugural address had a somber tone:

INAUGURAL ADDRESS
Franklin Pierce
March 4, 1853
Source Document Excerpt

My Countrymen:

It a relief to feel that no heart but my own can know the personal regret and bitter sorrow over which I have been borne to a position so suitable for others rather than desirable for myself.

The circumstances under which I have been called for a limited period to preside over the destinies of the Republic fill me with a profound sense of responsibility, but with nothing like shrinking apprehension. I repair to the post assigned me not as to one sought, but in obedience to the unsolicited expression of your will, answerable only for a fearless, faithful, and diligent exercise of my best powers. I ought to be, and am, truly grateful for the rare manifestation of the nation's confidence; but this, so far from lightening my obligations, only adds to their weight. You have summoned me in my weakness; you must sustain me by your strength. When looking for the fulfillment of reasonable requirements, you will not be unmindful of the great changes which have occurred, even within the last quarter of a century, and the consequent augmentation and complexity of duties imposed in the administration both of your home and foreign affairs.

The Power of Inaction

Because of Pierce's personal tragedies, it is thought that Secretary of War Jefferson Davis, who would go on to achieve infamy as president of the ill-fated Confederate States of America, held the real political power in the executive branch. Davis's wife, Varina, stepped in to host White House events in Jane Pierce's stead, and Davis directed Pierce's handling of important issues.

Pierce set forth his approach to the slavery issue in his inaugural address:

INAUGURAL ADDRESS
Franklin Pierce
March 4, 1853
Source Document Excerpt

In expressing briefly my views upon an important subject rich has recently agitated the nation to almost a fearful degree, I am moved by no other impulse than a most earnest desire for the perpetuation of that Union which has made us what we are, showering upon us blessings and conferring a power and influence which our fathers could hardly have anticipated, even with their most sanguine hopes directed to a far-off future. The sentiments I now announce were not unknown before the expression of the voice which called me here. My own position upon this subject was clear and unequivocal, upon the record of my words and my acts, and it is only recurred to at this time because silence might perhaps be misconstrued. With the Union my best and dearest earthly hopes are entwined. Without it what are we individually or collectively? What becomes of the noblest field ever opened for the advancement of our race in religion, in government, in the arts, and in all that dignifies and adorns mankind? From that radiant constellation which both illumines our own way and points out to struggling nations their course, let but a single star be lost, and, if these be not utter darkness, the luster of the whole is dimmed. Do my countrymen need any assurance that such a catastrophe is not to overtake them while I possess the power to stay it? It is with me an earnest and vital belief that as the Union has been the source, under Providence, of our prosperity to this time, so it is the surest pledge of a continuance of the blessings we have enjoyed, and which we are sacredly bound to transmit undiminished to our children. The field of calm and free discussion in our country is open, and will always be so, but never has been and never can be traversed for good in a spirit of sectionalism and uncharitableness. The founders of the Republic dealt with things as they were presented to them, in a spirit of self-sacrificing patriotism, and, as time has proved, with a comprehensive wisdom which it will always be safe for us to consult. Every measure tending to strengthen the fraternal feelings of all the members of our Union has had my heartfelt approbation. To every theory of society or government, whether the offspring of feverish ambition or of morbid enthusiasm, calculated to dissolve the bonds of law and affection which unite us, I shall interpose a ready and stern resistance. I believe that involuntary servitude, as it exists in different States of this Confederacy, is recognized by the Constitution. I believe that it stands like any other admitted right, and that the States where it exists are entitled to efficient remedies to enforce the constitutional provisions. I hold that the laws of 1850, commonly called the "compromise measures," are strictly constitutional and to be unhesitatingly carried into effect. I believe that the constituted authorities of this Republic are bound to regard the rights of the South in this respect as they would view any

Inaugural Address
continued

other legal and constitutional right, and that the laws to enforce them should be respected and obeyed, not with a reluctance encouraged by abstract opinions as to their propriety in a different state of society, but cheerfully and according to the decisions of the tribunal to which their exposition belongs. Such have been, and are, my convictions, and upon them I shall act. I fervently hope that the question is at rest, and that no sectional or ambitious or fanatical excitement may again threaten the durability of our institutions or obscure the light of our prosperity. [5]

Pierce is one of the most famous of politicians known in the 1850s as a "doughface," a northerner who backed slavery. Without them, the Civil War would likely have occurred sooner, as famous figures like John Quincy Adams and Martin Van Buren were able to hold the fractured union together.[6] The most recent effort at moderation—the Compromise of 1850—had failed, and the Democratic Party hoped to again strike a temporary balance that would preserve peace.

Among the most pressing issues when Pierce became president was the Kansas–Nebraska Territory. It had not been decided if new territories would allow slavery. As Pierce stated in his inaugural address, he supported the right of slaveholders, as a states' rights and individual liberties advocate, and did not believe that the federal government should intervene.

The southern solution to the new controversy was the Kansas–Nebraska Act of 1854, which had the residents of Nebraska and Kansas deciding if the new states were to be slave or free. It was the same tactic taken by Zachary Taylor in his executive position on the status of California and New Mexico; Pierce, like Taylor, believed that the popular will should decide. Situations were different, however. While Taylor promoted popular will in the west, the Kansas–Nebraska Act of 1854 repealed the Missouri

Compromise of 1820, which prohibited slavery north of 36 degrees 30 minutes. This was one of the earliest compromise bills designed to prevent Civil War by balancing state interests, and was a concession that northern abolitionists were not prepared to make. What's more, Kansas and Nebraska were not the frontiers of California and New Mexico. They were states that directly bordered existing settled states and so would see the continuation or prohibition of slavery alongside states where the laws might be otherwise.

The situation deteriorated, leading to what's been called "Bleeding Kansas" or "Bloody Kansas," a mini version of the Civil War that was to come, as abolitionists and slaveholders clashed across the Kansas and Missouri border. The city of Lawrence, Kansas, founded by abolitionists after the passage of the Kansas–Nebraska Act, made it likely that Kansas was going to become a free state, so in the lead-up to the 1855 Kansas legislative elections, thousands of Missouri residents and slaveholders came into the state illegally hoping to shift the balance of power. In November 1855, an abolitionist was killed by a slavery supporter. Free-state advocate Jacob Branson was arrested, despite not being involved in the killing. Fellow advocates rescued Branson from jail and took him to the abolitionist city of Lawrence. Nearly 2,000 proslavery militants came to Lawrence and camped near the Wakarusa River, resulting in a week-long siege of the city, marking a "war" that lasted nearly a decade as Missouri militants burned and sacked the town of Lawrence. When free-state advocate John Brown and his sons murdered five pro-slavery settlers in Pottawatomie, this shocking incident spread through the national press and was used by pro-slavery advocates to accuse abolitionists of treasonous violations of federal law.[7]

The pro-slavery faction that streamed into Kansas called on the federal government to support their right to settlement. Governor Andrew Horatio Reeder was sympathetic to the anti-slavery position. When violence

began to erupt, Pierce reluctantly intervened, siding with the pro-slavery advocates in Washington, and appointed slavery sympathizer Wilson Shannon, as governor, which intensified the violence.

Ultimately, Kansas became a free state. When it became clear that the free-state advocates had a popular advantage, Pierce supported the minority pro-slavery position, resulting in ten years of violence.

Pierce, despite his failure to address the slavery issue, hoped to win a second term and relied on the proven strategy of the acquisition of new territory, in this case the annexation of Cuba from Spain. Cuban territory already had legal slavery, an agricultural economy, and convenient proximity to Florida, a stronghold of American slave-driven agriculture. Southern Democrats had long favored annexing Cuba and saw an opportunity to add a new slave state to the Union while Pierce was in office.

Pierce appointed Pierre Soulé, a Louisiana Senator, to secure the purchase or annexation of Cuba. Soulé threatened the Spanish government with the Ostend Manifesto, which declared that Spain needed to sell the island or the United States would see continued Spanish possession as a threat to national security. Spain allegedly had little control over the island, making it vulnerable to a slave revolt that could impact the U.S. slave industry. If this occurred, the manifesto warned, America might have to take military control of Cuba. After this information was leaked and published by partisan newspapers, northerners and European politicians alike issued a flood of criticism against Pierce, a further blow to his popularity.[8]

Pierce became the first and only president not to be offered the nomination by his own political party. His administration destroyed both his fortunes and that of Stephen A. Douglas, who'd been one of the chief authors of the Kansas–Nebraska Act of 1854. As public opinion turned against slavery, Pierce's legacy went from bad to worse, and he is, in the twenty-first century, regularly included as one of America's worst presidents. It did not help that he opposed the Civil War and was an outspoken opponent of Abraham Lincoln. When Pierce died, the *New York Herald* noted that he "was a man of something more than average ability. He possessed, however, none of the attributes of greatness, and was more of a cautious, studious, and watchful politician than a comprehensive, far-seeing or observant statesman."[9] Pierce died in obscurity in 1869 from alcoholism.

Buchanan's Blazing

With Pierce disowned by his own party and Stephen Douglas likewise compromised, the Democrats chose James Buchanan, a long-time hopeful for the 1856 Democratic nomination. Buchanan, also a doughface, sympathized with southern slaveholders though he came from the north and had gained respect among moderate northerners who favored compromise. Buchanan was one of the Democratic Party's only remaining options with widespread name recognition.

James Buchanan, from a Matthew Brady daguerreotype Library of Congress Prints and Photographs Division, via Wikimedia.

We the People

Buchanan was the last president of the eighteenth century, born on April 23, 1791, in rural Pennsylvania. His father, a wealthy businessman and Irish immigrant, sent Buchanan, second of eleven children, to Dickinson College, where he was twice nearly expelled on disciplinary measures. However, Buchanan graduated with honors and went on to study law and take a clerkship in Lancaster, Pennsylvania, where he later set up his own law practice. He volunteered for service in the War of 1812 but saw no action, and won a seat for Pennsylvania in the House of Representatives at 23. The only bachelor ever elected to the presidency, Buchanan never married but was rumored to have engaged in frequent flirtations.[10]

Buchanan won election to the House in 1820, and he became the Pennsylvania leader for the Jacksonian movement and minister to Russia under Jackson. Success in this diplomatic post led to him winning a seat on the U.S. Senate in 1833. By the mid-1840s, Buchanan, who was called "Little Giant" because of his short stature and oversized head, was a powerful Democratic elite and their chief commentator on constitutional law.[11]

Buchanan tried to secure the presidential nomination in 1852, but party bosses chose Pierce as more marketable. Pierce appointed Buchanan minister to England despite resentment over the nomination. There, Buchanan avoided the political blowback from the Kansas–Nebraska Act. In the 1856 election, however, Buchanan faced the rise of a new political coalition known as the Republican Party, then the progressive, liberal faction of American politics. The Republican Party began as a movement against slavery and was a coalition of former single-issue parties, like the Free Soil Party and the Liberty Party, joined by progressive former Whigs and Democrats. For their first nomination, they put forward Californian John C. Frémont, known as the "Pathfinder" for his adventurous forays into the American west. Frémont rose to fame during the Mexican-American War when, as a major, he led the expedition that took control of California. He controversially violated the chain of command and was convicted

in a court-martial for mutiny, though his conviction was later overturned by Polk. Choosing Frémont was very much in the tradition of the Whigs, who'd selected famous public figures without significant legislative experience, and Frémont fared well in the lead-up to the election.[12]

Complicating the election was the debut of America's first competitive third party, the single-issue anti-immigration "American Party," better known as the "Know-Nothing Party." The 1850s was a racially divided time in American culture history, and violent white supremacist mobs attacked Chinese railroad workers, Irish immigrants, Catholics, African Americans, and Native Americans. The threat of slavery potentially being outlawed highlighted racist and xenophobic impulses among the public and, therefore, led to a surge in anti-immigrant sentiment and the birth of the Know-Nothing Party, which united behind the candidacy of former President Millard Fillmore. Ultimately, the Democrats and Buchanan won the popular vote with 1,836,072 votes, to 1,342,345 for Frémont, and 873,053 for Fillmore. It was a significant victory, further legitimized by nearly 80 percent of eligible voters coming to the polls. However, the emergence of a third party that garnered nearly a million votes, and the fact that the Republican coalition took 1.3 million votes indicated that trust in the Democratic Party, America's largest and strongest political coalition, was tenuous. It would be up to the Democratic-led Congress and Buchanan to solidify support for their view of America's future.[13]

The Anti-Immigrant Strategy

The nativist political party known as the Know-Nothings began as a secret fraternal organization called the Order of the Star Spangled Banner. The group was founded in 1849, and quickly spread from city to city. Interest in nativism was fueled by propagandistic misinformation. Rumors spread of secret Catholic conspiracies to undermine Democracy and to hand control of America to the Catholic Pope. Fear of Catholicism was so pronounced, in fact, that there are numerous documented instances of mobs of Protestants attacking Catholics and even burning Catholic churches, typically resulting from a rumor that Catholics were participating in deviant sexual abuse. The charge of deviant sexuality is a hallmark of religious hatemongering, and an effort to portray members of the target group as unworthy of compassion because of their violation of religious sexual norms. Similarly, anti-immigration activists in 2019 have frequently alleged that immigrants are more likely to be deviant, "rapists" or "child abusers." Such claims have little legitimacy, but are an often-used tactic among individuals seeking to encourage racial, ethnic, or religious violence.

Many anti-immigration groups were secret societies, and this secrecy allowed members to shield themselves from public condemnation. When asked about their membership in the Order of the Star Spangled Banner, members would claim that they "knew nothing" about the organization, and this became the label used for the group even after they transitioned from secret nativist hate group to political party. Though they attempted to rebrand themselves as the American Party and to claim that they carried on the legacy of the Whig Party, they became a unique political entity, attracting white and protestant supremacists from many of the other political parties.

Over the course of their time in politics, the Know-Nothings were successful in engineering a near-complete takeover of the Massachusetts local government and won thousands of local government posts as well. There were a total of 43 Known-Nothing candidates elected to the U.S. House of Representatives and five Know-Nothing Senators. The Know-Nothings saw a boost from opposition to slavery, which angered white supremacists and helped cause a movement toward more extreme activism of the Know-Nothing Party. Despite this considerable success, the Know-Nothings never gained enough control to pass serious legislation. Their only national convention was in 1856, where they nominated Fillmore as their candidate, who finished third in the race.[a]

Works Used

a. Anbinder, Tyler G. *Nativism and Slavery: The Northern Know-Nothings and the Politics of the 1850s.* New York: Oxford U P, 1994.

An Unwanted Balance

In the lead-up to Buchanan's presidency, the Supreme Court ruled on the famous Dred Scott case, testing the constitutionality of slavery. Scott had lived in the Wisconsin Territory, where slavery was illegal, and sued for his freedom upon returning to Missouri on the basis that having been taken to a free state by his owner, he was thereafter free.

Buchanan learned from his friend Justice John Catron of Tennessee that the court was leaning toward denying Scott's challenge, and he wrote to Justices Catron and Robert Cooper Grier to steer the court toward a more sweeping ruling, one that would stand as a constitutional judgment on the permanent legality of slavery. Buchanan's hope was that both abolitionist and slave owner would submit to the authority of the Supreme Court and accept their ruling as the final interpretation on the legality of slavery.

Members of the Supreme Court were partisan, biased, and indebted to their political patrons, such as Buchanan.[14] Buchanan was able to craft his inaugural address with foreknowledge of the verdict, and he called on Americans to leave aside their disputes and wait for the guidance of the courts:

INAUGURAL ADDRESS
James Buchanan
March 4, 1857
Source Document Excerpt

In entering upon this great office I must humbly invoke the God of our fathers for wisdom and firmness to execute its high and responsible duties in such a manner as to restore harmony and ancient friendship among the people of the several States and to preserve our free institutions throughout many generations. Convinced that I owe my election to the inherent love for the Constitution and the Union which still animates the hearts of the American people, let me earnestly ask their powerful support in sustaining all just measures calculated to perpetuate these, the richest political blessings which Heaven has ever bestowed upon any nation. Having determined not to become a candidate for reelection, I shall have no motive to influence my conduct in administering the Government except the desire ably and faithfully to serve my country and to live in grateful memory of my countrymen.

We have recently passed through a Presidential contest in which the passions of our fellow-citizens were excited to the highest degree by questions of deep and vital importance; but when the people proclaimed their will the tempest at once subsided and all was calm.

The voice of the majority, speaking in the manner prescribed by the Constitution, was heard, and instant submission followed. Our own country could alone have exhibited so grand and striking a spectacle of the capacity of man for self-government.

What a happy conception, then, was it for Congress to apply this simple rule, that the will of the majority shall govern, to the settlement of the question of domestic slavery in the Territories. Congress is neither "to legislate slavery into any Territory or State nor to exclude it therefrom, but to leave the people thereof perfectly free to form and regulate their domestic institutions in their own way, subject only to the Constitution of the United States."

As a natural consequence, Congress has also prescribed that when the Territory of Kansas shall be admitted as a State it "shall be received into the Union with or without slavery, as their constitution may prescribe at the time of their admission."

A difference of opinion has arisen in regard to the point of time when the people of a Territory shall decide this question for themselves.

continued

This is, happily, a matter of but little practical importance. Besides, it is a judicial question, which legitimately belongs to the Supreme Court of the United States, before whom it is now pending, and will, it is understood, be speedily and finally settled. To their decision, in common with all good citizens, I shall cheerfully submit, whatever this may be, though it has ever been my individual opinion that under the Nebraska-Kansas act the appropriate period will be when the number of actual residents in the Territory shall justify the formation of a constitution with a view to its admission as a State into the Union. But be this as it may, it is the imperative and indispensable duty of the Government of the United States to secure to every resident inhabitant the free and independent expression of his opinion by his vote. This sacred right of each individual must be preserved. That being accomplished, nothing can be fairer than to leave the people of a Territory free from all foreign interference to decide their own destiny for themselves, subject only to the Constitution of the United States.[15]

In his address Buchanan framed the slavery debate as an issue of popular sovereignty. He delivered his speech on March 4, and the Supreme Court issued its ruling on March 6, with Chief Justice Roger B. Taney penning the majority (7–2) decision. The Supreme Court ruled that Congress did not have the constitutional authority to determine the legality of slavery in the territories, ruling that African Americans were not and could never be citizens of the United States and were, therefore, barred from constitutional protections regarding natural or civil rights. The court ruled that the Scott case was nullified on the basis that Scott, who had no legally recognized rights because he was both a slave and African American, could not sue in U.S. courts.

Legal scholars have called the Dred Scott decision one of the worst in the Court's history. It can also be argued that Buchanan's direct influence over the Supreme Court's ruling was a blatant violation of the Constitutional division of power and the system of checks and balances, and thus might be considered one of the clearest examples of the misuse of executive and judicial powers in the history of the Union. Moreover, the ruling made the national situation much worse.

The dissenting voices of Justice John McLean and Justice Benjamin Robbins Curtis rebutted the ruling in very different ways. McLean argued that once the Court ruled that the trial was invalid, it should have dismissed the entire case without ruling on the merits of the various claims within the case. He, therefore, felt that the Court's ruling as to the legal status of all African Americans was unjustified and unconstitutional. Justice Curtis offered a more substantive argument on the ruling that African Americans could not be citizens. He noted that there were black citizens, empowered to vote, in five of the thirteen states when the Constitution was ratified and that the power to determine who is allowed citizenship is afforded to Congress and is not otherwise specified in the Constitution:

DRED SCOTT V. SANFORD
Justice Benjamin Robbins Curtis dissenting
1857
Source Document Excerpt

Citizens of the United States at the time of the adoption of the Constitution can have been no other than citizens of the United States under the Confederation. By the Articles of Confederation, a Government was organized, the style whereof was, "The United States of America." This Government was in existence when the Constitution was framed and proposed for adoption, and was to be superseded by the new Government of the United States of America, organized under the Constitution. When, therefore, the Constitution speaks of citizenship of the United States, existing at the time of the adoption of the Constitution, it must necessarily refer to citizenship under the Government which existed prior to and at the time of such adoption.

Without going into any question concerning the powers of the Confederation to govern the territory of the United States out of the limits of the States, and consequently to sustain the relation of Government and citizen in respect to the inhabitants of such territory, it may safely be said that

continued

the citizens of the several States were citizens of the United States under the Confederation.

That Government was simply a confederacy of the several States, possessing a few defined powers over subjects of general concern, each State retaining every power, jurisdiction, and right, not expressly delegated to the United States in Congress assembled. And no power was thus delegated to the Governement of the Confederation, to act on any question of citizenship, or to make any rules in respect thereto. The whole matter was left to stand upon the action of the several States, and to the natural consequence of such action, that the citizens of each State should be citizens of that Confederacy into which that State had entered, the style whereof was, "The United States of America."

To determine whether any free persons, descended from Africans held in slavery, were citizens of the United States under the Confederation, and consequently at the time of the adoption of the Constitution of the United States, it is only necessary to know whether any such persons were citizens of either of the States under the Confederation, at the time of the adoption of the Constitution.

Of this there can be no doubt. At the time of the ratification of the Articles of Confederation, all free native-born inhabitants of the States of New Hampshire, Massachusetts, New York, New Jersey, and North Carolina, though descended from African slaves, were not only citizens of those States, but such of them as had the other necessary qualifications possessed the franchise of electors, on equal terms with other citizens.

. . .

The Constitution having recognized the rule that persons born within the several States are citizens of the United States, one of four things must be true:

First.

That the Constitution itself has described what native-born persons shall or shall not be citizens of the United States; or,

Second.

That it has empowered Congress to do so; or,

Third.

That all free persons, born within the several States, are citizens of the United States; or,

Fourth.

That it is left to each State to determine what free persons, born

Dred Scott v. Sanford
continued

within its limits, shall be citizens of such State, and thereby be citizens of the United States.

If there be such a thing as citizenship of the United States acquired by birth within the States, which the Constitution expressly recognizes, and no one denies, then these four alternatives embrace the entire subject, and it only remains to select that one which is true.

That the Constitution itself has defined citizenship of the United States by declaring what persons, born within the several States, shall or shall not be citizens of the United States, will not be pretended. It contains no such declaration. We may dismiss the first alternative, as without doubt unfounded.

Has it empowered Congress to enact what free persons, born within the several States, shall or shall not be citizens of the United States?

Before examining the various provisions of the Constitution which may relate to this question, it is important to consider for a moment the substantial nature of this inquiry. It is, in effect, whether the Constitution has empowered Congress to create privileged classes within the States, who alone can be entitled to the franchises and powers of citizenship of the United States. If it be admitted that the Constitution has enabled Congress to declare what free persons, born within the several States, shall be citizens of the United States, it must at the same time be admitted that it is an unlimited power. If this subject is within the control of Congress, it must depend wholly or its discretion. For, certainly, on limits of that discretion can be found in the Constitution, which is wholly silent concerning it; and the necessary consequence is, that the Federal Government may select classes of persons within the several States who alone can be entitled to the political privileges of citizenship of the United States. If this power exists, what persons born within the States may be President or Vice President of the United States, or members of either House of Congress, or hold any office or enjoy any privilege whereof citizenship of the United States is a necessary qualification, must depend solely on the will of Congress. By virtue of it, though Congress can grant no title of nobility, they may create an oligarchy, in whose hands would be concentrated the entire power of the Federal Government.[16]

The Court's ruling in *Scott* eliminated the hope of challenging slavery in the courts, making it clear that the slavery question could not be settled by negotiation. By the end of Buchanan's presidency, citizens on both sides of the debate were voicing their support for war.

Buchanan routinely ranks among the least popular presidents, often in the spot of "worst president." His administration's failures in the slavery debate are frequently cited as reasons for his low rating, but other efforts as chief executive fared a little better. Like Pierce before him, Buchanan tried to annex Cuba, with little more success than his predecessor. The country also plunged into an economic recession as Civil War anxiety gripped the nation. There was little doubt, as the 1860 election approached, that Buchanan would be a losing candidate. Though he was still offered a nomination, the party also forwarded two additional candidates, both of whom fared better than Buchanan.

After the states began seceding from the Union, Buchanan opined, in his final State of the Union Address, that the federal government had no constitutional power to prevent secession, even if secession might also be considered illegal under U.S. law.

STATE OF THE UNION
James Buchanan
December 3, 1860
Source Document Excerpt

How easy would it be for the American people to settle the slavery question forever and to restore peace and harmony to this distracted country! They, and they alone, can do it. All that is necessary to accomplish the object, and all for which the slave States have ever contended, is to be let alone and permitted to manage their domestic institutions in their own way. As sovereign States, they, and they alone, are responsible before God and the world for the slavery existing among them. For this the people of the North are not more responsible and have no more fight to interfere than with similar institutions in Russia or in Brazil.

Upon their good sense and patriotic forbearance I confess I still greatly rely. Without their aid it is beyond the power of any President, no matter what may be his own political proclivities, to restore peace and harmony among the States. Wisely limited and restrained as is his power under our Constitution and laws, he alone can accomplish but little for good or for evil on such a momentous question.

And this brings me to observe that the election of any one of our fellow-citizens to the office of President does not of itself afford just cause for dissolving the Union. This is more especially true if his election has been effected by a mere plurality, and not a majority of the people, and has resulted from transient and temporary causes, which may probably never again occur. In order to justify a resort to revolutionary resistance, the Federal Government must be guilty of "a deliberate, palpable, and dangerous exercise" of powers not granted by the Constitution.[17]

Buchanan's personal writings indicate he believed history would vindicate him and prove that his belief in limited governmental powers and strict adherence to a principle of independent states was the only constitutionally valid approach. However, with the Union victory in the Civil War, Buchanan left a legacy as one of America's least competent and least effective leaders.

CONCLUSION

Many of the political minds of the mid and late 1800s did not quite realize that there was no hope of mediating the slavery issue. The pro-slavery southerners recognized that they were essentially fighting for the continuation of their culture, while abolitionists viewed the enslavement of humans as a moral evil that could not be forgiven. Northerners who were sympathetic to slavery were long seen as the best option to serve as president, providing some degree of appeal to those on both sides, but this approach just postponed the inevitable conflict over the issue. By attempting to avoid this inescapable reality, Pierce and Buchanan rendered themselves impotent, and neither man was able to command sufficient political power or popular support to establish a strong presidential authority. America's next, and favorite, president, Abraham Lincoln, was brave enough to state, outright, that the question would need to be solved. Either slavery was legal everywhere, or it needed to be everywhere abolished. The next chapter details this great president and his use of presidential authority.

DISCUSSION QUESTIONS

♦ Why was Buchanan's correspondence with members of the Supreme Court a violation of constitutional principles?

♦ Should southern states have been allowed to manage slavery on their own, as Buchanan suggested? Why or why not?

♦ Jean H. Baker of Goucher College said, "Difficult times require forceful leadership that is sensitive to issues both of change and continuity." Give an example of how this relates to modern presidencies.

♦ Should a person with severe depression, like Franklin Pierce, be allowed to serve as president? Why or why not?

♦ Should information such as a president's mental health be private or should it be available to the public? Explain your answer.

Works Used

Baker, Jean H. "Franklin Pierce: Impact and Legacy." *Miller Center*. U of Virginia. 2019. millercenter.org/president/pierce/impact-and-legacy.

_____. *James Buchanan,* edited by Arthur M. Schlesinger, Jr. New York: Times Books, 2004.

Bennett, James Gordon, editor. *New York Herald*, vol. 17, no. 228, 17 August 1852. *LOC*, Library of Congress, Chronicling America, chroniclingamerica. loc.gov/lccn/sn83030313/1852–08–17/ed-1/seq-4.

Bergen, Anthony. "Franklin Pierce and the Consequences of Ambition." *Medium*. 23 Nov. 2015. medium.com/@Anthony_Bergen/franklin-pierce-and-the-consequences-of-ambition-577969fc81ca.

Buchanan, James. "March 4, 1857: Inaugural Address." *Miller Center*. U of Virginia. 2019. millercenter.org/the-presidency/presidential-speeches/march-4-1857-inaugural-address.

Eschner, Kat. "President James Buchanan Directly Influences the Outcome of the Dred Scott Decision." *Smithsonian.com*. 6 Mar. 2017. www.smithsonianmag.com/smart-news/president-james-buchanan-directly-influenced-outcome-dred-scott-decision-180962329/.

"Franklin Pierce's Murky Legacy as President." *Constitution Center*. Constitution Daily. 8 Oct. 2019. constitutioncenter.org/blog/franklin-pierces-murky-legacy-as-president.

Gibson, John. "A Time for Doughfaces?" *Medium*. 21 June 2019. medium.com/@johngibsonks/a-time-for-doughfaces-16f64381f5b5.

"James Buchanan. State of the Union 1860—3 December 1860." *American History*. U of Groningen. 2012. www.let.rug.nl/usa/presidents/james-buchanan/state-of-the-union-1860.php.

"Justice Curtis Dissenting." *American History*. University of Groningen. 2012. www.let.rug.nl/usa/documents/1826-1850/dred-scott-case/justice-curtis-dissenting.php.

Landis, Michael Todd. *Northern Men with Southern Loyalties: The Democratic Party and the Sectional Crisis*. Ithaca, NY: Cornell U P, 2014.

Pierce, Franklin. "Inaugural Address of Franklin Pierce." *Avalon Project*. Yale Law School. 2019. avalon.law.yale.edu/19th_century/pierce.asp.

"Presidential Election of 1852: A Resource Guide." *LOC*. Library of Congress. 23 Oct. 2018. www.loc.gov/rr/program/bib/elections/election1852.html.

"Presidential Election of 1856: A Resource Guide." *LOC*. Library of Congress. 23 Oct. 2018. www.loc.gov/rr/program/bib/elections/election1856.html.

Reiber, Beth. "It Wasn't Called Bleeding Kansas for Nothing." *Unmistakably Lawrence*. 26 July 2018. unmistakablylawrence.com/history-heritage/bleeding-kansas/.

Strauss, Robert. *Worst. President. Ever.: James Buchanan, the POTUS Rating Game and the Least of the Lesser Presidents*. Guilford, CT: LP P, 2016.

Walther, Eric. *The Shattering of the Union*. New York: Rowman & Littlefield, 2004.

Weigley, Russell F. "Old Fuss and Feathers." *New York Times*. Books. 11 Jan. 1998. movies2.nytimes.com/books/98/01/11/reviews/980111.11weiglet.html.

We the People

Introduction

During the Civil War, Abraham Lincoln violated the limits of presidential authority more than any president who came before him. Lincoln refused to obey the rulings of the Supreme Court, he issued executive orders that superseded both state and congressional authority, and he directed his armies against sovereign state militias. Lincoln's administration saw an extraordinary reimagining of presidential power, but this occurred in the midst of an unprecedented national emergency. The secession of core southern states threatened the economic and material prosperity of the entire nation, and the steps taken by Lincoln have been judged necessary, based on the threat that America faced at the time. Though there were many reasons for the Civil War, slavery was the most important and the most polarizing. For years, a dedicated population of American reformers had fought against the evil of slavery, and Lincoln was the first American president with the fortitude and bravery to take up this cause. The Emancipation Proclamation stands as perhaps the most morally impactful executive order issued in American history and, though Lincoln was not initially an abolitionist, his role in bringing about the end of slavery is the sole reason that Lincoln is perhaps America's most cherished leader.

We the People

Topics covered in this chapter include:
- Civil War
- Writ of Habeas Corpus
- The Emancipation Proclamation
- Thirteenth Amendment

This Chapter Discusses the Following Source Documents:
Address before the Young Men's Lyceum of Springfield, Illinois, January 27, 1838
House Divided Speech, June 16, 1858
Message to Congress, Abraham Lincoln, July 4, 1861
The Merryman Case, Chief Justice Taney decision, June 4, 1861

We the People

Emancipation
Abraham Lincoln (1861–1865)

Abraham Lincoln is perhaps the nation's most popular president. A 2019 survey ranked American presidents on the ability to complete an agenda while in office, the ability to garner popular support, and the overall impact of a presidential term on the country and public perceptions of well-being. Abraham Lincoln ranked first on the list among Democrat/Liberal, Republican/Conservative, or independent participants.[1]

Washington and Lincoln eclipse other presidents in terms of popularity because both men's presidencies coincided with the most important movements in U.S. history: the founding of the nation and the end of slavery. Even those with limited knowledge of politics or history can single out these two leaders as important forces in shaping America. That the end of slavery is now equal to the founding of the nation speaks to the evolution of American morality. While there are still millions of Americans who harbor racist perceptions of African Americans and other non-white individuals, mainstream American morality has shifted toward the perception that the "natural rights" that Jefferson so passionately championed in the Declaration of Independence should apply to all persons, regardless of race, sex, or creed.

Abraham Lincoln, by Alexander Gardner, via Wikimedia.

Log Cabin Intellectual

Abraham Lincoln was born on February 12, 1809 in Hodgenville, Kentucky. Both his parents were illiterate, and the family was desperately poor, but young Abraham was intellectually curious and encouraged in his reading and studies as a child. Abraham worked on the family farm until age 17, when he got a job operating a ferryboat on the Mississippi River. At age 21, his family relocated to Illinois and Lincoln moved to the town of New Salem, where he found work as a clerk in a general store. A tall (6'4"), lanky young man with a thin, strong frame, Lincoln worked odd jobs and became popular thanks to his wit and easygoing nature.

In 1831, Lincoln signed on for the Illinois militia during the Black Hawk War. He was selected as captain of his regiment and spent the next several months fighting Native Americans in the Illinois bush. He also became a member of the Independent Spy Corps, a company that tried, unsuccessfully, to locate Chief Black Hawk in Wisconsin. When he returned to New Salem, Lincoln studied law, passing the state bar in 1836. He joined the Whig Party and became a well-known local member, serving as a secretary for local functions. Even though Lincoln was a Whig, Andrew Jackson appointed him postmaster of New Salem. He spent the next two years in the role, while working to supplement his salary by chopping wood, splitting rails, and handling small legal cases on the side.

The sport of wrestling has no single origin. Wrestling has emerged independently in cultures around the world, from the far east to the Americas, where many Native Americans wrestled for sport in the centuries before European arrival. Wrestling in the European tradition can be traced to ancient Greece and Rome and to the Persian societies that preceded them. In America, wrestling became a popular sport in the pioneer villages and communities of the British. Different towns held local matches and typically selected a local champion and neighboring towns would then pit their champions against one another. Prior to the origin of boxing, near the end of the nineteenth century, wrestling was the fighting sport of choice in America.

By the 1700s, wrestling was sufficiently evolved in America that there were many well-known institutions that included wrestling training as a form of physical education. Typically, the "collar and elbow" style was taught, based on a starting position in which opponents stand face-to-face, each with a hand on the back of the other's neck and the opposite hand on their opponent's elbow. George Washington learned this style of wrestling at the Reverend James Maury's Academy in Fredericksburg, Virginia and became a local collar and elbow champion in Virginia. It is reported that at age 47, and as commander of the Continental Armies, Washington was still skilled enough to defeat seven challengers from the Massachusetts Volunteers contingent of his army.

Though wrestling had become an acceptable past-time for the children of the aristocracy, like Washington, in the smaller towns and cities, wrestling was still a rough sport, with frequent fouling and injuries, and interference from the crowds. In the early 1800s, individual bouts between champions often ended in fighting mobs as supporters of opponents clashed over the outcome of the bout.

The most famous political wrestler is the other most famous president, Abraham Lincoln, who became an Illinois wrestling champion in the early 1830s while in his early twenties. Lincoln's tall, wiry frame was deceiving, as years of hard farm labor, wood chopping, and rail splitting had made him uncommonly strong. After moving to New Salem, Illinois, Lincoln famously engaged in a wrestling bout with Jack Armstrong, a local man known as a bully who was also the county wrestling champion. Accounts of the match vary, but it is widely reported that Lincoln used his superior reach to outwrestle Armstrong from the beginning. When Armstrong fouled Lincoln, the future president reportedly lifted Armstrong from the ground and threw him down, knocking the young man unconscious, after which Armstrong's friends and supporters nearly rushed Lincoln as a violent mob. Lincoln frequently forwent the more formal collar and elbow style for the frontier style, called "catch-as-catch-can," which was more hand-to-hand combat than pure, stylized wrestling. He became famous for his roughness and tenacity. It is said that Lincoln lost only one match, to a soldier from another unit during the Black Hawk War.

Many future presidents also wrestled, including Andrew Jackson, Zachary Taylor, Ulysses S. Grant, Chester A. Arthur, Theodore Roosevelt, and William Howard Taft, who wrestled at Yale University at a weight of 225 and was known as "Big Bill." Taft, the fourth generation of wrestlers in his family, even became known for mastering an expert move known as the "Flying Marc," used to flip one's opponent to the ground. Wrestling might deserve the status as the most presidential of the American sports, due to the many past presidents who wrestled in their youth, and some well into their adult lives. Wrestling also serves as a mirror of American evolution, from a rough-and-tumble frontier sport to the pastime of aristocratic sons and political legacy-holders.[a]

Works Used

a. Dellinger, Bob. "Wrestling in the USA." *NWHOF*. National Wrestling Hall of Fame. 2011. nwhof.org/stillwater/resources-library/history/wrestling-in-the-usa/.

While serving in local politics Lincoln developed a homespun political strategy that served him well for the rest of his life. When he ran for a seat on the state legislature in 1834, Lincoln eschewed partisanship and avoided the traditional party speeches. Instead, he traveled from house to house meeting families and speaking to them about their perception of politics in the region. His novel approach gained him the support not only of the Whigs, but of Democrats as well, and he easily won the 1834 election, followed by three successful reelection campaigns. Like most white Americans at the time, Lincoln was racist and did not believe in giving African Americans equal rights, but he opposed the institution of slavery, which he saw as immoral. In 1838, abolitionist publisher Elijah Parish Lovejoy was killed defending his printing press from a mob of pro-slavery agitators in Alton, Illinois. Lincoln delivered a speech condemning vigilantism at the Young Men's Lyceum in Illinois that stands as one of his earliest recorded speeches.

ADDRESS BEFORE THE YOUNG MEN'S LYCEUM OF SPRINGFIELD, ILLINOIS

Abraham Lincoln
January 27, 1838
Source Document Excerpt

I know the American People are *much* attached to their Government;—I know they would suffer *much* for its sake;—I know they would endure evils long and patiently, before they would ever think of exchanging it for another. Yet, notwithstanding all this, if the laws be continually despised and disregarded, if their rights to be secure in their persons and property, are held by no better tenure than the caprice of a mob, the alienation of their affections from the Government is the natural consequence; and to that, sooner or later, it must come.

Here then, is one point at which danger may be expected.

The question recurs, "how shall we fortify against it?" The answer is simple. Let every American, every lover of liberty, every well wisher to his posterity, swear by the blood of the Revolution, never to violate in the least particular, the laws of the country; and never to tolerate their violation by others. As the patriots of seventy-six did to the support of the Declaration of Independence, so to the support of the Constitution and Laws, let every American pledge his life, his property, and his sacred honor;—let every man remember that to violate the law, is to trample on the blood of his father, and to tear the character of his own, and his children's liberty. Let reverence for the laws, be breathed by every American mother, to the lisping babe, that prattles on her lap—let it be taught in schools, in seminaries, and in colleges; let it be written in Primers, spelling books, and in Almanacs;—let it be preached from the pulpit, proclaimed in legislative halls, and enforced in courts of justice. And, in short, let it become the *political religion* of the nation; and let the old and the young, the rich and the poor, the grave and the gay, of all sexes and tongues, and colors and conditions, sacrifice unceasingly upon its altars.[2]

Lincoln won an election to the House of Representatives in 1846 and served during James Polk's polarizing presidency. He was one of a group of Whig politicians who opposed the Mexican-American War and who accused Polk of misrepresenting his reasons for declaring war. Lincoln's criticism of the administration was apt, but the war effort was popular in Illinois, and so Lincoln lost support and left politics.

Returning to his law practice, Lincoln became one of the most well-known lawyers in Illinois and participated in a number of high-profile cases. Though he campaigned for Whig candidates, Lincoln left the party to join the emerging Republican Party in 1856. This new political move-ment was united around ending slavery and included abolitionist Whigs as well as members of the Free Soil Party, the Liberty Party, and a number of former Democrats who opposed slavery or its expansion. Lincoln and the Republicans united against the Kansas-Nebraska Act passed under President Pierce and supported the admission of Kansas as a free state. They further opposed Democratic efforts to annex Cuba, which would have become a new slave-state for the south.

Symbol of a Movement

During the Buchanan administration, Lincoln competed for a seat on the U.S. Senate with Senator Stephen A. Douglas of Illinois, a third-term Democrat. The Republican Party was just starting to define its nation-al identity, and Lincoln's debates with Douglas provided an opportunity to cement those distinctions in the minds of voters across the country. Douglas was a star of the Democratic establishment and one of their greatest orators, but his opposition to the Lecompton Constitution, which would have made Kansas a slave state was controversial. Democrats had called for the issue of slavery to be decided according to popular sovereignty. Many backed the Lecompton Constitution, arguing that the settlers of the state had decided to allow slavery, but it was widely known that this was not accurate. The population of the Kansas territory, prior to the Kansas-Nebraska Act, was predominantly anti-slavery. The

Lecompton Treaty was the result of President Pierce having assigned a pro-slavery governor to the territory combined with thousands of Missouri slave-supporters who flooded into Kansas to ensure that the state became a slave state. These Missourians had voted illegally in the legislative debate over the new constitution, and Douglas held that the Lecompton Constitution was not legitimately representative of the popular will.

Lincoln needed a more dramatic stance to have an impact, and he began their debates with his now famous "House Divided" speech, on June 16, 1858:

HOUSE DIVIDED SPEECH
Abraham Lincoln
Springfield, Illinois
June 16, 1858
Source Document Excerpt

Mr. President and Gentlemen of the Convention.

If we could first know *where* we are, and *whither* we are tending, we could then better judge *what* to do, and *how* to do it.

We are now far into the *fifth* year, since a policy was initiated, with the *avowed* object, and *confident* promise, of putting an end to slavery agitation.

Under the operation of that policy, that agitation has not only, *not ceased*, but has *constantly augmented*.

In *my* opinion, it *will* not cease, until a *crisis* shall have been reached, and passed.

"A house divided against itself cannot stand."

I believe this government cannot endure, permanently half *slave* and half *free*.

I do not expect the Union to be *dissolved*—I do not expect the house to *fall*—but I *do* expect it will cease to be divided.

It will become *all* one thing or *all* the other.

Either the *opponents* of slavery, will arrest the further spread of it, and place it where the public mind shall rest in the belief that it is in the course of ultimate extinction; or its *advocates*

House Divided Speech
continued

will push it forward, till it shall become alike lawful in *all* the States, *old* as well as *new*—*North* as well as *South*.

Have we no *tendency* to the latter condition?

Let any one who doubts, carefully contemplate that now almost complete legal combination—piece of *machinery* so to speak—compounded of the Nebraska doctrine, and the Dred Scott decision. Let him consider not only *what* work the machinery is adapted to do, and *how well* adapted; but also, let him study the *history* of its construction, and trace, if he can, or rather *fail,* if he can, to trace the evidence of design and concert of action, among its chief architects, from the beginning.

But, so far, *Congress* only, had acted; and an *indorsement* by the people, *real* or apparent, was indispensable, to *save* the point already gained, and give chance for more.

The new year of 1854 found slavery excluded from more than half the States by State Constitutions, and from most of the national territory by congressional prohibition.

Four days later, commenced the struggle, which ended in repealing that congressional prohibition.

This opened all the national territory to slavery, and was the first point gained.

This necessity had not been overlooked; but had been provided for, as well as might be, in the notable argument of *"squatter sovereignty,"* otherwise called *"sacred right of self government,"* which latter phrase, though expressive of the only rightful basis of any government, was so perverted in this attempted use of it as to amount to just this: That if any *one* man, choose to enslave *another,* no *third* man shall be allowed to object.

That argument was incorporated into the Nebraska bill itself, in the language which follows: *"It being the true intent and meaning of this act not to legislate slavery into any Territory or state, not to exclude it therefrom; but to leave the people thereof perfectly free to form and regulate their domestic institutions in their own way, subject only to the Constitution of the United States."*

Then opened the roar of loose declamation in favor of "Squatter Sovereignty," and "Sacred right of self-government."

"But," said opposition members, "let us be more *specific*—let us *amend*

continued

the bill so as to expressly declare that the people of the territory may exclude slavery." "Not we," said the friends of the measure; and down they voted the amendment.

While the Nebraska Bill was passing through congress, a *law case* involving the question of a negroe's freedom, by reason of his owner having voluntarily taken him first into a free state and then a territory covered by the congressional prohibition, and held him as a slave, for a long time in each, was passing through the U.S. Circuit Court for the District of Missouri; and both Nebraska bill and law suit were brought to a decision in the same month of May, 1854. The negroe's name was "Dred Scott," which name now designates the decision finally made in the case.

Before the *then* next Presidential election, the law case came *to,* and was argued *in,* the Supreme Court of the United States; but the *decision* of it was deferred until *after* the election. Still, *before* the election, Senator Trumbull, on the floor of the Senate, requests the leading advocate of the Nebraska bill to state *his opinion* whether the people of a territory can constitutionally exclude slavery from their limits; and the latter answers: "That is a question for the Supreme Court."

The election came. Mr. Buchanan was elected, and the *indorsement,* such as it was, secured. That was the *second* point gained. The indorsement, however, fell short of a clear popular majority by nearly four hundred thousand votes, and so, perhaps, was not overwhelmingly reliable and satisfactory.

The *outgoing* President, in his last annual message, as impressively as possible, *echoed back* upon the people the weight and *authority* of the indorsement.

The Supreme Court met again; *did not* announce their decision, but ordered a re-argument.

The Presidential inauguration came, and still no decision of the court; but the *incoming* President, in his inaugural address, fervently exhorted the people to abide by the forthcoming decision, *whatever might be.*

Then, in a few days, came the decision.

The reputed author of the Nebraska Bill finds an early occasion to make a speech at this capital indorsing the Dred Scott Decision, and vehemently denouncing all opposition to it.

The new President, too, seizes the early occasion of the Silliman letter to *indorse* and strongly *construe* that decision, and to express his *astonishment* that any different view had ever been entertained.

House Divided Speech
continued

At length a squabble springs up between the President and the author of the Nebraska Bill, on the *mere* question of *fact,* whether the Lecompton constitution was or was not, in any just sense, made by the people of Kansas; and in that squabble the latter declares that all he wants is a fair vote for the people, and that he *cares* not whether slavery be voted *down* or voted *up.* I do not understand his declaration that he cares not whether slavery be voted down or voted up, to be intended by him other than as an *apt definition* of the *policy* he would impress upon the public mind—the *principle* for which he declares he has suffered much, and is ready to suffer to the end.

And well may he cling to that principle. If he has any parental feeling, well may he cling to it. That principle, is the only *shred* left of his original Nebraska doctrine. Under the Dred Scott decision, "squatter sovereignty" squatted out of existence, tumbled down like temporary scaffolding—like the mould at the foundry served through one blast and fell back into loose sand— helped to carry an election, and then was kicked to the winds. His late *joint* struggle with the Republicans, against the Lecompton Constitution, involves nothing of the original Nebraska doctrine. That struggle was made on a point, the right of a people to make their own constitution, upon which

he and the Republicans have never differed.

The several points of the Dred Scott decision, in connection with Senator Douglas' "care-not" policy, constitute the piece of machinery, in its *present* state of advancement. This was the third point gained.

The *working* points of that machinery are:

First, that no negro slave, imported as such from Africa, and no descendant of such slave can ever be a *citizen* of any State, in the sense of that term as used in the Constitution of the United States.

This point is made in order to deprive the negro, in every possible event, of the benefit of this provision of the United States Constitution, which declares that—

"The citizens of each State shall be entitled to all privileges and immunities of citizens in the several States."

Secondly, that "subject to the Constitution of the United States," neither *Congress* nor a *Territorial Legislature* can exclude slavery from any United States Territory.

This point is made in order that individual men may *fill up* the territories with slaves, without danger

continued

of losing them as property, and thus to enhance the chances of *permanency* to the institution through all the future.

Thirdly, that whether the holding a negro in actual slavery in a free State, makes him free, as against the holder, the United States courts will not decide, but will leave to be decided by the courts of any slave State the negro may be forced into by the master.

This point is made, not to be pressed *immediately*; but, if acquiesced in for a while, and apparently *indorsed* by the people at an election, *then* to sustain the logical conclusion that what Dred Scott's master might lawfully do with Dred Scott, in the free State of Illinois, every other master may lawfully do with any other one, or one *thousand* slaves, in Illinois, or in any other free State.

Auxiliary to all this, and working hand in hand with it, the Nebraska doctrine, or what is left of it, is to *educate* and *mould* public opinion, at least *Northern* public opinion, to not *care* whether slavery is voted *down* or voted *up*.

This shows exactly where we now *are*; and *partially*, also, whither we are tending.

It will throw additional light on the latter, to go back, and run the mind over the string of historical facts already stated. Several things will *now* appear less *dark* and *mysterious* than they did *when* they were transpiring. The people were to be left "perfectly free" "subject only to the Constitution." What the Constitution had to do with it, outsiders could not *then* see. Plainly enough *now*, it was an exactly fitted *niche*, for the Dred Scott decision to afterward come in, and declare the *perfect freedom* of the people, to be just no freedom at all.

Why was the amendment, expressly declaring the right of the people to exclude slavery, voted down? Plainly enough *now*, the adoption of it would have spoiled the niche for the Dred Scott decision.

Why was the court decision held up? Why even a Senator's individual opinion withheld, till *after* the presidential election? Plainly enough *now*, the speaking out *then* would have damaged the *"perfectly free"* argument upon which the election was to be carried.

Why the *outgoing* President's felicitation on the indorsement? Why the delay of a reargument? Why the incoming President's *advance* exhortation in favor of the decision?

These things *look* like the cautious *patting* and *petting* of a spirited horse, preparatory to mounting him, when it is dreaded that he may give the rider a fall.

House Divided Speech
continued

And why the hasty after indorsements of the decision by the President and others?

We can not absolutely *know* that all these exact adaptations are the result of preconcert. But when we see a lot of framed timbers, different portions of which we know have been gotten out at different times and places and by different workmen—Stephen, Franklin, Roger, and James, for instance—and when we see these timbers joined together, and see they exactly make the frame of a house or a mill, all the tenons and mortices exactly fitting, and all the lengths and proportions of the different pieces exactly adapted to their respective places, and not a piece too many or too few—not omitting even scaffolding—or, if a single piece be lacking, we can see the place in the frame exactly fitted and prepared to yet bring such piece in—in *such* a case, we find it impossible not to believe that Stephen and Franklin and Roger and James all understood one another from the beginning, and all worked upon a common *plan* or *draft* drawn up before the first lick was struck.

It should not be overlooked that, by the Nebraska Bill, the people of a *State*, as well as *Territory*, were to be left "perfectly free" "*subject only to the Constitution.*"

Why mention a *State*? They were legislating for *territories*, and not *for* or *about* States. Certainly the people of a State *are* and *ought* to be subject to the Constitution of the United States; but why is mention of this *lugged* into this merely *territorial* law? Why are the people of a *territory* and the people of a *state* therein *lumped* together, and their relation to the Constitution therein treated as being *precisely* the same?

While the opinion of *the Court*, by Chief Justice Taney, in the Dred Scott case, and the separate opinions of all the concurring Judges, expressly declare that the Constitution of the United States neither permits Congress nor a Territorial legislature to exclude slavery from any United States territory, they all *omit* to declare whether or not the same Constitution permits a *state*, or the people of a State, to exclude it.

Possibly, this is a mere *omission*; but who can be *quite* sure, if McLean or Curtis had sought to get into the opinion a declaration of unlimited power in the people of a *state* to exclude slavery from their limits, just as Chase and Macy sought to get such declaration, in behalf of the people of a territory, into the Nebraska bill—I ask, who can be quite *sure* that it would not have been voted down, in the one case, as it had been in the other.

continued

The nearest approach to the point of declaring the power of a State over slavery, is made by Judge Nelson. He approaches it more than once, using the precise idea, and *almost* the language too, of the Nebraska act. On one occasion his exact language is, "except in cases where the power is restrained by the Constitution of the United States, the law of the State is supreme over the subject of slavery within its jurisdiction."

In what *cases* the power of the *states* is so restrained by the U.S. Constitution, is left an *open* question, precisely as the same question, as to the restraint on the power of the *territories* was left open in the Nebraska act. Put *that* and *that* together, and we have another nice little niche, which we may, ere long, see filled with another Supreme Court decision, declaring that the Constitution of the United States does not permit a *state* to exclude slavery from its limits.

And this may especially be expected if the doctrine of "care not whether slavery be voted *down* or voted *up*," shall gain upon the public mind sufficiently to give promise that such a decision an be maintained when made.

Such a decision is all that slavery now lacks of being alike lawful in all the States.

Welcome, or unwelcome, such decision *is* probably coming, and will soon be upon us, unless the power of the present political dynasty shall be met and overthrown.

We shall *lie down* pleasantly dreaming that the people of *Missouri* are on the verge of making their State *free*; and we shall *awake* to the *reality*, instead, that the *Supreme* Court has made *Illinois* a *slave* State.

To meet and overthrow the power of that dynasty, is the work now before all those who would prevent that consummation.

This is *what* we have to do.

But *how* can we best do it?

There are those who denounce us *openly* to their *own* friends, and yet whisper *us softly*, that *Senator Douglas* is the *aptest* instrument there is, with which to effect that object. *They* wish us to *infer* all, from the facts, that he now has a little quarrel with the present head of the dynasty; and that he has regularly voted with us, on a single point, upon which, he and we, have never differed.

They remind us that *he* is a great man, and that the largest of *us* are very small ones. Let this be granted. But "a *living* dog is better than a *dead lion*." Judge Douglas, if not a dead

House Divided Speech
continued

lion for this work, is at least a *caged* and *toothless* one. How can he oppose the advances of slavery? He don't *care* anything about it. His avowed *mission is impressing* the "public heart" to *care* nothing about it.

A leading Douglas Democratic newspaper thinks Douglas' superior talent will be needed to resist the revival of the African slave trade.

Does Douglas believe an effort to revive that trade is approaching? He has not said so. Does he *really* think so? But if it is, how can he resist it? For years he has labored to prove it a *sacred right* of white men to take negro slaves into the new territories. Can he possibly show that it is *less* a sacred right to *buy* them where they can be bought cheapest? And, unquestionably they can be bought *cheaper in Africa* than in *Virginia*.

He has done all in his power to reduce the whole question of slavery to one of a mere *right of property*; and as such, how can *he* oppose the foreign slave trade—how can he refuse that trade in that "property" shall be "perfectly free"—unless he does it as a *protection* to the home production? And as the home *producers* will probably not *ask* the protection, he will be wholly without a ground of opposition.

Senator Douglas holds, we know, that a man may rightfully be *wiser to-day* than he was *yesterday*—that he may rightfully *change* when he finds himself wrong.

But can we, for that reason, run ahead, and *infer* that he *will* make any particular change, of which he, himself, has given no intimation? Can we *safely* base our action upon any such *vague* inference?

Now, as ever, I wish not to *misrepresent* Judge Douglas' *position*, question his *motives*, or do ought that can be personally offensive to him.

Whenever, *if ever*, he and we can come together on *principle* so that *our great cause* may have assistance from *his great ability*, I hope to have interposed no adventitious obstacle.

But clearly, he is not *now* with us—he does not *pretend* to be—he does not *promise* to *ever* be.

Our cause, then, must be intrusted to, and conducted by its own undoubted friends—those whose hands are free, whose hearts are in the work—who *do care* for the result.

Two years ago the Republicans of the nation mustered over thirteen hundred thousand strong.

continued

We did this under the single impulse of resistance to a common danger, with every external circumstance against us.

Of *strange, discordant*, and even, *hostile* elements, we gathered from the four winds, and *formed* and fought the battle through, under the constant hot fire of a disciplined, proud, and pampered enemy.

Did we brave all *then* to *falter* now?—now—when that same enemy is *wavering,* dissevered and belligerent?

The result is not doubtful. We shall not fail—if we stand firm, we shall not fail.

Wise councils may *accelerate* or *mistakes delay* it, but, sooner or later the victory is sure to come.[3]

Lincoln's House Divided speech is considered one of the most important speeches in American history. In other debates, Lincoln warned that pursuing the path of popular sovereignty would lead to mass violence, with citizens in states across the union fighting in scattered conflicts while the federal government refused to intervene. He argued further that the Declaration of Independence, and the "natural rights" to life, liberty, and the pursuit of happiness described in that document, must apply equally to men of all races and that slavery violated this fundamental tenet of American society.

Lincoln denounced the Dred Scott decision as a conspiracy to extend the institution of slavery. Portrait of Dred Scott by Louis Schultze, via Wikimedia.

Though he drew significant attention and became the most famous Republican of the era, Lincoln lost the Senate race to Douglas. Over the ensuing months, Lincoln laid the groundwork for a presidential bid. Though he did not waiver from his absolutist opposition to slavery as a legal institution, Lincoln did not believe that African Americans should be afforded equal rights. He appealed to others who opposed slavery as a political force but might not have supported someone who advocated for full equality. By avoiding the stance of the radical abolitionists, Lincoln marketed himself as almost a moderate, though one committed to ending slavery.

With the Democratic Party in a state of near collapse, pro-slavery advocates did their best to drum up racist sentiment and fear. Drawings of Lincoln surrounded by overtly racist depictions of black people circulated through the pro-slavery press, and journalists and pundits threatened the public with incredible doomsday claims. [4]

In the lead-up to the 1860 election, the Democratic Party was divided. One faction backed Stephen Douglas, who favored a more moderate approach, while a new faction of absolutist Southern Democrats backed John Breckenridge, who supported expanding slavery into all the states. The situation was complicated further by a new third party, known as the Constitutional Union Party, which had no real platform but favored returning to the status quo, in which slavery remained legal but was prohibited from expanding into free states. With the nation divided and four large-scale parties at play, Lincoln led the Republicans to a qualified victory, earning 1,865,908 votes, making him the overall winner of popular votes. However, Douglas earned 1,380,202, and the Southern Democrats earned an 848,019 for Breckenridge, which indicates that Democratic unity might have prevented the Republican victory. The outsider Constitutional Union Party, which nominated John Bell, carried 590,901 votes, which reduced support for both Douglas and Breckinridge. The election

of 1860 saw 81.8 percent of eligible voters heading to the polls, making it the most popular public election in U.S. history.[5]

The Uncivil War

In February of 1861 seven states—South Carolina, Mississippi, Florida, Alabama, Georgia, Louisiana, and Texas—passed resolutions calling for secession from the Union. They formed the Confederate States of America (CSA), adopting a constitution that prohibited any law that limited or banned slavery, and elected Mississippi white supremacist Jefferson Davis as their president. The Civil War began on April 12, 1861, when Confederates opened fire on Fort Sumter in South Carolina, which was claimed by Union troops but within the territory claimed by the CSA. This forced Lincoln to commit to the war when he'd barely taken office. On April 15, Lincoln called for 75,000 volunteers to serve in the U.S. Army. As Union troops and ships engaged the South at Fort Sumter, the Civil War had officially begun.

The events of the subsequent five years are among the most widely analyzed in American history. Nearly 5 million Americans served as soldiers, and hundreds of thousands were killed, making the Civil War the deadliest and most devastating conflict in American history. For many years, the official death toll for the war was typically listed at around 618,000—360,000 from the North and 258,000 from the South—but more recent analysis by historian David Hacker indicates that the number was likely closer to 750,000. Hacker told the *New York Times,* "wars have profound economic, demographic and social costs. We're seeing at least 37,000 more widows here, and 90,000 more orphans. That's a profound social impact."[6]

Lincoln has been described as having invented the idea of "emergency powers" or "presidential war powers" used by subsequent presidents during times of crisis to assume powers beyond those in the Constitution. The Civil War called for a new interpretation of authority, as there was no

constitutional precedent depicting executive, judicial, or legislative power in the case of a civil war.

Southerners viewed Lincoln's presidency as unconstitutional. He had no popular mandate, having received less than 50 percent of the popular vote total, and his election was viewed as an attempt by congressional opponents of slavery to override the constitutional protections of property. Writing in the *Journal of the Abraham Lincoln Association*, scholar Herman Belz says:

> *What was to be done to contain the explosive situation? Where in the system of countervailing powers were responsible officers to be found capable of ordering the fragmented country to the end of preserving the Constitution and the Union? Discussion of the right of state secession as a theoretical issue was no longer in point. As a practical matter, the secession ordinances and the seizure of federal property that accompanied them plunged the country into a pre-constitutional condition of interstate anarchy. For the nation to survive, reconstruction of the Union was a constitutional imperative.*[7]

Lincoln first redefined presidential authority by calling for volunteers in the attack on Fort Sumter when Congress was not in session, declaring war without congressional authority. This violated the Constitutional division of powers, which provides Congress alone with the ability to declare war. Lincoln's declaration of war was later justified as a necessary emergency action, though supporters of the CSA would accuse him of unconstitutional action. Lincoln's statement to Congress on July 4, 1861, explained his actions:

MESSAGE TO CONGRESS
Abraham Lincoln
July 4, 1861
Source Document Excerpt

Fellow-Citizens of the Senate and House of Representatives:

Having been convened on an extraordinary occasion, as authorized by the Constitution, your attention is not called to any ordinary subject of legislation.

At the beginning of the present Presidential term, four months ago, the functions of the Federal Government were found to be generally suspended within the several States of South Carolina, Georgia, Alabama, Mississippi, Louisiana, and Florida, excepting only those of the Post-Office Department.

. . .

The forts remaining in the possession of the Federal Government in and near these States were either besieged or menaced by warlike preparations, and especially Fort Sumter was nearly surrounded by well-protected hostile batteries, with guns equal in quality to the best of its own and outnumbering the latter as perhaps ten to one. A disproportionate share of the Federal muskets and rifles had somehow found their way into these States, and had been seized to be used against the Government. Accumulations of the public revenue lying within them had been seized for the same object. The Navy was scattered in distant seas, leaving but a very small part of it within the immediate reach of the Government. Officers of the Federal Army and Navy had resigned in great numbers, and of those resigning a large proportion had taken up arms against the Government. Simultaneously and in connection with all this the purpose to sever the Federal Union was openly avowed. In accordance with this purpose, an ordinance had been adopted in each of these States declaring the States respectively to be separated from the National Union. A formula for instituting a combined government of these States had been promulgated, and this illegal organization, in the character of Confederate States, was already invoking recognition, aid, and intervention from foreign powers.

Finding this condition of things and believing it to be an imperative duty upon the incoming Executive to prevent, if possible, the consummation of such attempt to destroy the Federal Union, a choice of means to that end became indispensable. This choice was made, and was declared in the inaugural address. The policy chosen looked to the exhaustion of all peaceful measures before a resort to any

continued

stronger ones. It sought only to hold the public places and property not already wrested from the Government and to collect the revenue, relying for the rest on time, discussion, and the ballot box. It promised a continuance of the mails at Government expense to the very people who were resisting the Government, and it gave repeated pledges against any disturbance to any of the people or any of their rights. Of all that which a President might constitutionally and justifiably do in such a case, everything was forborne without which it was believed possible to keep the Government on foot.

On the 5th of March, the present incumbent's first full day in office, a letter of Major Anderson, commanding at Fort Sumter, written on the 28th of February and received at the War Department on the 4th of March, was by that Department placed in his hands. This letter expressed the professional opinion of the writer that reenforcements could not be thrown into that fort within the time for his relief rendered necessary by the limited supply of provisions, and with a view of holding possession of the same, with a force of less than 20,000 good and well-disciplined men. This opinion was concurred in by all the officers of his command, and their memoranda on the subject were made inclosures of Major Anderson's letter. The whole was immediately laid before Lieutenant-General Scott, who at once concurred with Major Anderson in opinion. On reflection, however, he took full time, consulting with other officers, both of the Army and the Navy, and at the end of four days came reluctantly, but decidedly, to the same conclusion as before. He also stated at the same time that no such sufficient force was then at the control of the Government or could be raised and brought to the ground within the time when the provisions in the fort would be exhausted. In a purely military point of view this reduced the duty of the Administration in the case to the mere matter of getting the garrison safely out of the fort.

It was believed, however, that to so abandon that position under the circumstances would be utterly ruinous; that the necessity under which it was to be done would not be fully understood; that by many it would be construed as a part of a voluntary policy; that at home it would discourage the friends of the Union, embolden its adversaries, and go far to insure to the latter a recognition abroad; that, in fact, it would be our national destruction consummated. This could not be allowed. Starvation was not yet upon the garrison, and ere it would be reached Fort Pickens might be reenforced. This last would be a clear indication of policy, and would better enable the country to accept the evacuation of Fort Sumter as a

Message to Congress
continued

military necessity. An order was at once directed to be sent for the landing of the troops from the steamship Brooklyn into Fort Pickens. This order could not go by land, but must take the longer and slower route by sea. The first return news from the order was received just one week before the fall of Fort Sumter. The news itself was that the officer commanding the Sabine, to which vessel the troops had been transferred from the Brooklyn, acting upon some quasi armistice of the late Administration (and of the existence of which the present Administration, up to the time the order was dispatched, had only too vague and uncertain rumors to fix attention), had refused to land the troops. To now reenforce Fort Pickens before a crisis would be reached at Fort Sumter was impossible, rendered so by the near exhaustion of provisions in the latter-named fort. In precaution against such a conjuncture the Government had a few days before commenced preparing an expedition, as well adapted as might be, to relieve Fort Sumter, which expedition was intended to be ultimately used or not, according to circumstances. The strongest anticipated case for using it was now presented, and it was resolved to send it forward. As had been intended in this contingency, it was also resolved to notify the governor of South Carolina that he might expect an attempt would be made to provision the fort, and that if the attempt should not be resisted there would be no effort to throw in men, arms, or ammunition without further notice, or in case of an attack upon the fort. This notice was accordingly given, whereupon the fort was attacked and bombarded to its fall, without even awaiting the arrival of the provisioning expedition.

. . .

So viewing the issue, no choice was left but to call out the war power of the Government and so to resist force employed for its destruction by force for its preservation. . .

The Constitution provides, and all the States have accepted the provision, that "the United States shall guarantee to every State in this Union a republican form of government." But if a State may lawfully go out of the Union, having done so it may also discard the republican form of government; so that to prevent its going out is an indispensable means to the end of maintaining the guaranty mentioned; and when an end is lawful and obligatory the indispensable means to it are also lawful and obligatory.

It was with the deepest regret that the Executive found the duty of employing the war power in defense of the Government forced upon him. He could but perform this duty

continued

or surrender the existence of the Government. No compromise by public servants could in this case be a cure; not that compromises are not often proper, but that no popular government can long survive a marked precedent that those who carry an election can only save the government from immediate destruction by giving up the main point upon which the people gave the election. The people themselves, and not their servants, can safely reverse their own deliberate decisions.

. . .

And having thus chosen our course, without guile and with pure purpose, let us renew our trust in God and go forward without fear and with manly hearts.[8]

Clearly, Lincoln did not take this decision lightly but felt that the secession crisis required an emergency decision, which he justified by his presidential oath.

The next challenge to Lincoln's leadership came from Chief Justice Roger B. Taney, who took issue with Lincoln's decision to declare martial law and to suspend the right of habeas corpus in areas captured by Union forces. Habeas corpus, one of the oldest principles of egalitarian law, means that any individual has the right to challenge being arrested or detained and can ask for independent arbitration through a court or officer of the courts. The principle of *habeas corpus* was enshrined in the U.S. Constitution which states, "the Privilege of the Writ of Habeas Corpus shall not be suspended, unless when in Cases of Rebellion or Invasion the public Safety may require it."

Lincoln ordered General Winfield Scott to suspend habeas corpus when arresting individuals near railroads connecting Philadelphia to Washington, out of fear that soldiers entering from Maryland might use the railroads to threaten Washington. A lawyer for one of those individuals, Taney then issued a written rebuke of Lincoln's actions, arguing that the

Constitution authorized Congress, and not the president, to suspend habeas corpus in times of emergency:

THE MERRYMAN CASE
Decision of Chief Justice Taney
June 4, 1861
Source Document Excerpt

"The clause in the Constitution which authorizes the suspension of the privilege of the writ of habeas corpus is in the ninth section of the first article. This article is devoted to the Legislative Department of the United States, and has not the slightest reference to the Executive Department. . . It is the second article of the Constitution that provides for the organization of the Executive Department, and enumerates the powers conferred on it, and prescribes its duties. And if the high power over the liberty of the citizens, now claimed, was intended to be conferred on the President, it would, undoubtedly, be found in plain words in this article. But there is not a word in it that can furnish the slightest ground to justify the exercise of the power.

. . .

With such provisions in the Constitution, expressed in language too clear to be misunderstood by any one, I can see no ground whatever for supposing that the President, in any emergency or in any state of things, can authorize the suspension of the privileges of the writ of *habeas corpus*, or arrest a citizen, except in aid of the judicial power. He certainly does not faithfully execute the laws if the takes upon himself legislative power by suspending the writ of *habeas corpus*, and the judicial power also, by arresting and imprisoning a person without due process of law."[9]

Lincoln did not respond immediately to Taney's decision, but waited to do so by addressing Congress. His famous defense is used to justify extraordinary powers during war time.

MESSAGE TO CONGRESS

Abraham Lincoln

July 4, 1861

Source Document Excerpt

Soon after the first call for militia, I felt it my duty to authorize the Commanding General, in proper cases, according to his discretion, to suspend the previlege of the writ of habeas corpus—or, in other words, to arrest, and detain, without resort to the ordinary processes and forms of law, such individuals as he might deem dangerous to the public safety. At my verbal request, as well as by the Generals own inclination, this authority has been exercised but very sparingly—Nevertheless, the legality and propriety of what has been done under it, are questioned; and I have been reminded from a high quarter that one who is sworn to "take care that the laws be faithfully executed" should not himself be one to violate them—So I think. Of course I gave some consideration to the questions of power, and propriety, before I acted in this matter—

The whole of the laws which I was sworn to see take care that they should be faithfully executed, were being resisted, and failing of execution to be executed, in nearly one third of the states. Must I have allowed them to finally fail of execution, even had it been perfectly clear that by the use of the means necessary to their execution, some provision of one single law, made

in such extreme tenderness of the citizens liberty, that more rogues than honest men practically more of the guilty than the innocent, find shelter under it, should, to a very limited extent, be violated? some single law, made in such extreme tenderness of the citizens liberty, that practically, it relieves more of the guilty, than the innocent, should, to a very limited extent, be violated? To state the question more directly, are all the laws, but one, to go unexecuted, and the government itself go to pieces, lest that one law be violated? Even in such a case I should consider my official oath broken if I should allow the government to be overthrown, when I might think the disregarding the single law would tend to preserve it—But, in this case I was not, in my own judgment, driven to this ground— In my opinion I violated no law—The provision of the Constitution that "The previlege of the writ of habeas corpus, shall not be suspended unless when, in cases of rebellion or invasion, the public safety may require it" is equivalent to a provision—is a provision—that such previlege may be suspended when, in cases of rebellion, or invasion, the public safety does require it. I decided that we have a case of rebellion, and that the public safety does require the qualified

Message to Congress
continued

suspension of the previlege of the writ of habeas corpus, which I authorized to be made. Now it is insisted that Congress, and not the executive, is vested with this power—But the Constitution itself, is silent as to which, or who, is to exercise the power; and as the provision plainly was made for a dangerous emergency, I can not bring myself to believe that the framers of that instrument intended that in every case the danger should run course until Congress could be called together, the very assembling of which

~~might be prevented, and in as was in~~ of which might be prevented, as was intended in this case, by the rebellion—

I enter upon no more extended argument; as an opinion, at some length, will be presented by the Attorney General—

Whether there shall be any legislation upon the subject, and if any, what, I submit entirely to the better judgment of Congress.[10]

In 1863, Congress authorized Lincoln to suspend habeas corpus whenever he felt necessary for the remainder of the conflict. Whether Lincoln was justified in assuming Congressional power when he first ordered habeas corpus to be suspended is still a matter of considerable constitutional debate. Strict constitutional interpretation seems to suggest that Lincoln's actions violated separation of powers, though the extreme nature of the Civil War calls into question traditional interpretations.[11]

Lincoln's next controversial move regarding expanding executive power was in issuing the Emancipation Proclamation—an executive order emancipating all slaves currently held in the Confederate states. Further, it provided a grand purpose for the Union campaign, authorizing the military to free enslaved persons whenever they arrived.[12]

The Emancipation Proclamation at the National Underground Railroad Freedom Center.
Engraving by W. Roberts, Library of Congress Prints and Photographs Division, via Wikimedia.

The Emancipation Proclamation has been cherished as an expression of the Union's commitment to equal rights and equality but was also a political strategy and weapon against the Confederacy. It did not apply to slaves in the "border states" that had not yet seceded from the Union, but only to states that had already seceded. Thus, it was meant as a punishment to Confederate states and a warning to the border states. Lincoln hoped that the Emancipation Proclamation would encourage more slaves to leave the South seeking their freedom, and he declared that the Union Army would begin to enlist black men as regular soldiers and would welcome any escaped slave who made it to Union territory. Tens of thousands fled to the North, and more than 180,000 black soldiers, former slaves and freemen, fought for the Union. The loss of labor weakened the South, and the addition of volunteer soldiers bolstered the North.

The Emancipation Proclamation was also a shrewd tactic in terms of foreign relations. Britain and France had been trading partners of the United States for many years, despite the United States allowing legal slavery while both France and Britain had outlawed slavery years before. French and British ministers met with leaders of the CSA, presenting the possibility that they might recognize the Confederacy. By issuing the Emancipation Proclamation, Lincoln framed the battle as a struggle between forces seeking to keep slaves and those fighting to abolish it, causing France and Britain, where public and political sentiment opposed slavery, to abandon recognition of the Confederacy and reaffirm their alliance with the Union.

Lincoln justified the emancipation of slaves in the Confederate states as an expression of his Congressionally approved war powers, but he was uncertain whether or not the states would find his order unconstitutional. He further worried that the courts might find the proclamation violated constitutional rights to property without due process. When Lincoln approached the 1864 campaign, therefore, he promoted a new strategy to

legitimize the proclamation, calling on Congress to pass an amendment outlawing slavery everywhere in America. Lincoln used all of his influence to promote this measure to Congress, who put the amendment to the states for ratification in January of 1865; the states ratified it that December.

The Emancipation Proclamation was undoubtedly a military tactic, but it fundamentally changed the nature of the war. From the moment that Lincoln issued this executive order, the march of the Union Army became one of liberation. As they approached towns and villages, slaves revolted and left their homes to join the advancing army. African Americans began to view the Union forces as heroic liberators. The Emancipation Proclamation provided a fundamental moral grounding for the war that drew support from beyond America's borders and depicted the war as among the great struggles for equality against the forces of evil and oppression. In issuing the Emancipation Proclamation, Lincoln claimed powers beyond what the Constitution grants, even during a time of emergency. Lincoln recognized this, and promoted the Thirteenth Amendment to legitimize his actions; he called on the Union and Congress to amend the Constitution to prohibit slavery forever.

The Power of the War-Time President

Lincoln's actions that can be classified as an overreach of presidential authority expanded the powers of the office, thereby establishing precedent that other presidents have exploited. Lincoln declared martial law, usurped the powers of Congress in issuing the Emancipation Proclamation and in declaring war, and ignored the authority of the judiciary and their constitutionally mandated role to limit presidential power. While not an empirical defense of these actions, the extraordinary circumstances of the Civil War made it difficult for the government to operate within the standards of constitutional law, and those same constitutional restraints may have made it near impossible for Lincoln to respond effectively to the threat of Southern secession.

Following the war, former Confederates and Confederate sympathizers have viewed Lincoln and the Civil War as the tyrannical actions of an oppressive government, arguing that Lincoln and the Union violated the spirit of the Constitution in using the military to prohibit states from voluntarily leaving the union or enforcing a legislative ban against slavery. Prior to the Thirteenth Amendment, which prohibits slavery at the Constitutional level, scholars had precedent for the position that the Constitution did not empower Congress, or the president, to decide for the states on the issue of slavery, no matter how abhorrent some might view it.

It is also true that America's favorite president was a flawed man who harbored many of the same prejudices that allowed slavery to endure for millennia. Some claim that the Emancipation Proclamation was a political stunt and military tactic, rather than the profound statement on American egalitarianism it has become. Many of Lincoln's most perceptively heroic accomplishments were undertaken for practical reasons and only partially reflected his own commitment to the natural rights of humankind. Whatever the criticisms levied at Lincoln and the Civil War, however, it is true that prior to the Civil War, humans were kept in bondage, bred, and sold as property. Women were raped, and children sold like livestock. Men and women were beaten and subjected to any number of horrors. Slavery was perhaps as close to empirical evil as it is possible to come. Whatever methods were used to end it, and whatever faults of the men and women who saw this through, for millions of Americans the Civil War was a just and righteous struggle in U.S. history.

CONCLUSION

Abraham Lincoln helped to redefine the "emergency powers" of the war-time presidency. The exception of national emergency was frequently used, after the fact, to excuse Lincoln's actions that violated presidential authority. Despite the argument that, in his case, the ends justified the means, there is little doubt that Lincoln greatly exceeded his constitutional authority in not only waging war against the seceding states, but in other ways as well. Lincoln did, for his part, attempt to balance his military aims with the traditional powers of his office, by consulting with Congress and seeking consensus on his extraordinary use of the military. Though there were no opinion polls to document public opinion on his presidency, it is likely that Lincoln's popularity was below 50 percent during his time in office. In the South, he was portrayed as a tyrant unleashing unbridled African American revenge on the white population. In the North, he was often blamed for leading the nation into a desperate, bloody war. For America's African Americans, however, it is difficult to argue against Lincoln's war. Whatever constitutional violations occurred, and however many died in defense of slavery, the southern slave industry was among the greatest evils in world history and its destruction is viewed by many as one of the proudest moments in American history. The next chapter shows a polar opposite president in the unpopular Andrew Johnson, the first to be impeached in American history.

DISCUSSION QUESTIONS

- ♦ How did Lincoln violate the separation of powers in suspending the Writ of Habeas Corpus?
- ♦ Should Confederate troops and leaders be celebrated as patriots? Why or why not?
- ♦ Why did the Emancipation Proclamation only free slaves in the southern states, instead of freeing them across the country?
- ♦ What did Lincoln consider the "political religion" of America? Did he uphold this belief during the Civil War? How or how not?
- ♦ How did pro-slavery politicians make it difficult to fight against slavery through state law?

Works Used

Belz, Herman. "Lincoln's Construction of the Executive Power in the Secession Crisis." *Journal of the Abraham Lincoln Association.* vol. 27, no. 1, Winter 2006. pp. 13–38. *JSTOR*, www.jstor.org/stable/20149090.

Bomboy, Scott. "Lincoln and Taney's Great Writ Showdown." *National Constitution Center.* Constitution Daily. 28 May 2019. constitutioncenter. org/blog/lincoln-and-taneys-great-writ-showdown.

Cummings, William. "Survey of Scholars Places Trump as Third Worst President of All Time." *USA Today.* 13 Feb. 2019. www.usatoday.com/ story/news/politics/onpolitics/2019/02/13/siena-presidential-ranking-survey/2857075002/.

Gugliotta, Guy. "New Estimate Raises Civil War Death Toll." *New York Times.* 2 Apr. 2012. www.nytimes.com/2012/04/03/science/civil-war-toll-up-by-20-percent-in-new-estimate.html.

Lincoln, Abraham. "Emancipation Proclamation." *Our Documents.* National Archives. 2018. www.ourdocuments.gov/doc. php?flash=false&doc=34&page=transcript.

_____. "House Divided Speech, June 16, 1858" *Abraham Lincoln Online*. 2018. www.abrahamlincolnonline.org/lincoln/speeches/house.htm.

_____. "Lincoln's Response to Congress, July 4, 1861." *Gilder Lehrman*. Gilder Lehrman Institute of American History. 2012. www.gilderlehrman. org/sites/default/files/inline-pdfs/Lincoln%20Response.pdf.

_____. "Lyceum Address." *Abraham Lincoln Online*. 2018. www. abrahamlincolnonline.org/lincoln/speeches/lyceum.htm.

_____. "Message to Congress in Special Session, July 4, 1861 *Miller Center*. U of Virginia. millercenter.org/the-presidency/presidential-speeches/july-4-1861-july-4th-message-congress.

McPherson, James M. *Battle Cry of Freedom: The Civil War Era*. New York: Oxford U P, 1988.

Murphy, Justin D., editor. *American Civil War: Interpreting Conflict through Primary Documents*. Santa Monica, CA: ABC–CLIO. 24 June 2019.

Novkov, Julie. *The Supreme Court and the Presidency: Struggles for Supremacy*. Washington D.C.: Sage P, 2013.

"Presidential Election of 1860: A Resource Guide." *LOC*. Library of Congress. 23 Oct. 2018. www.loc.gov/rr/program/bib/elections/election1860.html.

Introduction

Andrew Johnson is certainly one of the least respected presidents in history. He is remembered primarily as the first president to be impeached and as the man who failed to follow in Lincoln's large, popular footsteps. Johnson attempted to chart his own path for Reconstruction, the process by which southern states would be brought back into the Union. In doing so, he usurped congressional power. His attempt to consolidate a political base was also foolishly construed, trusting too much in the power of white supremacism and underestimating the popular appeal of abolition.

We the People

Topics covered in this chapter include:
- Reconstruction
- The assassination of Abraham Lincoln
- The Freedman's Bureau
- Tenure of Office Act
- The Command of the Army Act
- Impeachment

This Chapter Discusses the Following Source Documents:

Mr. Johnson's Views and His Anxiety to Save the Union

Speech to the Citizens of Washington, Andrew Johnson, February 22, 1866

State of the Union, Andrew Johnson, December 3, 1867

Articles of Impeachment, Article X, 1868

Reconstruction Halted
Andrew Johnson (1865–1869)

On April 14, 1865, six days after General Robert E. Lee surrendered to Union forces, marking the end of the Civil War, President Abraham Lincoln was assassinated at Ford's Theatre by John Wilkes Booth, a former member of Confederate militia the Richmond Grays. Angered by the Union's warrantless arrests of secession supporters in Maryland, Booth planned to kidnap Lincoln and trade him for southern prisoners of war. After the Confederacy surrendered, however, Booth decided to assassinate Lincoln and other high-ranking government figures. After shooting Lincoln, Booth yelled "Sic semper tyrannis" ("thus ever to tyrants") and fled the scene. After a 12-day manhunt, Booth was found hiding on a Virginia farm and was killed.[1]

At approximately the same time that Booth shot Lincoln, accomplice Lewis Powell attacked Secretary of State William Henry Seward at his Lafayette Square home, slashing Seward's throat twice but failing to kill him. George Atzerodt had been tasked with killing Vice President Andrew Johnson but lost his nerve, while David Herold aided Booth's escape from Ford's theater. The fourth co-conspirator was Mary Surratt, who owned the boarding house where the attacks were planned. The case was controversial. Vice President Andrew Johnson refused to grant clemency, however, making Surratt the first woman executed by the federal government. The four co-conspirators were all found guilty of "treasonable conspiracy" and sentenced to death by hanging.[2]

Lincoln's death left the presidency to Vice President Andrew Johnson, a Jacksonian Democrat and strong proponent of states' rights, who was judged a poor successor to Lincoln. Johnson's controversial behavior and pro-slavery policies resulted in one of the most contentious presidencies in American history.

Climbing to the Top

Andrew Johnson was born in Raleigh, North Carolina, in 1808, into a poor family. Parents, Jacob and Mary were illiterate, and the family scraped by. Johnson's father died when he was around three, after which his mother worked as a weaver to support Andrew and his older brother William. Struggling, Mary apprenticed her sons to local tailor James Selby. After several years Andrew and William ran away, and Selby put out a ransom for their arrest. Andrew tried to purchase his freedom from Selby, but they could not come to terms. To escape arrest, Andrew fled to Greeneville, Tennessee, where, at 17, he set up his own tailor shop. In Greeneville, he met an educated young woman named Eliza McCardle who took an interest in him, teaching him to read and write. They were married in 1827, when McCardle had just turned 16.[3]

Andrew Johnson, by Mathew Brady, Library of Congress Prints and Photographs Division, via Wikimedia.

In 1829, Johnson was elected as alderman. His progression from Greenville alderman to the presidency, showed him to be one of the most politically qualified candidates in history. Johnson served two terms in the state legislature beginning in 1834. In 1840, he was elected to the state senate, and two years later he was elected to the U.S. House of Representatives, where he sat from 1843 to 1853. From 1853 to 1857 he served as governor of Tennessee. At the outbreak of the Civil War, Johnson was unanimously chosen by the state legislature to represent Tennessee in the U.S. Senate. After the war, Lincoln picked him as military governor of Tennessee, and then as his second-term vice president as a conciliatory measure to the South. When Johnson assumed the presidency, he had held office at every level of state and federal government.[4]

Divergent Jacksonian

Being from Tennessee, Johnson could hardly have avoided the influence of Andrew Jackson, the state's favorite son. The Tennessee government emulated Jackson's philosophy, as did Johnson. He opposed national improvements or federal intervention in the economy, supported the expansionist efforts that led to the annexation of Texas, Oregon, California, and New Mexico, and remained sharply aligned with the Jacksonians.

However, there were differences. While Jackson became an elitist, Johnson grew up resenting these people and the way that they used their wealth to disadvantage the poor. Coming from the destitute upland region, Johnson fought against measures that would have benefitted the wealthy, becoming popular with working-class laborers and Catholics and the Irish.

While Johnson fought for the rights of poor white families, and non-Protestant immigrants, he was a slave owner and believed that ownership of slaves was protected by private property laws. He supported the Kansas-Nebraska Act and the Fugitive Slave Law of 1850 and aligned with the pro-slavery section of the Democratic Party. During the Civil War most

southern Democrats supported secession, but Johnson foresaw that secession would lead to control by the elite southern planting aristocracy. He criticized secession and made an unusual argument—that the Union needed to be preserved in order to protect the institution of slavery.

MR. JOHNSON'S VIEWS AND HIS ANXIETY TO SAVE THE UNION
Andrew Johnson
Source Document Excerpt

"What protection would it be to us to dissolve this Union? What protection would it be to us to convert this nation into two hostile powers, the one waring with the other? Whose property is at stake? Whose interest in endangered? Is it not the property of the border states? Suppose Canada were moved down upon our border, and the two separated section, then different nations, were hostile: what would the institution of slavery be worth on the border? Every man who has common sense will see that the institution would take up its march and retreat, as certainly and as unerringly as general laws can operate. Yes, it would commence to retreat the very moment this Government was converted into hostile powers, and you made the line between the slaveholding and non-slaveholding States the line of division."

"Then, what remedy do we get for the institution of slavery? Must we keep up a standing army? Must we keep up forts bristling with arms along the whole border? This is a question to be considered, one that involves the future; and no step should be taken without mature reflection. Before this Union is dissolved and broken up, we in Tennessee, as one of the slave States, want to be consulted; we want to know what protection we are to have; whether we are simply to be made outposts and guards to protect the property of others, at the same time that we sacrifice and lose our own. We want to understand this question."

. . .

"Here, in the centre of the Republic, is the seat of Government, which was founded by Washington, and bears his immortal name. Who dare appropriate it exclusively? It is within the borders of the States I have enumerated, in whose limits are found the graves of Washington, of Jackson, of Polk, of Clay. From them is it supposed that we will be torn away? No, sir; we will cherish these endearing associations with the hope, if this Republic shall be broken, that we may speak words of peace and

Mr. Johnson's Views and His Anxiety to Save the Union continued

reconciliation to a distracted, a divided, I may add, a maddened people. Angry waves may be lashed into fury on the one hand; on the other blustering winds may rage; but we stand immovable upon our basis, as on our own native mountains—presenting their craggy brows, their unexplored caverns, their summits 'rock-ribbed and as ancient as the sun'—we stand speaking peace, association, and concert, to a distracted Republic.[5]

Johnson argued that abandoning the Union would not save slavery because the resulting power vacuum and unstable state relations would destroy society. His hostility toward the southern aristocracy is clear, as is his distrust of their leadership. Johnson saw secession as cultural suicide, especially for states like Tennessee, which would become border states between the South and what was left of the Union.

Johnson's approach to Lincoln's authority was also unusual. Many Southerners contended that Lincoln was illegitimate because he had not won the popular vote. Johnson, who believed in the Constitution and the rule of law, argued that Lincoln had won more Electoral College votes than the other candidates combined. Though Johnson was a proponent of eliminating or altering the Electoral College to better reflect the popular vote, he nevertheless reasoned that under current law Lincoln had undoubtedly won the presidency.

Johnson was the only southern Senator who did not resign his seat in the U.S. Senate upon Lincoln's election. When Tennessee seceded from the Union, he was trapped in Washington and unable to return home. Effigies of Johnson were burned by angry mobs, his wife and children were driven from the state, and his home and property confiscated. While Southern leadership depicted him as a coward, in the North he was a hero. He was celebrated for his honesty and dedication to the Constitution, even honored by radical Republicans for risking his family's safety and his property for his beliefs.

When Tennessee was retaken, Lincoln appointed Johnson as military governor; Johnson arrested anti-Union journalists, agitators, and even members of the clergy, often without due process or trial. He removed all officers who would not publicly declare their opposition to secession and issued punitive taxes on the wealthy to pay for Reconstruction. When Lincoln issued the Emancipation Proclamation, Tennessee was under Union control. Johnson convinced Lincoln to exempt Tennessee from the immediate emancipation of slaves and spent his time promoting the voluntary release of slaves by all slave owners in the state, freeing his own slaves in 1863.

Approaching the 1864 election, Lincoln convinced Republican delegates to nominate Johnson to replace Hannibal Hamlin as his vice president to repair relations between the North and the South. Johnson gave Lincoln appeal among Catholic, Irish, and poor voters, and, though a Democrat, Johnson had become one of Lincoln's most ardent supporters. He not only supported the Emancipation Proclamation, but believed that the defeat of the Confederacy needed to be total and their fault needed to be acknowledged. When General William Sherman captured Atlanta in September, just before the election, Republicans united behind Lincoln and the swell of popular support followed. Lincoln won 2.2 million popular votes compared with 1.8 for Democratic candidate George B. McClellan, a Civil War general dismissed by Lincoln for failing to aggressively engage Southern forces. With 212 electoral votes to 21 for McClellan, Lincoln's victory was decisive.

1864 poster for the Lincoln and Johnson ticket, by Currier and Ives, Library of Congress Prints and Photographs Division, via Wikimedia.

In 1864, Johnson gave a speech regarding his candidacy for vice president, making his stance on slavery clear:

SPEECH TO THE CITIZENS OF WASHINGTON

Andrew Johnson
February 22, 1866
Source Document Excerpt

There was another portion of our countrymen who were opposed to this peculiar institution in the South, and who went to the extreme of being willing to break up the Government to get clear of it. (Applause.) I am talking to you to-day in the common phrase, and assume to be nothing but a citizen, and one who has been fighting for the Constitution and to preserve the Government. These two parties have been arrayed against each other; and I stand before you to-day, as I did in the Senate in 1860, in the presence of those who were making war on the Constitution, and who wanted to disrupt the Government, to denounce, as I then did in my place, those who were so engaged, as traitors. I have never ceased to repeat, and so far as my efforts could go, to carry out, the sentiments I then uttered. (Cheers.) I have already remarked that there were two parties, one for destroying the Government to preserve slavery, and the other to break up the Government to destroy slavery. The objects to be accomplished were different, it is true, so far as slavery is concerned, but they agreed in one thing, and that was the breaking up of the Government. They agreed in the destruction of the Government, the precise thing which I have stood up to oppose. *Whether the disunionists come from South Carolina or the North I stand now where I did then*, to vindicate the Union of these States and the Constitution of the country. (Applause.)

The rebellion or treason manifested itself in the South. I stood by the Government. I said I was for the Union with slavery, or I was for the Union without slavery. In either alternative, I was for my Government and the Constitution. (Applause.)

. . .

When I reached Washington for the purpose of being inaugurated as Vice-President of the United States I had a conversation with Mr. Lincoln. We were talking about the condition of affairs and in reference to matters in my own State. I said that we had called a convention, had amended our

Speech to the Citizens of Washington
continued

Constitution by abolishing slavery in the State a State not embraced in his proclamation. All this met his approbation and gave him encouragement, and in talking upon the amendment to the Constitution, he said: "When the amendment to the Constitution is adopted by three-fourths of the States, we shall have all, or pretty nearly all. I am in favor of amending the Constitution, if there was one other adopted." Said I, "What is that, Mr. President?" Said he, "I have labored to preserve this Union. I have toiled four years; I have been subjected to calumny and misrepresentation, yet my great desire has been to preserve the Union of these States intact under the Constitution as they were before." "But," said I, "Mr. President, what amendment do you refer to?" He said he thought there should be an amendment to the Constitution which would compel all the States to send their Senators and Representatives to the Congress of the United States. Yes, compel them. The idea was in his mind that it was a part of the doctrine of secession to break up the Government by States withdrawing their Senators and Representatives from Congress; and, therefore, he desired a Constitutional amendment to compel them to be sent.

How now does the matter stand? In the Constitution of the country, even that portion of it which provides for the amendment of the organic law, says that no State shall, without its consent, be deprived of its representation in the Senate. And now what do we find? We find the position taken that States shall not be represented; that we may impose taxes; that we may send our tax-gatherers to every region and portion of a State; that the people are to be oppressed with taxes; but when they come here to participate in legislation of the country, they are met at the door, and told, "No! you must pay your taxes; you must bear the burdens of the Government; but you must not participate in the legislation of the country, which is to affect you for all time." Is this just? ("No, no.") Then, I say, let us admit into the councils of the nation those who are unmistakably and unequivocally loyal those men who acknowledge their allegiance to the Government and swear to support the Constitution. It is all embraced in that. The amplification of an oath makes no difference, if a man is not loyal. But you may adopt whatever test oath you please to prove their loyalty. Let him be unquestionably loyal, owing his allegiance to the Government and willing to support it in its hour of peril and of need, and I am willing to trust him. I know that some do not attach so much importance to this principle as I do. But one principle we carried through. The Revolution was fought that there should be no taxation

continued

without representation. I hold to that principle, laid down as fundamental by our fathers. If it was good then, it is now. If it was a rule to stand by then, it is a rule to stand by now. It is a fundamental principle that should be adhered to as long as governments last.

. . .

Then, in conclusion, let me ask this vast concourse, this sea of upturned faces, to join with me in standing round the Constitution of our country. It is again unfolded and the people are invited to read, to understand, and to maintain its provisions. Let us stand by the Constitution of our fathers, though the heavens themselves may fall. Let us stand by it, though faction may rage. Though taunts and jeers may come, though vituperation may come in its most violent character, *I will be found standing by the Constitution as the chief rock of our safety*, as the palladium of our civil and religious liberty. Yes, let us cling to it as the mariner clings to his last plank when night and tempest close around him. Accept my thanks for the indulgence you have given me in making the extemporaneous remarks I have upon this occasion. Let us go forward, forgetting the past and looking to the future, and try to restore our country. Trusting in Him who rules on high that ere long our Union will be restored, and that we will have peace, not only on earth, but especially with the people of the United States, and good-will, I thank you, my countrymen, for the spirit you have manifested on this occasion. When your country is gone, and you are about, look out and you will find the humble individual who now stands before you weeping over its final dissolution.[6]

After the election, Lincoln delivered his second inaugural address, considered by many one of the best speeches in American history:

Fellow-Countrymen, at this second appearing to take the oath of the Presidential office there is less occasion for an extended address than there was at the first. Then a statement somewhat in detail of a course to be pursued seemed fitting and proper. Now, at the expiration of four years, during which public declarations have been constantly called forth on every point and phase of the great contest which still absorbs the attention and engrosses the energies of the nation, little that is new could be presented. The progress of our arms, upon which all else chiefly depends, is as well known to the public as to myself, and it is, I trust, reasonably satisfactory and encouraging to all. With high hope for the future, no prediction in regard to it is ventured.

On the occasion corresponding to this four years ago all thoughts were anxiously directed to an impending civil war. All dreaded it, all sought to avert it. While the inaugural address was being delivered from this place, devoted altogether to saving the Union without war, insurgent agents were in the city seeking to destroy it without war—seeking to dissolve the Union and divide effects by negotiation. Both parties deprecated war, but one of them would make war rather than let the nation survive, and the other would accept war rather than let it perish, and the war came.

One-eighth of the whole population were colored slaves, not distributed generally over the Union, but localized in the southern part of it. These slaves constituted a peculiar and powerful interest. All knew that this interest was somehow the cause of the war. To strengthen, perpetuate, and extend this interest was the object for which the insurgents would render the Union even by war, while the Government claimed no right to do more than to restrict the territorial enlargement of it. Neither party expected for the war the magnitude or the duration which it has already attained. Neither anticipated that the cause of the conflict might cease with or even before the conflict itself should cease. Each looked for an easier triumph, and a result less fundamental and astounding. Both read the same Bible and pray to the same God, and each invokes His aid against the other.

It may seem strange that any men should dare to ask a just God's assistance in wringing their bread from the sweat of other men's faces, but let us judge not, that we be not judged. The prayers of both could not be answered. That of neither has been answered fully. The Almighty has His own purposes. "Woe unto the world because of offenses; for it must needs be that offenses come, but woe to that man by whom the offense cometh." If we shall suppose that American slavery is one of those offenses which, in the providence of God, must needs come, but which, having continued through His appointed time, He now wills to remove, and that He gives to both North and South this terrible war as the woe due to those by whom the offense came, shall we discern therein any departure from those divine attributes which the believers in a living God always ascribe to Him? Fondly do we hope, fervently do we pray, that this mighty scourge of war may speedily pass away. Yet, if God wills that it continue until all the wealth piled by the bondsman's two hundred and fifty years of unrequited toil shall be sunk, and until every drop of blood drawn with the lash shall be paid by another drawn with the sword, as was said three thousand years ago, so still it must be said "the judgments of the Lord are true and righteous altogether."

"With malice toward none, with charity for all, with firmness in the right as God gives us to see the right, let us strive on to finish the work we are in, to bind up the nation's wounds, to care for him who shall have borne the battle and for his widow and his orphan, to do all which may achieve and cherish a just and lasting peace among ourselves and with all nations."[a]

Works Used

a. Lincoln, Abraham. "Lincoln's Second Inaugural." *NPS*. National Park Service. 22 May 2015. www.nps. gov/linc/learn/historyculture/lincoln-second-inaugural.htm.

Johnson's debut as the new Vice President was far less memorable. Ill from typhoid fever, Johnson spent the night before his inauguration drinking whiskey with his friend John W. Forney. The next morning, a blustery, rainy, and cold day in Washington, Johnson had more whiskey to fortify himself against the cold. Then, in the crowded Senate Chamber, Johnson rose to give his speech, and was clearly inebriated. His face was flushed, he had trouble standing, and he delivered an angry speech railing against secessionists and touting his own rise from humble origins to take on the planter aristocracy.[7]

According to the press, Lincoln wore an expression of "unutterable sorrow" during Johnson's speech, while other members of Congress could be seen averting their eyes or hanging their heads. Eventually, Johnson was convinced to take the oath of office and stop his speech. When it was time to swear in newly elected Senators, he became so confused that he had to turn the job over to a Senate clerk. Michigan Republican Zachariah Chandler wrote to his wife, "The inauguration went off very well except that the Vice President Elect was too drunk to perform his duties & disgraced himself & the Senate by making a drunken foolish speech. I was never so mortified in my life, had I been able to find a hole I would have dropped through it out of sight." There was talk of impeaching Johnson after his speech, and some interest in a condemnation, but Lincoln reportedly supported Johnson, who went into hiding out of embarrassment for several weeks, saying, "It has been a severe lesson for Andy, but I do not think he will do it again."[8]

An Inauspicious Start

Six weeks after his inauguration as vice president, Johnson became the nation's seventeenth president, entering office without the government's full support. The day prior to his death, Lincoln was presented with a proposal for a "reconstruction program" to rebuild the southern states, questioning how to deal with newly freed slaves, how to punish the Confederacy, and how to guide the restructuring of state laws to reflect the

Thirteenth Amendment. Crafted by the military and by Secretary of War Edwin Stanton, the plan called for a full military occupation of the South. The radical Republican faction, then in control of Congress but needing support from millions of new black voters, favored an absolutist system of black suffrage. Lincoln likely would have been convinced to adopt an aggressive plan, but not Johnson. Falling back on his commitment to states' rights, Johnson believed that the states should simply write clauses to their constitutions prohibiting slavery and swear oaths of allegiance to the restored Union, actions that would allow states to decide how to expand suffrage to African Americans.

Johnson's use of presidential authority was controversial. He instituted his own plan for Reconstruction without Congress, and appointed new governors and ordered them to oversee new drafts of the states' constitutions. Johnson decided that each southerner needed to personally sign an oath of loyalty to receive amnesty, and further ordered that four classes of individuals would not receive automatic pardons, but needed to apply for special presidential pardons: military officers who had occupied leadership roles in the Confederacy; high-ranking Confederate politicians; former federal officials who had supported secession; and any individual who aided the south and had property worth more than $20,000. This last category, again, reflected Johnson's special enmity toward the wealthy. With these relatively liberal requirements, Johnson personally pardoned thousands of former Confederates, including many high-ranking members of the Confederate elite. Historians agree that Johnson's deep-seated racism factored into his lenient handling of the South.

When Congress returned to session, most Republicans declared Johnson's handling of Reconstruction an abuse of his executive power. A new Joint Committee of Reconstruction was created, and Congress voted not to recognize Johnson's decision to readmit the Confederate states or the pardons given to Confederate representatives. In place of Johnson's plan,

Congress instituted a military Reconstruction program that would force the states, under supervision, to recognize the civil rights of their black populations. Johnson, in turn, opposed a bill that extended the Freedmen's Bureau, also known as the Bureau of Refugees, Freemen, and Abandoned Lands, which provided federal assistance to former slaves.

Many of the nearly four million freed slaves, were left homeless and largely stateless, with no possessions. The Freemen's Bureau was all that stood in the way of starvation for many of these families. Through branch offices, the bureau distributed clothing, ran hospitals and homeless camps, helped individuals to locate lost family members, provided basic education, performed legal marriages for freed slaves, offered job opportunities, created and supervised labor contracts between white employers and former slaves, provided legal assistance, investigated racial violence, and worked to secure abandoned territory, which they used to resettle individuals left destitute and homeless by the war. The Freedman's Bureau was an especially important institution for black soldiers who'd served in the Union Army, helping them to secure their pay and pensions.[9] When Congress voted to reauthorize the popular Freedmen's Bureau, Johnson vetoed the bill.[10]

Cartoon of Johnson eliminating the Freedmen's Bureau, by Thomas Nast, via Wikimedia.

Congress and Johnson clashed again over the Civil Rights Act of 1866, which defined all individuals born in the United States (except Native Americans) as citizens who would thereafter be entitled to own property, to make and enter into contracts, to testify in court, and to enjoy full protection of the law and due process. It further made the federal court the arbiter of all civil rights litigation, an important provision considering that racist and partisan southern jurists would, in many cases, have been unlikely to rule fairly in civil rights cases. The Civil Rights Act passed through both houses of Congress, but Johnson again used his veto power to oppose it, arguing that it was a violation of states' rights and sovereignty.

With his aggressive vetoes, Johnson had taken up the mantle of his hero Andrew Jackson, but, unlike Jackson, Johnson was not popular with the public. The Republican-controlled Congress was also able to override his most important vetoes, including the bill to extend the Freemen's Bureau and the Civil Rights Act, the latter being the first time that Congress overrode a presidential veto on an important piece of legislation.

Many Republicans knew that the Supreme Court might later invalidate the Civil Rights Act. The radical Republicans solved this by drafting the Fourteenth Amendment, which guaranteed due process at the constitutional level. Johnson also opposed the Fourteenth Amendment, as did many southern leaders. The 1866 elections did not go well for Johnson, who launched a "swing around the circle" speaking tour promoting his moderate Reconstruction policies; by the time he reached Ohio, things began to fall apart. Johnson began addressing hecklers in the crowd, replying to "hang Jeff Davis," with "Why don't you hang Thad Stevens and Wendell Phillips?" referring to Pennsylvania Representative Thad Stevens, a Republican leader and abolitionist, and Wendell Phillips, a famous abolitionist. Reporters from the *New York Times* and *New York Herald* described Johnson's behavior as "mortifying," and the situation continued to degenerate. His arrival led to a riot in Indianapolis that forced him to cancel his speech and go into hiding.[11] Newspapers claimed that Johnson was sullying the reputation of the office and acting in an unpresidential manner.

Johnson's tour ended with him in far worse political shape than when he began. Hundreds around the country viewed him as a cantankerous ideologue who was failing to finish the job that Lincoln had started. The elections resulted in the Republicans controlling two-thirds of both houses of Congress and with the power to shape Reconstruction. The Joint Committee on Reconstruction passed the Reconstruction Act of 1867, which placed the southern states under martial law. Each state was divided into districts, overseen by congressionally appointed military governors. To rejoin the Union, states needed to submit to federal authority, to ratify the Fourteenth Amendment, and to guarantee voting rights for black males in new state constitutions. Johnson attempted to veto the act but was overridden.

In March of 1867, Congress passed resolutions limiting Johnson's presidential powers. They refused him the power to make military decisions except through General Ulysses S. Grant. They also passed the "Tenure of Office Act," which prohibited the president from removing federal officials without Senate approval. Johnson felt he had been unconstitutionally deprived of authority and accused Congress of "despotism." In his 1867 State of the Union address, Johnson's racism was on full display:

STATE OF THE UNION
Andrew Johnson
December 3, 1867
Source Document Excerpt

The great difference between the two races in physical, mental, and moral characteristics will prevent an amalgamation or fusion of them together in one homogeneous mass. If the inferior obtains the ascendency over the other, it will govern with reference only to its own interests for it will recognize no common interest—and create such a tyranny as this continent has never yet witnessed. Already the Negroes are influenced by promises of confiscation and plunder. They are taught to regard as an enemy every white man who has any respect for the rights of his own race. If this continues it must become worse and worse, until all order will be subverted, all industry cease, and the fertile fields of the South grow up into a wilderness. Of all the dangers which our nation has yet encountered, none are equal to those which must result from the success of the effort now making to Africanize the half of our country.[12]

Johnson had underestimated the level of support for African American suffrage. Blocked by Congress, Johnson challenged their authority by dismissing Secretary of War Edwin Stanton without congressional approval, knowing that this would force Congress to assess whether or not he had violated the Tenure of Office Act. Congress refused the dismissal, but Johnson again tried to remove Stanton in early 1868. Several days later, the House of Representatives voted to impeach Johnson by a vote of 126 to 47, though the House had not yet formalized any charges against him. Days after already voting to impeach, the House issued a series of 11 impeachment charges, including accusations that Johnson had violated the Command of the Military Act and the Tenure of Office Act. However, the articles of impeachment revealed that Congress thought Johnson had engaged in behavior unfit for a president. Such a charge could not, on its own, be reason for impeachment, but the fact that the

House voted to include the article shows how unpopular Johnson had become. As members of the House described in their charges:

ARTICLES OF IMPEACHMENT
Article X
1868
Source Document Excerpt

That said Andrew Johnson, President of the United States, unmindful of the high duties of his office and the dignity and proprieties thereof, and of the harmony and courtesies which ought to exist and be maintained between the executive and legislative branches of the government of the United States, designing and intending to set aside the rightful authority and powers of Congress, did attempt to bring into disgrace, ridicule, hatred, contempt and reproach the Congress of the United States, and the several branches thereof, to impair and destroy the regard and respect of all the good people of the United States for the Congress and legislative power thereof, (which all officers of the government ought inviolably to preserve and maintain,) and to excite the odium and resentment of all the good people of the United States against Congress and the laws by it duly and constitutionally enacted; and in pursuance of his said design and intent, openly and publicly, and before divers assemblages of the citizens of the United States convened in divers parts thereof to meet and receive said Andrew Johnson as the Chief Magistrate of the United States, did, on the eighteenth day of August, in the year of our Lord one thousand eight hundred and sixty-six, and on divers other days and times, as well before as afterward, make and deliver with a loud voice certain intemperate, inflammatory and scandalous harangues, and did therein utter loud threats and bitter menaces as well against Congress as the laws of the United States duly enacted thereby, amid the cries jeers and laughter of the multitudes then assembled and in hearing, which are set forth in the several specifications hereinafter written

· · ·

Which said utterances, declarations, threats, and harangues, highly censurable in any, are peculiarly indecent and unbecoming in the Chief Magistrate of the United States, by means whereof said Andrew Johnson has brought to high office of the President of the United States into contempt, ridicule, and disgrace, to the great scandal of all good citizens, whereby said Andrew Johnson, President of the United States, did commit, and was then and there guilty of a high misdemeanor in office.[13]

On May 16, the Senate vote to convict Johnson failed, just one short of the two-thirds majority required, with 35 voting to convict and 19 voting to acquit.

A Powerless Man Empowered

Johnson entered office on the popularity of Lincoln, and Lincoln's assassination thrust Johnson, into the presidency. Johnson attempted to institute his own view of Reconstruction. Though he had been decidedly pro-Union and pro-Lincoln during the war, Johnson was a former slave owner and a product of southern society, where faith in the inherent inferiority of non-whites was part of the cultural fabric of white society. Even before Congress had reconvened in December of 1865, many former slave states had already begun passing "black codes," laws that limited the rights of black persons. In some states, black people were required to carry certificates of employment or risk being jailed as vagrants. In others, laws were passed requiring black people to submit to a curfew. In some states, laws explicitly prohibited black people to sit on juries, to vote, or to associate with whites. The purpose of these laws was to maintain the African American population in a state very similar to slavery. Under Johnson's plan, such laws would have been legal.

While it is true that Congress usurped presidential authority with the passage of the Tenure of Office Act and the Command of the Army Act, Johnson usurped Congressional power when he endeavored to decide how states would reenter the Union. This led to a power struggle between the Republican Senate and the presidency. As Johnson had not been elected president, and failed to generate popular support, the weight of his arguments was reduced. With a commanding majority in Congress, the Republicans were able to restrict Johnson's authority, and his impeachment was a political move designed to delegitimize his leadership without turning the presidency over to Vice President Benjamin Wade.

Johnson's impeachment also left a lasting mark on the presidency. Until the early 1900s, America was a "weak presidency" system in which Congress wielded most of the power. The reform presidencies of the early twentieth century returned the executive office to its former power. The impeachment of Johnson also established an important precedent for Congressional impeachment proceedings—a president, while he or she may be impeached, should not be removed from office unless guilty of high crimes or other gross violations of the office of the president.

CONCLUSION

Andrew Johnson stands as an example of a president who failed in nearly every conceivable way. The public shock, sadness, and outrage over the assassination of Lincoln would have provided Johnson with considerable leeway to set a national agenda, had he followed in the footsteps of Lincoln. However, Johnson's decision to attempt to assume unilateral control over Reconstruction established a hostile relationship with Congress from the start, and limited any potential for Johnson to accomplish legislative goals. Congress impeached Johnson, but left him in office, where he was essentially powerless for the remainder of his term. Had Johnson commanded the trust or faith of the American people, he might have been able to break free from congressional constraints, but he lacked the charisma of Lincoln, and misjudged the popularity of his own racially prejudiced views. Ultimately, Johnson's presidency led to an increase in power for the legislature and for several decades, presidential power was limited by a powerful congressional movement. The next chapter profiles President Ulysses S. Grant, a famous Civil War hero whose presidency was stymied by following on the heels of Andrew Johnson.

DISCUSSION QUESTIONS

♦ How did Congress usurp presidential authority with the Tenure of Office Act? Was this justified?

♦ Why was Johnson's treatment of southern soldiers and military leaders controversial?

♦ What was unusual about the Congressional override of Johnson's veto on the Civil Rights Act of 1865?

♦ Could Johnson be classified as a "populist" politician before his rise to the presidency? Why or why not?

Works Used

"African American Records: Freemen's Bureau." *National Archives*. 19 Sept. 2016. www.archives.gov/research/african-americans/freedmens-bureau.

"Andrew Johnson, 16th Vice President (1865)." *U.S. Senate*. 2019. www.senate.gov/about/officers-staff/vice-president/VP_Andrew_Johnson.htm.

"Article X." *NPS*. National Park Service. Andrew Johnson. National Historic Site Tennessee. 14 Apr. 2015. www.nps.gov/anjo/learn/historyculture/article-x.htm.

"Assassination of President Abraham Lincoln." *LOC*. Library of Congress. 2016. www.loc.gov/collections/abraham-lincoln-papers/articles-and-essays/assassination-of-president-abraham-lincoln/.

Fox, Justin. "Trump's 2018 Hasn't Been as Bad as Andrew Johnson's 1866." *Bloomberg*. 21 Nov. 2018. www.bloomberg.com/opinion/articles/2018-11-21/trump-s-2018-hasn-t-been-a-disaster-like-andrew-johnson-s-1866.

Gordon-Reed, Annette. *Andrew Johnson: The American Presidents Series*. New York: Times Books, 2011.

"John Wilkes Booth." *NPS*. National Park Service. 17 June 2015. www.nps.gov/people/john-wilkes-booth.htm.

Johnson, Andrew. "Speech to the Citizens of Washington."
    Teachingamericanhistory. 2018. teachingamericanhistory.org/library/
    document/speech-to-the-citizens-of-washington/.

_____. "State of the Union 1867—3 December 1867." *American History*.
    University of Groningen, 2012. www.let.rug.nl/usa/presidents/andrew-
    johnson/state-of-the-union-1867.php.

_____. "Veto of the Freemen's Bureau Bill." *Teachingamericanhistory*.
    2018. teachingamericanhistory.org/library/document/veto-of-the-
    freedmens-bureau-bill/.

"Overview of Andrew Johnson's Life." *NPS*. National Park Service. 8 Aug.
    2019. www.nps.gov/anjo/learn/historyculture/overview.htm.

Rayner, Kenneth. *Life and Times of Andrew Johnson*. New York: D. Appleton
    and Company, 1866, p. 117–19. babel.hathitrust.org/cgi/pt?id=loc.
    ark:/13960/t0zp44s4s&view=2up&seq=12&size=125.

"Transcript of Vice President Andrew Johnson's Inaugural Address." *Ball
    State University*. 2019. dmr.bsu.edu/digital/collection/BrcknCivCol/id/188.

Introduction

Ulysses Simpson Grant was among the most famous of the Union's Civil War heroes. A soft-spoken and considerate man who did not seek leadership, Grant was an abolitionist and a prominent critic of military overreach. After the disgrace of Johnson, Grant seemed an ideal, moderate candidate, but had the misfortune of entering office during a time when Congress had greatly limited presidential authority. Grant supported the radical path to Reconstruction, which essentially saw the South under martial law, and he was one of the only presidents who actually dispatched troops to oppose white supremacist militants attempting to prevent African Americans from exercising their newly won civil rights. Grant also tried, and failed, to establish a system that would have led to citizenship for the nation's Native Americans, being foiled by corrupt legislators in league with real estate developers and white supremacist lobbyists. In the end, Grant's achievements were overshadowed by widespread corruption during his administration and his reputation damaged by his failure to reform the executive branch.

Topics covered in this chapter include:

- Fifteenth Amendment
- Fourteenth Amendment
- The Peace Plan
- African American voting
- Reconstruction
- The Panic of 1873

This Chapter Discusses the Following Source Documents:

Inaugural Address, Ulysses S. Grant, March 4, 1869

Special Message on the 15th Amendment, Ulysses S. Grant, March 30, 1870

Corrupt Bargains
Ulysses S. Grant (1869–1877)

With the end of Andrew Johnson's presidency, the U.S. government entered the era of "Congressional government," with a procession of comparatively weak presidents largely dominated by Congress, starting with Ulysses S. Grant, a war hero who followed the radical Republican line, and ending with the illegitimate election of Rutherford B. Hayes, who was selected in a Congressional back-door deal, trading a Republican presidency for the end of military Reconstruction in the South and the beginning of the segregation era.

The Great American General

Ulysses S. Grant was born in Ohio, the eldest of six children, into an upper working-class family. His father, Jesse, was a successful tanner and an outspoken member of the Ohio community. Grant, by contrast, is typically described as shy and reserved. Though afforded little in the way of formal education, Grant loved to read and taught himself mathematics. As a youth, he worked with his father in the tannery. Although he complained of being covered in animal blood, working with animals did awaken in him a passion for working with horses. A naturally gifted horse trainer, he was able to handle even extremely feral animals.

Ulysses S. Grant, by Mathew Brady, Library of Congress Prints and Photographs Division, via Wikimedia.

His father sent him to private schools and then appealed to Ohio Senator Thomas Hamer, a former friend, who agreed to appoint Ulysses to West Point Military Academy in New York. Grant was born Hiram Ulysses Grant, not Ulysses S. Grant. When Senator Hamer wrote Grant's appointment to West Point, he listed Ulysses under his mother's maiden name, as Ulysses Simpson and Grant began using "Simpson" as his middle name, becoming Ulysses S. Grant.[1]

Grant was initially stationed near St. Louis, Missouri, in Jefferson Barracks, as part of the Fourth Infantry, where he met future wife Julia Dent, the sister of his West Point friend and roommate Frederick Dent. Grant spent two years fighting in the Mexican-American War as a lieutenant, where he received several commendations for bravery, though he would later criticize the war. Transferred to Michigan and New York, and then to Oregon and California, Grant began to dislike military life and distrust the chain of command. He resigned from the army in 1854 to try his hand at farming. An opponent of slavery, Grant freed the slave he was given by his father-in-law, and hired free black men to work on his farm. With four children, however, the Grants struggled to get by and nearly lapsed into poverty.[2]

The Civil War changed everything. Grant was called up to lead a volunteer regiment in Illinois and performed so well that he was promoted to Brigadier General. The first four years of the war went poorly for the Union. Though they had superior weaponry, the need to invade such a vast territory resulted in many hard-fought but losing battles, as additional states slipped away from the Union and joined the South. Grant proved one of the Union's most effective leaders. In 1862, he led successful charges to capture Fort Henry and Fort Donelson in Tennessee. Grant's successful capture of Fort Donelson involved the first unconditional surrender of an entire Confederate army, and Grant carried this habit forward, becoming the first general to ignore the formalized

process of surrender. Grant became an immediate celebrity when news of Donelson reached the press, and, after another series of victories, Lincoln named Grant commander of all Union forces. He was leading the army that forced General Robert E. Lee's surrender in Richmond, Virginia, and effectively ended the war. A national hero, in the wake of the war Grant was named General of the Armies, a rank that had been unfilled since George Washington occupied the position in the Revolutionary War.[3]

A Controversial Administrator

After Lincoln's assassination led to the unsuccessful presidency of Andrew Johnson, the executive and Congress were in a state of constant conflict. Grant was Johnson's Secretary of War, but he found himself increasingly at odds with Johnson over his approach to Reconstruction. His personal views more closely resembled the radical Republicans, who believed that the federal government needed to manage the process of helping former slaves transition to citizenship. They feared that southern societies would continue to oppress newly freed slaves, which is exactly what happened. Johnson refused to follow the congressional views on Reconstruction and was nearly impeached for attempting to force his own Reconstruction agenda through. In the lead-up to the 1868 election, Grant was chosen on the first ticket as the Republican candidate. Though he had not sought the nomination, Grant felt it his duty to honor it, though he did not promote himself for the office. Nonetheless, with public opinion decidedly favoring the Republicans, Grant earned 3 million votes to 2.7 million for Horatio Seymour, the Democratic candidate, and captured the lion's share of the states with 214 electoral to 80 for his opponent.[4] The 1868 election was one of the more popular in history, with roughly 80 percent of the voting age population showing up at the polls. The Republicans preserved their dominance in Congress as well, and with a strong popular mandate, the party was empowered to enact its approach to Reconstruction.

Historians have criticized Grant for the level of governmental corruption during his time in office. Grant refused to give out political appointments in order to build political leverage and took a principled stance on composing his cabinet and on forming political partnerships, resulting in some effective appointments. However, Grant did not take an aggressive approach to ferreting out corruption or removing ineffective or unscrupulous men. As a result, there were so many controversies under his administration that the term "Grantism" was used to refer to political corruption.

One of the most significant controversies during the Grant presidency involved the Union Pacific Railroad. Massachusetts Representative Oakes Ames, an early investor in and proponent of the Central Pacific Railroad, was chosen by Lincoln to oversee the Union Pacific Railroad, which was falling behind schedule in 1864. Ames invested in Crédit Mobilier, a fraudulent construction company created to inflate railroad construction costs. The excess money, paid by the government to build the railroad, was then used by Ames to bribe his fellow legislators, thus easing the way for railroad-related legislation. Vermont Representative Luke P. Poland led an investigation into the matter in 1872, revealing that many members of Congress, including Vice President Schuyler Colfax, had been bribed. The Republican-controlled Congress only punished one Democrat; indeed, Ames received only a censure but was not removed from office.[5]

Another major controversy, known as the "Black Friday" scandal, involved the 1869 attempt to corner the gold market by financial speculators Jim Fisk and Jay Gould, who purchased huge amounts of gold and gold futures. The two men, who worked with Abel Rathbone Corbin, Grant's brother-in-law, used Corbin to gain access to Grant, and tried to dissuade Grant from selling government gold, which would lower the price of gold stock. Corbin also convinced Grant to appoint Daniel Butterfield as assistant U.S. treasurer, who was bribed by Fisk and Gould, agreeing to warn them if the government was preparing to sell gold. Grant became suspicious of Corbin and ordered the government sale of $4 million in gold.

Within minutes, the price of gold fell, causing widespread panic as thousands of investors found their stock losing value. Butterfield was removed from his post, but Gould and Fisk escaped without punishment. News of the scandal painted Grant as a president unable to control his own White House or even his family from exploiting the government for profit.[6]

Other minor controversies during Grant's time in office, contributed to showing Grant as an ineffective political manager. Despite his celebrated military career, Grant was not a political man and tried to rely on personal relationships instead of partisan engineering. He was never tied to any corrupt practices, but corruption within Congress prevented prosecution of those involved in the Black Friday and Union Pacific scandals, thereby mitigating any efforts he took to address the issue.

Granting Equality

Although Grant is described as a relatively weak president when it came to establishing policy, he played a major role in Reconstruction by promoting the Fifteenth Amendment, which allowed African American men access to the elective franchise. In his first inaugural address, Grant expressed two surprising sentiments in the realm of racial equality:

INAUGURAL ADDRESS
Ulysses S. Grant
March 4, 1869
Source Document Excerpt

The proper treatment of the original occupants of this land—the Indians one deserving of careful study. I will favor any course toward them which tends to their civilization and ultimate citizenship.

The question of suffrage is one which is likely to agitate the public so long as a portion of the citizens of the nation are excluded from its privileges in any State. It seems to me very desirable that this question should be settled now, and I entertain the hope and express the desire that it may be by the ratification of the fifteenth article of amendment to the Constitution.[7]

At the time, racism was rampant. Though many in the North supported emancipation, far less white Americans believed in racial equality. Few believed that African Americans should have full political rights, even if a slight majority supported the end of slavery. Similarly, many white Protestant Americans saw threats anywhere that non-white, non-Christian, or non-Protestant people tried to assume equal rights. There were mob attacks on Catholics, Jews, and Irish people in America's cities. African Americans were facing terrorist violence in the South, and Native Americans were being pushed further and further west by settlers. In the realm of Native American policy, there was considerable support at the time for all-out genocide, and some in Congress called for the army to eliminate the remaining Native Americans.

Grant's writings portray a man who believed in racial, ethnic, and religious equality. He argued against the prejudice directed at Jewish and Catholic immigrants, Native Americans, African Americans, and Asian immigrants and, while in office, attempted to use the power of the presidency to further this ideal. Had he asserted his authority more forcefully, his presidency could have been impactful. Grant, however, typically capitulated when Congress assumed control.

Grant's failing to challenge Congress is especially apparent in his efforts to improve the fortunes of Native Americans. Grant's commitment to Native American rights began in the Mexican-American War, when he saw the devastation of Native American culture across the southwest. Around 1860, when he was at home working as a clerk in his father's leather goods store, he met a young Native American man named Ely Samuel Parker, who was working as an engineer for the state. Parker and Grant became close during the Civil War, during which Grant appointed Parker to the post of Brigadier General. After Grant won the presidency, Parker and his white wife, Minnie Orton Sackett, were frequent visitors to the White House, and the Grant family and Parker became well-known in political circles.

Grant and Parker formulated a plan to resolve the Native American situation that later became known as the "Peace Plan," because it contrasted with proposals calling for war against the remaining tribes. Grant named Parker Commissioner of Indian Affairs, becoming the first president to appoint a person of color to a federal post. Together, Parker and Grant sought a complete overhaul of American Indian policy by setting aside federal territories, known as reservations, protected by federal troops. They also intended to provide Native Americans assistance in farming, construction, and land management. Grant removed many political appointees serving as Indian agents and replaced them with advocates for racial equality. The goal was to transition Native Americans from military wards of the state to full citizenship, with voting rights, over the course of 3–5 years.

Grant's Commissioner of Indian Affairs, Ely Parker, was the first person of color appointed to a federal position. By Mathew Brady, via Wikimedia.

Though well-intentioned, racism and Congressional interference undid Grant's plans. Board of Indian Affairs Chairman William Welsh worked with Congress to force Parker from office by creating an elaborate set of false embezzlement charges against him. Though Parker was exonerated, white supremacist Congressmen used this incident as an excuse to pass a law giving the Bureau of Indian Affairs complete authority over the Indian service. Parker resigned in 1871, and the situation deteriorated. The Bureau of Indian Affairs appointed whites to key posts, countered the efforts of negotiators to engage in peaceful settlements, and attempted to move Native Americans by force. An uprising followed, and Grant was forced to commit federal forces to a series of brutal wars against Native American tribes, including the Great Sioux War of 1876. Grant's peace policy failed due to his inability to oppose Congressional directives.[8]

This happened again regarding Grant's efforts on behalf of African American suffrage. Grant mentioned the Fifteenth Amendment in his inaugural address, and after assuming office, he personally campaigned for it. When it was ratified in 1870, Grant issued a statement on the importance of the event:

SPECIAL MESSAGE ON THE 15TH AMENDMENT

Ulysses S. Grant
March 30, 1870
Source Document Excerpt

To the Senate and House of Representatives:

It is unusual to notify the two Houses of Congress by message of the promulgation, by proclamation of the Secretary of State, of the ratification of a constitutional amendment. In view, however, of the vast importance of the fifteenth amendment to the Constitution, this day declared a part of that revered instrument, I deem a departure from the usual custom justifiable. A measure which makes at once 4,000,000 people voters who were heretofore declared by the highest tribunal in the land not citizens of the United States, nor eligible to become so (with the assertion that "at the time of the Declaration of Independence the opinion was fixed and universal in the civilized portion of the white race, regarded as an axiom in morals as well as in politics, that black men had no rights which the white man was bound to respect"), is indeed a measure of grander importance than any other one act of the kind from the foundation of our free Government to the present day.

Institutions like ours, in which all power is derived directly from the people, must depend mainly upon their intelligence, patriotism, and industry. I call the attention, therefore, of the newly enfranchised race to the importance of their striving in every honorable manner to make themselves worthy of their new privilege. To the race more favored heretofore by our laws I would say, Withhold no legal privilege of advancement to the new citizen. The framers of our Constitution firmly believed that a republican government could not endure without intelligence and education generally diffused among the people. The Father of his Country, in his Farewell Address, uses this language:

Promote, then, as an object of primary importance, institutions for the general diffusion of knowledge. In proportion as the structure of a government gives force to public opinion, it is essential that public opinion should be enlightened.

. . .

Special Message on the 15th Amendment
continued

I repeat that the adoption of the fifteenth amendment to the Constitution completes the greatest civil change and constitutes the most important event that has occurred since the nation came into life. The change will be beneficial in proportion to the heed that is given to the urgent recommendations of Washington. If these recommendations were important then, with a population of but a few millions, how much more important now, with a population of 40,000,000, and increasing in a rapid ratio. I would therefore call upon Congress to take all the means within their constitutional powers to promote and encourage popular education throughout the country, and upon the people everywhere to see to it that all who possess and exercise political rights shall have the opportunity to acquire the knowledge which will make their share in the Government a blessing and not a danger. By such means only can the benefits contemplated by this amendment to the Constitution be secured.

U. S. GRANT.[9]

Grant also attempted to use his office to follow through on the promise of African American citizenship. He was instrumental in the passage of a series of laws, known as the Enforcement Acts, which empowered the military to enforce voting rights in the South. In October of 1871, Grant sent federal troops into South Carolina after reports arose of armed terrorist groups, largely the Ku Klux Klan, attacking African Americans. Nine South Carolina counties were temporarily placed under martial law. Federal troops arrested hundreds of Ku Klux Klan terrorists and broke up Klan chapters in several states, but the intervention of federal troops soon became a political lightning rod.

Grant's use of federal troops in the South was portrayed as a violation of states' rights. Congressional Republicans soon began to council Grant against intervention, and he often capitulated. He did not always commit federal troops for reports of violence against African Americans, and in other cases, he refrained from arresting or prosecuting those involved. Grant's failure to push his own agenda or to fight Congress with regard to enforcing Reconstruction left him largely ineffective.

The African American vote propelled Grant to victory for a second term, in which he received 3.6 million votes to 2.8 million for Democrat Horace Greeley. This was the first presidential election to include African American men, and thus could be viewed as the most legitimate in U.S. history to that point, though more than half the population (women and members of other non-white races) were still prohibited from voting, making this election not a true measure of popular support.[10] There was also a major decline in voter participation, with only 72 percent of voting age Americans going to the polls as opposed to nearly 81 percent in 1868. This was partly because few of the newly enfranchised African Americans voted (with only eight states allowing African Americans to vote), and because many white voters abstained, some believing that Grant was unbeatable or because of their personal objection to black enfranchisement.

Deconstructing Reconstruction

By the time the 1876 election arrived, the Republican Party was no longer facing a promising political situation. Reconstruction was controversial. Scandals in the Grant administration portrayed the party as corrupt and untrustworthy, and the 1872 Black Friday scandal had been linked to a series of other instances of irresponsible speculation that ultimately led to the Panic of 1873, a major financial collapse that affected both North America and Europe.

The panic was entwined with the railroad industry. Following the Civil War, there was a major push for railroad construction, and between 1866 and 1873, 35,000 miles of track were laid across the country. Railroad companies were the largest employers and a major target for investors, both private and corporate. Many banks were heavily invested in the industry. In September of 1873, Jay Cooke & Company, a banking firm managing

the government investment in the railroads, collapsed, setting off a chain of events that spread across the country. Railroad growth had involved a heavy amount of capital investment, with slow returns. When the banks began to fail, the railroads failed with them. This left millions without income and unable to pay bank loans, which placed banks on the verge of collapse. In total, 89 of the country's 364 railroads went into bankruptcy, and 18,000 businesses failed in two years. By 1876, unemployment had risen to 14 percent. Grant proved a poor manager, and the Republican party tried to address the panic by funneling funds into businesses instead of providing debt relief to the workers, which failed to ease the crisis.[11]

The Republican candidate in 1876 was Rutherford B. Hayes, a Civil War hero and a well-liked moderate reformer who served in the House of Representative and as governor of Ohio for two terms. Ohio was a swing state, and the choice of Hayes was strategic, giving the Republicans an advantage in a state that might have otherwise been captured by the Democrats. The Democrats nominated Samuel J. Tilden of New York, who ran on a platform of governmental reform. Tilden was an expert political organizer and soon gathered significant support, drawing right-leaning Republican voters to the party in several key states. In the election, Tilden won the popular vote, with 4,288,191 votes to 4,033,497 for Hayes. Approximately 83 percent of voters turned out to the polls, making it the most popular election in U.S. history. It is thought that the surge in voter participation occurred in part because of a large number of African American voters, encouraged by aggressive enforcement of Reconstruction and federal authorities who prevented violence and voter intimidation against African Americans. This helped the Republicans, but not enough to win the popular vote after two terms in office and in the midst of a severe depression.[12]

Rutherford B. Hayes, by Mathew Brady, Library of Congress Prints and Photographs Division, via Wikimedia.

𝔚𝔢 𝔱𝔥𝔢 𝔓𝔢𝔬𝔭𝔩𝔢

While Tilden was the clear popular vote winner, receiving more than 200,000 more votes, the Electoral College vote was so closely divided that neither candidate could claim a clear electoral victory. The Republicans claimed that the Democratic victories were the result of violence and voter intimidation against African Americans, making Hayes the legitimate winner. There were reports of widespread instances in which white mobs or armed white men intimidated or attacked black people trying to vote in the South. The Democrats, meanwhile, used their victories in state elections in the Pacific Northwest to skew elections in Oregon and Washington for Tilden, though Hayes may have actually won the electoral votes in those states. Ultimately, it was a deadlock that continued for months, and Congress eventually appointed a committee to decide the issue. The committee, consisting of five senators, five representatives, and five Supreme Court justices, was supposed to contain 7 Democrats, 7 Republicans, and 1 independent. However, the committee was made up of 8 Republicans and 7 Democrats, and the members voted along partisan lines. Hayes won the vote as part of a secret agreement wherein Hayes would be granted the presidency, and Republicans would end Reconstruction in the South.[13]

The political bargain that ended Reconstruction was seen as a positive result by many white Americans living in the 1870s. Reconstruction had become increasingly unpopular as whites in the North complained of the cost, constant controversies, and political unrest, while those in the South complained that they had been subject to an oppressive military regime led by Northern Republicans, and denied their appropriate level of independence and sovereignty. Reconstruction was depicted as a just ending for the Civil War drama until twentieth-century historians changed the narrative.

In 1935, African American scholar W.E.B. Du Bois wrote a seminal revisionist history, *Black Reconstruction in America*, which explored how

Reconstruction impacted black Americans. Even before the military Reconstruction program initiated by the Republican Congress and the Grant administration, a series of laws called "Black Codes" were put into place curtailing the rights of southern black people. African Americans were subject to special curfews and prohibited from visiting white-owned establishments or neighborhoods. Some argued that African Americans had little exposure to civilized life and needed to be controlled until they could become more civilized. Others argued that African Americans, if treated equally, would treat white persons violently, perhaps repaying debts from slavery. Others believed that many African Americans were inherently prone to violence. [14]

In addition, new domestic terrorist organizations like the Ku Klux Klan arose. These groups were often started by, or attracted, former Confederate officers and other white supremacists. These terrorist organizations used violence and intimidation to keep black people subservient and poor. They destroyed businesses and terrorized owners; they killed thousands of black men, women, and children with impunity, and few were arrested or in any way punished.

When the illegitimate election of 1876 resulted in the bargain that ended Reconstruction, the segregation era began. For most of the next century, African Americans were marginalized, disenfranchised, and disadvantaged to the point that in the twenty-first century, the fates of African American men and women are still influenced by institutionalized racial prejudice. Historian Eric Foner explained in his award-winning 1988 book *Reconstruction*, that the Reconstruction era was an "unfinished revolution." The idea of emancipation, of converting the previously captive population of America to citizens was truly revolutionary, but the revolution prematurely ended due to political bargaining and the influence of America's white supremacists.

CONCLUSION

In the wake of Grant's presidency, a contested election between Samuel Tilden and Rutherford B. Hayes resulted in Tilden winning a narrow popular vote victory, while neither candidate commanded the lead in the Electoral College. Hayes was essentially appointed to office by Congress, in return for the Republican Party agreeing to end martial law in the South. This resulted in white supremacists severely limiting African American political agency and keeping African Americans in a state of servitude and dependence in other ways. Grant was one of the few presidents willing to use the authority of his office to defend the rights of non-white individuals, but his presidency was overshadowed by an extremely strong iteration of Congress, with the power to limit his effectiveness and ability to establish an executive agenda with regard to domestic policy. The corrupt bargain that led to Hayes being installed in the presidency was the final failure of the radical Republican approach to Reconstruction and of any legitimate effort to integrate African Americans into citizenship. The next chapter discusses an era of presidents (Hayes, Garfield, and Arthur) who worked to reform government and helped to restore the power of the presidency still reeling from the extreme actions of Andrew Johnson.

DISCUSSION QUESTIONS

♦ Why have Grant's policies with regard to Native Americans become controversial?

♦ Would the scandals of Grant's presidency impact public opinion on a modern president? Why or why not?

♦ Why is the Grant administration important in the history of racial diversity in government?

♦ Was the legislature justified in trading the end of reconstruction policies for Hayes's election? Why or why not?

Works Used

"Black Friday, September 24, 1869." *PBS*. American Experience. 2019. www.pbs.org/wgbh/americanexperience/features/grant-black-friday/.

Bunting, Josiah III. *Ulysses S. Grant*. New York: Times Books, 2004.

Chernow, Ron. *Grant*. New York: Penguin Books, 2017.

Grant, Ulysses. "First Inaugural Address of Ulysses S. Grant." *The Avalon Project*. Yale Law School. 2008. avalon.law.yale.edu/19th_century/grant1.asp.

Grant, Ulysses. "Special Message—March 30, 1870." *NPS*. National Park Service. Ulysses S. Grant. 27 Feb. 2019. www.nps.gov/ulsg/learn/historyculture/grant-and-the-15th-amendment.htm.

Greene, Robert II. "The Legacy of *Black Reconstruction*." *Jacobin*. www.jacobinmag.com/2018/08/web-du-bois-black-reconstruction-civil-rights.

Morris, Roy Jr. *Fraud of the Century: Rutherford B. Hayes, Samuel Tilden, and the Stolen Election of 1876*. New York: Simon & Schuster, 2003.

"Oakes Ames." *PBS*. American Experience. 2019. www.pbs.org/wgbh/americanexperience/features/tcrr-ames/.

"Presidential Election of 1868: A Resource Guide." *LOC*. Library of Congress. 2018. www.loc.gov/rr/program/bib/elections/election1868.html.

"Presidential Election of 1872: A Resource Guide." *LOC*. Library of Congress. 2018. www.loc.gov/rr/program/bib/elections/election1872.html.

"Presidential Election of 1876: A Resource Guide." *LOC*. Library of Congress. 2018. www.loc.gov/rr/program/bib/elections/election1876.html.

Simpson, Brooks D. *Ulysses S. Grant: Triumph Over Adversity, 1822–1865*. Minneapolis, MN: Zenith P, 2000; 2014.

Stockwell, Mary. "Ulysses Grant's Failed Attempt to Grant Native Americans Citizenship." *Smithsonian.com*. Smithsonian Institution. 9 Jan. 2019. www.smithsonianmag.com/history/ulysses-grants-failed-attempt-to-grant-native-americans-citizenship-180971198/.

"The Panic of 1873." *PBS*. American Experience. 2019. www.pbs.org/wgbh/americanexperience/features/grant-panic/.

Introduction

Rutherford B. Hayes, James Garfield, and Chester A. Arthur, along with Benjamin Harrison (who is covered in the next chapter), have been called the "lost presidents," because their achievements and time in office were largely forgotten by the time America entered the early 1900s. Though each president was connected to important achievements, and all four together helped to restore the power of the presidency after the brief period of congressional rule after Andrew Johnson, none are connected to achievements sufficiently dramatic to secure a prominent place in history. The period from Hayes to Arthur, however, was marked by one of the most serious governmental reform efforts in history.

Hayes's greatest legacy was his effort to reform the civil service and to fight against the corrupt political "machines" that dominated the political process. He also helped to reestablish presidential authority and independence regarding political appointments. Garfield's presidency started off with promise and, like Hayes, he was committed to governmental reform. His assassination left the nation in mourning once again, and led to the formation of the Secret Service. Chester Arthur was supposed to be the voice supporting big business—at least, that's what big business leaders expected of him when he took office—but Arthur proved more independent than the political bosses thought. He largely completed most of the reform efforts begun under Hayes.

We the People

Topics covered in this chapter include:
- Panic of 1873
- Civil Service reform
- Presidential appointments
- The "War of the Riders"
- Roscoe Conkling

This Chapter Discusses the Following Source Documents:

Veto of Army Appropriations Bill, Rutherford B. Hayes, April 29, 1879

Greenberger, Scott S. "The Man the Presidency Changed." *Politico*, September 11, 2017

We the People

The Lost Presidents
Rutherford B. Hayes, James Garfield, and Chester A. Arthur (1877–1885)

American novelist Thomas Wolfe wrote in his 1935 book *From Death to Morning:*

> *"Garfield, Arthur, Harrison, and Hayes—time of my father's time, blood of his blood, life of his life, had been living, real, and actual people in all the passion, power, and feeling of my father's youth. And for me they were the lost Americans: their gravely vacant and bewhiskered faces mixed, melted, swam together in the sea-depths of a past intangible, immeasurable, and unknowable at the buried city of Persepolis.*
>
> *And they were lost."*[1]

Historians have used this quote to describe forgotten leaders in America's past: Rutherford B. Hayes, James A. Garfield, Chester A. Arthur, and Benjamin Harrison, men whose time in the oval office is largely ignored. The end of the Grant administration's two terms left America in a state of upheaval. The Panic of 1873 was a great American fiscal disaster that left millions destitute. White supremacist resistance to Reconstruction was growing. The administrations of Hayes, Garfield, Arthur, and Harrison were shaped by the end of the Civil War and the effort to rebuild, and by one of the most tumultuous periods of partisan competition in history. Nonetheless, after the failure of Johnson and the docility of Grant, the presidency of Hayes led to a resurgence of executive power that in many ways restored the independence of the office, a pattern that continued under the other "lost presidents."

Harvard War Hero

Rutherford B. Hayes was the son of a wealthy whiskey distiller from Ohio; his father's early death left his mother to raise Hayes and his sister, Fanny, and the family did well enough to send Hayes to Harvard Law School, where he graduated in 1845. He became a well-known criminal lawyer in Ohio and a prominent member in the state's intellectual circles. Hayes built his political career by taking a very moderate path. He was a member of the anti-slavery Whig Party coalition, which sought to limit the spread of slavery, but did not side with the abolitionists. His views on slavery were in part shaped by his wife, Lucy Ware Webb, who was a devout Christian abolitionist. In 1855 he defended a young slave named Rosetta Armstead, who had been accused of being a runaway slave after asserting her freedom when brought by her owner to Ohio, a free state. Hayes's successful defense brought him to prominence among anti-slavery politicians, and he thereafter served as city attorney for Cincinnati.

Hayes enlisted in the Civil War and became a member of the Ohio Volunteer regiment. Future president William McKinley served as one of Hayes's sergeants and remembered of Hayes, "his whole nature seemed to change with battle. From the sunny, agreeable, kind, generous gentle gentleman . . . he was, when the battle was once on, intense and ferocious." In the battle of Cedar Creek in 1864, Hayes was shot in the head by a bullet that passed through another soldier. He was promoted to major general and awarded for bravery.[2]

While still in the army, Hayes was nominated for a seat in the U.S. House of Representatives. Hayes responded: "Your suggestion about getting a furlough to take the stump was certainly made without reflection. An officer fit for duty who at this crisis would abandon his post to electioneer for a seat in Congress ought to be scalped. You may feel perfectly sure I shall do no such thing."[3] His words became his campaign speech, and he was still in the army serving under General Philip Sheridan when he learned he'd won the election. He served in the House until 1866, then resigned

to run in the 1867 gubernatorial elections. Though he supported a controversial bill that would provide voting rights to African Americans, losing the support of many white supremacists, Hayes proved able to garner just enough support to win the governorship, by a margin of less than 3,000 votes, and became popular enough to win a second term.

Editorial cartoon of Hayes kicking Chester A. Arthur out of the New York Custom House. By Frederick Burr Opper, Library of Congress Prints and Photographs Division, via Wikimedia.

The Feminist Press

The question of women's rights was a significant, though arguably secondary, issue during the Hayes administration's time in the White House. Lucy Hayes, who was the first First Lady with a college degree, supported the suffrage movement, though she was criticized in the press for not doing so more openly. Discussions of suffrage came to prominence in part because of the new generation of pioneering female reporters. The proliferation of women reporters is visible in coverage of the Hayes White House and, specifically, in the amount of coverage afforded Lucy Hayes. A number of women reporters wrote "society" or "culture" columns that covered Lucy's outfits, White House social events, or the First Lady's famous Sunday "sings," where members of the Washington elite and friends from Ohio gathered in the White House parlor. Hayes was an accomplished singer who accompanied herself on guitar, and though she championed no specific cause, she was held up as an exemplar of feminine morality. It was thanks to dedicated coverage that the term "First Lady" came into general use, as reporters increasingly used the term as an honorific for Lucy Hayes.

A few of the new breed of female reporters, especially Mary Clemmer Ames, refused to limit themselves to covering issues typically seen as "women's issues." While Ames wrote about women's suffrage and the women's rights movement in general, she also delivered impressive rebukes of Gilded Age excess and "cronyism" through her column: "A Woman's Letter from Washington." Ames was a critic of the Grant administration and the corruption that became widespread in Washington and viewed the incoming Hayes administration as a welcome change. Disappointed when many female government employees were dismissed from their roles and for the way that Hayes allowed Reconstruction in the South to regress, Ames became a critic. Though she had once believed that the Republican Party would usher in a new egalitarian age, she'd come to believe that the traditionalist males had no genuine intention of advancing that agenda. In one article she wrote, "Nothing could be more foolish than for a woman to be a partisan. She owes nothing to either party. As a citizen, both are condescending, shabby and mean to her." Ames was one of the few outspoken female journalists of her era, and she paved the way for many others. Though it was still difficult for women and though Ames often voiced opinions that might have offended future feminists, her career was proof that a woman could handle serious political reporting. During her tenure her paper, the *Washington Independent*, saw its zenith in both popularity and influence in Washington and around the country.[a]

Works Used

a. Beasley, Maurine Hoffman. "Mary Clemmer Ames: A Victorian Woman Journalist." *RBhayes*. Hayes Historical Journal, vol. ii, no. 1, 1978. www.rbhayes.org/research/hayes-historical-journal-mary-clemmer-ames/.

The Return of Presidential Power

Needing an unblemished candidate to carry their party after the scandals of the Grant administration, Hayes became the Republican presidential candidate for 1876. He failed to win the popular vote, but was appointed to office through a political bargain between the Republicans and Democrats that ended Reconstruction. Despite the questionable legitimacy of his electoral win, for which some angry Democrats called him "Rutherfraud," Hayes entered office seeking to unite the parties and to address the ills of the fractured nation.

One measure of presidential power concerns the extent to which a president aligns with the political party that helped him win. The Constitution provides the president with powers that can be used to counter partisanship. Whereas Johnson had been dominated completely by Congress, and Grant proved unwilling to challenge congressional influence, Hayes proved from the beginning that he would take a more independent approach. His cabinet appointments included a number of controversial Republicans who challenged leading party lines, as well as a former Confederate and Democrat, appointed as Postmaster General as a conciliatory gesture to southern Democrats.

Hayes faced several important battles over authority that helped to restore some of the independence characteristic of the presidency lost to the office since Lincoln. One involved Hayes's early efforts at Civil Service reform. Since Andrew Jackson, political appointments to federal posts were handled according to the "spoils system," in which appointments were used to reward supporters or to bribe individuals toward partisan support. Appointees who were not chosen for ability left many federal offices staffed by incompetent individuals. Hayes believed that one of the keys to reform was the "divorce of the legislature from the nominating power." Hayes stated, "With this, reform can and will successfully proceed. Without it, reform is impossible."[4]

In 1877 Hayes nominated Theodore Roosevelt Sr., Edwin Merritt, and L. Bradford Prince to replace officers of the New York Custom House, who had been gifted appointments by Republican senators. New York Senator Roscoe Conkling attempted to block two of those appointments, citing "senatorial courtesy," which is not constitutional law but a custom in which appointments to a state needed to be cleared by the ranking senator of the president's party within the state. Hayes wrote in his diary about the conflict:

"The political event of the last week is the opposition of Conkling to the New York appointments. This is a test case. The Senators generally prefer to confirm Merritt and Graham. But many, perhaps a majority, will not oppose Conkling on the question. Senatorial courtesy, the senatorial prerogative, and the fear of Conkling's vengeance in future control them. He is, like Butler, more powerful because he is vindictive and not restrained by conscience. The most noticeable weakness of Congressmen is their timidity. They fear the use to be made of their 'record.' They are afraid of making enemies. They do not vote according to their convictions from fear of consequences."[5]

Hayes did not budge on the appointments, and he wrote a message to Congress accusing the previous appointees, Arthur and Cornell, of conducting themselves in their offices to further the goals of a political "machine," rather than as faithful servants of the people. During the lame duck session of Congress in 1878, several Democrats aided Hayes in pushing past Conkling's obstruction and pushing through the Congressional block on Hayes's appointments. Though the Democrats did this for political leverage, it was nonetheless a major win for Hayes.[6]

Hayes's most important victory in terms of reestablishing presidential authority came in what historians have called the "War of the Riders" or

the "Rider War." The 1879 elections gave the Democrats major victories, sufficient to control both houses of Congress. The result was predictable because Republican control of the presidency and Congress under Grant had been tied, in the minds of the public, to the recession. Further, Democrats were gaining power again, driven by a wave of white supremacist sentiment in the South and North. Hayes thus faced a hostile Congress determined to eliminate what few vestiges of Reconstruction remained. One of these was the Federal Elections Law of 1871, which gave the government the right to appoint federal supervisors to districts where there had been allegations of irregularity or potential fraud. The government had used this power, under Grant, to investigate instances of white supremacists attempting to prohibit African American voters, but the law had also been used to justify federal supervision in northern cities, such as when federal investigators responded to massive voter fraud in 1868 linked to the Tammany Hall political organization that supported state Democrats.

The new Democratic Congress recognized that Hayes would veto any direct attempt to eliminate the Federal Elections Law, so they used riders, or addendums tacked on to another piece of legislation, especially to those "must-pass" appropriation bills that would provide funding for running the federal government. Riders called for the repeal of election laws, barred civil or military officers from protecting federal elections from fraud or violence, and repealed other provisions granting federal authority to oversee elections. In April of 1879, when Democrats attempted to attach a rider to an appropriations bill needed to fund the U.S. Army and to pay troops and officers, Hayes issued a veto, accompanied by his strong message that the actions being taken by Congress violated the spirit of the Constitution:

VETO OF
ARMY APPROPRIATIONS BILL
RUTHERFORD B. HAYES
April 29, 1879
Source Document Excerpt

It is the question whether or not the House of Representatives has a right to say, "We will grant supplies only upon condition that grievances are redressed. We are the representatives of the taxpayers of the Republic. We, the House of Representatives, alone have the right to originate money bills. We, the House of Representatives, have alone the right to originate bills which grant the money of the people. The Senate represents States; we represent the taxpayers of the Republic. We, therefore, by the very terms of the Constitution, are charged with the duty of originating the bills which grant the money of the people. We claim the right, which the House of Commons in England established after two centuries of contest, to say that we will not grant the money of the people unless there is a redress of grievances."

Upon the assembling of this Congress, in pursuance of a call for an extra session, which was made necessary by the failure of the Forty-fifth Congress to make the needful appropriations for the support of the Government, the question was presented whether the attempt made in the last Congress to ingraft by construction a new principle upon the Constitution should be persisted in or not. This Congress has ample opportunity and time to pass the appropriation bills, and also to enact any political measures which may be determined upon in separate bills by the usual and orderly methods of proceeding. But the majority of both Houses have deemed it wise to adhere to the principles asserted and maintained in the last Congress by the majority of the House of Representatives. That principle is that the House of Representatives has the sole right to originate bills for raising revenue, and therefore has the right to withhold appropriations upon which the existence of the Government may depend unless the Senate and the President shall give their assent to any legislation which the House may see fit to attach to appropriation bills. To establish this principle is to make a radical, dangerous, and unconstitutional change in the character of our institutions. The various departments of the Government and the Army and the Navy are established by the Constitution or by laws passed in pursuance thereof. Their duties are clearly defined and their support

Veto of Army Appropriations Bill
continued

is carefully provided for by law. The money required for this purpose has been collected from the people and is now in the Treasury, ready to be paid out as soon as the appropriation bills are passed. Whether appropriations are made or not, the collection of the taxes will go on. The public money will accumulate in the Treasury. It was not the intention of the framers of the Constitution that any single branch of the Government should have the power to dictate conditions upon which this treasure should be applied to the purpose for which it was collected. Any such intention, if it had been entertained, would have been plainly expressed in the Constitution.

That a majority of the Senate now concurs in the claim of the House adds to the gravity of the situation, but does not alter the question at issue. The new doctrine, if maintained, will result in a consolidation of unchecked and despotic power in the House of Representatives. A bare majority of the House will become the Government. The Executive will no longer be what the framers of the Constitution intended—an equal and independent branch of the Government. It is clearly the constitutional duty of the President to exercise his discretion and judgment upon all bills presented to him without constraint or duress from any other branch of the Government. To say that a majority of either or both of the Houses of Congress may insist upon the approval of a bill under the penalty of stopping all of the operations of the Government for want of the necessary supplies is to deny to the Executive that share of the legislative power which is plainly conferred by the second section of the seventh article of the Constitution. It strikes from the Constitution the qualified negative of the President. It is said that this should be done because it is the peculiar function of the House of Representatives to represent the will of the people. But no single branch or department of the Government has exclusive authority to speak for the American people. The most authentic and solemn expression of their will is contained in the Constitution of the United States. By that Constitution they have ordained and established a Government whose powers are distributed among coordinate branches, which, as far as possible consistently with a harmonious cooperation, are absolutely independent of each other. The people of this country are unwilling to see the supremacy of the Constitution replaced by the omnipotence of any one department of the Government.

. . .

Believing that this bill is a dangerous violation of the spirit and meaning of the Constitution, I am compelled to return it to the House in which it

continued

originated without my approval. The qualified negative with which the Constitution invests the President is a trust that involves a duty which he can not decline to perform. With a firm and conscientious purpose to do what I can to preserve unimpaired the constitutional powers and equal independence, not merely of the Executive, but of every branch of the Government, which will be imperiled by the adoption of the principle of this bill, I desire earnestly to urge upon the House of Representatives a return to the wise and wholesome usage of the earlier days of the Republic, which excluded from appropriation bills all irrelevant legislation. By this course you will inaugurate an important reform in the method of Congressional legislation; your action will be in harmony with the fundamental principles of the Constitution and the patriotic sentiment of nationality which is their firm support, and you will restore to the country that feeling of confidence and security and the repose which are so essential to the prosperity of all of our fellow-citizens.[7]

Hayes refused to capitulate to Democratic demands, allowing the government, the military, and the judiciary to go unfunded. Eventually the Democrats issued another funding bill for the executive, legislative, and army, without riders, and Hayes signed them, but he continued to veto any bill that came attached with riders. Hayes's strategy was to appeal directly to public opinion, writing his veto messages for public consumption, filled with appeals to the masses. He also traveled more widely and more often than any previous president, giving politically charged speeches about the need for cooperation and compromise. He endeared himself to the public for his forthright demeanor and offended few because he often chose a middle ground. Empowered by public support, therefore, he bypassed Congressional authority. By refusing to pass any appropriations bill with riders, he risked being seen as an obstructionist president. This is how Democratic Congressmen portrayed him, but Hayes was more popular than they were, and more successful in building political coalitions. In the end, the Democrats were forced to surrender every single rider.[8]

Tides of Power

Historians have not been kind to Hayes, whose presidency was connected with the failure of Reconstruction, the beginning of the Jim Crow era, the Chinese Exclusion Act, and a new Native American policy that led to "forced acculturation" and other human rights abuses. What is not often clear is that the power of the white supremacist lobby gave Hayes few good choices, and the choices he did make reflected an effort to prevent the worst abuses. He fought to retain federal oversight of elections in the South and to protect the civil rights of African Americans. Hayes fought to make the Chinese Exclusion Act a reduction, rather than a complete prohibition, on Chinese immigration; and his Native American policies, though they led to prejudicial acculturation abuses, should be considered against the more radical proposals of the era, such as genocide. While not a champion of Native American rights, Hayes's efforts were meant to follow the Peace Policy initiated by Grant, and to prevent open violence and hostilities.

Hayes reinstated presidential independence and power and helped to restore the image of the presidency in the eyes of the public. His greatest victories were Civil Service reform, in which he defied the Senate and his own party, and winning the War of the Riders against the Democrats. There is little doubt that Hayes would have won a second term had he sought it, but he instead endorsed James Garfield, a former Republican Representative who championed his fight against corruption. Though he proved willing to fight either Republicans or Democrats, Hayes's success was beneficial for his party. The rider scandal portrayed the Democrats as attempting to sneak through a radical, racist policy, and they lost support. In the legislative elections of 1880, the Republicans gained control of both houses, and maintained the presidency as Garfield campaigned under the rubric of continuing Hayes's legacy.

A Legacy Cut Short

James Garfield is one of the lesser known presidents. Born in a poor family in Ohio, he might have been the poorest man ever to become president. He funded his own college education, working as a janitor and part-time teacher, and studied law at Williams College. Garfield then taught English, classical languages, history, and mathematics. A committed abolitionist, Garfield was elected to the Ohio legislature in 1856, the youngest member to that point, and became an outspoken opponent of slavery. In the Civil War, he enlisted and served in the Ohio infantry, rising to Major General and becoming the youngest officer to hold this rank. Garfield was one of a number of war heroes who was elected without returning home from the front to campaign. He left the army in 1863 to take a seat on the U.S. House of Representatives and joined with the radical Republicans. There, he favored direct military intervention to promote equal rights, the seizure of Confederate property, and the exile or execution of southern leaders. Gradually, over eight terms in office, Garfield moderated his approach and aligned with the compromise Republicans. He was minority leader of the House while Hayes was in office and became a dedicated Hayes supporter.[9]

James Garfield, Library of Congress Prints and Photographs Division, via Wikimedia.

When Hayes declined a second term, Garfield was chosen as the replacement candidate. To win the northern states, he needed to appeal to two different factions within the Republican Party. The "Stalwarts," led by New York Senator Conkling, wanted a more aggressive retributive policy toward the South and was in conflict with Hayes over efforts to fight Civil Service corruption linked to Conkling's political machine. The other faction, sometimes known as "Half-Breeds," were more apt to embrace the moderate political approach. Garfield's vice-presidential running mate, Chester A. Arthur, was a protégé of Conkling's, who did not support Garfield. Garfield visited Conkling in New York, as well as members of the other Republican factions, and promised that all of the factions would be represented in his appointments. This political bargain was known as the "Treaty of Fifth Avenue," and Conkling agreed to support Garfield. In one of the closest elections in history, Garfield and Vice President Chester A. Arthur won 4,452,611 votes to 4,445,256 for Democratic opponents Winfield Hancock and William English. Garfield, the youngest president at 49, gave a promising inaugural address in which he vowed to fight corruption and to continue the legacy of Hayes.[10]

Though Garfield's electoral victory was not a dramatic popular mandate, Republican victories in Congress gave him power to set a limited national agenda. He began addressing corruption in the Civil Service, although his appointments indicated that he also participated in the patronage system. Though he benefitted from the Treaty of Fifth Avenue, Garfield proved in his first 100 days in office that he had no intention of being controlled by Conkling's political engine. He boldly appointed Conkling's political rival William Robertson to the New York Customs House, the cornerstone of Conkling's political empire. Conkling objected and tried to block the nomination. Garfield wrote of the issue:

_____ "This brings on the contest at once and will settle the question whether the President is the registering clerk of the Senate or the Executive of the United States. Summed up in a single sentence this is the question: shall the principal port of entry in which more than ninety percent of our custom duties are collected be under the control of the administration or under the local control of the factional senator."[11]

Conkling convinced his allies in Congress to approve those nominations who were his friends and refuse to confirm the nomination of Robertson. Congress was then scheduled to adjourn, which would leave the Customs House post unfilled and Conkling's power unchecked. Garfield out-played Conkling, however, by withdrawing all nominations except for Robertson. This left Congress with two choices—either approve Robertson, after which Garfield would resubmit the other names, or adjourn without making any appointments. Conkling and the other senator from New York resigned from the Senate in protest, confident that the state legislature would re-elect them, but the legislature did not, sensing that public opinion was against Conkling's long-time political machine. Both were replaced, and Robertson was approved, ending Conkling's dominance over the New York Customs House and state politics.

On July 2, 1881, Garfield was assassinated while entering a Washington, DC, train station with his wife Lucretia and five young children. Charles Guiteau, a 40-year-old failed lawyer and former bill collector, fired two shots at Garfield, the second of which struck him in the back and eventually killed him. While being hauled away by police, Guiteau shouted, "I am a Stalwart of Stalwarts! Arthur (Vice President Chester Alan Arthur) is President now!"

Garfield hung on for 79 days, during which the country eagerly followed his health through news dispatches. Garfield died from an infection as doctors probed his back to remove the bullet.

Guiteau had previously met Garfield in March of 1881 seeking a consul position to Paris but was denied and ultimately banned from the president's office due to inexplicable and coercive behavior. At his trial, Guiteau claimed a religious duty to kill Garfield in order to heal the nation's political discord, giving credence to his defense attorneys' claim that he was insane, but he was sentenced to death and hanged in 1882. Historians now believe that Guiteau may have, in fact, been insane and not a political assassin.[12]

Garfield's assassination encouraged the passage of the Pendleton Civil Service Act of 1883, which mandated that government jobs be awarded on merit rather than political affiliation. This was among the most important pieces of anti-corruption legislation in the nineteenth century, as it provided the federal government with new power to challenge political patronage.[13]

Replacement Reformer

Chester A. Arthur entered the White House as a result of Garfield's death. The fifth child of an abolitionist Baptist preacher born in New York, he had a comfortable childhood and graduated from Union College. His position in a prominent New York law firm gave him a name for himself, arguing several high-profile cases involving fugitive slaves. Arthur joined the state militia in 1858, at the beginning of the Civil War, and rose to the rank of brigadier general while running a provisioning operation that housed thousands of soldiers. Though he never served in battle, he had a distinguished military career despite marrying a Virginia native with family in the Confederacy. Retiring from duty in 1863, Arthur became a wealthy lawyer, also benefitting by working for Republican boss Conkling, becoming one of his leading supporters. Conkling saw to it that Arthur received a high-paying position in the New York City Tax Commission, and then Grant, bowing to party demands, appointed Arthur to head the Port of New York Customs House. While there is no evidence of Arthur taking bribes or improper payouts, he did collect bribes for Senator Conkling.

Chester A. Arthur, via Wikimedia.

Hayes suspended Arthur from the Customs House when he launched his fight against Conkling's political machine. When Hayes declined a second term, Conkling's political allies convinced Garfield to allow Arthur to become his running mate. Garfield accepted as a way of building needed support among the Stalwarts. Garfield proved less of a pushover than the Stalwarts hoped, and his early fight against Conkling's control in New York essentially ended Conkling's career. When Garfield died after less than 200 days in office, Arthur's ascension to presidency was seen by the Stalwarts as the best-possible scenario. However, rising to the presidency awakened new sensibilities in Arthur. In this article from *Politico*, biographer Scott Greenberger explores how becoming president led Arthur to abandon his role as a party faithful and embrace a larger one.

THE MAN
THE PRESIDENCY CHANGED
By SCOTT S. GREENBERGER
Politico
September 11, 2017

What a forgotten commander in chief can teach Donald Trump.

Eight months in, it's hard to argue that the presidency has changed Donald Trump.

The bombastic former reality television star hasn't been sobered by daily intelligence briefings, or by North Korean nukes. In Houston, confronted with human suffering on an unimaginable scale, he mostly talked about himself. He continues to boast about his crowd sizes, his gilded Manhattan apartment and his golf courses. Other presidents were awed by the history of the house they inhabited—Trump called it "a real dump."

On the eve of the election, Barack Obama warned voters that the presidency doesn't change a person. "Who you are, what you are, it doesn't change after you occupy the Oval Office," he said. "It magnifies who you are. It shines a spotlight on who you are."

But a virtually forgotten American president was an exception to Obama's

The Man the Presidency Changed
continued

rule. Like Trump, he was a wealthy New Yorker, disparaged by big-city intellectuals as unqualified, unfit and corrupt. Fellow Republicans were shocked when he landed on the threshold of the highest office in the land—but no more shocked than he was.

The majority of Americans viewed his ascension with dread, and leading newspapers feared for the future of the republic. The *Chicago Tribune* lamented "a pending calamity of the utmost magnitude." The *New York Times* called him "about the last man who would be considered eligible" for the presidency. Newspapers in Charleston and Louisville said he was a criminal who belonged in jail—or worse.

Chester Alan Arthur, the nation's 21st president, surprised them all.

Arthur didn't start out as a corrupt machine politician. As a young lawyer, he won the case that desegregated New York City's streetcars. During the Civil War, when many were enriching themselves on government contracts, he was an honest and efficient quartermaster for the Union Army.

But in the years following the war, Arthur's quest for power and wealth led him down a darker path. He attached himself to Senator Roscoe Conkling, the all-powerful boss of the New York Republican machine. At Conkling's urging, in 1871, President Ulysses S. Grant appointed Arthur collector of the New York Custom House, the largest single federal office in the nation and a valuable font of jobs and favors that was rotten with corruption.

When the Custom House fined merchants for violations, "Chet" Arthur took a cut. He lived in a world of Tiffany silver, fine carriages and grand balls, and had his Prince Albert coats and high hats imported from London. When an old college classmate told him his Custom House deputy was corrupt, Chet waved him away. "You are one of those goody-goody fellows who set up a high standard of morality that other people cannot reach," he said.

Arthur held on to his lucrative post until 1878, when reform-minded President Rutherford B. Hayes, a fellow Republican, fired him.

But in June 1880, GOP leaders resurrected Arthur's political career. When Republicans gathered in Chicago to pick their presidential nominee, James Garfield, a longtime congressman, upset former President Grant and emerged as the surprise choice. Party elders were desperate to appease Conkling, a Grant supporter, in order to secure his help in winning New York. The second place on the ticket seemed to be a safe spot for one of Conkling's flunkeys. They

continued

chose Arthur, and the Republicans triumphed in November.

But on the morning of July 2, 1881, a deranged office-seeker shot Garfield in a Washington railroad station. Garfield survived the shooting, but he was mortally wounded. For months, as he lay dying in the White House, Americans prayed for their fallen leader and trembled at the thought of Conkling's stooge leading the nation. Prominent diplomat and historian Andrew Dickson White later wrote, "It was a common saying of that time among those who knew him best, 'Chet Arthur President of the United States! Good God!'"

Arthur had never coveted the presidency, and could not conceive of leading the country. When newspapers accused him of conspiring to kill Garfield, he avoided appearing in public, fearing his own life might be in danger. His friends worried he was on the verge of an emotional collapse.

Under siege, Arthur leaned on Conkling and his cronies from the New York machine. The *New York Times* acknowledged that Arthur's loyalty to his friends was understandable, and had carried him far. But it warned that qualities praiseworthy in a private citizen or local pol could destroy a presidency. "If he is to prove equal to the great position he occupies he must know principles rather than individuals." The *Chicago Tribune* suggested that Arthur could earn "the loyal and powerful allegiance of those true hearts now mourning for the death of Garfield," but only "on one simple condition—that he be President of the Nation and not the chief of a faction."

At the end of August 1881, as Garfield's condition deteriorated, Arthur received a letter from a fellow New Yorker, a bedridden 31-year-old woman named Julia Sand. That letter, the first of nearly two dozen letters Sand wrote to Arthur, helped awaken the conscience of the man destined to become president.

"The hours of Garfield's life are numbered—before this meets your eye, you may be President," Sand wrote. "The people are bowed in grief; but—do you realize it?—not so much because he is dying, as because you are his successor."

"But making a man President can change him!" Sand continued boldly. "Great emergencies awaken generous traits which have lain dormant half a life. If there is a spark of true nobility in you, now is the occasion to let it shine . . . Reform!"

***

As Arthur was poised to take over the presidency, America stood at a critical juncture, in the midst of what Mark Twain famously dubbed "The

The Man the Presidency Changed
continued

Gilded Age." Rapid industrialization was creating vast fortunes—but also rampant waste, fraud and corruption. As the gap between rich and poor yawned ever wider, the Protestant ethic that had guided the nation since its birth was shunted aside in an orgy of speculation and consumerism. Financial titans such as Cornelius Vanderbilt, Jim Fisk and Jay Gould bribed legislators and siphoned government loans, land and subsidies even as they preached the values of self-reliance and a laissez-faire economy.

The Grand Old Party, the party that had saved the Union, was being corroded by greed and cronyism, dominated by political machines and bosses who enriched themselves at the public's expense. Under the so-called spoils system, politicians doled out government jobs to loyal party hacks, regardless of their qualifications. "Where did the public good enter into all this maze of personal intrigue, this wilderness of stunted natures where no straight road is to be found, but only the tortuous and aimless travels of beasts and things that crawl?" the heroine muses in *Democracy: An American Novel,* Henry Adams' 1880 book set in Washington.

The nation's intellectual elite believed that without civil service reform, American democracy was doomed. They wanted to root out patronage and award federal jobs based on competitive examinations, not political connections or contributions. Now, after more than a decade of struggle, they watched in horror as Conkling's puppet prepared to bring the worst features of New York machine politics into the White House. It seemed unlikely, if not impossible, that Arthur would disavow the spoils system that had been the whole basis of his political career.

And yet, that is exactly what he did.

Vice President Arthur had not hesitated to use his position to help his New York cronies, and Conkling and his associates looked forward to reaping the benefits of his elevation. But they underestimated the impact of Garfield's suffering and death on their old friend. President Arthur was determined to show the country he was no mere ward heeler.

In his first Annual Message to Congress—now known as the State of the Union—the erstwhile party hack shocked the nation by proclaiming his support for civil service reform and asking for money to revive the moribund Civil Service Commission, which would craft rules for hiring, promoting and firing federal workers and oversee the exams given to aspiring employees. Congressmen from both parties rejected Arthur's plea.

continued

It took huge Republican losses in the 1882 elections, interpreted by many as a rebuke to machine politics, to change the mood on Capitol Hill. After the elections, Arthur acknowledged that party leaders often coerced government employees into making "voluntary" political contributions—the "assessments" he had enthusiastically collected as Custom House chief. He called on Congress to ban such contributions, and urged passage of the reformers' civil service overhaul, which had been languishing in legislative purgatory for several years.

"One hears it said on the streets and in the hotels that the President has heard the verdict of the people and been guided by it," one New York reporter wrote. Prodded by Arthur, Congress finally approved the reform bill. Arthur signed the Pendleton Civil Service Reform Act in January 1883 and faithfully implemented it.

Julia Sand continued to write to Arthur throughout 1882 and 1883. The president heeded much of her advice—and even paid her a surprise visit at her home at 46 East 74th Street to thank her for believing in him. Ashamed of his pre-White House political career, Arthur ordered most of his papers burned upon his death—but he spared Sand's letters, which reside at the Library of Congress.

Arthur would not serve a second term. He had earned the enmity of his old machine buddies without winning reformers' trust, so he had no natural base of support. He also secretly suffered from Bright's disease, a debilitating kidney ailment that may have dampened his enthusiasm for serving another four years. In any case, the GOP did not nominate him in 1884.

By the time Arthur left the White House in March 1885, however, the public's perception of him had been transformed. "No man ever entered the Presidency so profoundly and widely distrusted as Chester Alan Arthur, and no one ever retired from the highest civil trust of the world more generally respected, alike by political friend and foe," newspaper editor Alexander K. McClure wrote.

In 1899, many of Arthur's surviving friends gathered in Madison Square in Manhattan to dedicate a statute to the late president. The featured speaker was Elihu Root, Arthur's personal lawyer, whom the president had tapped to be U.S. attorney for the Southern District of New York and who went on to serve in the administrations of William McKinley and Theodore Roosevelt.

Root began by recalling the summer of 1881—Garfield lingering

The Man the Presidency Changed
continued

on his deathbed, the strife within the Republican Party, the horror and rage many Americans felt when an assassin's bullet put Arthur on the threshold of the presidency. "Dark suspicions and angry threatenings filled the public mind, and for the moment there was doubt—grave doubt—and imminent peril that the orderly succession of power under the Constitution might not take its peaceful course," Root said.

But in Arthur, Root continued, "our ever fortunate Republic had again found the man for the hour." Arthur recognized that the moment Garfield died, he was "no longer a leader of a faction, but the president of the whole people, conscious of all his obligations and determined to execute the people's will."

Some hold out hope that Trump will come to a similar realization. Last month, fellow liberals blasted Senator Dianne Feinstein of California when she counseled patience and suggested that Trump could be a good president if he learned and changed.

So far, Trump's reaction to criticism or crisis has been to return to his base, to draw sustenance from the hard-core supporters who propelled him to the presidency. Campaign-style rallies may make him feel better in the short term, but if he wants his presidency to be judged a success in the long term, he'd be wise to heed the lessons of Chester A. Arthur.

"For the vice presidency, I was indebted to Mr. Conkling," Arthur said to one New York crony who complained about his transformation in office. "But for the presidency of the United States, my debt is to the Almighty."[14]

Though Arthur might be the most overlooked of the forgotten presidents, largely because he assumed the office through an assassination and not by winning an election, his presidency demonstrated an important aspect of the executive office. That is, though elected often along partisan lines, the president is a representative of all the American people. It is within a president's power to fight against the most destructive abuses of partisanship. Arthur, despite his history, chose to embrace a large role, attempting to represent what he saw as the welfare of all Americans. Called by some historians the "surprise president" for his shift in executive approach after taking office, Arthur was not nominated for another term, but did work to ensure Garfield's legacy, at least in terms of Civil Service reform.

Hayes, Garfield, and Arthur were successful administrators who helped to revive the idea of an independent, strong executive branch, and each was responsible for significant achievements in combating corruption and the patronage system. Their presidencies are also forgotten because they failed to address issues that have since taken on monumental importance, such as institutionalized white supremacy in the state and federal governments. As such, these men can be judged, by modern standards, as failures regarding civil rights and as complicit in the rise of white supremacy during the late nineteenth and early twentieth centuries.

CONCLUSION

The presidencies of the first three "lost presidents" were impactful on many levels. They each played an important role in the governmental reform movement and in restoring presidential independence after Congress acted to limit the power and independence afforded to Presidents Johnson and Grant. The political, bureaucratic battles fought by Hayes, Garfield, and Arthur might seem unimportant in the broader scheme, but they were important steps toward ending the corrupt party politics that had dominated the American political system since Andrew Jackson. It is true, however, that none of the three managed to formulate an effective response to the nation's civil rights issues, and over the course of the Hayes, Garfield, and Arthur administrations, the mistreatment and marginalization of African Americans and Native Americans intensified. The next chapter profiles reformer President Cleveland, as he continued to strengthen the power of the president, as well as Benjamin Harrison.

DISCUSSION QUESTIONS

♦ Why did Thomas Wolfe call Hayes, Garfield, Arthur, and Harrison the "Forgotten Presidents?"

♦ Why was civil service reform needed when Hayes entered office?

♦ How did Hayes demonstrate political independence in his presidency?

♦ Should important issues be included as "riders" to other pieces of legislation? Why or why not?

♦ How did each of these presidents help to restore power to the office of the presidency?

Works Used

Ackerman, Kenneth D. *Dark Horse*. Viral History P, 2011.

Ackerman, Kenneth D. "The Garfield Assassination Altered American History, But Is Woefully Forgotten Today." *Smithsonian.com.*, Smithsonian Institution. 2 Mar. 2018. www.smithsonianmag.com/history/garfield-assassination-altered-american-history-woefully-forgotten-today-180968319/.

Banner, James M. Jr. *Presidential Misconduct: From George Washington to Today*. New York: The New P, 2019.

Bellamy, Jay. "A Stalwart of Stalwarts." *Archives*. National Archives. Prologue Magazine, vol. 48, no 3, Fall 2016. www.archives.gov/publications/prologue/2016/fall/guiteau.

Getchell, George H. *Our Nation's Executives and Their Administrations: The Continental and National Congress*. New York: Getchell & Fuller, 1885.

Greenberger, Scott S. "The Man the Presidency Changed." *Politico*. 11 Sept. 2017. www.politico.com/magazine/story/2017/09/11/chester-arthur-presidency-donald-trump-215593.

Hayes, Rutherford. "April 29, 1879: Veto of Army Appropriations Bill." *Miller Center*. University of Virginia. 2019. millercenter.org/the-presidency/presidential-speeches/april-29-1879-veto-army-appropriations-bill.

Hoogenboom, Ari. "Rutherford B. Hayes: Impact and Legacy." *Miller Center*. University of Virginia. 2019. millercenter.org/president/hayes/impact-and-legacy.

"Presidential Election of 1880: A Resource Guide." *LOC*. Library of Congress. 23 Oct. 2018. www.loc.gov/rr/program/bib/elections/election1880.html.

Robertson, James. *After the Civil War: The Heroes Villains, Soldiers, and Civilians Who Changed America*. Washington DC: National Geographic P, 2015.

Trefousse, Hans. *Rutherford B. Hayes*. New York: Times Books, 2002.

Williams, Charles Richard. *The Life of Rutherford Birchard Hayes*. New York: Houghton Mifflin, 1913.

Wolfe, Thomas. *The Complete Short Stories of Thomas Wolfe*. New York: Simon and Schuster, 1989.

Zarkaria, Fareed. *From Wealth to Power: The Unusual Origins of America's World Role*. Princeton, NJ: Princeton U P, 1998, p. 110.

Introduction

Grover Cleveland was another political reformer, focused on reforming the corrupt party system, and thus followed in the legacy of the three presidents who preceded him. He was also a president with an extremely scandalous past and whose personal behavior while in the White House likewise led to more scandal. Cleveland was essentially forced out of office in a corrupt election that led to the presidency of the honest and well-meaning Benjamin Harrison, but Cleveland returned to office four years later, becoming the first and only president to serve non-consecutive terms. In terms of presidential power, Cleveland managed to eliminate some of the congressional constraints that had been placed on the presidency, such as the Tenure of Office Act of 1867, and thus contributed to the gradual strengthening of the office of the presidency that occurred over the course of the early twentieth century. Harrison, for his part, tried to deal with the nation's severe financial troubles but could not, in a single administration, effectively undo years of regulatory apprehension and financial mismanagement. His greatest achievement, the Pan-American Conference of 1889, marks the first early experiment in global governance and so stands as an important milestone in the making of international Americanism.

Topics covered in this chapter include:

- Governmental corruption
- Tenure of Office Act
- Frederick Douglass
- Civil Service reform

This Chapter Discusses the Following Source Documents:
"How They Got There." *St. Paul Daily Globe*, June 16, 1889
Ackerman, S. J. "The Vote That Failed." *Smithsonian Magazine*,
    November 1998

We the People

Popularity and Political Corruption
Grover Cleveland and Benjamin Harrison (1885–1897)

The fight against corruption dominated politics at the end of the twentieth century, and moderate reformer Grover Cleveland entered office as the new face of the Democratic Party. After taking on the powerful Tammany Hall political machine of New York, Cleveland shot to fame and to the White House, where he became controversial for both his political approach and his private life. He was removed from office after his first term, but Cleveland returned to the White House later, carried by a surge in popular support.

Uncle Jumbo's Anti-Corruption Campaign

Born in the small town of Caldwell, New Jersey, in 1837 Grover Cleveland was the fifth of nine children of Yale-educated minister Richard Cleveland and Ann Neal Cleveland, the daughter of a Maryland bookshop owner. Cleveland was unable to attend college because of his father's early death, which left him to support the family when he was only 16. Although old enough to enlist during the Civil War, Cleveland opted to pay $300 for a substitute to represent him, taking advantage of a clause in the Enrollment Act of 1863.[1] Despite his lack of college education, Cleveland passed the New York bar and began practicing law. As a young man, Cleveland was an avid hunter and fisherman and spent much of his time in saloons and restaurants carousing with male companions and young ladies. With his sizable girth, earning him the nickname "Big Steve," Cleveland was a difficult figure to miss in the New York social scene.

Grover Cleveland, U.S. National Archives and Records Administration, via Wikimedia.

In 1881, the Buffalo City Democratic Committee asked Cleveland to run for mayor; despite little name recognition, he won the election with a promise to tackle legal corruption. Cleveland followed through, conducting a major sweep that revealed graft within the sanitation and transportation departments. He was elected governor in 1882, where he became known as "Uncle Jumbo," and served for two years, gaining national fame. The press covered his efforts to take on the Tammany Hall network, a corrupt faction of the Democratic Party in New York. This was a political risk, given that it was the Tammany Hall network that had supported Cleveland's rise to power, but Cleveland emerged from the fight with significant national support in the Democratic Party and well positioned for a national role.

Cleveland was chosen by the Democrats as their candidate for the 1884 election, following the popular but marginalized Republican administration under Chester A. Arthur. The Republicans chose Maine's James G. Blaine, a long-time fixture in executive politics who had been Secretary of State to both Garfield and Arthur, a U.S. Senator, and Speaker of the House. Cleveland's lack of exposure in the national sphere was an advantage, as Blaine had become a divisive figure in the Republican Party. Blaine suffered from the public perception of Republican corruption, and as he had traded his political influence for cash in the past, these charges were not baseless. Cleveland ran his campaign portraying Blaine and the Republicans as a corrupt network of elites, and this resonated with Americans frustrated by income and wealth inequality even though corruption was common in both parties, especially at the state level. Cleveland appealed to the people with his easygoing style, and since he was relatively unknown, he had few skeletons in his closet. The Republicans highlighted his well-known philandering and relationships with women, but this did little to diminish his supporters.[2]

The 1884 election was close, with roughly 78 percent of voters turning out. Cleveland won with 4.9 million votes and 219 electoral votes to 4.8 million and 182 electoral votes for Blaine. Democrats continued their dominance of the House of Representatives, as they had under Arthur, though Republicans picked up 23 seats and significantly reduced Democratic control, while the Democrats lost two additional seats in the Republican Senate, giving the Republicans a larger lead in the upper chamber. The election was in no way a sweep for the reinvigorated Democrats, but it returned them to the White House after two Republican administrations. Cleveland entered the White House without a dramatic public mandate and without control of Congress.[3]

#MeToo in the Nineteenth Century

On July 21, 1884, the *Buffalo Evening Telegraph* ran a story about Cleveland from his time as governor in upstate New York. According to the article, a woman named Maria Halpin had given birth to a child and listed Cleveland as the last name. She was subsequently taken to a mental asylum, and the child was adopted by another family. Cleveland admitted to having sexual relations with Halpin and acknowledged that he might have fathered the child. His campaign portrayed the affair, however, as relatively innocent. According to Cleveland, Halpin had been a flirtatious woman who frequently associated with Cleveland and his friends. When she turned up pregnant, he did not know if the child was his but supported her, helped name the child, and helped find an adoptive family.

However, in October of 1884, the *Chicago Tribune* located Halpin. Halpin, a 38-year-old widow at the time of the incident, claimed that Cleveland had pursued her for some time, and she had agreed to join him for dinner. After escorting her to her home, Halpin stated that Cleveland had forced his way in and raped her, after which he threatened her if she should go to the authorities. Halpin felt she needed to approach Cleveland about her pregnancy, and according to her, Cleveland did nothing to help. Instead, once her son was born, state officials arrived, removed her son from her custody, and committed her to an insane asylum. The *Tribune* interviewed doctors from the institution, who confirmed that Halpin was not mentally ill and had not needed to be institutionalized. Dr. William G. King, attending physician at Providence Asylum, told reporters he remembered the incident well, and that Halpin had been committed without any legal paperwork. She was released after a few days and attempted to charge Cleveland with assault and the abduction of her son. Her attorney, Milo Whitney, was presented with a document indicating that Halpin had agreed to surrender her son, Oscar Folsom Cleveland, and in return was paid $500. Whitney reported that the document was not signed by Halpin.

The New York press ran numerous stories about the affair, along with commentary on Cleveland's other well-known affairs. Pastor Henry Crabbe of Buffalo's United Presbyterian Church said in an interview with the *Buffalo Evening Standard*, "I am very sorry to say that he is a corrupt, licentious man. He has never been married, and is notoriously bad with women. Cleveland is well known here, and it is a reproach to the city that he ever got into the Gubernatorial chair. I most sincerely and earnestly pray that he will not be our next President. His public life is revealing his true character. It may be said these stories are put into circulation for political effect, but the trouble is they cannot be refuted."

Cleveland's critics came up with the chant, "Ma, ma, where's my Pa?," but supporters argued that his behavior, however morally compromised, was nothing more than the indiscretions common to young men, a weak argument given that Cleveland was over 40 at the time he allegedly raped Halpin. His supporters countered "Ma, ma, where's my pa?" with a slogan of their own: "Gone to the White House, ha ha ha!" Even credible accusations of rape, child abduction, and blackmail were not enough to dash Cleveland's political career.[a]

Works Used

a. Serratore, Angela. "President Cleveland's Problem Child." *Smithsonian.com*. Smithsonian Institution. 26 Sept. 2013. https://www.smithsonianmag.com/history/president-clevelands-problem-child-100800/.

Anti-Welfare Conservatism

The conservative, business-minded Cleveland was an unremarkable executive in most respects. Though he came into office as an anti-corruption reformer, he made little actual progress in this regard. His most significant contribution was his expansion of Civil Service Commission rules dictating that federal positions must be filled under the merit system put into place by Republican reformers; this prohibited government officials from filling certain posts because of party affiliation.

Cleveland did not play a major role in the creation of the most notable government organizations to emerge during his two terms in the White House. These included the Interstate Commerce Commission (ICC)—established in 1887 to manage trade disputes arising from increased connectivity between states—as well as the Department of Labor and the Department of Agriculture.

Cleveland's presidency also coincided with the gift of the Statue of Liberty from France, and he led the dedication ceremonies, though his legacy runs contrary to the spirit of the gift and the symbolism that the Statue of Liberty has taken on since. One of Cleveland's most remembered actions was his signing of the Chinese Exclusion Act of 1888 prohibiting Chinese immigration, the most overtly racist immigration bill in the nation's history to that point. Cleveland was, like many white upper-class Americans, a white supremacist. He did nothing to address ongoing civil rights violations in the southern states and demonstrated little interest in multiculturalism. Although he supported immigration from Europe, he felt that Chinese people were too different from white Americans to successfully assimilate, stating:

_____ *"The experiment of blending the social habits and mutual race idiosyncrasies of the Chinese laboring classes with those of the great body of the people of the United States has been proved by the experience of twenty years, and ever since the Burlingame treaty of 1868, to be in every sense unwise, impolitic, and injurious to both nations."*[4]

Cleveland did, however, support transitioning Native Americans to citizenship, and he supported a law proposed by Massachusetts Senator Henry L. Dawes that called for federally controlled territory occupied by Native Americans to be split into individual allotments and given to families to farm. The effort was legitimately intended to help Native Americans assimilate into society and was inspired by a popular book written by historian Helen Hunt Jackson, *A Century of Dishonor*, that documented the federal government's mistreatment of Native Americans. The effort failed because it was designed from a prejudicial white perspective urging Native Americans to adopt white, nuclear-family-oriented, land-use customs. As the collective use of tribal lands is an important part of Native American culture, forcing Native Americans to become individual land "owners" did further damage to their efforts to preserve their culture. Cleveland supported the act and touted himself as a defender of Native Americans, a stance that was becoming increasingly popular in the press, but this was disingenuous. Business lobbyists had been pressuring the federal government to remove additional land reserved for Native Americans for public sale and the Dawes Act allowed this to happen. Much of the land not given to Native Americans was split up and sold to businessmen and the railroads, further reducing and degrading Native American territory.[5]

Cleveland also helped to establish the modern anti-welfare form of conservatism, arguing that the power to provide welfare assistance was beyond the scope of the federal government and that tax revenues should not be used in such a way. He vetoed a bill that would have provided pensions for Civil War Union veterans, citing the number of fraudulent claims; he vetoed a bill that would have provided a military pension to any individual who served 90 or more days during wartime; and he vetoed the Texas Seed Bill, intended to provide monetary relief to Texas farmers affected by a severe drought. Cleveland's business-over-labor stance, also a hallmark of modern conservatism, was demonstrated by his handling of the labor rights movement—when the American Railway Union led a strike against the Pullman Railway Company in May of 1894, he dispatched federal troops to arrest the strike leaders.[6]

Cleveland was involved in one major constitutional amendment that sought to change the line of succession for the presidency in order to guarantee continuity in the office, prompted by the death of Vice President Thomas Hendricks shortly after Cleveland took office. At the time, the order of presidential succession had been decided in an 1879 law stating that, should the president and vice president both die or be otherwise unable to serve, the president pro tempore of the Senate would take charge, followed by the speaker of the House. Cleveland wrote to Congress following Hendricks's death asking that this law be changed so that a member of the presidential cabinet would assume the presidency, in the order in which they were appointed, and Congress passed this law. In the 1940s, it was argued that the line of succession should include only elected, not appointed, individuals, and a new law was passed, calling for succession from president, to vice president, to speaker of the House, to president pro tempore of the Senate, and only then to the heads of executive departments.[7]

Cleveland's most notable action regarding presidential authority came with his personal effort to eliminate the Tenure of Office Act of 1867, which Congress had passed to dominate former President Andrew Johnson. The bill prohibited the president from removing any individual from office who had received congressional approval without the approval of the Senate. Clearly a political effort to control Johnson, who had tried to usurp congressional power, the law, Cleveland argued, violated the separation of powers and was unconstitutional. Though there was some resistance from the Republican-controlled Senate, the law was ultimately repealed, returning the nation to the previous power structure, in which the executive branch assumed full control to appoint and remove appointed federal officials.

The Popular President

Cleveland's somewhat controversial personal life proved a significant benefit to him while in office. In May of 1886, Cleveland announced his engagement to 21-year-old Frances Folsom, who was 27 years his junior and the daughter of his former law partner. Folsom's father died when she was young, and Cleveland had become the young woman's guardian, so he was essentially marrying his adopted daughter. In 1889, the *St. Paul Daily Globe* published an article entitled "How They Got There—Prominent and Wealthy Men Who Have Captured Pretty Girls":

HOW THEY GOT THERE
PRESIDENT CLEVELAND
St. Paul Daily Globe
June 16, 1889
Source Document Excerpt

As a young man Grover Cleveland was extremely fond of children. In the bachelor apartments over his law office in Buffalo the walls were covered with photographs of bright and beautiful babes. He was particularly interested in the pretty little daughter of his partner and closest friend, Oscar Folsom, and it is said that the portrait of the lovely child at five years old, arrayed in a white dress with a big blue sash, held the place of honor in his collection.

When Oscar Folsom died he made Cleveland a co-trustee with Mrs. Folsom of their only child, and, true to his trust, Cleveland watched over the rearing and education of the girl with tenderest solicitude.

As the child grew to womanhood the bonds of affection drew the girl and her guardian closer and finally strengthened into the bonds of love.

continued

An old schoolmate of Mrs. Cleveland's tells the tale of Cleveland's proposal. When little Frances was eight years old she was sitting on 'Uncle Grover's' lap one day entertaining him with childish prattle of what she should do when she grew up into 'a big lady.' It was about the time of Nelly Grant's marriage in the White House, which had formed a topic of family talk.

'I'm going to have a nice white satin dress and get married in the White House, too,' she lisped.

'But I thought you were going to marry me, and I should wait for you,' laughingly returned Mr. Cleveland.

'Of course it will be you, for you will grow up to be president then,' said the child, knowingly.

When Cleveland was elected Mrs. Folsom and her daughter were preparing to go to Europe, and on calling to say good-by, Mr. Cleveland claimed from Miss Folsom the fulfillment, on her return, of the promise made when a child. He had performed his part of the bargain, and she had only to fulfill her's and become a White House bride.[8]

The marriage was controversial but benefited Cleveland in a number of ways. It silenced critics who accused him of philandering. And the marriage, which was the first time that a president was married in the White House, was also a major media event. Newspapers across the country covered the lead-up to the wedding, the ceremony, and the newly married couple for a long time afterward. Folsom became the most popular woman in America, and one of the most popular in the world, arguably the first celebrity First Lady. Women copied her dress and hairstyle. Most everyone described her as ravishingly beautiful, and journalists fondly described her friendly warmth as a new White House hostess. As America's youngest First Lady, Folsom also lent to her obese, cigar-smoking husband an air of youthfulness and vigor.

In 1888, Cleveland was re-nominated as the Democratic Party presidential candidate. The Republicans chose Benjamin Harrison, a Civil War

general, Indiana Senator, and the grandson of former president William Henry Harrison. The campaign was one of the most civil to date, with the two men battling over issues but with not much in the way of personal attacks. The results were close, with Cleveland winning the popular vote by 48.6 percent to Harrison's 47.9 percent. Despite the popular vote, Harrison won 233 electoral votes to Cleveland's 168, accomplished by Republican political agents in Indiana and other swing states manipulating the election to give Harrison an electoral advantage. This 1998 article from *Smithsonian Magazine* describes how corruption led to Harrison's controversial electoral victory:

THE VOTE THAT FAILED
S.J. Ackerman
Smithsonian Magazine
November 1998

By the gaudy standards of 19th-century American political ballots, it's not terribly impressive: a flimsy 3-by-13-inch oblong paper. Except for the typographical flourish at the top, the Smithsonian's 1888 Republican ballot from Hendricks County, Indiana, is a pretty ordinary version of the ballots Americans all over the country used to cast.

It lists the nominees for President and Vice President, followed by candidates for Indiana's 15 members of the Electoral College—the slightly arcane body that still actually elects our chief executives—and finally, the candidates for state and local offices. Indiana Democrats dealt with comparable tickets, each with its own distinctive graphics and design. Back then many ballots sported a more elaborate mix of slogans, typefaces, pictures and colors than the one shown here. Yet G.O.P. ballots from Indiana in 1888 may be the most significant in American politics. They were distributed wholesale to rascals who were divided into "blocks of five" and paid to cast them illegally. The public reaction to the scandal helped to change electoral history and establish the secret ballot.

In Colonial times Americans mostly declared their votes at the polls, out loud and in public. In 1888, voters in some states, notably Kentucky, still did so. The cerebral Pilgrims wrote their votes, a process that Rhode Islanders

continued

streamlined into what was known as a prox (or ticket) printed by each faction. By 1888 each party in each ward of most states produced its own ticket.

This method and the ward bosses who used it thrived because district ballot designs made secrecy impossible. In some states, politicos could buy votes confident of knowing whether the voters stayed bought; they could watch at the polls as their conspicuously marked ballots descended into glass-sided ballot boxes. Sometimes voters handed their votes to election clerks for deposit, inviting further fiddling with the results. Apparently, ballot fraud was so common it developed its own vocabulary. "Colonizers" were groups of bought voters who moved en masse to turn the voting tide in doubtful wards. "Floaters" flitted like honeybees wafting from party to party, casting ballots in response to the highest bidder. "Repeaters" voted early and, sometimes in disguise, often. In Indiana, the absence of any voter registration especially invited such doings.

By September 1888, Indiana Republicans knew that native-son Presidential nominee Benjamin Harrison was in trouble. Harrison was a Hoosier and a high-tariff man, the darling of big business. His party was rich, rich, rich, but to win in the Electoral College where it counted, he needed to carry New York, the home state of President Grover Cleveland, and, for insurance (and honor), his own state.

Both states looked bad for Harrison. "Grover the Good" had won in 1884 despite sneers that he was a draft dodger and a womanizer. Famously charged with having had an illegitimate son several years earlier, the bachelor candidate did not deny it.

Cleveland's integrity and reform policies (promoting low tariffs and a civil service overhaul) impressed voters. The Republican campaign taunt "Ma! Ma! Where's my Pa? Gone to the White House, Ha! Ha! Ha!" proved prophetic. Warned at various times that his stand on tariffs would cost him votes—in his day tariffs paid the government's bills (there was no income tax)—Cleveland eventually shot back, "What is the use of being elected or re-elected unless you stand for something?"

Yet one of the most brilliant triumphs of his first term was marrying his pretty 21-year-old ward, Frances Folsom, the daughter of his late law partner. Poised yet unaffected, "Frank" became our first style-setting, superstar First Lady. Everywhere she went, she drew adoring crowds. Women copied her hairdo and, on the mere rumor that she was against them, banished the bustles encumbering their dresses.

The Vote That Failed
continued

Cleveland, with a respectable record and a spectacular First Lady, became the first Democrat renominated for President since 1840. Then the robber barons began flooding Republican coffers with campaign boodle. In New York, Republican National Chairman Matt Quay spent lavishly to buy the support of renegade Democratic bosses in the big cities. The Republicans, it would seem, managed to finagle enough votes to control the election. Harrison was confident he would carry Cleveland's home state, where Cleveland was expected to run well behind his party's victorious gubernatorial nominee. But Indiana still looked like a big problem.

For one thing, the state was already famous for ballot chicanery, which the Republican state platform roundly condemned. Ten years before, a U.S. marshal named W. W. Dudley had rounded up scores of Democrats accused of violating election laws. But at the time the special prosecutor, future Presidential candidate Benjamin Harrison ("Little Ben"), managed to secure only one conviction. Now, ten years later, "Little Ben" was at the top of one ballot, running for President, with Dudley as treasurer of the Republican National Committee. To Republican delegations trekking to Indianapolis, Harrison made honest voting—"a pure, free ballot . . . the jewel above price"—a leitmotif of his campaign. He exhorted one and all to free Indiana elections "from the taint of suspicion." But Dudley had other ideas. He was buying ballots wholesale. In a fabulously indiscreet circular on Republican National Committee stationery he instructed local leaders in Indiana: "Divide the floaters into blocks of five, and put a trusted man with necessary funds in charge," being sure to "make him responsible that none get away and all vote our ticket."

Near the campaign's close a suspicious Indiana railway postal agent intercepted one of the incriminating missives. Newspaper headlines followed. Dudley and Quay rallied to blast the Democratic "forgery," and Dudley slapped libel suits on the newspapers that printed it. The vote buying rolled on. Party faithful even brought voters over from Pennsylvania, which was safely in Harrison's column. With the whole nation watching, Dudley brazenly bought blocks of votes in Indiana. But instead of going to prison, where his personal knowledge of Dudley's doings could have put him, Harrison went to Washington.

As President he boosted the already staggering protective tariff and depleted the U.S. Treasury with an orgy of pork barrel boondoggles approved by what Democrats called his Billion

continued

Dollar Congress. He turned Cleveland's civil service into a joke. Meanwhile, in defeat Cleveland flourished. He practiced law in New York. Frank gave birth to "Baby Ruth," a celebrated tyke whose name was bequeathed to a candy bar. Cleveland was content, save for a nagging sense of duty about balloting. Normally he dodged banquets and barbecues requesting "a few words," but when the Merchants' Association of Boston offered a forum, he rose to the occasion. In 1888, the city of Louisville, Kentucky, and the Commonwealth of Massachusetts had adopted the secret ballot system of New South Wales, then a territory in Australia. In a single year, 1889, nine states adopted the Australian method, including Indiana. There was a chance that the reform would catch on nationwide.

The most celebrated martyr to ballot fraud and vote buying, Cleveland lashed out against the "vile, unsavory" forms of self-interest that "fatten upon corruption and debauched suffrage." He called upon good citizens everywhere, to rise above "lethargy and indifference," to "restore the purity of their suffrage." And they did. A ballot-reform landslide swamped the nation's legislatures. By the 1892 elections, citizens in 38 states voted by secret ballot. That year, they also returned Grover Cleveland and Frank to the White House. [9]

The Last of the Forgotten Leaders

Despite the corruption that landed Benjamin Harrison in the White House, he played no role in the fraudulent actions, and he tried to do well by his country. Harrison has been perceived as one of the lesser presidents, largely because of a lack of major events during his time in office and the fact that his presidency ended in a recession. Novelist Thomas Wolfe described him as one of America's four "forgotten" leaders, alongside Garfield, Hayes, and Arthur. It could be argued, however, that Harrison's performance indicates a man with substantial skill and conviction who was marginalized by party politics.

We The People

Benjamin Harrison, Library of Congress Prints and Photographs Division, via Wikimedia.

Born in Ohio in 1833 to a wealthy family, Harrison was part of a true political dynasty. He was the great-grandson of Colonel Benjamin Harrison (a signatory of the Declaration of Independence), grandson of former president William Henry Harrison, and the son of Congressman Scott Harrison. Harrison attended Miami University in Ohio, where he studied law. He had a legal career in Indiana and campaigned for the Republican Party beginning with its first candidate, John C. Frémont. During the Civil War, he served in the Indiana Infantry, rising from lieutenant to brigadier general serving under General William Sherman. Harrison served in the Senate from 1881 to 1887, during which time he championed the party's platform on Civil War veteran pensions (vetoed by Cleveland), high tariffs, and wilderness conservation, which was one of the emerging issues in the Republican platform.

While many Republicans of the era touted support for civil rights and equality, few supported legitimate equal rights or endeavored to end the oppression of African Americans in the South, and nearly the entire Democratic Party (which was the conservative party of the era) was dominated by white supremacist thought. Harrison diverged considerably from this pattern, breaking with party leadership by opposing the Chinese Exclusion Act, claiming it was prejudicial and bigoted. Harrison also gave several speeches that voiced his personal belief in equal rights for African Americans, and he appointed Frederick Douglass, the famed abolitionist and Civil Rights leader, to serve as minister to Haiti, which was the most significant government role given to an African American at that time.[10]

Harrison argued that civil rights for African Americans was a matter of basic legal and constitutional principles, and not of activism or secularism. In his inaugural address, he stated:

> _"I have altogether rejected the suggestion of a special executive policy for any section of our country. It is the duty of the Executive to administer and enforce, in the methods and by the_

> *instrumentalities pointed out and provided by the Constitution, all the laws enacted by Congress. These laws are general, and their administration should be uniform and equal."*

Once in office, Harrison promoted a three-pronged approach, contending that civil rights was a matter of law and order, capitalism, and republicanism. He frequently gave speeches where the subtext advocated civil rights without directly mentioning African Americans. This was part of a strategy to portray civil rights issues—such as the government's duty to intervene in cases of mob violence or terrorism against African Americans—as a matter of general law and order, rather than of intervention in states' rights issues. There were times, however, when he confronted the issue more directly. In the final year of his presidency, for example, Harrison addressed this issue head on in his final message to Congress on December 6, 1892:

> *"The frequent lynching of colored people accused of crime is without the excuse, which has sometimes been urged by mobs for a failure to pursue the appointed methods for the punishment of crime, that the accused of an undue influence over courts and juries. Such acts are a reproach to the community where they occur, and so far as they can be made the subject of Federal jurisdiction the strongest repressive legislation is demanded. A public sentiment that will sustain the officers of the law in resisting mobs and in protecting accused persons in their custody should be promoted by every possible means. . . No lesson needs to be so urgently impressed upon our people as this, that no worthy end or cause can be promoted by lawlessness."*[11]

Had Harrison been able to impose his beliefs on Congress, he might have been remembered as a civil rights reformer, but bills he endorsed to end abuses did not make it through Congress, blocked by the white supremacist majority.

Harrison can also be remembered as the first president to put America on a path toward globalization. While presidents between Lincoln and Harrison were relatively domestically focused in their agendas, Harrison and Secretary of State James G. Blaine initiated an aggressive globalist agenda, and in doing so, carved out a new international role for the presidency. One of Harrison's biggest global accomplishments was his role in convening the Pan-American Conference in 1889, an early inter-governmental organization that presaged the United Nations. Harrison also negotiated a protectorate relationship between the United States and the Samoan Islands, which required tense negotiations with Germany and Great Britain. Further, Harrison sought to use the international market to improve the U.S. economy, leading the nation into reciprocal trade agreements with important trading partners. These actions not only served as important stepping-stones toward our modern international relations and trade, but validated that the U.S. president could have an increasingly dominant role in America's economy through diplomacy and diplomatic imperialism.

A Popular Resurgence

Although a recession hit the nation during Harrison's time in office, it can be argued that he was not completely responsible. The failure of the British banking system was largely responsible for the failure of the gold standard, but financial insecurity marginalized Harrison while in office and detracted from his popularity. Cleveland, after leaving office and returning to his law practice, became even more popular than he had been as president. He and his wife welcomed their first child, Ruth, in 1891, and the press covered her birth and the family's changing fortunes more vigorously than they covered Harrison's presidency. The Curtiss Candy Company named their candy bar, "Baby Ruth," after Ruth Cleveland, though

Ruth Cleveland died of diphtheria in 1901, and the candy bar didn't become popular until 1921. The Clevelands were enormous celebrities after Cleveland left office, and he spent much of this time preparing for another run for the White House. Legend has it that Frances Cleveland told White House staff, upon their leaving the residence, that they would return in four years, which was exactly what happened.

Cleveland again won the Democratic nomination for the 1892 election, and the Republican Party was compromised by the new People's Party, a coalition of western populists aligned with agricultural lobbyists. The populists detracted from Republican support, claiming only 8 percent of the popular vote and 22 electoral votes. Cleveland won with 46 percent of the popular vote and 277 electoral votes to Harrison's 43 percent of the vote and 145 electoral votes. Cleveland, thus, became the first and only president to serve two non-continuous terms in office. In addition to the presidency, the Democratic Party captured both houses of Congress in an upset that saw the Republicans fall into the minority position.[12]

Soon after Cleveland's reelection, the Panic of 1893 hit, the worst financial crisis in the nation's history; Cleveland blamed it on Harrison and the Republicans. Cleveland's business-oriented measures at economic reform were ineffective, and federal debt expanded significantly.

During Cleveland's second term, he was diagnosed with oral cancer, which he hid from the public with the cooperation of his political circle. He insisted on keeping his condition secret, even from Vice President Adlai Stevenson. In June of 1893, Cleveland underwent surgery aboard the yacht, *Oneida*, under the guise of suffering a toothache. In August, veteran reporter Elisha Jay Edwards of the *Philadelphia Press* published an exposé, "The President a Very Sick Man," in which he provided an accurate account of what had transpired off the coast of New York. Edwards was tipped off by a doctor who heard about a secret operation and tracked down others who verified the story. Despite his reporting being

a great piece of investigative journalism, the Cleveland administration refused to admit the facts, and instead launched a campaign to discredit Edwards, calling him a liar and a disgrace to journalism. Edwards's career was ruined, and he was maligned as a dishonest muckraker. In 1917, one of the physicians involved in the operation reported the story to the *Saturday Evening Post*, offering regret for what had been done to Edwards, who was inundated with letters of support from the public.

Today, presidents are not required by law to disclose information about their health, an issue frequently debated by politicians, political scientists, and the public. Given that popular support for a president may be contingent on how fit for office he is seen to be, it can be argued that presidential health should be public information. Cleveland was not the only president to hide a serious medical problem while in office, and the tradition of presidents sharing their physical health with the public only started happening in the 1970s. Presidents and their staff have reasoned that the perception of medical problems would result in a loss of support. Whether or not Cleveland had a right to hide his condition, discrediting a journalist, too, constitutes a criminal act and, thus, a misuse of presidential authority.

CONCLUSION

Grover Cleveland's personal life, his marriage to his much-younger "ward," accusations of rape during his governorship, and his decision to hide a life-threatening illness from the American people are the great controversies of his time in office. As a president, he helped to reestablish presidential power, but he lacked the vision to see how the government's lack of regulation would lead to financial turmoil. Cleveland's return to power after being essentially ousted from office demonstrates the power of public interest and support, which was in no small part the result of his wife, who became America's first major celebrity first lady. Cleveland's scandals in many ways made him more popular and more interesting to the public, presaging controversial presidents in later years. Harrison had the misfortune of coming to office through party corruption and of facing financial uncertainty caused by his predecessors. Though he, too, attempted to assert his authority he was prevented from doing so by the powerful forces protecting business interests and white supremacist control of the southern states.

DISCUSSION QUESTIONS

- ♦ Was Cleveland justified in hiding his surgery for mouth cancer? Why or why not?
- ♦ In your opinion, why didn't Cleveland's past accusation of rape impact his popularity?
- ♦ Would Cleveland's past and marriage be interpreted differently in the #*MeToo* era? Why or why not?
- ♦ How did Harrison contribute to the effort for civil rights and equality?
- ♦ How did Cleveland demonstrate that he was a "pro-business" politician while he was in office?

Works Used

Ackerman, S. J. "The Vote That Failed." *Smithsonian.com*. Smithsonian Institution. Nov. 1998. www.smithsonianmag.com/history/the-vote-that-failed-159427766/.

Brown, Everett S., and Ruth C. Silva. "Presidential Succession and Inability." *The Journal of Politics*, vol. 11, no. 1, 1949, pp. 236–56. *JSTOR*, www.jstor.org/stable/2126507.

Cleveland, Grover. "October 1, 1888: Message Regarding Chinese Exclusion Act." *Miller Center*. University of Virginia. 2019. millercenter.org/the-presidency/presidential-speeches/october-1-1888-message-regarding-chinese-exclusion-act.

Graff, Henry F. *Grover Cleveland*. New York: Times Books, 2002.

"How They Got There." *The St. Paul Daily Globe*. June 16, 1889. p. 12. Chroniclingamerica. LOC. Library of Congress. chroniclingamerica.loc.gov/lccn/sn90059522/1889-06-16/ed-1/seq-12/.

Medhurst, Martin J. *Before the Rhetorical Presidency*. Texas A & M University, 2008.

Meier, Michael T. "Civil War Draft Records: Exemptions and Enrollments." *Archives*. Prologue Magazine. National Archives, vol. 26, no. 4, Winter 1994. www.archives.gov/publications/prologue/1994/winter/civil-war-draft-records.html.

"On This Day, the Pullman Strike Changes Labor Law." *National Constitution Center*. Constitution Daily. 11 May 2019. constitutioncenter.org/blog/on-this-day-the-pullman-strike-changes-labor-law.

Pevar, Stephen. "The Dawes Act: How Congress Tried to Destroy Indian Reservations." *OUP Blog*. Oxford U P, 2019. blog.oup.com/2012/02/dawes-act-congress-indian-reservations/.

"Presidential Election of 1884: A Resource Guide." *LOC*. Library of Congress. 23 Oct. 2018. www.loc.gov/rr/program/bib/elections/election1884.html.

"Presidential Election of 1892: A Resource Guide." *LOC*. Library of Congress. 23 Oct. 2018. www.loc.gov/rr/program/bib/elections/election1892.html.

Sinkler, George. "Benjamin Harrison and the Matter of Race." *Indiana Magazine of History*, vol. 65, no. 3, 1969, pp. 197–213. *JSTOR*, www.jstor.org/stable/27789595.

Introduction

President William McKinley set America down a path that proved ultimately disastrous, what historians later called "American imperialism." Under McKinley, America captured and attempted to manage Puerto Rico, Cuba, Guam, and the Philippines, leading to some of the most morally questionable military actions in our nation's history. The resurgence of colonialism did not ultimately benefit the United States. At the time, however, McKinley gained significant popular support by alleging national security concerns and even humanitarian goals as reasons for America's territorial expansion. McKinley's use of presidential power in successfully crafting his imperialist agenda despite significant levels of congressional opposition was a result of shrewd coalition building within Congress and McKinley's successful effort to win public trust.

Topics covered in this chapter include:
- Spanish-American War
- Occupation of Cuba
- Occupation of the Philippines
- The Philippine-American War
- Anti-Imperialist League
- National Labor Union
- Anarchist Movement
- American Communist Movement
- Presidential assassination

This Chapter Discusses the Following Source Documents:

Turner, Frederick Jackson. "The Significance of the Frontier in American History," July 12, 1893

Twain, Mark. "To the Person Sitting in Darkness." *North American Review*, February 1901

A State of Anarchy
William McKinley (1897–1901)

As the turn of the century approached, America was struggling through one of the worst depressions in history, the Panic of 1893. Cleveland's efforts to address the crisis had failed, and he left office with a relatively low approval rating. As the election of 1896 approached, Republican songwriter Charles Evarts Williams published the following, criticizing the Democrats; it was played frequently during the campaign of Republican William McKinley.

_____ *Where, O where is Grover Cleveland*

Where, O where is Grover Cleveland

Where, O where is Grover Cleveland

Way down on Potomac's shore.

Is he gunning for Duck O' Mallard

Is he humming a Jingo ballad

Dining ev'ry day on lobster salad

Way down on Potomac's shore.[1]

The Democrats nominated William Jennings Bryan, a Nebraska congressman and skilled speaker who attacked the gold standard, opposed protective tariffs and was generally anti-immigration. They attempted to paint Republicans as subordinate to the demands of big business, and highlighted the fact that much of McKinley's financial support came from businesses who favored protective tariffs. During the campaign, Republicans focused on such issues as the acquisition of Hawaii and a proposal on an equal-pay-for-equal-work law to protect women workers. Like the Democrats, they were critical of immigration, but proposed a more moderate ban on illiterate immigrants—a popular debate of the day, with both sides claiming that immigration should be limited to the best and brightest.

William McKinley, by Harriet Anderson Stubbs Murphy, via Wikimedia.

Bryan ultimately lost support for his opposition to the gold standard, which many Democrats favored; he also lost support among progressives who felt he was too tied to traditionalist conservative interests and agriculture. The election was a sweep for the Republicans, 7.1 million popular votes and 271 electoral votes to 6.3 million popular votes and 176 electoral votes for Bryan's Democratic/Populist coalition, with 80 percent of the voting age population turning out to the polls. The Republicans also maintained control of Congress, though they lost 31 seats in the House. A gain of two seats in the Senate solidified their control and gave McKinley a strong mandate to set a new Republican agenda.[2]

Ohio Imperialist

The New Orleans *Picayune*, a Democratic newspaper, said of McKinley:

> *"McKinley appears a little under middle height, and this defect of under size is increased by the exceeding squareness and solidity both of form and face. His forehead, smooth and white, overhangs eyes deep-set under bushy eyebrows of jet black. He has a trick, when asking a question, of lifting those eyebrows so that the latent fire in his eyes flashes forth suddenly and sharp."[3]*

McKinley gained a reputation, in life and office, as a superb if somewhat stodgy orator. Born in 1843 in a small town in Ohio, McKinley was the seventh of eight children in a moderately poor family. When the Civil War began, McKinley joined the Ohio Volunteer Infantry, where he served on the staff of Colonel Rutherford B. Hayes, who he considered a mentor. He emerged from the war with the rank of brevet major and returned to Ohio to study and practice law. McKinley's first public office was as county prosecutor in Canton, Ohio, where he won election to the Republican Party. McKinley won a seat in Congress in 1876. In 1889 he became chair of the powerful House Ways and Means Committee. Republicans of the time were firmly aligned with protective tariffs, which pleased domestic business owners but were often unpopular with consumers, as tariffs typically raise prices. When Republicans pushed through the McKinley Tariff of 1890, McKinley and a number of other Republicans lost their seats in the 1890 elections. McKinley returned to Ohio, where he won a close race for governor in 1891.

As president, McKinley left his most lasting mark in expansionism and American imperialism. In part, this was a function of the approaching new century, bringing with it a hunger for newness, change, and transformation. The western frontier was nearly entirely settled, and frontier towns were becoming urban and industrialized. At the World's Fair in Chicago, historian Frederick Jackson Turner delivered a famous speech that has come to be called the "frontier thesis"—the idea that America's greatness is necessarily tied to the capability for discovery, expansion, and the exploration of new frontiers. The following excerpts demonstrate Turner's mourning at the death of an American ideal that had shaped the nation:

THE SIGNIFICANCE OF THE FRONTIER IN AMERICAN HISTORY
Frederick Jackson Turner
July 12, 1893
Source Document Excerpt

In a recent bulletin of the Superintendent of the Census for 1890 appear these significant words: "Up to and including 1880 the country had a frontier of settlement, but at present the unsettled area has been so broken into by isolated bodies of settlement that there can hardly be said to be a frontier line. In the discussion of its extent, its westward movement, etc., it can not, therefore, any longer have a place in the census reports." This brief official statement marks the closing of a great historic movement. Up to our own day American history has been in a large degree the history of the colonization of the Great West. The existence of an area of free land, its continuous recession, and the advance of American settlement westward, explain American development.

continued

Behind institutions, behind constitutional forms and modifications, lie the vital forces that call these organs into life and shape them to meet changing conditions. The peculiarity of American institutions is, the fact that they have been compelled to adapt themselves to the changes of an expanding people—to the changes involved in crossing a continent, in winning a wilderness, and in developing at each area of this progress out of the primitive economic and political conditions of the frontier into the complexity of city life. Said Calhoun in 1817, "We are great, and rapidly—I was about to say fearfully—growing!" So saying, he touched the distinguishing feature of American life. All peoples show development; the germ theory of politics has been sufficiently emphasized. In the case of most nations, however, the development has occurred in a limited area; and if the nation has expanded, it has met other growing peoples whom it has conquered. But in the case of the United States we have a different phenomenon. Limiting our attention to the Atlantic coast, we have the familiar phenomenon of the evolution of institutions in a limited area, such as the rise of representative government; the differentiation of simple colonial governments into complex organs; the progress from primitive industrial society, without division of labor, up to manufacturing civilization. But we have in addition to this a recurrence of the process of evolution in each western area reached in the process of expansion. Thus American development has exhibited not merely advance along a single line, but a return to primitive conditions on a continually advancing frontier line, and a new development for that area. American social development has been continually beginning over again on the frontier. This perennial rebirth, this fluidity of American life, this expansion westward with its new opportunities, its continuous touch with the simplicity of primitive society, furnish the forces dominating American character. The true point of view in the history of this nation is not the Atlantic coast, it is the Great West. Even the slavery struggle, which is made so exclusive an object of attention by writers like Professor von Holst, occupies its important place in American history because of its relation to westward expansion.

. . .

In this advance, the frontier is the outer edge of the wave—the meeting point between savagery and civilization. Much has been written about the frontier from the point of view of border warfare and the chase, but as a field for the serious study of the economist and the historian it has been neglected.

. . .

The Significance of the Frontier in American History
continued

From the conditions of frontier life came intellectual traits of profound importance. The works of travelers along each frontier from colonial days onward describe certain common traits, and these traits have, while softening down, still persisted as survivals in the place of their origin, even when a higher social organization succeeded. The result is that to the frontier the American intellect owes its striking characteristics. That coarseness and strength combined with acuteness and inquisitiveness; that practical, inventive turn of mind, quick to find expedients; that masterful grasp of material things, lacking in the artistic but powerful to effect great ends; that restless, nervous energy; that dominant individualism, working for good and for evil, and withal that buoyancy and exuberance which comes with freedom—these are traits of the frontier, or traits called out elsewhere because of the existence of the frontier. Since the days when the fleet of Columbus sailed into the waters of the New World, America has been another name for opportunity, and the people of the United States have taken their tone from the incessant expansion which has not only been open but has even been forced upon them. He would be a rash prophet who should assert that the expansive character of American life has now entirely ceased. Movement has been its dominant fact, and, unless this training has no effect upon a people, the American energy will continually demand a wider field for its exercise. But never again will such gifts of free land offer themselves. For a moment, at the frontier, the bonds of custom are broken and unrestraint is triumphant. There is not *tabula rasa*. The stubborn American environment is there with its imperious summons to accept its conditions; the inherited ways of doing things are also there; and yet, in spite of environment, and in spite of custom, each frontier did indeed furnish a new field of opportunity, a gate of escape from the bondage of the past; and freshness, and confidence, and scorn of older society, impatience of its restraints and its ideas, and indifference to its lessons, have accompanied the frontier. What the Mediterranean Sea was to the Greeks, breaking the bond of custom, offering new experiences, calling out new institutions and activities, that, and more, the ever retreating frontier has been to the United States directly, and to the nations of Europe more remotely. And now, four centuries from the discovery of America, at the end of a hundred years of life under the Constitution, the frontier has gone, and with its going has closed the first period of American history.[4]

For most of the country's history, American politicians on both sides favored an isolationist approach to foreign policy. Westward expansion was not seen as globalist or imperialist, though today it is more realistically depicted that way. Americans fought an imbalanced war with Mexico to claim half of Mexico's territory, threatened war with Europe to claim a larger piece of the country's northern boundary, and killed hundreds of thousands of Native Americans, members of their own sovereign nations, to claim new territory. Politicians framed these efforts as part of a domestic security and economic policy. Turner's speech about the end of the frontier struck a chord with many Americans, many of whom wanted more frontier to conquer.

At the time, politicians and the public were being presented with arguments suggesting that America should expand its global influence by exerting control of contested properties, such as Puerto Rico, Cuba, and the Philippines. This divided the country into two camps: imperialists and anti-imperialists. Anti-imperialists included author Mark Twain, former president Benjamin Harrison, and Democratic candidate William Jennings Bryan, who warned that expansion would be costly, lead America into unnecessary international conflict, and detract from domestic issues, such as the labor movement, exploitation of African Americans, and domestic economy. Imperialists—like McKinley, Theodore Roosevelt, and Massachusetts Senator Henry Cabot Lodge—believed that the nation should seek greatness by asserting itself in the international sphere by building a stronger military with greater naval power and acquiring overseas colonies to spread the American ideal across the globe. The appeal of new vistas to conquer and explore resonated with the American people and gave McKinley widespread popular support to pursue a more aggressive path toward American imperialism.

McKinley began with Cuba, an expansion possibility that had arisen during the Cleveland administration. Years of oppressive rule by Spain led

to a Cuban revolt in 1895, just before McKinley's win. Spain sent a massive military force to Cuba and reportedly rounded up more than 300,000 into military camps. America had considerable economic interests in Cuba, and a number of Americans lived and worked on the island. There was an economic lobby calling for the United States to end violence in the state, while others supported Cuba based on Cuban oppression by the Spanish government. This created an unusual coalition calling for U.S. intervention. Some Americans even traveled to Cuba to aid the revolutionary cause.

Re-election poster for McKinley, 1900, via Wikimedia. McKinley set the United States on a path to imperialism, beginning with Cuba.

McKinley's administration pressured Spain to resolve the crisis, and in late 1897 the Spanish government proposed a system of limited autonomy and released citizens from military detainment. However, in January 1898 loyalists to Spain became violent and attacked rebel sympathizers in riots in Havana in retaliation for Spain's accessions. McKinley ordered the battleship *U.S.S. Maine* to Havana harbor to symbolically represent America's interest in restoring peace. The *New York Journal* then published a letter, reportedly intercepted by Cubans and written by Enrique Dupuy de Lôme of Spain, which suggested that the Spanish government considered McKinley weak and had no intention of good-faith negotiations with the United States.[5]

The De Lôme letter had hawks in Congress and the public gearing up for war; the situation worsened in February when the *Maine* suffered an explosion and sunk, killing 266 crew members. Despite no evidence of attack, many suspected Spanish misconduct, strengthening calls for war. Activists used the slogan, "Remember the Maine! To Hell with Spain!" An investigation discovered that the *Maine* likely hit a Spanish mine, and though this was not an intentional attack, pro-war agitation grew more intense. Negotiators searched for a diplomatic solution, but Spain was unwilling to budge, and McKinley was increasingly influenced by calls for war. In April, Congress granted McKinley the authority to intervene in Cuba. Spain declared war on April 23, in response to an American blockade. The U.S. Congress also declared war, but anti-imperialists passed the Teller Amendment, which established an anti-imperialist objective, stating that the United States, "hereby disclaims any disposition of intention to exercise sovereignty, jurisdiction, or control over said island except for pacification thereof, and asserts its determination, when that is accomplished, to leave the government and control of the island to its people." This was enough to convince some of the anti-imperialists in Congress to back military engagement.[6]

The war lasted just over three months, and McKinley fully occupied his role as commander in chief. He set up a war room in the White House, with maps of the battlefield, from which he could communicate with his generals in the field. Major naval victories led to a ground assault in which Theodore Roosevelt, then a colonel, led his "Rough Riders" to capture Santiago. U.S. naval forces then captured Jamaica and Puerto Rico, without significant resistance. In the midst of war fever, McKinley promoted a resolution to annex Hawaii, long contested in Congress. With war ongoing, and a surge of nationalism among the public, Congress conceded to the annexation. In total, fewer than 400 Americans were killed in the battle, with roughly twice as many Spanish troops losing their lives.

The Paris Peace Treaty of December 1898 gave the United States control of Puerto Rico, Guam, and the Philippine Islands, for which the United States paid $20 million to the Spanish government. Cuba was not an occupied territory, but it did remain a protectorate into the 1930s. Despite criticism from the anti-imperialists in Congress, McKinley's war had given him the power of public opinion. Driven by a predictable surge in public support afforded to nearly every president (except in the modern era) who declared war, McKinley's popularity had never been higher, and his opponents, both Republicans and Democrats, realized that too much opposition might destroy their political aspirations as well.

McKinley had not violated constitutional limits on presidential power, but through shrewd use of political influence, he dominated Congress and forced the legislature to avoid any aggressive attempts at limiting his authority. This demonstrated forceful executive power; he greatly expanded presidential authority and America's role in the world by transforming the nation into a colonial power. McKinley proved able to maintain his influence even as America's experiment in imperialism almost immediately took a dark turn.

A nationalist movement in the Philippines, led by Emilio Aguinaldo, opposed American occupation. Riots and demonstrations spread across the country, and McKinley sent thousands of troops and naval ships to keep the peace. It took until 1902 for the Philippine government to put down the insurrection. Compared to the Spanish-American War, the Filipino insurgency proved far less sanitized. Nearly 5,000 Americans lost their lives in the revolt, more than 200,000 Filipinos were killed, and citizens and towns were left devastated. The McKinley administration did its best to stifle news of the Philippine-American War and disseminated propaganda linking the violence to terrorist groups. In truth, American troops were guilty of what would today be called war crimes, including arson, villages destroyed and pillaged, women raped, and torture against insurgents. This was a far cry from the allegedly noble intentions of America's intervention in Cuba, claimed to be necessary to counter Spanish atrocities, and closer to oppression against a people fighting for independence and autonomy.

McKinley's influence enabled him to remain unsullied from the accusations levied against him by anti-imperialists, but their views soon became accepted as standards of human rights. One of the few members of Congress to stand up to McKinley was George Frisbie Hoar, a Republican from Massachusetts:

> *"You have devastated provinces. You have slain uncounted thousands of peoples you desire to benefit. You have established reconcentration camps . . . . You make the American flag in the eyes of a numerous people the emblem of sacrilege in Christian churches, and of the burning of human dwellings, and of the horror of the water torture."*[7]

Mark Twain, perhaps the most visible opponent of imperialism at the turn of the century wrote his seminal satire, "To the Person Sitting in Darkness" as a rebuke of American imperialists and their agenda:

TO THE PERSON SITTING IN DARKNESS

Mark Twain
February 1901
Source Document Excerpt

Shall we? That is, shall we go on conferring our Civilization upon the peoples that sit in darkness, or shall we give those poor things a rest? Shall we bang right ahead in our old-time, loud, pious way, and commit the new century to the game; or shall we sober up and sit down and think it over first? Would it not be prudent to get our Civilization-tools together, and see how much stock is left on hand in the way of Glass Beads and Theology, and Maxim Guns and Hymn Books, and Trade-Gin and Torches of Progress and Enlightenment (patent adjustable ones, good to fire villages with, upon occasion), and balance the books, and arrive at the profit and loss, so that we may intelligently decide whether to continue the business or sell out the property and start a new Civilization Scheme on the proceeds?

Extending the Blessings of Civilization to our Brother who Sits in Darkness has been a good trade and has paid well, on the whole; and there is money in it yet, if carefully worked— but not enough, in my judgment, to make any considerable risk advisable. The People that Sit in Darkness are getting to be too scarce—too scarce and too shy. And such darkness as is now left is really of but an indifferent quality, and not dark enough for the game. The most of those People that Sit in Darkness have been furnished with more light than was good for them or profitable for us. We have been injudicious.

The Blessings-of-Civilization Trust, wisely and cautiously administered, is a Daisy. There is more money in it, more territory, more sovereignty, and other kinds of emolument, than there is in any other game that is played. But Christendom has been playing it badly of late years, and must certainly suffer by it, in my opinion. She has been so eager to get every stake that appeared on the green cloth, that the People who Sit in Darkness have noticed it—they have noticed it, and have begun to show alarm. They have become suspicious of the Blessings of Civilization. More—they have begun to examine them. This is not well. The Blessings of Civilization are all right, and a good commercial property; there could not be a better, in a dim light. In the right kind of a light, and at a proper distance, with the goods a little out of focus, they furnish this desirable exhibit to the Gentlemen who Sit in Darkness. . .[8]

Twain became vice president of the Anti-Imperialist League and one of the most influential critics of the McKinley administration; yet with a new era approaching, Americans' new imperialist agenda offered a sense of newness and adventure and returned some of the popular sentiment of manifest destiny.

Labor and Violence

The National Labor Union was founded in 1866, and this began a more organized effort to achieve workers' rights, a movement that reflected the inequality that plagued America in the nineteenth century and continues to be today one of America's most significant issues. The labor movement organized workers against company owners who wanted better pay, reasonable working hours, health and safety guarantees, and compensation for work-related injuries. In the late 1800s, most Republicans and Democrats were pro-business, as political power and influence were linked directly to a candidate's ability to generate campaign funds, funds that were easier to get from corporate donations. Wealthy citizens, who were also able to contribute more, had greater influence over politicians, while working-class individuals commanded little in the way of political power.

The creation of labor unions in the late 1800s shifted that balance, giving workers the power of a political lobby. However, with most politicians closely aligned to business owners, labor rights activists had a difficult road. Companies hired thugs to break up strikes and demonstrations. Corrupt politicians and police officials used legal force to prohibit labor meetings and to break strikes, and politicians excused this conduct by portraying labor activists as anti-government radicals and agitators. Some in the labor movement began gravitating toward alternative political philosophies, including communism and socialism.

Beginning in the late 1800s, another anti-capitalist movement began gaining steam in the United States: anarchism. Anarchist philosophy holds

that it is not necessary to have a broader government within a society; instead, smaller groups of people will form social compacts to facilitate the exchange of goods. The philosophy is not especially robust, but anarchism appealed to a number of those in the working class who believed that the corruption of the American government was a function of government itself, which was the evil that was preventing the advance of human rights.

Labor activists in the late 1800s had legitimate grievances, but years of organized resistance had done little to secure workers' rights. As the labor movement evolved, clashes between labor and police or labor and management-hired thugs became more violent. The infamous Haymarket Square Riot in Chicago saw a group of allegedly anarchist individuals detonate a bomb killing eight people after police began arresting protestors. This resulted in a major crackdown on anarchism and reported police abuses of anarchists.

McKinley occasionally broke with the Republican Party line, which was pro-business and anti-labor. While Governor of Ohio, he pushed for a state arbitration program that could be used to settle disputes. This, coupled with personal losses in the Panic of 1893 that damaged McKinley's personal fortune, gave him strong support from the labor movement heading into the 1896 election. Once elected, McKinley tried to court support from labor by appointing prominent labor leaders to federal positions, including Ohio's Terence V. Powderly to lead the department of immigration. It was a symbolic nod to the labor movement, rather than a sign of real policy change. Despite not being a strong pro-labor leader, McKinley gained popular support, even among labor activists, during the Spanish-American War, and achieved an historic win in the 1900 election, which saw a drop in voters from nearly 80 percent four years earlier to 74 percent. McKinley won by an even larger margin in his second election, receiving 7.2 million votes to 6.3 million votes for Jennings Bryan, whom

the Democrats, again, chose as their candidate. The legislative elections were no better for Democrats, with Republicans leading by 24 seats in the Senate and 46 seats in the House. Thanks to the war surge, the Republicans again dominated the government.

In September of 1901, McKinley was assassinated by Leon F. Czolgosz at the Pan-American Exposition in Buffalo, New York, while standing in a greeting line shaking hands. The 28-year-old Czolgosz, an unemployed mill worker, had a history of involvement with anarchist activists. The incident resulted in the government banning anarchists from entering the United States, and police raiding anarchist meetings and harassing communist and socialist organizations. Czolgosz's attack was likewise exploited by industrialists and their political allies to discredit the labor movement.[9]

McKinley died at the crest of his public popularity and has been judged by historians as a relatively successful executive who made effective use of his powers and who, in many ways, dramatically changed the direction of American foreign policy. Critics argue that by ignoring the labor and civil rights movements and putting the United States on the path of imperialism, his actions had political and ethical repercussions into the modern era, such as the 2018 controversy over federal responsibility in Puerto Rico after the devastation caused by Hurricane Maria.

CONCLUSION

Though the era of overt American imperialism was relatively short-lived, the United States has never ceased imperialistic activities. Numerous military and covert actions have been undertaken to secure American interests in a variety of developing countries. Later presidents would utilize intelligence services to conduct secret operations in nations with diplomatic, military, or economic importance. Though such actions are frequently controversial, as were McKinley's imperialist policies in the early 1900s, American concern with imperialist policies has never reached the critical stage where politicians who pursue this course suffer sufficiently on the political sphere to discourage them. McKinley's presidency changed the course of American foreign policy, and historians have since judged him a capable executive, if not particularly gifted with forethought about how the national agenda he helped to create would impact the world after his death. McKinley's assassination, by a mentally-ill young man who felt McKinley had failed the labor movement, led to the ascension of Theodore Roosevelt, who became one of America's best-known and well-liked presidents, as the next chapter illustrates.

DISCUSSION QUESTIONS

♦ Were American military actions in the Philippines justified? Why or why not?

♦ Did McKinley violate constitutional limits on presidential power? Explain your answer.

♦ What was the meaning of Mark Twain's essay, "To the Person Sitting in Darkness?"

♦ Explain the basis of Frederick Turner's "frontier thesis?"

Works Used

E.A.S. (arranger), and Charles Evarts Williams (lyricist). Lyrics to Democracy's Lament. Bangor, Maine: Chas. E. Williams, 1896. *LOC*, Library of Congress, www.loc.gov/item/ihas.200155624/.

Fallows, Samuel. *Life of William McKinley, Our Martyred President*. Chicago, IL: Regan Printing House, 1901.

Meiser, Jeffrey W. *Power and Restraint: The Rise of the United States, 1898–1941*. Washington DC: Georgetown U P, 2015.

Miller, Scott. *The President and the Assassin: McKinley, Terror, and the Empire at the Dawn of the American Century*. New York: Random House, 2011; 2013.

"Presidential Election of 1896: A Resource Guide." *LOC*. Library of Congress. Oct. 23, 2018. www.loc.gov/rr/program/bib/elections/election1896.html.

"Transcript of the De Lôme Letter (1898)." *Our Documents*. 2019. www.ourdocuments.gov/doc.php?flash=false&doc=53&page=transcript.

Turner, Frederick Jackson. "The Significance of the Frontier in American History." *National Humanities Center*. nationalhumanitiescenter.org/pds/gilded/empire/text1/turner.pdf.

Twain, Mark. "To the Person Sitting in Darkness." (originally published in *North American Review*, February 1901.) *Investigating History*, City University of New York, investigatinghistory.ashp.cuny.edu/module7A.php.

Welch, Richard E. "American Atrocities in the Philippines: The Indictment and the Response." *Pacific Historical Review*, vol. 43, no. 2, May 1974, pp. 233-53, *JSTOR*, www.jstor.org/stable/3637551.

Introduction

Theodore Roosevelt is one of the most beloved American presidents. He possessed both the ability to capture the public trust and to form functional working relationships with other politicians, traits that enabled him to command significant presidential power. Roosevelt entered office the top celebrity of the short and celebrated Spanish-American War, and carried with him a reputation as a rugged reformer. Even before the presidency, running as McKinley's vice president, Roosevelt mastered the campaign trail with a tireless tour of American cities that brought his political vision to millions of Americans. In office, Roosevelt made his biggest mark as a domestic reformer, and was the first president to take the workers' rights movement seriously. Roosevelt used the power of the presidency to mediate domestic disputes, setting a precedent that future presidents would likewise follow. On the foreign front, Roosevelt established an important foreign policy approach in which the United States would assume unilateral responsibility to police the Americas, and he followed through on this militarily and diplomatically. Lastly, Roosevelt left a tremendous impact on America's legacy of natural resource conservation and was the most ecologically-minded of all U.S. presidents. Even with the massive weight of the oil, railroad, lumber, and coal industries opposing his agenda, Roosevelt established new national parks, monuments, and wildlife preserves, and helped inspire in Americans the idea that the nation's natural beauty was the American corollary of the great cultural landmarks of the old world, and needed to be preserved for future generations, just like ancient castles and cathedrals were protected by government trusts.

Roosevelt was followed by Taft, who sought to follow in Roosevelt's footsteps, but lacked his conviction and personality. Taft lost hold of the Republican political machine and was too weak to stand against

his opponents in Congress. Though initially following Roosevelt's lead in domestic affairs, completing big-business and anti-trust reforms that Roosevelt started, Taft's decisions weren't as popular and he didn't command the same level of legislative or popular support as his predecessor. Though not a poor president, Taft left little impression on the office, or the public.

Topics covered in this chapter include:
- Spanish-American War
- National Park System
- National Monuments
- Sherman Antitrust Act
- The Depression of 1897
- The Anthracite Coal Strike of 1902

This Chapter Discusses the Following Source Documents:
Roosevelt Corollary to the Monroe Doctrine, 1904
Seventh Annual Message, Theodore Roosevelt, December 3, 1907

Natural American History
Theodore Roosevelt and
William Howard Taft (1901–1913)

Teddy Roosevelt became president after the assassination of William McKinley. A self-assured leader, Roosevelt brought new ideas and considerable vigor to the White House and established a reform-oriented agenda that kicked off the progressive era of the early 1900s. Roosevelt became so popular among the public that the Republicans had no choice but to back him as their candidate for his second term. In the 1904 election Roosevelt earned 7.6 million votes and 336 electoral votes to 5 million and 140 electoral votes for Democratic challenger Alton B. Parker.[1]

Theodore Roosevelt, by Pach Bros, Library of Congress Prints and Photographs Division, via Wikimedia.

Public opinion was Roosevelt's chief weapon, and he frequently traveled to speak directly with the people. Andrew Jackson had used a similar tactic, employing public opinion to discourage legislators from opposing his policy directives, but Roosevelt was far more effective. His level of public support was robust, though women were still prohibited from voting and "Jim Crow" laws significantly curtailed African American political power. For all his often-touted egalitarian principles, Roosevelt was racist and embraced the theory of social Darwinism, which proposed a hierarchy of race in which white Europeans were the "most evolved." Roosevelt did nothing to challenge the exploitation of African Americans in the South and was silent on women's rights. He was, however, the first president to engage in a progressive economic agenda.

A Curious Mind

Theodore Roosevelt was born in 1858 in New York City. A frail, asthmatic child, Roosevelt's passion for adventure and physical fitness began in his teenage years, when he engaged in a strenuous physical regimen to overcome the limitations of his sickly childhood. He became quite fit, was an avid swimmer, wrestler, boxer, and devoted sportsman, and spent much of his life hunting, fishing, riding horses, and exploring the outdoors. His interest in animals led Roosevelt to Harvard College where he planned to study natural history and zoology but switched to law.[2]

He married Alice Lee, whom he met at Harvard, in 1880, and returned to New York to attend law school but instead ran for office. He was elected to the state assembly for two terms beginning in 1882. In 1884, tragedy struck when Roosevelt's mother and wife both died on the same day (February 12), hours apart, his mother from typhoid fever and his wife from kidney disease shortly after giving birth to their daughter. A depressed Roosevelt abandoned politics, left his infant daughter in the care of his sister, and retreated to the Badlands of North Dakota, where he purchased two ranches. For more than two years, Roosevelt hunted and fished in the wilderness and became a respected member of the community. Many of his adventures are recorded in his book, *Ranch Life and the Hunting Trail*, published in 1888, including a six-day pursuit and capture of armed men who stole a boat from his ranch. Though he fit into the frontier well, his intellectual roots were obvious, evidenced by this description of the boat thieves:

> *"They had quite a stock of books, some of a rather unexpected kind. Dime novels and the inevitable 'History of the James Brothers' . . . As for me, I had brought with me 'Anna Karénina,' and my surroundings were quite grey enough to harmonize well with Tolstoï."*[3]

Roosevelt returned to New York in 1886, where he married childhood girlfriend Edith Carow, and began a productive second career, writing and publishing books on history and nature. His first, *The Naval War of 1812*, was followed by *The Life of Thomas Hart Benton* (1887), and his beloved four-volume history of the frontier, *The Winning of the West*, which took from 1889 to 1896 to finish. Meanwhile he published articles, essays, and many of his personal stories in magazines and newspapers. Roosevelt's reintroduction to politics came in 1888, after he campaigned for Benjamin Harrison and was rewarded by an appointment to the Civil Service Commission. In 1895, he was appointed president of the New York City Police Board and in 1897, thanks in part to his knowledge of military history, Roosevelt was appointed by President McKinley to serve as Assistant Secretary of the Navy.

During the Spanish-American War, Roosevelt volunteered for service and served as commander of the 1st Volunteer Cavalry unit. Nicknamed the "Rough Riders," Roosevelt's division was one of the most irregular in military history. Roosevelt recruited officers from the Ivy Leagues in the north, frontier lawmen, cowboys, and prospectors from the west, and police officers and a group of Native American scouts. This colorful contingent charged up San Juan Hill near Santiago, Cuba, suffering heavy losses but ultimately claiming victory in an attack featured in newspapers across the country. Roosevelt and the "Rough Riders" were perfect media fodder, and the newspapers made them all national heroes. The Republican Party in New York pushed Roosevelt to enter the gubernatorial race, which he won thanks to the help of Thomas C. Platt, the corrupt head of a powerful Republican political machine. Once in office, however, Roosevelt demonstrated a commitment to anti-corruption reform. He refused to participate in the patronage system that distributed political offices as bribes and passed bills against the party platform. The Republicans, seeking to protect their patronage system, consulted with national Republican leadership, and they conspired to eliminate his reforms by essentially promoting him to the vice presidency. As Platt described:

> _____ *"Roosevelt had from the first agreed that he would consult me on all questions of appointments, Legislature or party policy. He religiously fulfilled his pledge, although he frequently did just what he pleased. . . . I may add that instead of 'shelving' Roosevelt, I must plead guilty to the charge of 'kicking him upstairs.'"*[34]

Roosevelt had little interest in the vice presidency but realized that the nomination process had been rigged to assure he would become the candidate. This action was more fateful than those responsible could have imagined, leading to one of the most reform-oriented presidencies of all time. Platt seemed to recognize that Roosevelt's nomination, whatever its political motivation, changed the presidency.

> _____ *"No candidate for Vice-President in the whole history of this Republic ever made such a canvass in a national campaign as did Roosevelt in the campaign that has recently closed. The reason is simple. No Theodore Roosevelt was ever before nominated.*

When before has any Vice-Presidential candidate ever become the central figure, the leading general, the field marshal of a national political campaign? Those who thought that Roosevelt made a mistake in accepting the nomination for Vice-President will do well to remember that in the campaign just closed Governor Roosevelt had increased his prestige, power and popularity one hundred fold. Early in the campaign he became the national Republican leader who on every occasion was pitted against Bryan and who vanquished the Democratic Presidential candidate off every field. He answered all of Bryan's questions. Bryan could answer none of his. Besides all this, Roosevelt broke all records as a campaigner. He traveled more miles, visited more States, spoke in more towns, made more speeches and addressed a larger number of people than any man who ever went on the American stump. He beat Bryan all through the campaign, and he beat him on election day. What more could he have done if he had been the candidate for President? Is it not plain that the man makes the office, not the office the man?"[5]

Roosevelt's 1900 vice presidential campaign is the most famous in history. Traveling more than 21,000 miles, Roosevelt spoke in 567 cities in 24 states, and it's estimated that more than 3 million Americans turned out to watch him speak. Political columnists joked that it was Roosevelt's candidacy more than McKinley's, a portent of things to come. When McKinley was killed in September of 1901, Roosevelt was suddenly thrust into the presidency, becoming the youngest man to serve in the office. In the early days of his presidency, Roosevelt promised to fulfill McKinley's objectives, but it soon became clear that he had no intention of doing so. This began the most progressive presidency in U.S. history, and marked a turning point in the history of the executive office.

The Most Powerful Man in America

When Roosevelt entered the White House in 1901, the United States was a nation desperately in need of reform. The laboring class was languishing in economic inequality, and there were few in the political sphere with the power or will to change the status quo. One of Roosevelt's first major actions was to use the Sherman Antitrust Act of 1890 to block the 1901 merger of the Great Northern and Northern Pacific railroad companies, which would have created a railroad monopoly covering much of the country. The merger was the brainchild of robber barons like J.P. Morgan, E.H. Harriman, and James J. Hill. This placed Roosevelt at odds with the business elite and the Republican political machine, but he pushed ahead with his decision, which reached the Supreme Court in 1904, where the Court ruled in favor of Roosevelt and his use of the Antitrust Act.

Because the railroads were the center of local, national, and international commerce, railroad regulation was one of the major goals of the Roosevelt administration. Large companies supported politicians who opposed railroad regulation, and railroads offered substantial discounts to larger companies shipping their products, making it impossible for smaller companies to compete. Roosevelt and allied progressives in Congress tried twice to address this, first with the Elkins Act of 1903 and later with a bill to authorize the Interstate Commerce Commission (ICC) to regulate pricing on interstate shipping. Business-centric politicians tried to weaken the bill by calling for judicial review, recognizing that the appointed justices would likely rule in favor of business. Roosevelt faced a common issue—his goals were opposed by a majority in Congress, both within his and the opposition party. To break this deadlock, Roosevelt traveled the country speaking directly to the public. Politicians saw his popularity rising and saw support from their own constituents on railroad regulation. In the end, Roosevelt succeeded in placing significant regulation on railroad pricing.

Roosevelt's overall reform agenda is often summarized by his efforts regarding the 1902 anthracite coal shortage resulting from a miner's strike in Pennsylvania. Recognizing that he was not constitutionally empowered to intervene in a strike unless it threatened national security or safety, Roosevelt invited mine owners and labor representatives to the White House to participate in negotiations. Roosevelt wrote to the mine owners:

"We are upon the threshold of winter with an already existing coal famine, the future terrors of which we can hardly yet appreciate. The evil possibilities are so far-reaching, so appalling, that it seems to me that you are not only justified in sinking, but required to sink for the time being, any tenacity as to your respective claims in the matter at issue between you.

In my judgment the situation imperatively requires that you meet upon the common plane of the necessities of the public. With all the earnestness there is in me I ask that there be an immediate resumption of operations in the coal mines in some such way as will without a day's unnecessary delay meet the crying needs of the people.

I do not invite discussion of your respective claims and positions. I appeal to your patriotism, to the spirit that sinks personal considerations and makes individual sacrifices for the general good."[6]

Previous presidents had used federal power to break strikes, including Andrew Jackson, who sent federal troops to break a construction workers' strike in 1834; Rutherford B. Hayes, who sent troops to avoid a mail strike; and Grover Cleveland, who used troops to break the Pullman Strike of 1894. However, Roosevelt knew that the depression of 1897 had led to worsening conditions for workers in the industry. The coal-miners' strikes that had occurred resulted in few substantive improvements. Mine owners used cheap immigrant labor, and workers who joined unions might be dismissed.

Roosevelt's proposed summit failed, and he commented to his allies that he was at a loss. Part of his solution was unprecedented: he threatened government occupation and operation of the mines unless a negotiation was reached. With this ultimatum, workers realized that they might not have employment and owners realized they were risking ownership of the mine. Both sides agreed to a deal, and Roosevelt created a commission to handle arbitration, resulting in moderate concessions to the workers in return for the resumption of work.

The anthracite coal crisis of 1902 was an important moment for labor unions. It was the first nationally recognized victory for the unions and confirmed the effectiveness of labor organization. Longtime president of the American Federation of Labor (AFL–CIO) Samuel Gompers said that the anthracite strike was the most important moment in the history of the labor movement. However, the coal strike was also an enormously important change for the presidency. Roosevelt established that, in situations that might legitimately lead to a public crisis, the presidency can utilize powers to act for the people. Presidents since would use their power to initiate investigations and engage in negotiation and arbitration in national and local issues. It is unknown if Roosevelt would have followed through on his threat to assume control of the mines, and unclear how Congress might have reacted to this unprecedented use of executive authority, but Roosevelt's handling of the situation was transformative in terms of executive powers and function. Historian for the *Department of Labor* Jonathan Grossman said of this event, "This meeting marked the turn of the U.S. Government from strikebreaker to peacemaker in industrial disputes."[7]

Global Police

One of the other areas in which Roosevelt also explored uncharted presidential domain was in expanding the American empire. Faced with the aftermath of the Spanish-American War and the management of America's first colonies, Roosevelt's most lasting impact on foreign affairs was his handling of several issues.

First, in 1902 Germany and Britain blockaded Venezuela after dictator Cipriano Castro refused to pay debts owed to both nations; Roosevelt pressured England, Germany, and Venezuela into accepting American negotiation attempts and rejected the right of England and Germany to engage in a naval blockade in the western hemisphere. In January of 1903, Castro asked Roosevelt to intervene, and he hosted a series of negotiations that resulted in Venezuela agreeing to reserve custom duties until the country's debt had been repaid.[8]

Second, in 1904, the Latin American nation of Santo Domingo (now the Dominican Republic) was unable to repay debts to France, Germany, and Italy. As European powers threatened military action, Roosevelt insisted that the United States had the right to intervene based on the Monroe Doctrine, a declaration stating that the United States would prohibit any future colonial occupation from Europe in the region. This was question-able legal ground. Journalist Richard Weightman argued in a February 18, 1905, issue of the *Chicago Daily Tribune* that "learned lawyers in Congress insist that the United States is not required by traditional policy to help republics out of its financial difficulties,"[9] criticizing Roosevelt's actions in Santo Domingo and Venezuela as an overreach of presidential authority. To deal with his objectors, Roosevelt issued an executive order adding what came to be called the "Roosevelt Corollary to the Monroe Doctrine." In his 1904 message to Congress, Roosevelt explains his justi-fication for this shift in American foreign policy in the Americas:

ROOSEVELT COROLLARY TO THE MONROE DOCTRINE
1904
Source Document Excerpt

To the Senate and House of Representatives:

The Nation continues to enjoy noteworthy prosperity. Such prosperity is of course primarily due to the high individual average of our citizenship, taken together with our great natural resources; but an important factor therein is the working of our long-continued governmental policies. The people have emphatically expressed their approval of the principles underlying these policies, and their desire that these principles be kept substantially unchanged, although of course applied in a progressive spirit to meet changing conditions.

Foreign Policy

In treating of our foreign policy and of the attitude that this great Nation should assume in the world at large, it is absolutely necessary to consider the Army and the Navy, and the Congress, through which the thought of the Nation finds its expression, should keep ever vividly in mind the fundamental fact that it is impossible to treat our foreign policy, whether this policy takes shape in the effort to secure justice for others or justice for ourselves, save as conditioned upon the attitude we are willing to take toward our Army, and especially toward our Navy. It is not merely unwise, it is contemptible, for a nation, as for an individual, to use high-sounding language to proclaim its purposes, or to take positions which are ridiculous if unsupported by potential force, and then to refuse to provide this force. If there is no intention of providing and keeping the force necessary to back up a strong attitude, then it is far better not to assume such an attitude.

The steady aim of this Nation, as of all enlightened nations, should be to strive to bring ever nearer the day when there shall prevail throughout the world the peace of justice. There are kinds of peace which are highly undesirable, which are in the long run as destructive as any war. Tyrants and oppressors have many times made a wilderness and called it peace. Many times peoples who were slothful or timid or shortsighted, who had been enervated by ease or by luxury, or misled by false teachings, have shrunk in unmanly fashion from doing duty that was stern and that needed self-sacrifice, and have sought to hide from their own minds their shortcomings, their ignoble motives, by calling them love of peace. The peace of tyrannous terror, the peace of craven weakness,

continued

the peace of injustice, all these should be shunned as we shun unrighteous war. The goal to set before us as a nation, the goal which should be set before all mankind, is the attainment of the peace of justice, of the peace which comes when each nation is not merely safe-guarded in its own rights, but scrupulously recognizes and performs its duty toward others. Generally peace tells for righteousness; but if there is conflict between the two, then our fealty is due first to the cause of righteousness. Unrighteous wars are common, and unrighteous peace is rare; but both should be shunned. The right of freedom and the responsibility for the exercise of that right can not be divorced. One of our great poets has well and finely said that freedom is not a gift that tarries long in the hands of cowards. Neither does it tarry long in the hands of those too slothful, too dishonest, or too unintelligent to exercise it. The eternal vigilance which is the price of liberty must be exercised, sometimes to guard against outside foes; although of course far more often to guard against our own selfish or thoughtless shortcomings.

If these self-evident truths are kept before us, and only if they are so kept before us, we shall have a clear idea of what our foreign policy in its larger aspects should be. It is our duty to remember that a nation has no more right to do injustice to another nation, strong or weak, than an individual has to do injustice to another individual; that the same moral law applies in one case as in the other. But we must also remember that it is as much the duty of the Nation to guard its own rights and its own interests as it is the duty of the individual so to do. Within the Nation the individual has now delegated this right to the State, that is, to the representative of all the individuals, and it is a maxim of the law that for every wrong there is a remedy. But in international law we have not advanced by any means as far as we have advanced in municipal law. There is as yet no judicial way of enforcing a right in international law. When one nation wrongs another or wrongs many others, there is no tribunal before which the wrongdoer can be brought. Either it is necessary supinely to acquiesce in the wrong, and thus put a premium upon brutality and aggression, or else it is necessary for the aggrieved nation valiantly to stand up for its rights. Until some method is devised by which there shall be a degree of international control over offending nations, it would be a wicked thing for the most civilized powers, for those with most sense of international obligations and with keenest and most generous appreciation of the difference between right and wrong, to disarm. If the great civilized nations of the present day should completely disarm,

Roosevelt Corollary to the Monroe Doctrine
continued

the result would mean an immediate recrudescence of barbarism in one form or another. Under any circumstances a sufficient armament would have to be kept up to serve the purposes of international police; and until international cohesion and the sense of international duties and rights are far more advanced than at present, a nation desirous both of securing respect for itself and of doing good to others must have a force adequate for the work which it feels is allotted to it as its part of the general world duty. Therefore it follows that a self-respecting, just, and far-seeing nation should on the one hand endeavor by every means to aid in the development of the various movements which tend to provide substitutes for war, which tend to render nations in their actions toward one another, and indeed toward their own peoples, more responsive to the general sentiment of humane and civilized mankind; and on the other hand that it should keep prepared, while scrupulously avoiding wrongdoing itself, to repel any wrong, and in exceptional cases to take action which in a more advanced stage of international relations would come under the head of the exercise of the international police. A great free people owes it to itself and to all mankind not to sink into helplessness before the powers of evil.

Arbitration Treaties—Second Hague Conference

We are in every way endeavoring to help on, with cordial good will, every movement which will tend to bring us into more friendly relations with the rest of mankind. In pursuance of this policy I shall shortly lay before the Senate treaties of arbitration with all powers which are willing to enter into these treaties with us. It is not possible at this period of the world's development to agree to arbitrate all matters, but there are many matters of possible difference between us and other nations which can be thus arbitrated. Furthermore, at the request of the Interparliamentary Union, an eminent body composed of practical statesmen from all countries, I have asked the Powers to join with this Government in a second Hague conference, at which it is hoped that the work already so happily begun at The Hague may be carried some steps further toward completion. This carries out the desire expressed by the first Hague conference itself.

Policy Toward Other Nations of the Western Hemisphere

It is not true that the United States feels any land hunger or entertains any projects as regards the other nations of the Western Hemisphere save such as are for their welfare. All

continued

that this country desires is to see the neighboring countries stable, orderly, and prosperous. Any country whose people conduct themselves well can count upon our hearty friendship. If a nation shows that it knows how to act with reasonable efficiency and decency in social and political matters, if it keeps order and pays its obligations, it need fear no interference from the United States. Chronic wrongdoing, or an impotence which results in a general loosening of the ties of civilized society, may in America, as elsewhere, ultimately require intervention by some civilized nation, and in the Western Hemisphere the adherence of the United States to the Monroe Doctrine may force the United States, however reluctantly, in flagrant cases of such wrongdoing or impotence, to the exercise of an international police power. If every country washed by the Caribbean Sea would show the progress in stable and just civilization which with the aid of the Platt Amendment Cuba has shown since our troops left the island, and which so many of the republics in both Americas are constantly and brilliantly showing, all question of interference by this Nation with their affairs would be at an end. Our interests and those of our southern neighbors are in reality identical. They have great natural riches, and if within their borders the reign of law and justice obtains, prosperity is sure

to come to them. While they thus obey the primary laws of civilized society they may rest assured that they will be treated by us in a spirit of cordial and helpful sympathy. We would interfere with them only in the last resort, and then only if it became evident that their inability or unwillingness to do justice at home and abroad had violated the rights of the United States or had invited foreign aggression to the detriment of the entire body of American nations. It is a mere truism to say that every nation, whether in America or anywhere else, which desires to maintain its freedom, its independence, must ultimately realize that the right of such independence can not be separated from the responsibility of making good use of it.

In asserting the Monroe Doctrine, in taking such steps as we have taken in regard to Cuba, Venezuela, and Panama, and in endeavoring to circumscribe the theater of war in the Far East, and to secure the open door in China, we have acted in our own interest as well as in the interest of humanity at large. There are, however, cases in which, while our own interests are not greatly involved, strong appeal is made to our sympathies. Ordinarily it is very much wiser and more useful for us to concern ourselves with striving for our own moral and material betterment here at home than to concern ourselves with trying to better the condition of

Roosevelt Corollary to the Monroe Doctrine
continued

things in other nations. We have plenty of sins of our own to war against, and under ordinary circumstances we can do more for the general uplifting of humanity by striving with heart and soul to put a stop to civic corruption, to brutal lawlessness and violent race prejudices here at home than by passing resolutions and wrongdoing elsewhere. Nevertheless there are occasional crimes committed on so vast a scale and of such peculiar horror as to make us doubt whether it is not our manifest duty to endeavor at least to show our disapproval of the deed and our sympathy with those who have suffered by it. The cases must be extreme in which such a course is justifiable. There must be no effort made to remove the mote from our brother's eye if we refuse to remove the beam from our own. But in extreme cases action may be justifiable and proper. What form the action shall take must depend upon the circumstances of the case; that is, upon the degree of the atrocity and upon our power to remedy it. The cases in which we could interfere by force of arms as we interfered to put a stop to intolerable conditions in Cuba are necessarily very few. Yet it is not to be expected that a people like ours, which in spite of certain very obvious shortcomings, nevertheless as a whole shows by its consistent practice its belief in the principles of civil and religious liberty and of orderly freedom, a people among whom even the worst crime, like the crime of lynching, is never more than sporadic, so that individuals and not classes are molested in their fundamental rights—it is inevitable that such a nation should desire eagerly to give expression to its horror on an occasion like that of the massacre of the Jews in Kishenef, or when it witnesses such systematic and long-extended cruelty and oppression as the cruelty and oppression of which the Armenians have been the victims, and which have won for them the indignant pity of the civilized world.[10]

The Roosevelt Corollary is one of the most impactful, but controversial, foreign policy directives in history. There was considerable resistance to it, but subsequent presidents have made use of the corollary to justify aggressive foreign policy maneuvers. The precedent established by Roosevelt was used to justify military actions against Cuba in 1906, Nicaragua in 1909 and 1912, Mexico in 1914 and 1916, and Haiti in 1915.

Roosevelt's position was that the United States would not only prohibit European colonialism, but would behave as if all of Latin America was a protectorate territory, asserting U.S. rights to intervene and "police" affairs in the region. The validity of this approach has been much debated and U.S. intervention was, on the whole, unsuccessful, leading to further devolution of Latin American governments or the emergence of authoritarian regimes. Further, the morality of what amounts to the United States dictating policies to sovereign nations is highly questionable.

Military dominance was a major focus of Roosevelt's, who promoted efforts to expand U.S. naval forces. Even after his presidency, U.S. naval forces patrolled the coasts of the Americas, as an unofficial police force. The Roosevelt Corollary was abandoned by the next Roosevelt in office, Franklin D. Roosevelt, who favored a less militant approach to American foreign relations, helping to alleviate hostility toward American intervention. However, Teddy Roosevelt became the first U.S. president to be awarded the Nobel Peace Prize for his efforts to mediate a dispute between Russia and Japan, meeting with representatives in 1905 in Portsmouth, New Hampshire. Some historians believe that without an arbitrating voice the situation might have deteriorated into large-scale warfare.

The American Cathedral

Roosevelt's most lasting contribution to the United States came through his interest in wilderness, wildlife, and America's natural environment. From his early childhood interest in zoology and natural history through his experiences living in the American frontier as a cattle rancher in a rapidly disappearing landscape, Roosevelt had come to believe that America's natural landscape was a key part of the American psyche and identity. He believed strongly that much of what differentiated Americans from their ancestors in Europe was the physical, ecological nature of America and the experience of exploring its rugged beauty.

While America's first national park, Yellowstone, was created under the Grant administration in 1872, Roosevelt is the president most associated with the park system and the preservation of America's wilderness. Roosevelt, his friend John Muir, and other conservationists worked to create five new national parks, Crater Lake in Oregon, Wind Cave in South Dakota, Sullys Hill in North Dakota, Platt National Park in Oklahoma, and Mesa Verde in Colorado, in addition to adding thousands of acres to Yosemite National Park in California. Roosevelt's personal connection to the outdoors is evident in his decision to establish a park near where he lived and grazed cattle in the North Dakota Badlands. Roosevelt also created the U. S. Forest Service (USFS), through which he established 150 national forests, 51 federally protected bird preserves, and four national game reserves. It was Roosevelt who helped to bring together sport hunters and fishermen, conservation-minded politicians, scientists and ecologists, and the American public to build a massive surge of interest in protecting America's natural landscapes.[11]

Like fellow conservationist Muir, Roosevelt argued that America's natural environment was part of the legacy of the nation, comparable in many ways to the ancient ruins, cathedrals, churches, and works of art in Europe. Roosevelt was so passionately committed to the preservation of America's natural monuments that he delivered a now famous speech in which he suggested to the American people that conservation was not simply an aesthetic choice but a "national duty" of citizenship.[12]

Roosevelt helped to touch off a national park craze, and parks were visited by millions of Americans, necessitating laws to protect the land from tourist misuse. Despite the parks' popularity, some politicians felt that the program was a waste of federal attention and revenues. Had the process of creating new national parks been less contentious in Congress, Roosevelt would likely have established many more.

Roosevelt found a way around this in 1906, after Congress passed the Antiquities Act, which gave Congress the power to protect important archaeological sites on public lands. The act allowed a sitting president to establish a new protected monument without congressional approval. Meant to preserve landmarks such as houses or buildings owned or used by famous Americans, Roosevelt used the act to establish 18 new national monuments, which were essentially new national parks. Among the most famous are Washington's Mount Olympus, the Devil's Tower in Wyoming, Muir Woods in California, and Arizona's cherished Grand Canyon.[13]

Roosevelt's use of the Antiquities Act was seen by some as an overreach of presidential authority, but the program was immensely popular with the American people. The national park and national monuments system was also one of the most innovative ideas in American history, marking the first time that segments of the natural environment were set aside for public, rather than private, use. Popular across the lines of partisanship and ideology, documentary filmmaker Ken Burns called the national park system America's "best idea."[14]

A Transformative Presidency

Roosevelt was a master of presidential authority, making liberal use of executive orders, wielding his strong public approval to convince legislators to support his agenda, and establishing an effective and persuasive rapport with the American people. In the election for his second term, Roosevelt secured the largest popular vote lead in history. However, the percentage of voters participating also dropped, with 66 percent turning out to the polls as compared to around 74 percent in 1900. Roosevelt's election was, in fact, a turning point, and voter turnout for presidential elections would never again reach 70 percent.

Roosevelt remains one of the most popular presidents of all time. Historians and political scientists have given him marks for accomplishing his goals and demonstrating the effective use of presidential power, and students of history still respond to his unique style of leadership. Roosevelt was so transformative because he perceived a fundamental role for government, regulating the free market to balance the interests of individuals against the general welfare. In his message to Congress in December of 1905, Roosevelt said this of the role of government:

SEVENTH ANNUAL MESSAGE
Theodore Roosevelt
December 3, 1907
Source Document Excerpt

"If the folly of man mars the general well-being, then those who are innocent of the folly will have to pay part of the penalty incurred by those who are guilty of the folly. A panic brought on by the speculative folly of part of the business community would hurt the whole business community; but such stoppage of welfare, though it might be severe, would not be lasting. In the long run, the one vital factor in the permanent prosperity of the country is the high individual character of the average American worker, the average American citizen, no matter whether his work be mental or manual, whether he be farmer or wage-worker, business man or professional man.

"In our industrial and social system the interests of all men are so closely intertwined that in the immense majority of cases a straight-dealing man, who by his efficiency, by his ingenuity and industry, benefits himself, must also benefit others. Normally, the man of great productive capacity who becomes rich by guiding the labor of many other men does so by enabling them to produce more than they could produce without his guidance; and both he and they share in the benefit, which comes also to the public at large. The superficial fact that the sharing may be unequal must never blind us to the underlying fact that there is this sharing, and that the benefit comes in some degree to each man concerned. Normally, the wageworker, the man of small means, and the average consumer, as well as the average producer, are all alike helped by making conditions such that the man of exceptional business ability receives an exceptional reward for his ability. Something can be done by legislation to help the general prosperity; but no such help of a permanently beneficial character can be given to the less able and less fortunate save as the

continued

results of a policy which shall inure to the advantage of all industrious and efficient people who act decently; and this is only another way of saying that any benefit which comes to the less able and less fortunate must of necessity come even more to the more able and more fortunate. If, therefore, the less fortunate man is moved by envy of his more fortunate brother to strike at the conditions under which they have both, though unequally, prospered, the result will assuredly be that while damage may come to the one struck at, it will visit with an even heavier load the one who strikes the blow. Taken as a whole, we must all go up or go down together.

"Yet, while not merely admitting, but insisting upon this, it is also true that where there is no governmental restraint or supervision some of the exceptional men use their energies, not in ways that are for the common good, but in ways which tell against this common good. The fortunes amassed through corporate organization are now so large, and vest such power in those that wield them, as to make it a matter of necessity to give to the sovereign—that is, to the Government, which represents the people as a whole—some effective power of supervision over their corporate use. In order to insure a healthy social and industrial life, every big corporation should be held responsible by, and be accountable to, some sovereign strong enough to control its conduct. I am in no sense hostile to corporations. This is an age of combination, and any effort to prevent all combination will be not only useless, but in the end vicious, because of the contempt for law which the failure to enforce law inevitably produces. We should, moreover, recognize in cordial and ample fashion the immense good effected by corporate agencies in a country such as ours, and the wealth of intellect, energy, and fidelity devoted to their service, and therefore normally to the service of the public, by their officers and directors. The corporation has come to stay, just as the trade union has come to stay. Each can do and has done great good. Each should be favored so long as it does good. But each should be sharply checked where it acts against law and justice.

"The makers of our National Constitution provided especially that the regulation of interstate commerce should come within the sphere of the General Government. The arguments in favor of their taking this stand were even then overwhelming. But they are far stronger to-day, in view of the enormous development of great business agencies, usually corporate in form. Experience has shown conclusively that it is useless to try to get any adequate regulation and supervision of these great corporations by State action. Such regulation and

Seventh Annual Message
continued

supervision can only be effectively exercised by a sovereign whose jurisdiction is coextensive with the field of work of the corporations—that is, by the National Government. I believe that this regulation and supervision can be obtained by the enactment of law by the Congress. Our steady aim should be by legislation, cautiously and carefully undertaken, but resolutely persevered in, to assert the sovereignty of the National Government by affirmative action.

"This is only in form an innovation. In substance it is merely a restoration; for from the earliest time such regulation of industrial activities has been recognized in the action of the lawmaking bodies; and all that I propose is to meet the changed conditions in such manner as will prevent the Commonwealth abdicating the power it has always possessed, not only in this country, but also in England before and since this country became a separate nation.

"It has been a misfortune that the National laws on this subject have hitherto been of a negative or prohibitive rather than an affirmative kind, and still more that they have in part sought to prohibit what could not be effectively prohibited, and have in part in their prohibitions confounded what should be allowed and what should not be allowed. It is generally useless to try to prohibit all restraint on competition, whether this restraint be reasonable or unreasonable; and where it is not useless it is generally hurtful. The successful prosecution of one device to evade the law immediately develops another device to accomplish the same purpose. What is needed is not sweeping prohibition of every arrangement, good or bad, which may tend to restrict competition, but such adequate supervision and regulation as will prevent any restriction of competition from being to the detriment of the public, as well as such supervision and regulation as will prevent other abuses in no way connected with restriction of competition.[15]

Presidential Justice

Theodore Roosevelt promised, while campaigning for his second term, that he would not seek a third term in office. Although he regretted this promise, he kept his word and promoted his long-time friend and political protégé William Howard Taft to succeed him. Taft had good intentions and a judicious mind but lacked the charisma and leadership skill of Roosevelt. In the 1913 elections, Roosevelt returned to the fold with the new "Bull Moose Party," and competed with Taft for the presidency—so breaking his word. With Republicans split, a new Democratic progressive, Woodrow Wilson, claimed victory for the Democrats and altered the course of American history.

William Howard Taft was born in 1857 in Cincinnati, Ohio, a member of a political and legal legacy. His father had been Secretary of War for Ulysses Grant and a minister to Austria-Hungary and Russia—a major figure in the Republican Party. Taft attended Yale University, where he graduated second in his class, and then studied law at the University of Cincinnati. Rising within the judicial circuit, he became a solicitor general and then judge in the superior courts, later serving on the Sixth Circuit Court of Appeals. President McKinley pulled Taft into national politics when he tapped him to serve as president of a commission overseeing the Philippines after the U.S. annexed the Philippine Islands in the Spanish-American War. Taft was reluctant to accept the post but did so on the promise of an appointment to the Supreme Court.[16]

William Howard Taft, Library of Congress Prints and Photographs Division, via Wikimedia.

Taft did well as administrator of the Philippines and was chosen by Roosevelt to serve as his Secretary of War. When Roosevelt left office, he personally selected Taft, over the objections of some Republican strategists, as his replacement. With Roosevelt's endorsement, he commanded a significant lead. In the 1908 election Taft drew 7.6 million votes to 6.4 million for Democratic challenger William Jennings Bryan, continuing the Republican dominance of the office. The Republicans held the Senate, though they lost one seat, and controlled the House, though the Democrats gained five seats. Taft entered the presidency with a public mandate and executive support but failed to exert his authority sufficiently to establish dominance over Congress, as Roosevelt had. His four years in office were dominated by the legislature, and most of Taft's initiatives were undone. The most cited example is Taft's unsuccessful effort to lower tariffs, which was defeated by Congress, losing Taft the support of radical and moderate progressives.[17]

Large While in Charge

William Howard Taft was America's most overweight president. When he entered the office, Taft ate a twelve-ounce steak nearly every morning for breakfast. White House records indicate that he could also down nearly a pound of bacon and dozens of pancakes in a single meal. At his heaviest, Taft weighed in at over 330 pounds, and he was frequently sluggish after a meal. Some historians have suggested that Taft's weight problem contributed to his problems in the presidency, as he preferred sedentary activities to the touring and campaigning that more successful presidents engaged in. His weight was the subject of frequent jokes in the press and even among friends. There is a famous anecdote from Taft's time as military governor of the Philippines in which Taft wrote to Elihu Root, who would later become his Secretary of State. Taft told Root, then head of the War Department,

"Rode twenty miles up the mountain today. Feeling fine."

To which Root responded,

"How is the horse?"

Taft also famously had a good nature and was a man of good humor, and this humorous exchange became one of his favorite anecdotes.[a]

Taft was concerned about how his weight would affect his health, and in December of 1905, he wrote to English physician Nathaniel Yorke-Davies, a recognized expert in dietary issues. There is a trove of letters between Yorke-Davies and Taft documenting the president's efforts to stick to a diet. According to these, Taft was supposed to have 2–3 gluten biscuits and 6 ounces of lean meat for breakfast, followed by 4 ounces of meat, 4 ounces of vegetables (without butter), 3 ounces of fruit, 1 biscuit, and 1 glass of sugarless wine. For dinner, he was allowed 4 ounces of fish, 5 ounces of meat, 8 ounces of vegetables, 4 ounces of fruit, plain salad and two biscuits.

Taft reportedly lost 60 pounds on the diet, but the weight loss was slow, and he never achieved anything that might be thought of as a slim physique. Taft's weight has been the subject of historical criticism, derision, sympathy, and humor, at times diverging considerably from the facts. A widely circulated story, for instance, alleging that Taft was once stuck in the White House bathtub, is untrue. Had it happened, however, it is possible that Taft's good humor would have allowed him to share the story himself to amuse his frequent dinner guests.

Works Used

a. Blythe, Samuel G. "The Bigness of Big Bill." *Saturday Evening Post*. 13 June 1908. www. saturdayeveningpost.com.

A Transitional Man

Much of what was accomplished during Taft's single term in office occurred with little influence from Taft himself. The Sixteenth Amendment, establishing an income tax, was a congressional prerogative, though Taft signed the bill into law. Taft also signed the Seventeenth Amendment, which called for direct popular election to the Senate, with little resistance. Taft did, however, successfully attack monopolies early in his presidency, challenging the trust formed by Standard Oil Company and U.S. Steel, though the latter brought him into conflict with Roosevelt. Notably, Taft was the first to suggest that the president, rather than the federal departments, should submit a national budget to Congress. Legislators rejected this proposal at the time, but in the 1920s this became the standard formula, with the creation of a new executive budget office.

Perhaps one of the greatest mistakes of Taft's career was his decision to replace Gifford Pinchot, an experienced conservationist, with pro-business Richard Ballinger to head the Department of the Interior. Ballinger had convinced Taft that Roosevelt had set aside too much land for conservation and that some of it would be better utilized if opened to commercial development. Pinchot criticized Ballinger in the press, and Taft's removal of Pinchot created a rift between Taft and Roosevelt. As Roosevelt considered his conservation advancements one of his proudest presidential achievements, he opposed Taft's reelection in 1912 and created his "Bull Moose Party" to campaign for the presidency.[18]

In the 1912 election, Taft and Roosevelt split the Republican vote. Roosevelt might have won if Taft had dropped out, which would have forced Republicans to support Roosevelt's progressive coalition, but New Jersey Governor Woodrow Wilson, tapped by the Democrats to lead a new progressive Democratic movement, captured 42 percent of the popular vote, and took 435 of the 531 electoral votes. The labor movement saw the emergence of the first non-capitalist political party to compete in a U.S.

election with the American Socialist Party, which promoted candidate Eugene Debs. Though the Socialist Party received no electoral votes, Debs garnered a full 6 percent of the popular vote.[19]

Taft has never been considered a particularly good president. Unable to exert the kind of power that Roosevelt wielded and vulnerable to influence from the big business sector, he alienated progressives in his own party, leading to the creation of more radical Democratic opposition. He remains an important figure for historians, however, as his presidency demonstrated the broader shift in political alignment that saw the Republican Party becoming more conservative, and the Democratic Party become more progressive. This led to a period of political transition. Many Southern democrats were still conservative, so needed to decide whether to remain with their party, which was locally conservative, or switch to the Republican Party, which became more conservative on the national level. Northern liberal Republicans had to make similar choices. As politicians on both sides debated whether to switch, voters were left confused by the evolution of the political system. For several years, both parties contained both political and conservative elements, which had a dramatic impact on policies both from the legislature and the executive branch into the latter half of the twentieth century.

CONCLUSION

Roosevelt broke the presidential mold. His extraordinary life captured the imagination of the American public and he was one of America's most beloved celebrities while in office. Much of U.S. history with regard to Latin America can be traced to his important reformulation of America's role in the hemisphere. The nation would be a far different place without the monuments and parks he preserved, with places like the Grand Canyon and Washington's Mount Olympus serving as an enduring testimony to his vision and commitment. Taft failed to continue the Roosevelt legacy, but was a well-meaning executive. Though there were no major accomplishments to his presidency, Taft did leave one lasting change on the presidency—it was during his administration that the tradition of the presidential budget first became established. Taft was followed by Woodrow Wilson, one of America's most influential presidents, whose extraordinary use of presidential power is discussed in the next chapter.

DISCUSSION QUESTIONS

♦ How was Roosevelt's use of the Antiquities Act a questionable exercise of presidential authority?

♦ How did Roosevelt make novel use of the presidency in terms of his diplomatic relations with Russia?

♦ What was Roosevelt's fundamental belief about the role of the government? Do you agree with this position? Why or why not?

♦ Do you agree with the preservation of America's natural history and landscape, as Roosevelt did, or should such land be developed for housing and business? Explain your answer.

Works Used

"1912 Electoral Vote Tally, February 12, 1913." *National Archives*. 15 Aug. 2016. www.archives.gov/legislative/features/1912-election.

Gompers, Samuel, John McBride, and William Green. *The American Federationist.. AFL-CIO*. American Federation of Labor and Congress of Industrial Organizations, vol. 9, 1902.

Grossman, Jonathan. "The Coal Strike of 1902—Turning Point in U.S. Policy." *Monthly Labor Review*, vol. 98, no. 10, 1975, pp. 21-28. *JSTOR*, www.jstor.org/stable/41839484.

Lee, Ronald F. "Antiquities Act." *NPS*. National Parks Service. Archaeology Program. 8 Dec. 2019. www.nps.gov/archeology/pubs/Lee/index.htm.

Lurie, Jonathan. *William Howard Taft: The Travails of a Progressive Conservative*. New York: Cambridge U P, 2012.

Miller, Char. *Gifford Pinchot and the Making of Modern Environmentalism*. Washington: Island P, 2001.

Morris, Edmund. *The Rise of Theodore Roosevelt*. New York: The Modern Library, 2001.

Platt, Thomas Collier. *The Autobiography of Thomas Collier Platt*. New York: B.W. Dodge & Company, 1910.

"Presidential Election of 1904: A Resource Guide." *LOC*. Library of Congress. 23 Oct. 2018. www.loc.gov/rr/program/bib/elections/election1904.html.

Roosevelt, Theodore. "December 3, 1907: Seventh Annual Message." *Miller Center*. University of Virginia. 2019. millercenter.org/the-presidency/presidential-speeches/december-3-1907-seventh-annual-message.

Roosevelt, Theodore. "Roosevelt Corollary to the Monroe Doctrine." 1904. *Digital History*. 2019 www.digitalhistory.uh.edu/disp_textbook.cfm?smtID=3&psid=1259.

_____. "Conservation as a National Duty." 13 May 1908. *Voices of Democracy*, The US Oratory Project.

"Roosevelt Pursues the Boat Thieves." *NPS*. National Park Service. 10 Apr. 2015. www.nps.gov/thro/learn/historyculture/roosevelt-pursues-boat-thieves.htm.

Rosen, Jeffrey. *William Howard Taft: The American Presidents Series: The 27th President*, edited by Arthur M. Schlesinger, Jr. and Sean Wilentz. New York: Times Books, 2018.

"The National Parks: America's Best Idea." *PBS*. 2009. www.pbs.org/nationalparks/.

"Theodore Roosevelt and Conservation." *NPS*. National Park Service. 16 Nov. 2017. www.nps.gov/thro/learn/historyculture/theodore-roosevelt-and-conservation.htm.

"Venezuela Debt Crisis." *Theodorerooseveltcenter*. Dickinson State University. 2019. www.theodorerooseveltcenter.org/Learn-About-TR/TR-Encyclopedia/Foreign-Affairs/Venezuela-Debt-Crisis.aspx.

Weightman, Richard. "Monroe Doctrine Not Involved in the Santo Domingo Affair." *Chicago Daily Tribune*.18 Feb. 1905, p. 8.projects.leadr.msu.edu/usforeignrelations/files/original/02e257b121fea966e429509a3a41d14c.pdf.

Introduction

Woodrow Wilson was one of the country's most influential presidents. It was under Wilson that the Democratic Party began shifting more aggressively toward a reform-oriented agenda. He initiated social welfare programs that became the hallmark of the Democratic Party political agenda. Wilson's achievements were made possible by his skill in speaking directly to the people and his ability to form coalitions within Congress behind his various policy proposals. The most dramatic event of his presidency was, of course, World War I, and Wilson's position on the issue changed considerably during his time in office. He advocated neutrality during his first term, and ran on that achievement during his second election. When it became clear, however, that America could not avoid the violence in Europe, Wilson's administration essentially invented the American propaganda industry to promote the war effort. It was during and after the war that Wilson became the first chief executive to call for the organization of global governance, international agreements both military and economic that would, in theory, prevent anything like World War I from happening again.

Topics covered in this chapter include:

- Invasion of Haiti
- World War I
- Tariff reform
- League of Nations
- Presidential propaganda

This Chapter Discusses the Following Source Documents:

Message Regarding Tariff Duties, Woodrow Wilson, April 8, 1913

War Message to Congress, Woodrow Wilson, April 2, 1917

Fourteen Points, Woodrow Wilson, January 8, 1918

The Dawn of Internationalism
Woodrow Wilson (1913–1921)

President Woodrow Wilson is one of the most influential presidents in American history. During his presidency, the Democratic Party saw a major shift toward a reform-oriented platform, and Congress enacted one of the most significant economic programs to date. Wilson's presidency helped usher in a social welfare focus for the federal government, and he championed victories for the labor movement. Wilson was also the first president to put his full support behind the idea of collectivism on the world stage as a way to ensure world peace and to spread the perceptive benefits of American democracy. However, Wilson's era also saw the expansion of American imperialism with dramatic humanitarian impact. He authorized violations of civil liberties in wartime, and his prejudice prevented him from perceiving the social justice issues of his era.

Southern Progressivism

Thomas Woodrow Wilson, who later dropped the "Thomas" in favor of his middle name, was born in 1856 in Virginia, the son of a Presbyterian minister. A child during the Civil War, his family lived in Georgia and were southern sympathizers with his mother opening their home to Confederate soldiers. Wilson's racial views were apparent by his decision to screen *Birth of a Nation* at the White House. This film by David Mark Griffith portrays the Ku Klux Klan as heroes, and white actors dressed in blackface portray African Americans as sexually depraved criminals. It has been said that after the screening Wilson stated, "It's like writing history with lightning. My only regret is that it is all so terribly true."[1]

Woodrow Wilson, by Harris & Ewing, Library of Congress Prints and Photographs Division, via Wikimedia.

Although some historians have questioned the veracity of this quote, Wilson's racism has been documented in other ways, including his embracing eugenics, a false theory of white supremacy, and by turning a blind eye to segregation in the South. When he ran for office, he promised to support civil rights and campaigned for African American voters but did not follow through once in office. Wilson also allowed federal departments to be segregated, causing the removal of African Americans from their federal jobs.

Wilson attended the College of New Jersey, which later became Princeton University, and then entered the University of Virginia to study law. He set up his own practice in Atlanta before enrolling in Johns Hopkins University to pursue a doctorate in history and political science. Wilson's graduate research and PhD dissertation, *Congressional Government: A Study in American Politics*, provide insights into his presidency. His research criticized the devolution of the presidency and the dominance of Congress in the wake of the Civil War and suggested that a system resembling the parliamentary systems of Europe might be more beneficial. In such systems, the leader of the majority party in the legislature also serves as head of government, which can, in principle, avoid situations where Congress and the presidency are paralyzed by a deadlock.

Wilson was a professor of politics and history at Bryn Mawr College in Pennsylvania, and then at Wesleyan University, where he received tenure before transferring to Princeton. During his teaching career, Wilson published more than 10 books, including political histories and biographies and scholarly examinations of major political issues. He became president of Princeton in 1902 and set upon modernizing the institution. This brought him to the attention of the New Jersey Democrats, who asked Wilson to consider running for governor in 1910. Wilson accepted and won, and immediately broke with the Democratic Party platform. He prohibited corporate political contributions, created a system forcing candidates to disclose financial information, and set limits on political spending. Wilson also engaged in a robust system of labor reforms, passing a worker's compensation law to help families of workers killed or injured on the job, and created a public utility commission to set fair rates for utilities.[2]

Democratic Party luminary William Jennings Bryan of Nebraska, one of the most important figures in the Democratic Party and American political history, is largely forgotten because he lost the presidential election three times. Bryan was a committed populist and championed the direct election of Senators and the income tax and was an early proponent of international law and governance. He is credited as a pioneer of Democratic liberalism and with helping to steer the Democratic Party toward a more progressive agenda. Impressed by Wilson's work as governor, Bryan was one of the Democratic Party leaders who promoted Wilson for the presidency.

Wilson ran on a platform focused largely on controlling big business. Whereas Roosevelt, running through his "Bull Moose Party," focused on eliminating perceptively bad trusts, Wilson believed that all trusts were malignant and that eliminating all corporate monopolies would allow free market forces to correct other issues. He positioned himself as a moderate progressive, forcing Roosevelt's progressives to adopt a more radical platform. In the lead-up to the election, Roosevelt threw his support behind women's suffrage, a minimum wage law for women, and establishing a national social security system and national health service. When the election came, many Republicans simply abstained, unwilling to vote for Roosevelt and realizing that Taft, the more conservative Republican candidate, had little chance. This was enough to give Wilson the advantage, and he won with 41.9 percent of the popular vote, while Roosevelt took 27.4 percent and Taft the remaining 23 percent. Wilson's victory was more convincing on the electoral level, claiming most of the states. Wilson was re-elected in 1916.[3]

The Reform Agenda

Wilson has been credited with initiating a new kind of activist presidency, by which the president acts as the advocate of the people. His study of parliamentary politics led him to believe that an effective head of government needed to form political coalitions within Congress, and this is how he approached setting his national agenda. Wilson spent considerable time meeting with members of Congress in groups and singly to build support for his national agenda, and his relationship with Congress was perhaps one of the strongest in history. For example, on April 8, 1913, Wilson appeared in a joint session of Congress to personally address the nation's legislators on the issue of tariff reform. This was the first time that a president had appeared before Congress for an address of this kind since John Adams.

MESSAGE REGARDING TARIFF DUTIES

Woodrow Wilson
April 8, 1913
Source Document Excerpt

Mr. Speaker, Mr. President, Gentlemen of the Congress:

I am very glad indeed to have this opportunity to address the two Houses directly and to verify for myself the impression that the President of the United States is a person, not a mere department of the Government hailing Congress from some isolated island of jealous power, sending messages, not speaking naturally and with his own voice—that he is a human being trying to cooperate with other human beings in a common service. After this pleasant experience I shall feel quite normal in all our dealings with one another.

I have called the Congress together in extraordinary session because a duty was laid upon the party now in power at the recent elections which it ought to perform promptly, in order that the burden carried by the people under existing law may be lightened as soon as possible and in order, also, that the business interests of the country may not be kept too long in suspense as to what the fiscal changes are to be to which they will be required to adjust themselves. It is clear to the whole country that the tariff duties must be altered. They must be changed to meet the radical alteration in the conditions of our economic life which the country has witnessed within the last generation. While the whole face and method of our industrial and commercial life were being changed beyond recognition the tariff schedules have remained what they were before the change began, or have moved in the direction they were given when no large circumstance of our industrial development was what it is to-day. Our task is to square them with the actual facts. The sooner that is done the sooner we shall escape from suffering from the facts and the sooner our men of business will be free to thrive by the law of nature (the nature of free business) instead of by the law of legislation and artificial arrangement.

We have seen tariff legislation wander very far afield in our day—very far indeed from the field in which our prosperity might have had a normal growth and stimulation. No one who looks the facts squarely in the face or knows anything that lies beneath the surface of action can fail to perceive the principles upon which recent tariff legislation has been based. We long ago passed beyond the modest notion of "protecting" the industries of the country and moved boldly forward to the idea that they were entitled to the direct patronage of the Government.

continued

For a long time—a time so long that the men now active in public policy hardly remember the conditions that preceded it—we have sought in our tariff schedules to give each group of manufacturers or producers what they themselves thought that they needed in order to maintain a practically exclusive market as against the rest of the world. Consciously or unconsciously, we have built up a set of privileges and exemptions from competition behind which it was easy by any, even the crudest, forms of combination to organize monopoly; until at last nothing is normal, nothing is obliged to stand the tests of efficiency and economy, in our world of big business, but everything thrives by concerted arrangement. Only new principles of action will save us from a final hard crystallization of monopoly and a complete loss of the influences that quicken enterprise and keep independent energy alive.

It is plain what those principles must be. We must abolish everything that bears even the semblance of privilege or of any kind of artificial advantage, and put our business men and producers under the stimulation of a constant necessity to be efficient, economical, and enterprising, masters of competitive supremacy, better workers and merchants than any in the world. Aside from the duties laid upon articles which we do not, and probably cannot, produce, therefore, and the duties laid upon luxuries and merely for the sake of the revenues they yield, the object of the tariff duties henceforth laid must be effective competition, the whetting of American wits by contest with the wits of the rest of the world.

It would be unwise to move toward this end headlong, with reckless haste, or with strokes that cut at the very roots of what has grown up amongst us by long process and at our own invitation. It does not alter a thing to upset it and break it and deprive it of a chance to change. It destroys it. We must make changes in our fiscal laws, in our fiscal system, whose object is development, a more free and wholesome development, not revolution or upset or confusion. We must build up trade, especially foreign trade. We need the outlet and the enlarged field of energy more than we ever did before. We must build up industry as well, and must adopt freedom in the place of artificial stimulation only so far as it will build, not pull down. In dealing with the tariff the method by which this may be done will be a matter of judgment, exercised item by item. To some not accustomed to the excitements and responsibilities of greater freedom our methods may in some respects and at some points seem heroic, but remedies may be heroic and yet be remedies. It is our business to make sure that they are genuine remedies. Our object is clear. If our motive is above just challenge and only an occasional error of judgment

Message Regarding Tariff Duties
continued

is chargeable against us, we shall be fortunate.

We are called upon to render the country a great service in more matters than one. Our responsibility should be met and our methods should be thorough, as thorough as moderate and well considered, based upon the facts as they are, and not worked out as if we were beginners. We are to deal with the facts of our own day, with the facts of no other, and to make laws which square with those facts. It is best, indeed it is necessary, to begin with the tariff. I will urge nothing upon you now at the opening of your session which can obscure that first object or divert our energies from that clearly defined duty. At a later time I may take the liberty of calling your attention to reforms which should press close upon the heels of the tariff changes, if not accompany them, of which the chief is the reform of our banking and currency laws; but just now I refrain. For the present, I put these matters on one side and think only of this one thing—of the changes in our fiscal system which may best serve to open once more the free channels of prosperity to a great people whom we would serve to the utmost and throughout both rank and file.

I thank you for your courtesy.[4]

Wilson's approach to Congress was strategic. His speech drew more media attention than usual because of the novelty, introducing a greater share of the public to Wilson's personal view on tariffs, one of the most controversial economic issues of the era. This was the kind of campaign that a prime minister might run, and it successfully created a cooperative coalition with the legislature while simultaneously promoting his position directly to the people. Legislators who opposed him, therefore, risked appearing to oppose what Wilson cleverly positioned as a fight for the common benefit to eliminate the unfair advantages of wealth.

Utilizing this unique strategy, the Wilson administration's economic reforms were sweeping. Congress created the Federal Reserve and empowered it to control interest rates, which ranks as one of the greatest economic changes in the nation's history. Wilson's administration also aggressively promoted federal oversight to eliminate unfair business practices, resulting in the creation of a new federal Department of Labor, in March of 1913. His administration also saw the establishment of eight-hour workdays in the industrial sector, and he campaigned against child labor. Wilson's efforts at economic reform were significant and far-reaching.[5]

Wilson and the World

On the global stage, Wilson and Secretary of State Bryan pursued an agenda to promote democracy on a global scale. Through speeches and writings, Wilson and Bryan promoted a new era of peaceful negotiations between nations and international collectivism. In practice, however, the approach had mixed results.

Wilson avoided certain conflicts and followed through on a promise to set the Philippines on a path to independence. He successfully avoided war with Mexico after Mexican forces clashed with American forces near the border, negotiating an end to the conflict, though American troops remained in case the conflict escalated. These comparative successes clash with Wilson's handling of revolutionary conflict in Haiti and the Dominican Republic. These revolutionary movements weakened established governments, and Wilson rapidly authorized occupation. In Haiti, Wilson sent U.S. Marines partly to keep peace after the assassination of President Jean Vilbrun Guillaume Sam and partly to prevent Germany from capturing Haiti and its strategic naval position. Haiti remained under U.S. control until the 1930s and the Dominican Republic until the 1920s. Though ostensibly acting as peacekeepers in the tradition of Roosevelt's corollary to the Monroe Doctrine, in both cases the United States asserted its own interests while undermining native freedom and self-determination. In Haiti, for example, U.S. agents manipulated elections to create a pro-American government, introduced racial segregation, censored the media, and created forced labor camps for political rebels.[6]

The most dramatic foreign affairs issue of Wilson's two terms in the White House was World War I. When war broke out in Europe, Wilson promised that he would keep America neutral. This was still Wilson's position in 1916, when he ran for re-election, with supporters touting that Wilson had kept America out of the war. Wilson was committed to peace on a personal level, but it is also true that neutrality was a financial benefit to American businesses who supported neutrality because it allowed them to sell supplies to both sides in the conflict. In fact, U.S. companies continued selling arms to Germany and the other central powers until just before America joined the war.

Politically, neutrality was a prudent course for Wilson because the diverse origins of the American people meant that they were conflicted about the war. Many Americans of German descent supported neutrality because they believed that German aggression was justified. By contrast, many Americans of British descent actively promoted intervention, wanting America to help Britain stand up to Germany's imperialist expansion. The U.S. press was undecided on the issue as well. While some journalists and publications clearly advocated for neutrality or intervention, much of the coverage was detached. As late as 1916, for instance, the *New York Times* published a friendly interview with a German U-Boat captain who visited the U.S. coast to gather supplies.[7]

When German submarines torpedoed the British ship *Lusitania* near the coast of Ireland in 1915, resulting in the death of 128 American soldiers, it marked the beginning of the end of American neutrality. Wilson warned Germany to allow safe passage of merchant ships and Germany refused, forcing Wilson into an uncomfortable position. In 1917, Wilson asked Congress to declare war. His message to Congress on April 2, 1917, famously set the stage for modern military diplomacy in Wilson's stated belief that America should function so as to make the world "safe for democracy":

WAR MESSAGE TO CONGRESS
Woodrow Wilson
April 2, 1917
Source Document Excerpt

I have called the Congress into extraordinary session because there are serious, very serious, choices of policy to be made, and made immediately, which it was neither right nor constitutionally permissible that I should assume the responsibility of making. On the 3d of February last, I officially laid before you the extraordinary announcement of the Imperial German Government that on and after the 1st day of February it was its purpose to put aside all restraints of law or of humanity and use its submarines to sink every vessel that sought to approach either the ports of Great Britain and Ireland or the western coasts of Europe or any of the ports controlled by the enemies of Germany within the Mediterranean.

. . .

The present German submarine warfare against commerce is a warfare against mankind.

It is a war against all nations. American ships have been sunk, American lives taken, in ways which it has stirred us very deeply to learn of, but the ships and people of other neutral and friendly nations have been sunk and overwhelmed in the waters in the same way. There has been no discrimination. The challenge is to all mankind. Each nation must decide for itself how it will meet it. The choice we make for ourselves must be made with a moderation of counsel and a temperateness of judgment befitting our character and our motives as a nation. We must put excited feeling away. Our motive will not be revenge or the victorious assertion of the physical might of the nation, but only the vindication of right, of human right, of which we are only a single champion.

When I addressed the Congress on the 26th of February last, I thought that it would suffice to assert our neutral rights with arms, our right to use the seas against unlawful interference, our right to keep our people safe against unlawful violence. But armed neutrality, it now appears, is impracticable. Because submarines are in effect outlaws when used as the German submarines have been used against merchant shipping, it is impossible to defend ships against their attacks as the law of nations has assumed that merchantmen would defend themselves against privateers or cruisers, visible craft giving chase upon the open sea.

War Message to Congress
continued

It is common prudence in such circumstances, grim necessity indeed, to endeavor to destroy them before they have shown their own intention. They must be dealt with upon sight, if dealt with at all. The German Government denies the right of neutrals to use arms at all within the areas of the sea which it has proscribed, even in the defense of rights which no modern publicist has ever before questioned their right to defend. The intimation is conveyed that the armed guards which we have placed on our merchant ships will be treated as beyond the pale of law and subject to be dealt with as pirates would be. Armed neutrality is ineffectual enough at best; in such circumstances and in the face of such pretensions it is worse than ineffectual; it is likely only to produce what it was meant to prevent; it is practically certain to draw us into the war without either the rights or the effectiveness of belligerents. There is one choice we can not make, we are incapable of making: we will not choose the path of submission and suffer the most sacred rights of our nation and our people to be ignored or violated. The wrongs against which we now array ourselves are no common wrongs; they cut to the very roots of human life.

With a profound sense of the solemn and even tragical character of the step I am taking and of the grave responsibilities which it involves, but in unhesitating obedience to what I deem my constitutional duty, I advise that the Congress declare the recent course of the Imperial German government to be in fact nothing less than war against the government and people of the United States; that it formally accept the status of belligerent which has thus been thrust upon it, and that it take immediate steps not only to put the country in a more thorough state of defense but also to exert all its power and employ all its resources to bring the government of the German Empire to terms and end the war.

. . .

While we do these things, these deeply momentous things, let us be very clear, and make very clear to all the world what our motives and our objects are. My own thought has not been driven from its habitual and normal course by the unhappy events of the last two months, and I do not believe that the thought of the nation has been altered or clouded by them. I have exactly the same things in mind now that I had in mind when I addressed the Senate on the 22d of January last; the same that I had in mind when I addressed the Congress on the 3d of February and on the 26th of February. Our object now, as then, is to vindicate the principles of peace and justice in the life of the world as against

continued

selfish and autocratic power and to set up amongst the really free and self-governed peoples of the world such a concert of purpose and of action as will henceforth ensure the observance of those principles. Neutrality is no longer feasible or desirable where the peace of the world is involved and the freedom of its peoples, and the menace to that peace and freedom lies in the existence of autocratic governments backed by organized force which is controlled wholly by their will, not by the will of their people. We have seen the last of neutrality in such circumstances. We are at the beginning of an age in which it will be insisted that the same standards of conduct and of responsibility for wrong done shall be observed among nations and their governments that are observed among the individual citizens of civilized states.

. . .

We are accepting this challenge of hostile purpose because we know that in such a government, following such methods, we can never have a friend; and that in the presence of its organized power, always lying in wait to accomplish we know not what purpose, there can be no assured security for the democratic governments of the world. We are now about to accept [the] gage [the challenge] of battle with this natural foe to liberty and shall, if necessary, spend the whole force of the nation to check and nullify its pretensions and its power. We are glad, now that we see the facts with no veil of false pretense about them, to fight thus for the ultimate peace of the world and for the liberation of its peoples, the German peoples included: for the rights of nations great and small and the privilege of men everywhere to choose their way of life and of obedience.

The world must be made safe for democracy. Its peace must be planted upon the tested foundations of political liberty. We have no selfish ends to serve. We desire no conquest, no dominion. We seek no indemnities for ourselves, no material compensation for the sacrifices we shall freely make. We are but one of the champions of the rights of mankind. We shall be satisfied when those rights have been made as secure as the faith and the freedom of nations can make them.[8]

American intervention in the war shifted the tide, gave a serious advantage to the allies, and resulted in the defeat of Germany and the central powers. When the war ended, Wilson was set to lead the peace negotiations and delivered a now famous speech in Congress on January 8, 1918, calling for a "new diplomacy" to govern American foreign affairs:

FOURTEEN POINTS
Woodrow Wilson
January 8, 1918
Source Document Excerpt

It will be our wish and purpose that the processes of peace, when they are begun, shall be absolutely open and that they shall involve and permit henceforth no secret understandings of any kind. The day of conquest and aggrandizement is gone by; so is also the day of secret covenants entered into in the interest of particular governments and likely at some unlooked-for moment to upset the peace of the world. It is this happy fact, now clear to the view of every public man whose thoughts do not still linger in an age that is dead and gone, which makes it possible for every nation whose purposes are consistent with justice and the peace of the world to avow nor or at any other time the objects it has in view.

We entered this war because violations of right had occurred which touched us to the quick and made the life of our own people impossible unless they were corrected and the world secure once for all against their recurrence. What we demand in this war, therefore, is nothing peculiar to ourselves. It is that the world be made fit and safe to live in; and particularly that it be made safe for every peace-loving nation which, like our own, wishes to live its own life, determine its own institutions, be assured of justice and fair dealing by the other peoples of the world as against force and selfish aggression. All the peoples of the world are in effect partners in this interest, and for our own part we see very clearly that unless justice be done to others it will not be done to us. The programme of the world's peace, therefore, is our programme; and that programme, the only possible programme, as we see it, is this:

I. Open covenants of peace, openly arrived at, after which there shall be no private international understandings of any kind but diplomacy shall proceed always frankly and in the public view.

continued

II. Absolute freedom of navigation upon the seas, outside territorial waters, alike in peace and in war, except as the seas may be closed in whole or in part by international action for the enforcement of international covenants.

III. The removal, so far as possible, of all economic barriers and the establishment of an equality of trade conditions among all the nations consenting to the peace and associating themselves for its maintenance.

IV. Adequate guarantees given and taken that national armaments will be reduced to the lowest point consistent with domestic safety.

V. A free, open-minded, and absolutely impartial adjustment of all colonial claims, based upon a strict observance of the principle that in determining all such questions of sovereignty the interests of the populations concerned must have equal weight with the equitable claims of the government whose title is to be determined.

VI. The evacuation of all Russian territory and such a settlement of all questions affecting Russia as will secure the best and freest cooperation of the other nations of the world in obtaining for her an unhampered and unembarrassed opportunity for the independent determination of her own political development and national policy and assure her of a sincere welcome into the society of free nations under institutions of her own choosing; and, more than a welcome, assistance also of every kind that she may need and may herself desire. The treatment accorded Russia by her sister nations in the months to come will be the acid test of their good will, of their comprehension of her needs as distinguished from their own interests, and of their intelligent and unselfish sympathy.

VII. Belgium, the whole world will agree, must be evacuated and restored, without any attempt to limit the sovereignty which she enjoys in common with all other free nations. No other single act will serve as this will serve to restore confidence among the nations in the laws which they have themselves set and determined for the government of their relations with one another. Without this healing act the whole structure and validity of international law is forever impaired.

VIII. All French territory should be freed and the invaded portions restored, and the wrong done to France by Prussia in 1871 in the matter of Alsace-Lorraine, which has unsettled the peace of the world for nearly fifty years, should be righted, in order that peace may once more be made secure in the interest of all.

Fourteen Points
continued

IX. A readjustment of the frontiers of Italy should be effected along clearly recognizable lines of nationality.

X. The peoples of Austria-Hungary, whose place among the nations we wish to see safeguarded and assured, should be accorded the freest opportunity to autonomous development.

XI. Rumania, Serbia, and Montenegro should be evacuated; occupied territories restored; Serbia accorded free and secure access to the sea; and the relations of the several Balkan states to one another determined by friendly counsel along historically established lines of allegiance and nationality; and international guarantees of the political and economic independence and territorial integrity of the several Balkan states should be entered into.

XII. The turkish portion of the present Ottoman Empire should be assured a secure sovereignty, but the other nationalities which are now under Turkish rule should be assured an undoubted security of life and an absolutely unmolested opportunity of autonomous development, and the Dardanelles should be permanently opened as a free passage to the ships and commerce of all nations under international guarantees.

XIII. An independent Polish state should be erected which should include the territories inhabited by indisputably Polish populations, which should be assured a free and secure access to the sea, and whose political and economic independence and territorial integrity should be guaranteed by international covenant.

XIV. A general association of nations must be formed under specific covenants for the purpose of affording mutual guarantees of political independence and territorial integrity to great and small states alike.

In regard to these essential rectifications of wrong and assertions of right we feel ourselves to be intimate partners of all the governments and peoples associated together against the Imperialists. We cannot be separated in interest or divided in purpose. We stand together until the end.

For such arrangements and covenants we are willing to fight and to continue to fight until they are achieved; but only because we wish the right to prevail and desire a just and stable peace such as can be secured only by removing the chief provocations to war, which this programme does remove. We have no jealousy of German greatness, and there is nothing in this

continued

programme that impairs it. We grudge her no achievement or distinction of learning or of pacific enterprise such as have made her record very bright and very enviable. We do not wish to injure her or to block in any way her legitimate influence or power. We do not wish to fight her either with arms or with hostile arrangements of trade if she is willing to associate herself with us and the other peace-loving nations of the world in covenants of justice and law and fair dealing. We wish her only to accept a place of equality among the peoples of the world,—the new world in which we now live,—instead of a place of mastery.[9]

The importance of Wilson's "fourteen points" cannot be overstated as the beginning of international government, a movement that resulted in the establishment of the United Nations (UN). Wilson proposed a similar organization, the League of Nations, which would accept membership of all democratic states and would lead the effort to disarm global offensive militaries and to end global colonialism. Wilson's perception of the Civil War may have informed his approach to the peace that would end the First World War. He believed, as many southern Americans did, that the punitive treatment of the South after the Civil War was morally flawed. In place of punishing the people of the central power states, Wilson promoted "peace without victory," the idea of moving ahead, forgiving the offenses of the war, and working toward building a coalition to promote peace and prevent future wars.

However noble the idea of the League of Nations might have been, it was unrealistic. Prejudice and self-interest dominated government and ultimately, most of Wilson's fourteen points were abandoned in the negotiations of the Treaty of Versailles. Back home, Wilson faced a Republican majority in the Senate, many of whom were committed to isolationism and believed that deeper involvement in foreign affairs would hurt American independence and economic freedom. Wilson tried to bypass Congress by taking his ideas directly to the American people in an ambitious tour that involved speeches in 29 cities, the exertion of which contributed to his declining health. In Colorado, on September 25, Wilson suffered a major stroke that left him partially paralyzed. He returned to Washington essentially immobilized and remained that way for the rest of his term.

Opponents in Congress won, and the United States did not join the League of Nations. Historians have wondered what might have occurred if Wilson's vision of the League of Nations became a reality—would a robust international government have been able to forestall the Second World War? It is likely that the more ameliorative conditions favored by Wilson would have left the former central powers nations in better economic condition and thus prevented the rise of militant nationalism in Germany and Russia.

Writing for the CATO think tank in 2014, historian Jim Powell suggested that Wilson's greatest mistake was entering the war in the first place. Had this not happened, Powell believes there would likely have been a negotiated settlement. With America's participation, however, the central powers were thoroughly crushed, and vengeful politicians proceeded to disadvantage aggressor nations to the point that radicalism emerged again, in the form of the Nazi Party, resulting in the Second World War.[10]

America's First Woman President

During his second term Wilson shifted his political stance on the topic of women's suffrage and promoted passing the Nineteenth Amendment granting women the right to vote. Though Wilson, therefore, occupies an important position in the history of women's rights, the decision to support suffrage was a practical political decision based on the fact that Wilson was attempting to convince the nation that intervention in the war was the best course for the nation. He was facing considerable resistance, and his efforts were further diminished by the increasingly radical protests of women's suffrage activists. The women's suffrage movement, which began in the 1840s, had reached a new stage in which a new generation of women activists, frustrated by years of little political gain, decided to try new tactics. These included the first protest in front of the White House, and eventually months-long protests at the White House and other demonstrations of civil disobedience. Wilson promoted women's suffrage to end this very visible new wave of opposition to his presidency, and thus it was the radical activists of the women's rights movement who turned the tide of history, demonstrating popular power to influence the president.

Wilson's presidency was a landmark moment in women's history in a darker, more tragic sense as well. After he suffered his stroke in 1919, Wilson was confined to his bed. At the time, his wife, Edith Bolling Galt, maintained that her husband was still well enough to make important decisions and that she would act as his secretary, an intermediary between Wilson and his cabinet and between the executive and Congress. The public and most government representatives never learned how disabled Wilson was or the degree to which his physical and mental faculties remained intact. Even when Edith Wilson later wrote her autobiography in 1938, she maintained that she was simply a messenger delivering Wilson's directives to the nation. Historians, however, have found that this was not the case. In fact, rather than acting in a secretarial capacity, Edith Wilson made most if not all executive decisions between her husband's stroke in 1919 and the end of his second term, in 1921, on her own. She was, in effect, president of the United States for the remainder of her husband's time in office. Though Edith Wilson wasn't forced to make any major executive decisions during this time, she did on occasion exercise authority. One of the most notable examples came when the Secretary of State conducted a cabinet meeting without Wilson's approval. Edith Wilson called this a breach of duty and had him removed from his position.

It would be many years until a woman would be considered for the role of chief executive, but Edith Wilson, in secret, occupied the office for more than a year and was, unbeknownst to nearly everyone, the most powerful woman in the nation for a brief moment in history.[a]

Works Used

a. Markel, Howard. "When a Secret President Ran the Country." *PBS*. News Hour. 2 Oct. 2015. www.pbs. org/newshour/health/woodrow-wilson-stroke.

Edith Galt holding a document steady for Woodrow Wilson to sign. Historians believe that she took over all of Wilson's executive duties after his stroke. By Harris & Ewing, Library of Congress Prints and Photographs Division, via Wikimedia.

The Power of Information

While Woodrow Wilson has been given ample credit for his progressive economic policies and forward-thinking views on globalism, his use of presidential power was somewhat controversial. To gain public support for American intervention in the war, Wilson enlisted the help of George Creel, a writer for the tabloid press. Creel was the early-twentieth-century equivalent of a writer for Breitbart or InfoWars, crafting what we call "fake news" today. Wilson and Creel created the Committee on Public Information, ostensibly to disseminate information about the war effort, but which was essentially America's first federal propaganda department.[11]

The committee created posters, handouts, newspaper and magazine articles, and funded propaganda films by some of the nation's most prominent filmmakers. The committee trained actors to pose as citizens, striking up conversations with other citizens to deliver scripted stories to inspire patriotic interest in American intervention. The committee hired fiction writers to craft novels and short stories demonstrating virtues of Americanism and evils of German imperialism. Posters featured illustrations of Germans as monstrous creatures, and fabricated stories told of enemy soldiers raping and murdering women and children. The 2016 allegations linking Hillary Clinton to a child sex trafficking ring is a modern example of this technique.

Wilson's propaganda machine did successfully increase public support for American intervention but also encouraged prejudice and violence. Some states passed laws prohibiting Americans from speaking foreign languages or banning the playing of German music, including Bach or Beethoven. Libraries burned books by German authors or by Americans of German descent. People with Germanic-sounding names were often attacked and even killed. In one instance, German immigrant Robert Paul Prager was hanged by an angry mob in Missouri after being forced to march down the street while draped in the American flag and singing patriotic songs.[12]

Creel and his propagandists attacked the American socialist and communist movements as well, portraying them as un-American and cowardly subversives plotting to undermine the government. This led to widespread police oppression of socialists and communists and, in some cases, to mob violence. The Wilson administration passed the Espionage and Sedition Acts, which made it illegal to criticize the government or the war effort under penalty of imprisonment or hefty fines. Further, Wilson directed the Post Office to censor the public mail, leading to hundreds of publications being banned or not distributed.[13]

With the aid of propagandists, the legislature, and the courts, Wilson dramatically curtailed First Amendment rights, leading to widespread persecution and governmental oppression. Wilson's efforts raise questions about the use of presidential authority. Is it acceptable for a president, or any other elected representative of the people, to purposefully encourage bigotry and violence? Should an elected representative be limited to promoting accurate information to the public, or is it permissible to use questionable methods to accomplish political goals? On a more fundamental level, does the power temporarily afforded to a president or other leader, but ultimately residing with the people, include the power to mislead the people?

Whether a president should be allowed to misinform the public is, again, in the news with the presidency of Donald Trump, who has frequently put forward false claims designed to promote the idea that he is a successful and beloved leader or to downplay criticism. Trump's critics argue that this damages public trust and undermines public welfare. Trump's frequent use of false information has engendered widespread opposition to his presidency and has caused him to be faced with record levels of criticism. Wilson suffered little of this during his time in office. The relative paucity of reliable information and the authoritarian tactics taken by Wilson's regime meant that Wilson was more or less unopposed. The fact that Trump has been unable to achieve similar levels of success reflects the fact that Trump does not have Wilson's public appeal or Wilson's capability to form effective congressional coalitions. Further, today, Americans have greater access to information, and many view the government skeptically. Nonetheless, governmental use of propaganda remains controversial, and historians have suggested that Wilson's complicity detracts from his legacy.

CONCLUSION

While Wilson's accomplishments were significant, much of what he hoped to achieve, with the League of Nations and his view for America's place on the world stage, did not come to pass. In looking back on his presidency, there are several areas in which Wilson's performance raises questions about presidential power. First, Wilson's propaganda machine raises questions about whether it is appropriate for a president to willfully misinform the populace. Second, the fact that Wilson withheld from the American people his debilitating injury, with his wife essentially serving as his stand-in for months of his presidency, raises questions about whether a president has the right to withhold vital information about his or her health that might impact their effectiveness in office. On the domestic stage, Wilson began a change in Democratic Party politics that ultimately saw the Democratic Party become the more progressive, humanitarian party in American politics. This left the Republicans to become the more conservative, business-oriented party, as shown by the discussion of Presidents Harding, Coolidge and Hoover in the next chapter.

DISCUSSION QUESTIONS

♦ Did Wilson's propaganda department violate presidential power? Why or why not?

♦ Are Wilson's "Fourteen Points" still relevant today?

♦ Was the Wilson Administration justified in its occupation of Haiti? Why or why not?

♦ Does Wilson's racial prejudice detract from his legacy? Why or why not?

Works Used

Ambar, Saladin. "Woodrow Wilson: Life Before the Presidency." *Miller Center*. University of Virginia. 2019. millercenter.org/president/wilson/life-before-the-presidency.

Benbow, Mark E. "Birth of a Quotation: Woodrow Wilson and 'Like Writing History with Lightning.'" *The Journal of the Gilded Age and Progressive Era*. vol. 9, no. 4, Oct. 2010, pp 509–533. *JSTOR*, www.jstor.org/stable/20799409.

Berg, A. Scott. *Wilson*. New York: G.P. Putnam's Sons, 2013.

Cull, Nicholas J. "Master of American Propaganda." *PBS*. American Experience. www.pbs.org/wgbh/americanexperience/features/the-great-war-master-of-american-propaganda/.

Daly, Christopher B. "How Woodrow Wilson's Propaganda Machine Changed American Journalism." *Smithsonian.com*. Smithsonian Institution. 28 Apr. 2017. www.smithsonianmag.com/history/how-woodrow-wilsons-propaganda-machine-changed-american-journalism-180963082/.

Dunphy, John J. "The Lynching of Robert Prager: A World War I Hate Crime." *Medium*. 17 Nov. 2018. medium.com/@johnjdunphy/the-lynching-of-robert-prager-a-world-war-i-hate-crime-11b7a5e567a.

"German U-Boat Reaches Baltimore, Having Crossed Atlantic in 16 Days; Has Letter from Kaiser to Wilson." *New York Times.* 10 July 1916.

Powell, Jim. "Woodrow Wilson's Great Mistake." *Cato.* Cato Institute. 2 June 2014. www.cato.org/policy-report/mayjune-2014/woodrow-wilsons-great-mistake.

"Presidential Election of 1912: A Resource Guide," *LOC*. 23 Oct. 2018. www.loc.gov/rr/program/bib/elections/election1912.html.

"U.S. Invasion and Occupation of Haiti, 1915–34." *U.S. Department of State*. Office of the Historian. history.state.gov/milestones/1914-1920/Haiti.

Wilson, Woodrow. "April 8, 1913: Message Regarding Tariff Duties." *Miller Center*. University of Virginia. 2019. millercenter.org/the-presidency/presidential-speeches/april-8-1913-message-regarding-tariff-duties.

_____. "President Woodrow Wilson's Fourteen Points." 8 Jan. 1918. *Avalon Project*. Yale Law School. 2018. avalon.law.yale.edu/20th_century/wilson14.asp.

_____. "War Message to Congress." 2 April 1917. Brigham Young University, 28 May 2009. wwi.lib.byu.edu/index.php/Wilson's_War_Message_to_Congress.

Introduction

The three Republican presidents in between Woodrow Wilson and Franklin Delano Roosevelt were pioneers of Republican Party conservatism. They championed the idea that the country needed to return to a better time, something that Warren Harding, the first of the three, called "readjustment." The Harding presidency is remembered largely for scandals of corruption and ominous corporate entanglements. He was followed by Calvin Coolidge, or "Silent Cal," a relatively weak and inactive president whose reputation for being stingy with words ironically coincided with the first presidency conducted over the radio waves. Last came Herbert Hoover, a complicated man remembered both for his philosophy of "rugged individualism," and as the president who oversaw the nation at the beginning of the Great Depression. Each of these early twentieth-century Republicans approached presidential power in unique ways, but none are remembered as particularly strong executives. In many ways, the three presidencies chart an evolution in conservative thought, and a desire to retreat from the rapid changes brought about by industrialization and the war.

Topics covered in this chapter include:
- Great Depression
- Oil industry lobby
- Presidential corruption

The Conservative Shift
Warren Harding, Calvin Coolidge, and Herbert Hoover (1921–1933)

Following Woodrow Wilson's two terms as president, the Republican Party needed a reinvention. For years, their power base had been in the north, and the party's platform was in many cases as liberal as the political tides allowed (though still conservative by modern standards). The Republicans first championed government reform and made the abolition of slavery a nation-defining political issue. Wilson began a new progressive identity for the Democratic Party, moving away from the states' rights southern Democrats of the Jacksonian era. In response, the Republican Party focused on the collective discomfort caused by progressive reforms enacted under Wilson. The pace of change left many Americans with a sense that they couldn't keep up with how quickly America's culture was changing. The Republican Party, therefore, became the party of tradition and continuity. Republican presidential candidates would frequently market themselves as wanting to "return" America to some past state.

Between the progressive era reforms of Woodrow Wilson and the transformative presidency of Franklin D. Roosevelt in the 1930s, three Republican presidents—Warren Harding, Calvin Coolidge, and Herbert Hoover—held office. None are fondly remembered, and none left a lasting mark on the office, but all three helped to define the new Republican conservatism.

The Ohio Gang

Warren Harding came from Ohio, long a seed bed for Republican politicians, the son of two doctors. His mother, Phoebe Harding, had been granted a license to practice medicine in the state after assisting her husband, George Harding, as a midwife. Warren attended Ohio Central College and worked in a law office, sold insurance policies, and wrote

articles for local newspapers, eventually establishing the *Marion Star*, which became known for nonpartisan political coverage.[1]

Warren G. Harding, by Harris & Ewing, via Wikimedia.

Harding became popular as an Ohio businessman and won election to the Ohio State Senate in 1899, where he served for two terms. In 1914, Harding ran for the U.S. Senate against Attorney General Timothy Hogan. Anti-Catholic sentiment enabled Harding to win in a landslide. As a Senator, Harding had no significant bills attached to his name. His middle-of-the-road legislative style did not impress or offend, and he had few enemies in Congress as Wilson's second term came to an end. In the 1920 election, Harding was chosen because he came from the swing state of Ohio. With Massachusetts Republican Calvin Coolidge as his running mate, Harding ran on a straight party-platform ticket; he opposed involvement in Wilson's League of Nations, immigration, and the rising internationalism. Harding's campaign slogan was "A Return to Normalcy"—an attempt to paint Wilson's presidency as extreme. Harding was running against Ohio liberal James Cox, who was also in the newspaper business, but had been governor of Ohio, an office that Harding failed to win.

Harding's campaign speech on "readjustment" demonstrates how the Republicans attempted to regain traction by capitalizing on Americans' insecurity about their changing world:

"READJUSTMENT" ADDRESS
WARREN G. HARDING
May 14, 1920
Source Document Excerpt

My countrymen, there isn't anything the matter with the world's civilization except that humanity is viewing it through a vision impaired in a cataclysmal war. Poise has been disturbed, and nerves have been wracked, and fever has rendered men irrational. Sometimes there have been draughts upon the dangerous cup of barbarity. Men have wandered far from safe paths, but the human procession still marches in the right direction. Here in the United States we feel the reflex, rather than the hurting wound itself, but we still think straight; and we mean to act straight; we mean to hold firmly to all that was ours when war involved us and seek the higher attainments which are the only compensations that so supreme a tragedy may give mankind.

America's present need is not heroics, but healing; not nostrums, but normalcy; not revolution, but restoration; not agitation, but adjustment; not surgery, but serenity; not the dramatic, but the dispassionate; not experiment, but equipoise; not submergence in internationality but sustainment in triumphant nationality. It's one thing to battle successfully against the world's domination by a military autocracy because the infinite God never intended such a program; but it's quite another thing to revise human nature and suspend the fundamental laws of life and all of life's requirements.

The world calls for peace. America demands peace, formal as well as actual, and means to have it so we may set our own house in order. We challenged the proposal that an armed autocrat should dominate the world, and we choose for ourselves to cling to the representative democracy which made us what we are.

This republic has its ample task. If we put an end to false economics which lure humanity to utter chaos, ours will be the commanding example of world leadership today. If we can prove a representative popular government under which the citizenship seeks what it may do for the government and country, rather than what the country may do for individuals, we shall do more to make democracy safe for the world than all armed conflict ever recorded.

The world needs to be reminded that all human ills are not curable by legislation, and that quantity of statutory enactments and excess of

continued

government offer no substitute for quality of citizenship. The problems of maintained civilization are not to be solved by a transfer of responsibility from citizenship to government and no eminent page in history was ever drafted to the standards of mediocrity. Nor, no government worthy of the name which is directed by influence on the one hand or moved by intimidation on the other. My best judgement of America's need is to steady down, to get squarely on our feet, to make sure of the right path. Let's get out of the fevered delirium of war with the hallucination that all the money in the world is to be made in the madness of war and the wildness of its aftermath. Let us stop to consider that tranquility at home is more precious than peace abroad and that both our good fortune and our eminence are dependent on the normal forward stride of all the American people. We want to go on, secure and unafraid, holding fast to the American inheritance, and confident of the supreme American fulfillment.[2]

Many Americans wanted to return to "normalcy," and Harding easily won the election, earning 16.1 million popular votes and 404 electoral votes, to 9.1 million and 127 for Cox.[3] The Republican Party did very well in the election, gaining 10 seats to control the Senate and 63 seats to control the House, as well as 7 gubernatorial seats nationwide. The election was one of many in which a lengthy period of control by one party, under a powerful president, was followed by partisan shift across the nation.

The Republican Party was well positioned after the 1920 elections, but Harding had no real vision for how to return America to normalcy, and confessed to friends that he felt ill-prepared for the office. Lacking a coherent plan to set a national agenda, Harding never challenged Congress significantly, or strayed from the agenda set by Republican Party bosses; in general, he performed in the office as if it was a more or less symbolic head of state position. Some historians have argued that Harding was a needed transitional president after the political strife of the Wilson administration and World War I, and others have praised him for forward-thinking ideas about racial equality, though he never attempted to act on those ideas. In general, Harding is maligned as among the weakest, least effective presidents, and frequently ranks at the bottom of presidential lists.

Despite this, Harding was initially quite popular among the people and was the first president elected when more than half of the population had been empowered to vote, so perhaps the first president elected with a legitimate popular vote. However, with just 49 percent of eligible voters casting votes (the lowest turnout of the preceding century), Harding never had a clear public mandate. He served as an apt and uncontroversial candidate for the new Republican message: to preserve traditional Americanism.

Harding's presidency was made possible thanks to contributions from the oil industry. Harding was not himself particularly dishonest, but he failed to break with the corrupt Republican power base of his state, the "Ohio Gang." Members of Harding's circle committed bribery, extortion, bootlegging, black mail, jury tampering, misappropriations of federal funds, and worse. The oil industry had been slowly gaining more political influence by making unreported donations to candidates who then supported legislation that benefitted the oil tycoons. By the time Harding was in office, the oil lobby was more powerful than the Republican Party, and few Republicans made decisions that would put them at odds with the industry's leadership.[4]

Even today, Republicans regularly utilize campaign contributions from oil companies and routinely oppose efforts to preserve land or prohibit oil exploration. *Open Secrets* reports, for instance, that oil companies donated 43 million to Republican politicians in 2018, whereas only 6.2 million was donated to Democratic politicians.[5] Donald Trump is a Republican politician who has personally invested millions in oil industry companies and received donations from those same companies in his controversial 2016 presidential bid. Another Republican, Maine Senator Susan Collins, received more donations from Texas-based oil companies than from Maine resident companies combined in her 2018 election bid.[6]

The standard Republican Party platform, since Harding, has opposed environmental regulation, research and protection, and prioritized corporate interests over public welfare. While it is not clear whether these actions are based on the large contributions that oil companies make to Republican candidates, many believe this to be true.

The First Fall Guy

One of the most egregious political miscreants of the Ohio Gang was Albert Fall, who was named Secretary of the Interior under Warren G. Harding despite having no qualifications. Fall's appointment was engineered by Republican Party bosses to reduce regulation on land use, thus giving oil companies new opportunities for profit. Such deregulation initiatives were presented as an important to free-market democracy, but powerful economic leaders bribed Republican Party politicians to increase their personal wealth.

Albert Fall was a political pawn whose appointment was one of the aims of the oil companies. Once in office, he took a $500,000 bribe to turn over control of the oil reserves in Teapot Dome in Wyoming to Mammoth Oil Company, run by friend Harry Sinclair. Other land was given to Pan American Petroleum and Transport Company, for which Fall received $100,000. Though these deals were conducted in secret, journalists uncovered evidence of bribery. Before long, the Teapot Dome scandal went nationwide.

Senator Robert M. La Follette of Wisconsin called for an investigation, later joined by Democratic Senator Thomas Walsh of Montana, and it was discovered that Mammoth and the Pan American Petroleum Company had both given generous donations to Fall. Fall was convicted of bribery and sentenced to a year's imprisonment, becoming the first cabinet officer sentenced to prison. Fall did not implicate other individuals involved in the scheme, and most of the Ohio Gang escaped without punishment. Fall took nearly sole responsibility, and this became the origin of the term "fall guy"—someone who accepts punishment that might be better applied to others.[a]

Work Used

a. Craig, Bryan. "Making the Teapot Dome Scandal Relevant Again." *Miller Center*. University of Virginia. 11 Apr. 2017. millercenter.org/issues-policy/us-domestic-policy/making-teapot-dome-scandal-relevant-again.

Harding died in office on June 20, 1923. The official cause of death was listed as a heart attack, brought on by an enlarged heart and a bout of food poisoning. It was rumored, however, that he had been poisoned by his wife, First Lady Florence Harding, who reportedly refused to allow an autopsy. A 1930 book held that she poisoned him because his administration was facing corruption charges, and she felt that she should lead the nation, largely a sensationalist account. Harding's death left the presidency to Vice President Calvin Coolidge, a business-minded conservative who helped to bring the new Republican Party platform to its fullest expression.

"Keep Cool with Coolidge"

Calvin Coolidge was born in Vermont, the son of a storekeeper who also owned a farm. He attended Amherst College in Massachusetts, where he joined the Republican Club and formed friendships that would later impact his political career. Coolidge had a slow rise to national prominence, from City Council to chairman of the Republican Party of Massachusetts to the state legislature. In 1918, Coolidge became governor, narrowly defeating Democrat Richard Long, and proved to be an able politician. He supported progressive reforms, including a broad overhaul of the government that drew support both from progressives and small-government conservatives in both parties. When the Republicans put forward Harding for the presidency, Coolidge looked like a good choice for the vice presidency, drawing on his appeal with northern moderate progressives and business-centric conservatives.

Calvin Coolidge, by Notman Studio, Library of Congress Prints and Photographs Division, via Wikimedia.

The story of Coolidge's rise to the presidency starts with him being informed of Harding's passage while at his family's farm house, which lacked a telephone. The news came in the middle of the night, and soon the farmhouse was swarmed by the press. Coolidge's father, who was a justice of the peace, obtained a copy of the Constitution and delivered the oath of office to his son, who then returned to bed. Coolidge's calm, unflappable demeanor was the hallmark of his legacy and earned him the nickname "Silent Cal." When a White House dinner guest told Coolidge that she bet she could get him to say more than two words, he reportedly replied, "You lose."[7]

Coolidge finished Harding's term in office, then ran for election in 1924, the first in which campaigning was conducted largely by radio broadcast. Coolidge and other politicians gave impassioned speeches that were broadcast across the country, resulting in a personal connection with candidates. This also changed the nature of political speeches, which were shortened to fit the new medium. The ability to broadcast political coverage and news also provided a huge boon for the radio industry, which was already among the fastest-growing in the nation. In 1924, the Radiola company introduced the following ad:

"SPEECHES MUST BE SHORT": RADIO AND THE BIRTH OF THE MODERN PRESIDENTIAL CAMPAIGN

Matt Novak

May 3, 2017

Source Document Excerpt

No "influence" needed this year for a gallery seat at the big political conventions! Get it all with a Radiola Super-Heterodyne.

When the delegates march in—their banners streaming; when the bands play and the galleries cheer—be there with the "Super-Het." Hear the pros and cons as they fight their way to a "platform" for you. Hear the speeches for the "favorite sons." The sudden stillness when the voice of a great speaker rings out. The stamp and whistle and shrill of competitive cheering. Hear the actual nomination of a president.

It used to be all of the delegates' wives and the "big" folks of politics. Now it's for everybody. Listen in. Get it all! With the newest Radiola.[8]

Radio's coverage of politics also made the political process more public, including the political party conventions and the nomination of vice-presidential candidates. With the hunger for content (as much for entertainment as information), radios became an essential part of the political process.

Despite the excitement that millions felt at listening to presidential speeches in their homes, there was a slight drop in voter turnout to 48.9 percent, from 49.2 percent in the 1920 election. The Republicans advised the nation to "Keep Cool with Coolidge," meaning that Coolidge would, like Harding, maintain a steady course. Meanwhile, the Democratic candidate was John Davis of West Virginia, while Robert La Follette of Wisconsin ran on a new Progressive Party ticket. Coolidge was the winner, with 15.7 million popular votes and 382 electoral votes to 8.3 million popular

votes and 136 electoral votes for Davis, and 4.8 million popular votes and 13 electoral votes for La Follette.

In office, Coolidge was a symbolic leader for a dominant Republican Party agenda. He traveled widely and frequently posed for photos, for which he was thought to be the "most photographed person on earth." In terms of presidential authority, Coolidge was a believer in the "less is more" school of thought. Rarely did he try to impose his will on Congress, and he never exerted the authority of his office in a controversial way. Though he rarely ranks in lists of the worst presidents, he has never been singled out for greatness. Political biographer William Allen White, author of the 1938 Coolidge biography *A Puritan in Babylon*, wrote that America had decided to "erect this pallid shrunken image of its lost ideals and bow down before it in subconscious repentance for its inequities."[9] Some historians have suggested that America needed the temperate symbolic leadership of a serious, unenthusiastic, and uncontroversial figure like Coolidge to adjust to the many changes brought about by the Wilson administration. Under the leadership of congressional Republicans, America retreated from the global sphere, reduced restrictions on businesses, and stepped back on economic reform.

Most of Coolidge's achievements were economic in nature, and have been judged faulty by modern economists. He favored lower taxes and reduced regulation and spoke frequently about balancing the budget. Secretary of the Treasury Andrew Mellon is credited with the idea of "trickle down" economics, in which the wealthy get tax breaks which then encourages them to spend more, and this money trickles down to the middle and laboring classes. In practice, this system never engenders economic growth at the lower level. Coolidge was fortunate to take the helm of the country in a time of prosperity, brought about largely by Wilson's policies. The policies that Coolidge and the Republican Congress were putting into place, such as deregulating businesses and cutting

taxes for corporations, would shortly contribute to the worst financial collapse in U.S. history, which began in 1929, the year that Coolidge left office. Coolidge opposed filtering federal money into agriculture, as well as other debt-relief bills to combat early signs of the depression. As a result, many farmers were left without support when rural banks closed due to stock market speculation and poor investment. On the international front, the Coolidge administration's decision to retreat from global affairs was one of many factors that contributed to the rise of Nazi Germany and World War II.

Hoover: The Last Republican Pioneer

The last of the conservative Republican pioneers was Herbert Hoover. Things were looking bad as America approached the 1928 election, and Coolidge had decided not to run again, citing the unofficial two-term rule that had become traditional in Republican circles. Iowa Republican Herbert Hoover, who had worked closely with Wilson during his administration, was announced as the presidential candidate at the Republican convention in Kansas City.

Hoover was born into a Quaker family and grew up in rural Iowa. He went to Stanford University in California, where he earned a degree in geology and later became a mining magnate. Hoover married Lou Henry, the only female geology student in his Stanford class, who gained a reputation as an activist during her later tenure as First Lady. After their 1899 marriage, the Hoovers traveled to China, both becoming fluent in Mandarin; over the next decade they traveled the world. Lou became fluent in eight languages, and during Hoover's presidency, she and her husband would frequently converse in Mandarin to be secretive. Lou Hoover was the first First Lady to speak on the radio and one of the first to advocate for social justice issues. She once caused controversy when she invited the wife of an African American congressman, Jesse DePriest, to the White House for tea, despite racist objections.

Herbert Hoover, Library of Congress Prints and Photographs Division, via Wikimedia.

During World War I, Hoover was tapped by the Wilson administration to lead the U.S. Food Administration, and his laudable performance made him one of the few Republicans with whom President Wilson regularly conferred. Hoover was even invited to travel with Wilson to the Versailles peace conference that officially ended the war. As the Great Depression loomed in 1928, the Republican Party needed to shift gears again. Coolidge was seeing a drop in public support, accused of not doing enough to prevent the economic problems that were emerging. Hoover thus ran on an aggressive economic platform, promising to "put a chicken in every pot and two cars in every garage."

The Anti-Catholic President

At the time, prohibition divided America. The Democrats put forward New York's Al Smith, an outspoken opponent of prohibition. Hoover gained an advantage because Smith was Catholic, one of many groups targeted as enemies of America by the Ku Klux Klan. When Smith toured the South, white supremacists burned crosses, and conservative preachers warned that voting for him would lead directly to eternal damnation. Smith's opposition to prohibition was also viewed as evidence of his alignment with wickedness. In New York, Hoover supporters spread a leaflet that read:

When Catholics rule the United States

And the Jew grows a Christian nose on his face

When Pope Pius is head of the Ku Klux Klan

In the land of Uncle Sam

Then Al Smith will be our president

And the country not worth a damn.

A Junior Senator from Alabama, James Thomas Heflin, gave a memorable speech defining the election as a contest between "Romanism," or the Roman Catholic Church, and Christianity:

WARNING AGAINST THE "ROMAN CATHOLIC PARTY": CATHOLICISM AND THE 1928 ELECTION
James Thomas Heflin
January 1928
Source Document Excerpt

Mr. President, in the name of all that is dear to us as a free people I call on my countrymen to wake up. The climax of this move is Al Smith's candidacy for President. Wake up, Americans! Gird your loins for political battle, the like of which you here not seen in all the tide of time in this country. Get ready for this battle. The Roman Catholics of every country on the earth are backing his campaign. Already they are spending money in the South buying up newspapers, seeking to control the vehicles that carry the news to the people. They are sending writers down there from New York and other places to misrepresent and slander our State, all this to build a foundation on which to work for Al Smith for President. The Roman Catholic edict has gone forth in secret articles, "Al Smith is to be made President." Doctor McDaniel said: "Of all countries the Pope wants to control this country." "The Knights of Columbus slogan," said Doctor Chapman, . . . "is make America Catholic." Here they tell you in their book that they will force the propaganda of Protestants to cease, they will lay the heavy hand of a Catholic state upon you and crush the life out of Protestantism in America.[10]

While Smith was accused of wanting to turn America over to the papacy, his Irish wife was likewise maligned by the political press; journalists mocked her accent, attire, and breeding. This was the first time that a non-Protestant competed for the office since Thomas Jefferson. Prejudice, especially in the South, provided an advantage for Hoover and led to his winning more than 58 percent of the popular vote.[11] This was the beginning also of a major shift among white supremacist voters towards the Republican Party. The high stakes of the contest drew more voters, with 56 percent of eligible voters turning out, the highest percentage of the decade.[12] Along with Hoover's victory came a Republican majority in Congress. The Republican Party claimed 8 seats to control the Senate and 32 seats to control the House, leaving them in near total control of the growing financial disaster.

A Depressing Presidency

As president, Hoover is perhaps best known for helping to define the philosophy of "rugged individualism" that he saw as key to American identity. He campaigned as the defender of a way of life and a political philosophy that had been abandoned during the war, one that the Republican Party was attempting to bring back. As he described it:

"RUGGED INDIVIDUALISM" CAMPAIGN SPEECH
Herbert Hoover
October 22, 1928
Source Document Excerpt

During [World War I] we necessarily turned to the government to solve every difficult economic problem. The government having absorbed every energy of our people for war, there was no other solution. For the preservation of the state the Federal Government became a centralized despotism which undertook unprecedented responsibilities, assumed autocratic powers, and took over the business of citizens. To a large degree, we regimented our whole people temporally into a socialistic state. However justified in war time, if continued in peace-time it would destroy not only our American system but with it our progress and freedom as well.

When the war closed, the most vital of issues both in our own country and around the world was whether government should continue their wartime ownership and operation of many [instruments] of production and distribution. We were challenged with a. . . choice between the American system of rugged individualism and a European philosophy of diametrically opposed doctrines—doctrines of paternalism and state socialism. The acceptance of these ideas would have meant the destruction of self-government through centralization. . . [and] the undermining of the individual initiative and enterprise through which our people have grown to unparalleled greatness.

The Republican Party [in the years after the war] resolutely turned its face away from these ideas and war practices. . . . When the Republican Party came into full power it went at once resolutely back to our fundamental conception of the state and the rights and responsibility of the individual. Thereby it restored confidence and hope in the American people, it freed and stimulated enterprise, it restored the government to a position as an umpire instead of a player in the economic game. For these reasons the American people have gone forward in progress. . . . [13]

Hoover's solution to the Depression was to call for Americans to rely on "volunteerism," a system in which cooperation between the government and private entities would ensure strong economic growth and might address the impact of the Depression. The philosophy marks a sharp departure from the laissez-faire doctrine that had long governed the thinking of fiscal conservatives, having more in common with later fiscal progressive thinking. Volunteerism was an attempt to incorporate social justice with a small, decentralized government, focusing on individualism and free enterprise—cornerstones of conservatism—by portraying volunteerism as a form of "public service." Communities, business leaders, and government officials would work together to find regional solutions to specific issues. In Hoover's words, this was "self-government by the people outside of the Government."[14]

Hoover hoped that the American people would come together to address the crisis without the need for aggressive federal intervention, but the strategy was ineffective. Republicans in Congress passed legislation limiting international trade to aid local business, but this only deepened the problem. Consumer spending continued to plummet, driven by job losses and business closures, which led to a cycle of further business closures, rising unemployment and even lower consumer spending. Hoover eventually recognized the need for more aggressive government intervention, but the relief package his administration passed focused on businesses rather than working-class poverty and so did nothing to stop the downward spiral.

Hoover was not a man of limited skill or a blind patron of big business. His attempt to lead the country through the Depression demonstrated greater strength of character than the passive approach of Coolidge or Harding. However, Hoover did not break with the party platform, relying on his Republican legislators and cabinet members, and they proved unfit for the challenge. Some historians argue that Hoover's attempts

to address the crisis were not entirely to blame for the collapse of the economy. Whether or not this is true, the broader philosophy of non-intervention was partly to blame for the economic downturn. Predatory and irresponsible business practices contributed to the problem, and the interconnectedness of the industrial economy meant that depression in any sector necessarily affected the entire economic network. Lack of regulation left no systems in place to stop the depression from infecting the entire economy, and the philosophy of limited intervention was insufficient to address the problem once it began.

While Hoover has been criticized for his handling of the Great Depression, much of the blame belongs to his predecessors, Coolidge and Harding. Further, during his troubled administration he engaged in a goodwill tour through Latin America, visiting ten countries and meeting with regional leaders to discuss a change in American policy, pledging to reduce military interference. This was the beginning of a major shift toward the "Good Neighbor Policy" adopted under Franklin D. Roosevelt with regard to Latin America, and signaled the end of America's brief experiment with imperialism.

Conservatives in Retreat

The three presidents between Woodrow Wilson and Franklin D. Roosevelt were all marked by limited presidential authority. Although Hoover was more aggressive than Silent Cal or Warren Harding, his presidency was unremarkable in comparison to the one that followed; FDR left a mark on American culture still evident in the twenty-first century. By the early 1930s, the political parties had shifted roles. The Republicans had become the party for fiscal and social conservatism, but their failure to address the Great Depression would propel an emboldened Democratic Party, driven by claims of radical reform, into a long period of executive power.

CONCLUSION

Neither Harding, Coolidge, nor Hoover feature on lists of the most effective or impactful presidents, but they are important figures in the evolution of American politics. In the post-World War I world, many Americans were left feeling fearful of the international world and nostalgic for the comparative pre-war illusion of stability and security. Harding and Coolidge attempted to appeal to this sentiment directly, offering an agenda of isolationism and stability and both followed through on this by essentially being figureheads rather than active shapers of national policy. Hoover was more open to international engagement and not as hostile toward the reform-minded Democratic Party platform of the era, but he arrived in the presidency in the midst of a deepening financial crisis caused, in part, by poor economic management of his predecessors. In all, the performance of America's first three Republican Party conservatives left much to be desired and they proved ill-prepared for the task of managing the nation's increasingly complex economy. It is unsurprising that America's experiment in moderate, conservative stewardship ended with the election of the most radically progressive president to that point, who struggled to heal the ailing economy and leadership during the Second World War. The discussion of the presidency of Franklin Roosevelt in the next chapter makes it clear why he is one of the nation's most cherished leaders.

DISCUSSION QUESTIONS

♦ How did Coolidge and Harding contribute to the Great Depression?

♦ Could "volunteerism" be used to address economic problems in modern America? Why didn't this strategy work in the Hoover administration?

♦ How did Hoover's foreign relations efforts presage the shift in foreign policy that was to come?

♦ How did Harding's presidency mark a change in the Republican Party?

Works Used

"1928 Presidential General Election Results." *US Election Atlas*. 2019. uselectionatlas.org/RESULTS/national.php?year=1928.

"Calvin Coolidge: Thirtieth President 1923–1929." *Clinton White House*. clintonwhitehouse4.archives.gov/WH/glimpse/presidents/html/cc30.html.

Cummins, Joseph. "Dirty Campaigning in the Roaring Twenties: Herbert Hoover vs. Al Smith." *Mental Floss*. 17 Oct. 2008. www.mentalfloss.com/article/19897/dirty-campaigning-roaring-twenties-herbert-hoover-vs-al-smith.

Dean, John W. *Warren G. Harding*. New York: Times Books, 2004.

Gangitano, Alex, and Miranda Green. "Collins Received More Donations from Texas Fossil Fuel Industry Than from Maine Residents." *The Hill*. 16 Apr. 2019. thehill.com/business-a-lobbying/439145-texas-fossil-fuel-industry-bests-maine-residents-for-donations-to-susan.

Harding, Warren. "May 14, 1920: Readjustment." *Miller Center*. University of Virginia. millercenter.org/the-presidency/presidential-speeches/may-14-1920-readjustment.

Heflin, James Thomas. "Warning Against the 'Roman Catholic Party': Catholicism and the 1928 Election," *History Matters*. Congressional Record. 28 Jan. 1928. historymatters.gmu.edu/d/5073/.

Hoover, Herbert. "Principles and Ideals of the United States Government." *Teaching American History*. Ashbrook Center. 2019. teachingamericanhistory.org/library/document/principles-and-ideals-of-the-united-states-government/.

Hoover, Herbert. "Rugged Individualism." *Digital History*. 2019. www.digitalhistory.uh.edu/disp_textbook.cfm?smtID=3&psid=1334.

Mallon, Thomas. "Less Said." *The New Yorker*. 3 Mar. 2013. www.newyorker.com/magazine/2013/03/11/less-said.

Novak, Matt. "'Speeches Must Be Short': Radio and the Birth of the Modern Presidential Campaign." *Pacific Standard*. 2 Oct. 2012. psmag.com/news/airwaves-1924-the-first-presidential-campaign-over-radio-47615.

"Oil & Gas: Long-Term Contribution Trends." *Open Secrets*. 21 Nov. 2019. www.opensecrets.org/industries/totals.php?ind=E01++.

Payne, Phillip G. *Dead Last: The Public Memory of Warren G. Harding's Scandalous Legacy*. Athens, OH: Ohio U P, 2009.

"Presidential Election of 1920: A Resource Guide." *LOC*. Library of Congress. Web Guides. 23 Oct. 2018. www.loc.gov/rr/program/bib/elections/election1920.html.

Introduction

Few presidents before or since have been as influential as Franklin Delano Roosevelt. Roosevelt's combination of widespread public appeal and his skill in forming strong, bi-partisan working relationships made him powerful enough to set a dramatic domestic agenda, and the advent of World War II provided him with the power to reshape America's role in the international sphere. He was elected to office four times, a testament to his popular appeal, and though he is sometimes maligned as setting America on the path to the "welfare state," this was a manifestation of Roosevelt's strong belief that government should bring people together toward common goals and ensure that as many Americans as possible benefitted from the collective efforts of America's labors. This is the core of progressivism in the modern world as well, and Roosevelt can therefore be credited as the architect of the modern progressive movement. In terms of presidential powers, Roosevelt fundamentally reshaped the presidency, adding new offices, new duties, and, in general, creating a presidency with a more robust role in shaping the nation's legislative agenda.

Topics covered in this chapter include:

- World War II
- The United Nations
- The Economy Act of 1933
- The Brownlow Committee
- The Reorganization Act of 1939
- The Great Depression
- The New Deal

This Chapter Discusses the Following Source Documents:

Executive Order 8248, Franklin Delano Roosevelt, September 8, 1939

First Inaugural Address, "The Only Thing We Have to Fear Is Fear Itself," Franklin Delano Roosevelt, 1933

On the Bank Crisis, Franklin Delano Roosevelt, March 12, 1933

On Drought Conditions, Franklin Delano Roosevelt, September 6, 1936

On the European War, Franklin Delano Roosevelt, September 3, 1939

On the Declaration of War with Japan, Franklin Delano Roosevelt, December 8, 1941

Eulogy in Commons for the Late President Roosevelt, Winston Churchill, April 17, 1945

We the People

New Ideas
Franklin Delano Roosevelt (1933–1945)

Franklin Delano Roosevelt (FDR) was a defining figure in American history. He held the office for 12 years, the longest in American history, and his sweeping reforms fundamentally changed the role of the government in the economy, redefining the relationship between the president and the American people.

East Coast Progressivism

Roosevelt was born in Hyde Park, New York, into moderate wealth in 1882. Schooled in exclusive private academies, he was groomed for leadership and inspired by the successes of his cousin Theodore Roosevelt, whose reform-oriented Republican administration served as a model for much of what Franklin tried to accomplish. Roosevelt attended Harvard College, became editor of the school's student newspaper, and joined the Democratic Party student organization. At Harvard, Roosevelt met Anna Eleanor Roosevelt, Teddy's niece and so a distant cousin. They married in 1905 and had six children, one of whom died in infancy. Roosevelt attended Columbia Law School; and though he never finished his degree, worked as a lawyer in New York.

Franklin Delano Roosevelt, Google Art Project, via Wikimedia.

Roosevelt was elected to the state senate and became a supporter for Woodrow Wilson's presidential campaign; once Wilson won, Roosevelt was appointed Assistant Secretary of the Navy, a post once held by Teddy. Roosevelt's success helped him become the vice-presidential candidate in 1920, alongside Democrat James Cox. Though they lost the election to Warren Harding, FDR gained significant recognition to be considered one of the Democratic Party's rising leaders.[1]

Roosevelt's political career stalled in 1921 when he contracted polio. He was paralyzed from the waist down, and though he made an impressive recovery, never fully regained the use of his legs and used a wheelchair for the rest of his life. Though he remained active in politics, the administrations of Warren Harding, Calvin Coolidge, and Herbert Hoover were marked by Republican dominance. In the 1922 elections, which were nearly a sweep for the Republican Party, Roosevelt achieved a narrow victory to become governor of New York, a prestigious office that frequently led to the presidency. Roosevelt was governor when the economy slowed in 1929, exposing problems with the stock market. On two infamous days, "Black Thursday" (October 24) and "Black Tuesday" (October 29), brokers tried to unload declining stocks, beginning a multi-year decline in the stock market and investor losses of some $75 billion. In the early 1930s, five percent of America's population controlled one-third of the nation's monetary resources, worsening the situation as most Americans had no personal savings to weather the financial crisis.[2]

In Washington, Hoover and the Republican-led Congress addressed the problem by calling on Americans to help one another (volunteerism) and by investing in corporations, hoping to forestall further job losses. This was unsuccessful, because consumers lacked the resources to support the nation's corporations. In New York, Roosevelt lowered agricultural taxes and passed a public works bill to help the unemployed. What little federal funds were available were used to create relief systems for the

homeless and families thrown into poverty. Roosevelt was reelected as governor in 1930, but the Republican hold on the federal government was crumbling, and Roosevelt was well positioned to make a run for the presidency.

Despite critics who maintained that his disability and radical policies would prevent his success, Roosevelt won the Democratic Party nomination in 1932 and promised sweeping changes to the economic sector. He called for labor protections, insurance for elderly Americans, unemployment assistance, and a series of public works projects, bold strategies that he marketed as a "New Deal" for America. Roosevelt easily won the election, earning 22.8 million votes to 15.7 million for Hoover, and the Democrats picked up 12 seats to control the Senate and a whopping 97 seats to control the House.[3] The magnitude of Roosevelt's win provided a strong public mandate, which he used to aggressively push social and economic reform.

The Executive Office

Presidencies are about personality as much as political ideology, and Roosevelt brought with him strong progressive tendencies, tempered by respect for both conservative and liberal viewpoints. He was neither a radical liberal nor a fiscal or social conservative, which informed his use of presidential powers.

A basic presidential power, established by George Washington's military style, is creating the presidential cabinet. For years, cabinet positions were part of a patronage system used to reward or bribe political party members. Roosevelt instead chose nearly all of his cabinet based on merit, possible because Democratic dominance in Congress gave him sufficient influence. He chose individuals from diverse backgrounds and with opposing ideologies, similar to Thomas Jefferson in inviting debate within the executive branch. His core staff included a number of liberal

Democrats and independents with a history of labor activism. Worker-rights activist Francis Perkins was appointed Secretary of Labor, the first woman to hold a cabinet post.[4]

Workers' rights activist Frances Perkins, the first woman appointed to a presidential cabinet. Library of Congress Prints and Photographs Division, via Wikimedia.

Immediately upon entering office, Roosevelt championed the Economy Act of 1933, which gave him the authority to reorganize the executive branch. The bill, which also tried to address the federal budget by eliminating some federal agencies and reducing salaries, was opposed by liberals, but Roosevelt pushed it through with help from conservatives in both parties. Critics argue that Roosevelt misused the emergency reorganization provisions of the bill by dramatically expanding the size of the White House staff, through new agencies and investigatory committees.[5] In the early years of his presidency, Roosevelt often had multiple advisors and staff working on the same problem. Critics called his approach inefficient and wasteful, but Roosevelt appreciated the wide variety of options that this approach created.

Still feeling limited by the nature of his office, Roosevelt created the Committee on Administrative Management in 1936 to examine the function of the executive branch. Generally known as the Brownlow Committee, it comprised political scientist and specialist in administrative organization Louis Brownlow, University of Chicago political science professor Charles Merriam, and Columbia University expert in public administration Luther Gulick. In a 1937 report, which began famously with the statement, "The President Needs Help," Brownlow, Gulick, and Merriam provided 37 recommendations for how to shape a more streamlined, yet robust, presidential department.[6]

It took nearly all of Roosevelt's presidency to achieve his goal of reorganizing the office, bringing him into conflict with politicians on both sides. The Reorganization Act of 1939 required congressional approval for permanent changes to the cabinet and the executive branch. Also created was the position of presidential assistant, authorizing the president to hire up to six personal assistants to help manage the federal departments. The act also created the Executive Office of the President (EOP), which brought a number of independent government branches under executive

control. The EOP would head up a number of councils and offices, including the personal offices of the vice president and president, the Security Council, and the Council of Economic Advisors.

Roosevelt engaged in three separate reorganization plans, each of which created several new federal agencies, typically by consolidating formerly independent agencies. For instance, the Federal Security Agency was formed by combining aspects of the Office of Education, the Social Security Board, the U.S. Employment Service, and several other divisions. The function of the offices under the presidency was further established through the controversial executive order 8248, issued by Roosevelt on September 8, 1939, in which he explains the function of the new EOP subdivisions:

EXECUTIVE ORDER 8248
Franklin Delano Roosevelt
September 8, 1939
Source Document Excerpt

The functions and duties of the divisions of the Executive Office of the President are hereby defined as follows:

1. *The White House Office.*—In general, to serve the President in an intimate capacity in the performance of the many detailed activities incident to his immediate office. To that end, The White House Office shall be composed of the following principal subdivisions, with particular functions and duties as indicated:

(a) *The Secretaries to the President.*—To facilitate and maintain quick and easy communication with the Congress, the individual members of the Congress, the heads of executive departments and agencies, the press, the radio, and the general public.

(b) *The Executive Clerk.*—To provide for the orderly handling of documents and correspondence within The White House Office, and to organize and supervise all clerical services and procedure relating thereto.

(c) *The Administrative Assistants to the President.*—To assist the President in such matters as he may direct, and at the specific request of the President, to get information and to condense

Executive Order 8248
continued

and summarize it for his use. These Administrative Assistants shall be personal aides to the President and shall have no authority over anyone in any department or agency, including the Executive Office of the President, other, than the personnel assigned to their immediate offices. In no event shall the Administrative Assistants be interposed between the President and the head of any department or agency, or between the President and any one of the divisions in the Executive Office of the President.

2. *The Office of Management and Budget.*—(a) To assist the President in the preparation of the Budget and the formulation of the fiscal program of the Government.

(b) To supervise and control the administration of the Budget.

(c) To conduct research in the development of improved plans of administrative management, and to advise the executive departments and agencies of the Government with respect to improved administrative organization and practice.

(d) To aid the President to bring about more efficient and economical conduct of Government service.

(e) To assist the President by clearing and coordinating departmental advice on proposed legislation and by making recommendations as to Presidential action on legislative enactments, in accordance with past practice.

(f) To assist in the consideration and clearance and, where necessary, in the preparation of proposed Executive orders and proclamations, in accordance with the provisions of Executive Order No. 7298 of February 18, 1936.

(g) To plan and promote the improvement, development, and coordination of Federal and other statistical services.

(h) To keep the President informed of the progress of activities by agencies of the Government with respect to work proposed, work actually initiated, and work completed, together with the relative timing of work between the several agencies of the Government; all to the end that the work programs of the several agencies of the Executive branch of the Government may be coordinated and that the monies appropriated by the Congress may be expended in the most economical manner possible with the least possible overlapping and duplication of effort.

[Sec. 2 amended by Executive Order 12608 of Sept. 9, 1987, 52 FR 34617, 3 CFR, 1987 Comp., p. 245]

continued

3. *The National Resources Planning Board.*—(a) To survey, collect data on, and analyze problems pertaining to national resources, both natural and human, and to recommend to the President and the Congress long-time plans and programs for the wise use and fullest development of such resources.

(b) To consult with Federal, regional, state, local, and private agencies in developing orderly programs of public works and to list for the President and the Congress all proposed public works in the order of their relative importance with respect to (1) the greatest good to the greatest number of people, (2) the emergency necessities of the Nation, and (3) the social, economic, and cultural advancement of the people of the United States.

(c) To inform the President of the general trend of economic conditions and to recommend measures leading to their improvement of stabilization.

(d) To act as a clearing house and means of coordination for planning activities, linking together various levels and fields of planning.

4. [Revoked]

[Sec. 4 revoked by Executive Order 10452 of May 1, 1953, 18 FR 2599, 3 CFR, 1949–1953 Comp., p. 940]

5. *The Office of Government Reports.*—-(a) To provide a central clearing house through which individual citizens, organizations of citizens, state or local governmental bodies, and, where appropriate, agencies of the Federal Government, may transmit inquiries and complaints and receive advice and information.

(b) To assist the President in dealing with special problems requiring the clearance of information between the Federal Government and state and local governments and private institutions.

(c) To collect and distribute information concerning the purposes and activities of executive departments and agencies for the use of the Congress, administrative officials, and the public.

(d) To keep the President currently informed of the opinions, desires, and complaints of citizens and groups of citizens and of state and local governments with respect to the work of Federal agencies.

(e) To report to the President on the basis of the information it has obtained possible ways and means for reducing the cost of the operation of the Government.[7]

Roosevelt's reinvention of the executive branch is one of the most significant changes in presidential authority in American history, leading to a meaningful change in the basic relationship between the president and Congress. With a more robust staff of experts, Roosevelt and future presidents were able to more directly create proposals for new legislation, tipping the balance of federal power toward the executive branch.

What's the Deal with Roosevelt?

Roosevelt's approach to executive management resulted in a remarkably versatile administration, and the New Deal program Roosevelt spearheaded to address the Depression turned into a series of broad policy directives typically divided into phases—the "First New Deal," the "Second New Deal," and the "Third New Deal." In practice, the New Deal is not viewed as a coherent series of policies, but rather as an evolving series of strategies that changed as new information emerged, or as the economic system began to change, and as Roosevelt reorganized the executive. As Republican journalist William Allen White described it, Roosevelt and the American people had come to believe that the government needed to become an "agency for human welfare," an overarching theme of the New Deal programs.

Another innovation of the Roosevelt presidency involved participation in the legislative process. Since Roosevelt, the press often focuses on a president's first 100 days in office as an arbitrary, but important, measure of how successful he or she will be in terms of working with Congress and establishing a national agenda. This idea started with Roosevelt, whose first months in the White House became known as the "Hundred Days" because of the strength with which he established his administration's dominance over Congress and his ability to set the national agenda.[8]

This aggressive approach was key to Roosevelt's strategy. In the first years of his presidency, this dominance was instrumental in passing

legislation to address unemployment. This involved the Federal Emergency Relief Administration, Civilian Conservation Corps, and Civil Works Administration, which hired unemployed Americans through federal contracts. Most of Roosevelt's efforts to combat unemployment and homelessness met with objections—similar to those being raised today—from conservatives. It was argued that giving work to civilians was little more than government handouts and would discourage individuals from looking for work in the private sector, weakening the economy over the longer term. Conservatives typically opted to provide tax breaks and federal assistance to large corporations to create jobs, but this did not restore consumer spending. The New Deal attempted to reverse this and attempted to provide revenues to low-income individuals to stimulate consumer spending, which would then support corporate America from the ground up.

For example, the Civilian Conservation Corps (CCC) provided more than 300,000 federally funded jobs. Workers in the program, known as "Roosevelt's Tree Army," worked on conservation and infrastructure projects, planting millions of trees, and building and maintaining park facilities and equipment.

Poor soil conservation practices in the Great Plains region resulted in a sharp decline in farm revenues during the Depression, ultimately leading to the Dust Bowl—millions of acres of dry soil swept into clouds of dust that covered miles of farmland. The CCC traveled to farms to help initiate soil improvement and conservation methods, and it became part of the broader effort to address natural disasters.[9] Roosevelt's initial New Deal programs included an aggressive effort to help struggling farmers keep their land and earn higher wages. The Agricultural Adjustment Act doubled farm income between 1932 and 1935, and the Rural Electrification Administration (REA) delivered electricity to farming communities for the first time. Soil conservation was another key goal, and the administration

formulated a comprehensive plan to increase soil quality earning Roosevelt the legacy of "father of soil conservation."

Similar New Deal systems were aimed at addressing the urban sphere. The Public Works Administration (PWA), run by the Department of the Interior, hired Americans for a series of public works project, including the construction of San Francisco's Golden Gate Bridge and New York City's Triborough Bridge, large-scale construction programs that employed thousands and facilitated transport, shipping, and the movement of labor in those regions.

Though Roosevelt earned praise for his aggressive efforts to combat the Depression, he drew criticism as well. A failed program was the National Recovery Administration (NRA), designed to address problems in the industrial sector. It was hoped that the NRA would develop workplace standards to regulate competition, price-setting, and labor wages. With the exception of establishing a federal prohibition on child labor, however, the program was largely a failure.

The idea behind the NRA was for business leaders to craft new regulations regarding wages and setting prices, supervised by the NRA. Businesses in compliance would display a "Blue Eagle" logo in their windows. FDR believed that the self-regulating function of the free market would breed success, but business leaders used political influence to prevent any attempt to control their behavior, creating regulations that benefitted larger companies and hurt small competitors. Corporations ignored union demands and only complied with regulations regarding fair wages and treatment of workers when they absolutely needed to.[10]

The failures of the first era of the New Deal led to a more aggressive system of legislation and executive policies, often called the Second New Deal, whose key legislative accomplishments were the Social Security Act (SSA), the Works Progress Administration (WPA), and the National Labor

Don't Be Fooled by Figures

I. SPENDING UNDER REPUBLICANS

Under Hoover the national debt rose 3½ billion (net). In the last 2¼ years the gross debt increased nearly 5 billions. **Yearly Deficits Were 59 Per Cent of Expenditures in 1932; 46 Per Cent in 1933.**

WHAT DID PRESIDENT HOOVER BUY?

A six-billion-dollar loss in farm income, bank failures, foreclosed homes, shut-down factories, government bonds at low levels, national panic. The depression was bought and the people sold.

Our Yearly National Income Dropped 40 Billion
Our Federal Revenues Fell 2 Billion

THIS WAS REPUBLICAN PROSPERITY

II. SPENDING UNDER DEMOCRATS

Under President Roosevelt the gross national debt has increased about thirteen billion (including the 2 billion bonus). Against this, however, the Government has 2 billion in gold profit, a 2 billion increase in the General Treasury Fund, and another 2 billion investment in bank stocks, loans and other repayable assets so that the *net* increase is cut down to 7 billion. It costs less to carry this heavier debt because easier credit and able treasury financing have saved approximately 1 per cent in interest rates. **Yearly Deficits Were 56 Per Cent of Expenditures in 1934; 48 Per Cent in 1935**

WHAT HAS PRESIDENT ROOSEVELT BOUGHT?

A 1935 gross farm income of over 8 billion—a 2.8 billion rise since 1932.

Reemployment of 5 million workers. A payroll gain of 59 per cent since 1933.

The highest volume of industrial production since 1930.

Less than 50 bank failures in 1935 compared with more than 1,400 in 1932.

1936 dividends at a 5-year peak.

Government bonds at their top prices, the best test of treasury soundness.

Our National Income, as Estimated for 1936, Will Have Grown Some 21 Billion in 4 Years
Federal Revenues Are Running More Than Double the Receipts in 1933

THIS IS DEMOCRATIC PROSPERITY

III. BALANCING THE BUDGET

When President Roosevelt took office he faced a grave national crisis. He could stand on his platform and cut expenditures. Or he could draw heavily on government funds to feed the starving and aid banks and business. He chose the latter course as *the only road to recovery*. If the Government could shoulder a war debt of 25 billion to save Europe, President Roosevelt felt that it must use its credit even more freely to save its suffering people in a national catastrophe. Had government help come sooner and on a more adequate scale, it would have taken less spending and lending to stop the depression.

ORDINARY EXPENSES MET

In no fiscal year have the ordinary expenses of government under President Roosevelt exceeded revenues. Increases have been caused by farm aid, new construction and additions to regular recurring items such as veterans' benefits, pensions, national defense and the like.

EMERGENCIES BROUGHT RISE

RELIEF is the great human cost which has run up government expenses. As good times return, this item is being lowered.

DECREASING THE DEFICIT

President Roosevelt's program calls for a steadily decreasing deficit each year. In 1935 the deficit was 400 million less than in 1934; had it not been for the soldiers' bonus and the loss of AAA taxes, the deficit would have declined again in the fiscal year 1936. For 1937 there will be a drop below 1936, as estimated by the Treasury, of over 3 billion (to $2,675,700,000).

The gross national debt per capita was $250 after the war. Today it is $255 (including a bonus charge of over $15 apiece). We reduced the debt then. We can do it again.

The First Step to Reduce NATIONAL Debt is to Lighten PERSONAL Debt

Follow PRESIDENT ROOSEVELT Forward

Democratic party re-election handout promoting Roosevelt's economic policy. By Democratic National Campaign Committee, via Wikimedia.

We the People

Relations Act (NLRA). These three pieces of legislation committed the federal government as caretaker for Americans, ensuring a basic level of financial support. The WPA provided jobs through a wide-ranging series of projects, including building new schools, airports, shipping depots, and hospitals, in both urban and rural areas. The NLRA gave unions the legal right to organize and bargain with corporations and gave the federal government the power to defend this right. Union membership swelled with support from the federal government. The SSA remains among the most controversial piece of legislation ever developed by the U.S. Congress and executive branch, calling for the federal government to provide basic care for the elderly, disabled, dependent children, and the unemployed.

Like the first phase of the New Deal, the second phase was controversial. In some cases, business-centric conservatives diluted key pieces of legislation, and bureaucratic ineptitude and manipulation prevented even distribution of federal welfare benefits. Farm laborers, women, and minorities found it more difficult to gain assistance, and so the more marginalized segments of the population recovered more slowly.

While the New Deal fundamentally changed the relationship between the federal government and the American people, recovery from the Depression was slow until World War II created a massive nation-wide industrial and public effort to support the war. Government-enforced rationing of power, food, and other amenities made poverty look like patriotic duty. The surge of nationalism saw individuals and corporations making sacrifices for the good of their country. The war proved to be the economic stimulus that America needed; America emerged from the war years into a boom economy, with many of the New Deal programs still in place in hopes of ensuring that America would never again suffer such a devastating financial collapse.

America's Father

Those presidents who have been judged as America's greatest tend to have at least one common ability, to bring Americans together and cultivate a sense of trust and faith in America. Presidents who fail to break away from partisan politics and support legislation that only appeals to core supporters, alienated the rest of the population. Those presidents adjudged to be great leaders overcome partisanship and political ideology and engender respect, at least, among a majority of the American people. Roosevelt did this, leaving a legacy that looms large.

When Roosevelt entered office, with the Great Depression worsening by the week, Americans were in a state of panic. Roosevelt capitalized on radio broadcasts as no politician had in the past; throughout his presidency he communicated directly with the American people. This began with his inaugural address in 1933, which was broadcast into homes and businesses across the country:

FIRST INAUGURAL ADDRESS
"THE ONLY THING WE HAVE TO FEAR IS FEAR ITSELF"

Franklin Delano Roosevelt
1933
Source Document Excerpt

I am certain that my fellow Americans expect that on my induction into the Presidency I will address them with a candor and a decision which the present situation of our people impel. This is preeminently the time to speak the truth, the whole truth, frankly and boldly. Nor need we shrink from honestly facing conditions in our country today. This great Nation will endure as it has endured, will revive and will prosper. So, first of all, let me assert my firm belief that the only thing we have to fear is fear itself—nameless, unreasoning, unjustified terror which paralyzes needed efforts to convert retreat into advance. In every dark hour of our national life a leadership of frankness and vigor has met with that understanding and support of the people themselves which is essential to victory. I am convinced that you will again give that support to leadership in these critical days.

In such a spirit on my part and on yours we face our common difficulties. They concern, thank God, only material things. Values have shrunken to fantastic levels; taxes have risen; our ability to pay has fallen; government of all kinds is faced by serious curtailment of income; the means of exchange are frozen in the currents of trade; the withered leaves of industrial enterprise lie on every side; farmers find no markets for their produce; the savings of many years in thousands of families are gone.

More important, a host of unemployed citizens face the grim problem of existence, and an equally great number toil with little return. Only a foolish optimist can deny the dark realities of the moment.

Yet our distress comes from no failure of substance. We are stricken by no plague of locusts. Compared with the perils which our forefathers conquered because they believed and were not afraid, we have still much to be thankful for. Nature still offers her bounty and human efforts have multiplied it. Plenty is at our doorstep, but a generous use of it languishes in the very sight of the supply. Primarily this is because the rulers of the exchange of mankind's goods have

continued

failed, through their own stubbornness and their own incompetence, have admitted their failure, and abdicated. Practices of the unscrupulous money changers stand indicted in the court of public opinion, rejected by the hearts and minds of men.

True they have tried, but their efforts have been cast in the pattern of an outworn tradition. Faced by failure of credit they have proposed only the lending of more money. Stripped of the lure of profit by which to induce our people to follow their false leadership, they have resorted to exhortations, pleading tearfully for restored confidence. They know only the rules of a generation of self-seekers. They have no vision, and when there is no vision the people perish.

The money changers have fled from their high seats in the temple of our civilization. We may now restore that temple to the ancient truths. The measure of the restoration lies in the extent to which we apply social values more noble than mere monetary profit.

Happiness lies not in the mere possession of money; it lies in the joy of achievement, in the thrill of creative effort. The joy and moral stimulation of work no longer must be forgotten in the mad chase of evanescent profits. These dark days will be worth all they cost us if they teach us that our true destiny is not to be ministered unto but to minister to ourselves and to our fellow men.

Recognition of the falsity of material wealth as the standard of success goes hand in hand with the abandonment of the false belief that public office and high political position are to be valued only by the standards of pride of place and personal profit; and there must be an end to a conduct in banking and in business which too often has given to a sacred trust the likeness of callous and selfish wrongdoing. Small wonder that confidence languishes, for it thrives only on honesty, on honor, on the sacredness of obligations, on faithful protection, on unselfish performance; without them it cannot live.

Restoration calls, however, not for changes in ethics alone. This Nation asks for action, and action now.[11]

Roosevelt's casual communications with the American people became known as "fireside chats." Through them, Roosevelt kept the American people informed about specific problems facing the country and how his administration was seeking to address them. On March 12, 1933, he talked to the public about the banking system, simply and effectively:

ON THE BANK CRISIS
Franklin Delano Roosevelt
March 12, 1933
Source Document Excerpt

I want to talk for a few minutes with the people of the United States about banking—with the comparatively few who understand the mechanics of banking but more particularly with the overwhelming majority who use banks for the making of deposits and the drawing of checks. I want to tell you what has been done in the last few days, why it was done, and what the next steps are going to be. I recognize that the many proclamations from State Capitols and from Washington, the legislation, the Treasury regulations, etc., couched for the most part in banking and legal terms should be explained for the benefit of the average citizen. I owe this in particular because of the fortitude and good temper with which everybody has accepted the inconvenience and hardships of the banking holiday. I know that when you understand what we in Washington have been about I shall continue to have your cooperation as fully as I have had your sympathy and help during the past week.[12]

When drought swept through the Great Plains, leaving thousands homeless and out of work, Roosevelt again took to the radio to assuage fears and to reassure the nation that their government was at work on the problem:

ON DROUGHT CONDITIONS
Franklin Delano Roosevelt
September 6, 1936
Source Document Excerpt

I have been on a journey of husbandry. I went primarily to see at first hand conditions in the drought states; to see how effectively Federal and local authorities are taking care of pressing problems of relief and also how they are to work together to defend the people of this country against the effects of future droughts.

I saw drought devastation in nine states. I talked with families who had lost their wheat crop, lost their corn crop, lost their livestock, lost the water in their well, lost their garden and come through to the end of the summer without one dollar of cash resources, facing a winter without feed or food—facing a planting season without seed to put in the ground.

That was the extreme case, but there are thousands and thousands of families on western farms who share the same difficulties.

I saw cattlemen who because of lack of grass or lack of winter feed have been compelled to sell all but their breeding stock and will need help to carry even these through the coming winter. I saw livestock kept alive only because water had been brought to them long distances in tank cars. I saw other farm families who have not lost everything but who, because they have made only partial crops, must have some form of help if they are to continue farming next spring.

I shall never forget the fields of wheat so blasted by heat that they cannot be harvested. I shall never forget field after field of corn stunted, earless and stripped of leaves, for what the sun left the grasshoppers took. I saw brown pastures which would not keep a cow on fifty acres.

Yet I would not have you think for a single minute that there is permanent disaster in these drought regions, or that the picture I saw meant depopulating these areas. No cracked earth, no blistering sun, no burning wind, no grasshoppers, are a permanent match for the indomitable American farmers and stockmen and their wives and children who have carried on through desperate days, and inspire us with their self-reliance, their tenacity and their courage. It was their fathers' task to make homes; it is their task to keep those homes; it is our task to help them with their fight.[13]

When World War II began, being called the "European War" in the American press, Americans were divided on whether or not to intervene. Like Wilson had at the beginning of World War I, Roosevelt initially chose to pursue a neutral path, and as with his championing of the New Deal, he took this decision directly to the American people:

ON THE EUROPEAN WAR
Franklin Delano Roosevelt
September 3, 1939
Source Document Excerpt

MY FELLOW AMERICANS AND MY FRIENDS:

Tonight my single duty is to speak to the whole of America.

Until four-thirty this morning I had hoped against hope that some miracle would prevent a devastating war in Europe and bring to an end the invasion of Poland by Germany.

For four long years a succession of actual wars and constant crises have shaken the entire world and have threatened in each case to bring on the gigantic conflict which is today unhappily a fact.

It is right that I should recall to your minds the consistent and at time successful efforts of your Government in these crises to throw the full weight of the United States into the cause of peace. In spite of spreading wars I think that we have every right and every reason to maintain as a national policy the fundamental moralities, the teachings of religion (and) the continuation of efforts to restore peace—(for) because some day, though the time may be distant, we can be of even greater help to a crippled humanity.

It is right, too, to point out that the unfortunate events of these recent years have, without question, been based on the use of force (or) and the threat of force. And it seems to me clear, even at the outbreak of this great war, that the influence of America should be consistent in seeking for humanity a final peace which will eliminate, as far as it is possible to do so, the continued use of force between nations.

It is, of course, impossible to predict the future. I have my constant stream of information from American representatives and other sources throughout the world. You, the people of this country, are receiving news through your radios and your newspapers at every hour of the day.

continued

You are, I believe, the most enlightened and the best informed people in all the world at this moment. You are subjected to no censorship of news, and I want to add that your Government has no information which it (hesitates to) withholds (from you) or which it has any thought of withholding from you.

At the same time, as I told my Press Conference on Friday, it is of the highest importance that the press and the radio use the utmost caution to discriminate between actual verified fact on the one hand, and mere rumor on the other.

I can add to that by saying that I hope the people of this country will also discriminate most carefully between news and rumor. Do not believe of necessity everything you hear or read. Check up on it first.

You must master at the outset a simple but unalterable fact in modern foreign relations between nations. When peace has been broken anywhere, the peace of all countries everywhere is in danger.

It is easy for you and for me to shrug our shoulders and to say that conflicts taking place thousands of miles from the continental United States, and, indeed, thousands of miles from the whole American Hemisphere, do not seriously affect the Americas—and that all the United States has to do is to ignore them and go about (our) its own business. Passionately though we may desire detachment, we are forced to realize that every word that comes through the air, every ship that sails the sea, every battle that is fought does affect the American future.

Let no man or woman thoughtlessly or falsely talk of America sending its armies to European fields. At this moment there is being prepared a proclamation of American neutrality. This would have been done even if there had been no neutrality statute on the books, for this proclamation is in accordance with international law and in accordance with American policy.

This will be followed by a Proclamation required by the existing Neutrality Act. And I trust that in the days to come our neutrality can be made a true neutrality.

It is of the utmost importance that the people of this country, with the best information in the world, think things through. The most dangerous enemies of American peace are those who, without well-rounded Information on the whole broad subject of the past, the present and the future, undertake to speak with assumed authority, to talk in terms of glittering generalities, to give to the nation assurances or prophecies which are of little present or future value.

On the European War
continued

I myself cannot and do not prophesy the course of events abroad—and the reason is that because I have of necessity such a complete picture of what is going on in every part of the world, that I do not dare to do so. And the other reason is that I think it is honest for me to be honest with the people of the United States.

I cannot prophesy the immediate economic effect of this new war on our nation but I do say that no American has the moral right to profiteer at the expense either of his fellow citizens or of the men, the women and the children who are living and dying in the midst of war in Europe.

Some things we do know. Most of us in the United States believe in spiritual values. Most of us, regardless of what church we belong to, believe in the spirit of the New Testament—a great teaching which opposes itself to the use of force, of armed force, of marching armies and falling bombs. The overwhelming masses of our people seek peace—peace at home, and the kind of peace in other lands which will not jeopardize our peace at home.[14]

As the situation in Europe deteriorated, Roosevelt broadcasted several more fireside chats on national security, naval security, and, general updates on the state of America's national defense. After the Japanese attack on Pearl Harbor, Roosevelt again took to the radio:

ON THE DECLARATION OF WAR WITH JAPAN

Franklin Delano Roosevelt
December 9, 1941
Source Document Excerpt

MY FELLOW AMERICANS:

The sudden criminal attacks perpetrated by the Japanese in the Pacific provide the climax of a decade of international immorality.

Powerful and resourceful gangsters have banded together to make war upon the whole human race. Their challenge has now been flung at the United States of America. The Japanese have treacherously violated the longstanding peace between us. Many American soldiers and sailors have been killed by enemy action. American ships have been sunk; American airplanes have been destroyed.

The Congress and the people of the United States have accepted that challenge.

Together with other free peoples, we are now fighting to maintain our right to live among our world neighbors in freedom, in common decency, without fear of assault.

I have prepared the full record of our past relations with Japan, and it will be submitted to the Congress. It begins with the visit of Commodore Parry to Japan eighty-eight years ago. It ends with the visit of two Japanese emissaries to the Secretary of State last Sunday, an hour after Japanese forces had loosed their bombs and machine guns against our flag, our forces and our citizens.

I can say with utmost confidence that no Americans today or a thousand years hence, need feel anything but pride in our patience and in our efforts through all the years toward achieving a peace in the Pacific which would be fair and honorable to every nation, large or small. And no honest person, today or a thousand years hence, will be able to suppress a sense of indignation and horror at the treachery committed by the military dictators of Japan, under the very shadow of the flag of peace borne by their special envoys in our midst.

The course that Japan has followed for the past ten years in Asia has paralleled the course of Hitler and Mussolini in Europe and in Africa. Today, it has become far more than a parallel. It is actual collaboration so well calculated that all the continents of the world, and all the oceans, are

On the Declaration of War with Japan
continued

now considered by the Axis strategists as one gigantic battlefield.

In 1931, ten years ago, Japan invaded Manchukuo—without warning.

In 1935, Italy invaded Ethiopia—without warning. In 1938, Hitler occupied Austria—without warning.

In 1939, Hitler invaded Czechoslovakia—without warning.

Later in '39, Hitler invaded Poland—without warning. In 1940, Hitler invaded Norway, Denmark, the Netherlands, Belgium and Luxembourg—without warning.

In 1940, Italy attacked France and later Greece—without warning.

And this year, in 1941, the Axis Powers attacked Yugoslavia and Greece and they dominated the Balkans—without warning. In 1941, also, Hitler invaded Russia—without warning. And now Japan has attacked Malaya and Thailand—and the United States—without warning.

It is all of one pattern.

We are now in this war. We are all in it—all the way. Every single man, woman and child is a partner in the most tremendous undertaking of our American history. We must share together the bad news and the good news, the defeats and the victories—the changing fortunes of war.[15]

Roosevelt was beloved as a president and as a commander in chief, largely due to the direct relationship he cultivated with the American people. Roosevelt's fireside chats went beyond speeches and press releases of past presidents, creating a new bar for communicating with the people. Through his chats, Roosevelt adopted a more intimate relationship with Americans, transforming himself from political celebrity to father-like figure, speaking to Americans in common terms, asking for their understanding and support as his administration faced some of the most difficult issues in American history. Historian William E. Leuchtenburg believes that Roosevelt cultivated the idea of the president as the "caretaker" of the American people, an entirely new presidential model.[16]

At the same time that Roosevelt entered the presidency, the science of public opinion polling was also beginning to emerge. The method was pioneered by George Gallup, whose Gallup polls used scientific representative sampling to produce a more-accurate-than-before picture of public opinion. Roosevelt utilized this emerging technology to improve his presidency. His became the first administration to conduct its own opinion polls on a wide variety of issues, which guided how Roosevelt approached issues and campaigned for public support, an approach that is commonplace today.[17] While there is little direct data to demonstrate Roosevelt's approval rating during his presidency, his electoral results demonstrate a president who was uncommonly skilled in gaining and maintaining public trust. After winning his 1932 election with 56.9 percent of the vote, he was able to win the 1936 election by an even higher margin—61 percent—and then increased his dominance in his historic third term by capturing 62.5 percent of the vote.

Falling Short of the Mark

Franklin Roosevelt died from a cerebral hemorrhage while in office, on April 12, 1945. He collapsed while sitting for a portrait, just after winning his fourth election. Roosevelt's health had been failing for some time, and medical examinations had discovered a variety of heart-related problems, but Roosevelt nonetheless committed to a fourth term in office, hoping to see the war to its conclusion, but died just months from achieving this goal. English Prime Minister Winston Churchill delivered a eulogy at Roosevelt's funeral:

EULOGY IN COMMONS FOR THE LATE PRESIDENT ROOSEVELT
Winston Churchill
April 17, 1945
Source Document Excerpt

I conceived an admiration for him as a statesman, a man of affairs, and a war leader. I felt the utmost confidence in his upright, inspiring character and outlook and a personal regard—affection I must say—for him beyond my power to express to-day. His love of his own country, his respect for its constitution, his power of gauging the tides and currents of its mobile public opinion, were always evident, but, added to these, were the beatings of that generous heart which was always stirred to anger and to action by spectacles of aggression and oppression by the strong against the weak. It is, indeed, a loss, a bitter loss to humanity that those heart-beats are stilled for ever. President Roosevelt's physical affliction lay heavily upon him. It was a marvel that he bore up against it through all the many years of tumult—and storm. Not one man in ten millions, stricken and crippled as he was, would have attempted to plunge into a life of physical and mental exertion and of hard, ceaseless political controversy. Not one in ten millions would have tried, not one in a generation would have succeeded, not only in entering this sphere, not only in acting vehemently in it, but in becoming indisputable master of the scene. In this extraordinary effort of the spirit over the flesh, the will-power over physical infirmity, he was inspired and sustained by that noble woman his devoted wife, whose high ideals marched with his own, and to whom the deep and respectful sympathy of the House of Commons flows out to-day in all fullness. There is no doubt that the President foresaw the great dangers closing in upon the pre-war world with far more prescience than most well-informed people on either side of the Atlantic, and that he urged forward with all his power such precautionary military preparations as peace-time opinion in the United States could be brought to accept. There never was a moment's doubt, as the quarrel opened, upon which side his sympathies lay.[18]

Roosevelt left an enduring legacy as one of the most progressive and transformative presidents. The social welfare systems that he put in place dramatically changed the American government, for better and worse. Roosevelt legitimized the political view that a government must actively promote egalitarian ideals. He introduced socialist ideals into the American system—ideals that are today both celebrated and lamented—that established a role for the central government as the arbiter of economic justice.

However, Roosevelt ignored civil rights and, in some cases, accepted legislation that contributed to racial and gender discrimination. After the Japanese attack on Pearl Harbor, for example, Roosevelt allowed tens of thousands of Japanese-American citizens to be deprived of their rights without due process and placed in internment camps, one of the most shameful periods in American history.

There is little doubt that Roosevelt transformed both America and the presidency. The fact that he was able to achieve this, while winning four presidential elections and maintaining a high level of popular support throughout, is enough to place him among the most accomplished leaders in American history. That he enjoyed such high levels of popular and political success in the face of the two most devastating periods of the twentieth century, the Great Depression and World War II, suggests a man of uncommon skill and native capacity for leadership.

CONCLUSION

Roosevelt is a great hero to American progressives, but is often depicted as a villain in the conservative movement. His aggressive economic policies, although garnering mixed results, greatly improved the welfare of the working class. Though he had significant failings as a president, Roosevelt also demonstrated the most successful formula for achieving strong presidential authority. He mastered the art of gaining public trust and simultaneously proved a strong proponent of coalition politics. Future political scientists would criticize Roosevelt for making the presidency too powerful, and this is a matter of perspective, but it is true that Roosevelt was among the most influential presidents in establishing the modern presidency and the modern interpretation of presidential authority.

DISCUSSION QUESTIONS

♦ How did Roosevelt change the administrative offices of the presidency? Where these beneficial changes?
♦ In what ways did Roosevelt's use of radio and polling strengthen his popular appeal?
♦ What are some of the infrastructural legacies of the Roosevelt administration?
♦ How did Roosevelt's economic policies and approach to the Great Depression differ from the strategies utilized by Herbert Hoover?

Works Used

Black, Conrad. *Franklin Delano Roosevelt: Champion of Freedom*. New York: PublicAffairs P, 2003.

Breitman, Jessica. "Francis Perkins: Honoring the Achievements of FDR's Secretary of Labor." *FDR Library*. 2016. www.fdrlibrary.org/perkins.

Churchill, Winston. "Prime Minister Churchill's Eulogy in Commons for the Late President Roosevelt." 17 Apr. 1945. www.ibiblio.org/pha/policy/1945/1945-04-17a.html.

"Civilian Conservation Corps." *NPS*. National Park Service. 10 Apr. 2015. www.nps.gov/thro/learn/historyculture/civilian-conservation-corps.htm.

Dallek, Robert. *Franklin D. Roosevelt: A Political Life*. New York: Penguin, 2018.

Dickinson, Matthew J. *Bitter Harvest: FDR, Presidential Power and the Growth of the Presidential Branch*. New York: Cambridge U P, 1996.

Edwards, Sebastian. *American Default: The Untold Story of FDR, the Supreme Court, and the Battle over Gold*. Princeton, NJ: Princeton U P, 2019.

Himmelberg, Robert F. *The Origins of the National Recovery Administration: Business, Government, and the Trade Association, 1921–1933*. New York: Fordham U P, 1993.

Leuchtenburg, William E. "Franklin D. Roosevelt: Impact and Legacy." *Miller Center*. University of Virginia. 2019. millercenter.org/president/fdroosevelt/impact-and-legacy.

Roosevelt, Franklin. "Executive Order 8248—Executive Orders." *Archives*. National Archives. www.archives.gov/federal-register/codification/executive-order/08248.html.

_____. "The Only Thing We have to Fear Is Fear Itself": FDR's First Inaugural Address. 4 Mar. 1933. *History Matters*. historymatters.gmu.edu/d/5057/.

_____. "On Drought Conditions." 6 Sept. 1936. *FDR Library*. Marist University. docs.fdrlibrary.marist.edu/090636.html.

_____. "On the Bank Crisis." 12 Mar. 1933. *FDR Library*. Marist University. docs.fdrlibrary.marist.edu/031233.html.

_____. "On the Declaration of War with Japan." 9 Dec. 1941. *FDR Library*. Marist University. docs.fdrlibrary.marist.edu/120941.html.

_____. "On the European War." 3 Sept. 1939. *FDR Library*. Marist University. docs.fdrlibrary.marist.edu/090339.html.

Walsh, Kenneth T. "The First 100 Days: Franklin Roosevelt Pioneered the 100-Day Concept." *U.S. News*. 12 Feb. 2009. www.usnews.com/news/history/articles/2009/02/12/the-first-100-days-franklin-roosevelt-pioneered-the-100-day-concept.

_____. "The Most Consequential Elections in History: Franklin Delano Roosevelt and the Election of 1932." *US News*. 10 Sept. 2008. www.usnews.com/news/articles/2008/09/10/the-most-consequential-elections-in-history-franklin-delano-roosevelt-and-the-election-of-1932.

Waxman, Olivia B. "President Trump's Approval Rating Is at a Near-Record Low. Here's What to Know About the History of Those Numbers." *Time*. 24 Jan. 2019. time.com/5511118/presidential-approval-ratings-history/.

Introduction

Harry Truman came to power after the death of Franklin Roosevelt, just after the beginning of Roosevelt's fourth term in office. He faced the challenge of ending World War II, and did so by becoming the only American president and world leader in history to use weapons of mass destruction against an enemy state, killing hundreds of thousands of civilians in the process. The end of World War II marked the beginning of a period of state development focused on demonstrating, maintaining, and advancing America's military superiority, but also by the continuation of progressive domestic policies. By modern standards, Truman walked a line between pro-military conservatism and pro-public welfare progressivism. The nation's proactive military strategy following the conclusion of World War II was the beginning of new and more morally complex problems, such as the Korean War, which set the stage for the Vietnam Conflict, the invasion of Iraq (twice) and many other complex military operations that followed. The anti-communist terror that swept the nation in the 1940s was a destructive social force and the government's embrace of this spectral threat was self-defeating. On the domestic front, Truman was the first Democratic Party politician to actively speak to black voters and his presidency marked a historic shift, with African Americans and minority voters increasingly identifying with the Democratic Party, and the Republican Party, once a hotbed of progressivism, becoming more staunchly aligned with traditionalism and white interests.

Topics covered in this chapter include:
- World War II
- The Cold War
- The Bombings of Hiroshima and Nagasaki
- The Truman Doctrine
- African American alignment with the Democratic Party

This Chapter Discusses the Following Source Documents:
Statement on Hiroshima, Harry S. Truman, August 6, 1945
The Truman Doctrine, Harry S. Truman, March 12, 1947
Address before the NAACP, Harry S. Truman, June 29, 1947

Extreme Solutions
Harry S. Truman (1945–1953)

Harry S. Truman came to office after the death of Franklin Roosevelt and faced the challenge of living up to Roosevelt's legacy, while carving a path of his own. Truman is a highly ranked president of the modern era, though he also pushed a series of policy agendas that drew America deeper into the Cold War and dominated military policy into the twenty-first century.

Midwestern Progressivism

Born in the small town of Lamar, Missouri, in 1884, Harry Truman spent much of his youth working on his family's struggling farm. Denied entrance to the army because of poor eyesight, Truman entered the National Guard. When World War I broke out, Truman's National Guard unit was called into action, and he became a captain in the 129th Artillery Regiment, leading his unit into battle in France. Returning home to Independence, Missouri, Truman married and opened a clothing store. In 1922, Thomas Pendergast, head of the Kansas City Democratic Party political machine, helped Truman get elected as a judge for the county courts and, in 1934, as a U.S. Senator in a race marked by widespread voter fraud. Senator Truman became a strong ally of Franklin Roosevelt and gained a reputation as a defender of the labor movement.[1]

Harry S. Truman, by National Archives and Records Administration, via Wikimedia.

In the 1940s, Pendergast was imprisoned for corruption. Truman faced a divided Missouri electorate, but nonetheless retained his Senate seat by campaigning energetically in Missouri's cities. Voters from St. Louis and Kansas City saw him through to victory. When World War II hit, Truman came to national prominence as the head of the Truman Committee, a White House–created task force that sought to prevent corruption and misallocation of military revenues. In 1944 Franklin Roosevelt was preparing for his fourth bid for the presidency, his strong public approval ratings falling during his third term and facing a strong candidate in Republican New York governor Thomas Dewey. Vice President Henry Wallace was also turning into something of a political liability, as his controversial views had drawn criticism from moderates. Roosevelt dropped him from the ticket, and Democratic Party bosses picked Truman to replace him, counting on his strong support among midwestern urbanites and his moderate image. With Truman as his second, Roosevelt won a historic fourth term in the presidency, though his health was already failing. Roosevelt died in April of 1945 from a cerebral hemorrhage, leaving the presidency to Truman.[2]

Ending the War

Truman entered office at the end of World War II. Allied forces had already beaten Germany, and Japan—while not surrendering—had lost the military might to attack. Truman's advisers warned that securing a Japanese surrender might require a full-scale invasion that would lead to massive U.S. casualties. Meanwhile a top-secret military operation known as the Manhattan Project produced the first atomic bomb, which the military establishment favored using on Japan to accomplish a number of goals.

First, they hoped that an atomic attack would be so devastating that Japan would surrender without the need for a costly invasion. Second, it was the beginning of the Cold War and Russian military aggression was becoming a looming threat in the international sphere. American hawks were eager to demonstrate America's military might to Russia. Japan

could not defend itself against the bomb, and, further, anti-Japanese sentiment was still rampant, as Japan had become the first nation since Britain (in the war of 1812) to attack U.S. soil. Given these considerations, Truman became the first president to endorse the use of an atomic weapon on a military enemy.

On August 6, 1945, the B-29 bomber *Enola Gay* dropped an atomic bomb nicknamed "little boy" on Hiroshima. Truman, after not receiving full unconditional surrender after three days, authorized the use of a second bomb on Nagasaki on August 9. By August 14, the Japanese had agreed to unconditional surrender, ending World War II.[3]

There is nothing out of the ordinary about a president, acting as commander in chief, authorizing the use of a new military weapon against a confirmed enemy during war when that enemy has attacked the United States directly. There was little public outcry following Truman's decision, and Gallup polls in 1945 found that approximately 85 percent of Americans approved of the use of nuclear weapons. Use of the weapons was presented as necessary and justified against the inhuman evil of the Japanese empire. During the war Roosevelt ordered thousands of Japanese Americans to be imprisoned without due process, setting the stage for the majority of the American people to embrace the use of atomic weapons against Japan. Over the years, opinions gradually changed. In 1991, 63 percent of Americans said that the decision was justified, and in 2015 the percentage dropped to 56. However, 73 percent of Americans still believe that there is no need for a formal U.S. apology to Japan.[4]

According to twenty-first century estimates, the atomic bomb killed nearly 80,000 instantly in Hiroshima. Tens of thousands more died from radiation poisoning, increasing the total to 190,000 in Hiroshima alone. While some political scientists have attempted to argue that the first atomic bomb was a prudent decision, there is less support for the bombing of Nagasaki. It was well known that Japan was debating surrender. The second bomb killed some 70,000 instantly, with the total death toll reaching well over 100,000. In total, about 300,000 were killed, the vast majority civilians, and nearly 50,000 children in Nagasaki alone.[5]

Hiroshima after the bombing, by U.S. Navy Public Affairs Resources, via Wikimedia.

The fact that tens of thousands of Japanese civilians were killed or severely injured in the bombing helped to shift public opinion on this key moment in American history. American physicist Karl T. Compton, who was part of the committee who advised Truman, wrote an article for the *Atlantic* arguing that Japan would never have surrendered without the bomb, leading to many more months or years of violence.[6] Modern historians have argued that it would have been possible to secure an eventual Japanese surrender, without the need for an invasion, if America and the allies had not demanded unconditional surrender. Truman argued that the bombing of Hiroshima and Nagasaki was an act of vengeance:

STATEMENT ON HIROSHIMA
Harry S. Truman
August 6, 1945
Source Document Excerpt

Sixteen hours ago an American airplane dropped one bomb on Hiroshima, an important Japanese Army base. That bomb had more power than 20,000 tons of T.N.T. It had more than two thousand times the blast power of the British "Grand Slam" which is the largest bomb ever yet used in the history of warfare.

The Japanese began the war from the air at Pearl Harbor. They have been repaid many fold. And the end is not yet. With this bomb we have now added a new and revolutionary increase in destruction to supplement the growing power of our armed forces. In their present form these bombs are now in production and even more powerful forms are in development.

It is an atomic bomb. It is a harnessing of the basic power of the universe. The force from which the sun draws its power has been loosed against those who brought war to the Far East.[7]

Truman's use of the atomic bomb was well within his presidential powers, but some suggest it might be considered a war crime or a crime against humanity. As of 2019, the use of weapons of mass destruction remains controversial. Powerful political players in nations with arsenals of mass destruction have argued against using them based on official lists of "war crimes" as defined by the United Nations courts, but many disagree. Official designations of war crimes within the United Nations have been problematic and inconsistent. Consider, for instance, the remarks made by Barbara Bedont of the Women's International League for Peace and Freedom at a 1998 meeting to discuss war crimes and the jurisdiction of the International Criminal Court:

_____ *"The inclusion of certain weapons systems under the definition of war crimes is an issue which tests the commitment to creating an impartial judicial system. A provision in the statute has a list including chemical weapons but excludes weapons such as landmines and blinding laser weapons. More significantly, the list excludes nuclear weapons, the threat or use of which are generally prohibited under customary international law, as determined by the International Court of Justice. This would create an absurd result whereby, under the statute's provision, the Court would have jurisdiction if someone killed one civilian with a poisoned arrow or dum-dum bullet, but would not be able to act if the person incinerated a hundred thousand civilians with a nuclear weapon. Those options which only prohibit a selective list of weapons are unacceptable. The world community has a responsibility to future victims of yet to be invented weapons to provide a means to deter their use."*[8]

In the 1995 book *The Decision to Use the Atomic Bomb and the Architecture of an American Myth*, Gar Alperovitz determines that the idea that the atomic bomb was necessary is a myth, created to justify a controversial military attack to the American people. Alperovitz argues that military leaders recognized that the use of the bomb was unnecessary and that the decision to use it was motivated to strengthen the American position in negotiating with the Soviet Union. Further, Alperovitz found evidence suggesting it was Truman's decision to attack an urban target, Hiroshima, which resulted in tens of thousands more civilian casualties, to demonstrate the full destructive power of the weapon to Russia.[9]

Was the goal of gaining an advantage in the growing Cold War justification for killing 300,000 people and the wholesale destruction of two cities? Truman's authorization of the atomic attack stands as the most extreme and controversial use, or abuse, of presidential military power.

A New Internationalism

At the end of World War II, Truman led the nation in the establishment of a new international regime. A series of key negotiations resulted in the North Atlantic Treaty Organization (NATO) and the creation of the United Nations. Historians consider these organizations the fulfillment of President Woodrow Wilson's goals with the League of Nations in the wake of World War I. America's motivation in creating these organizations was, in part, fear about Russia, China, and the rise of global communist authoritarianism. The Truman administration addressed this in two ways.

First, in 1947 Truman addressed the first controversies of the Cold War—Russian aggression in Greece and in Turkey. At the time, Greece was involved in a civil war, with Great Britain's support, involving an uprising from the Greek Communist Party. Similarly, military instability threatened democracy in Turkey, where Britain had also been providing aid. When it was clear that Britain wanted to withdraw military aid from both nations, the question was whether the United States would step in. It was the deterioration of U.S. relations with the Soviet Union that motivated Truman's decision. The Soviet Union had refused demands to withdraw troops from Iran and was pressuring the Iranian government to grant the Soviet Union access to oil, they were supporting the Greek Communist Party, and they were attempting to force the Turkish government to allow them a naval base at the Turkish Straits. Truman delivered a speech to Congress in support of U.S. intervention, specifically of giving aid to both Turkey and Greece:

THE TRUMAN DOCTRINE
Harry S. Truman
March 12, 1947
Source Document Excerpt

Mr. President, Mr. Speaker, Members of the Congress of the United States:

The gravity of the situation which confronts the world today necessitates my appearance before a joint session of the Congress. The foreign policy and the national security of this country are involved.

One aspect of the present situation, which I wish to present to you at this time for your consideration and decision, concerns Greece and Turkey.

The United States has received from the Greek Government an urgent appeal for financial and economic assistance. Preliminary reports from the American Economic Mission now in Greece and reports from the American Ambassador in Greece corroborate the statement of the Greek Government that assistance is imperative if Greece is to survive as a free nation.

I do not believe that the American people and the Congress wish to turn a deaf ear to the appeal of the Greek Government.

Greece is not a rich country. Lack of sufficient natural resources has always forced the Greek people to work hard to make both ends meet. Since 1940, this industrious and peace loving country has suffered invasion, four years of cruel enemy occupation, and bitter internal strife.

When forces of liberation entered Greece they found that the retreating Germans had destroyed virtually all the railways, roads, port facilities, communications, and merchant marine. More than a thousand villages had been burned. Eighty-five per cent of the children were tubercular.

The Truman Doctrine
continued

Livestock, poultry, and draft animals had almost disappeared. Inflation had wiped out practically all savings.

As a result of these tragic conditions, a militant minority, exploiting human want and misery, was able to create political chaos which, until now, has made economic recovery impossible.

Greece is today without funds to finance the importation of those goods which are essential to bare subsistence. Under these circumstances the people of Greece cannot make progress in solving their problems of reconstruction. Greece is in desperate need of financial and economic assistance to enable it to resume purchases of food, clothing, fuel and seeds. These are indispensable for the subsistence of its people and are obtainable only from abroad. Greece must have help to import the goods necessary to restore internal order and security, so essential for economic and political recovery.

The Greek Government has also asked for the assistance of experienced American administrators, economists and technicians to insure that the financial and other aid given to Greece shall be used effectively in creating a stable and self-sustaining economy and in improving its public administration.

The very existence of the Greek state is today threatened by the terrorist activities of several thousand armed men, led by Communists, who defy the government's authority at a number of points, particularly along the northern boundaries. A Commission appointed by the United Nations security Council is at present investigating disturbed conditions in northern Greece and alleged border violations along the frontier between Greece on the one hand and Albania, Bulgaria, and Yugoslavia on the other.

Meanwhile, the Greek Government is unable to cope with the situation. The Greek army is small and poorly equipped. It needs supplies and equipment if it is to restore the authority of the government throughout Greek territory. Greece must have assistance if it is to become a self-supporting and self-respecting democracy.

The United States must supply that assistance. We have already extended to Greece certain types of relief and economic aid but these are inadequate.

There is no other country to which democratic Greece can turn.

No other nation is willing and able to provide the necessary support for a democratic Greek government.

The British Government, which has been helping Greece, can give no further financial or economic aid after March 31. Great Britain finds itself under the necessity of reducing or

continued

liquidating its commitments in several parts of the world, including Greece.

We have considered how the United Nations might assist in this crisis. But the situation is an urgent one requiring immediate action and the United Nations and its related organizations are not in a position to extend help of the kind that is required.

It is important to note that the Greek Government has asked for our aid in utilizing effectively the financial and other assistance we may give to Greece, and in improving its public administration. It is of the utmost importance that we supervise the use of any funds made available to Greece; in such a manner that each dollar spent will count toward making Greece self-supporting, and will help to build an economy in which a healthy democracy can flourish.

No government is perfect. One of the chief virtues of a democracy, however, is that its defects are always visible and under democratic processes can be pointed out and corrected. The Government of Greece is not perfect. Nevertheless it represents eighty-five per cent of the members of the Greek Parliament who were chosen in an election last year. Foreign observers, including 692 Americans, considered this election to be a fair expression of the views of the Greek people.

The Greek Government has been operating in an atmosphere of chaos and extremism. It has made mistakes. The extension of aid by this country does not mean that the United States condones everything that the Greek Government has done or will do. We have condemned in the past, and we condemn now, extremist measures of the right or the left. We have in the past advised tolerance, and we advise tolerance now.

Greece's neighbor, Turkey, also deserves our attention.

The future of Turkey as an independent and economically sound state is clearly no less important to the freedom-loving peoples of the world than the future of Greece. The circumstances in which Turkey finds itself today are considerably different from those of Greece. Turkey has been spared the disasters that have beset Greece. And during the war, the United States and Great Britain furnished Turkey with material aid.

Nevertheless, Turkey now needs our support.

Since the war Turkey has sought financial assistance from Great Britain and the United States for the purpose of effecting that modernization necessary for the maintenance of its national integrity.

The Truman Doctrine
continued

That integrity is essential to the preservation of order in the Middle East.

The British government has informed us that, owing to its own difficulties can no longer extend financial or economic aid to Turkey.

As in the case of Greece, if Turkey is to have the assistance it needs, the United States must supply it. We are the only country able to provide that help.

I am fully aware of the broad implications involved if the United States extends assistance to Greece and Turkey, and I shall discuss these implications with you at this time.

One of the primary objectives of the foreign policy of the United States is the creation of conditions in which we and other nations will be able to work out a way of life free from coercion. This was a fundamental issue in the war with Germany and Japan. Our victory was won over countries which sought to impose their will, and their way of life, upon other nations.

To ensure the peaceful development of nations, free from coercion, the United States has taken a leading part in establishing the United Nations. The United Nations is designed to make possible lasting freedom and independence for all its members. We shall not realize our objectives, however, unless we are willing to help free peoples to maintain their free institutions and their national integrity against aggressive movements that seek to impose upon them totalitarian regimes. This is no more than a frank recognition that totalitarian regimes imposed on free peoples, by direct or indirect aggression, undermine the foundations of international peace and hence the security of the United States.

The peoples of a number of countries of the world have recently had totalitarian regimes forced upon them against their will. The Government of the United States has made frequent protests against coercion and intimidation, in violation of the Yalta agreement, in Poland, Rumania, and Bulgaria. I must also state that in a number of other countries there have been similar developments.

At the present moment in world history nearly every nation must choose between alternative ways of life. The choice is too often not a free one.

One way of life is based upon the will of the majority, and is distinguished by free institutions, representative government, free elections, guarantees of individual liberty, freedom of speech and religion, and freedom from political oppression.

continued

The second way of life is based upon the will of a minority forcibly imposed upon the majority. It relies upon terror and oppression, a controlled press and radio; fixed elections, and the suppression of personal freedoms.

I believe that it must be the policy of the United States to support free peoples who are resisting attempted subjugation by armed minorities or by outside pressures.

I believe that we must assist free peoples to work out their own destinies in their own way.

I believe that our help should be primarily through economic and financial aid which is essential to economic stability and orderly political processes.

The world is not static, and the status quo is not sacred. But we cannot allow changes in the status quo in violation of the Charter of the United Nations by such methods as coercion, or by such subterfuges as political infiltration. In helping free and independent nations to maintain their freedom, the United States will be giving effect to the principles of the Charter of the United Nations.

It is necessary only to glance at a map to realize that the survival and integrity of the Greek nation are of grave importance in a much wider situation. If Greece should fall under the control of an armed minority, the effect upon its neighbor, Turkey, would be immediate and serious. Confusion and disorder might well spread throughout the entire Middle East.

Moreover, the disappearance of Greece as an independent state would have a profound effect upon those countries in Europe whose peoples are struggling against great difficulties to maintain their freedoms and their independence while they repair the damages of war.

It would be an unspeakable tragedy if these countries, which have struggled so long against overwhelming odds, should lose that victory for which they sacrificed so much. Collapse of free institutions and loss of independence would be disastrous not only for them but for the world. Discouragement and possibly failure would quickly be the lot of neighboring peoples striving to maintain their freedom and independence.

Should we fail to aid Greece and Turkey in this fateful hour, the effect will be far reaching to the West as well as to the East.

We must take immediate and resolute action.

I therefore ask the Congress to provide authority for assistance to Greece and Turkey in the amount of $400,000,000 for the period ending

The Truman Doctrine
continued

June 30, 1948. In requesting these funds, I have taken into consideration the maximum amount of relief assistance which would be furnished to Greece out of the $350,000,000 which I recently requested that the Congress authorize for the prevention of starvation and suffering in countries devastated by the war.

In addition to funds, I ask the Congress to authorize the detail of American civilian and military personnel to Greece and Turkey, at the request of those countries, to assist in the tasks of reconstruction, and for the purpose of supervising the use of such financial and material assistance as may be furnished. I recommend that authority also be provided for the instruction and training of selected Greek and Turkish personnel.

Finally, I ask that the Congress provide authority which will permit the speediest and most effective use, in terms of needed commodities, supplies, and equipment, of such funds as may be authorized.

If further funds, or further authority, should be needed for purposes indicated in this message, I shall not hesitate to bring the situation before the Congress. On this subject the Executive and Legislative branches of the Government must work together.

This is a serious course upon which we embark.

I would not recommend it except that the alternative is much more serious. The United States contributed $341,000,000,000 toward winning World War II. This is an investment in world freedom and world peace.

The assistance that I am recommending for Greece and Turkey amounts to little more than 1 tenth of 1 per cent of this investment. It is only common sense that we should safeguard this investment and make sure that it was not in vain.

The seeds of totalitarian regimes are nurtured by misery and want. They spread and grow in the evil soil of poverty and strife. They reach their full growth when the hope of a people for a better life has died. We must keep that hope alive.

The free peoples of the world look to us for support in maintaining their freedoms.

If we falter in our leadership, we may endanger the peace of the world—and we shall surely endanger the welfare of our own nation.

Great responsibilities have been placed upon us by the swift movement of events.

I am confident that the Congress will face these responsibilities squarely.[10]

This speech established the "Truman Doctrine," which asserts that the United States will take an active role in promoting democratic republicanism on the global stage and use its economic and military influence to prevent the spread of Communism. The Truman Doctrine was the first step toward the militarization of the Cold War, military proliferation and, eventually, to the threat of global nuclear annihilation. American public opinion on the Truman Doctrine differs based on agreement with broader Cold War efforts to combat Communism. The decision to commit the United States to the military opposition of Communism led to America's involvement in the Korean War, and was also justification for American military operations in Vietnam, leading to one of the most controversial wars in American history. In any case, the Truman Doctrine represents a major expression of presidential authority that dominated American foreign policy objectives through the 1990s. The American military has also used Communist aggression as the basis to gain economic advantages, including access to foreign oil and foreign trading partners.[11]

The Truman administration, with Britain, arranged for the creation of the state of Israel from the former state of Palestine, thus beginning America's long-term military and economic support of Israel. Though well-intentioned, the creation of Israel included many of the problems typical of nation building. The population of Palestine was divided among Jewish residents and Muslims, so the creation of a Jewish state marginalized the Muslim population. A coalition of Muslims fought back against the forced military partition of the nation, and the U.S.–backed Israeli Jewish soldiers. To this day, the state of Israel has been plagued by controversy and instability, and Palestinians remain in a condition of statelessness, making this one of the world's greatest unsolved human rights crises.

Another lasting impact that Truman had on the American presidency was the reorganization of the American military complex. Under the National Security Act of 1947, the Army, Navy, and Air Force were united under

the joint supervision of the Department of Defense (originally the National Military Establishment). The act also established a new cabinet post, secretary of defense, charged with overseeing the Defense Department, and the National Security Council (NSC), a research office designed to provide data to the secretary of defense and the president on matters involving national security or foreign policy. Members of the NSC include the vice president, secretary of state, secretary of defense, secretary of energy, and possibly advisors from other branches. Today's NSC includes representatives from the Department of Homeland Security, and typically includes U.S. representatives to the United Nations.[12]

Truman's reorganization of the military-industrial complex also created the Central Intelligence Agency (CIA). To this point, intelligence and espionage activities were under the supervision of the American military, and each branch of the military service had its own intelligence division. The CIA was an innovative organization, a civilian intelligence organization independent from the military chain of command and thus able to investigate and engage in intelligence and espionage operations beyond the military purview. Truman and a group of advisors, several from Missouri and so known as the "Missouri Gang," were those most responsible for creating this new intelligence organization.

The impetus for the CIA was the growing tensions of the Cold War, but it was involved in many unrelated activities. The CIA gained a reputation as one of the world's most controversial intelligence organizations. Declassified information revealed that the CIA was involved in activities that could be seen as violating both U.S. statutory and constitutional law, and international regulations regarding conduct toward allied and enemy states. The establishment of the CIA also dramatically increased the power of the presidency, giving the president near-total control over a vast intelligence network that could shape both domestic and international politics. This issue frequently became controversial, most notably in the way that the Nixon administration used the CIA to conduct illegal surveillance on American citizens and political rivals in violation of constitutional limits on executive authority.[13]

Domestic Dilemmas

Harry Truman is well-known for his handling of foreign affairs, but he also left a mark on the nation in the domestic sphere. Truman carried on Roosevelt's New Deal approach and later pioneered his own take on this formula, in the "Fair Deal" package he released in 1949, which catered to some of the long-standing demands of progressives, including increasing the federal minimum wage, expanding the social security program, and creating a new federally funded housing program.

Truman was also the first modern president to speak out about racial prejudice and discrimination. His most visible efforts in this regard was his support of changes to immigration laws that would eliminate the "quota system" used to restrict the immigration of non-white and non-Christian people. Truman managed modest changes to the immigration system, but it was his decision to speak out on the inequities of racist immigration legislation that stands out from his progressive predecessors in the White House.

Truman entered office with a relatively high approval rating, bolstered by sympathy after the death of Roosevelt, with a majority of Americans wishing to see Roosevelt's agenda carried out. Truman had an average approval of 55.6 percent for his entire first term (April 1945 to January 1949), according to Gallup poll data. The high point was 87 percent in June of 1945. However, toward the end of his first term, Truman's approval slid, partly because a number of southern Democrats defected from the party to endorse Strom Thurmond and his newly established "Dixiecrat" party. His Republican opponent, Thomas Dewey, was a moderate candidate who promised to continue with the successful economic initiatives of the New Deal but wanted to walk back the more activist tendencies of the

Democrats. Dewey had strong support among northern white suprema-cists and business-centric conservatives. Freed from having to moderate his views on civil rights, or having to attract moderate Republicans, Tru-man made a serious pitch for the African American vote.

Truman had already established stronger than average credentials as a believer in civil rights. In 1947, he became the first president to speak before the National Association for the Advancement of Colored People (NAACP):

ADDRESS BEFORE THE NAACP
Harry S. Truman
June 29, 1947
Source Document Excerpt

I should like to talk to you briefly about civil rights and human freedom. It is my deep conviction that we have reached a turning point in the long history of our country's efforts to guarantee freedom and equality to all our citizens. Recent events in the United States and abroad have made us realize that it is more important today than ever before to insure that all Americans enjoy these rights.

When I say all Americans I mean all Americans.

The civil rights laws written in the early years of our Republic, and the traditions which have been built upon them, are precious to us. Those laws were drawn up with the memory still fresh in men's minds of the tyranny of an absentee government. They were written to protect the citizen against any possible tyrannical act by the new government in this country.

But we cannot be content with a civil liberties program which emphasizes only the need of protection against the possibility of tyranny by the Government. We cannot stop there.

We must keep moving forward, with new concepts of civil rights to safeguard our heritage. The extension of civil rights today means, not protection of the people against the Government, but protection of the people by the Government.

We must make the Federal Government a friendly, vigilant defender of the rights and equalities of all Americans. And again I mean all Americans.[14]

In 1948, Truman campaigned in the black neighborhoods of Harlem and met with black political leaders and activists. With Congress controlled by the Republican Party, Truman was unable to get any of his initiatives passed and used this to accuse the Republican Party of engaging in obstructionist tactics at the expense of public welfare. Wanting to prove his worthiness to African American voters, Truman issued executive orders (EO). On July 26, 1948, Truman issued the famous EO 9981, prohibiting segregation in the American military.[15] Another EO prohibited discrimination in appointing or hiring to civil service positions. Though he could do little to dictate to states how to handle the civil rights issue, Truman's use of executive orders to reform federal branches, including the military and the civil service, was inspired.

African American voters were essential to the surprise reelection of Truman, who defeated Dewey by such a narrow margin that one Chicago newspaper prematurely printed a front-page headline reading "Dewey Defeats Truman."[16]

Ending segregation in the armed forces and discrimination in the civil service were an important and controversial use of presidential power that forever altered the official governmental stance on race. By the late 1940s, it was difficult for a politician to openly push a racist agenda, though many supported racism in subtle ways. Most politicians claimed to support civil rights, and fear of African American political reprisal was ingrained. None but the most openly racist legislators, who drew their power from white supremacist districts, would openly call for racist policies. By prohibiting federally sanctioned racism by executive order, Truman forced the issue. Those who wished to reestablish the white supremacist order would have to attack the executive orders themselves.

Although Truman did little to address institutionalized racism, he was the first president to openly support addressing the civil rights issue and helped to energize African American voters. Truman's administration

marks the beginning of African American voters aligning with the Democratic Party, which saw an exodus of white supremacists. In addition, Truman's speeches on civil rights and his direct actions were precursors of the civil rights era that began in the 1950s.

CONCLUSION

Truman's presidency saw highs and lows of public opinion. He managed major advances in ending discriminatory federal policies, but also contributed to a massive increase in the power of the military-industrial complex and did not address the dangerous paranoia about Communism that dominated domestic policy for the next half century. In terms of presidential power, Truman was less visible than Roosevelt, but still managed to gain public support, especially among African American and minority voters, and he, like Roosevelt, formed strong congressional coalitions and worked across traditional party lines. In many ways, Truman's presidency was transitional. The subsequent Eisenhower administration marked a return of conservative leadership and saw covert military action become a more important part of the presidential arsenal, with dangerous and disastrous consequences. Truman's work in building military power became a standard part of the Republican Party approach moving forward, which then led to the Democratic Party aligning more substantially with disarmament and diplomacy over military action. The next chapter focuses on Dwight D. Eisenhower, a war hero who approached the presidency as such.

DISCUSSION QUESTIONS

- ◆ Is the power to use weapons of mass destruction appropriate for a president? Why or why not?
- ◆ How did Truman help change political support for the Democratic Party?
- ◆ How did Truman contribute to the Cold War that followed his presidency?
- ◆ What are some examples of standard conservative political priorities in the Truman administration's policy agenda?

Works Used

Alperovitz, Gar. *The Decision to Use the Atomic Bomb*. New York: Vintage Books, 1996.

"Article 3: Life, Liberty, & Security of Person." *UDHR*. Universal Declaration of Human Rights. Columbia University. ccnmtl.columbia.edu/projects/mmt/udhr/article_3.html.

Compton, Karl T. "If the Atomic Bomb Had Not Been Used." *The Atlantic*. Dec. 1946. www.theatlantic.com/magazine/archive/1946/12/if-the-atomic-bomb-had-not-been-used/376238/.

Ferrell, Robert H. *Truman and Pendergast*. Columbia, MO: U of Missouri P, 1999.

Gardner, Michael R. *Harry Truman and Civil Rights: Moral Courage and Political Risks*. Edwardsville, IL: Southern Illinois U P, 2003.

Hall, Michelle. "By the Numbers: World War II's Atomic Bombs." *CNN*. 6 Aug. 2013. www.cnn.com/2013/08/06/world/asia/btn-atomic-bombs/index.html

McCullough, David. *Truman*. New York: Simon & Schuster, 1992.

Miscamble, Wilson D. *The Most Controversial Decision: Truman, the Atomic Bombs, and the Defeat of Japan*. New York: Cambridge U P, 2011.

"National Security Act of 1947." *Office of the Historian*. Department of State. 2016. history.state.gov/milestones/1945-1952/national-security-act.

Schroeder, Richard E. *The Foundation of the CIA: Harry Truman, the Missouri Gang, and the Origins of the Cold War*. Columbia, MO: U of Missouri P, 2017.

Stokes, Bruce. "70 Years after Hiroshima, Opinions Have Shifted on Use of Atomic Bomb." Pew Research Center, 4 Aug. 2015. https://www.pewresearch.org/fact-tank/2015/08/04/70-years-after-hiroshima-opinions-have-shifted-on-use-of-atomic-bomb/.

Truman, Harry. "Truman Doctrine: President Harry S. Truman's Address before a Joint Session of Congress, March 12, 1947." *Avalon Project*. Yale Law School. avalon.law.yale.edu/20th_century/trudoc.asp.

_____. "Address Before the National Association for the Advancement of Colored People." 29 June 1947. *Voices of Democracy*. The U.S. Oratory Project. U of Maryland. voicesofdemocracy.umd.edu/harry-s-truman-naacp-speech-text/.

_____. "Transcript of Executive Order 9981: Desegregation of the Armed Forces (1948)." *Our Documents*. www.ourdocuments.gov/doc.php?flash=true&doc=84&page=transcript.

_____. "Truman Doctrine." *Avalon Project*. Yale Law School. Retrieved from https://avalon.law.yale.edu/20th_century/trudoc.asp.

_____. "Truman Statement on Hiroshima." 6 Aug. 1945. Atomic Heritage Foundation. www.atomicheritage.org/key-documents/truman-statement-hiroshima.

"Use of Weapons of Mass Destruction Should Be Included in Criminal Court's Definition of War Crimes, Say Several Conference Speakers." *UN*. United Nations. 18 June 1998. www.un.org/press/en/1998/19980618.12882.html.

Introduction

Dwight David "Ike" Eisenhower was a career military officer whose rapid rise to the chief executive position harked back to the candidacies of the William Henry Harrison and Zachary Taylor. His public service experience was limited, but he was a World War II hero who came to represent the sense of national insecurity that gripped America as the Cold War deepened and the threat of the Holocaust matriculated through society. Eisenhower was a grandfatherly figure, symbolizing trust in tradition and conservatism. He appeared calm and collected, and offered a vague promise of American greatness yet to come. Eisenhower offered little innovation in domestic policy and strove to find a moderate path that allowed him to win allies on both sides of the political aisle. Americans at the time were unaware of how Eisenhower used the powers of his office. As a career military strategist and leader, and a man who'd deeply embraced paranoia about Russian designs for world domination, Eisenhower actively utilized his military powers primarily through the newly founded CIA, a domestic agency that nonetheless became the most important military arm of the government in the Cold War era. The Eisenhower presidency marked the beginning of the shadow war between the United States, Russia, and China, with increasingly aggressive espionage efforts and secret military operations afoot. Eisenhower's use of the CIA remains controversial, and he has been credited with worsening Russian-U.S. relations and deepening America's involvement in Indochina and thus in the Vietnam War.

Topics covered in this chapter include:

- The Korean War
- The Vietnam War
- The Central Intelligence Agency
- *Brown v. Board of Education*

This Chapter Discusses the Following Source Documents:
White House Statement, Dwight D. Eisenhower, May 11, 1960
Farewell Address, Dwight D. Eisenhower, 1961

The Cold War Hero
Dwight D. Eisenhower (1953–1961)

Where Roosevelt and Truman established the modern Democratic party presidency, the modern Republican party presidency was established by Dwight D. Eisenhower, an enormously popular president who saw America through the end of the Korean War and presided over a period of relative economic prosperity. Though initially a low-ranking modern president, historians have come to see Eisenhower as an important moderate whose policies, while not dramatic, helped define the modern presidential style.

Midwestern Soldier

Dwight Eisenhower was born in Texas, but lived for much of his life in the small town of Abilene, Kansas, where his father worked as a mechanic for a local ice cream manufacturer. Eisenhower's small-town, midwestern background would later become one of his most valuable assets, allowing him to market himself to the American people as a person who understood traditional American values and to appeal to voters attracted to the "common man" presidential archetype.[1]

Dwight D. Eisenhower, by White House, Eisenhower Presidential Library, via Wikimedia.

Eisenhower attended West Point Military Academy, graduating in the lower middle of his class. Though he wanted to serve in a combat position in World War I, Eisenhower was relegated to troop training duties. When the war ended, he was stationed at Fort Meade in Maryland, where he befriended another famous American military general, George S. Patton. Eisenhower and Patton were both experts in tank technology, and the two researched and discussed strategies for better integrating tanks into combat, given lessons learned from the war. Both men felt that the trench warfare common in World War I produced a high casualty rate and that tanks, integrated into infantry strategy, would lessen casualties. While both Patton and Eisenhower published articles promoting tank use in warfare, Patton—who was wealthy with connections to high-ranking military leaders—did not suffer for his outspoken ideas, whereas Eisenhower was targeted as a potential troublemaker.

Eisenhower's article "A Tank Discussion" appeared in the November 1920 issue of *Infantry Journal* and was primarily a review of existing tank technology and its uses in World War I. It suggested replacing the divisional machine gun battalion with tanks. Infantry Chief Charles Farnsworth found Eisenhower's suggestions unacceptable and potentially insubordinate, accusing Eisenhower of violating "solid infantry doctrine" and warned that if he continued to publish, Farnsworth would see him court-martialed. Fortunately for Eisenhower, Brigadier General Fox Connor was impressed by Eisenhower's articles and invited him to serve with his division in Panama.[2]

After serving in Panama for more than a year, Eisenhower attended the Command and General Staff College in Leavenworth, Kansas, where he graduated first in his class. He continued writing for military publications but was more circumspect. He wrote an article about his time in Leavenworth and then a guidebook for World War I battlefields at the request of retired General John Pershing. When he returned to the United States,

Eisenhower was appointed as an aide to Army Chief of Staff Douglas MacArthur, the most prominent military man in the nation.

When World War II broke out, Eisenhower was promoted to brigadier general, and he helped develop the U.S. response to the Japanese attack on Pearl Harbor. Army Chief of Staff George Marshall promoted Eisenhower to lead the allied troop invasion in North Africa and later to coordinate the U.S. invasion of Italy. In 1944, Eisenhower was promoted to command the Allied invasion of Western Europe, by which time he had earned the rank of four-star general. Eisenhower's most famous command was during the Allied invasion of Normandy on June 6, 1944, known as "D-Day." His role in this historic battle made him a national hero and one of the most famous figures of the war.[3]

Eisenhower's visibility continued to rise, and in 1945 he was asked to relieve his long-time friend George Patton of command. Eisenhower was also one of Harry Truman's advisors at the Potsdam Conference, where Truman met with Soviet Premier Josef Stalin and British Prime Minister Winston Churchill to determine the Allied course for ending the war against the Japanese empire. Eisenhower did not believe that the nuclear attack on Japan was necessary and felt that Japanese surrender could be achieved without high casualty rates. Truman decided to take the advice of Secretary of War Henry L. Stimson and others, who were primarily interested in utilizing Japan as an example of American military superiority as a threat to Russia.

Eisenhower with the 101st Airborne Division the day before the famous D-Day invasion. By U.S. Army photographer, Library of Congress Prints and Photographs Division, via Wikimedia.

General Dysfunction

General George Patton came from a family of soldiers, one of considerable wealth. At the height of his military career, Patton had a stable of horses and a lavish estate. Though he became one of the most beloved heroes of the war to the American people, those who worked closely with Patton remembered him as a difficult and, at times, intemperate man whose overriding interest was in glorifying his own reputation. Eisenhower had befriended a young Patton when the two men were academic officers interested in promoting tank warfare as the future for the military. Patton went on to achieve this, becoming the champion of the tank during World War II, but his behavior both in and out of combat caused problems for his superiors. Eisenhower, who later rose to command above his old friend, supported Patton and thought of him as an indispensible asset, but he also called him a "problem child." Commander Omar Bradley, a close associate of Patton's, said he was "full of temper, bluster, inclined to treat the troops and subordinates as morons. He was primarily a showman. The show always seemed to come first."

Patton's need for personal glory and his difficulty getting along with others prevented him from being promoted to Command of the Pacific, and he was instead assigned to serve as the military governor of Bavaria. Part of the occupation campaign in Germany was the "de-Nazification" of the country, which entailed outreach programs to promote democracy and expose the failings of Nazi ideology, as well as punishing Nazi war criminals publicly.

Historians have learned from Patton's journals and conversations that he was a Nazi sympathizer. In his journal, he referred to the Jewish refugees housed in Bavaria as "lower than animals," and as "a subhuman species without any of the cultural or social refinements of our times." His writings reveal a similar level of racism with regard to other nonwhites, such as Arabs, whom he called "a mixture of all the worst races of the world." Reports from Bavaria convinced Truman to visit, and he arrived to find thousands of Jewish refugees confined to camps and living in inhumane conditions. Even more troubling to Truman was that Patton had assigned former SS officers to guard the refugee population. Newspapers back in the United States covered the issue, and Patton destroyed his own reputation in speaking to the press, making unfounded claims about a conspiracy between the press and the Communists to undermine him. Eisenhower decided to keep a closer watch on Patton, bugging his phone, and through this he heard Patton trying to covertly push a new war with the Soviet Union utilizing German troops, whom he called "the only decent people left in Europe." Eisenhower relieved Patton from duty in disgrace.

Patton's death, three months after being removed from Bavaria, in many ways preserved his reputation. In the post-war world, Patton's outspoken nature, combined with rabid white supremacist tendencies and ignorance, made him a divisive figure. His death eliminated the possibility that many more years of violent anti-Communist commentary might have further eroded the myth of his heroism.[a]

Work Used

a. Allen, Arthur. "The Problem with Trump's Admiration of General Patton." *Politico*. 26 Dec. 2016www.politico.com/magazine/story/2016/12/trump-general-patton-admiration-214545.

After the war, Eisenhower was elected president of Columbia University, while still a frequent advisor on national security issues. His military retirement was short-lived, however, and when North Korea attempted to invade South Korea, Eisenhower was asked to serve as Supreme Commander of the North Atlantic Treaty Organization (NATO) forces in Europe during the Korean War. In 1948, Eisenhower also was asked by President Truman to run on a joint ticket and surprisingly suggested that Eisenhower should run for the presidency, while Truman would run as his vice president. Truman's approval rating had fallen toward the end of his first term, and it looked nearly impossible for him to win a second term in office. Eisenhower, however, turned down the offer and resisted offers from the Republican Party to support his candidacy for the presidency as well.

After his unexpected re-election in 1948, Truman's popularity never fully rebounded. The Korean War soon became a stalemate and political quagmire, and Truman had problems with his military command, resulting in the enormously unpopular decision to relieve General Douglas MacArthur as leader of the UN forces. Republicans capitalized on this by highlighting their party's support for the military and ability to achieve victory in the Korean conflict. Eisenhower was, again, approached about running for president. He had strong ties to Democratic and well as Republican legislators and was widely respected among the public. For the Republicans, Eisenhower would also provide a way to attract internationalist voters; other candidates, including Ohio Senator Robert Taft, who was then the frontrunner, were campaigning for a return to isolationism. Eisenhower eventually agreed to have his name added to the ticket. Before long, Eisenhower was the clear leader, with California Senator Richard M. Nixon as his running mate.

Eisenhower proved a masterful campaigner. He refrained from competing with Democratic Candidate Adlai Stevenson and focused instead on criticizing Truman's strategy in Korea and failure to combat the rise of Communism. Further, Eisenhower capitalized on allegations of corruption in

Truman's administration, which were largely false, but allowed him to use the popular strategy of running as an anti-corruption candidate. This tactic nearly backfired, however, when Richard Nixon was accused of having misused campaign contributions. Nixon gave a televised speech denying the allegations and used his family dog "Checkers" for comedic effect, arguing that though Checkers had been a gift from a supporter, he would not be willing to surrender the dog. The televised statement was a huge hit, and the accusation of corruption turned into a campaign success. Nixon's televised speech was one of many televised appearances for both him and Eisenhower, and the 1952 campaign was the first in which television, rather than radio, proved key to electoral victory. The campaign slogan "I Like Ike" became one of the most familiar campaign slogans in presidential history.

Historians have criticized Eisenhower for capitalizing on the panic-inducing anti-Communist rhetoric of Junior Senator Joseph McCarthy, whose personal campaign to purge Communism from the United States turned into government-sanctioned oppression of free speech and free association. McCarthy had attacked Truman and claimed that Communists had infiltrated the Truman campaign. Eisenhower did not attempt to correct this false accusation and benefitted from the perception that the Truman administration might have been compromised. Though they had once been allies and colleagues, Truman and Eisenhower's relationship soured during the 1952 campaign and never recovered. Eisenhower was successful, winning 55 percent of the popular vote to 44 percent for Stevenson. However, it wasn't an overwhelming victory for the resurgent Republican Party, who picked up two seats for moderate control of the Senate, and 22 seats to control the House, but by a relatively narrow margin. Eisenhower entered office with a public mandate but without the full support of Congress and in the midst of intense political discord.

The Hidden Hand of the Presidency

Over the course of his two terms in office, Eisenhower maintained high public approval, with Gallup polls estimating an average of 65 percent approval between 1953 and 1961. Approval during his first term averaged 69.6 percent, and his lowest approval rating was around 48 percent, far higher than Truman's (or those presidents who followed) ratings at the low point in his presidency. Despite his high public approval, his performance was not always perfect.

On the foreign front, Eisenhower helped to escalate Cold War tensions with military threats and failure to live up to international agreements. The most questionable use of presidential power under the Eisenhower administration concerned the CIA and covert warfare tactics to gain a Cold War advantage. The full extent of Eisenhower's use of the CIA , which was utilized in ways that violated standards of presidential power, was not known until years after his presidency and so had little impact on public opinion.

The French, who controlled what was called "Indochina" (which consists of modern Vietnam, Laos, and Cambodia), were fighting against a Communist uprising in Vietnam. Truman contributed arms and funds to the French effort to preserve their hold on the region, and Eisenhower did the same. In 1954, French and Vietminh leaders signed the Geneva Accords, an agreement meant to end hostilities in the region and calling for the division of the country along the seventeenth parallel, with the Communist Vietminh controlling the northern section and the French controlling the south. Democratic elections were expected to later determine which government would control the entire country.[4]

The United States did not sign the agreement, but the Eisenhower administration released statements claiming that they would seek to see it upheld. For many years, official U.S. records held that Vietnamese forces, supported by China, violated the Geneva Accords and forced

U.S. military action. However, the Pentagon papers, leaked in the 1960s made it clear that this was not the case. The Eisenhower administration had never intended to adhere to the accords and immediately set about covert military operations against the North Vietnamese, including contaminating the oil supply and sabotaging railroads. The reports indicate that the administration misled both Congress and the American people with regard to U.S. activities in Vietnam. These secrets would be kept to prevent Americans from concluding that continued U.S. military operations were, in part, responsible for the escalation of tensions in the region, resulting in one of the least-popular wars in American history.[5]

In the escalating tensions with Russia, the death of Premier Joseph Stalin brought hope of a détente, and Eisenhower claimed he was seeking peace with the rival power under Premier Nikita Khrushchev. The first United States–Soviet Summit took place in Geneva in July 1955 and resulted in a slight easing of tensions. Eisenhower, however, covertly ordered CIA reconnaissance mission planes to fly over Russia. After Russia occupied Hungary in 1956, Eisenhower resisted calls for military intervention and won support back home for avoiding a potentially devastating war that might have led to the world's first nuclear war. Further, the Eisenhower administration shifted its talking points on Russia, promoting a nuclear nonproliferation agreement. For a brief time, it appeared as if this might occur, with Khrushchev visiting the United States in 1959 for a meeting at Camp David with Eisenhower and French and British officials.[6]

The Camp David summit appeared promising, but a military controversy derailed progress. On May 1, one of the CIA's U-2 spy planes went missing. Eisenhower claimed that an unarmed "weather surveillance" plane had gone missing, but on May 7, the Soviets revealed that the pilot, Gary Powers, had been captured after being shot down by Russian anti-aircraft weapons. Camera equipment on the plane was recovered and analyzed, and Khrushchev demanded an apology from the United States, but Eisenhower refused. On May 11, he instead issued a press release

acknowledging the spy program, and his personal knowledge of it. Eisenhower defended the necessity of the program:

WHITE HOUSE STATEMENT
Dwight D. Eisenhower
May 11, 1960
Source Document Excerpt

No one wants another Pearl Harbor. This means that we must have knowledge of military forces and preparations around the world, especially those capable of massive surprise attack.

Secrecy in the Soviet Union makes this essential. In most of the world no large-scale attack could be prepared in secret. But in the Soviet Union there is a fetish of secrecy and concealment. This is a major cause of international tension and uneasiness today. Our deterrent must never be placed in jeopardy. The safety of the whole free world demands this.

As the Secretary of State pointed out in his recent statement, ever since the beginning of my administration I have issued directives to gather, in every feasible way, the information required to protect the United States and the Free World against surprise attack and to enable them to make effective preparations for defense.

He then defended the lack of Congressional oversight into the activities:

White House Statement
continued

These have a special and secret character. They are so-to-speak "below the surface" activities.

They are secret because they must circumvent measures designed by other countries to protect secrecy of military preparations.

They are divorced from the regular, visible agencies of government which stay clear of operational involvement in specific detailed activities.

These elements operate under broad directives to seek and gather intelligence short of the use of force—with operations supervised by responsible officials within this area of secret activities."[7]

Eisenhower then stated that the United States would not cease its intelligence gathering activities. The Russian capture of Powers and the U-2 was a major embarrassment to Eisenhower, and his response was to justify his decisions. Khrushchev had been promoting a policy of "peaceful coexistence" with the United States, and the upcoming peace accords were intended to result in a concrete policy to prevent further military escalation. Had Eisenhower apologized publicly, and promise (even disingenuously) to cease surveillance, Khrushchev might have been able to claim a political victory and most likely would have continued with the accords. Because Eisenhower remained defiant, Khrushchev chose a political victory by withdrawing from the agreements and claiming that the United States was not participating in good faith.[8]

Eisenhower's use of the CIA went deeper than diplomatically disastrous spy missions over Russia and his covert escalation of what became the Vietnam War; he also authorized the CIA to help overthrow the elected Prime Minister of Iran, Mohammed Mosaddegh, after Mosaddegh kicked Britain out of the nation's oil industry. The British attempted to use economic sanctions to restore their access to Iranian oil. Eisenhower used the excuse of a potential alliance between Mosaddegh and Iranian Communist groups as justification for authorizing a CIA operation to stage a coup to relieve Mosaddegh from power and replace him with Shah Mohammed Reza Pahlavi. Eisenhower gained an equal share of control of the Iranian oil industry, along with restoring British control, but also undermined the democratic will of the Iranian people. Shah Reza Pahlavi, who proved an ally of the United States in their efforts against Communism, was also an autocratic dictator who restricted civil liberties and personal rights and controlled the Iranian people under threat of military and police violence.[9]

Another controversial CIA operation authorized by Eisenhower was the political destabilization of Guatemala in 1954. The poverty-stricken Central American nation had recently elected Jacobo Árbenz Guzmán, who

was secretly a Marxist and demonstrated a willingness to work with Communist reformers. Eisenhower authorized the CIA to support a military revolutionary group to overthrow Guzmán. The Guatemalan government accused the United States of involvement in the coup. Eisenhower denied involvement and secretly worked to install a new president, Carlos Castillo Armas, who agreed to oppose Communism in support of the United States. Armas quickly turned out to have dictatorial tendencies, using police violence to suppress communism, restricted freedom of speech and the press, and passed laws restricting voting rights. Eisenhower also authorized the CIA to train a group of Guatemalan militants for an invasion of Cuba, which led to the "Bay of Pigs" disaster in 1961.[10]

Eisenhower was the first president to utilize the CIA as a tool for forcing regime change in support of U.S. interests, a use of presidential authority that remains controversial today. In Guatemala and Iran, the Eisenhower administration subverted the Democratic process in order to install leaders more favorable to America. History shows that this interpretation of presidential authority and the results of Eisenhower's covert efforts to shape world politics were not favorable to U.S. interests. The escalation of hostilities in Vietnam drew America into a disastrous and unpopular war, while U.S. diplomatic failures with Russia deepened Cold War tensions, raising the threat of nuclear war. In Iran and Guatemala, violence and dictatorial regimes emerged, and both nations remain problematic for the United States in the modern era.

Eisenhower, at the end of his second term, delivered a farewell address in which he cautioned about the military-industrial complex that he had helped to create through the arms race with the Soviet Union:

FAREWELL ADDRESS
Dwight D. Eisenhower
1961
Source Document Excerpt

A vital element in keeping the peace is our military establishment. Our arms must be mighty, ready for instant action, so that no potential aggressor may be tempted to risk his own destruction.

Our military organization today bears little relation to that known by any of my predecessors in peace time, or indeed by the fighting men of World War II or Korea.

Until the latest of our world conflicts, the United States had no armaments industry. American makers of plowshares could, with time and as required, make swords as well. But now we can no longer risk emergency improvisation of national defense; we have been compelled to create a permanent armaments industry of vast proportions. Added to this, three and a half million men and women are directly engaged in the defense establishment. We annually spend on military security more than the net income of all United State corporations.

This conjunction of an immense military establishment and a large arms industry is new in the American experience. The total influence—economic, political, even spiritual—is felt in every city, every state house, every office of the Federal government. We recognize the imperative need for this development. Yet we must not fail to comprehend its grave implications. Our toil, resources and livelihood are all involved; so is the very structure of our society.

In the councils of government, we must guard against the acquisition of unwarranted influence, whether sought or unsought, by the military-industrial complex. The potential for the disastrous rise of misplaced power exists and will persist.

We must never let the weight of this combination endanger our liberties or democratic processes. We should take nothing for granted only an alert and knowledgeable citizenry can compel the proper meshing of huge industrial and military machinery of defense with our peaceful methods and goals, so that security and liberty may prosper together.

Akin to, and largely responsible for the sweeping changes in our industrial-military posture, has been the technological revolution during recent decades.

Farewell Address
continued

In this revolution, research has become central; it also becomes more formalized, complex, and costly. A steadily increasing share is conducted for, by, or at the direction of, the Federal government.

Today, the solitary inventor, tinkering in his shop, has been overshadowed by task forces of scientists in laboratories and testing fields. In the same fashion, the free university, historically the fountainhead of free ideas and scientific discovery, has experienced a revolution in the conduct of research. Partly because of the huge costs involved, a government contract becomes virtually a substitute for intellectual curiosity. For every old blackboard there are now hundreds of new electronic computers.

The prospect of domination of the nation's scholars by Federal employment, project allocations, and the power of money is ever present and is gravely to be regarded.

Yet, in holding scientific research and discovery in respect, as we should, we must also be alert to the equal and opposite danger that public policy could itself become the captive of a scientific-technological elite.

It is the task of statesmanship to mold, to balance, and to integrate these and other forces, new and old, within the principles of our democratic system-ever aiming toward the supreme goals of our free society."[11]

Eisenhower's warning about the influence of money on military development was not heeded. Military expenditures accounted for around half of the budget during Eisenhower's time in office, and expenditures would rise further in future presidencies.

A Mixed Record

Eisenhower's domestic policies were less controversial than his foreign policy decisions; and since Americans knew little about their government's foreign policy activities, it was Eisenhower's domestic agenda that dominated press coverage. As is typical of conservative presidents, Eisenhower criticized the "big government" interventionist policies of Truman, but he also did not sway to the extreme right, calling for the

elimination of all New Deal economic initiatives. Eisenhower established a new Republicanism that he called "Modern Republicanism," with a focus on the free market, yet preserving activist controls on the economy put into place by his Democratic predecessors. Eisenhower even acted to expand some of the existing welfare programs, marketing these efforts as an attempt to help common Americans left behind by the pace of progress—an approach that also worked well for future moderate Republicans.

On the primary social issue of the era, civil rights, Eisenhower did not speak out as had his predecessor Truman, but he was forced to act in the highly visible riots that followed the Supreme Court ruling in *Brown v. Board of Education*, which struck down school segregation. In the South, white supremacists gathered to forcibly prevent the desegregation of schools, leading to violence in Little Rock, Arkansas, in 1957. Governor Orval Faubus called in the National Guard to prevent African American students from entering the formerly segregated Central High School. Eisenhower convinced Faubus to allow the students to enter the school. However, when the National Guard left, a mob gathered at the school, and Eisenhower became the first president since Grant to send federal troops into a state to maintain order. Explaining his position to the American people, he avoided political rhetoric and did not give a strong defense of civil rights; instead he argued that he had an obligation to preserve law and order and that the American people did not have the right to violate the ruling of the courts. Soldiers remained in Little Rock for an entire school year, allowing one African American student to graduate from the high school; the following year, Governor Faubus subverted the federal government's orders by closing all of the city's public schools, thereby preventing integration.[12]

Eisenhower left office with a high approval rating, but his status quickly fell once the full extent of his covert activities was revealed. A 1962 poll

of historians, for instance, ranked Eisenhower 22nd out of 34 presidents. In the years since, however, Eisenhower's reputation has improved. In C-Span's third Presidential Historians Survey of 2017, Eisenhower was ranked fifth out of 43 presidents. According to those who took part, Eisenhower excelled in moral authority.[13] Examples included Eisenhower's call for adherence to law and order after the riots that followed *Brown v. Board* and his enforcement of humanitarian convictions in the reconstruction after World War II, removing his one-time close friend Patton from command. In a separate 2019 poll of political scientists, Eisenhower ranked 7th out of all 44 living presidents.[14] Overall, he was praised not for what he accomplished, but for resisting the urge to act in ways that might have made matters worse. This includes resisting the influence of hawks who wanted to push for a war with the Soviet Union and resisting the influence to take a more aggressive strategy in Korea and Indochina. Many modern experts appreciate that Eisenhower tried to moderate between the progressives and conservatives of his era, a skill that has become increasingly rare in America's modern political landscape.

CONCLUSION

Eisenhower's presidency remains controversial in the twenty-first century. Though he is frequently highly rated, especially among conservative commanders-in-chief, it is argued that certain decisions led America down dangerous paths. His high approval rating of the American public was due in large part because his presidency was free from major controversies, but historians and political scientists assess him less kindly. Eisenhower's use of the CIA for operations that were extremely military in character could be seen as a violation of presidential authority. Further, modern historians believe that some of his administration's foreign policy maneuvers were ethically and morally problematic. Eisenhower's presidency ended as America was becoming embroiled in another war and, although Eisenhower's Republican successor, Richard Milhouse Nixon, had the support of older conservatives, young Senator John F. Kennedy built a political base of young voters and voters of color, and was strong enough to return the Democratic Party to the White House for what became one of the most enduringly famous and analyzed presidencies in American history, as shown in the following chapter.

DISCUSSION QUESTIONS

♦ Did Eisenhower violate the powers of the presidency with his use of the CIA? Why or why not?

♦ Are there any modern-day groups who are feared in the same way that Soviets were feared in the 1950s? Explain your answer.

♦ What did Eisenhower mean when he warned Americans about the "military industrial complex" in his farewell address?

♦ Is it beneficial for a president to have civilians in leadership positions in addition to those with military experience? Why or why not?

Works Used

"Agreement on the Cessation of Hostilities in Viet-Nam, 20 July 1954." *Mt. Holyoke*. 2019. www.mtholyoke.edu/acad/intrel/genevacc.htm.

Ambrose, Stephen E. *The Supreme Commander: The War Years of General Dwight D. Eisenhower*. New York: Anchor Books, 1970.

Beschloss, Michael. *Mayday: Eisenhower, Khrushchev, and the U-2 Affair*. Open Road Media, 2016.

Butterfield, Fox. "Pentagon Papers: Eisenhower Decisions Undercut the Geneva Accords, Study Says." *New York Times*. 5 July 1971. www.nytimes.com/1971/07/05/archives/pentagon-papers-eisenhower-decisions-undercut-the-geneva-accords.html.

Eisenhower, Dwight. "Statement by the President Regarding U-2 Incident, May 11, 1960." *Dwightdeisenhower*. IKE Eisenhower Foundation. www.dwightdeisenhower.com/404/U-2-Spy-Plane-Incident.

_____. "Transcript of President Dwight D. Eisenhower's Farewell Address (1961)." *Our Documents*. 2019. www.ourdocuments.gov/doc.php?flash=false&doc=90&page=transcript.

Gillett, Rachel, and Allana Akhtar. "These Are the Top 20 US Presidents (and Why You Won't Find Trump on the List)." *Business Insider*. 4 July 2019. www.businessinsider.com/the-top-20-presidents-in-us-history-according-to-historians-2017-2.

Glass, Andrew. "Eisenhower Approves Coup in Iran, Aug. 19, 1953." *Politico*. 19 Aug. 2018. www.politico.com/story/2018/08/19/eisenhower-green-lights-coup-in-iran-aug-19-1953-788012.

Morgan, Thomas. "The Making of a General: Ike, the Tank, and the Interwar Years." *Army History*. Army Historical Foundation. 20 Jan. 2015. armyhistory.org/the-making-of-a-general-ike-the-tank-and-the-interwar-years/.

Pach, Chester J. Jr. "Dwight D. Eisenhower: Domestic Affairs." *Miller Center*. University of Virginia. 2019. millercenter.org/president/eisenhower/domestic-affairs.

Rabe, Stephen G. *Eisenhower and Latin America: The Foreign Policy of Anticommunism*. U of North Carolina P, 1988.

Smith, Jean Edward. *Eisenhower: In War and Peace*. New York: Random House, 2012.

"U-2 Overflights and the Capture of Francis Gary Powers, 1960." *Office of the Historian*. U.S. Department of State. history.state.gov/milestones/1953-1960/u2-incident.

Weiss, Brennan. "RANKED: The Greatest US Presidents, According to Political Scientists." *Business Insider*. 16 Feb. 2019. www.businessinsider.com/greatest-us-presidents-ranked-by-political-scientists-2018-2.

Introduction

John Fitzgerald Kennedy's assassination gave his life and presidency a unique mystique. Kennedy edged out the establishment candidate, Richard Nixon, thanks to his popularity with women, young voters, and voters of color and is arguably the first candidate whose election demonstrated the power of marginalized and often ignored classes of voters. He was part of a powerful Massachusetts political family and was Catholic, a major political disadvantage, as anti-Catholic prejudice was still prominent. Although his mandate was one of progressive change, Kennedy was thrust into a deepening Cold War environment. On the domestic front, Kennedy invested in space technology and he spoke out about civil rights issues. On the Cold War front, his administration endured the scandal of the Bay of Pigs fiasco and the Cuban Missile Crisis, emerging unscathed and perhaps more popular thanks to his dexterous handling of the issues. After Kennedy's assassination, Vice President Lyndon Baines Johnson inherited a strong mandate to complete what Kennedy had started and he is responsible for some of the most important pieces of civil rights legislation in American history, including the Voting Rights Act, Medicaid, and Medicare. His domestic vision, which he called the "Great Society," was not as successful as that of previous pioneers of social reform and Johnson suffered significantly from his perceived failure to prevent the escalation of the Vietnam War. Though he in many ways championed the causes important to the youth movement and minorities, he also failed them in terms of foreign policy, and thus Johnson lost public trust and political power during his second term.

Topics covered in this chapter include:

- Civil Rights Act
- Voting Rights Act
- Vietnam War
- Bay of Pigs
- Cuban Missile Crisis
- The Space Race
- Great Society Program
- Gulf of Tonkin Resolution

This Chapter Discusses the Following Source Documents:
Civil Rights Address, John F. Kennedy, June 11, 1963
Moon Speech, John F. Kennedy, September 12, 1962

We the People

Civil Rights and Human Rights
John F. Kennedy and Lyndon B. Johnson (1961–1969)

The Eisenhower administration marked the beginning of the era of the secret presidency, in which presidents used the power of American intelligence services to complete foreign policy objectives. This secrecy continued under John F. Kennedy, Lyndon B. Johnson, and Richard Nixon—all of whom relied heavily on covert efforts to meet foreign policy goals, frequently with less-than-ideal results.

The Youth Vote

John F. Kennedy was born into a wealthy Boston, Irish-Catholic family. His father, Joe, made a fortune in the stock market through investment in the Hollywood film industry, and this influence won him an appointment as ambassador to Britain under Franklin Roosevelt. John "Jack" Kennedy was plagued with medical problems, including Addison's disease, and spinal fusion to treat a back injury, both of which resulted in chronic pain. His health issues were kept secret to avoid compromising Kennedy's public image.[1] Whether a president has the right to withhold significant health information, remains controversial.

John F. Kennedy, by Cecil Stoughton, National Archives and Records Administration, via Wikimedia.

Despite his chronic illness, Kennedy attended Harvard University, and his senior thesis on England's military preparedness during the Second World War became the bestselling book *Why England Slept.* After graduation, Kennedy was refused entrance to the U.S. Navy due to his health, but his father's influence gained him command of a PT boat in the South Pacific during World War II. In August of 1943, a Japanese ship rammed Kennedy's boat and Kennedy led 10 survivors to a tiny island where they were later rescued. Assessments of this incident include the belief that there were no seamen posted on watch at the time of the attack, which would mean that Kennedy was negligent. However, Kennedy led 10 survivors on a three-mile swim to safety, dragging a wounded seaman by his life jacket, and the Navy chose to highlight his heroism and take the good publicity it created for the war effort. Kennedy was awarded a Purple Heart and Navy Medal for Valor.

After discharge from the Navy and a brief career as a journalist, Kennedy was elected to the House of Representatives, thanks, in part, to his father's political pull. After serving two terms, he defeated Republican Henry Lodge Jr. for a seat in the U.S. Senate. As a Congressman, Kennedy had a poor attendance record and was not especially active, though he was attached to a bill providing federal loans for housing and public education. Over his seven years as a U.S. Senator, Kennedy sponsored labor reform bills and a Democratic minimum wage bill, and used his time in the Senate to advance his visibility for the presidency. Kennedy became one of the most vocal critics of Eisenhower's stance on the Cold War race against Russia.[2]

Kennedy lost a bid for the vice-presidential nomination with Democratic candidate Adlai Stevenson in 1956, but this campaign raised his public profile. In 1960, Kennedy beat out challenger Hubert Humphrey to claim the Democratic nomination. This is one of the most studied elections in history because it was the first modern contest to capture the attention of young voters and because of the tremendous social turmoil in the nation at the time. Much of this change was due to the spread of television and news coverage that created a new awareness of the civil rights and youth movements, and greater visibility for the key issues of the era.

Kennedy, though only four years younger than Nixon, portrayed himself as the candidate of youthful vigor and liberalism and promised to move away from the stodgy conservatism of the Eisenhower era. It has been said that Kennedy won because, in televised debates, he appeared energetic and healthy while rival Nixon appeared frail and old. It seemed that those who watched the debate favored Kennedy, whereas those who listened thought Nixon had won the debate, although there were no comparative studies of radio and television audiences. Combined with his liberalism, Kennedy had a strong lead among youthful voters.[3] During the campaign, he concentrated on states with the highest number of electoral votes, while Nixon attempted to visit as many states as possible to demonstrate equal commitment.

Kennedy lacked support with traditionalists and white supremacists, who favored Nixon, and also faced a unique challenge in being only the second Catholic candidate for the presidency. Anti-Catholic prejudice, which had played a major role in Al Smith's defeat in 1928, had subsided significantly by the time Kennedy ran for office, but certain legislators and political ideologues questioned Kennedy's loyalty. In his September 1960 address to the Houston Minister's Conference, Kennedy spoke about the separation of church and state and argued against political attacks on the basis of religion, "Contrary to common newspaper usage, I am not the Catholic candidate for president. I am the Democratic Party's candidate for president, who happens also to be a Catholic. I do not speak for my church on public matters, and the church does not speak for me."[4]

Kennedy's advantage with young voters was barely enough to win the presidency, earning 34,220,984 votes (49.72 percent) to 34,108,157 (49.55) votes for Nixon.[5] Research shows that roughly 64 percent of the voting age population turned out to vote, an improvement over 60 percent in the previous election. The Democratic Party maintained control of the Senate and House, giving Kennedy significant congressional support even if he lacked a strong popular mandate.

Expansive Powers

Kennedy's presidency is famous for several major changes. The final shift in the federal stance on civil rights culminated in the Civil Rights Act of 1964, which prohibits discrimination based on race, religion, gender, or ethnicity and is the strongest defense of civil liberties ever issued by the federal government. Progress on civil rights was also made in key legal battles that eroded segregation, long used to curtail the rights of African Americans. Kennedy did not intend to use his presidency for civil rights activism, but the escalation of hostilities in the South forced his hand. When African American Air Force veteran James Meredith attempted to enroll at the then all-white University of Mississippi, he was denied entrance and took the issue to the courts, which ruled in favor of the school. However, Governor Ross Barnett allowed Meredith to enroll, and riots ensued, killing two and injuring hundreds. Kennedy dispatched federal marshals to keep the peace, an action he took again after white supremacists bombed a church in Birmingham, Alabama, killing four young children.

Though Kennedy hoped to wait until his second term to propose a new civil rights law, the intensification of violence convinced him that he needed to act. The Kennedy administration put forward their proposal for a Civil Rights Act in June of 1963, and Kennedy promoted this landmark effort in a June 11, 1963, televised address that ranks among his most famous speeches:

CIVIL RIGHTS ADDRESS
John F. Kennedy
June 11, 1963
Source Document Excerpt

This Nation was founded by men of many nations and backgrounds. It was founded on the principle that all men are created equal, and that the rights of every man are diminished when the rights of one man are threatened.

Today, we are committed to a worldwide struggle to promote and protect the rights of all who wish to be free. And when Americans are sent to Vietnam or West Berlin, we do not ask for whites only. It ought to be possible, therefore, for American students of any color to attend any public institution they select without having to be backed up by troops. It ought to to be possible for American consumers of any color to receive equal service in places of public accommodation, such as hotels and restaurants and theaters and retail stores, without being forced to resort to demonstrations in the street, and it ought to be possible for American citizens of any color to register and to vote in a free election without interference or fear of reprisal. It ought to to be possible, in short, for every American to enjoy the privileges of being American without regard to his race or his color. In short, every American ought to have the right to be treated as he would wish to be treated, as one would wish his children to be treated. But this is not the case.

The Negro baby born in America today, regardless of the section of the State in which he is born, has about one-half as much chance of completing a high school as a white baby born in the same place on the same day, one-third as much chance of completing college, one-third as much chance of becoming a professional man, twice as much chance of becoming unemployed, about one-seventh as much chance of earning $10,000 a year, a life expectancy which is 7 years shorter, and the prospects of earning only half as much.

This is not a sectional issue. Difficulties over segregation and discrimination exist in every city, in every State of the Union, producing in many cities a rising tide of discontent that threatens the public safety. Nor is this a partisan issue. In a time of domestic crisis men of good will and generosity should be able to unite regardless of party or politics. This is not even a legal or legislative issue alone. It is better to settle these matters in the courts than on the streets, and new laws are needed at every level, but law alone cannot make men see right. We are confronted primarily with a moral issue. It is as old as the Scriptures and is as clear as the American Constitution.

continued

The heart of the question is whether all Americans are to be afforded equal rights and equal opportunities, whether we are going to treat our fellow Americans as we want to be treated. If an American, because his skin is dark, cannot eat lunch in a restaurant open to the public, if he cannot send his children to the best public school available, if he cannot vote for the public officials who will represent him, if, in short, he cannot enjoy the full and free life which all of us want, then who among us would be content to have the color of his skin changed and stand in his place? Who among us would then be content with the counsels of patience and delay?[6]

Another major transformation credited to Kennedy's administration was America's earnest entrance into the "space race," a competition between the United States and the Soviet Union to develop and test space technology. The space race was part of the Cold War, and interest in space technology was as much about national security as about scientific exploration. Kennedy specifically promoted the race to send a manned mission to the moon, helping to create the idea that exploration of the final frontier could initiate a new era of global peace. In a September 1962 speech at Rice University, Kennedy said:

MOON SPEECH
John F. Kennedy
September 12, 1962
Source Document Excerpt

We set sail on this new sea because there is new knowledge to be gained, and new rights to be won, and they must be won and used for the progress of all people. For space science, like nuclear science and all technology, has no conscience of its own. Whether it will become a force for good or ill depends on man, and only if the United States occupies a position of pre-eminence can we help decide whether this new ocean will be a sea of peace or a new terrifying theater of war. I do not say the we should or will go unprotected against the hostile misuse of space any more than we go unprotected against the hostile use of land or sea, but I do say that space can be explored and mastered without feeding the fires of war, without repeating the mistakes that man has made in extending his writ around this globe of ours.

There is no strife, no prejudice, no national conflict in outer space as yet. Its hazards are hostile to us all. Its conquest deserves the best of all mankind, and its opportunity for peaceful cooperation many never come again. But why, some say, the moon? Why choose this as our goal? And they may well ask why climb the highest mountain? Why, 35 years ago, fly the Atlantic? Why does Rice play Texas?

We choose to go to the moon. We choose to go to the moon in this decade and do the other things, not because they are easy, but because they are hard, because that goal will serve to organize and measure the best of our energies and skills, because that challenge is one that we are willing to accept, one we are unwilling to postpone, and one which we intend to win, and the others, too.

It is for these reasons that I regard the decision last year to shift our efforts in space from low to high gear as among the most important decisions that will be made during my incumbency in the office of the Presidency.[7]

Kennedy's use of presidential powers regarding civil rights and the space race was in keeping with those who came before him. The struggle with the Soviet Union and the ongoing communist controversy also delivered the biggest tests of Kennedy's presidency. Kennedy agreed to an ill-fated invasion of Cuba, known as the "Bay of Pigs." The invasion was a failure, resulting in the death of more than 100 and the capture of the remaining invasion force. Kennedy was embarrassed by his failure, but took full responsibility, saying, "Victory has a thousand fathers and defeat is an orphan . . . I am the responsible officer of the government."[8]

In September of 1962, the Cold War again took center stage when it became clear that the Soviet Union, under the leadership of Nikita Khrushchev, decided to station ballistic missiles in Cuba. This incident, known as the "Cuban Missile Crisis," realized the fears of those who had pushed for the invasion of Cuba. With potential consequences that included global nuclear war, the Kennedy administration responded to the issue without input from Congress. Kennedy convened a council of his closest advisors, known as the Executive Committee of the National Security Council (ExComm), which did not include any legislators. Kennedy and ExComm centered on a naval blockade of Cuba, which they called a "quarantine" rather than a "blockade" to downplay its military nature. To gain popular support for any further military action, Kennedy took the issue directly to the people on October 22, 1962, explaining that Soviet aggression demanded action. Thirteen days later, the gamble payed off when the United States and the Soviet Union reached an agreement. Publicly for Kennedy it was a major win, as he claimed that his decisive action convinced the Soviet Union not to place armaments in Cuba. Privately, the Kennedy administration made serious concessions to Russia, which included removing arms from both Italy and Turkey.[9]

The use of executive power in the Kennedy administration was expansive, especially in assuming unilateral control over the Bay of Pigs operation and the Cuban Missile Crisis. Both times, Kennedy's unsanctioned use of military power could have been considered extreme and inappropriate at the beginning of a presidency. The public's embrace of Kennedy demonstrates a change from politics of today, when presidential power is being questioned. Following the Cuban Missile Crisis, Kennedy had a 74 percent approval rating, which reached a high of 83 percent in April of 1961, the same month of the aborted Bay of Pigs invasion. Over the course of his three years in office, his approval rating remained around or above 70 percent.[10] Kennedy's ability to maintain high levels of public approval was due to his facility for public speaking and tendency to involve the American people in his failures and successes. With such command of public opinion, his assumption of broad executive power met with tentative resistance from Congress. Some historians have concluded that Kennedy's approval rating can be seen as a public mandate with regard to executive dominance, even unilateral action, in foreign policy.

Transition of Power

Kennedy's presidency was cut short by his assassination on November 22, 1963. One of the most controversial assassinations in American history, historians, filmmakers, and conspiracy theorists have long wondered whether Kennedy's assassination was orchestrated by his political enemies, but little evidence exists to support this. Lyndon Johnson, Kennedy's vice president, stepped into the presidency in the midst of a number of highly charged political dramas. Cold War tensions were ratcheting higher with the American intervention in Vietnam. Kennedy increased the number of American service members from 600 to more than 16,000 in an effort to stave off a Communist takeover of Saigon, and Johnson inherited this conflict along with questions about how to counter the Soviet advance elsewhere in the world.[11] Likewise, Johnson was left with an unfulfilled domestic agenda on civil rights, and it was he who needed to push through Kennedy's Civil Rights Act.

Lyndon Baines Johnson was born in Texas into a family that traced its roots back to the settlement of the state. His father was a member of the state legislature, and divided his time between politics and farming. His family suffered serious financial troubles, and this informed his later approach to the presidency. After a series of part-time jobs and an arrest after a drunken brawl, Johnson got a degree in education from the Southwest Texas State Teachers College, later working in impoverished communities, primarily with Latino students. He entered politics during the Great Depression, when he was galvanized to do something to address the nation's financial situation. In 1931, he became an aide to Congressman Richard Kleberg. It was also during this time that he married Claudia Alta Taylor, better known by her nickname, "Lady Bird."[12]

Lyndon B. Johnson, by Arnold Newman, White House Press Office, via Wikimedia.

In 1937, Johnson won election to the House of Representatives and became the Congressional Inspector in the Pacific Theatre during World War II. Johnson flew in one combat mission, receiving a Silver Star. In 1949, after a hostile campaign, he won a seat in the Senate by a narrow margin against Coke "Mr. Texas" Stevenson. Johnson's victory may have involved some electoral fraud, and he entered the Senate with less than a comfortable level of public support. In his book *Master of the Senate*, historian Robert Caro argues that Johnson might be considered one of the most, if not the most, effective senators in U.S. history. Over the course of his more than ten years in office, Johnson saw the Democratic Party rise and fall in prominence, and he served in most of the essential congressional roles. His effectiveness was based on his ability to campaign to other senators and representatives, and Caro described Johnson as using whatever means he needed to secure a majority vote for one of the many bills he helped steer through Congress. By the end of Eisenhower's presidency, Johnson was a favorite for the Democratic Party nomination, but he was passed up in favor of Kennedy as party bosses were hoping to exploit Kennedy's youthful image. Johnson was nominated for the vice presidency to reassure those skeptical about Kennedy's relative inexperience.[13]

Hope and Shame

Lyndon Johnson had the fortune, and misfortune, of following in the footsteps of Kennedy. After Kennedy's assassination, Johnson retained Kennedy's inner circle of advisors and promised continuity as he took over the office. The collective anguish over Kennedy's assassination had far-reaching consequences. In the political sphere, there was a short-lived but important shift toward fulfilling Kennedy's legacy. Those among the public and in Congress who had long opposed Kennedy and his politics temporarily softened on those issues. Some suggest that there was a sense of shame among Kennedy's critics, and a desire to distance themselves from anything that would achieve its ends through such violent means. Johnson received an early advantage in pushing through his executive agenda, so long as that agenda was in keeping with Kennedy's. Kennedy's popularity also contributed to Johnson's favorability when he ran for president in 1964 and was part of the reason that he was able to secure such a dramatic victory, winning 43.1 million votes (61 percent) to 27.1 million (38 percent) for Republican challenger Barry Goldwater.[14]

On the domestic front, Kennedy's memory and Johnson's capacity for shrewd political bargaining resulted in the passage of the Civil Rights Act, establishing the U.S. government as the arbiter between the people and the states on matters involving civil rights and civil liberties. In 1965, during a civil rights march in Selma, Alabama, white supremacist police used dogs, tear gas, and clubs to attack African American protestors, an incident that was broadcast live on television across America. The public reaction to the Selma footage was dramatic, and the graphic images provided the best possible argument for those calling for federal intervention in the South. With a temporary public mandate, Johnson pushed for legislation that would allow the federal government to intervene to protect voting rights. This led to the passage of the Voting Rights Act of 1965,[15] one of the most important efforts to reform the U.S. voting system. The act prohibited some of the common methods that were used to disenfranchise voters, and allowed federal agents to directly intervene to protect against intimidation or state-government interference. The Voting Rights Act was more effective than any previous measure meant to counter the systematic racism that had impacted African Americans in the South. Within a year, black voter turnout had increased markedly, and over the course of the next half decade African Americans nearly reached parity with white voters in many southern states.

After winning a landslide reelection in 1964, Johnson proposed a sweeping series of reforms modeled after Woodrow Wilson and Theodore Roosevelt that he called the "Great Society" program, meant to address wealth inequality. The program was partially successful and resulted in the Medicare and Medicaid systems, which provided medical assistance to the elderly and the disabled. The package also increased federal assistance to public education, long held up over the inclusion of religious schools, which might be misconstrued as federal endorsement of a particular religion.[16]

Part of Johnson's Great Society vision was his "War on Poverty." The Johnson administration's solution was to create a series of Community Action Agencies (CAAs), with a combination of federal and local input, that would be responsible for dispensing aid from federal programs to various cities and counties. The CAAs became controversial as local leaders and federal legislators competed for control. Johnson's political opponents claimed that the system was rife with corruption, though there is little evidence of this. Controversy surrounding the CAAs tarnished the reputation of Johnson's entire War on Poverty program, despite a number of key successes in other areas. Overall, Johnson's efforts to increase assistance to the marginalized was a success, and the poverty rate decreased by nearly half over the next decade in response to Johnson's expansion of the federal welfare system.[17]

One of the major results of Johnson's domestic agenda was the complete rebirth of the Democratic Party. Prior to Johnson, the vast majority of Democratic Party politicians and voters were white. Johnson's advocacy for civil rights and Voting Rights Act, and his efforts to reform the economy, won him and the Democratic Party significant allegiance from African Americans and other people of color. Johnson's presidency marked a turning point for the Democratic Party, and the Democratic Party became more diverse, with African American voters preferring Democratic candidates and increasingly joining the party as politicians at the local and national level, culminating in Barack Obama's 2008 election to the presidency.

However, none of Johnson's accomplishments on the domestic front were enough to save him from his failures in foreign policy. The Vietnam War, as inherited from Kennedy, was a quagmire. Under Johnson "police action," Vietnam became a full-fledged military operation. After Vietnamese soldiers attacked U.S. ships in the Gulf of Tonkin, Johnson asked Congress for permission to escalate the conflict, which was approved by a vote of 98 to 2.[18] The escalation went against Johnson's campaign promise to seek an early end and lasting peace, but he had come to believe, like Kennedy and Eisenhower, that it was important to contain the spread of communism in Asia. This goal proved nearly impossible, however, without United States engaging in a full-scale takeover of the country. By the time Johnson left office, there were more than 500,000 American troops in Vietnam who seemed to be making little progress. A full-scale invasion or a nuclear attack might invite a new global war, but retreat would leave South Vietnam vulnerable to a full takeover and be politically disastrous.[19]

Johnson took a middle-of-the-road path—slow escalation punctuated by sporadic bombing campaigns—which proved no better for him politically than more aggression or more diplomacy would have been. Part of the reason for Johnson's declining public image was due to the way the media covered the war. During Vietnam, the media highlighted brutality and casualties of the conflict, and were less likely to engage in the kind of pro-government propagandizing that helped to build public support during World War II and the Korean War. The shift in journalistic approach combined with changing tastes of consumers created a generational transformation. Vietnam became the first war presented to the American people in more realistic detail, which failed to help build or maintain popular support of the war.

With casualty rates rising and little hope of victory, Johnson became the enemy of the counterculture peace movement. Anti-war protestors

chanted "Hey, hey, LBJ, how many kids did you kill today?" Politicians, emboldened by the shift in public support, attacked Johnson's policies openly in Congress while Republican political hopefuls blamed the failures of the war effort on his leadership. Because Johnson had acted alone in making key decisions about the American response to Vietnam, he had little defense, and by the end of his presidency, Johnson's popularity had plummeted severely. In February 1964, Lyndon Johnson had a 79 percent approval rating, and by August of 1968, Gallup measured his public approval at 35 percent.[20] In 1968, Johnson announced that he would not run for another term as president.

Regarding presidential power, Johnson was less apt than Kennedy to take unilateral actions, though he did exercise considerable independent power. In the Vietnam conflict, he fell back on the system of shared powers when he asked Congress to authorize escalating American action in Vietnam, resulting in the Gulf of Tonkin Resolution. Johnson acted without congressional oversight in deciding to authorize a March 1965 bombing campaign in North Vietnam[21] and also to increase the number of troops stationed in the region by 100,000. Both of these actions lost him support within the legislature. Over the course of his time in office, Johnson went from having support of moderates in both parties to only that of the more liberal Democrats, with little to no bipartisan support or support of the more conservative Democrats.

In contrast, Kennedy committed major military blunders, such as the Bay of Pigs fiasco, without congressional oversight and yet emerged not only unscathed but with increased popular approval. Kennedy's skill in marketing himself gave him power to assume greater independence from Congress. Johnson was not able to get the people on his side, and, therefore, could not wield popular support to bend Congress to his will.

Together, Kennedy and Johnson presided over a period of nearly unilateral presidential action regarding foreign affairs. This culmination of a

gradual increase of presidential power began with Woodrow Wilson and ended with Lyndon Johnson, during which time the executive branch increased in both size and scope, with presidents taking a more active and often dominant role in setting legislative priorities. World Wars I and II created rapid growth of the military-industrial complex; coupled with civilian intelligence services like the CIA; this gave the presidency increased powers to take sole control of the nation's foreign affairs. Whether or not this expansion of presidential powers was good for the country is still a matter of debate in the twenty-first century. Kennedy and Johnson, like Eisenhower before them, made liberal use of the CIA to engage in covert operations with important consequences for U.S. foreign relations, operations that typically occurred without judicial or congressional oversight. Since then, political analysts and the American public have debated whether it is appropriate for a president to exercise such a high level of independent power. When Richard Nixon entered office, many legislators were determined that he would not wield unmitigated power. Nixon thus marked a limited resurgence of Congressional power and in conservatism, largely in response to the perceived failings of Johnson's foreign policies and social justice efforts.

Kennedy's assassination spared him from the political turmoil that the Vietnam War became, and it is difficult to evaluate his unfinished presidency. Historians tend to rank Kennedy highly in terms of his overall capability to capture public attention, to work with Congress, and to accomplish his administration's goals. Though Johnson left office one of the most hated presidents of his era, his reputation has seen a renaissance. A 2019 survey of political scientists found John F. Kennedy ranked 16 out of 45 in terms of "presidential greatness," while Johnson ranked higher, as America's 10th greatest president.[22] Kennedy and Johnson both presided over a period of intense social and political transformation, and it is perhaps fitting that they changed the presidency and the American government's role in the lives of the people.

CONCLUSION

Kennedy and Johnson, like Eisenhower, served in a time of nearly unilateral presidential power in the field of foreign affairs. The secret activities of these presidents, however, especially in their use of the CIA to conduct important foreign affairs operations was becoming controversial, and this would lead to Congress reasserting authority under the Nixon administration which followed President Johnson. Even though Kennedy is remembered as one of the most progressive presidents, Johnson did far more to advance the cause of civil rights in America, and it was his administration that created a lasting link between the Democratic Party and the African American voting population that endured into the modern era. The next chapter profiles the two least-liked presidents in modern history—Nixon and Ford— and scandalous misuse of presidential power.

DISCUSSION QUESTIONS

♦ Would Kennedy's presidency have had the same enduring appeal if Kennedy had not been assassinated? Explain your answer.

♦ How did Kennedy avoid losing popular support after the Bay of Pigs controversy?

♦ Why was Johnson conflicted about how to proceed with the Vietnam War? How would you have advised him to proceed?

♦ How important is space exploration to American culture? To global culture? Why?

Works Used

"1960 Presidential General Election Results." *U.S. Election Atlas*. 2019. uselectionatlas.org/RESULTS/national.php?year=1960.

"1964 Presidential General Election Results." *U.S. Election Atlas*. 2019. uselectionatlas.org/RESULTS/national.php?year=1964.

Bailey, Martha J., and Nicolas J. Duquette. "How Johnson Fought the War on Poverty: The Economics and Politics of Funding at the Office of Economic Opportunity." *Journal of Economic History*. vol. 74, no. 2. 2014, pp 351–88. *US National Library of Medicine*. National Institutes of Health.www.ncbi.nlm.nih.gov/pmc/articles/PMC4266933/.

Brown, David. "JFK's Addison's Disease." *The Washington Post*. 6 Oct. 6, 1992. www.washingtonpost.com/archive/lifestyle/wellness/1992/10/06/jfks-addisons-disease/aceb473c-a5dc-4199-9453-d3fcd3b18312/.

Caro, Robert A. *Master of the Senate: The Years of Lyndon Johnson III*. New York: Vintage Books, 2002.

Glass, Andrew. "LBJ Approves 'Operation Rolling Thunder,' Feb. 13, 1965." *Politico*. 13 Feb. 2019. www.politico.com/story/2019/02/13/lbj-operation-rolling-thunder-feb-13-1965-1162618.

Greenberg, David. "Rewinding the Kennedy-Nixon Debates." *Slate*. 24 Sept. 2010. slate.com/news-and-politics/2010/09/did-jfk-really-win-because-he-looked-better-on-television.html.

Goodwin, Doris Kearns. *Lyndon Johnson and the American Dream*. Open Road Media, 2015.

"John F. Kennedy's Pre-Presidential Voting Record & Stands on Issues." CQ Fact Sheet on John F. Kennedy, Congressional Quarterly, Inc. , 1960. *JFK Library*. www.jfklibrary.org/learn/about-jfk/life-of-john-f-kennedy/fast-facts-john-f-kennedy/voting-record-and-stands-on-issues.

Kennedy, John F. "Address to the Greater Houston Ministerial Association." *JFK Library*. 12 Sept. 1960, www.jfklibrary.org/learn/about-jfk/historic-speeches/address-to-the-greater-houston-ministerial-association.

Kennedy, John F. "Civil Rights Address." *American Rhetoric*. 11 June 1963. americanrhetoric.com/speeches/jfkcivilrights.htm.

Kennedy, John F. "Moon Speech—Rice Stadium." *NASA*. 12 Sept. 1962. er.jsc.nasa.gov/seh/ricetalk.htm.

Kennedy, John F. "News Conference 10, April 21, 1961." *JFK Library*. 2019. www.jfklibrary.org/archives/other-resources/john-f-kennedy-press-conferences/news-conference-10.

"Medicare and Medicaid." *LBJ Library*. 2019. www.lbjlibrary.org/press/media-kit/medicare-and-medicaid.

"Military Advisors in Vietnam: 1963." *JFK Library*. 2019. www.jfklibrary.org/learn/education/teachers/curricular-resources/high-school-curricular-resources/military-advisors-in-vietnam-1963.

Moise, Edwin E. *Tonkin Gulf and the Escalation of the Vietnam War*. Chapel Hill, NC: The U of North Carolina P, 1996.

Nathan, James. *The Cuban Missile Crisis Revisited*. New York: Palgrave, MacMillan, 1992.

"Presidential Approval Ratings—Gallup Historical Statistics and Trends." *Gallup*. 2019. news.gallup.com/poll/116677/presidential-approval-ratings-gallup-historical-statistics-trends.aspx.

"Voting Rights Act." *Our Documents*. 2019. www.ourdocuments.gov/doc.
php?flash=false&doc=100.

Watson, W. Marvin, and Sherwin Markman. *Chief of Staff: Lyndon Johnson
and His Presidency*. New York: MacMillan, 2014.

Weiss, Brennan. "RANKED: The Greatest US Presidents, According to
Political Scientists." *Business Insider*. 18 Feb. 2019. www.businessinsider.
com/greatest-us-presidents-ranked-by-political-scientists-2018-2.

Introduction

Richard Milhouse Nixon had a profoundly negative impact on American perceptions of the presidency. He was an unscrupulous politician who pushed forward policies to maximize benefit to himself and his allies, and he frequently lied to Congress and the American people. Over the course of his term, Nixon used the intelligence community to spy on American citizens and members of Congress without due process, committed secret military operations without congressional oversight, and used the powers of the presidency to gain an advantage on his political rivals, all in violation of presidential power and authority. Though he was popular while in office, Nixon's presidency crumbled with the Watergate controversy and the release of the Pentagon Papers, which were leaked documents that revealed secret military operations ongoing since Eisenhower. While public opinion gradually turned against him, it was his loss of support in the legislature that ultimately led to his resignation. President Gerald Ford followed, a decent and intelligent man who had the misfortune of following Nixon's scandalous presidency. Ford's decision to pardon Nixon for his crimes lost him any support he might have had among progressives, and his presidency is among the least respected in American history.

Topics covered in this chapter include:
- World War II
- The Cold War
- The Bombings of Hiroshima and Nagasaki
- The Truman Doctrine
- African American alignment with the Democratic Party

This Chapter Discusses the Following Source Documents:

Recording of a Meeting Between the President and H.R. Haldeman in the Oval Office, June 23, 1972

DeVeaux, Amelia Thomson. "It Took A Long Time For Republicans to Abandon Nixon." *Five Thirty Eight*, October 9, 2019

Thieves and Liars
Richard Nixon and Gerald Ford (1969–1977)

Richard Nixon was the first president to resign from office, making his presidency historic. Nixon's fall from power led to a decline in American trust of the presidency and government as a whole.

The Denigrative Method

Nixon was born in 1913 in Yorba Linda, California, into a modest family. He was a top student at Duke University's law school before joining a California law firm. Enlisting in the U.S. Navy during World War II at age 29, Nixon served as lieutenant and commander in the naval reserve.[1] Returning to California, Nixon ran for a congressional seat in 1946 against Jerry Voorhis, a five-time incumbent, hiring political strategist Murray Chotiner, who helped him develop an aggressive campaign style. In *Nixon Agonistes: The Crisis of the Self-Made Man,* historian Gary Wills explains:

"It is the denigrative method: find the opposition's weak point and then just *lean* on it all through the race. In such a contest, the first blow means a great deal. Once a man is on the defensive, he must explain—and explanation is not nearly as effective as accusation. Besides, by the time your opponent has explained A, you can have B and C ready for him to explain.

What if one's opponent is launching attacks on you? Refuse to be put on the defensive. Just don't answer. If, after a while, that becomes impossible, contrive a way to turn the tables and make an *attack* out of your explanation."[2]

Nixon's campaign against Voorhis exemplified this strategy of accusation. He won his first election and became a member of the House of Representatives Un-American Activities Committee. Nixon's role in the investigation of suspected communist spy Alger Hiss brought him national attention.

Richard Nixon, by Department of Defense, via Wikimedia.

In 1950, Nixon used his fame from the Hiss case to run for the Senate, where he faced feminist activist Helen Gahagan Douglas. Nixon accused Douglas of communist sympathies, calling her the "Pink Lady," remarking that she was "pink right down to her underwear." The Nixon-Douglas campaign is remembered as a low-point in California politics. Misogyny was the primary strategy for Republicans. When Douglas visited the USC campus for a speech, she was sprayed with seltzer and covered with hay. Those responsible acted illegally on behalf of Nixon (and were later implicated as part of Nixon's White House scandal). Nixon's campaign attempted to inspire anti-Semitism by broadcasting that Douglas was married to a Jewish man. Nixon launched a telephone campaign that featured anti-Douglas messages such as "Did you know Helen Gahagan Douglas was a Communist?" Nixon won election to the Senate as well as the nickname, "Tricky Dick," which stuck with him through the remainder of his career.[3]

In 1952, Eisenhower selected Nixon as his vice-presidential candidate. During the campaign, the *New York Post* claimed that Nixon was misusing federal campaign funds for personal gain. Nixon delivered a televised address defending his use of campaign funds, claiming, however, that he would never give up one campaign gift, a cocker spaniel puppy named "Checkers." The Checkers story showed Nixon's softer side. Eisenhower and Nixon achieved a landslide victory.

Nixon gained valuable credentials through meetings with foreign dignitaries and when Eisenhower's presidency ended, Nixon was the clear successor. However, he faced a reinvigorated Democratic Party and John F. Kennedy. Plus, the 1960 campaign saw Nixon in uncomfortable territory, as the defender of the Eisenhower's mixed record. Kennedy was more attractive, carried more weight with women, youth, and African Americans, and was a more effective speaker. Despite this, it was a close election, with Kennedy defeating Nixon by one of the smallest margins in history.

Nixon later said of the campaign:

_____ *"The way the Kennedy's played politics and the way the media let them get away with it left me angry and frustrated. From this point on, I had the wisdom and wariness of someone who had been burned by the power of the Kennedys and their money and by the license they were given by the media. I vowed that I would never again enter an election at a disadvantage by being vulnerable to them—or anyone—on the level of political tactics."[4]*

_____

Following his loss, Nixon suffered another defeat when he ran for governor of California, saying:

_____ *"I leave you gentlemen now, and you will write it. You will interpret. That's your right. But as I leave you I want you to know— just think how much you're going to be missing. You won't have Nixon to kick around anymore, because gentlemen, this is my last press conference, and it will be the one in which I have welcomed the opportunity to test wits with you. I have always respected you. I have sometimes disagreed with you. But unlike some people, I've never cancelled a subscription to a paper, and also I never will.*

I believe in reading what my opponents say, and I hope that what I have said today will at least make television, radio, and the press, first recognize the great responsibility they have to report all the news and, second, recognize that they have a right and responsibility, if they're against a candidate, give him the shaft, but also recognize if they give him the shaft, put one lonely reporter on the campaign who will report what the candidate says now and then. Thank you, gentleman, and good day."[5]

_____

Nixon the President

Nixon chose not to run for president in 1964, when Johnson won a landslide victory thanks to Kennedy's assassination. Nixon resurfaced in the 1968 presidential race, winning the Republican Party nomination from Ronald Reagan with a new team of consultants and a new media image. A Republican victory was nearly assured thanks to the Vietnam War, which had tarnished the reputation of both Johnson and the Democratic Party. Democratic opponent Hubert Humphrey climbed in the polls when the Johnson administration announced that it was nearing a peace agreement in Vietnam. Nixon secretly dispatched campaign operatives to convince key South Vietnamese leaders to delay a peace agreement. Announcement of the peace talks was postponed until after the election, and Nixon won a close popular vote victory, 31.8 million votes compared to 31.3 for Humphrey, with independent candidate George Wallace claiming 9.9 million votes. After his victory, Nixon urged South Vietnamese leaders to engage in the peace talks.

Nixon served two terms in office and was a moderately popular, yet divisive, president. Over the course of his first term, he averaged 56 percent approval, with a peak of 69 percent approval just after his election. Nixon's overall average approval rating is low (49 percent) due to the Watergate Scandal during his second term, dropping to 24 percent, making him one of the worst-rated presidents.[6] In office, he faced a divided public and a host of national issues: unemployment and poverty rates were rising; significant public backlash to the ongoing Vietnam War; and a surge of interest in environmental protection. Documents uncovered from Nixon's personal correspondence reveal a self-serving man who broadcasted misinformation.

For example, Nixon has been credited with a host of environmental reforms, including the Environmental Protection Agency (EPA), the National Oceanic and Atmospheric Administration (NOAA), and key legislative

initiatives to address air and water pollution. During his second term, Nixon supported the Marine Mammal Protection Act of 1972 and the Endangered Species Act of 1973, landmark legislative efforts to preserve biodiversity. However, documents and recordings from the Nixon era indicate that he promoted what he saw as weak bills in order to prevent more aggressive environmental legislation.

Economically, Nixon outwardly supported legislative efforts to address poverty and unemployment, but his actions were equally self-serving. The Family Assistance Program (FAP) was supposed to provide a national minimum income, but the proposal was both radical enough to generate opposition from conservatives, and weak enough to be criticized by progressives. White House Chief of Staff Bob Haldeman wrote, "About Family Assistance Plan, [President] wants to be sure it's killed by Democrats and that we make a big play for it, but don't let it pass, can't afford it." Nixon would get credibility among liberals, but also political leverage as he could blame Democrats for the plan's failure to pass.[7]

Nixon's political strategy won him electoral victory in 1972, and 47 million popular votes to 29 million for Democrat George McGovern. Problems began for Nixon when leaked documents, known as the Pentagon Papers, threatened to expose secret details regarding presidential use of the CIA and covert policies that contributed to escalation in Vietnam. Commissioned by Secretary of Defense Robert McNamara in 1967 under President Johnson, the report revealed that presidents Truman through Johnson purposefully misled the American people regarding American activities in Vietnam. Though Nixon himself was not implicated in the Pentagon Papers, he realized that increased scrutiny of secret government activities might result in revelations about his use of the CIA. From Nixon's writings, it is clear he believed he was the victim of a "left-wing" conspiracy theory aiming to delegitimize his presidency.[8]

Nixon created the Special Investigations Unit (SIU), charged with un-covering and eliminating conspiratorial evidence that might be used to implicate him. This organization was tasked with covering up a secret 1969 bombing of Cambodia and Laos intended to gain American control of Laos and the destruction of Khmer Rouge rebels in Cambodia. The bombing campaign used 540,000 tons of bombs and killed between 150,000 to 500,000.[9]

The SIU, nicknamed "The Plumbers," included some of those same individuals who harassed Helen Douglas during her Senate run against Nixon, as well as former FBI agents and Republican political operatives. Ex-CIA agent Howard Hunt and ex-FBI agent G. Gordon Liddy were tasked with discrediting Daniel Eisenberg, former Pentagon aide and intelligence operative who leaked the Pentagon Papers to the press. Hunt recruited Cuban expatriates to break into the Democratic National Committee HQ at the Watergate Hotel in Washington, DC, some of whom were arrested and named Liddy and Hunt. Nixon's misuse of presidential power became known, and investigators quickly found a trail of money that led back to his administration. Two days after the Watergate Hotel arrests, Nixon and chief aide Bob Haldeman had a discussion that was recorded and proved to be what prosecutors called the "smoking gun" in the case for Nixon's impeachment.

RECORDING OF A MEETING BETWEEN THE PRESIDENT AND H.R. HALDEMAN IN THE OVAL OFFICE

June 23, 1972
Source Document Excerpt

HALDEMAN: okay—that's fine. Now, on the investigation, you know, the Democratic break-in thing, we're back to the—in the, the problem area because the FBI is not under control, because Gray doesn't exactly know how to control them, and they have, their investigation is now leading into some productive areas, because they've been able to trace the money, not through the money itself, but through the bank, you know, sources—the banker himself. And, and it goes in some directions we don't want it to go. Ah, also there have been some things, like an informant came in off the street to the FBI in Miami, who was a photographer or has a friend who is a photographer who developed some films through this guy, Barker, and the films had pictures of Democratic National Committee letter head documents and things. So I guess, so it's things like that that are gonna, that are filtering in. Mitchell came up with yesterday, and John Dean analyzed very carefully last night and concludes, concurs now with Mitchell's recommendation that the only way to solve this, and we're set up beautifully to do it, ah, in that and that . . . the only network that paid any attention to it last night was NBC . . . they did a massive story on the Cuban . . .

PRESIDENT: That's right.

HALDEMAN: thing.

PRESIDENT: Right.

HALDEMAN: That the way to handle this now is for us to have Walters call Pat Gray and just say, "Stay the hell out of this . . . this is ah, business here we don't want you to go any further on it." That's not an unusual development, . . .

PRESIDENT: Um huh.

HALDEMAN: . . . and, uh, that would take care of it.

PRESIDENT: What about Pat Gray, ah, you mean he doesn't want to?

HALDEMAN: Pat does want to. He doesn't know how to, and he doesn't have, he doesn't have any basis for doing it. Given this, he will then have the basis. He'll call Mark Felt in, and the two of them . . . and Mark Felt wants to cooperate because . . .

PRESIDENT: Yeah.

continued

HALDEMAN: he's ambitious . . .

PRESIDENT: Yeah.

HALDEMAN: Ah, he'll call him in and say, "We've got the signal from across the river to, to put the hold on this." And that will fit rather well because the FBI agents who are working the case, at this point, feel that's what it is. This is CIA.

PRESIDENT: But they've traced the money to 'em.

HALDEMAN: Well they have, they've traced to a name, but they haven't gotten to the guy yet.

PRESIDENT: Would it be somebody here?

HALDEMAN: Ken Dahlberg.

PRESIDENT: Who the hell is Ken Dahlberg?

HALDEMAN: He's ah, he gave $25,000 in Minnesota and ah, the check went directly in to this, to this guy Barker.

PRESIDENT: Maybe he's a . . . bum. He didn't get this from the committee though, from Stans.

HALDEMAN: Yeah. It is. It is. It's directly traceable and there's some more through some Texas people in— that went to the Mexican bank which they can also trace to the Mexican bank. . . they'll get their names today. And (pause)

PRESIDENT: Well, I mean, ah, there's no way . . . I'm just thinking if they don't cooperate, what do they say? They, they, they were approached by the Cubans. That's what Dahlberg has to say, the Texans too. Is that the idea?

HALDEMAN: Well, if they will. But then we're relying on more and more people all the time. That's the problem. And ah, they'll stop if we could, if we take this other step.

PRESIDENT: All right. Fine.

HALDEMAN: And, and they seem to feel the thing to do is get them to stop?

PRESIDENT: Right, fine.

HALDEMAN: They say the only way to do that is from White House instructions. And it's got to be to Helms and, ah, what's his name...? Walters.

PRESIDENT: Walters.

HALDEMAN: And the proposal would be that Ehrlichman (coughs) and I call them in

PRESIDENT: All right, fine.

HALDEMAN: and say, ah . . .

We the People

Recording of a Meeting between the President and H.R. Haldeman in the Oval Office
continued

PRESIDENT: How do you call him in, I mean you just, well, we protected Helms from one hell of a lot of things.

HALDEMAN: That's what Ehrlichman says.

PRESIDENT: Of course, this is a, this is a Hunt, you will—that will uncover a lot of things. You open that scab there's a hell of a lot of things and that we just feel that it would be very detrimental to have this thing go any further. This involves these Cubans, Hunt, and a lot of hanky-panky that we have nothing to do with ourselves. Well what the hell, did Mitchell know about this thing to any much of a degree?

HALDEMAN: I think so. I don't think he knew the details, but I think he knew . . .

PRESIDENT: You call them in. Good. Good deal! Play it tough. That's the way they play it and that's the way we are going to play it.

HALDEMAN: O.K. We'll do it . . .

PRESIDENT: When you get in these people when you . . . get these people in, say: "Look, the problem is that this will open the whole, the whole Bay of Pigs thing, and the President just feels that" ah, without going into the details . . . don't, don't lie to them to the extent to say there is no involvement, but just say this is sort of a comedy of errors, bizarre, without getting into it, "the President believes that it is going to open the whole Bay of Pigs thing up again. And, ah because these people are plugging for, for keeps and that they should call the FBI in and say that we wish for the country, don't go any further into this case, period!"[10]

The scandal started before the 1972 election, and the Nixon administration stopped it leaking until right after the election. At the Senate Watergate hearings former Haldeman aide Alexander Butterfield revealed that the White House had employed a secret recording system. Prosecutor Archibald Cox issued a subpoena for the tapes and Nixon then fired Cox, and forced Attorney General Elliot Richardson to resign. This purge of executive staff, known as the "Saturday Night Massacre," backfired. There was an outpouring of public criticism, and Nixon's approval rating plummeted. The Supreme Court ordered Nixon in 1974 to release his secret recordings and the tapes, including the "smoking gun." Facing certain impeachment and without the support to keep him in office, Nixon resigned on August 8, 1974.

Watergate and the subsequent trials were only one example of Nixon's misuse of presidential power. Nixon secretly used the CIA to investigate the anti-war movement and student activists, and to spy on officials of allied foreign governments, and he also secretly bombed Laos and Cambodia. The creation of the SIU was an overreach of presidential authority, and the use of public funds to support his activities was a breach of both constitutional powers and the public trust. Nixon is often described as one of the most corrupt presidents in American history. Revelations of Nixon's misdeeds have sealed his reputation, but there have been other presidents who have engaged in serious abuses of power and violated the public trust in ways that have not been made public.

It is difficult not to draw similarities between Richard Nixon and current President Donald Trump. Both men used a denigrative style of political campaigning and obfuscation and false information to distract from accusations of misconduct. Donald Trump's supporters, both within the Republican Party and the public, remain loyal despite the current impeachment investigation. In this article from *FiveThirtyEight*, Amelia Thomson-DeVeaux explores how Republicans in Nixon's time also remained faithful until Nixon's resignation.

IT TOOK A LONG TIME FOR REPUBLICANS TO ABANDON NIXON

Amelia Thomson-DeVeaux

FiveThirtyEight

October 9, 2019

On July 23, 1974, Rep. Lawrence Hogan, Sr., a Republican on the House Judiciary Committee, bought airtime on TV networks across his home state of Maryland. He had a big announcement to share: Hogan was the first Republican on the House Judiciary Committee to publicly say he would vote to impeach Nixon. It was just over two weeks before Nixon would announce his resignation, and the Judiciary Committee was poised to approve three articles of impeachment against the president—except nobody knew that yet.

Today, as another impeachment drama unfolds, it's easy to see Republicans like Hogan, who were willing to break ranks with their party, as a fundamental difference between Watergate and today. And it's true that Republicans are currently staying in President Trump's corner. But while we tend to focus on the bipartisan rebellion that led to Nixon's resignation, it's also worth understanding *how* public opinion and the party eventually turned against the president.

Support for impeachment had grown slowly over the course of 1974, but there still wasn't an overwhelming public consensus behind it until right before Nixon left office in early August. And Republican support for Nixon had remained mostly strong, even in the face of a scandal that consumed his second term. As the truth about the scope of Nixon's misconduct emerged, though, impeachment became increasingly popular and the president lost even his most fervent defenders in Congress. Of course, there are many differences between the Nixon impeachment and the Democrats' current inquiry, which is still in its early stages, and each impeachment investigation will unfold differently. But as today's Republicans are scrutinized for signs that they might turn on Trump, it's important to remember that even in Watergate, it took more than a year of investigation—and a *lot* of evidence against Nixon—to reach the point where Republicans like Hogan were voting for impeachment.

Impeachment Wasn't Popular until Right before Nixon Resigned

When the House of Representatives voted in February 1974 to give the House Judiciary Committee subpoena power to investigate Nixon, it did not have the weight of public opinion

continued

behind it. According to a poll conducted by Gallup just days before the vote, only 38 percent of Americans were in favor of impeachment. And although a solid majority of Americans did eventually come to support impeachment, that moment didn't arrive until quite late in the game.

But this didn't mean the public wasn't souring on Nixon as the Watergate scandal unfolded. After winning a sweeping victory in the 1972 election, the president began his second term with an approval rating around 60 percent, according to FiveThirtyEight's tracker of presidential approval. Then that spring saw a stunning 30-point drop in Nixon's support starting around when one of the people charged with breaking into the Democratic National Committee headquarters confessed to a judge that he and the other conspirators had been pressured to stay silent.

Support for Nixon continued to plunge throughout the long summer of 1973, while former White House lawyer John Dean testified in Senate hearings that the president had been involved in a cover-up of the burglary and a White House aide confirmed in closed-door testimony that Nixon had set up a secret White House taping system. And by the time of October's

Saturday Night Massacre—where Nixon ordered the firing of special prosecutor Archibald Cox, who had been demanding those tapes, and the closing of the special prosecutor's investigation—his approval rating had plunged to 27 percent, which is about where it stayed until Nixon resigned.

As Nixon's approval ratings fell, support for impeachment was rising more gradually, reaching solid majority support by early August 1974. That was right in the midst of the crucial two-week period when the Supreme Court ordered Nixon to turn over the White House tapes, the House Judiciary Committee voted to approve three articles of impeachment and Nixon released the transcript of what became known as the "smoking gun" tape, which showed that he had helped orchestrate the cover-up. His support among his allies (who had included some conservative southern Democrats as well as Republicans) had already started to erode significantly, but it was the "smoking gun" tape that finally forced his resignation on August 8, before the House could vote on impeachment. At that point, the public was clearly behind impeachment, although a significant minority of Americans—including most Republicans—still didn't think Nixon should be removed from office.

It Took A Long Time for Republicans to Abandon Nixon
continued

Most Republicans in Congress Took a Long Time to Break with Nixon

So why did it take most Republicans so long to break with Nixon? There was a growing bipartisan sense of alarm about his actions, especially in the wake of the Saturday Night Massacre, as a handful of Republicans in Congress called for Nixon's resignation. Even some party leaders and staunch Nixon defenders, like Sen. Barry Goldwater, criticized the president's handling of the scandal, although their rebukes still fell short of calling for impeachment. The House's vote to formally open an impeachment inquiry in February 1974 was almost unanimous.

Republicans generally saw the inquiry as legitimate, but that didn't mean they had lost faith in Nixon. "Many remained vocal in support of the president, saying he was innocent," said Timothy Naftali, a presidential historian at New York University and the former director of the Nixon presidential library. "Others were more judicious, waiting for the evidence to come out."

Eventually, several of the more moderate Republicans on the House Judiciary Committee, including Hogan, were convinced by the evidence against Nixon and voted for at least one of the articles of impeachment in July 1974. .

. .Three of the articles of impeachment passed with varying levels of support from Republicans and conservative Democrats, although a significant number of conservative Republicans remained in Nixon's camp. The final two articles of impeachment, which centered on the secret bombing of Cambodia that began in 1969 and charges of tax fraud against Nixon, were not approved.

Some of the Republican defense of Nixon probably boiled down to party loyalty, according to Jeffrey Engel, a presidential historian at Southern Methodist University. "For a long time, they just weren't going to pull the trigger on a duly elected president from their own party," he said. Republicans also faced pressure from a small but powerful group of activists who were vehemently opposed to Nixon's impeachment and were aggressively lobbying their representatives not to abandon him. "Increasingly, [Republican leadership] thought it would be better for the party if Nixon could be persuaded to go," said Mark Nevin, a history professor at Ohio University Lancaster who has studied Republican support for Nixon at the end of his presidency. "But nobody wanted to be the one who pushed him out."

It also took a while for all of the evidence to emerge, and ultimately,

continued

the *scope* of Nixon's wrongdoing helped convince some of the Judiciary Committee Republicans to break ranks, in spite of pressure from leadership to maintain a united front in support of Nixon. "It wasn't a single act that moved them—it was the pattern of corruption by the president," Naftali said. Nixon's support was crumbling by the time the Judiciary Committee voted on impeachment, but he didn't lose the full support of his party until the "smoking gun" tape clearly implicated him in the Watergate cover-up, at which point he lost even the Republicans on the committee who had voted against impeachment. Two days after the transcript of the tape became public, Goldwater led a delegation to the White House to tell Nixon it was over.

It's hard to imagine what such a "smoking gun" would look like today, in part because the Democrats' investigations are still in the information-gathering stage, but it does seem that we haven't arrived there yet. One important difference between the Nixon era and today: Trump hasn't really denied the allegations against him, while several historians told me that many Republicans probably believed Nixon was telling the truth about his lack of involvement in the cover-up. The shock of discovering just how much Nixon had misled them was also an important factor.

"It was an enormous betrayal for some of Nixon's allies when they realized that he had been lying the whole time," Engel said. "Because it meant they had been lying too."

Partisanship Can Be a Powerful Barrier to Impeachment

One of the oft-cited lessons of Watergate is that impeaching a president requires a bipartisan effort. And in the end, it did. Republicans voted with Democrats to subpoena Nixon and to approve the articles of impeachment, which was a significant political risk. But focusing only on that part of the saga doesn't account for how strongly many Republicans defended their president throughout most of the investigation. "The Nixon case shows that seemingly intractable partisan disagreement over impeachment can give way if the president's conduct is bad enough and the proof of it is clear enough," said Joshua Matz, a constitutional lawyer and the co-author of "To End a Presidency: The Power of Impeachment." "But it also shows that this is a high barrier, and it didn't happen until awfully late in the process."

At several points, according to Nevin's research, Goldwater and other prominent Republicans considered pushing Nixon to resign, but instead continued to defend him because they were afraid of a backlash from

It Took A Long Time for Republicans to Abandon Nixon
continued

his supporters. "Some Republicans were actually relieved when the tape came out because it was so obviously obstruction that you couldn't come to any other conclusion," Nevin said. "It freed them from having to make what would have been a very difficult decision."

Today some Republicans may be facing a similar dilemma: Do they ignore party allegiance and turn on the president, or double down on party loyalty?

One complicating factor here is that if Republicans were to abandon Trump, history does not suggest that Trump loyalists would easily forgive them for joining the Democrats' impeachment effort. Even though most Americans did eventually support removing Nixon from office, Republican voters were mostly not part of that consensus. Days before he resigned, a Gallup poll found that only 31 percent of Republicans thought Nixon should no longer be president. And some of those supporters deeply resented their representatives for their role in ousting Nixon, which may even have contributed to the Democratic landslide in the 1974 midterm elections.

Of course, looking back on what happened in Watergate can't tell us whether Trump will survive this particular scandal. Some Republicans have started to criticize Trump's behavior, but none have taken the momentous step of supporting an impeachment inquiry. So Trump's removal certainly doesn't seem likely now. But if nothing else, history offers a good reminder about how challenging it is to predict the future. After all, until a few weeks before his resignation, Nixon's fate wasn't a foregone conclusion either.[11]

Another "Least Popular" President

Upon Nixon's resignation, Vice President Gerald Ford assumed the presidency. The Nixon administration had been hopelessly tainted, and there was little hope that Ford would be able to resurrect his party's reputation. Upon taking office, Gallup polls saw Ford's approval rating at 70 percent, but over the course of his partial term Ford averaged 47 percent approval—higher than Nixon's second-term average of 34 percent—but still ranking him as one of the least popular presidents. Historians describe

Ford as a pleasant and good-natured man, who was unprepared and unable to capitalize on his unexpected rise to the nation's highest office.

Gerald Ford, by David Hume Kennerly, via Wikimedia.

Born Leslie Lynch King, Jr. in Omaha, Nebraska, his mother's second marriage to Gerald Robert Ford saw Leslie King officially change his name to Gerald Randolph Ford, Jr. after college. Ford majored in economics at the University of Michigan, which he attended, in part, on his skill as a football player. He was recruited by both the Green Bay Packers and the Detroit Lions while in college, but he declined the offers, working instead as an assistant football coach at Yale University while completing a law degree. After briefly working as a lawyer in Michigan, Ford became involved in the Michigan Republican Party. He enlisted in the U.S. Navy at the outbreak of World War II, served on an aircraft carrier for four years, and returned to practice law in Michigan.

Ford won election to the House of Representatives in 1948 in a Republican-dominated district and served twelve terms, becoming a stalwart of the anti-Communist movement. By the mid-1960s, Ford was one of the highest-ranking Republicans in Congress and supported Nixon's run for the presidency in 1968. Despite his loyalty to Nixon, the Republican Party neglected Ford, who considered retiring from Congress before the tumultuous final years of the Nixon administration catapulted him to national prominence. Vice President Spiro Agnew resigned in October of 1973, in the midst of the Watergate Scandal, when it was discovered that he had taken bribes both as vice president and as governor of Maryland. Nixon selected Ford to replace Agnew because he was one of the last Republicans to remain loyal. Eight months after Ford was confirmed by Congress Nixon resigned, making Ford the first and only president who was not elected to office. At his inauguration, he said:

_____ *"I am acutely aware that you have not elected me as your President by your ballots, and so I ask you to confirm me as your President with your prayers. And I hope that such prayers will also be the first of many.*

If you have not chosen me by secret ballot, neither have I gained office by any secret promises. I have not campaigned either for the Presidency or the Vice Presidency. I have not subscribed to any partisan platform. I am indebted to no man, and only to one woman—my dear wife—as I begin this very difficult job."[12]

Ford entered the presidency with most Americans giving him the benefit of the doubt, a trust he lost when he pardoned Richard Nixon a month later. This action brought Ford severe criticism from the public, political scientists, and politicians; and he was, thereafter, unable to achieve any wins that might have restored his reputation with the public. His economic policies were unsuccessful at addressing the increasingly severe recession, which had also evolved to include a serious energy problem.

A Presidential Misstep

While Americans who lived through the Ford presidency remembered him as a benign if not particularly effective executive, Ford's legacy has been less than flattering. He developed, for instance, a reputation for clumsiness that stayed with him throughout his life and became one of the most common ways he was lampooned while in office. In December 1975, a rainy day, Ford slipped while descending the steps from Air Force One, a misstep that was recorded on video and circulated through the media. He had another high-profile trip while ascending the steps of Air Force One on another occasion and newspapers also circulated a report of Ford falling while skiing on a brief retreat from office. In his 1976 campaign, Ford missed a doorway and bumped his head while giving a speech on a train platform. The sketch comedy series Saturday Night Live capitalized on Ford's apparent clumsiness with comedian Chevy Chase portraying Ford in a series of cold open sketches in which Chase, an accomplished physical comic, would trip, stumble, or bungle some other physical activity. Ford was likely the only president lampooned with slapstick more often than through political criticism. One of the most common jokes told about him during his presidency was that Ford's vice president was a "banana peel" away from becoming president.

Ford's reputation for clumsiness might have begun long before his presidency. While serving on the *USS Monterey* during World War II, Ford was nearly washed overboard when the ship was hit by a typhoon in December of 1944. This tropical storm resulted in the destruction of three destroyers and over 800 deaths. When the *Monterey* was hit, Ford was on deck. High winds caused the ship to roll 25 degrees, and Ford lost his footing and slid towards the edge of the deck. Apparently, Ford's foot got caught on the railing of a drain, which saved him from being thrown from the deck of the ship but also became part of his legacy of clumsiness. In 2017, the U.S. Navy unveiled a new, $12.8 billion aircraft carrier dubbed the

USS Gerald R. Ford in Ford's honor and featuring a statue of Ford standing on the railing of the ship's drain that saved his life and contributed to his uncoordinated reputation.[a]

Work Used

a. Mieczkowski, Yanek. *Gerald Ford and the Challenges of the 1970s*. Louisville, KY: U P of Kentucky, 2005.

On the foreign policy front, Ford achieved one victory when he sent troops to rescue hostages captured by the Cambodian Khmer Rouge. Analysts later criticized the operation, as 41 American soldiers were killed in an operation that rescued only 39 captured sailors. Ford's decision to dispatch troops was also seen by some in Congress as a violation of presidential authority.

One of the most important consequences of the Nixon presidency was the passage of the War Powers Resolution of 1973, an act intended to place a further check on the ability of a president to unilaterally commit American troops or military assets to an armed conflict without consulting Congress. Ford's decision to dispatch troops to deal with the Khmer Rouge was, therefore, not out of line with previous presidential authority as exercised by Nixon, Johnson, Kennedy, Eisenhower, or Truman, and met with the approval of the American people, but it was a violation of presidential power according to the newly established War Powers Act.

Ford had the ignominious honor of being the first president to be treated as a less than serious figure, obvious in frequent jokes about his alleged clumsiness and lack of intelligence, despite his status as one of only three presidents with a graduate degree from an Ivy League university. This treatment of Ford suggests an erosion of faith in the presidency and the government, brought about by years of perceived failure to address long-standing social, economic, and foreign policy issues coupled with the Watergate revelations. Reverence for the presidency ended with Nixon and the office would never again achieve the air of a sacred institution.

CONCLUSION

Nixon's presidency had a dramatic impact on public perception of politics over the longer term. Though many presidents have misled and lied to the public and members of Congress while pursuing secret agendas, the revelation that Nixon had misused his authority for personal gain, to protect himself from perceptions of criminality, and to spy on political opponents showed a government could not be trusted. These events did not cause an immediate souring of public opinion toward the presidency, and many conservatives and Republicans remained committed to Nixon even after his abuses of power were revealed. As time went on, however, public opinion of Nixon and his actions nosedived and never recovered. The next chapter reveals one of the most respected public figures. President Jimmy Carter was faced with major challenges—from restoring public trust in the office of the president to addressing the economic problems left by the Nixon administration.

DISCUSSION QUESTIONS

♦ How do Nixon's abuses of presidential power compare to those allegedly committed by Donald Trump?

♦ How might Gerald Ford have retained a higher level of public support after taking office?

♦ How did the War Powers Act represent an attempt to rebalance federal powers?

♦ Would Nixon have been impeached and removed from office if he hadn't resigned? Explain your answer.

Works Used

Cowie, Jefferson. *Stayin' Alive: The 1970s and the Last Days of the Working Class*. New York: The New P, 2010.

Cuddy, Brian. "Was It Legal for the U.S. to Bomb Cambodia?" *New York Times*. 12 Dec. 2017. www.nytimes.com/2017/12/12/opinion/america-cambodia-bomb.html.

Ford, Gerald R. "Gerald R. Ford's Remarks Upon Taking the Oath of Office as President." *Ford Library Museum*. 2019. www.fordlibrarymuseum.gov/library/speeches/740001.asp.

Matthews, Christopher. *Kennedy & Nixon: The Rivalry that Shapes Postwar America*. New York: Touchstone Books, 1996.

Mitchell, Greg. *Tricky Dick and the Pink Lady: Richard Nixon vs Helen Gahagan Douglas-Sexual Politics and the Red Scare, 1950*. New York: Random House, 1998.

Nixon, Richard. "The Last Press Conference." *Nixon Foundation*. 2019. www.nixonfoundation.org/2017/11/55-years-ago-last-press-conference/.

"Presidential Approval Ratings—Gallup Historical Statistics and Trends." *Gallup*. 2019. news.gallup.com/poll/116677/presidential-approval-ratings-gallup-historical-statistics-trends.aspx.

"Richard Milhouse Nixon." *Naval History and Heritage Command*. U.S. Navy. www.history.navy.mil/research/histories/biographies-list/bios-n/nixon-richard.html.

Rudenstine, David. *The Day the Presses Stopped: A History of the Pentagon Papers Case*. Berkeley, CA: U of California P, 1996.

Thomson-DeVeaux, Amelia. "It Took A Long Time for Republicans to Abandon Nixon." *FiveThirtyEight*. 9 Oct. 2019. fivethirtyeight.com/features/it-took-a-long-time-for-republicans-to-abandon-nixon/.

"Transcript of a Recording of a Meeting Between the President and H.R. Haldeman in the Oval Office on June 23, 1972, from 10:04 to 11:39 AM," *PBS*. www.pbs.org/newshour/extra/app/uploads/2013/11/Smoking-Gun-Transcript-v-2.pdf.

Wills, Garry. *Nixon Agonistes: The Crisis of the Self-Made Man*. Open Road Media, 2017.

Introduction

James Earl "Jimmy" Carter is one of America's most respected public figures. A lifelong champion of equal rights and integration, Carter was an activist president who had the misfortune of entering office at a time when trust of the presidency had been badly damaged by the misdeeds of Richard Nixon. Carter faced an uphill battle to maintain public support, to work with Congress, and to address the economic problems he inherited from the previous administration. Though he succeeded in significant federal reforms and took a personal role in promoting more responsible consumerism, Carter lacked the power to challenge the economic establishment and ended up appearing as a weak and ineffectual president, a perception furthered by demonstrably negative press coverage. Lacking sufficient support to enact the reform agenda he'd envisioned, Carter nonetheless made a major mark in becoming the first president to successfully arbitrate on the foreign stage since Theodore Roosevelt.

Topics covered in this chapter include:

- Cold War
- Israel-Egypt Peace Process
- Consumerism and the oil crisis
- Resource conservation

This Chapter Discusses the Following Source Document:
Energy and the National Goals—A Crisis of Confidence, Jimmy
  Carter, July 15, 1979

We the People

Moralistic Progressivism
Jimmy Carter (1977–1981)

Jimmy Carter is one of the most admired men to hold the office of president. Entering office on the heels of the Nixon administration's collapse and in the midst of an energy and economic crisis, the road to public approval was long and difficult, and Congress was set on limiting presidential power. Carter's single term in the office is largely remembered as a failure, but once leaving office, he mounted one of the most successful post-presidential careers in history, becoming respected across partisan lines.

Farming for Civil Rights

James Earl "Jimmy" Carter was born in Georgia into a middle-class family that owned a peanut farm and a general store near the town of Plains, Georgia. Carter graduated as valedictorian of his high school and immediately enlisted for military service. He was admitted to the Naval Academy in Annapolis, Maryland, in 1943 and graduated at the top of his class. After marrying Rosalynn Smith, Carter served in the naval submarine service. Even in the U.S. Navy, Carter's attitude toward civil rights was evident. While his submarine was moored near Bermuda, his crew was invited to attend a "whites only" party on the island; Carter convinced his crew not to attend in protest.[1] He returned home in 1953 upon his father's cancer diagnosis to help revive the family farm.

Jimmy Carter, by Department of Defense, via Wikimedia.

Back in Plains, Carter refused to join a White Citizens' Council group in the aftermath of the controversial *Brown v. Board of Education* Supreme Court ruling that segregation was unconstitutional, despite customers' threats to boycott his business.[2] Even though Carter never bowed to the white supremacist movement, his farm prospered, and he became a powerful member of the local community.

Carter entered the race for the Georgia State Senate, and though he was defeated, proved that his loss was due to voter fraud, and was awarded the election. Carter continued fighting for racial integration, and he and his wife were two of only three people who voted to integrate their Baptist Church. Carter openly criticized laws in the state. He felt that such laws at the national level were meant to discourage integration or African American political power.

Carter ran for governor in 1964 and lost to Lester Maddox, a white supremacist who refused African Americans access to his restaurant, Pickrick. In July of 1964, three African American divinity students attempted to enter Pickrick. Maddox met them in the parking lot armed with an ax handle and bashed their car. He sold ax handles to his customers as a symbol of integration resistance.[3] Carter ran for governor a second time, resolving to end white supremacist hold on his city and state and positioned himself as a segregationist. Although he never openly stated that he supported segregation, he campaigned against public bussing. The strategy was so successful that the progressive press refused to endorse him. Carter won a close race, winning 49 percent of the vote and surprised his constituents by giving a speech calling for the end of segregation. It was a bold, strategic move that won him national acclaim. Carter's inaugural address as Georgia's new governor was carried in the national press. As governor, Carter increased African American participation in the state government and opposed any measure to reinstate segregation of schools or businesses.

Governor Carter positioned himself for the presidency, though he had not built a strong national profile. When he announced his candidacy for the 1976 presidential race, the *Atlanta Constitution* ran the headline, "Jimmy Who Is Running for What!?" Carter's lack of national attention was a function of the way he chose to run his campaign. With no major corporate contributions and little in the way of funding, Carter was running as a relatively unknown dark horse in a sea of major contenders. His strategy began with an effort to win the Iowa state vote for the nomination, which he did, giving him the power to compete for the party's nomination.[4] In many ways, Carter's lack of national recognition meant that he had few enemies on the national field and that he was able to appeal to a growing segment of the American people disillusioned with government insiders after the Watergate scandal. Carter portrayed himself as an outsider, and his relatively underfunded campaign seemed to back this up.

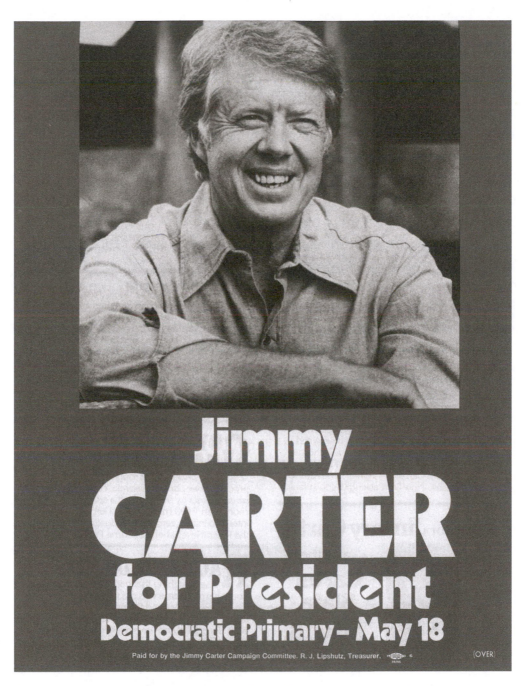

Jimmy Carter's presidential campaign was not financed by major corporations. Via Wikimedia.

Carter won the Democratic nomination and entered the race against Ford with a major lead. However, he nearly lost his advantage after a *Playboy* magazine interview in which he stated, "I've looked on a lot of women with lust. I've committed adultery in my heart many times." It was a shockingly honest admission that drew major public and media scrutiny. Carter had been urged to do the interview by members of his campaign staff, responding to criticisms that he was too "pious" to be president. Carter lost his polling lead against Ford, but after several weeks, the controversy died down and some members of the electorate even felt that Carter had perhaps made himself slightly more relatable.[5] It was a close election, but Carter won 40.8 million votes to Ford's 39.1 million. Only 55 percent of the electorate voted in the election, a 2 percent reduction from the previous election.[6] The low voter turnout was another sign that the electorate had become increasingly disillusioned with the presidency. Nevertheless, the Democratic Party held both the Senate and the House, and Carter entered the presidency with a narrow popular mandate and significant congressional support.

A Partially Empowered President

As president, Carter had a poor relationship with both Congress and the press; by extension, his perception among the people soured as well. He entered office with a reform agenda and made good on this promise by fighting with Congress over bills he described as wasteful and perhaps even corrupt. Carter initiated environmental efforts, but legislators altered or defeated most of Carter's domestic efforts, making him look ineffectual. Carter's inability to push through more of his national agenda was the result of his limited public support, which gave him limited leverage over the legislature.

The most significant domestic issue of his presidency was the energy crisis, a complex issue resulting from a steady increase in oil imports during previous administrations. Between 1973 and 1976, oil imports rose

by more than 65 percent, and the United States had become the global leader in oil consumption, utilizing more than twice as much oil per capita than Europe. Carter was the first president to legitimately try to promote an energy reform, creating the Department of Energy to manage domestic supplies and to research alternative energy. The situation became a crisis when the Organization of Petroleum Exporting Countries (OPEC) raised prices on domestic oil by more than 300 percent, creating a huge spike in gas prices and long lines at gas stations. By and large, Carter's energy policies were a success, reducing foreign oil consumption from 48 percent in 1976 to 40 percent in 1980, but the media and legislators did not credit him with the win. For consumers, high oil prices and shortages were the most visible part of the equation. Congressional solutions were shaped by an energy industry that had more control over the legislature than the president. For instance, when Carter vetoed a bill repealing an import fee on foreign oil, Congress overrode the veto, one of the few times in history that the majority party overrode a veto from their own president. Oil industry lobbyists watered down Carter's efforts to promote renewable energy development, action in which legislators were complicit, leaving Carter looking powerless and ineffective.

One of the most significant foreign policy issues of Carter's presidency was also the most damaging. The 1979 revolution in Iran led to more than 50 American staff of the U.S. embassy in Tehran being taken hostage. Militants stormed the American embassy and took 66 American hostages, offering to trade them for an apology from the American government for the removal of their prime minister, and a trial for puppet dictator Shah Pahlavi. Carter's attempt at secret negotiations to rescue the hostages failed, so he authorized a secret rescue operation. One of the eight rescue helicopters crashed in the Iranian desert, killing eight soldiers. Plus, Iranian militants hid the hostages in separate areas, making rescue more difficult. Carter's use of military power, without congressional authorization, was in line with many of the nation's past administrations, but the

passage of the War Powers Act after the Watergate scandal caused legislators, and the media, to accuse Carter of recklessness. Eventually, Carter defused the situation by promising to not interfere in Iranian politics and arranging independent mediation to settle financial disputes between the two countries. In return, the Iranian militants released the American hostages. This situation, less than a year before Carter's re-election, was a major blow, and his popularity plummeted again.[7]

In 1979, historian Gebhard Schweigler wrote that Carter seemed like a "president without power" for most of his administration except in his unexpected return to presidential arbitration. Following the Yom Kippur War of 1973, Egypt and Israel were stuck in political deadlock during which Israel fought a brief, but brutal, series of battles with Egypt and Syria. In September of 1978, Carter invited Israeli Prime Minister Menachem Begin and Egyptian President Anwar Sadat to meet with him at Camp David to discuss a peace agreement. Largely due to Carter's efforts—leveraging U.S. aid, and agreeing to help Israel rebuild military bases in return for Israel's ceding control of the Sinai Peninsula to Egypt—an agreement between Egypt and Israel was eventually reached.[8]

The historic Camp David Accords, signed on September 17, 1978, were a major victory in the field of international diplomacy. Hostilities between Egypt and Israel had been ongoing since the creation of the Israeli state. Carter's management of this difficult negotiation was a significant expression of presidential power; he was the first president to make such effective diplomatic use of the executive office since Theodore Roosevelt negotiated the end of the Russo-Japanese War of 1905. Carter's public approval rating went up thanks to his efforts at Camp David, but while Begin and Sadat were both awarded the Nobel Peace Prize of 1979, Carter's role was scarcely recognized.

Losing the Presidency

Carter's average approval rating during his time in office was around 45 percent, which is lower than Ford's or Nixon's. In early 1977 Carter was polling at 75 percent, and by June 1979 it had fallen to 28 percent.[9] What Carter lacked most was public image. Despite significant accomplishments and successes that rival presidents whose time in office was longer and popularity higher, he failed to persuade the American people, or legislators, to support his vision for America's future.

Carter was often depicted as "moralistic" and "holier than thou," and his commitment to the principles of Christian activism and equal rights often put him at odds with Congress. His refusal to compromise on the bills he introduced cost him support, and when he did reach out to the American people, his forthright manner was sometimes perceived as arrogant or cold.

A key moment in Carter's presidency came after a televised speech about the energy crisis, called both the "malaise" speech and the "crisis of confidence" speech. Although the speech was initially well received, Carter's subsequent purge of several cabinet members created the perception of an administration in crisis, and the short-lived goodwill that Carter engendered with this speech disappeared. Moreover, although the speech was initially viewed in a positive light, it became one of the most frequently criticized political speeches of Carter's career.

ENERGY AND THE NATIONAL GOALS—A CRISIS OF CONFIDENCE

Jimmy Carter
July 15, 1979
Source Document Excerpt

Good Evening:

This a special night for me. Exactly three years ago, on July 15, 1976, I accepted the nomination of my party to run for President of the United States. I promised you a President who is not isolated from the people, who feels your pain, and who shares your dreams, and who draws his strength and his wisdom from you.

During the past three years I've spoken to you on many occasions about national concerns, the energy crisis, reorganizing the government, our nation's economy, and issues of war and especially peace. But over those years the subjects of the speeches, the talks, and the press conferences have become increasingly narrow, focused more and more on what the isolated world of Washington thinks is important. Gradually, you've heard more and more about what the government thinks or what the government should be doing and less and less about our nation's hopes, our dreams, and our vision of the future.

Ten days ago, I had planned to speak to you again about a very important subject—energy. For the fifth time I would have described the urgency of the problem and laid out a series of legislative recommendations to the Congress. But as I was preparing to speak, I began to ask myself the same question that I now know has been troubling many of you: Why have we not been able to get together as a nation to resolve our serious energy problem?

It's clear that the true problems of our nation are much deeper—deeper than gasoline lines or energy shortages, deeper even than inflation or recession. And I realize more than ever that as President I need your help. So, I decided to reach out and to listen to the voices of America.

I invited to Camp David people from almost every segment of our society—business and labor, teachers and preachers, governors, mayors, and private citizens. And then I left Camp David to listen to other Americans, men and women like you. It has been an extraordinary ten days, and I want to share with you what I've heard.

First of all, I got a lot of personal advice. Let me quote a few of the typical comments that I wrote down.

continued

This from a southern governor: "Mr. President, you are not leading this nation—you're just managing the government."

"You don't see the people enough anymore."

"Some of your Cabinet members don't seem loyal. There is not enough discipline among your disciples."

"Don't talk to us about politics or the mechanics of government, but about an understanding of our common good."

"Mr. President, we're in trouble. Talk to us about blood and sweat and tears."

"If you lead, Mr. President, we will follow."

Many people talked about themselves and about the condition of our nation. This from a young woman in Pennsylvania: "I feel so far from government. I feel like ordinary people are excluded from political power."

And this from a young Chicano: "Some of us have suffered from recession all our lives."

"Some people have wasted energy, but others haven't had anything to waste."

And this from a religious leader: "No material shortage can touch the important things like God's love for us or our love for one another."

And I like this one particularly from a black woman who happens to be the mayor of a small Mississippi town: "The big shots are not the only ones who are important. Remember, you can't sell anything on Wall Street unless someone digs it up somewhere else first."

This kind of summarized a lot of other statements: "Mr. President, we are confronted with a moral and a spiritual crisis."

Several of our discussions were on energy, and I have a notebook full of comments and advice. I'll read just a few.

"We can't go on consuming forty percent more energy then we produce. When we import oil we are also importing inflation plus unemployment."

"We've got to use what we have. The Middle East has only five percent of the world's energy, but the United States has twenty-four percent."

And this is one of the most vivid statements: "Our neck is stretched over the fence and OPEC has a knife."

"There will be other cartels and other shortages. American wisdom and

Energy and the National Goals—A Crisis of Confidence
continued

courage right now can set a path to follow in the future."

This was a good one: "Be bold, Mr. President. We may make mistakes, but we are ready to experiment."

And this one from a labor leader got to the heart of it: "The real issue is freedom. We must deal with the energy problem on a war footing."

And the last that I'll read: "When we enter the moral equivalent of war, Mr. President, don't issue us BB guns."

These ten days confirmed my belief in the decency and the strength and the wisdom of the American people, but it also bore out some of my longstanding concerns about our nation's underlying problems.

I know, of course, being President, that government actions and legislation can be very important. That's why I've worked hard to put my campaign promises into law, and I have to admit, with just mixed success. But after listening to the American people, I have been reminded again that all the legislation in the world can't fix what's wrong with America. So, I want to speak to you first tonight about a subject even more serious than energy or inflation. I want to talk to you right now about a fundamental threat to American democracy.

I do not mean our political and civil liberties. They will endure. And I do not refer to the outward strength of America, a nation that is at peace tonight everywhere in the world, with unmatched economic power and military might.

The threat is nearly invisible in ordinary ways.

It is a crisis of confidence.

It is a crisis that strikes at the very heart and soul and spirit of our national will. We can see this crisis in the growing doubt about the meaning of our own lives and in the loss of a unity of purpose for our nation.

The erosion of our confidence in the future is threatening to destroy the social and the political fabric of America.

The confidence that we have always had as a people is not simply some romantic dream or a proverb in a dusty book that we read just on the Fourth of July. It is the idea which founded our nation and has guided our development as a people. Confidence in the future has supported everything else—public institutions and private enterprise, our own families, and the very Constitution of the United States. Confidence has defined our course and has served as a link between generations. We've always believed in something called

continued

progress. We've always had a faith that the days of our children would be better than our own.

Our people are losing that faith, not only in government itself but in the ability as citizens to serve as the ultimate rulers and shapers of our democracy. As a people we know our past and we are proud of it. Our progress has been part of the living history of America, even the world. We always believed that we were part of a great movement of humanity itself called democracy, involved in the search for freedom; and that belief has always strengthened us in our purpose. But just as we are losing our confidence in the future, we are also beginning to close the door on our past.

In a nation that was proud of hard work, strong families, close-knit communities, and our faith in God, too many of us now tend to worship self-indulgence and consumption. Human identity is no longer defined by what one does, but by what one owns. But we've discovered that owning things and consuming things does not satisfy our longing for meaning. We've learned that piling up material goods cannot fill the emptiness of lives which have no confidence or purpose.

The symptoms of this crisis of the American spirit are all around us. For the first time in the history of our country a majority of our people believe that the next five years will be worse than the past five years. Two-thirds of our people do not even vote. The productivity of American workers is actually dropping, and the willingness of Americans to save for the future has fallen below that of all other people in the Western world.

As you know, there is a growing disrespect for government and for churches and for schools, the news media, and other institutions. This is not a message of happiness or reassurance, but it is the truth and it is a warning.

These changes did not happen overnight. They've come upon us gradually over the last generation, years that were filled with shocks and tragedy.

We were sure that ours was a nation of the ballot, not the bullet, until the murders of John Kennedy and Robert Kennedy and Martin Luther King, Jr. We were taught that our armies were always invincible and our causes were always just, only to suffer the agony of Vietnam. We respected the Presidency as a place of honor until the shock of Watergate.

We remember when the phrase "sound as a dollar" was an expression of absolute dependability, until ten years of inflation began to shrink our dollar and our savings. We believed that our

Energy and the National Goals—A Crisis of Confidence continued

nation's resources were limitless until 1973 when we had to face a growing dependence on foreign oil.

These wounds are still very deep. They have never been healed.

Looking for a way out of this crisis, our people have turned to the Federal Government and found it isolated from the mainstream of our nation's life. Washington, D.C., has become an island. The gap between our citizens and our government has never been so wide. The people are looking for honest answers, not easy answers; clear leadership, not false claims and evasiveness and politics as usual.

What you see too often in Washington and elsewhere around the country is a system of government that seems incapable of action. You see a Congress twisted and pulled in every direction by hundreds of well-financed and powerful special interests.

You see every extreme position defended to the last vote, almost to the last breath by one unyielding group or another. You often see a balanced and a fair approach that demands sacrifice, a little sacrifice from everyone, abandoned like an orphan without support and without friends.

Often you see paralysis and stagnation and drift. You don't like it, and neither do I. What can we do?

First of all, we must face the truth, and then we can change our course. We simply must have faith in each other, faith in our ability to govern ourselves, and faith in the future of this nation. Restoring that faith and that confidence to America is now the most important task we face. It is a true challenge of this generation of Americans.

One of the visitors to Camp David last week put it this way: "We've got to stop crying and start sweating, stop talking and start walking, stop cursing and start praying. The strength we need will not come from the White House, but from every house in America."

We know the strength of America. We are strong. We can regain our unity. We can regain our confidence. We are the heirs of generations who survived threats much more powerful and awesome than those that challenge us now. Our fathers and mothers were strong men and women who shaped a new society during the Great Depression, who fought world wars and who carved out a new charter of peace for the world.

We ourselves are the same Americans who just ten years ago put a man on the moon. We are the generation that dedicated our society to the pursuit of human rights and equality. And we are the generation that will win the war on the energy

continued

problem and in that process, rebuild the unity and confidence of America.

We are at a turning point in our history. There are two paths to choose. One is a path I've warned about tonight, the path that leads to fragmentation and self-interest. Down that road lies a mistaken idea of freedom, the right to grasp for ourselves some advantage over others. That path would be one of constant conflict between narrow interests ending in chaos and immobility. It is a certain route to failure.

All the traditions of our past, all the lessons of our heritage, all the promises of our future point to another path—the path of common purpose and the restoration of American values. That path leads to true freedom for our nation and ourselves. We can take the first steps down that path as we begin to solve our energy problem.[10]

Kevin Mattson, author of the book *What the Heck Are You Up To, Mr. President?,* told National Public Radio (NPR), "Carter goes out there and he essentially condemns the American way of life. He says our consumerism, our materialism have really gotten in the way of this problem."[11] The initial positive reaction to the speech indicates, to Mattson, that a good portion of the American people were receptive to being called out on their faults. But the message of the speech was twisted in the weeks that followed. Critics accused Carter of arrogance or even of passing the blame onto the American people for the energy crisis, and this perception dominated public opinion in the years that followed. With dismal public approval, Carter was no match for the telegenic campaign of Ronald Reagan, who presented a promise to lead a rebirth of American moderate conservatism, and mastered the art of political rhetoric and jingoism. Next to this trained and experienced actor, Carter seemed moribund and unexciting. After losing the election, Carter began using his fame to participate in numerous human rights and charitable causes. He founded the Carter Center at Atlanta's Emory University and became the most prominent advocate and spokesperson for the Habitat for Humanity charity. On several

occasions, future presidents called upon Carter to participate in particularly sensitive State Department negotiations, recognizing his documented skill in this regard. In 2002, Carter was finally recognized with a Nobel Peace Prize. In his acceptance speech, Carter admonished the American people on their failure to commit to human rights and on the continuation of racism. At the end of his speech, he admonished America's leaders for pursuing military solutions instead of diplomatic ones.

Energy and the National Goals—A Crisis of Confidence continued

War may sometimes be a necessary evil. But no matter how necessary, it is always an evil, never a good. We will not learn how to live together in peace by killing each other's children.

The bond of our common humanity is stronger than the divisiveness of our fears and prejudices. God gives us the capacity for choice. We can choose to alleviate suffering. We can choose to work together for peace. We can make these changes—and we must.[12]

Carter refused to pander to popular perceptions of American exceptionalism and was willing to call attention to the nation's political failures and to the failure of the American people to live up the ideals they so often claimed as American values. This tendency for blunt honesty and Carter's frequent failure to compromise hindered his presidency, but served him well in the years that followed his presidency, giving him perhaps the most successful post-presidential career in American history. Though he has rarely been ranked among America's most effective presidents, his enduring commitment to making America a better nation, and the world a better place, saw him achieve a stature that few presidents before or after approached.

CONCLUSION

Carter's personal style, and moralistic stance on many issues, made him a less relatable president to those members of the American public who sought reassurance rather than moral rectitude. Although this weakened Carter's presidency, he also suffered from the timing of his presidency, coming as it did amidst a severe downturn in public perception of politics in general, and the presidency specifically, following the Nixon presidency and all that entailed. Historians and political scientists have since recognized Carter's sincere efforts and the value of some of his policy proposals but his failure to form strong partnerships in Congress and to maintain the trust of the people reduce estimates of his "presidential greatness." Nevertheless, Carter enjoyed the most successful post-presidency career, becoming a symbol of American goodness and humanitarianism in the decades after he left office. The next chapter follows the very popular President Ronald Reagan.

DISCUSSION QUESTIONS

♦ Was Carter correct in his assessment of the energy situation that he presented in his "crisis of confidence" speech? Why or why not?

♦ How does Carter's personality and personal convictions play into his use of presidential power?

♦ How did actions of the Nixon administration impact media treatment of Carter during his presidency?

♦ Does Carter's stance on civil rights improve his reputation? Why or why not?

♦ Is it fair for a president to be judged on the state of economy during his or her first and second year in office? Why or why not?

Works Used

"1976 Presidential General Election Results." *US Election Atlas*. 2019. uselectionatlas.org/RESULTS/national.php?year=1976.

Berman, Ari. *Give Us the Ballot: The Modern Struggle for Voting Rights in America*. New York: Farrar, Straus and Giroux, 2015.

Berman, Ari. "Op-Ed: How Jimmy Carter Championed Civil Rights — and Ronald Reagan Didn't." *Los Angeles Times*. 3 Sept. 2015. www.latimes.com/opinion/op-ed/la-oe-0906-berman-carter-civil-rights-20150906-story.html.

Carter, Jimmy. "Energy and the National Goals—A Crisis of Confidence." *American Rhetoric*. 2019. www.americanrhetoric.com/speeches/jimmycartercrisisofconfidence.htm.

Carter, Jimmy. "Nobel Lecture." *Nobel Prize*. 10 Dec. 2002. www.nobelprize.org/prizes/peace/2002/carter/lecture/.

Emerson, Bo. "When Jimmy Carter Lusted in His Heart." *AJC*. Atlanta Journal Constitution. 28 Sept. 2017. www.ajc.com/news/when-jimmy-carter-lusted-his-heart/kzdD5pLXvT3qnf5RyJlIiK/.

"Examining Carter's 'Malaise Speech,' 30 Years Later." *NPR*. 12 July 2009. www.npr.org/templates/story/story.php?storyId=106508243.

Farber, David R. *Taken Hostage: The Iran Hostage Crisis and America's First Encounter with Radical Islam*. Princeton U P, 2005.

Frank, Jeffrey. "The Primary Experiment: Jimmy Who?" *The New Yorker*. Condé Nast. 1 May 2015. www.newyorker.com/news/daily-comment/the-primary-experiment-jimmy-who.

Kucharsky, David. *The Man from Plains*. New York: Harper & Row, 1976.

Morris, Kenneth E. *Jimmy Carter, American Moralist*. Athens, GA: U of Georgia P, 1996.

"Presidential Approval Ratings—Gallup Historical Statistics and Trends." *Gallup*. 2019. news.gallup.com/poll/116677/presidential-approval-ratings-gallup-historical-statistics-trends.aspx.

Schweigler, Gebhard. "Carter's Dilemmas: Presidential Power and Its Limits." *The World Today*, vol. 35, no 2, 1979, pp. 46–55. *JSTOR*, www.jstor.org/stable/40395096.

Introduction

Ronald Reagan does not boast one of the most significant records of achievement. His administration's economic reforms have been judged faulty and his foreign policy accomplishments were moderate at best. However, Reagan was a very popular president and has remained popular, in part because there are no other conservative presidents of the modern era who managed the same level of cross-ideological appeal, and in part due to nostalgia for the 1980s. The perception of the 1980s as a period of economic greatness belies the reality of high poverty rates, especially in minority communities, increased friction between the government and the populace, and the beginning of the era of mass incarceration, created by faulty drug control policies enacted for popular appeal rather than guided by experts in the field.

Topics covered in this chapter include:
- End of the Cold War
- The Iran Hostage Crisis
- The Iran-Contra controversy
- "Say No To Drugs"

This Chapter Discusses the Following Source Document:
Hart, Benjamin. "Concerns About Reagan's Mental Health Were Handled Very Differently Than Concerns About Trump's." *New York Magazine*, January 14, 2018

Acting Like a President
Ronald Reagan (1981–1989)

Ronald Reagan broke the presidential mold in many ways. A successful radio personality turned actor, Reagan came into office during a time of low public opinion of the office of the presidency. His presidency marks a turning point for the Republican Party, and many modern American conservatives adhere to what has since been called "Reagan Republicanism."

Presidential Player

Reagan was born in 1911 in Tampico, Illinois, and grew up in a Democratic household. His father, Jack, worked for Franklin Roosevelt's Works Progress Administration and campaigned on behalf of democratic candidates. Reagan lived a middle-class life, and his father suffered from alcoholism. He attended Eureka College, where he earned a degree in economics and sociology.

Ronald Reagan, via Wikimedia.

Reagan's first job after college was as a sportscaster for radio station WOC in Iowa. He achieved success in the broadcasting world, eventually covering college basketball and major league baseball. Reagan traveled to California in 1937, while following the Chicago Cubs as an announcer, and hired a talent agent. He was offered a fairly lucrative contract from Warner Brothers studio and appeared in 52 films by 1957.[1]

During World War II, Reagan became a second lieutenant in the U.S. Army Cavalry Reserves and was assigned to the army's entertainment unit, where he narrated recruitment films and appeared in propaganda pictures such as *Rear Gunner* (1943) and *Jap Zero* (1943). He was also cast in the musical *This Is the Army* (1943), produced by famed director Irving Berlin and a fundraiser for war-related charitable causes. His first marriage, to actress Jane Wyman, ended in divorce, and in 1952 Reagan married Nancy Davis.

Film critics generally rank Reagan as a poor to middling actor, yet he left an important behind-the-scenes legacy in the film industry based on the skills that fans would admire during his presidency. In 1960, Reagan was president of the Screen Actors Guild (SAG), and he led a group of big-name SAG actors in a strike that resulted in the creation of the residual system, wherein union actors are entitled to residual payments. Reagan also helped to negotiate terms by which working actors were eligible to receive pensions and health insurance.[2]

Reagan started his career in national politics working for the Nixon campaign in 1960, delivering speeches and writing articles. He then worked on the presidential campaign of Arizona Senator and Republican Party presidential candidate Barry Goldwater in 1964. Barry Goldwater was a conservative political theorist who has been credited with reinventing the Republican Party with his own 1964 campaign, in which he lost to Lyndon Johnson. He and Reagan are often seen as creating a new Republican base, one which opposed civil rights legislation established by Johnson, allegedly on constitutional grounds. Reagan turned a blind eye to the way that his policies impacted African Americans. In 1971, while Reagan was governor of California, the United Nations voted to recognize the People's Republic of China, over U.S. objections. Reagan called President Nixon to complain about this. The tape of his conversation was released in 2019, with Reagan calling the delegates of African countries that voted to recognize China "monkeys" who were "uncomfortable wearing shoes."[3]

Reagan won election as governor of California in 1966 running on a platform light on policy but heavy on charm. He was a moderate governor, preferring compromise to ideological posturing. As such, Reagan won endorsements by a number of more liberal organizations, like the Urban Institute and state environmentalist groups. He retired from the governorship in 1967 and began writing speeches and articles, and stayed in the media with frequent appearances on television and radio. In 1976, he fought against the Republican nomination, but party bosses backed incumbent Gerald Ford.[4]

Reagan won the Republican nomination for the 1980 election against Jimmy Carter. Dissatisfaction with government and a hunger for a political shake-up was stronger than Carter's incumbent advantage or popular appeal. Reagan promised to expand military spending to ensure that America beat Russia in the Cold War, to cut taxes and reduce environmental regulation to promote business, and generally attacked "big government." In debates with Carter, Reagan emerged the clear victor, his acting and speaking experience a major advantage. His outsider status was a clear advantage in an environment of distrust of government, and he was able to portray Carter as a government stooge.

The campaign of independent John Anderson, a progressive liberal whose policies were left of Carter's, was another blow to the Carter campaign. However, even without Anderson's entrance to the race, it was unlikely that Carter would have won. Reagan won 43.9 million votes to 35.4

million for Carter and 5.7 million for Anderson. Though the Democrats maintained control of the House, Republicans gained 34 house seats and took 12 seats to control the Senate for the first time in a decade. The electoral margin, and the accompanying legislative victories, gave Reagan a clear mandate, and he entered office on the promise to be the great conservative reformer of his time.[5]

The Great Economic Strategist

Reagan's two-term presidency, 1980 to 1989, was seen by many Republicans as a golden age. Reagan was the most popular Republican president of the modern era and marked a resurgence of American conservatism after the embarrassment of Nixon. There is a mythos surrounding the Reagan presidency, despite it not ranking among the most successful in terms of achieving campaign objectives.

One of Reagan's most common promises was to reduce the size of the government. The small-government, states-rights approach had long been popular among conservatives, but Reagan expanded the role and size of the federal government. Government employment rose from 4.9 million to 5.3 million. Reagan came into office with a federal budget of $599 billion in revenue, versus $678 billion in spending (a deficit of $79 billion), and left office with a federal budget of $909 billion in revenue, $1.1 trillion in spending (a deficit of $155 billion).[6]

One of the things that Reagan is most often praised for is cutting taxes, and his Economic Tax Recovery Act has been cited by Republicans as *the* template for fiscal conservatism. Taxes on large corporations fell by around 24 percent, but middle-class and working-class families saw little to no benefit. Affluent families at the top of the income bracket saw their incomes rise by around 9 percent, while middle-class families saw, at best, a 1 percent increase. Families at the bottom end of the income spectrum saw an average decline in income of 8 percent. The Reagan administration exacerbated income inequality that continues to rank among America's most pressing economic issues in the twenty-first century.

Another Reagan legacy is the reduction in federal spending on housing and rental subsidies, which decreased from $26 billion to $8 billion. With homelessness rates rising, there was a surge in media coverage, and Reagan put the onus back on society itself when, in 1981, he suggested that if "every church and synagogue would take in 10 welfare families," the problem could be solved. Peter Drier, director of the Urban and Environmental Policy Department at Occidental College in Los Angeles, states: "Every park bench in America—everywhere a homeless person sleeps—should have Ronald Reagan's name on it."[7]

Two years into his presidency, more than 17,000 businesses had gone under and unemployment had hit a record high. The Reagan tax cuts were eliminated, and the economic situation began to improve, enough so that by 1984 Reagan was able to claim credit for a strong year of economic growth. Some say that credit rightfully belongs to Paul Volker, an appointee of Jimmy Carter and chairman of the Federal Reserve, whose plan to control inflation began to take effect while Reagan was in office.[8]

The Reagan administration also took initiative to combat the drug problem by treating drug use as a crime. This approach is considered by some an ineffective and often counterproductive way to address the issue. Previous presidents invested in this strategy with little result, and Reagan increased penalties for drug possession, sales, smuggling, and abuse, and also launched the "Just Say No" to drugs campaign. Abuse and addiction rates rose substantially over the course of Reagan's two terms, while increased penalties worsened America's mass incarceration problem.[9] The approach also led to the militarization of police, and this led to a dramatic increase in the violence surrounding the drug trade, with a spike in drug-related murders and injuries and attacks on police.[10]

Diplomacy and Détente

Internationally, Reagan has been described as the most openly anti-Communist president. His strategy was to abandon the détente policy in place under Nixon, Ford, and Carter, and aggressively push Russia toward a bargain. To force negotiation with the Soviet Union, Reagan proposed a massive increase in military spending and the nation's nuclear arsenal, increasing federal debt and spending.

Perhaps Reagan's crowning achievement in foreign policy came with his historic peace negotiations with reform-minded Russian leader Mikhail Gorbachev. Reagan was openly hostile toward the Soviet Union during his first term, calling Russia an "evil empire." He drew acclaim, criticism, and mockery for his proposal to build an orbital weapons system to counter nuclear assault. During his second term, a series of meetings between Reagan and Gorbachev led to substantive diplomatic improvements and, ultimately, to the first nuclear non-proliferation agreements. The achievement was seen by many as having ended the Cold War, but Reagan has said that most of the credit belongs to Gorbachev.[11]

Reagan was in office when mutual mass destruction was already assured in the case of open war between the United States and Russia. The continual hostilities between the United States and Russia (i.e., Russia's misinformation campaign to support Donald Trump's presidential campaign in 2016), prove that competition for global supremacy and economic dominance between the United States and Russia is ongoing. While Reagan did not actually solve any of the political problems between the United States and Russia, the Reagan era was when most Americans stopped taking the idea of nuclear war seriously, explaining why Reagan is as popular in presidential polls in the twenty-first century as when he was in office.

The second prong of Reagan's anti-communist effort was to utilize overt and covert military means to support anti-communist movements. In

Central America, the administration funded brutal civil wars in El Salvador, Nicaragua, and Guatemala. Elizabeth Oglesby, associate professor of Latin American studies at the University of Arizona, said of these clandestine U.S. efforts in an interview with *Vice*, "Hundreds of thousands of people were displaced in the 1980s. People were fleeing violence and massacres and political persecution that the United States was either funding directly or at the very minimum, covering up and excusing."[12] The political instability that exists in this region today is a direct result of these policies, most notably the Reagan administration's efforts to counter the rise of Marxist populism.

The biggest scandal of the Reagan presidency, the "Iran-Contra" affair, is an example of how Reagan used presidential power. Until the 1970s, the Central American nation of Nicaragua was controlled by a brutal dictatorship. In the 1970s, a leftist, semi-communist revolutionary group, the Sandinistas, overthrew the dictatorship. The United States, in support of the deposed dictatorial, non-communist government, gave arms and funds to support the anti-Sandinista group known as Contras. The Reagan administration got these funds by secretly and illegally selling weapons to Iran, who was in a war with Iraq. When this arrangement was leaked to the press, there was widespread outrage at participating in two human rights crises, illegally selling arms, and using the proceeds to support an oppressive regime.

If Reagan was fully aware of this arrangement, he is guilty of willfully violating the law. Reagan apologized for his government's actions, maintaining that he had no personal knowledge of these events. If this is true, then Reagan is guilty of poor executive management and of failing to control his administration. The Iran-Contra affair, while the biggest scandal of his presidency, did not seriously damage Reagan's popularity among his supporters.

A frequently repeated myth about the Reagan presidency claims that Reagan's election frightened Iran into releasing American hostages taken captive in 1979. Writing in *Vox*, Amanda Taub says:

——————— *"The story goes that on the day of his inauguration, in January 1981, President Reagan convinced the Iranian regime to free the American Embassy hostages more or less just by glaring harshly in the direction of Tehran, which quailed in the face of his unyielding toughness and released the Americans immediately."*[13]

Carter's team negotiated the release of the American hostages even though the deal was completed on the day of Reagan's inauguration. Historians have proven that the Ayatollah Khomeini delayed releasing the American hostages until Reagan's taking office to deprive the Carter administration of credit.

Presidential Empowerment?

C-Span's 2017 Presidential Historians Survey of 90 historians and biographers rated Ronald Reagan 9th out of 44 American presidents, based on his achievements in "public persuasion."[14] According to Gallup, his overall average approval rating was about 53 percent. His approval rating improved over time, with 50.3 in his first term and 55 percent in his second. Reagan's highest level of approval was around 68 percent, which he achieved twice, and his low was around 35 percent, in the midst of the recession. In Reagan's first election he won 50.7 percent of the popular vote, with 54 percent of the voting age population turning out to the polls. In his second, he won 59 percent of the vote, also with 55 percent turning out to the polls. This is a strong level of popular support, though neither of his elections resulted in a major surge of voter interest.[15] Reagan is far more popular after his presidency and death than he was when in office, and this reflects both the imperfect collective memory of the American people, deteriorating perceptions of government in the years since, and

the fact that Reagan has been remembered for the high points in his career, rather than for his failures.

Was Reagan a powerful president? In terms of helping to establish a power base for the Republican Party, Reagan proved powerful. Reagan helped to bring together the white supremacist, fiscal conservative, moderate libertarian, and conservative hawks to create a more powerful political base for Republicanism. He was not, however, an independent executive, and his administration was a period of party rather than presidential agenda.

Nevertheless, Reagan's popularity gave him privilege, if not exactly presidential power, that many other presidents lacked, shaping the way Americans treated his failures. Major violations of presidential power, such as in the Iran-Contra Deal and secret CIA activities in Latin America and the Middle East, were treated as mistakes rather than violations of the public trust. In this article from *New York* magazine's Intelligencer, Benjamin Hart discusses how issues surrounding Reagan's mental health were handled and how this differs from how issues surrounding the mental health of Donald Trump, a far less-popular president, have been handled.

CONCERNS ABOUT REAGAN'S MENTAL HEALTH WERE HANDLED VERY DIFFERENTLY THAN CONCERNS ABOUT TRUMP'S

Benjamin Hart

New York Magazine

January 14, 2018

After a long period on the fringes of the national conversation, the matter of President Trump's mental health has taken center stage since the publication of Michael Wolff's blockbuster book *Fire and Fury*. The book includes testimonials from former White House chief strategist Steve Bannon and others that paint a picture of the president as a semi-literate ball of rage with a nonexistent attention span who is cognitively declining before our eyes.

In response to the fallout, Trump called himself a "very stable genius" on Twitter and held an open meeting that seemed designed to prove his mental acuity, two moves that only drew more attention to the state of his addled brain.

A lot about this administration is unprecedented—or as Trump might say, "unpresidented." But in the case of a president's fitness to serve, recent history may act as a very rough guide. To grapple with the idea that the man running the United States may not be in full possession of his faculties, one need only turn back the clock about 30 years to President Reagan's second term.

In 1994, Reagan revealed in a letter that he was suffering from early-stage Alzheimer's Disease. He died in 2004.

Whether Reagan was suffering clear symptoms from Alzheimer's while in office has been a subject of fevered debate for many years. In 2011, his son Ron Reagan wrote in his book *Reagan at 100* that he felt "something was amiss" with his father's mind during his second term, though the younger Reagan later clarified that this did not mean that the president was suffering from dementia during that time. The book drew a fierce backlash from conservative Reagan defenders, including the former president's other son, Michael, who insisted that his father was perfectly capable throughout his White House tenure—a conclusion that had previously been reached by Reagan's four personal doctors and other memoirists who were close to him. (A sketchily sourced Bill O'Reilly book released in 2015 was renounced by the president's inner circle.)

Concerns about Reagan's Mental Health Were Handled Very Differently Than Concerns about Trump's
continued

But multiple journalists have testified to a complicated reality: a slowly diminishing executive who leaned increasingly heavily on advisers, disengaged from day-to-day affairs, and sometimes had difficulty distinguishing fantasy from reality.

The way these accounts were handled at the time highlight the differences between the 1980s and our own turbulent era, and the differences between Reagan and Trump. Here's a look back at how key segments of the political world handled Reagan's mental state.

Democrats Pounced, Then Left the Issue Alone

As Ronald Reagan ascended the national stage in the late 1970s, the former Hollywood star and governor of California had already honed his reputation as the avuncular "cowboy," a persona he would perfect in the White House. He was a man who thought in broad strokes, but was prone, even before he became president, to forgetting stories and details, tendencies his opponents attacked as proof that he was too old to lead. Reagan was no spring chicken, after all; at 69, he was the oldest person ever to be elected president when he won in 1980. (Trump, elected at 70, broke the mark in 2016.) Reagan addressed such concerns head-on. He vowed to resign the office if he was ever found mentally unfit by White House doctors.

Democrats most seriously exploited concerns about Reagan's age four years later, when the president appeared confused at multiple points during his first debate with Walter Mondale in 1984.

"Reagan showed his age," Tony Coelho, chair of the Democratic Congressional Campaign Committee, said afterward. "The age issue is in the campaign now and people like me can talk about it, even if Mondale can't."

Reagan appeared much sharper in the second debate, subduing his opponent with a famous, rehearsed quip: "I will not make age an issue of this campaign. I am not going to exploit, for political purposes, my opponent's youth and inexperience."

He won a landslide victory in the fall, and there was no concerted effort by Democrats to question his fitness again.

While it's overdoing it to cast the 1980s as some sort of bipartisan paradise compared to our hyperpolarized era—again, there was plenty of discussion about Reagan's fitness from 1980 onward—it is true

continued

that a different, more genteel set of political norms applied. There's also the matter of public opinion. Unlike Trump, Reagan was more liked than disliked by Americans for a large chunk of his time in office, and it's easy to see how a systematic campaign to paint him as incapacitated could have backfired.

And yet, not all of the old rules have gone by the wayside. Even as President Trump behaves in unhinged ways, even as his speech undergoes a noticeable reduction in clarity and complexity, even as his own advisers confide in reporters that they worry about his stability, and even as the general public conversation about it has grown louder—there has not, until recently, been a serious effort from Democrats to question the president's basic faculties. Whether this has been out of a fear of overreach, a sense of political propriety, or other factors is hard to say, though it's difficult to imagine congressional Republicans holding their fire with a similarly erratic Democratic president.

In any case, it's a reality that seems to be changing. Forsaking the so-called Goldwater rule that forbids diagnosing presidents from afar, Democratic lawmakers recently invited a Yale University psychiatrist to testify about Trump's deterioration; she warned the group, which included a Republican senator, that the president is "going to unravel." A Democratic congress member introduced a gimmicky resolution to require future presidents to disclose the results of medical tests before an election.

But amid the nonstop chaos, it's notable that it's still Democratic backbenchers, not senior leaders, or even senators, who have sounded the mental-health alarm. (The highest-profile move in that direction has come from a Republican.)

If that reality changes, it will be yet another sign that we're in uncharted waters.

The Media Mostly Played Nice

Peak media speculation about Reagan's fitness came after his disastrous 1984 debate performance. The New York *Times* reported that the "age issue" dominated headlines in print publications and on national TV news in the aftermath. A *Wall Street Journal* headline that week went farther than most: "Reagan Debate Performance Invites Open Speculation on His Ability to Serve."

But they cropped up again amid the Iran-*contra* scandal, when Reagan claimed to have forgotten key details about his administration's selling of arms to Iran to fund Nicaraguan rebels.

In 1987, *The New Republic* ran the headline: "Is Reagan Senile?" But the takeaway was more about Reagan's

Concerns about Reagan's Mental Health Were Handled Very Differently Than Concerns about Trump's
continued

seemingly calculated forgetfulness than possible dementia. And the idea that Reagan was actually dangerously unfit never gained traction in the mainstream media. (Of course, there was also no internet at the time, making it far more difficult to stoke the kind of wild medical speculation that hurt Hillary Clinton's 2016 campaign.)

If reporters had been fully forthcoming about their experiences with Reagan, the press could have been much worse. In her 2000 book *Reporting Live,* CBS's Lesley Stahl recounted a startling interaction with Reagan in 1986—she described him as "vacant" and "a doddering space cadet"—that left her questioning the president's mental fitness. She came close to reporting the full incident, she told *Mother Jones's* David Corn, but decided against it when the president quickly "recovered." In later years, advisers and others would observe that while Reagan grew markedly less interested in the quotidian tasks of the presidency as the years went on, to the point of almost entirely disengaging, he still had the ability to turn on the telegenic charm he was famous for and appear perfectly lucid when needed.

The press often portrayed Reagan as doddering, but he usually came off in the end as benevolent or, in the case of a famous *Saturday Night Live* sketch, menacing—not incapacitated.

In 2018, questions of Trump's mental fitness are far more out in the open than they ever were with Reagan, thanks to two factors: Trump's clearly aberrant behavior and the public town square that is the internet, which feeds a constant speculation loop. There is certainly no shortage of national commentators proclaiming Trump unwell. For instance, CNN's Brian Stelter opened an August show by asking if the president was mentally ill. In May, Joe Scarborough called the president "a man in decline" on MSNBC. During the campaign and after, armchair psychiatrists diagnosed the president with narcissistic personality disorder.

Legacy media outlets like the New York *Times* and Washington *Post* have, for the most part, been more cautious in their assessments—for now. Whether their standards will hold depends on whether the president's behavior grows even more unhinged, which seems like a safe bet.

Reagan's Staff Had Faith in the President

During his presidency and after, Reagan's inner circle mostly testified to the president's intelligence and ability

continued

to retain information. When Howard Baker became chief of staff in 1987, he recalled a decade later, "It did not take me a day to figure out that this man was sharp, well organized, fully capable, and the same person that I knew from previous years."

But *The New Yorker*'s Jane Mayer wrote in 2011 that "by early 1987, several top White House advisers were so concerned about Reagan's mental state that they actually talked among themselves about invoking the Twenty-fifth Amendment of the Constitution, which calls for the Vice-President to take over in the event of the President's incapacity." She recalled that "they told stories about how inattentive and inept the president was. He was lazy; he wasn't interested in the job. They said he wouldn't read the papers they gave him—even short position papers and documents. They said he wouldn't come over to work—all he wanted to do was to watch movies and television at the residence."

And in his biography of the president, journalist Lou Cannon wrote: "The sad, shared secret of the Reagan White House was that no one in the presidential entourage had confidence in the judgment or the capacities of the president."

Here it is useful to examine the single biggest difference between the final years of Reagan's presidency and the unprecedented situation we find ourselves in now. That is Reagan's temperament, which was steady and reassuring even under duress—closer to President Obama's cool demeanor than Trump's impetuous-schoolchild routine. Even though Reagan could seem checked out to a degree that probably would have frightened the public, his aides did not alert reporters that they were alarmed by their boss's mental state, in part because they did not fear that a true disaster would arise from his condition.

But Trump's White House is leakier than a sieve, and while elected Republicans are fearful of crossing Trump in public, the president's purported allies and confidants have no compunction about telling reporters what they really think of the president.

Whether Reagan was ever seriously impaired in office or not, his natural aplomb, both in public and private settings, gave him cover for his lapses. Trump, on the other hand, seems only to grow less tolerant, more impulsive, and more dangerous as he hurtles through his early 70s. His instability is right out in the open for everyone to see, and only his hardiest defenders—the Kellyanne Conways of the world—can consistently stick up for him without occasionally taking him to task.

And yet almost the entire Republican Party has decided to come to terms,

Concerns about Reagan's Mental Health Were Handled Very Differently Than Concerns about Trump's continued

in every important way, with their maniac-in-chief. In the end, it will be the *actions* of Trump's allies, not their words, that determine whether or for

how long their manifestly unfit leader will despoil the presidency. Don't hold your breath.[16]

While not one of America's most powerful or dynamic presidents, Reagan left a lasting mark on America and on Republican politics in general, to the point that conservative politicians in the twenty-first century rarely if ever criticize his presidency and almost always pay homage to his legacy. It is likely that opinions on Reagan will change markedly in the future. His political legacy is currently buoyed by nostalgic and imperfect memories of the 1980s, but fondness for the 1980s and appreciation of its key presidential figure will likely not endure the generational shift of power.

CONCLUSION

Reagan is one of the most overrated presidents of the modern era—his actual accomplishments do not align with the level of public affection that he is afforded. His popularity was due, in part, to the fact that Reagan was a celebrity rather than a career public servant. He was skilled in oration and a practiced performer and presented himself as a traditionalist "everyman," though the reality of his life bore little resemblance to that of the average American. Some of the Reagan Era policies were dramatic failures, including his administration's economic efforts and anti-drug campaign. The failures of Reagan Era policy demonstrate the difference in effectiveness between leaders who pursue politically expedient solutions and those who pursue solutions based on expert knowledge and experience.

DISCUSSION QUESTIONS

- ♦ How did the Reagan administration's drug policy fail?
- ♦ Why didn't Reagan suffer a more significant loss of support after the Iran Contra controversy?
- ♦ What are some of the factors that contribute to Reagan's continued popularity?
- ♦ How did Reagan Era economic policies contribute to current economic issues?

Works Used

"1980 Presidential General Election Results." *U.S. Election Atlas*. uselectionatlas.org/RESULTS/national.php?year=1980&off=0&elect=0&f=0.

Alexander, Michelle. *The New Jim Crow*. New York: The New P, 16 Jan. 2012.

Brands, H.W. *Reagan: The Life*. New York: Anchor Books, 2015.

Cannon, Lou. *Governor Reagan: His Rise to Power*. New York: Public Affairs, 2003.

Cullen, James. "The History of Mass Incarceration." *Brennan Center*. 20 July 2018. www.brennancenter.org/our-work/analysis-opinion/history-mass-incarceration.

Federman, Wayne. "What Reagan Did for Hollywood." *The Atlantic*. Atlantic Monthly Group. 14 Nov. 2011. www.theatlantic.com/entertainment/archive/2011/11/what-reagan-did-for-hollywood/248391/.

Hart, Benjamin. "Concerns about Reagan's Mental Health Were Handled Very Differently Than Concerns about Trump's." *Intelligencer*. 14 Jan. 2018. nymag.com/intelligencer/2018/01/how-reagans-mental-health-concerns-were-handled.html.

Kazdin, Cole. "The Violence Central American Migrants Are Fleeing Was Stoked by the US." *Vice*. 27 June 2018. www.vice.com/en_us/article/qvnyzq/central-america-atrocities-caused-immigration-crisis.

Naftali, Tim. "Ronald Reagan's Long-Hidden Racist Conversation with Richard Nixon." *The Atlantic*. Atlantic Monthly Group. 30 July 2019. www.theatlantic.com/ideas/archive/2019/07/ronald-reagans-racist-conversation-richard-nixon/595102/.

"Presidential Approval Ratings—Gallup Historical Statistics and Trends." *Gallup*. 2019. news.gallup.com/poll/116677/presidential-approval-ratings-gallup-historical-statistics-trends.aspx.

Richman, Sheldon L. "The Sad Legacy of Ronald Reagan." *The Free Market*. No 10. 1988. mises.org/library/sad-legacy-ronald-reagan-0.

Roberts, Chris. "The Great Eliminator: How Ronald Reagan Made Homelessness Permanent." *SF Weekly*. 29 June 2016. www.sfweekly.com/news/the-great-eliminator-how-ronald-reagan-made-homelessness-permanent/.

Rottinghaus, Brandon and Justin S. Vaught. "How Does Trump Stack Up Against the Best—and Worst—Presidents?" *The New York Times*. 19 Feb. 2018. www.nytimes.com/interactive/2018/02/19/opinion/how-does-trump-stack-up-against-the-best-and-worst-presidents.html.

Samuelson, Robert J. *The Great Inflation and Its Aftermath: The Past and Future of American Affluence*. New York: Random House, 2010.

Talbott, Strobe. "Reagan and Gorbachev: Shutting the Cold War Down." *Brookings*. 1 Aug. 2004. www.brookings.edu/articles/reagan-and-gorbachev-shutting-the-cold-war-down/.

Taub, Amanda. "The Republican Myth of Ronald Reagan and the Iran Hostages, Debunked." *Vox*. 25 Jan. 2016. www.vox.com/2016/1/25/10826056/reagan-iran-hostage-negotiation.

Introduction

Summing up the presidencies of George Herbert Walker Bush and William Jefferson Clinton is a difficult task. Both men presided over dramatic military actions, both sought to implement reform economic policies, and both faced (in different ways) the rise of anti-U.S. sentiment in the Arab world, which would ultimately lead to the War on Terror era of the 2000s. Bush came into office thanks to the popularity of Reagan. He was a moderate president who followed a neoconservative agenda, and was moderately successful in working across party lines. His handling of the Gulf War is outwardly a demonstration of appropriate and balanced presidential military power, but his administration's covert efforts to manipulate public opinion raise serious questions about presidential conduct. Clinton was a great economic reformer and one of the most conservative-friendly progressives in presidential history. His policies were largely middle of the road, and he was successful in building coalitions with conservative politicians. The Clinton presidency ended dramatically, however, with the revelation that he'd misused his authority to hide an affair with White House intern Monica Lewinsky. Clinton's sexual misconduct led to him becoming just the second president in history to be impeached, though he managed to retain high levels of public support despite the scandal.

Topics covered in this chapter include:
- Transition from President Reagan to President Bush
- Bush's secret agenda
- Monica Lewinsky scandal
- Presidential impeachment
- The Gulf War

This Chapter Discusses the Following Source Document:
Collins, Bruce. "Clinton Impeachment: 20 Years On, Will Donald Trump Now Face the Same Fate?" *The Conversation*. December 19, 2018.

Crime and Punishment
George H.W. Bush and Bill Clinton (1989–2001)

The 1990s were a tumultuous time in national politics. The end of the Reagan administration gave rise to George H.W. Bush, a career politician and political strategist who became a key player for the neoconservative movement. Bush was followed by Bill Clinton, who achieved a great deal on the economic and domestic front but suffered from personal scandals so serious that he became only the second president in history to be impeached.

The Bush Legacy Begins

George H.W. Bush was born in Massachusetts into a wealthy family and attended Phillips Andover Academy, a prestigious boarding school whose graduates enjoy access to a strong network within America's corporate and political elite. Bush served in the U.S. Navy from 1942 until 1945, becoming a naval pilot, then the youngest in the Navy. His military achievements were significant, flying 58 combat missions, and he was honored after being shot down by Japanese aircraft in 1944, earning him a Distinguished Flying Cross.[1] Following his military service, Bush graduated from Yale University with a degree in economics. He moved to Texas and began a career in the oil industry, receiving a job through a family friend. By 1954, Bush had been promoted to president of one of the oil company's subsidiaries.[2]

George H.W. Bush, via Wikimedia.

While in Texas, Bush was Harris County chairman for the Republican Party, gaining recognition on the national Republican stage. His 1964 bid for the Senate failed, but in 1966 and again in 1968 he won a seat in the House of Representatives. In Congress, Bush took a moderate stance. He was a hawk when it came to Vietnam but also supported some of Johnson's social policies. Bush lost another bid for the Senate in 1970, but Nixon appointed him Ambassador to the United Nations. In 1973, he became chairman of the Republican Party. Under Ford, Bush was named U.S. envoy to the People's Republic of China and, after two years in that role, was invited to lead the Central Intelligence Agency (CIA). Bush ran for the presidency in 1979, but the election went to Ronald Reagan, who offered Bush the vice presidency.

In 1988, with Reagan retired, Bush won the nomination despite strong competition from more conservative candidates Bob Dole and evangelical Pat Robertson. Democrat opponent Mike Dukakis was unable to overcome Bush's incumbent advantage and the benefit received from Reagan's end-of-term popularity. The Reagan administration's policies had contributed to a dramatic rise in crime rates in American cities, and Bush proposed continuing the Reagan-era "tough on crime" stance, and this became his most notable campaign position. A controversial example of this strategy was a series of advertisements run by the Bush team that highlighted the crimes of Willie Horton, an African American convicted of murder who received a furlough from prison while Dukakis was Governor of Massachusetts. While out on furlough, Horton raped a white woman and stabbed her partner. The Bush campaign used this as evidence that Dukakis was "soft on crime" and supported a "revolving door" policy.

Bush's running mate, Dan Quayle, was criticized often during the campaign as unintelligent because of his tendency to make unfortunate statements. His poor performance in debates against Democratic vice-presidential candidate Lloyd Bentsen created some of the most famous

moments of the campaign. In one famous debate, Quayle suggested that he had a similar level of expertise to John F. Kennedy when Kennedy was elected president. His opponent Bentsen replied, "Senator, I served with Jack Kennedy: I knew Jack Kennedy; Jack Kennedy was a friend of mine. Senator, you're no Jack Kennedy."[3]

Bush was victorious, winning 53 percent of the popular vote and promising to continue the Reagan legacy. The election was one of the least popular in the twentieth century, attracting just 53 percent of eligible voters. Democrats picked up seats to control both houses of Congress. Bush thus entered office with a mild mandate and a hostile Congress.

President Bush the First

President George H.W. Bush is remembered as a moderate Republican willing to compromise, but he did make regular use of his veto power, issuing 44 vetoes during his four years in office.[4] The Reagan administration's fiscal policies left him with a serious budget issue and a recession. Bush capitulated to the Democratic-controlled Congress and agreed to some tax increases. Bush was forced to address another of Reagan's failed economic strategies when the savings and loan industry collapsed after years of deregulation had left the industry vulnerable to fraud and poor management. Lacking the power to craft a unilateral solution, Bush was forced to compromise with Congress, in the form of a $100 billion bailout.[5] Bush's most popular domestic achievements included an updated Clean Air Act and the Americans with Disabilities Act, which prohibited discrimination against persons based on physical or mental disabilities. In both cases, the bills that passed were a result of bipartisan cooperation, and these achievements helped to make Bush far more popular with moderate progressives.

The most dramatic development of the Bush presidency was the Persian Gulf War. In August of 1990, Iraq invaded Kuwait, and the United States intervened to prevent Iraq from taking control of Kuwait's oil reserves.

The United States, Britain, and the Soviet Union joined in condemning the invasion; the United States sent troops into Saudi Arabia and called for Iraq to withdraw from Kuwait. Economic sanctions did little to convince Iraqi President Saddam Hussein to withdraw, and the UN Security Council authorized member states to take military action. Bush requested full authorization of military action from Congress, signaling a return to the cooperative military relationship that had existed between Congress and the executive branch prior to the era of unilateral presidential military action. The conflict, Operation Desert Storm, began on January 17, 1991, with a U.S.–led coalition commanding the charge, soldiers from Saudi Arabia, Egypt, France, and Britain joining the United States, and financial support from Japan and Germany. The coalition reached Kuwait City on February 27, and a ceasefire was declared the next day.

The Iraqi military was clearly outmatched by the United States, and the war was over quickly, with 148 U.S. casualties and a death total of 290 for the allied nations. At least 1,000 Kuwaitis were killed, 60,000 to 200,000 Iraqi soldiers killed, and 100,000 to 200,000 civilian deaths.[6] After the war, a Gallup Poll in 1992 found that 66 percent of Americans thought the operation was worth it, while 32 percent disagreed. A decade later, in 2001, opinion had changed little.[7] The war boosted Bush's approval ratings to 89 percent, but by the summer of the following year, it had plummeted to 29 percent.

Bush made a concerted effort to handle the Gulf War effort within the confines of traditional presidential authority. His efforts in building a strong international coalition and in gaining UN and congressional support demonstrate a restrained, traditionalist approach to presidential military powers. This may have been the most prudent strategy for Bush, who lacked a stable lead in popular approval and who faced an opposition Congress. The fact that Bush did not act unilaterally is part of the reason that public approval for the war has remained high.

However, the Bush administration participated in questionable efforts to gain popular support for the war effort. The public was initially divided on the invasion of Kuwait. PR firm Hill & Knowlton, whose COO Craig Fuller was George Bush's former chief of staff, was hired for $10.7 million to gain public support. The firm found that wartime atrocities would be the most effective way to anger the public and to build support for war, and engineered fake testimony before the Congressional Human Rights Caucus in October 1990 during which a woman named Nayira claimed she'd been a volunteer at a Kuwaiti hospital and saw Iraqi troops ripping babies out of incubators and leaving them to die on the floor. Bush and Republican legislators repeated this story for weeks and sent video of Nayira to 700 television stations, which helped push the needle on public approval firmly in favor of U.S. intervention.[8]

Further, the Bush administration claimed that the Iraqi government's invasion of Kuwait was the beginning of an imperialistic campaign that would spread to other countries. In truth, the Iraqi invasion of Kuwait was part of a complicated and long-lasting feud between the two countries. Back in the United States, the Bush administration knew that Americans would have little interest in invading for the sole reason of saving Kuwaitis and so the claim was that Saddam Hussein would continue his imperialist military agenda, invading American allies like Saudi Arabia.[9] Bush first committed troops to the region on the claim that the Iraqi military was gathered at the border of Saudi Arabia, and an invasion was imminent. Research found no evidence to support this.

The Persian Gulf War was devastating to the Middle East and helped set the stage for the rise of Islamic radicalism in the years that followed. The United States preserved interest in Kuwaiti oil and access to Kuwait as a strategic military position, but the cost in human lives was severe and U.S. military forces were accused of presenting false depictions of U.S.

activities and attempting to cover up instances where poor military strategy or execution led to large numbers of civilian casualties.

While most Americans were in favor of the war effort, and while Bush demonstrated adherence to the balance of powers in his political campaign before the war, it is also likely that Bush and his administration misused presidential power by misleading the American people, members of Congress, and members of the international community regarding the purpose and objectives of the war. Bush critics alleged that the Gulf War was a war for oil and access to oil imports. Had it not been for the Gulf War, however, Bush's average approval rating would likely have been below 50 percent for most of his presidency—financial problems inherited from the Reagan administration damaged his domestic record, and Bush lacked the charisma and appeal that Reagan commanded. Like Reagan, however, Bush helped to restore the image of the presidency and the global power of the office after the embarrassment of Nixon, and helped to sharpen and define the modern Republican political approach.

The Clinton Years

William Clinton was born in Hope, Arkansas, and raised by his mother and grandmother. His father died just before he was born, and his mother's second husband, Roger Clinton, was an abusive alcoholic. Bill Clinton excelled at school and put himself through Georgetown University. During college, he clerked for Arkansas Senator William Fulbright, and later won a Rhodes Scholarship and spent two years in Oxford, England, studying public policy and law. He then entered Yale Law School and worked for the Democratic Party on Senate campaigns. Clinton also taught classes in law and public policy at the University of Arkansas.

Bill Clinton, by Bob McNeely, White House, via Wikimedia.

Clinton lost a bid for the House of Representatives in 1974, but became Arkansas' state attorney general two years later. In 1978, at 32, he was elected governor of Arkansas by a large margin. His first term was marred by controversial decisions that placed Clinton at odds with the powerful timber industry, and he lost his reelection bid in 1980. He immediately returned to the campaign trail and spent two years convincing Arkansas residents to give him another shot, admitting his earlier failures and discussing different approaches. Clinton became Arkansas' governor again in 1982, 1984, 1986, and 1990. His chief accomplishments included increasing the diversity of the Arkansas state government and a successful series of educational reforms.[10]

When the 1992 presidential election came around, years of respectable leadership in Arkansas and his work with the Democratic Party made Clinton the frontrunner among prospective Democratic candidates. Moreover, his moderate record and strong personal charisma made him the Democratic Party's answer to Reagan. Reagan and Bush had painted the Democratic Party as a special interest party concerned only with women and people of color. Clinton changed the narrative, portraying the Republican Party as the party of big business and the wealthy. Further, poor Republican financial management had left the nation in a recession and facing a huge deficit, and this played well into Clinton's campaign strategy.

The entrance of billionaire independent candidate Ross Perot also did not bode well for the Republican Party. Perot claimed that the economy could be fixed by running the nation like a business. Like candidate Donald Trump, Perot argued that his experience in business was sufficient, despite having no previous governance or public service experience. Although he had no chance of winning, his was among the most influential third-party campaigns in American history. Clinton won 44.9 million votes (43 percent), Bush 39.1 million votes (37 percent) and Perot 19.7 million

votes (19 percent).[11] The election drew significantly more attention than the previous three elections, with 58 percent of voters turning out. The Democratic Party also managed to hold onto the Senate and the House, giving Clinton a legislative mandate.

President Clinton

Bill Clinton proved a very popular president, with an average of 55 percent approval over his two terms, and he was more popular overall during his second term, despite controversies. His overall popularity was higher than Reagan's during Reagan's two terms in office and substantially higher than any Republican since Dwight Eisenhower.[12] Bill Clinton's high level of public support was due to his overwhelmingly moderate approach, keeping the support of many centrists, even as opinion of his presidency shifted at the far left and right ends of the spectrum. For example, Clinton's economic reform policy included raising taxes on the wealthy, but also cut spending on federal welfare programs; NAFTA might have generated more controversy, but Clinton put his weight behind conservative reforms of the system, which allowed the program to pass without a partisan struggle; the administration's solution on the prohibition of homosexuals in the U.S. military was the non-committal "Don't ask, don't tell" policy, which he established by executive order, allowing homosexuals to serve, but not openly, and not be asked about their sexual orientation.

Clinton's ability to straddle the line between the right and left is most apparent in his handling of criminal justice. Research refuted the effectiveness of the law and order approach and validated rehabilitative methods. Clinton chose a conservative "get tough on crime" approach with a series of punitive laws aimed at combating the drug trade and other crimes. Experts believe that Clinton's approach was counterproductive and increased incarceration rates, especially for people of color, and Clinton has admitted as much.[13] Crime rates did fall significantly during the 1990s, but this was more closely related to economic efforts.

Senate floor proceedings during the impeachment trial of Bill Clinton, via Wikimedia.

Failure and Controversy

Clinton's capability to maintain strong support made him an effective executive and a strong Democratic counterpoint to the Reagan legacy, but his presidency was also marked by failure and controversy. Clinton's chief goal was to overhaul the national healthcare system with the addition of universal healthcare but the campaign, headed up by his wife, Hillary, was a failure. A shift toward the Republican Party in the 1994 election left Clinton facing a hostile Congress and unable to make progress on his healthcare agenda.

President Clinton was under investigation for a series of potentially illegal financial deals that occurred in Arkansas, involving a real estate development on the Whitewater River. Clinton called for independent counsel to investigate, with former judge and attorney Kenneth Starr the lead investigator. Starr found evidence of impropriety and his investigation broadened. At the same time, Paula Jones, a former employee of Governor Clinton, accused him of sexual harassment, leading Starr to discover the Clinton/Monica Lewinsky affair.

In addition to adultery, the affair with Lewinsky had the potential of sexual abuse, as Clinton's status as Lewinsky's employer constituted a complicating power dynamic. Starr proved that Clinton had lied about the affair during the investigation and had taken other steps to obstruct justice. In August, Clinton admitted to the affair publicly, though not to lying under oath. The Starr Report, stated that Clinton could be impeached for obstruction of justice, lying under oath, and abusing presidential powers.

Following the report televised House hearings drew millions of viewers and dominated the news cycle. As the hearing commenced, Clinton remained largely silent on the issue. Ultimately, the House adopted two articles of impeachment, obstruction of justice and perjury. The Senate did not have the votes to remove Clinton, who was acquitted on both counts in February 1999.

Tickets (presented to former president Gerald Ford) to Clinton's impeachment trial. By Gerald R. Ford Presidential Library, NARA, via Wikimedia.

The following *Conversation* article highlights the similarities and differences between the impeachment proceedings of Clinton and Donald Trump, as well as each president's reaction.

CLINTON IMPEACHMENT: 20 YEARS ON, WILL DONALD TRUMP NOW FACE THE SAME FATE?

Bruce Collins

The Conversation

December 19, 2018

Twenty years ago, Republicans in the US House of Representatives narrowly voted to impeach president Bill Clinton. It was December 19, 1998. Subsequently tried by the Senate in early 1999, he was found not guilty on one count of perjury, while senators divided 50-50 on the other count of obstruction of justice. This fell far short of the two thirds majority required to remove him from office. He survived, but many Americans now wonder whether Donald Trump might face impeachment now the Democrats have regained control of the House.

Clinton, after all, was the target of a politically-motivated investigation into his financial and personal affairs set up when the Republicans won the House in 1994. It was led by Kenneth Starr, a Republican nominated to a senior judgeship by Ronald Reagan, who served as US solicitor general under George H. W. Bush between 1989 and 1993.

Starr's exhaustive investigation into the personal and especially financial affairs of the Clintons in Arkansas prior to 1992 (when he was elected to the presidency) found no hard evidence of wrongdoing. But it intersected with a suit brought by Paula Jones against Clinton over his personal conduct, which led investigators to White House intern Monica Lewinsky and the president's alleged sexual relations with her. Clinton denied under oath in August 1998 that he'd had sexual relations with "that woman", and this denial led to the perjury charge.

The Clinton case revealed the challenging nature of impeachment. It is a political move, played to remove a head of state. But its outcome depends on the rules of black letter law. Did an incumbent commit "high crimes and misdemeanours" provable by the tests of hard evidence as required in a court of law?

continued

How it played out

When news of the Lewinsky affair broke in January 1998, Clinton reportedly believed he would be forced from office. But the legal case against him took months to assemble and by December the political dynamics had shifted. Hillary Clinton led in turning the tables against the investigation, arguing that they were victims of an unprincipled conservative conspiracy. In November 1998, Clinton also settled with Jones out of court, paying her US$850,000, which further eased the pressure on him.

The main shift, though, was political. The Republican House was led by speaker Newt Gingrich, who saw himself as a national party leader articulating a coherent Republican programme. In challenging Clinton, he insisted that the Republicans would make big gains in the November 1998 midterm elections – but their House majority actually fell. Gingrich also faced a sex scandal of his own. He resigned from the speakership in November 1998 – and, soon after, Congress. His successor resigned within weeks for similar reasons. The Republicans' claim to the moral high ground was further undermined by the Starr report's lengthy, prurient descriptions of Clinton's sexual encounters with Lewinsky.

Bill Clinton's approval ratings remained high. Tired of investigations grinding on for years, increasingly the public failed to see that perjury about personal encounters amounted to a high crime or misdemeanour. Meanwhile, the US economy continued to grow.

When the Senate's vote in February 1999 finally failed to unseat him, it ultimately reflected the public mood.

Trump's fate

Impeaching Trump would also depend on political calculations. If the grounds were an infringement of campaign finance laws by the alleged payments in 2016 to two women, the Democrats would be derided for double standards, and the Clinton brand, important in mainstream Democratic politics, would be savaged. How election expenses are defined when they affect personal matters is also not clear cut.

Impeachment could also result from Trump's alleged Russian connections. But the link, if found, would likely seem obscure and complex to a majority of Americans, who will ask where the smoking gun is.

Besides, by the time there are possible charges, attention will likely be focused on the 2020 election and

Clinton Impeachment: 20 Years On, Will Donald Trump Now Face the Same Fate?
continued

revisiting the details of 2016 might simply reinforce partisan tribalism unless the evidence is powerful and clear cut. Equally important, a Russian-focused inquiry could divert attention back to Hillary Clinton's emails and alleged ties to Russia, which the current nominee for US attorney general, William Barr, has said merits further review.

The Republican-controlled Senate will not convict the president unless an exceptionally clear case of criminality is assembled. And by attempting to remove Trump, the Democrats will be accused of ignoring America's real concerns and blamed for torpedoing the president's agenda.

Indeed, even if such an attempt succeeded, current vice-president Mike Pence as president would appeal to a deeply conservative Republican base and might stir Trump enthusiasts to vote in huge numbers against a party which destroyed their hero. Consequently, the Democrat House leadership is currently more interested in developing positive social, economic and foreign policies.

Cue: The Radical Democrats
Instead, the main proponents of Trump's impeachment seem to be more radical Democrats. Their opposition to all that Trump represents is undoubted. But internal party calculations may ultimately influence their tactics.

The field for the Democrats' next presidential candidate in 2020 is open. A recent poll in Iowa, the first state to hold a presidential primary in January 2020, showed that the leading candidates were former vice-president Jo Biden, and Vermont senator Bernie Sanders. There have also been suggestions that Hillary Clinton, who is younger than both, might enter the fray.

Impeachment may appeal to Democrats seeking a more radical alternative to Hillary Clinton as it would revive memories of the Clinton legacy's failings. For them, impeachment would ramp up the personal pressure on Trump, even though it would fail to remove him, and make launching a Clinton rerun more problematic. They are now the ones to watch.

Congressional Record

United States
of America

PROCEEDINGS AND DEBATES OF THE 106th CONGRESS, FIRST SESSION

Vol. 145   WASHINGTON, FRIDAY, FEBRUARY 12, 1999   No. 26

Senate

The Senate met at 9:36 a.m. and was called to order by the Chief Justice of the United States.

TRIAL OF WILLIAM JEFFERSON CLINTON, PRESIDENT OF THE UNITED STATES

The CHIEF JUSTICE. The Senate will convene as a Court of Impeachment. The Chaplain will offer a prayer.

PRAYER

The Chaplain, Dr. Lloyd John Ogilvie, offered the following prayer:

Gracious God, whose love for this Nation has been displayed so magnificently through our history, we praise You that Your presence fills this historic Chamber and enters into the minds of the Senators gathered here. Each of them is here by Your divine appointment. Together they claim Your promise, "Call upon Me in the day of trouble; I will deliver you."—Ps.50:15. We call upon You on this day of trouble in America as this impeachment trial comes to a close. You have enabled an honest, open debate of alternative solutions. Soon a vote will be taken. You have established a spirit of unity in the midst of differences. Most important of all, we know that we can trust You with the results. You can use what is decided and continue to accomplish Your plans for America. We entrust to Your care the President and his family. Use whatever is decided today to enable a deeper experience of Your grace in his life and healing in his family. We commit this day to You and thank You for the hope that fills our hearts as we place our complete trust in You. You are our Lord and Saviour. Amen.

The CHIEF JUSTICE. The Sergeant at Arms will make the proclamation.

The Sergeant at Arms, James W. Ziglar, made proclamation as follows:

Hear ye! Hear ye! Hear ye! All persons are commanded to keep silent, on pain of imprisonment, while the Senate of the United States is sitting for the trial of the articles of impeachment exhibited by the House of Representatives against William Jefferson Clinton, President of the United States.

THE JOURNAL

The CHIEF JUSTICE. If there is no objection, the Journal of proceedings of the trial are approved to date.

The majority leader is recognized.

Mr. LOTT. Thank you, Mr. Chief Justice.

ORDER OF PROCEDURE

Mr. LOTT. For the information of all Senators, later on today, the Secretary of the Senate will be putting at each Senator's desk something I think you will enjoy reading later. It is the prayers of the Chaplain during the impeachment trial. Subsequently, we plan to put it in a small pamphlet, because they truly have been magnificent. We thought you each would like to have copies.

The Senate will resume final deliberations now in the closed session. Thank goodness. At this point in the proceedings, there are approximately eight Members who still wish to speak or submit part of their speech into the RECORD.

Following those final speeches, the Senate will resume open session and proceed to the votes on the two articles of impeachment. I estimate that those votes will begin at approximately 11, 11:30. However, the exact time will depend on the length of the remaining speeches, and also we will have to have a few minutes to open the Chamber and the galleries so that our constituents and our families can enter the galleries if they would like to.

Following those votes, all Senators should remain at their desks as the Senate proceeds to several housekeeping items relating to the adjournment of the Court of Impeachment. So again, I emphasize, please, after the votes, don't rush out of the Chamber because we have some very important proceedings to attend to, and I think you will enjoy them if you will stay and participate.

Under the consent agreement reached last night, following those votes, a motion to censure may be offered by the Senator from California, Senator FEINSTEIN. If offered, Senator GRAMM will be recognized to offer a motion relative to the Feinstein motion, with a vote to occur on the Gramm motion. Therefore, Senators may anticipate an additional vote or votes following the votes on the articles.

I thank the Senators. And I believe we are ready to proceed to the closed session.

Mrs. BOXER. Will the majority leader yield for a question?

Mr. LOTT. Yes.

Mrs. BOXER. Will there be intervening debate or no debate on any of those votes?

Mr. LOTT. In the UC that was reached last night, I believe we have 2 hours, which will be equally divided, for Senators to submit statements at that point or to make speeches if they would like. So I presume—after the votes, yes.

Mrs. BOXER. That is the question. Yes.

Mr. LOTT. I presume we will go on for a couple hours—2 or 3 o'clock in the afternoon, yes.

UNANIMOUS-CONSENT AGREEMENT—PRINTING OF STATEMENTS IN THE RECORD AND PRINTING OF SENATE DOCUMENT OF IMPEACHMENT PROCEEDINGS

Mr. LOTT. I would like to clarify one other matter. Senators will recall the motion approved February 9, 1999, which permitted each Senator to place in the CONGRESSIONAL RECORD his or her own statements made during final deliberations in closed session.

I ask unanimous consent that public statements made by Senators subsequent to the approval of that motion, with respect to his or her own statements made during the closed session, be deemed to be in compliance with the Senate rules. This would permit a Senator to release to the public his or her

---

● This "bullet" symbol identifies statements or insertions which are not spoken by a Member of the Senate on the floor.

Printed on recycled paper.

The opening day of Clinton's impeachment trial detailed in the Congressional Record of February 12, 1999, via Wikimedia.

Politically, the impeachment hearings were a disaster for the Republican Party. In public opinion polls, though most Americans felt that Clinton's actions were wrong, they saw the affair as a personal matter, and few believed he should be removed from office. In the November 1998 elections, the Republicans gained no seats in the Senate and lost seats in the House, and Clinton's public opinion rating hit near-record levels for his presidency immediately after the impeachment process. The Republican Party politicians who were most active in attacking Clinton lost public approval, and there was a widespread impression that the attack was politically motivated.

The Clinton impeachment process raised important questions about presidential power. The initial crime of which Clinton was accused (and later admitted to) could be viewed as a consensual sexual act, as both Clinton and Lewinsky have claimed that it was such. However, the power dynamic between Clinton, 27 years Lewinsky's senior and the president of the United States, presents a strong case that Clinton's sexual behavior with Lewinsky is sexual abuse. In any case, a majority in the public and many legislators were inclined to view Clinton's sexual misconduct as a violation of his marital oaths and perhaps a demonstration of a moral and ethical lapse, but not as a crime worthy of removal from office. In the Senate hearings, it was argued that Clinton's lying under oath and his attempt to obstruct justice could still constitute a "high crime" because he violated his oath of office and the law, but the Senate rejected this interpretation. Clinton became the second president to be impeached, but was not convicted and removed from office.

Demonstrators opposing the impeachment of Clinton outside the Capitol in December 1998. By Elvert Barnes, via Wikimedia.

U.S. House of Representatives adopting articles of impeachment against Trump, December 18, 2019. *House Floorcast*, by Clerk of the U.S. House of Representatives, via Wikimedia.

Clinton is not the first president to lie to Congress or the American people. Reagan lied about conducting illegal arms deals with radical militant factions, and the Bush administration lied about the justification for the invasion of Iraq. In some ways, the lies told by these presidents might seem more serious, especially since the Reagan and Bush administrations' conduct contributed to vast human rights abuses, environmental and cultural devastation, and the loss of hundreds of thousands of lives. The stakes involved in Clinton's misconduct were significantly lower, and yet Clinton's obstruction and perjury happened in the midst of a direct investigation of his conduct and this creates a different legal context. The relative ease with which most forgave him is evidence that the American people, at that time, did not consider private marital or sexual misconduct grounds for removal.

Whether Clinton should have been impeached or removed from office remains a subject of debate. While Clinton's actions are now generally seen as morally or ethically flawed by most Americans, opinions on his presidency have remained more or less positive. In 2019, historians ranked Clinton 15th out of America's 45 presidents on the basis of his successful efforts to rehabilitate the American economy.[15] Clinton was one of the most moderate successful Democrats of the modern era, and his centrist approach gave him political pull across the aisle. The aggressive Republican-led effort to remove him from power backfired because the Republican Party was not united behind the efforts, partly because of Clinton's cross-party appeal.

Harper's Weekly illustration of impeachment trial of Johnson, 1868. By Theodore Russel Davis, via Wikimedia.

Judiciary Committee formal impeachment hearings against Nixon, May 9, 1974. By Thomas J. O'Halloran, Library of Congress, Prints and Photographs Reading Room, via Wikimedia.

CONCLUSION

While H.W. Bush's reputation has seen improvement since his time in office, opinion of Clinton has soured considerably. Evolving attitudes about sexual abuse and misconduct have led to a more serious condemnation of Clinton's abuses of power, leading to increasingly negative opinions on his overall performance in office. Interestingly, opinion on many of Clinton's other policy priorities have also deteriorated, including how his aggressive anti-crime bills deepened the problem of mass incarceration. After Clinton, America entered a period of dramatic partisan deadlock, with little willingness to cooperate between the political parties. As this evolved, the presidencies of Bush and Clinton have come notable for the degree to which both presidents were able to form bi-partisan coalitions to achieve results, a technique that has become increasingly infrequent in the modern era. The next chapter showcases the first presidencies of the twenty-first century, including H.W. Bush's son, George, and Barack Obama, America's first African American president.

DISCUSSION QUESTIONS

- ♦ Would the public react differently to Clinton's impeachment trial if it were happening in the 2010s? How so?
- ♦ Did the Bush administration abuse presidential power in misleading the public about the Gulf War? Explain your answer.
- ♦ Did the scandals of Bill Clinton's administration impact Hillary Clinton's campaign for the presidency? Explain your answer.
- ♦ Did the impeachment process against Clinton damage the credibility of the Republican Party? How?

Works Used

"1992 Presidential General Election Results." *US Election Atlas*. uselectionatlas.org/RESULTS/national.php?year=1992.

Calavita, Kitty, Henry N. Pontell, and Robert Tillman. *Big Money Crime: Fraud and Politics in the Savings and Loan Crisis*. U of California P. May 1999.

Collins, Bruce. "Clinton Impeachment: 20 Years On, Will Donald Trump Now Face the Same Fate?" *The Conversation*. 19 Dec. 2018. https://theconversation.com/clinton-impeachment-20-years-on-will-donald-trump-now-face-the-same-fate-109045.

"George Herbert Walker Bush." *Naval History and Heritage Command*. www.history.navy.mil/research/histories/biographies-list/bios-b/bush-george-h-w.html.

Gillett, Rachel, and Allana Akhtar. "These Are the Top 20 US Presidents (and Why You Won't Find Trump on the List)." *Business Insider*. 4 July 2019. www.businessinsider.com/the-top-20-presidents-in-us-history-according-to-historians-2017-2.

Holland, Joshua. "The First Iraq War Was Also Sold to the Public Based on a Pack of Lies." *Bill Moyers*. 27 June 2014. billmoyers.com/2014/06/27/the-first-iraq-war-was-also-sold-to-the-public-based-on-a-pack-of-lies/.

Maraniss, David. *First in His Class: A Biography of Bill Clinton*. New York: Simon & Schuster, 1995.

Meacham, Jon. *Destiny and Power: The American Odyssey of George Herbert Walker Bush*. New York: Random House, 2015.

Merica, Dan. "Bill Clinton Says He Made Mass Incarceration Issue Worse." *CNN*. 15 July 2015. www.cnn.com/2015/07/15/politics/bill-clinton-1994-crime-bill/index.html.

Moore, David W. "Americans Believe U.S. Participation in Gulf War a Decade Ago Worthwhile." *Gallup*. 26 Feb. 2001. news.gallup.com/poll/1963/americans-believe-us-participation-gulf-war-decade-ago-worthwhile.aspx.

"Presidential Approval Ratings—Gallup Historical Statistics and Trends." *Gallup*. 2019. news.gallup.com/poll/116677/presidential-approval-ratings-gallup-historical-statistics-trends.aspx.

"Remembering the Gulf War: The Key Facts & Figures." *Forces*. 7 Mar. 2017. www.forces.net/news/remembering-gulf-war-key-facts-figures#:~:targetText=According%20to%20the%20BBC%2C%20between,at%20between%20100%2C000%20and%20200%2C000.

Salameh, Mamdouh G. "Oil Wars." *USAEE Working Paper*. No. 14–163. SSRN. 1 May 2014. papers.ssrn.com/sol3/papers.cfm?abstract_id=2430960.

"Senator, You're No Jack Kennedy." *NPR*. 23 May 2006. www.npr.org/templates/story/story.php?storyId=5425248.

"Vetoes by President George H.W. Bush." *United States Senate*. www.senate.gov/reference/Legislation/Vetoes/BushGHW.htm.

Withers, Rachel. "George H.W. Bush's 'Willie Horton' Ad Will Always Be the Reference Point for Dog-Whistle Racism." *VOX*. 1 Dec. 2018. www.vox.com/2018/12/1/18121221/george-hw-bush-willie-horton-dog-whistle-politics.

Introduction

The presidencies of George W. Bush and Barack Obama were polarizing periods in American history. Bush entered office on a wave of conservative traditionalist sentiment in the wake of the tumultuous end to Clinton's presidency, but failed to win the popular vote and so entered office without a public mandate. This changed with the September 2001 terrorist attacks, which gave Bush the most significant boost in public opinion of any modern president and afforded his administration nearly unfettered foreign policy powers for the remainder of his two terms in office. Bush was followed by Barack Obama, the historic first African American to serve as president. His candidacy saw the greatest level of youth and minority involvement in the political process since John F. Kennedy. Obama was an effective economic leader and pursued a moderate foreign policy agenda guided by conservatives in the military establishment. Although he attempted to bridge the partisan divide, his efforts were stymied by one of the most obstructionist Republican Party legislatures in history.

Topics covered in this chapter include:

- 9/11 terrorist attacks
- George Bush's presidential power
- The Invasion of Iraq
- The Invasion of Afghanistan
- The Patriot Act
- The Great Recession

This Chapter Discusses the Following Source Document:
Richey, Warren. "Bush Pushed the Limits of Presidential Power."
Christian Science Monitor, January 14, 2009

Empire and Archetype
George W. Bush and Barack Obama (2001–2017)

The 2000s and 2010s were periods of profound change. George W. Bush ushered in a new era in traditionalist conservatism, marketed to voters as a "compassionate" approach to preserving conservative ideals. Bush is among the most controversial presidents, achieving both high peaks of public approval and deep valleys of scorn. The polarizing Bush presidency gave way to the historic presidency of Barack Obama, America's first African American president, whose tumultuous two terms in the White House defined the 2010s and reignited debates about race, power, and ideology across America.

The Bush Legacy Continued

George W. Bush was the eldest child of President George H.W. Bush and attended Phillips Andover Academy, an elite boarding school in Andover, Massachusetts, notable for producing economic and political leaders. Despite a less than stellar record, Bush was accepted at Yale University, in the footsteps of his father and grandfather, and became a member of the Skull and Bones society, a group catering to the nation's wealthy. Bush enlisted in the National Guard after his graduation, and trained as a pilot. He pursued an MBA at Harvard University and returned to Texas where he began working, like his father, in the oil industry.

We the People

George W. Bush, U.S. Department of Defense, via Wikimedia.

After Bush lost a bid for the House of Representatives, he became a key player in his father's 1988 bid for the presidency. After his father's victory, Bush invested in the Texas Rangers baseball team, which he sold for a profit of $15 million. With little political capital, Bush nonetheless challenged Democratic Texas Governor Ann Richards in 1994. The Bush name was a major advantage, and he proved a charming, if slightly awkward, speaker. His unexpected victory was a major blow to the struggling Texas Democratic Party, and he entered office with a strong public mandate for reform. Like his father, Governor Bush proved adept at compromise and working across partisan lines. He worked closely with Democratic Lieutenant Governor Bob Bullock to pass reform bills and managed a major overhaul of the education system, with new literacy rate standards and new requirements for students. He also initiated a series of tax reforms that reduced taxes on businesses and the wealthy.[1]

Controversial President

George W. Bush's 2000 presidential campaign is one of the most controversial in history. His opponent, Al Gore, promised a continuation of Clinton's moderate progressive agenda but with major changes in environmental policy. Bush attempted to swing moderate progressives, independents, and conservatives with his compassionate conservativism campaign, arguing that the fundamental principles of small government and deregulation would achieve the same goals as progressivist social welfare investment. On election night, the popular vote count was so close that a recount was initiated. Al Gore won the popular vote by what was then the largest margin of any losing candidate, but Bush had a slight advantage in the Electoral College. Irregularities in the vote count in Florida, where Bush's brother Jeb Bush was governor, became a major controversy, as many votes were not counted during the initial tally and other electoral improprieties had occurred. The recount effort went on for 36 days before the Supreme Court ruled to stop the recount because there was no fair way to recount the votes. Gore conceded the race, but Bush lost the popular vote by around 500,000, so entered office at a public deficit. Many Americans felt that the election had been rigged.[2]

The Florida recount became an issue of academic interest in the years following the election. Studies indicate that had the recount been completed, Bush would have probably won. However, studies of other voting irregularities in Florida indicate that Gore would have won the state had they not existed. The close and contentious election also brought national attention to the ways in which African American and poor voters were marginalized in state and national elections, including through gerrymandering, in which legislators draw districts so as to limit the political power of people of color and working-class Americans.[3]

Were it not for the terrorist attacks on the United States on September 11, 2001, George W. Bush might never have been elected to a second term. Entering office with approval ratings below 50 percent, Bush was often criticized for his policies and personal gaffes. After 9/11, Bush's approval rating surged to 90 percent, the highest for any modern president, reflecting the extreme nature of the incident. Millions watched the disaster, which was described as an act of war against the United States. Nationalism and patriotism surged, similar to after the Japanese attacked Pearl Harbor in World War II. The public support that Bush enjoyed was well beyond the typical "war-time president" bump that his father enjoyed during the Persian Gulf conflict, or that any of the Cold War presidents enjoyed during their efforts in Asia.[4]

Following 9/11, the Bush administration promoted an invasion of Iraq and Afghanistan, claiming that Afghanistan was a state sponsor of terrorist organizations and that Iraq might possess weapons of mass destruction, was linked to the radical group Al-Qaeda, and believed to have been behind the 9/11 attacks. These allegations were found to be without merit: Iraq did not possess weapons of mass destruction and had no meaningful links to Al-Qaeda. Studies found that the information about weapons of mass destruction reflected major failures of the intelligence community. However, the Bush administration misled the American people about the connections between Iraq and Al-Qaeda and exaggerated information about weapons of mass destruction, downplaying reports indicating that invasion of Iraq would do little to stem radical terrorism in the region.[5]

The Iraq and Afghanistan invasions were accomplished with little difficulty because of U.S. military strength. This was part of what the Bush administration called the "War on Terror," a series of initiatives meant to keep America safe from terrorist attacks and to combat domestic terrorist cells. With the massive surge in public support and panic over terrorism, Bush was able to push through legislation for a new domestic intelligence agency, unauthorized surveillance on American citizens, and a massive increase in presidential powers during war time. In the *Christian Science Monitor*, staff writer Warren Richey explores how Bush altered presidential powers during his presidency. Richey's commentary reflects the skepticism about the Bush administration's policies after his administration came to a close.

BUSH PUSHED THE LIMITS OF PRESIDENTIAL POWER

Warren Richey

The Christian Science Monitor

January 14, 2009

Source Document Excerpt

The presidential legacy of George W. Bush is perhaps best expressed in four words: He kept America safe.

Many legal scholars question President Bush's claim to unilateral power as commander in chief in the war on terror. And experts will long debate his aggressive approach to the fight against Al Qaeda—authorizing warrantless wiretaps within the US, secret kidnappings of terror suspects, coercive interrogation tactics, and military commissions with stripped-down legal protections.

But even Mr. Bush's harshest critics must concede that on his watch the country remained free of further terrorist atrocities following the 9/11 attacks.

The deeper question is at what price?

At the heart of the debate over Bush's legacy is a fundamental difference in outlook over what it means to remain faithful to the constitutional protections laid down by America's founding generation.

Critics say the Bush administration's expansive vision of executive power eclipsed the Constitution's mandated system of checks and balances. Some see the Bush years as lurching toward an imperial presidency, posing a direct threat to the essence of American liberty.

"The breadth of the theory that they were articulating is as broad as any theory of presidential power offered by any administration in history," says Gene Healy, a vice president at the Cato Institute in Washington and author of "The Cult of the Presidency: America's Dangerous Devotion to Executive Power."

Others disagree. "President Bush clearly had constitutional authority to make the military and counterterrorism decisions that he did," says Michael Paulsen, a constitutional scholar at the University of St. Thomas in Minneapolis. "I can think of none of President Bush's actions that fall outside those categories of relatively clear commander-in-chief clause power."

continued

Bush, Vice President Dick Cheney, and administration advisers insist that their actions have been fully consistent with the Constitution.

Historical Precedent for Bush Actions

Every president since George Washington has sworn an oath to "preserve, protect and defend the Constitution of the United States." But presidents have interpreted that sacred pledge in different ways.

Some read it narrowly, that the president must always act within the strict letter and spirit of the law and Constitution. Others viewed it more broadly, embracing a duty to protect the nation itself, even when specific actions might temporarily violate the Constitution or laws.

Abraham Lincoln interpreted his presidential oath as a pledge to preserve the Union and the government itself. In 1861 amid a mounting crisis over the possible secession of Maryland, he suspended the writ of habeas corpus, a protection reserved under the Constitution to Congress.

Had Lincoln called Congress into special session in Washington, just as Maryland pulled out of the Union, the entire government would have been located within the Confederacy and in grave danger.

Instead, Lincoln acted quickly and alone. Then, within months, once the crisis in Maryland subsided, he presented the issue to Congress and obtained its approval.

Bush administration members invoked the example of Lincoln as justification for their own assertions of executive authority in the war on terror. But some analysts say the Bush administration wrongly sought to act alone in controversial areas, rather than obtaining the guidance and support of Congress.

"Given the kind of conflict we're faced with today, we find ourselves in a situation where I believe you need strong executive leadership," Mr. Cheney said in a FOX News interview in December. "There are bound to be debates and arguments . . . about what kind of authority is appropriate in any specific circumstance. But I think that what we've done has been totally consistent with what the Constitution provides for."

Cheney noted that the president has 24-hour access to a briefcase containing all the codes necessary to launch a nuclear counterattack. "He could launch a kind of a devastating attack the world has never seen," the vice president said. "He doesn't have to check with anybody. He doesn't have to call Congress. He doesn't have to check

Bush Pushed the Limits of Presidential Power
continued

with the courts. He has that authority because of the nature of the world we live in."

Many scholars take issue with Cheney's view. They say he and others in the Bush administration have used the war on terror as an opportunity to try to establish more robust powers within the executive.

"The basic strategy was to assert that the president could do various things like [authorizing domestic] wiretaps, detaining enemy combatants, and setting up military commissions solely on his own, he didn't need congressional authorization," says Steven Calabresi, a constitutional scholar at the Northwestern University School of Law in Chicago and author of "The Unitary Executive: Presidential Power from Washington to Bush."

"The hope was that by President Bush doing those things on his own it would vindicate presidential power in those areas," Professor Calabresi says. "I think that strategy was a mistake both legally and politically."

Cheney's Strong Hand Seen

Others agree.

"Cheney is an executivist in the sense that he really thinks the president needs all that power and control to defend the country," says James Pfiffner, a political scientist at George Mason University in Fairfax, Va, and author of "Power Play: The Bush Presidency and the Constitution."

"There is a difference between power and authority," Professor Pfiffner says. "The president has the power to push the [nuclear] buttons, but he doesn't have the constitutional authority to do that. That rests with Congress."

Congress can delegate the power to the president to be prepared to respond immediately to a sudden attack. But the president does not possess the constitutional authority to launch and fight a war without congressional approval.

"Immediately repelling attacks is constitutionally entirely appropriate," Pfiffner says. "But Cheney wants to extend that and say that things are different now that we are under big threats, so you have to give all this power to the executive."

The effort did not fail, experts say. But it did not succeed either.

"I think probably the hopes of the president and vice president for creating a much stronger executive branch have been largely frustrated," says Bradford Berenson, a former associate White House counsel under Bush.

continued

"In the Bush years the hope for revivifying presidential power ended up foundering on some of the war on terror-related policies that Congress and the public ultimately perceived as too pro-executive or too unilateral," Mr. Berenson says.

Some analysts say it is only a matter of time before the Bush and Cheney position is vindicated.

"Over the long term the view will come to be that President Bush was largely successful in restoring the full constitutional powers of the president as commander in chief during time of war and crisis," says Professor Paulsen.

He says President Bush's terror policies were supported by Congress, including via legislation specially written to overturn Supreme Court decisions and amend domestic surveillance laws.

"Ironically, President Bush's use of war powers was much more fully supported by Congress than were President Clinton's," Paulsen says. President Clinton ordered offensive US military operations in Kosovo, he says, without any authorization from Congress.

Paulsen acknowledges that the administration lost several important cases in the US Supreme Court. But he says over time those decisions will be viewed as "far more questionable on legal grounds than President Bush's decisions."

Historians Like Activist Presidents

Cato's Healy agrees that history may be kind to Bush, but for a different reason. "Historians tend to overvalue presidents who provide a lot of drama and explosions," he says. "This is more a reflection of the perverse fascination with activist presidents who provide a lot of drama than it is on President Bush's actual performance, which I think has been quite awful."

Bush isn't the only president who sought to greatly expand his executive powers. Lincoln did it while trying to hold the union together and win a civil war. Franklin Roosevelt did it when he ordered the open-ended internment of American citizens of Japanese heritage during World War II. Harry Truman did it when he tried to use his commander in chief powers to take over the steel mills in 1952.

The Supreme Court precedent from the Truman debacle established the principle that presidents are at the zenith of their power when they act with Congress. It also established that presidential power is at its lowest ebb when the president acts alone in defiance of Congress.

Bush Pushed the Limits of Presidential Power
continued

Although the Supreme Court dealt the Bush administration setbacks in cases involving detainees and military commissions at the Guantánamo Bay prison camp, the high court has never directly ruled on the constitutionality of the administration's claims of unilateral commander in chief power. The terror cases were all decided on lesser legal arguments.

That means Bush's arguments are still available for future presidents. But the Bush experience could cut either way, analysts say. "If you think about lawyers in a future administration arguing about whether a similar claim [of executive power] is right or wrong, those who argue that it is wrong or at least unwise will be strengthened in their arguments [by Bush's record,]" Berenson says.

"I wouldn't say the Bush administration has done more harm than good to executive authority, but they have done less good then they hoped to," he says.

Will Other Presidents Expand Power?

Pfiffner sees a looming threat from the Bush example. "In general, executive power tends to ratchet up; it is less like a pendulum and more like a ratchet," he says. "Bush created precedents of constitutional claims to executive power that other presidents have not. So in that sense he has made the institution more powerful and future presidents can point to that and say Bush did it."

Ironically, future terror attacks may play the most decisive role in shaping how history views the Bush presidency.

"If we are attacked again and there is major loss of life, I think Bush's stock will soar and people will conclude that a lot of what he was doing was absolutely essential," says Professor Calabresi.

But he adds: "If there are no additional attacks and the whole terrorism threat seems to have fizzled out then I think people will be skeptical of what Bush did in fighting the war on terror and think it was unnecessary."

Several analysts echo an assessment made by former Bush legal adviser Jack Goldsmith in his book "The Terror Presidency." Mr. Goldsmith, now a law professor at Harvard, has said the administration could have gotten most of what it wanted had it reached out to Congress instead of trying to act unilaterally.

In his book, he writes: "When an administration makes little attempt to work with the other institutions of our government and makes it a public priority to emphasize that its aim is to expand its power, Congress, the courts,

continued

and the public listen carefully, and worry."

Professor Goldsmith says Bush failed to follow the lessons of Lincoln and Roosevelt, that greatness resides not in the ability to command but in the responsibility to persuade and inspire.

"[Bush] has been almost entirely inattentive to the soft factors of legitimation—consultation, deliberation, the appearance of deference, and credible expressions of public concern for constitutional and international values—in his dealings with Congress, the courts, and allies," Goldsmith writes.

In These Failings Are Important Lessons

"I think the enduring legacy of the Bush administration in the separation of powers realm will be a renewed appreciation of the fact that whatever the limits of unilateral executive authority may be, the executive is strongest when it is acting in partnership with the legislative branch," former White House associate counsel Berenson says. "That is the deepest, ultimate lesson from the administration."[6]

A Complicated Legacy

Despite the surge in nationalism and public support that accompanied Bush's declaration of war in Iraq and subsequent promotion of the War on Terror, Bush's average approval rating over two terms in office was around 49 percent. Such a rating, despite nearly two years of artificially inflated approval, demonstrates how unpopular Bush was outside of the anti-terrorist efforts. Bush's educational initiative, known as "No Child Left Behind," touted as the core of his domestic agenda, is widely considered a failure that deepened educational disparities rather than improving the education system.[7] Bush's tax reform efforts, which included major tax cuts in 2001 and 2003, were a major boon to high-income families but raised the average income for the bottom 20 percent of earners by just

1 percent, insufficient to keep up with inflation. The tax cuts reduced tax revenues and did not result in economic growth.[8] The Bush administration's failure to regulate contributed to the 2008 recession, and Bush left office with an approval rate of around 20 percent, which was the lowest for a departing president in the 70 years since Gallup began recording presidential approval.[9]

In surveys of political scientists and historians, George W. Bush tends to rank at the low end in terms of "greatness," reflecting how the public turned against him and the failure of his policy initiatives. A 2018 study conducted by the *New York Times* found George W. Bush ranked 30th out of 44 presidents. Bush ranked much higher when only right-leaning scholars voted, with Republican scholars ranking him 11th.[10] Interestingly, the election of Donald Trump, the least popular president of the twenty-first century, has had a major impact on public opinion of the George W. Bush presidency. From his low of 20–30 percent approval between 2008 to 2010, Bush's approval ratings rose moderately over the course of the 2010s and shot up to 60 percent following Trump's election. The change in Bush's approval rating reflects the strong negative feelings about Trump.[11]

Left and Civil Rights

Barack Hussein Obama II was born in Hawaii in 1961. The son of a Kenyan national, Barack Obama Sr., and a Kansas-born white woman, Ann Dunham, racism played a major role in young Barack's life. His father was forced to return to Kenya after completing his master's degree at Harvard University in what some historians claim is an example of institutionalized racism for his African heritage and relationships with white women.[12] He returned to see his son only once and was killed in a car accident in Kenya when Obama Jr. was 19 years old. Following his parent's divorce, Obama was raised by his mother and stepfather Lolo Soetoro, a native of Indonesia, spending parts of his childhood in Indonesia and Hawaii.

Barack Obama, by Pete Souza, White House, via Wikimedia.

Obama attended Occidental College in Los Angeles and then Columbia University, where he graduated with a degree in political science in 1983. Soon after, Obama relocated to Chicago, where he worked in predominantly black communities as part of the Developing Communities Project, a private-public investment program designed to help residents of low-income housing communities. In 1988, Obama attended Harvard Law School, where he graduated with a law degree and became the first African American editor of the *Harvard Law Review*, one of the nation's most respected legal journals. His first book, *Dreams from My Father: A Story of Race and Inheritance* (1995), was a memoir that discussed his search for identity and multicultural upbringing. Back in Chicago, Obama married Michelle Robinson, a Chicago native and alum of Harvard and Princeton, who was Obama's supervisor when he took an internship at the Sidley and Austin Law Firm in Chicago.[13]

Obama entered politics in 1996, when he ran for an Illinois state senate seat vacated by Democratic politician Alice Palmer. After winning the election, Obama engaged in what can be described as an activist career, passing more than 300 social service bills that created new state-funded programs for children, the elderly, and the underemployed. He lost a bid for the House of Representatives in 2000 to Representative Bobby Rush, a former leader in the Illinois Black Panther movement who had strong support in the state. In 2004, he won election to the Senate in one of the largest victories in the history of the state and became one of the rising stars of the Democratic Party. His 2004 address at the Democratic National Convention cemented his status as a future party leader. Obama attacked the perception of ideological, racial, and economic divisions in America and called for unity and a collective optimism with regard to the future. A second book, *The Audacity of Hope*, published in 2006, became Obama's manifesto on how he would choose to lead the nation, if ever elected.

Hope and Change

At the end of George W. Bush's presidency, the Republican Party was in major trouble. The War on Terror gradually transformed into a quagmire. The destabilization of the Middle East led to the growth of Islamic radicalism rather than the defeat of terrorism. The Bush administration struggled through a series of controversies and failed policy initiatives, and the recession of 2008 and 2009 was the death knell of the Bush administration and Republican Party's standing. Nevertheless, as an African American, Barack Obama remained a long-shot candidate and would test the influence of racism at the presidential level.

There was an attempt to allege that Obama was not born in the United States and that he was secretly Muslim—claims supported by Donald Trump. Despite blatant attempts to discredit his candidacy, Obama attracted higher numbers of young voters and people of color to his presidential race than any twentieth-century president. His 2009 win was a huge victory, with Obama winning 69.5 million votes to 60 million for Republican challenger John McCain.[14] Running on a platform of hope and change, Obama promised a new start and a new unity for Americans. Democrats also made moderate gains to control the Senate and the House, giving Obama a strong public mandate and a high level of legislative support.

Hope Constrained

Obama's candidacy and election were historic. In addition to becoming the first African American president in U.S. history, Obama excited voters, especially young voters and people of color, more than any other president since John F. Kennedy. Obama's campaign drew higher crowds than any other candidate in history, and he was awarded the Nobel Peace Prize solely on the basis of becoming America's first African American president.

Obama entered office in the middle of the Great Recession, an economic disaster caused in part by the mismanagement of the Bush administration and longer-term failure to regulate the economy that can be credited to Bush, Clinton, Bush Sr., and Reagan. Presidents entering office in the midst of an economic crisis rarely do well because the methods needed to combat such a crisis often have mixed results. The Obama administration's economic package was of a different character. The bill called for funds to be invested in alternative energy, education, and infrastructure projects, using the reinvestment to build and maintain long-term economic assets.[15] The Obama-era economic recovery initiative was broader than FDR's New Deal and included higher levels of investment in public welfare, outreach for the poor, and investment in research and technology. Further, Obama used his bailout of the automotive and health care industries to enact major changes. His sweeping system of health care reform, the Affordable Care Act, turned into a compromise between conservatives and progressives, but was nonetheless the most impactful effort at health-care reform in recent history, helping millions of previously uninsured Americans achieve at least a basic level of health-care.

On the foreign affairs front, Obama faced a difficult situation. The unpopular war that began under Bush continued, and Obama committed additional troops to Afghanistan, Syria, and Iraq, as the emergence of new radical groups threatened the installed governments in those countries. Obama's military legacy was decidedly mixed. His administration is credited with successfully combating the rise of the Syrian militant group ISIS in Syria and Iraq, but his tactics extended and deepened America's commitment to a war that many saw as never ending and unwinnable. His administration was more successful with Iran, reaching a multi-lateral international agreement to prevent their developing nuclear weapons in return for lessening sanctions. Though his administration failed to meet international climate goals, he has also been credited for his role in helping to reach a bilateral US–Chinese agreement that saw both nations pledge to reduce carbon emissions. The Obama administration also took part in the Paris Agreement, an international meeting on climate change, but Republican resistance prevented Obama from committing to a more serious pledge to meet climate goals.

Overall, Obama achieved more than most presidents over his eight years, but the degree of resistance he faced from within the legislature and in the public was unprecedented.[16] The Republicans took control of Congress midway through Obama's first term and adopted an obstructionist approach. Critics of Republican behavior during Obama's term have accused the legislature of emphasizing opposition to Obama over achieving any legislative results. During Obama's second term, after Republicans took control of the Senate, Obama often gave speeches bemoaning the lack of Republican cooperation.[17]

Obama left office having achieved strong economic growth and with major achievements in many domestic and foreign policy issues, but left amid highly divided public sentiment. Overall, his average approval rating sits at around 48 percent, which is lower than any president since Gerald Ford. His highest spike in public approval, at 69 percent just after his election, was balanced by a low of around 38, which he hit three times during his second term in office.[18] It can be argued, however, that Obama's public opinion ratings cannot be effectively used to legitimately judge his presidency because many Americans' attitudes about Obama are colored by racial prejudice rather than objective judgment of his performance or policies.

Certainly, not all criticisms of Obama and his policies are motivated by race, but many studies demonstrate how racial prejudice has affected opinions of Obama. A 2019 study published in *Politics, Groups, and Identity* found that the impact of racial prejudice on public opinion increased during the Obama years, to the extent that the Obama presidency became for some a representation of an existential threat to the dominance of white interests.[19] Likewise, a 2018 study published in *Environmental Politics* looked at what sociologists call the "spillover of racialization," which occurs when racist ideology fuels a shift of opinion on an unrelated topic. In this case, the researchers found that attitudes of white voters on climate change shifted as Barack Obama championed that issue, to the point that skepticism about climate change is now correlated with racial prejudice.[20] Numerous studies of voting statistics have found that racial resentment was a major factor influencing voting patterns in both 2008 and 2012, and further have shown that the most fervent Obama critics among the public rank highly on measurements of racial resentment.[21]

The sense that Obama's administration was a failed one is certainly not shared by experts in the field, no matter their political affiliation. A 2018 *New York Times* poll of political scientists and historians found Obama ranked 8th out of 44 percent. Scholars who identified as progressive or Democratic tended to rank Obama higher, with Obama ranking 6th according to these experts, but independent and scholars identifying as Republican also ranked him highly, with Obama ranking 12th among independents and 16th among Republican scholars.[22] In a 2019 poll of historians conducted by C-SPAN, Obama ranked 12th out of the nation's 44 presidents.[23]

CONCLUSION

Bush left office with one of the lowest levels of public opinion in recent history, but has seen his reputation gradually improve, especially after the election of Donald Trump inspired nostalgia for the less-polarizing manifestation of conservative ideology that existed in the early 2000s. Historians and political scientists, however, have not been as kind in their depictions of the Bush legacy. The dramatic Republican takeover of the legislature and the public panic over the War on Terror gave the Bush administration unfettered powers that were in some ways misused. Bush has also been criticized for purposefully misleading the American people with regard to his administration's activities, and for the widespread civilian surveillance that began amidst the panic over Islamic terrorism. Barack Obama came to office amidst a massive populist surge in civic interest, but his presidency and opinions of his presidency, were overshadowed by racial prejudice. At the end of his two terms in office, Obama stood as a hero to many Americans, and a villain to others, due to perceived abuse of power although some argue that this is based in racial prejudice. The Obama administration was marginalized by an uncooperative Congress, but still managed to achieve much in a short time, including successfully handling the biggest financial crisis since the Great Depression. Historians and political scientists rank Obama relatively highly among America's past presidents. The final chapter discusses the presidency of Donald Trump, whose first term will end in a matter of months. Impeached for abuse of power, Trump's fate is unknown at this time.

DISCUSSION QUESTIONS

♦ Did "racial resentment" impact public perception of the Obama presidency? Explain your answer.

♦ Did the Bush Administration violate presidential authority in the invasion of Iraq? Why or why not?

♦ How did Bush's overall approach to governance change between his gubernatorial administration and his presidential administration?

♦ How would you characterize Obama's use of presidential power?

♦ Do current opinion polls reflect a realistic depiction of Obama's accomplishments? Why or why not?

Works Used

"2000 Presidential General Election Results." *US Election Atlas*. 2019. uselectionatlas.org/RESULTS/national.php?year=2000&off=0&elect=0&f=0.

"2008 Presidential General Election Results." *US Election Atlas*. 2019. uselectionatlas.org/RESULTS/national.php?year=2008&off=0&elect=0&f=0.

"Barack Obama." *YouGov*. 2019. today.yougov.com/topics/politics/explore/ public_figure/Barack_Obama.

Benegal, Salil D. "The Spillover of Race and Racial Attitudes into Public Opinion about Climate Change." *Environmental Politics*, vol. 27, no. 4, 2018, Taylor and Francis online,www.tandfonline.com/doi/ abs/10.1080/09644016.2018.1457287?journalCode=fenp20.

"Bush's Final Approval Rating: 22 Percent." *CBS News*. 16 Jan. 12009. www. cbsnews.com/news/bushs-final-approval-rating-22-percent/.

Drehle, David Von. "Honor and Effort: What President Obama Achieved in Eight Years." *Time*. 22 Dec 2016. time.com/4616866/barack-obama- administration-look-back-history-achievements/.

García, Lily Eskelsen, and Otha Thornton. "'No Child Left Behind' Has Failed." *The Washington Post*. 13 Feb. 2015. www.washingtonpost.com/opinions/no-child-has-failed/2015/02/13/8d619026-b2f8-11e4-827f-93f454140e2b_story.html.

Garrow, David. *Rising Star: The Making of Barack Obama*. New York: Harper Collins, 2017.

Gillett, Rachel, and Allana Akhtar. "These Are the Top 20 US Presidents (and Why You Won't Find Trump on the List)." *Business Insider*. 4 July 2019. www.businessinsider.com/the-top-20-presidents-in-us-history-according-to-historians-2017-2.

Grunwald, Michael. "A New New Deal." *Time*. 5 Nov. 2008. //content.time.com/time/specials/packages/article/0,28804,1856381_1856380,00.html.

_____. "The Victory of 'No.'" *Politico*. 4 Dec. 2016. www.politico.com/magazine/story/2016/12/republican-party-obstructionism-victory-trump-214498.

Horton, Emily. "The Legacy of the 2001 and 2003 'Bush' Tax Cuts." *Center on Budget and Policy Priorities*. 23 Oct. 2017. www.cbpp.org/research/federal-tax/the-legacy-of-the-2001-and-2003-bush-tax-cuts.

Kessler, Glenn. "The Iraq War and WMDs: An Intelligence Failure or White House Spin?" *The Washington Post*. 22 Mar. 2019. www.washingtonpost.com/politics/2019/03/22/iraq-war-wmds-an-intelligence-failure-or-white-house-spin/.

Payson-Denney, Wade. "So, Who Really Won? What the Bush v. Gore Studies Showed." *CNN*. 31 Oct. 2015. www.cnn.com/2015/10/31/politics/bush-gore-2000-election-results-studies/index.html.

"Presidential Approval Ratings—Gallup Historical Statistics and Trends." *Gallup*. 2019. Overnews.gallup.com/poll/116677/presidential-approval-ratings-gallup-historical-statistics-trends.aspx.

Rice, Andrew. "Was Barack Obama Sr. 'Eased' Out of Harvard, and America, for Dating White Women?" *Politico*. 27 Apr. 2011. www.politico.com/states/new-york/albany/story/2016/05/was-barack-obama-sr-eased-out-of-harvard-and-america-for-dating-white-women-048282.

Richey, Warren. "Bush Pushed the Limits of Presidential Power." *Christian Science Monitor*. 14 Jan. 12009. www.csmonitor.com/USA/2009/0114/p11s01-usgn.html.

Rottinghaus, Brandon, and Justin S. Vaughn. "How Does Trump Stack Up Against the Best—and Worst—Presidents?" *New York Times*. 19 Feb. 2018. www.nytimes.com/interactive/2018/02/19/opinion/how-does-trump-stack-up-against-the-best-and-worst-presidents.html.

Smith, Jean Edward. *Bush*. New York: Simon & Schuster, 2016.

Struyk, Ryan. "George W. Bush's Favorable Rating Has Pulled a Complete 180." *CNN Politics*. 22 Jan. 2018. www.cnn.com/2018/01/22/politics/george-w-bush-favorable-poll/index.html.

Tesler, Michael. "Racial Attitudes Remain a Powerful Predictor of Obama Vote Preference." *YouGov*. 23 Jan. 2012. today.yougov.com/topics/politics/articles-reports/2012/01/23/racial-attitudes-remain-powerful-predictor-obama-v.

_____. "The Spillover of Racialization into Evaluations of Bo Obama." *YouGov*. 10 Apr. 2012. today.yougov.com/topics/politics/articles-reports/2012/04/10/spillover-racialization-evaluations-bo-obama.

Toobin, Jeffrey. *Too Close to Call: The Thirty-Six-Day Battle to Decide the 2000 Election.* New York: Random House, 2002.

Woodward, Bob. *Bush at War*. New York: Simon & Schuster, 2002.

Yadon, Nicole, and Spencer Piston "Examining Whites' Anti-Black Attitudes after Obama's Presidency." *Politics, Groups, and Identities*. vol. 7, no.4, 2019, Taylor and Francis online, www.tandfonline.com/doi/abs/10.1080/21565503.2018.1438953?journalCode=rpgi20.

Introduction

It is unfair to judge a presidential administration before that president has left office, and impossible to predict how history will ultimately judge Donald Trump. Barring a major shift in public opinion, however, Trump will most likely finish his first term as the most unpopular president since public opinion polling first began. Entering office despite losing the popular vote by the largest margin of any winning candidate in history, Trump had no public mandate. Though past presidents in similar situations attempted to broaden their appeal, Trump's tendency is to aim his policies at keeping the support of his base rather than to garner a higher level of public appeal. He has pursued a number of highly controversial policy proposals, including cancelling the DACA program, constructing a U.S.-Mexico border wall, and proposing to ban Muslim immigration into the United States. In 2019, federal employees revealed that Trump attempted to use his authority to gain an advantage over his potential political rival Joe Biden, in advance of the 2020 presidential election. This led to Donald Trump becoming the third president to be impeached by the House of Representatives.

Topics covered in this chapter include:

- 2016 election
- U.S.-Mexico border wall
- Presidential impeachment

This Chapter Discusses the Following Source Documents:

"Executive Secrecy: Keeping Information Secret from Congress,"
New York Times, 2019

Shepard, Steven. "Poll: As Impeachment Progresses, Voter Support
Remains Static." *Politico*, Decenber 11, 2019

America's Business
Donald Trump (2017–)

Donald Trump ran for office with no experience in the military, public office, or the civil service. His ability to energize and anger millions of Americans enabled him to defeat a suite of Republican challengers to gain the nomination, and his denigrative style of campaigning enabled him to win an Electoral College victory over Hillary Clinton, who won the popular vote.

The Platinum Spoon

Donald John Trump was born on June 14, 1946, in Queens, New York, the son of real estate developer Frederick Trump and Mary Anne MacLeod. Trump's family was wealthy, and he attended elite private schools and Fordham University, transferring to the Wharton School of Business at the University of Pennsylvania, where he graduated with a bachelor's degree in business. There is little information available about Trump's academic performance from his high-school or college years.

Donald Trump, by Shealah Craighead, White House, via Wikimedia.

Trump's behavior over the last decade suggests he was a poor to middling student.[1] Following college, Trump obtained a draft deferment for the Vietnam War based on bone spurs.[2] Daughters of a Queens podiatrist claimed that their father, who worked in a building owned by Trump Sr., gave Trump a doctor's note falsely claiming an injury at the request of his father.[3]

The *New York Times* has presented the most well-documented analysis of Trump's personal finances. He received a $200,000 salary from his father's company from age 3. At 17, his father gifted him a 52-unit apartment building. After college, Trump's annual salary was around $1 million. Fred Trump operated a real-estate empire, and records show he engaged in an illegal scheme to defraud the federal government out of millions in tax revenue, which included naming Donald banker, consultant, and landlord; numerous "loans" were recorded to Donald Trump by his father, none of which were ever repaid according to Fred Trump's New York tax and financial records. Fred purchased Donald's vehicles and offices, paid his employees and for the renovations of Trump's buildings, and gifted his son partnership in his own businesses. Donald Trump became CEO and shared his father's $300 million estate with his siblings.

Trump's personal rise to fame came via the wealthy social circles of 1980s New York, where he lived the life of a socialite. Trump proved to be a poor businessman, and IRS records indicate that between 1985 and 1994, Trump's empire lost money each year, more than any other individual in the United States. Four of Trump's businesses went bankrupt in the 1990s and evidence suggests that Trump's personal success in business is minimal and that his continued economic strength is primarily due to assets obtained from his father.[4] At the end of 2019, Trump was under investigation for potential tax fraud and other financial misdeeds.[5] In November 2019, it was revealed that Trump had illegally misused funds donated to the Trump Foundation to fund his political campaign and for

personal purchases, and he paid a $2 million dollar fine.[6] In 2018, Trump paid $25 million to settle a case involving a fake business education program, called "Trump University," that defrauded thousands of students of their tuition.[7]

The Man Without a Mandate

The 2016 election was plagued with irregularities, and there were states in which the vote totals were contested because of the disenfranchisement of poor and minority voters. In any case, Trump did not win the popular vote, losing by the greatest margin (nearly 3 million votes) of any winning candidate in history. Trump claimed that he would have won the popular vote if not for a large number of fraudulent votes, but a committee appointed by his administration to investigate this did not turn up any evidence to support this.[8]

As Trump is still in office, it is impossible to judge his leadership or performance as president. Though he entered office without a public mandate, Trump benefitted from a post-election bump in approval ratings as the public withheld judgment until he had had a chance to establish a new agenda. Trump's polarizing agenda quickly resulted in a loss of approval.

Based on the best available data from opinion polling and taking Trump's first 1,000+ days in office, Donald Trump is the least popular president since opinion polling began. Opinion polls do not exist before the twentieth century, but it is likely that Trump would have an extremely low ranking in terms of approval rating compared to these individuals as well due to the fact that, prior to the mid-twentieth century, most Americans felt a responsibility to support their president, regardless of how they voted. For this reason, it is unlikely that many former presidents had approval ratings as consistently low as Trump's over such a long period of time.

While there have been presidents whose approval ratings dipped below Trump's during their first 1,000 days, they all managed at least 50 percent

approval. Trump's rating peaked at 45 percent, for less than a month. For the remainder of his first 1,000 days it hovered between 40–42 percent. This unusually steady level of approval is indicative of a loyal, consistent base largely unaffected by details of Trump's performance or behavior.[9] However, in an editorial that went viral, outgoing editor of *Christianity Today* Mark Galli broke from one of Trump's most unified support bases, evangelical Christians, declaring, "None of the president's positives can balance the moral and political danger we face under a leader of such grossly immoral character." Calling for the president's removal from office, Galli admits that the majority of evangelicals will continue to support Trump.[10]

Presidential Performance?

Trump entered office with his Republican Party dominating both houses of Congress and so, for his first two years, enjoyed significant power to establish a national agenda. However, Trump's achievements over his first three years are relatively few in comparison to past presidents. He faces resistance from both his own party and the opposition party and has failed to win over public opinion on most of his policies. His administration's most notable accomplishment is the passage of a series of tax and economic reforms. The tax reform package was a standard conservative approach, providing tax relief for the wealthy and for corporations while limiting tax relief for the middle and working class. Economists have noted that the Trump tax changes have not "paid for themselves," as it typically claimed, and both corporate and individual tax revenues have fallen as a result. The ultimate impact on the economy will not be known for several years, but analysis of the administration's overall economic reforms indicates little overall benefit to the middle or working class.[11]

Trump has touted the strength of the U.S. economy, which is indeed in the midst of a boom period, but this has done little to win him the support of economists and many in the public, who argue that economic growth is the result of decisions made by previous presidents, notably Barack

Obama during the recovery from the 2008–2009 Great Recession. Under Trump, economic growth is lower per annum than it was under Obama, and the reduction in unemployment slowed also during Trump's time in office as compared to under the Obama administration. While the economy continues an upward trajectory, the pace of economic growth is slowing.[12]

The Trump administration has also greatly reduced regulation. This conservative philosophy says that regulations hurt business productivity and that the free-market will mandate "good behavior" from corporations without the need for government intervention. During periods of deregulation, corporate wealth increases sharply, but consumer interest is typically sacrificed. In many cases, lack of regulation or deregulation ultimately contributes to an economic recession, though this typically happens several years after the deregulatory movement begins. The Trump administration has reduced regulations on real estate, banking, investment trading, and several other industries, most notably on environmental protections, which has created the least environmentally-friendly government in modern history.[13] The Trump administration withdrew America's involvement in international efforts to combat climate change and has voiced skepticism about climate change, despite incontrovertible scientific consensus on the issue.

One of Trump's primary campaign promises was to reform the immigration system. To this end, he proposed a travel ban that would have barred entry to persons from Muslim-majority countries, but it was declared unconstitutional. The Trump administration authorized the separation of immigrant families detained at the border and then authorized the creation of detention centers housing children removed from their parents. Trump was ordered to reunite children with their parents, but failed to comply. He has also reduced visas for high-tech workers and individuals fleeing war or persecution in their home countries. Most of the Trump administration's efforts with immigration have failed or are controversial, and ongoing legal challenges reflect the disparity between Trump's approach and public opinion.

Donald Trump's administration has been chaotic. White House employee turnover has been extreme, and scandals are nearly constant. Trump has bribed a pornographic film star to prevent her from sharing details about their affair; his businesses have been under investigation for tax fraud and other improprieties; he has been forced to pay fines for operating a fraudulent university and misusing funds donated to charity; he has been accused of sexual misconduct with cases still pending due to presidential privilege from prosecution; and he has been the subject of an investigation into the 2016 Russian interference scandal.

The Controversial Chief Executive

Trump's use of executive authority has been controversial in a number of ways. Traditionally, presidential power comes from a president's ability to persuade. Presidents can gain public support for an agenda and use this to force legislators to adopt that agenda. Trump's public approval is too low for this approach. Many conservative legislators feel pressured to support him rather than risk losing support of Trump supporters in their home states or districts. One can argue, however, that Trump's overall lack of strong public support means that many politicians may stand to gain more from opposing him. Trump has also proven unskilled in achieving goals by forming coalitions within the legislature. Faced with a lack of traditional presidential power, he is forced to using the unilateral powers of the presidency, an approach that garners mixed results, due to strong legislative and popular opposition.

Trump's unique style of executive leadership has led to unique questions about presidential authority regarding: appointing family members without qualifications to key governmental positions; refusing to cooperate with official investigations; withholding tax returns.

In late 2019, the *New York Times* asked about the kind of reforms that might occur after Trump's time in office. One reform was regarding "executive secrecy." To what degree does a president have the right to withhold personal or professional information, and to what degree does Congress have the power to demand this information? The question of executive privilege and secrecy is not new. Numerous presidents have withheld personal information from the public and from Congress. For example, Woodrow Wilson withheld from Congress that he was disabled and unable to fulfill his duties. The following article offers politicians' views:

EXECUTIVE SECRECY
KEEPING INFORMATION SECRET FROM CONGRESS

New York Times

2019

Source Document Excerpt

Presidents of both parties have claimed that executive privilege applies not only to their own internal White House communications, but also to internal deliberations within government department and agencies that do not involve the president. The Trump legal team has further argued that congressional subpoenas whose primary goal is to uncover potential wrongdoing, rather than to inform bill writing, are invalid because they lack a legitimate legislative purpose.

The Question

Does executive privilege extend to agency deliberations that did not involve the White House? Does Congress have legitimate constitutional authority to issue subpoenas compelling disclosure of information about potential wrongdoing?

Michael Bennet
Senator from Colorado, 54

Executive privilege should not be used to shield advisors from Congressional inquiries. Unlike President Trump, I would make sure the privilege is exercised with great caution.

Joseph R. Biden Jr.
Former Vice President, 76

We have seen in this administration systematic abuses of claims of executive privilege. In the first

continued

instance, presidents should not seek to aggressively expand claims of presidential privilege to internal deliberations within government departments and agencies that do not involve the president or implicate in any meaningful way the president's confidentiality interests.

Cory Booker
Senator from New Jersey, 50

The Supreme Court has made clear that executive privilege is qualified. An alarming feature of this administration is the perception that it is absolute, and can extend to nearly all agency deliberations.

Steve Bullock
Governor of Montana, 53

The President must have some measure of executive privilege so as to obtain guidance and information from within the White House and the Administration. Executive privilege cannot be invoked to cloak illegal acts or criminal conduct.

Pete Buttigieg
Mayor of South Bend, Ind., 37

I believe claims of executive privilege have been made too loosely and casually in recent years. They should be limited to the original rationale of that doctrine: the need of any President to be able to rely on the candor and completeness of the advice received, and to avoid the self-censorship that may come with the risk that confidential advice could be disclosed.

Bill de Blasio
Mayor of New York City, 58

Congress has the constitutional authority to obtain necessary information to investigate potential wrongdoing within the executive branch. And the executive branch has the legal authority to withhold certain material because it is protected by executive privilege.

Tulsi Gabbard
Congresswoman from Hawaii, 38

No, executive privilege should not extend beyond White House internal communications. Yes, Congress has legitimate authority to compel disclosure of wrongdoing.

Kamala Harris
Senator from California, 54

Executive privilege can extend to agency deliberations that do not involve the White House, but it should not be a broad shield to prevent public scrutiny and oversight. Congress has legitimate constitutional authority to issue subpoenas compelling disclosure of information about potential wrongdoing.

Executive Secrecy
Keeping Information Secret from Congress
continued

Amy Klobuchar
Senator from Minnesota, 59

I believe that Congress does have a role to compel disclosure about potential wrongdoing, and I have always believed in the importance of Congressional investigations, the separation of powers, and our system of checks and balances. As President, I would continue to hold a limited view of executive privilege.

Beto O'Rourke
Former congressman from Texas, 47

Although the precise scope of the authorities of Congress and the president have been the subject of centuries of debate, it is my view that President Trump has overstated the appropriate scope of executive privilege and understated the scope of Congress's legitimate power to seek information, with harmful consequences for the balance of powers and the healthy functioning of our system of checks and balances.

Tim Ryan
Congressman from Ohio, 46

No.

Bernie Sanders
Senator from Vermont, 78

The Trump administration has gone much farther than its predecessors, and abused the power of executive privilege as applied to agency deliberations. This privilege should only be exercised in limited circumstances.

Mark Sanford
Republican former governor from South Carolina,

With every privilege comes responsibility, and in this regard, it is important that Congress not overstep its bounds in its authority for oversight of the Executive Branch. So to answer your question I do not believe in executive privilege agency deliberation, and I believe Congress has the right to issues subpoenas compelling disclosure.

Joe Sestak
Former congressman from Pennsylvania, 67

No, I do not believe executive privilege extends to agency deliberations, and so Congress does have legitimate constitutional authority to issue subpoenas compelling disclosure

continued

of information about potential wrongdoing. Executive privilege is nowhere to be found in the Constitution, and thus is a very limited principle.

Tom Steyer
Democratic businessman and activist, 62

The Supreme Court ruled in the 1970's that executive privilege is a right of the President, but that that right is qualified and not absolute. I believe that the fraud and failure we have in the White House has completely distorted the scope of executive privilege and the cronies he appointed to political positions is hiding behind executive privilege even though that right does not extend to their agencies or departments.

Joe Walsh
Republican former congressman from Illinois, 57

It's important to highlight the distinction between broad executive privilege and investigative privilege: Our system of checks and balances assigns Congress the responsibility to investigate executive-branch wrongdoing in order to support Congress's legislative actions. This is why our federal and state prosecutors have subpoena power.

Elizabeth Warren
Senator from Massachusetts, 70

Oversight and transparency are essential to preserving our system of checks and balances, and Congress has a responsibility to require transparency from executive branch officials and oversee their activities. The use of executive privilege has become, under the Trump Administration, exceedingly broad, extending to activities far beyond protecting internal deliberations that facilitate sound decision-making.

William F. Weld
Republican former governor of Massachusetts, 74

I think an otherwise proper assertion of executive privilege could extend to executive branch deliberations not involving the White House. On the other hand, the oversight responsibilities of Congress clearly warrant the issuance of subpoenas seeking evidence of potential wrongdoing.

Marianne Williamson
Self-help author, 67

Unlike the express Speech or Debate Clause privileging congressional deliberations, executive privilege is a constitutionally atextual and substantially invented concept vis-a-

Executive Secrecy
Keeping Information Secret from Congress
continued

vis Congress. The Supreme Court has never sustained the privilege regarding congressional oversight of the executive and the House Judiciary Committee voted an article of impeachment against President Nixon for resisting a congressional subpoena.[14]

Third To Be Impeached

In late 2019, a federal whistleblower alerted investigators that Trump and members of his team were engaged in activities that might constitute a violation of authority. The scandal hinged on whether or not Trump abused the power of his office when he pressured the newly elected president of Ukraine, Volodymyr Zelensky, to announce he was investigating the activities of Hunter Biden, son of former vice president and 2020 presidential contender Joe Biden, who was working at a Ukrainian company. Trump claimed that Biden's employment at this company involved illegal activities. It was thereafter revealed that the Trump administration had allegedly attempted to leverage military aid (already earmarked for the Ukraine) and a potential White House visit in return for Zelensky announcing publicly that his government was investigating the Bidens. A number of legislators and experts in the field of constitutional law issued statements to the effect that attempting to utilize presidential power for personal gain was a violation of constitutional limits on the presidency, and thus constituted an "abuse of power" that could potentially warrant impeachment.

The Democrat-led House of Representatives opened an impeachment hearing, and the public and legislators heard testimony from members of the civil service and constitutional legal scholars on the issue. The general consensus was that the Trump administration had attempted to use the

authority of the presidency to leverage personal political gains for Trump. The White House presented no evidence to refute the validity of these claims, but alleged that the investigation and impeachment proceedings were a political attack. The issue remained highly partisan. In this article from *Politico*, journalist Steven Shepard looks at the evolution of public opinion regarding the impeachment controversy:

POLL: AS IMPEACHMENT PROGRESSES, VOTER SUPPORT REMAINS STATIC

Steven Shepard
Politico
December 11, 2019

In nine surveys since early October, backing has ranged from 48 percent to 50 percent.

Over the past 2½ months, the House impeachment inquiry has brought a whirlwind of new information about President Donald Trump's handling of aid to Ukraine.

But as the House inches closer to just the third impeachment of a sitting president, a new POLITICO/Morning Consult poll shows public opinion of the inquiry is right where it started.

Half of registered voters, 50 percent, approve of the current impeachment inquiry, the poll shows. That's greater than the 42 percent who oppose it. Eight percent of voters don't have an opinion.

Since the official inquiry began on Sept. 24, POLITICO/Morning Consult polls have shown remarkable stability in public support for the probe. In nine surveys since early October, support has ranged from 48 percent to 50 percent, while opposition has been from 41 percent to 45 percent.

The numbers cast doubt on Republicans' claims that, as Democrats in the House majority have laid out their case, impeachment has become less popular. But they also show—despite wall-to-wall televised hearings and, at times, bombshell testimony—Democrats have failed to convert voters who were skeptical of the probe, including a small share of the electorate that disapproves of the president's job performance.

Views of the impeachment inquiry split sharply along party lines: Eighty-three percent of Democratic voters support the inquiry, while 81 percent

of Republicans oppose it. Among independent voters, 45 percent support the inquiry and 41 percent oppose it.

Public opinion of the next two steps in the impeachment process closely tracks with overall backing for the inquiry: Fifty-one percent of voters would support the House voting to impeach Trump, and 49 percent would support conviction and removal by the Senate.

The POLITICO/Morning Consult poll was conducted Dec. 6–8, prior to House Democrats' announcement Tuesday that they would pursue two articles of impeachment against Trump, charging him with abuse of power and obstruction of Congress.

While impeachment hasn't become more popular over the past two months, the president's stance—that his conduct was entirely appropriate—is shared by less than a third of voters. Only 29 percent say Trump "acted appropriately, and Congress shouldn't impeach him and remove him from office." By comparison, 46 percent say "Trump committed impeachable offenses, and Congress should remove him from office," while 16 percent say "Trump acted inappropriately, but Congress shouldn't impeach him and remove him from office."

Despite consistent plurality support for the impeachment inquiry, few voters expect him to be removed. Only 21 percent say it's "very" or "somewhat" likely he'll be impeached or removed.

The poll also shows a small slide for Trump's job approval rating, bringing the president to a new low in POLITICO/Morning Consult polling.

"Our polling indicates the impeachment inquiry may be taking a toll on the president's standing with the American public," said Tyler Sinclair, Morning Consult's vice president. "This week, President Trump's net approval rating has declined to its lowest point of his term, as 58 percent of voters disapprove and 39 percent approve of his performance."

Eight in 10 voters who disapprove of Trump's job performance, 80 percent, support the impeachment inquiry, while 13 percent oppose it. By comparison, only 8 percent of voters who approve of the job Trump is doing as president support the inquiry, and 87 percent oppose it.

The POLITICO/Morning Consult poll surveyed 1,994 registered voters and has a margin of sampling error of plus or minus 2 percentage points.[15]

The evidence suggesting that Trump committed the acts for which he is under investigation is robust, and there has been little effort to counter these charges. It does not appear that Trump defenders will attempt to argue that Trump did not try to utilize his office for personal gain, but rather will argue that this is not an impeachable offense.

Defenders have argued that there is or should be a high bar for impeachment. However, in the case against Bill Clinton, the charges were obstruction of justice and lying under oath. Trump has refused to testify, and so has not lied under oath, but he has made a number of public statements about the controversy and his role that have been proven false, and so is guilty of attempting to spread misinformation. Further, Trump has admitted that he ordered individuals who had been subpoenaed to testify to ignore those orders and to refuse to testify.

A formal impeachment inquiry against Trump was launched in September 2019, and in November 2019 a federal judge ruled—against historical precedent—that members of the executive branch are not immune from compulsory testimony in Congress, despite demands from the Trump administration that top-level White House staff defy subpoenas. On December 18, the House of Representatives impeached the president on two counts—obstruction of Congress (by a vote of 230–197) and abuse of power (229–198). This is the third time in history that a president has been impeached. Next steps involve a Senate trial, which will likely take a partisan path.[16] It remains unclear whether or not public opinion on Trump will change markedly in coming years.

The Power of the President

There have been presidents who failed to exercise presidential power or to capitalize on their political advantages, and there have been presidents who aggressively utilized the power of their office and who dominated the evolution of government during their presidencies. Trump belongs to

neither of these camps. His public approval, among a minority but passionate base, gives him influence, but he appears to lack the ability to capitalize on this. Some have accused Trump of attempting to expand the powers of the presidency with his actions, but the evidence suggests that this may not be the case.

When evaluating the Trump presidency, it is important to note that Trump had no prior experience in civil service or governance. It is possible that Trump's use of presidential power appears chaotic because Trump is utilizing the powers of his presidency as he learns about them or as they are brought to his attention by his advisors. Trump sparked controversy when he suggested via *Twitter* that he could simply pardon himself for any crime he'd committed while in office, or perhaps before. This is not legally correct, but Trump's claim may reflect a lack of knowledge more than a desire to abuse his power. In a 2018 *Atlantic* article, David Graham noted that Trump's controversial use of presidential power does not seem to be designed to increase the power of the presidency, but has primarily consisted of instances in which Trump attempted to utilize what he saw as his authority to protect himself or to provide himself with some form of political or personal profit.[17]

The prohibition against using political power for personal gain is a fundamental ethical principle that underlies democratic and representative governance and is enshrined in both constitutional passages and other forms of law. Some of the earliest reform movements were attempts to eliminate the patronage system, in which presidents and politicians used political appointments to increase their personal wealth and as bribes to gain political or economic support.

Regardless of why he used executive power as he did, Trump's first three years in office have not resulted in favorable ratings from experts. In a 2018 *New York Times* survey of historians and political scientists, Trump ranked last of 44 presidents in terms of performance and effectiveness.

Even among scholars of opposing political ideology, Trump achieved low ratings. Scholars identifying as independent ranked Trump 43rd out of 44 presidents, ahead of only James Buchanan, who failed to prevent the Civil War. Even scholars who identified as Republican or conservative only rated Trump 40th out of 44.[18]

The difficulty in judging Trump is that his administration claims that all criticism of his performance and presidency is part of a political conspiracy against him. For those Americans who believe this, all information on his presidency is untrustworthy, despite being shaped by false claims and misinformation. Likewise, it would have been impossible to gauge rational public opinion on issues like the Vietnam War when presidential administrations promoted false information about the war to the American people.

Trump's election has revealed deep ideological fissures within American society, and there is widespread disagreement regarding Trump's performance. Beyond partisan affiliation, a fundamental truth about the American political process is that the president and all members of the legislature are not chosen to lead the American people but to represent them. All political power arises from the people, and those chosen to hold office have a sworn constitutional duty to serve and represent the people who placed them into office.

CONCLUSION

As the impeachment process against President Trump unfolds, the Trump administration has depicted opposition to his policies, and presidency in general, as a manifestation of a conspiracy against him. More realistically, opposition to Trump is due to his failure to build on the traditional sources of presidential authority. As we have seen throughout this volume, the power of the presidency is based on a president's ability to gain public trust and approval, and to work effectively with other administrators and public servants. Trump has a poor record in this regard and, as of January 2020, has not managed to build his support base. This lack of public trust and failure to form working relationships explains the unprecedented level of opposition to Trump's presidency. The negative depiction of his performance in the popular press likewise reflects Trump's low levels of popular approval, as well as the fact that Trump's policies are not designed with reference to professional and expert opinion; thus media reports frequently include professional and expert criticism. Though the Trump administration has argued that his December 2019 impeachment is invalid, the allegations against him were made by respected members of his administration and the Civil Service, and there is no evidence to suggest that any of them made false statements or their concerns regarding presidential misconduct were false. Whether or not Americans believe that Trump's behavior warrants removal from office, the case for impeachment was strong and has been judged appropriate by the vast majority of experts in the field.

DISCUSSION QUESTIONS

♦ What does Trump's low popularity level reveal about the nature of presidential success and failure?

♦ Does Trump's lack of experience in public service impact the way that he has performed in his presidency? Explain your answer.

♦ How does the Trump impeachment process differ from that undertaken against Bill Clinton?

♦ How does Trump's actions regarding abuse of presidential power compare with that of other presidents?

♦ Was there anything that Trump could have done to avoid being impeached? What?

Works Used

Anapol, Avery. "Daughters of NY Podiatrist Allege He Helped Trump Avoid Vietnam War: New York Times." *The Hill*. 26 Dec. 2018. thehill.com/homenews/administration/422854-daughters-of-queens-podiatrist-and-fred-trump-tenant-say-father.

Blake, Aaron. "The Extensive Effort to Bury Donald Trump's Grades." *The Washington Post*. 5 Mar. 2019. www.washingtonpost.com/politics/2019/03/05/extensive-effort-bury-donald-trumps-grades/.

Bycoffe, Aaron, Ella Koeze, and Nathaniel Rakich. "Do Americans Support Impeaching Trump?" *FiveThirtyEight*. 17 Dec. 2019. projects.fivethirtyeight.com/impeachment-polls/.

Cassidy, John. "As a Businessman, Trump Was the Biggest Loser of All." *New Yorker*. 8 May 2019. www.newyorker.com/news/our-columnists/as-a-businessman-trump-was-the-biggest-loser-of-all.

"Executive Secrecy." *New York Times*. 2019. www.nytimes.com/interactive/2019/us/politics/executive-secrecy-executive-power.html.

Graham, David A. "The Strangest Thing About Trump's Approach to Presidential Power." *The Atlantic*. 7 June 2018. www.theatlantic.com/politics/archive/2018/06/the-strangest-thing-about-trumps-approach-to-presidential-power/562271/.

"How Unpopular Is Donald Trump?" *FiveThirtyEight*. 15 Dec. 2019. projects.fivethirtyeight.com/trump-approval-ratings/.

Mathis-Lilley, Ben. "President Pays Gigantic Fine for Stealing from Charity." *Slate*. 11 Dec. 2019. slate.com/news-and-politics/2019/12/trump-pays-2-million-fine-for-stealing-from-charity.html.

Norman, Jim. "Solid Majority Still Opposes New Construction on Border Wall." *Gallup*. 4 Feb. 2019. news.gallup.com/poll/246455/solid-majority-opposes-new-construction-border-wall.aspx.

Politi, Daniel. "Trump Says 'Probably Not' Prepared to Lose in 2020, Doesn't Believe He Lost Popular Vote." *Slate*. 23 June 2019. slate.com/news-and-politics/2019/06/trump-not-prepared-lose-reelection-lost-popular-vote.html.

Rottinghaus, Brandon, and Justin S. Vaughn. "How Does Trump Stack Up Against the Best—and Worst—Presidents?" *New York Times*. 19 Feb. 2018. www.nytimes.com/interactive/2018/02/19/opinion/how-does-trump-stack-up-against-the-best-and-worst-presidents.html.

Russonello, Giovanni. "The Supreme Court May Let Trump End DACA. Here's What the Public Thinks About It." *New York Times*. 15 Nov. 2019. www.nytimes.com/2019/11/15/us/politics/daca-supreme-court-polls.html.

Shepard, Steven. "Poll: As Impeachment Progresses, Voter Support Remains Static." *Politico*. 11 Dec. 2019. www.politico.com/news/2019/12/11/poll-impeachment-voter-support-081122.

"Trump Investigation Guide: Impeachment, Inquiries, Lawsuits." *Bloomberg*. 22 Nov. 2019. www.bloomberg.com/graphics/trump-investigations/.

"US Economy Under Trump: Is It the Greatest in History?" *BBC*. BBC News. 27 Sept. 2019. www.bbc.com/news/world-45827430.

Waldman, Paul. "Is It Time to Talk about Donald Trump's Draft Dodging?" *The Washington Post*. 28 May 2019. www.washingtonpost.com/opinions/2019/05/28/is-it-time-talk-about-donald-trumps-draft-dodging/.

Walters, Joanna. "Trump University: Court Upholds $25m Settlement to Give Students' Money Back." *The Guardian*. 6 Feb. 2018. www.theguardian.com/us-news/2018/feb/06/trump-university-court-upholds-25m-settlement-to-give-students-money-back.

Wilker, Noelle. "Harder to Breathe: Air Quality Has Worsened Since 2016." *CMU*. Carnegie Mellon University. 25 Nov. 2019. www.cmu.edu/news/stories/archives/2019/november/air-quality-worsens.html.

Wilkie, Christina. "President Trump Is Impeached in a Historic Vote by the House, Will Face Trial in the Senate." *CNBC*. 19 Dec. 2019. www.cnbc.com/2019/12/18/trump-impeached-by-house-for-high-crimes-and-misdemeanors.html.

Yglesias, Matthew. "What Trump Has Actually Done in His First 3 Years." *Vox*. 2 Dec. 2019. www.vox.com/policy-and-politics/2019/12/2/20970521/trump-administration-achievements.

Zimmerman, Jonathan. "Decades Later, My Fellow Democrats Should Admit Character Counts." *Wall Street Journal*. 23 Dec. 2019. www.wsj.com/articles/decades-later-my-fellow-democrats-should-admit-character-counts-11577144800.

On December 18, 2019, Donald Trump became the third president in 243 years to be impeached. It is fitting that this work—an examination of presidential authority throughout history—is published just as the House of Representatives exercises its constitutional role by formally condemning a president for abusing his authority.

The No Confidence Vote

In a parliamentary system, when a prime minister is seen as failing in his or her duties, members of the parliament may cast a "no confidence vote," indicating that they no longer believe the prime minister capable of fulfilling the office. In this case, a new public vote may be called to reconstitute the parliament and thereby replace the prime minister.

In the American system, a president cannot be replaced before the end of his or her four-year term, except through extraordinary means. However, after two years of a president's term in office, American voters have the opportunity to express their support for a president and his party by re-electing or replacing legislators, during the "midterm vote"

In the 2018 midterm election, the Republican Party maintained control of the Senate but suffered a major defeat in the House of Representatives, where the Democratic Party gained majority control. When Congress was created, the Framers envisioned the Senate as the representative body of America's wealthy and intellectual elite, and the House of Representatives was envisioned as a way to balance the will of the masses against the elite.

When a president is accused of misbehavior, both the House and Senate have specific roles to play. The House of Representatives, as the organ of the people, brings formal charges against a president, called

impeachment. While impeachment is a necessary step to removing a president from office, it does not automatically result in removal from office. Two presidents have been impeached but not removed from the presidency. The Senate chose to leave Andrew Johnson in office, knowing that he would be powerless after impeachment. In the case of Bill Clinton, Senators from both parties were divided on whether he should be removed from office, and voted to acquit.

When a federal whistleblower revealed that Trump used the power of his office to gain a political advantage over opponent Joe Biden, the House of Representatives investigated to determine if the president was guilty of crimes warranting impeachment. Trump refused to testify, and ordered federal witnesses to refuse to comply with House subpoenas. This tactic was part of the reason that he was impeached for obstructing justice in the investigation. Members of the House voted 230 to 197 in favor of abusing the power of the presidency, and 229 to 198 in favor of obstructing Congress.

No Conspiracies Allowed

Three years of public opinion polls indicate that Trump has never commanded majority popular support and, in fact, has the lowest approval rating over his first three years of any president since public opinion polling began. As discussed in this volume, many, many presidents have lost popular support or have entered office without a popular mandate, but went on to increase their popularity. Such presidents have become more popular through handling of key issues or because they campaigned directly to recruit more voters to their cause. This is not the case with President Trump.

How might past presidents have approached the current situation faced by Donald Trump? Thomas Jefferson, James Madison, and John Adams might have written eloquent letters published in the finest papers of their era. Franklin Roosevelt would have likely arranged fireside chats to speak to the American public, while Teddy Roosevelt might have embarked on a train tour across the country, speaking at political rallies, county fairs, Christmas pageants, and city council meetings. One common action they all would have taken is to have fought their case in Congress, which Donald Trump chose not to do. Had opinion polls showed significant opposition to impeachment, or had Trump chosen to handle the impeachment inquiry differently, it is likely that he might have avoided impeachment and perhaps been issued a less-impactful censure.

As we have seen throughout this work, a president's power depends on the quality, expertise, and effectiveness of his or her allies and the strength of the relationships that the president forms with other officers of the government. Trump's failure to build bi-partisan alliances and cultivate relationships with experienced experts are likewise factors in his impeachment.

Power and Purpose

In general, popular opinion of the presidency is less informative in the midst of a presidency than in the years after a president has left office. In addition, there are often factors at play that limit the legitimacy of public opinion. For instance, studies have shown that Barack Obama's rating is impacted by what's called "racial resentment"—factors unrelated to his performance. This typically results when a president takes on an unfamiliar and controversial role. When the first woman is elected president of the United States, for example, her approval rating is likely to be influenced by misogyny and gender stereotypes. In coming years, opinions on the performance of recent presidents will solidify, and the evaluation of President Trump will reflect a more dispassionate, rational view of his presidency and performance. Bill Clinton actually experienced a boost in public support during and

immediately after his impeachment, but his popular approval has since declined.

Scholars have argued that, in recent years, the independent power of the presidency has increased. As alarming as this might be, presidential authority remains a collaborative process that depends both on public support and effective working relationships. Presidents who do not form professional relationships, or win the public trust, will encounter too much resistance to effectively exercise their power. The impeachment process is the last resort of Congressional checks and balances on the office of the president That the American presidency is afforded limited independent power is not an accident, but a purposeful construction to avoid the inherent danger in allowing the presidency to become too independently powerful. Presidents who face low public opinion, or who are unable to convince the public or other legislators to support their agenda, should alter that agenda to more effectively reflect the public will.

Works Used

"Article 3." *UDHR*. Universal Declaration of Human Rights. Columbia University. http://ccnmtl.columbia.edu/projects/mmt/udhr/article_3.html.

Notes

Introduction

1. Tan, "Presidential Systems."
2. "Federalist No. 70 (1788)," *Bill of Rights Institute*.
3. Meacham, *The Soul of America*.
4. Longley, "Separation of Powers: A System of Checks and Balances."
5. Neustadt, *Presidential Power: The Politics of Leadership*.
6. Gilens and Page, "Testing Theories of American Politics: Elites, Interest Groups, and Average Citizens."

Chapter 1

1. Cain, "29 American Presidents Who Served in the Military."
2. McDonald, "Washington, George."
3. "Surveying Career," *Mount Vernon*.
4. "George Washington," *White House*.
5. Hoock, *Scars of Independence*.
6. "To George Washington from Lewis Nicola, 22 May 1782," *Founders Online*.
7. "From George Washington to Lewis Nicola," *Founders Online*.
8. Haggard, "The Nicola Affair."
9. Geist, "George Washington and the Evolution of the American Commander in Chief."
10. Washington, "Letter of the President of the Federal Convention."
11. Chernow, *Washington: A Life*.
12. "Washington's Inaugural Address of 1789, a transcription," *Archives*.
13. Yoo, "George Washington and the Executive Power."
14. Washington, "Washington's Farewell Address 1796."
15. Weinger, "Poll: George Washington Still Tops."

Chapter 2

1. "John Adams Biography," *National Park Service*.
2. Adams, "The Braintree Instructions."
3. "Articles of Confederation, 1777–1781." *U.S. Department of State*.
4. Illing, "How Meritocracy Harms Everyone—Even the Winners."
5. Carson, *The Measure of Merit*.

6. Jefferson, "From Thomas Jefferson to James Sullivan, 9 February 1797."
7. Prakash, "Stop Fighting It. America Is a Monarchy, and That's Probably for the Best."
8. Ellenbogen, "Another Explanation for the Senate: The Anti-Federalists, John Adams, and the Natural Aristocracy."
9. "John Jay's Treaty, 1794–95," *U.S. Department of State.*
10. "On This Day: The First Bitter, Contested Presidential Election Takes Place," *National Constitution Center.*
11. "The XYZ Affair and the Quasi-War with France, 1798–1800," *U.S. Department of State.*
12. Hemel and Posner, "The Logan Act and its Limits."
13. "Alien and Sedition Acts (1798)," *Our Documents.*
14. "Benjamin Franklin Bache," *Mount Vernon.*
15. Hamilton, "Letter from Alexander Hamilton, Concerning the Public Conduct and Character of John Adams."
16. "Residence Act," *LOC.*

Chapter 3

1. Meacham, *Thomas Jefferson: The Art of Power.*
2. "Declaration of Independence: A Transcription," *National Archives.*
3. Onuf, "Thomas Jefferson: Life Before the Presidency."
4. "To James Madison from Thomas Jefferson, 20 December 1787," *Founders Online.*
5. Dunn, *Jefferson's Second Revolution.*
6. Thompson and Pollitt, "Impeachment of Federal Judges: An Historical Overview."
7. Jefferson, "From Thomas Jefferson to Abigail Smith Adams, 13 June 1804."
8. "Marbury v. Madison," *Justia.*
9. Jefferson, "From Thomas Jefferson to Yusuf Qaramanli."
10. Jefferson, "First Annual Message to Congress, 8 December 1801."
11. "Barbary Wars," *U.S. Department of State.*
12. Madison, James. "From James Madison to Tobias Lear, 6 June 1804."
13. Jefferson, "From Thomas Jefferson to United States Congress, 13 January 1806."
14. "The Louisiana Purchase," *Monticello.*

Chapter 4

1. Grove, "The Man Who Was the Madison."
2. Dunaway, "The Virginia Conventions of the Revolution."
3. Madison, "Federalist No. 51."

4. "Five Items Congress Deleted from Madison's Original Bill of Rights," *Constitution Daily*.

5. Hunter, "The First Gerrymander? Patrick Henry, James Madison, James Monroe, and Virginia's 1788 Congressional Districting."

6. "The Chesapeake Affair of 1807," *Mariners Museum*.

7. "Naval Chronicle Vol XXVII," USS Constitution Museum Collection.

8. "Embargo of 1807," *Monticello*.

9. Stagg, "James Madison: Campaigns and Elections."

10. Hickey, *The War of 1812: A Forgotten Conflict*.

11. "Flight of the Madisons," *White House History*.

12. "War of 1812–1815," *U.S. Department of State*.

14. Buel, *America on the Brink*.

15. Madison, "March 3, 1817: Veto Message on the Internal Improvements Bill."

16. Stewart, "The Surprising Raucous Home Life of the Madisons."

17. "Becoming America's First Lady," *Montpelier*.

Chapter 5

1. Unger, *The Last Founding Father*.

2. Poston, *James Monroe: A Republican Champion*.

3. Preston, "James Monroe: Life Before the Presidency."

4. Preston, "James Monroe: Campaigns and Elections."

5. McNamara, "The Era of Good Feelings."

6. Unger, *The Last Founding Father*.

7. Sky, *The National Road and the Difficult Path to Sustainable National Investment*.

8. "The Monroe Doctrine," *Jamesmonroemuseum*.

Chapter 6

1. Feller, "Andrew Jackson."

2. Unger, *The Last Founding Father*.

3. Traub, "The Ugly Election That Birthed Modern American Politics."

4. Ratcliffe, *The One-Party Presidential Contest*.

5. Parsons, *The Birth of Modern Politics*.

6. Jordan, "Andrew Jackson Was a Rich Populist Who Bragged and Invited Scorn. Trump Draws New Interest in the 7th President."

7. Meacham, *American Lion: Andrew Jackson in the White House*.

8. McNamara, "The Spoils System: Definition and Summary."

9. Wilentz, *Andrew Jackson*.

10. Marszalek, *The Petticoat Affair*.

11. Jackson, "May 27, 1830: Veto Message Regarding Funding of Infrastructure Development."
12. Clay, *The Speeches of Henry Clay,* p. 408.
13. "Cherokee Nation v. Georgia," *LII.*
14. Donovan, "John Marshall Has Made His Decision, Now Let Him Enforce it."
15. Jackson, "Andrew Jackson's Speech to Congress on Indian Removal."
16. "Indian Removal," *PBS.*
17. Celano, "The Indian Removal Act: Jackson, Sovereignty and Executive Will."
18. Inskeep, "How Jackson Made a Killing in Real Estate."
19. "National General Election VEP Turnout Rates, 1789–Present," *Elect Project.*

Chapter 7

1. Sibley, *Martin Van Buren and the Emergence of American Popular Politics.*
2. "Presidential Election of 1836: A Resource Guide," *LOC.*
3. Sumner, *Andrew Jackson as a Public Man,* p. 382.
4. "History-Essays," *Lehrman Institute.*
5. Wilson, *The Presidency of Martin Van Buren.*
6. Moore, *Eighteen Minutes.*
7. Schroeder, "Annexation or Independence: The Texas Issue in American Politics, 1836–1845."
8. "William Henry Harrison," *White House.*
9. Watt, Spedding, Scott, *Cheap Print and Popular Song in the Nineteenth Century*, p. 77.
10. Shafer, *The Carnival Campaign.*
11. "Presidential Election of 1840: A Resource Guide," *LOC.*
12. Kelly, "Quotes from Martin Van Buren."
13. Harrison, "Inaugural Address of William Henry Harrison."
14. May, *John Tyler.*
15. Shafer, "'He Lies Like a Dog': The First Effort to Impeach a President Was Led by His Own Party."
16. "The First Congressional Override of a Presidential Veto," *House.*
17. Freehling, "John Tyler: Campaigns and Elections."
18. Freehling, "John Tyler: Impact and Legacy."

Chapter 8

1. Seigenthaler, *James K. Polk.*
2. Bicknell, *America 1844.*

3. O'Sullivan, "Annexation."

4. Polk, "Inaugural Address of James Knox Polk."

5. Polk, "May 11, 1846: War Message to Congress."

6. Lincoln, "Spot Resolutions."

7. Bomboy, "The Man Who Delivered California to the U.S. and Was Fired for It."

8. Guardino, *The Dead March*.

9. Uenuma, "During the Mexican-American War, Irish-Americans Fought for Mexico in the 'Saint Patrick's Battalion.'"

10. Greenberg, *A Wicked War*.

Chapter 9

1. Bauer, *Zachary Taylor: Soldier, Planter, Statesman of the Old Southwest*.

2. Holt, "Zachary Taylor: Life Before the Presidency."

3. "Presidential Election of 1848: A Resource Guide," *LOC*.

4. Han, *Hatred of American Presidents*.

5. Clay, *The Speeches of Henry Clay*, p. 470.

6. Clay, "Clay's Resolutions, January 29, 1850."

7. Feuerherd, "The Strange History of Masons in America."

8. Vaughn, *The Anti-Masonic Party in the United States: 1826–1843*.

9. Holt, "Millard Fillmore: Life Before the Presidency."

10. Webster and Everett, *The Writings and Speeches of Daniel Webster*, pp. 419–20.

11. McNamara, "The Christiana Riot."

12. "The Jerry Rescue," *New York History Net*.

13. Brooks, "What Can the Collapse of the Whig Party Tell Us About Today's Politics."

Chapter 10

1. Baker, "Franklin Pierce: Impact and Legacy."

2. Weigley, "Old Fuss and Feathers."

3. "Presidential Election of 1852: A Resource Guide," *LOC*.

4. Bennett, New York Herald, vol. 17, no. 228, 17 August 1852. *LOC*.

5. Pierce, "Inaugural Address of Franklin Pierce."

6. Gibson, "A Time for Doughfaces?"

7. Reiber, "It Wasn't Called Bleeding Kansas for Nothing."

8. Walther, *The Shattering of the Union,* p. 53.

9. "Franklin Pierce's Murky Legacy as President," *Constitution Center*.

10. Strauss, *Worst. President. Ever.*

11. Baker, *James Buchanan*.

12. Landis, *Northern Men with Southern Loyalties*.

13. "Presidential Election of 1856: A Resource Guide," *LOC*.

14. Eschner, "President James Buchanan Directly Influences the Outcome of the Dred Scott Decision."

15. Buchanan, "March 4, 1857: Inaugural Address."

16. "Justice Curtis Dissenting," *American History*.

17. "James Buchanan State of the Union 1860—3 December 1860," *American History*.

Chapter 11

1. Cummings, "Survey of Scholars Places Trump as Third Worst President of All Time."

2. Lincoln, "Lyceum Address."

3. Lincoln, "House Divided Speech."

4. McPherson, *Battle Cry of Freedom: The Civil War Era,* p. 244.

5. "Presidential Election of 1860: A Resource Guide," *LOC*.

6. Gugliotta, "New Estimate Raises Civil War Death Toll."

7. Belz, "Lincoln's Construction of the Executive Power in the Secession Crisis."

8. Lincoln, "Message to Congress in Special Session July 4, 1861."

9. Novkov, *The Supreme Court and the Presidency*, p. 233.

10. Lincoln, "Lincoln's Response to Congress."

11. Bomboy, "Lincoln and Taney's Great Writ Showdown."

12. Lincoln, "Emancipation Proclamation."

Chapter 12

1. "John Wilkes Booth," *NPS*.

2. "Assassination of President Abraham Lincoln," *LOC*.

3. "Overview of Andrew Johnson's Life," *NPS*.

4. Gordon-Reed, *Andrew Johnson*.

5. Rayner, *Life and Times of A. Johnson*, pp. 117-19.

6. Johnson, "Speech to the Citizens of Washington."

7. Transcript of Vice President Andrew Johnson's Inaugural Address.

8. "Andrew Johnson, 16th Vice President (1865)," *U.S. Senate*.

9. "African American Records: Freemen's Bureau," *National Archives*.

10. Johnson, "Veto of the Freemen's Bureau Bill."

11. Fox, "Trump's 2018 Hasn't Been as Bad as Andrew Jonson's 1866."

12. Johnson, "State of the Union 1867—3 December 1867."

13. "Article X," *NPS*.

Chapter 13

1. Bunting, *Ulysses S. Grant,* pp. 14–15.
2. Chernow, *Grant.*
3. Simpson, *Ulysses S. Grant: Triumph Over Adversity, 1822–1865.*
4. "Presidential Election of 1868: A Resource Guide," *LOC.*
5. "Oakes Ames," *PBS.*
6. "Black Friday, September 24, 1869," *PBS.*
7. Grant, "First Inaugural Address of Ulysses S. Grant."
8. Stockwell, "Ulysses Grant's Failed Attempt to Grant Native Americans Citizenship."
9. Grant, "Special Message–March 30, 1870."
10. "Presidential Election of 1872: A Resource Guide," *LOC.*
11. "The Panic of 1873," *PBS.*
12. "Presidential Election of 1876: A Resource Guide," *LOC.*
13. Morris, *Fraud of the Century.*
14. Greene, "The Legacy of *Black Reconstruction.*"

Chapter 14

1. Wolfe, *The Complete Short Stories of Thomas Wolfe,* p. 110.
2. Robertson, *After the Civil War.*
3. Getchell, *Our Nation's Executives and Their Administrations,* p. 328.
4. Banner, *Presidential Misconduct.*
5. Williams, *The Life of Rutherford Birchard Hayes,* p. 92.
6. Trefousse, *Rutherford B. Hayes,* pp. 105–107.
7. Hayes, "April 29, 1879: Veto of Army Appropriations Bill."
8. Hoogenboom, "Rutherford B. Hayes: Impact and Legacy."
9. Ackerman, *Dark Horse.*
10. "Presidential Election of 1880: A Resource Guide," *LOC.*
11. Zakaria, *From Wealth to Power,* p. 110.
12. Bellamy, "A Stalwart of Stalwarts."
13. Ackerman, "The Garfield Assassination Altered American History, But Is Woefully Forgotten Today."
14. Greenberger, "The Man the Presidency Changed."

Chapter 15

1. Meier, "Civil War Draft Records: Exemptions and Enrollments."
2. Graff, *Grover Cleveland.*

3. "Presidential Election of 1884: A Resource Guide," *LOC*.

4. Cleveland, "October 1, 1888: Message Regarding Chinese Exclusion Act."

5. Pevar, "The Dawes Act: How Congress Tried to Destroy Indian Reservations."

6. "On This Day, the Pullman Strike Changes Labor Law," *Constitution Center*.

7. Brown and Silva, "Presidential Succession and Inability."

8. "How They Got There," *The St. Paul Daily Globe,* p. 12.

9. Ackerman, "The Vote That Failed."

10. Sinkler, "Benjamin Harrison and the Matter of Race."

11. Medhurst, *Before the Rhetorical Presidency*, p. 279.

12. "Presidential Election of 1892: A Resource Guide," *LOC*.

Chapter 16

1. "Democracy's Lament," *LOC*.

2. "Presidential Election of 1896: A Resource Guide," *LOC*.

3. Fallows, *Life of William McKinley*, pp. 127–28.

4. Turner, "The Significance of the Frontier in American History, 1893."

5. "Transcript of the De Lôme Letter (1898)," *Our Documents*.

6. Meiser, *Power and Restraint,* p. 31.

7. Welch, "American Atrocities in the Philippines: The Indictment and the Response."

8. Twain, "To the Person Sitting in Darkness."

9. Miller, *The President and the Assassin*.

Chapter 17

1. "Presidential Election of 1904: A Resource Guide," *LOC*.

2. Morris, *The Rise of Theodore Roosevelt*.

3. "Roosevelt Pursues the Boat Thieves," *NPS*.

4. Platt, *The Autobiography of Thomas Collier Platt,* p. 397.

5. Platt, *The Autobiography of Thomas Collier Platt*, pp. 396–97.

6. Gompers, McBride, and Green, *The American Federationist,* vol. 9, p. 794.

7. Grossman, "The Coal Strike of 1902: Turning Point in U.S. Policy."

8. "Venezuela Debt Crisis," *Theodorerooseveltcenter*.

9. Weightman, "Monroe Doctrine Not Involved in the Santo Domingo Affair."

10. Roosevelt, "Roosevelt Corollary to the Monroe Doctrine."

11. "Theodore Roosevelt and Conservation," *NPS*.

12. Theodore Roosevelt: "Conservation as a National Duty" (13 May 1908)

13. "Antiquities Act." *NPS*.

14. "The National Parks: America's Best Idea," *PBS*.

15. Roosevelt, "December 3, 1907: Seventh Annual Message."
16. Rosen, *William Howard Taft.*
17. Lurie, *William Howard Taft.*
18. Miller, *Gifford Pinchot*, pp. 200–20.
19. "1912 Electoral Vote Tally, February 12, 1913," *National Archives.*

Chapter 18

1. Benbow, "Birth of a Quotation: Woodrow Wilson and 'Like Writing History with Lightning.'"
2. Ambar, "Woodrow Wilson: Life Before the Presidency."
3. "Presidential Election of 1912: A Resource Guide," *LOC.*
4. Wilson, "April 8, 1913: Message Regarding Tariff Duties."
5. Berg, *Wilson.*
6. "U.S. Invasion and Occupation of Haiti, 1915–34," *U.S. Department of State.*
7. "German U-Boat Reaches Baltimore, Having Crossed Atlantic in 16 Days; Has Letter from Kaiser to Wilson." *New York Times.*
8. Wilson, "War Message to Congress."
9. Wilson, "President Woodrow Wilson's Fourteen Points."
10. Powell, "Woodrow Wilson's Great Mistake."
11. Cull, "Master of American Propaganda."
12. Dunphy, "The Lynching of Robert Prager: A World War I Hate Crime."
13. Daly, "How Woodrow Wilson's Propaganda Machine Changed American Journalism."

Chapter 19

1. Dean, *Warren G. Harding.*
2. Harding, "May 14, 1920: Readjustment."
3. "Presidential Election of 1920: A Resource Guide," *LOC.*
4. Payne, *Dead Last: The public Memory of Warren G. Harding's Scandalous Legacy.*
5. "Oil and Gas: Long-Term Contribution Trends," *Open Secrets.*
6. Gangitano and Green, "Collins Receives More Donations from Texas Fossil Fuel Industry Than from Maine Residents."
7. "Calvin Coolidge Thirtieth President 1923–1929," *White House.*
8. Novak, "'Speeches Must Be Short': Radio and the Birth of the Modern Presidential Campaign."
9. Mallon, "Less Said."
10. Heflin. "Warning Against the 'Roman Catholic Party': Catholicism and the 1928 Election," *History Matters.*

11. Cummins, "Dirty Campaigning in the Roaring Twenties: Herbert Hoover vs. Al Smith."

12. "1928 Presidential General Election Results," *US Election Atlas*.

13. Hoover, "Rugged Individualism."

14. Hoover, "Principles and Ideals of the United States Government."

Chapter 20

1. Black, *Franklin Delano Roosevelt: Champion of Freedom*.

2. Dallek, *Franklin D. Roosevelt: A Political Life*.

3. Walsh, "The Most Consequential Elections in History: Franklin Delano Roosevelt and the Election of 1932."

4. "Frances Perkins," *FDR Library*.

5. Edwards, *American Default*.

6. Dickinson, *Bitter Harvest: FDR, Presidential Power and the Growth of the Presidential Branch*.

7. Roosevelt, "Executive Order 8248."

8. Walsh, "The First 100 Days: Franklin Roosevelt Pioneered the 100-Day Concept."

9. "Civilian Conservation Corps," *NPS*.

10. Himmelberg, *The Origins of the National Recovery Administration*.

11. Roosevelt, "FDR's First Inaugural Address."

12. Roosevelt, "On the Bank Crisis."

13. Roosevelt, "On Drought Conditions."

14. Roosevelt, "On the European War."

15. Roosevelt, "On the Declaration of War with Japan."

16. Leuchtenburg, "Franklin D. Roosevelt: Impact and Legacy."

17. Waxman, "President Trump's Approval Rating Is at a Near-Records Low. Here's What to Know About the History of Those Numbers."

18. Churchill, "Prime Minister Churchill's Eulogy in Commons for the Late President Roosevelt."

Chapter 21

1. Ferrell, *Truman and Pendergast*.

2. McCullough, *Truman*.

3. Miscamble, *The Most Controversial Decision: Truman, the Atomic Bombs, and the Defeat of Japan*.

4. Stokes, "70 Years after Hiroshima, Opinions Have Shifted on the Use of Atomic Bomb."

5. Hall, "By the Numbers: World War II's Atomic Bombs."

6. Compton, "If the Atomic Bomb Had Not Been Used."

7. Truman, "Truman Statement on Hiroshima."

8. "Use of Weapons of Mass Destruction Should be Included in Criminal Court's Definition of War Crimes, Say Several Conference Speakers," *UN*.

9. Alperovitz, *The Decision to Use the Atomic Bomb*.

10. Truman, "Truman Doctrine."

11. Truman, "Truman Doctrine".

12. "National Security Act of 1947," *Office of the Historian*.

13. Schroeder, *The Foundation of the CIA*.

14. Truman, "Address Before the National Association for the Advancement of Colored People."

15. Truman, "Transcript of Executive Order 9981: Desegregation of the Armed Forces (1948)."

16. Gardner, *Harry Truman and Civil Rights*.

Chapter 22

1. Smith, *Eisenhower: In War and Peace*.

2. Morgan, "The Making of a General: Ike, the Tank, and the Interwar Years."

3. Ambrose, *The Supreme Commander*.

4. "Agreement on the Cessation of Hostilities in Viet-Nam, July 20, 1954," *Mt Holyoke*.

5. Butterfield, "Pentagon Papers: Eisenhower Decisions Undercut the Geneva Accords, Study Says."

6. Beschloss, *Mayday: Eisenhower, Khrushchev, and the U-2 Affair*.

7. Eisenhower, "Statement by the President Regarding the U-2 Incident, May 11, 1960."

8. "U-2 Overflights and the Capture of Francis Gary Powers, 1960," *Office of the Historian*.

9. Glass, "Eisenhower Approves Coup in Iran, Aug. 19, 1953."

10. Rabe, *Eisenhower and Latin American: The Foreign Policy of Anticommunism*.

11. Eisenhower, "Transcript of President Dwight D. Eisenhower's Farewell Address (1961)."

12. Pach, "Dwight D. Eisenhower: Domestic Affairs."

13. Gillett and Akhtar, "These Are the Top 20 US Presidents (and Why You Won't find Trump on the List)."

14. Weiss, "RANKED: The Greatest US Presidents, According to Political Scientists."

Chapter 23

1. Brown, "JFK's Addison's Disease."
2. "John F. Kennedy's Pre-Presidential Voting Record & Stands on Issues," *JFK Library*.
3. Greenberg, "Rewinding the Kennedy-Nixon Debates."
4. Kennedy, "Address to the Greater Houston Ministerial Association."
5. "1960 Presidential General Election Results," *US Election Atlas*.
6. Kennedy, "Civil Rights Address."
7. Kennedy, "Moon Speech-Rice Stadium."
8. Kennedy, "News Conference 10, Apr 21, 1961."
9. Nathan, *The Cuban Missile Crisis Revisited*.
10. "Presidential Approval Ratings—Gallup Historical Statistics and Trends," *Gallup*.
11. "Military Advisors in Vietnam: 1963," *JFK Library*.
12. Goodwin, *Lyndon Johnson and the American Dream*. Open Road Media, 2015.
13. Caro, *Master of the Senate: The Years of Lyndon Johnson III*.
14. "1964 Presidential General Election Results," *US Election Atlas*.
15. "Voting Rights Act," *Our Documents*.
16. "Medicare and Medicaid," *LBJ Library*.
17. Bailey and Duquette, "How Johnson Fought the War on Poverty."
18. Moise, *Tonkin Gulf and the Escalation of the Vietnam War*.
19. Watson and Markman, *Chief of Staff: Lyndon Johnson and His Presidency*.
20. "Presidential Approval Ratings—Gallup Historical Statistics and Trends," *Gallup*.
21. Glass, "LBJ Approves 'Operation Rolling Thunder,' Feb. 13, 1965."
22. Weiss, "RANKED: The Greatest US Presidents, According to Political Scientists."

Chapter 24

1. "Richard Milhous Nixon," *Naval History and Heritage Command*.
2. Wills, *Nixon Agonistes*.
3. Mitchell, *Tricky Dick and the Pink Lady*.
4. Matthews, *Kennedy & Nixon*, p. 183.
5. Nixon, "The Last Press Conference."
6. "Presidential Approval Ratings—Gallup Historical Statistics and Trends," *Gallup*.
7. Cowie, *Stayin' Alive*, pp. 139–140.
8. Rudenstine, *The Day the Presses Stopped*.
9. Cuddy, "Was It Legal for the U.S. to Bomb Cambodia?"
10. "Transcript of a Recording of a Meeting Between the President and H.R. Haldeman in the Oval Office on June 23, 1972, from 10:04 to 11:39 AM," *PBS*.

11. Thomson-DeVeaux, "It Took a Long Time for Republicans to Abandon Nixon."
12. Ford, "Gerald R. Ford's Remarks Upon Taking the Oath of Office as President."

Chapter 25

1. Kucharsky, *The Man from Plains*, p. 33.
2. Berman, *Give Us the Ballot*, p. 114.
3. Morris, *Jimmy Carter: American Moralist*, p. 147.
4. Frank, "The Primary Experiment: Jimmy Who?"
5. Emerson, "When Jimmy Carter Lusted in His Heart."
6. "1976 Presidential General Election Results," *US Election Atlas*.
7. Farber, *Taken Hostage*.
8. Schweigler, "Carter's Dilemmas: Presidential Power and Its Limits."
9. "Presidential Approval Ratings—Gallup Historical Statistics and Trends," *Gallup*.
10. Carter, "Energy and the National Goals—A Crisis of Confidence."
11. "Examining Carter's 'Malaise Speech,' 30 Years Later," *NPR*.
12. Carter, "Nobel Lecture."

Chapter 26

1. Brands, *Reagan: The Life*.
2. Federman, "What Reagan Did for Hollywood."
3. Naftali, "Ronald Reagan's Long-Hidden Racist Conversation with Richard Nixon."
4. Cannon, *Governor Reagan: His Rise to Power*.
5. "1980 Presidential General Election Results," *US Election Atlas*.
6. Richman, "The Sad Legacy of Ronald Reagan."
7. Roberts, "The Great Eliminator: How Ronald Reagan Made Homelessness Permanent."
8. Samuelson, *The Great Inflation and Its Aftermath: The Past and Future of American Influence*.
9. Cullen, "The History of Mass Incarceration."
10. Alexander, *The New Jim Crow*.
11. Talbott, "Reagan and Gorbachev: Shutting the Cold War Down."
12. Kazdin, "The Violence Central American Migrants Are Fleeing Was Stoked by the US."
13. Taub, "The Republican Myth of Ronald Reagan and the Iran Hostages, Debunked."
14. Rottinghaus and Vaughn, "How Does Trump Stack Up Against the Best—and Worst—Presidents?"
15. "Presidential Approval Ratings—Gallup Historical Statistics and Trends," *Gallup*.

16. Hart, "Concerns About Reagan's Mental Health Were Handled Very Differently Than Concerns About Trump's."

Chapter 27

1. "George Herbert Walker Bush," *Naval History and Heritage Command*.
2. Meacham, *Destiny and Power*.
3. "Senator, You're No Jack Kennedy," *NPR*.
4. "Vetoes by President George H.W. Bush," *United States Senate*.
5. Calavita, Pontell, and Tillman, *Big Money Crime*.
6. "Remembering the Gulf War: The Key Facts & Figures," *Forces*.
7. Moore, "Participation in Gulf War a Decade Ago Worthwhile."
8. Holland, "The First Iraq War Was Also Sold to the Public Based on a Pack of Lies."
9. Salameh, "Oil Wars."
10. Maraniss, *First in His Class: A Biography of Bill Clinton*.
11. "1992 Presidential General Election Results," *US Election Atlas*.
12. "Presidential Approval Ratings—Gallup Historical Statistics and Trends," *Gallup*.
13. Merica, "Bill Clinton Says He Made Mass Incarceration Issue Worse."
14. Collins, *The Conversation*.
15. Gillet and Akhtar, "These Are the Top 20 US Presidents (and Why You Won't Find Trump on the List)."

Chapter 28

1. Smith, *Bush*.
2. Toobin, *Too Close to Call*.
3. Payson-Denney, "So, Who Really Won? What the Bush v. Gore Studies Showed."
4. Woodward, *Bush at War*.
5. Kessler, "The Iraq War and WMD's: An Intelligence Failure or White House Spin?"
6. Richey, "Bush Pushed the Limits of Presidential Power."
7. García and Thornton, "'No Child Left Behind' Has Failed."
8. Horton, "The Legacy of the 2001 and 2003 'Bush' Tax Cuts."
9. "Bush's Final Approval Rating: 22 Percent," *CBS News*.
10. Rottinghaus and Vaughn, "How Does Trump Stack Up Against the Best—and Worst—Presidents?"
11. Struyk, "George W. Bush's Favorable Rating Has Pulled a Complete 180."
12. Rice, "Was Barack Obama Sr. 'Eased' Out of Harvard, and America, for Dating White Women?"
13. Garrow, *Rising Star: The Making of Barack Obama*.

14. "2008 Presidential General Election Results," *US Election Atlas*.
15. Grunwald, "A New New Deal."
16. Drehle, "Honor and Effort: What President Obama Achieved in Eight Years."
17. Grunwald, "The Victory of 'No.'"
18. "Presidential Approval Ratings—Gallup Historical Statistics and Trends," *Gallup*.
19. Yadon, "Examining Whites' Anti-Black Attitudes after Obama's Presidency."
20. Benegal, "The Spillover of Race and Racial Attitudes into Public Opinion about Climate Change."
21. Tesler, "Racial Attitudes Remain a Powerful Predictor of Obama Vote Preference."
22. Rottinghaus and Vaughn, "How Does Trump Stack Up Against the Best—and Worst—Presidents?"
23. Gillett and Akhtar, "These Are the Top 20 US Presidents (and Why You Won't Find Trump on the List)."

Chapter 29

1. Blake, "The Extensive Effort to Bury Donald Trump's Grades."
2. Waldman, "Is It Time to Talk about Donald Trump's Draft Dodging?"
3. Anapol, "Daughters of NY Podiatrist Allege He Helped Trump Avoid Vietnam War: New York Times."
4. Cassidy, "As a Businessman, Trump Was the Biggest Loser of All."
5. "Trump Investigation Guide: Impeachment, Inquiries, Lawsuits," *Bloomberg*.
6. Mathis-Lilley, "President Pays Gigantic Fine for Stealing from Charity."
7. Walters, "Trump University: Court Upholds $25m Settlement to Give Students' Money Back."
8. Politi, "Trump Says 'Probably Not' Prepared to Lose in 2020, Doesn't Believe He Lost Popular Vote."
9. "How Unpopular Is Donald Trump?" *FiveThirtyEight*.
10. Zimmerman, "Decades Later, My Fellow Democrats Should Admit Character Counts."
11. Yglesias, "What Trump Has Actually Done in His First 3 Years."
12. "US Economy Under Trump: Is It the Greatest in History?" BBC.
13. Wilker, "Harder to Breathe: Air Quality Has Worsened Since 2016."
14. "Executive Secrecy," *New York Times*.
15. Shepard, "Poll: As Impeachment Progresses, Voter Support Remains Static."
16. Wilkie, Christina. "President Trump Is Impeached in Historic Vote."
17. Graham, "The Strangest Thing About Trump's Approach to Presidential Power."
18. Rottinghaus and Vaughn, "How Does Trump Stack Up Against the Best—and Worst—Presidents?"

Primary & Secondary Sources

Ackerman, S. J. "The Vote That Failed." *Smithsonian.com*. Smithsonian Institution. Nov. 1998. www.smithsonianmag.com/history/the-vote-that-failed-159427766/.

Adams, John. "Instructions Adopted by the Braintree Town Meeting." *Massachusetts Historical Society*. Papers of John Adams, vol 1. 2019. Adams Paper Digital Edition. www.masshist.org/publications/adams-papers/index.php/view/PJA01d073.

"Article X." *NPS*. National Park Service. Andrew Johnson. National Historic Site Tennessee. 14 Apr. 2015. www.nps.gov/anjo/learn/historyculture/article-x.htm.

Belz, Herman. "Lincoln's Construction of the Executive Power in the Secession Crisis." *Journal of the Abraham Lincoln Association*. vol. 27, no. 1, Winter 2006. pp. 13–38. *JSTOR*, www.jstor.org/stable/20149090.

Bennett, James Gordon, editor. *New York Herald*, vol. 17, no. 228, 17 August 1852. *LOC*, Library of Congress, Chronicling America, chroniclingamerica.loc.gov/lccn/sn83030313/1852–08–17/ed-1/seq-4.

Buchanan, James. "March 4, 1857: Inaugural Address." *Miller Center*. U of Virginia. 2019. millercenter.org/the-presidency/presidential-speeches/march-4-1857-inaugural-address.

_____. "James Buchanan. State of the Union 1860—3 December 1860." *American History*. U of Groningen. 2012. www.let.rug.nl/usa/presidents/james-buchanan/state-of-the-union-1860.php.

Carter, Jimmy. "Energy and the National Goals—A Crisis of Confidence." *American Rhetoric*. 2019. www.americanrhetoric.com/speeches/jimmycartercrisisofconfidence.htm.

_____. "Nobel Lecture." *Nobel Prize*. 10 Dec. 2002. www.nobelprize.org/prizes/peace/2002/carter/lecture/.

"Cherokee Nation v. Georgia." *LII*. Cornell Law School. 2019. www.law.cornell.edu/supremecourt/text/30/1#writing-USSC_CR_0030_0001_ZO.

Churchill, Winston. "Prime Minister Churchill's Eulogy in Commons for the Late President Roosevelt." 17 Apr. 1945. www.ibiblio.org/pha/policy/1945/1945-04-17a.html.

Clay, Henry. "Clay's Resolutions January 29, 1850." *Transcript of Compromise of 1850. Our Documents*. www.ourdocuments.gov/doc.php?flash=false&doc=27&page=transcript.

_____. *The Speeches of Henry Clay*, edited by Calvin Colton. New York: A.S. Barnes & Co, 1857.

Cleveland, Grover. "October 1, 1888: Message Regarding Chinese Exclusion Act." *Miller Center*. University of Virginia. 2019. millercenter.org/the-presidency/presidential-speeches/october-1-1888-message-regarding-chinese-exclusion-act.

Collins, Bruce. "Clinton Impeachment: 20 Years On, Will Donald Trump Now Face the Same Fate?" *The Conversation*. 19 Dec. 2018. https://theconversation.com/clinton-impeachment-20-years-on-will-donald-trump-now-face-the-same-fate-109045.

"Declaration of Independence: A Transcription." *National Archives*. July 26, 2019. www.archives.gov/founding-docs/declaration-transcript.

Eisenhower, Dwight. "Statement by the President Regarding U-2 Incident, May 11, 1960." *Dwightdeisenhower*. IKE Eisenhower Foundation. www.dwightdeisenhower.com/404/U-2-Spy-Plane-Incident.

_____. "Transcript of President Dwight D. Eisenhower's Farewell Address (1961)." *Our Documents*. 2019. www.ourdocuments.gov/doc.php?flash=false&doc=90&page=transcript.

"Executive Secrecy." *New York Times*. 2019. www.nytimes.com/interactive/2019/us/politics/executive-secrecy-executive-power.html.

Grant, Ulysses. "First Inaugural Address of Ulysses S. Grant." *The Avalon Project*. Yale Law School. 2008. avalon.law.yale.edu/19th_century/grant1.asp.

_____. "Special Message—March 30, 1870." *NPS*. National Park Service. Ulysses S. Grant. 27 Feb. 2019. www.nps.gov/ulsg/learn/historyculture/grant-and-the-15th-amendment.htm.

Greenberger, Scott S. "The Man the Presidency Changed." *Politico*. 11 Sept. 2017. www.politico.com/magazine/story/2017/09/11/chester-arthur-presidency-donald-trump-215593.

Hamilton, Alexander. "Letter from Alexander Hamilton, Concerning the Public Conduct and Character of John Adams, Esq. President of the United States, [24 October 1800]." *Founders Online*. National Archives. 2019. founders.archives.gov/documents/Hamilton/01-25-02-0110-0002.

Harding, Warren. "May 14, 1920: Readjustment." *Miller Center*. University of Virginia. millercenter.org/the-presidency/presidential-speeches/may-14-1920-readjustment.

Harrison, William Henry. "Inaugural Address of William Henry Harrison." *Avalon Project*. Lillian Goldman Law Library. avalon.law.yale.edu/19th_century/harrison.asp.

Hart, Benjamin. "Concerns about Reagan's Mental Health Were Handled Very Differently Than Concerns about Trump's." *Intelligencer*. 14 Jan. 2018. nymag.com/intelligencer/2018/01/how-reagans-mental-health-concerns-were-handled.html.

Hayes, Rutherford. "April 29, 1879: Veto of Army Appropriations Bill." *Miller Center*. University of Virginia. 2019. millercenter.org/the-presidency/presidential-speeches/april-29-1879-veto-army-appropriations-bill.

Heflin, James Thomas. "Warning Against the 'Roman Catholic Party': Catholicism and the 1928 Election," *History Matters*. Congressional Record. 28 Jan. 1928. historymatters.gmu.edu/d/5073/.

Hoover, Herbert. "Rugged Individualism." *Digital History*. 2019. www.digitalhistory.uh.edu/disp_textbook.cfm?smtID=3&psid=1334.investigatinghistory.ashp.cuny.edu/module7A.php.

"How They Got There." *The St. Paul Daily Globe*. June 16, 1889. p. 12. Chroniclingamerica. LOC. Library of Congress. chroniclingamerica.loc.gov/lccn/sn90059522/1889-06-16/ed-1/seq-12/.

Jackson, Andrew. "Andrew Jackson's Speech to Congress on Indian Removal." *National Park Service*. NPS. www.nps.gov/museum/tmc/MANZ/handouts/Andrew_Jackson_Annual_Message.pdf.

_____. "May 27, 1830: Veto Message Regarding Funding of Infrastructure Development." *Miller Center*. University of Virginia. 2019. millercenter.org/the-presidency/presidential-speeches/may-27-1830-veto-message-regarding-funding-infrastructure.

Jefferson, Thomas. "First Annual Message to Congress, 8 December 1801." *Founders Online*. National Archives. founders.archives.gov/documents/Jefferson/01-36-02-0034-0003.

_____. "From Thomas Jefferson to Abigail Smith Adams, 13 June 1804." *Founders Online*. National Archives. founders.archives.gov/documents/Adams/99-03-02-1280.

_____. "From Thomas Jefferson to James Sullivan, 9 February 1797." *Founders Online*. National Archives. 2016. founders.archives.gov/documents/Jefferson/01-29-02-0231.

_____. "From Thomas Jefferson to United States Congress, 13 January 1806." *Founders Online*. National Archives, 2019. founders.archives.gov/documents/Jefferson/99-01-02-3010.

_____. "To James Madison from Thomas Jefferson, 20 December 1787." *Founders Online*. National Archives. 2019. founders.archives.gov/documents/Madison/01-10-02-0210.

Johnson, Andrew. "Speech to the Citizens of Washington." *Teachingamericanhistory*. 2018. teachingamericanhistory.org/library/document/speech-to-the-citizens-of-washington/.

_____. "State of the Union 1867—3 December 1867." *American History*. University of Groningen, 2012. www.let.rug.nl/usa/presidents/andrew-johnson/state-of-the-union-1867.php.

"Justice Curtis Dissenting." *American History*. University of Groningen. 2012. www.let.rug.nl/usa/documents/1826-1850/dred-scott-case/justice-curtis-dissenting.php.

Kennedy, John F. "Civil Rights Address." *American Rhetoric*. 11 June 1963. americanrhetoric.com/speeches/jfkcivilrights.htm.

_____. "Moon Speech—Rice Stadium." *NASA*. 12 Sept. 1962. er.jsc.nasa.gov/seh/ricetalk.htm.

Lincoln, Abraham. "House Divided Speech, June 16, 1858" *Abraham Lincoln Online*. 2018. www.abrahamlincolnonline.org/lincoln/speeches/house.htm.

_____. "Lincoln's Response to Congress, July 4, 1861." *Gilder Lehrman*. Gilder Lehrman Institute of American History. 2012. www.gilderlehrman.org/sites/default/files/inline-pdfs/Lincoln%20Response.pdf.

_____. "Lyceum Address." *Abraham Lincoln Online*. 2018. www.abrahamlincolnonline.org/lincoln/speeches/lyceum.htm.

_____. "Message to Congress in Special Session, July 4, 1861 *Miller Center*. U of Virginia. millercenter.org/the-presidency/presidential-speeches/july-4-1861-july-4th-message-congress.

_____. "Spot Resolutions in the U.S. House of Representatives." *Teaching American History*. December 22, 1847. teachingamericanhistory.org/library/document/spot-resolutions-in-the-u-s-house-of-representatives/.

Madison, James. "Federalist No. 51." *Bill of Rights Institute*. billofrightsinstitute.org/founding-documents/primary-source-documents/the-federalist-papers/federalist-papers-no-51/.

_____. "March 3, 1817: Veto Message on the Internal Improvements Bill." *Miller Center*. 2019.millercenter.org/the-presidency/presidential-speeches/march-3-1817-veto-message-internal-improvements-bill.

Monroe, James. "The Monroe Doctrine." *Jamesmonroemuseum*. 2019. jamesmonroemuseum.umw.edu/about-james-monroe/research/articles/.

Nixon, Richard. "Transcript of a Recording of a Meeting Between the President and H.R. Haldeman in the Oval Office on June 23, 1972, from 10:04 to 11:39 AM," *PBS*. www.pbs.org/newshour/extra/app/uploads/2013/11/Smoking-Gun-Transcript-v-2.pdf.

Novak, Matt. "'Speeches Must Be Short': Radio and the Birth of the Modern Presidential Campaign." *Pacific Standard*. 2 Oct. 2012. psmag.com/news/airwaves-1924-the-first-presidential-campaign-over-radio-47615.

O'Sullivan, John. "Annexation." *The United States Magazine and Democratic Review*. vol. 17, no. 1, (July–August 1845), pp.5–10. pdcrodas.webs.ull.es/anglo/OSullivanAnnexation.pdf.

Pierce, Franklin. "Inaugural Address of Franklin Pierce." *Avalon Project*. Yale Law School. 2019. avalon.law.yale.edu/19th_century/pierce.asp.

Platt, Thomas Collier. *The Autobiography of Thomas Collier Platt*. New York: B.W. Dodge & Company, 1910.

Polk, James Knox. "Inaugural Address of James Knox Polk." March 4, 1845. *Avalon*. Yale Law School. avalon.law.yale.edu/19th_century/polk.asp.

_____. "May 11, 1846: War Message to Congress." *Miller Center*. U of Virginia. 2019. millercenter.org/the-presidency/presidential-speeches/may-11-1846-war-message-congress.

Rayner, Kenneth. *Life and Times of Andrew Johnson*. New York: D. Appleton and Company, 1866, p. 117–19. babel.hathitrust.org/cgi/pt?id=loc.ark:/13960/t0zp44s4s&view=2up&seq=12&size=125.

Richey, Warren. "Bush Pushed the Limits of Presidential Power." *Christian Science Monitor*. 14 Jan. 12009. www.csmonitor.com/USA/2009/0114/p11s01-usgn.html.

Roosevelt, Franklin. "Executive Order 8248—Executive Orders." *Archives*. National Archives. www.archives.gov/federal-register/codification/executive-order/08248.html.

_____. "On the Bank Crisis." 12 Mar. 1933. *FDR Library*. Marist University. docs.fdrlibrary.marist.edu/031233.html.

_____. "On the Declaration of War with Japan." 9 Dec. 1941. *FDR Library*. Marist University. docs.fdrlibrary.marist.edu/120941.html.

_____. "On Drought Conditions." 6 Sept. 1936. *FDR Library*. Marist University. docs.fdrlibrary.marist.edu/090636.html.

_____. "On the European War." 3 Sept. 1939. *FDR Library*. Marist University. docs.fdrlibrary.marist.edu/090339.html.

_____. "The Only Thing We have to Fear Is Fear Itself": FDR's First Inaugural Address. 4 Mar. 1933. *History Matters*. historymatters.gmu.edu/d/5057/.

Roosevelt, Theodore. "December 3, 1907: Seventh Annual Message." *Miller Center*. University of Virginia. 2019. millercenter.org/the-presidency/presidential-speeches/december-3-1907-seventh-annual-message.

_____. "Roosevelt Corollary to the Monroe Doctrine." 1904. *Digital History*. 2019 www.digitalhistory.uh.edu/disp_textbook.cfm?smtID=3&psid=1259.

Shepard, Steven. "Poll: As Impeachment Progresses, Voter Support Remains Static." *Politico*. 11 Dec. 2019. www.politico.com/news/2019/12/11/poll-impeachment-voter-support-081122.

Thomson-DeVeaux, Amelia. "It Took A Long Time for Republicans to Abandon Nixon." *FiveThirtyEight*. 9 Oct. 2019. fivethirtyeight.com/features/it-took-a-long-time-for-republicans-to-abandon-nixon/.

Truman, Harry. "Address Before the National Association for the Advancement of Colored People." 29 June 1947. *Voices of Democracy*. The U.S. Oratory Project. U of Maryland. voicesofdemocracy.umd.edu/harry-s-truman-naacp-speech-text/.

_____. "Truman Doctrine: President Harry S. Truman's Address before a Joint Session of Congress, March 12, 1947." *Avalon Project*. Yale Law School. avalon.law.yale.edu/20th_century/trudoc.asp.

_____. "Truman Statement on Hiroshima." 6 Aug. 1945. Atomic Heritage Foundation. www.atomicheritage.org/key-documents/truman-statement-hiroshima.

Turner, Frederick Jackson. "The Significance of the Frontier in American History." *National Humanities Center*. nationalhumanitiescenter.org/pds/gilded/empire/text1/turner.pdf.

Twain, Mark. "To the Person Sitting in Darkness." (originally published in *North American Review*, February 1901.) *Investigating History*, City University of New York.

"Use of Weapons of Mass Destruction Should Be Included in Criminal Court's Definition of War Crimes, Say Several Conference Speakers." *UN*. United Nations. 18 June 1998. www.un.org/press/en/1998/19980618.l2882.html.

Washington, George. "From George Washington to Lewis Nicola." 22 May 1782, *Founders Online*. National Archives. founders.archives.gov/documents/Washington/99-01-02-08501.

_____. "To George Washington from Lewis Nicola, 22 May 1782." *Founders Online*. National Archives. founders.archives.gov/?q=nicola%2C%20lewis&s=1111311111&sa=&r=51&sr=.

_____. "Letter of the President of the Federal Convention, Dated September 17, 1787, to the President of Congress, Transmitting the Constitution." *Avalon Project*. Yale Law School. 2008. avalon.law.yale.edu/18th_century/translet.asp.

"Washington's Farewell Address 1796." *Avalon*. Yale Law School. 2008. avalon.law.yale.edu/18th_century/washing.asp.

"Washington's Inaugural Address of 1789." *Archives*. National Archives and Records Administration. 2019. www.archives.gov/exhibits/american_originals/inaugtxt.html.

Webster, Daniel, and Edward Everett. *The Writings and Speeches of Daniel Webster*. (National Edition, vol. 13), pp. 419–20. Boston, MA: Little, Brown & Company, 1903.

Wilson, Woodrow. "April 8, 1913: Message Regarding Tariff Duties." *Miller Center*. University of Virginia. 2019. millercenter.org/the-presidency/presidential-speeches/april-8-1913-message-regarding-tariff-duties.

_____. "President Woodrow Wilson's Fourteen Points." 8 Jan. 1918. *Avalon Project*. Yale Law School. 2018. avalon.law.yale.edu/20th_century/wilson14.asp.

_____. "War Message to Congress." 2 April 1917. Brigham Young University, 28 May 2009. wwi.lib.byu.edu/index.php/Wilson's_War_Message_to_Congress.

Glossary

A

adjourn—formally end a meeting of a chamber or committee.

adjournment sine die—an adjournment that terminates an annual session of Congress. A "sine die" ("without day") adjournment sets no day for reconvening, so that Congress will not meet again until the first day of the next session. Requires the agreement of both chambers under the Constitution.

amendment—an amendment to the U.S. Constitution is an improvement, a correction, or a revision to the original content. To date, 27 amendments have been approved.

amendment exchange—also referred to as "amendments between the houses" or, colloquially, "ping-pong." A method for reconciling differences between the two chambers' version of a measure by sending the measure back and forth between them until both have agreed to identical language.

anarchism—an anti-authoritarian political and social philosophy that rejects hierarchies as unjust and advocates their replacement with self-managed, self-governed societies based on voluntary, cooperative institutions.

Anti-Federalism—eighteenth-century movement that opposed the creation of a stronger U.S. federal government and which later opposed the ratification of the 1787 constitution.

appropriation—an act of Congress that enables federal agencies to spend money for specific purposes.

aristocracy—the highest class in certain societies especially those holding hereditary titles or offices.

Articles of Confederation—the original constitution of the United States, ratified in 1781 and replaced by the U.S. Constitution in 1789. The Articles of Confederation and Perpetual Union was a much weaker document in terms of central government.

Articles of Impeachment—the written accusation sent by the U.S. House of Representatives to the Senate listing the crimes and misdemeanors the president allegedly committed.

B

bicameral—literally, "two chambers"; in a legislative body, having two houses (as in the House of Representatives and the Senate comprising the U.S. Congress.

big government—government that is regarded as infringing on the rights of individual citizens because of extensive bureaucracy and intrusive regulations.

bill—the primary form of legislative measure used to propose law. Depending on the chamber or origin, bills begin with a designation of either H.R. or S. If passed by both the House and the Senate and signed by the president, it becomes law.

Bill of Rights—the first ten amendments to the U.S Constitution, ratified in 1791 and guaranteeing such rights as freedom of speech, assembly, and worship.

bill summary—a short summary written by legislative analysts in the Congressional Research Service of the Library of Congress upon introduction of a bill or resolution. A final public summary is prepared upon enactment into law.

bipartisan—involving cooperation and compromise between two political parties.

bribery—the offering or receiving of an undue reward to influence behavior and incline a person to act contrary to duty and the known rules of honesty and integrity.

budget resolution—a measure that sets forth a congressional budget plan, in the form of a concurrent resolution; not a law-making vehicle and as such is not submitted to the president.

bully pulpit—a prominent public position, such as the presidency, that provides an opportunity for expounding one's views. Coined by Theodore Roosevelt when "bully" was used as an adjective meaning "excellent."

by request—a designation on a measure indicating that the member has introduced the measure on behalf of someone else (e.g., the president or an executive branch agency), or pursuant to statutory requirements, and may not necessarily support its provision.

C

cabinet—a group of advisers to the president consisting of the most senior appointed officers of the executive branch, who head the fifteen executive departments.

calendar—lists of measures, motions, and matters that are (or soon will be) eligible for consideration on the chamber floor. The House has four such calendars, published as one document; the Senate publishes two.

campaign—an organized effort to win an election.

caucus—a closed meeting of a group of persons belonging to the same political party or faction usually to select candidates or decide on policy.

checks and balances—a system that allows each branch of a government to amend or veto acts of another branch so as to prevent any one branch from exerting too much power.

cloture—method by which a supermajority (typically, three-fifths) of the Senate may agree to limit further debate and consideration of a question, generally used to end a filibuster.

coattails—the influence or pulling power of a popular movement or person, such a political candidate.

committee/subcommittee—may interact with a bill in a variety of ways. Bill may be referred to or discharged from a committee by the full chamber. Committees markup bill texts, hold hearings to learn more about a topic, or may express legislative interest.

committee chair—member of the majority party on a committee who has formal responsibility over the pane's agenda and resources, besides presiding at its meetings, and can, in some circumstances, act of the committee's behalf.

Committee of the Whole—device designed to allow greater participation in floor consideration of measures. It can be understood as the House assembled in a different form; it is a committee of the House composed of every Representative that meets in the House chamber. The House considers many major measures in the Committee of the Whole.

committee report—document accompanying a measure reported from a committee. It contains an explanation of the provisions of the measure, arguments for its approval, votes held in markup, individual committee members' opinions, cost estimates, and other information.

communications—written statements, messages or petitions sent to the Congress by the president of the United States, executive branch officials, or state or local governments. Types of communications include executive communications, presidential messages, petitions, and memorials.

companion measure—identical or substantially similar measured introduced in the other chamber.

concurrent resolution—a legislative measure used for the regulation of business within both chambers of Congress, not for proposing changes in law; not signed by the president and therefore not holding the weight of law.

conference committee—temporary joint committee created to resolve differences between House-passed and Senate-passed versions of a measure.

Congress—the bicameral legislature of the federal government of the United States, consisting of two chambers: the House of Representatives and the Senate.

Congressional Budget Office (CBO)—a legislative branch agency that produces independent analyses of budgetary and economic issues to support the Congressional budget process.

Congressional Research Service (CRS)—a division of the Library of Congress that works exclusively for the U.S. Congress, providing policy and legal analysis to committees and members of both the House and the Senate, regardless of party affiliation.

Congressional Record—the official record of the proceedings and debates of the U.S. Congress. For every day Congress is in session, an issue of the Congressional Record is printed by the Government Publishing Office. Each issue summarizes the day's floor and committee actions and records all remarks delivered in the House and the Senate.

Constitution—The Constitution of the United States is the supreme law of the United States of America. Originally comprising seven articles, it delineates the national frame of government.

Constitutional Convention—the gathering that drafted the U.S. Constitution in 1787 and designed a government with separate legislative, executive, and judicial branches.

continuing resolution—an appropriations act (typically in the form of a joint resolution) that provides stop-gap (or full-year) funds for federal agencies and programs to continue operations when the regular (or annual) appropriations acts have not been enacted by the beginning of the fiscal year.

cosponsor—Representatives or Senators who formally sign on to support a measure. Only the first-named member is the sponsor; all others are cosponsors, even those whose names appeared on the measure at the time it was submitted.

convention—a national meeting of the delegates of a political party for the purpose of formulating a platform and selecting candidates for office.

D

Daily Digest—section of the Congressional Record summarizing the day's floor and committee actions in each chamber, with page references to verbatim accounts of floor actions. It also lists the measures scheduled for action during each chamber's next meeting and the announcements of upcoming committee meetings.

dark horse—a political candidate with little name recognition who unexpectedly is nominated (usually as a compromise between factions) or wins election.

delegate—a representative to a party's national convention chosen by local voters to vote for a particular candidate. The number of delegates is determined by state population.

deposition—the written statement of a witness taken under oath in response to questions. This information may later be used in court as evidence.

détente—the easing of hostility or strained relations, especially between countries.

E

Electoral College—a body of electors established by the U.S. Constitution that forms every four years for the sole purpose of electing the president and vice president of the United States. Each state has as many Electoral College votes as it does Representatives and Senators. Electoral votes are awarded on the basis of the popular vote in each state, with 48 of 50 states awarding electoral votes on a winner-take-all basis; can result in a candidate being elected president without winning the national popular vote.

enacted—made into law.

en bloc—"all together"; when a committee or congressional chamber agrees to act concurrently on multiple measures (e.g, bills) or matters (e.g., nominations).

engrossed measure—official copy of a measure as passed by one chamber, including the text as amended by floor action.

enrolled measure—final official copy of a measure as passed in identical form by both chambers and then printed on parchment for presentation to the president.

errata—lists of errors in congressional publications.

executive agreement—an international agreement between the president and another country made by the executive branch and without formal consent by the Senate.

executive branch—the branch of federal and state government that is broadly responsible for implementing, supporting, and enforcing the laws made by the legislative branch and interpreted by the judicial branch.

executive business—nominations and treaties submitted by the president to the Senate for its "advice and consent"; the Senate treats such business separately from its legislative business.

executive calendar—the list of treaties and nominations that are (or soon will be) eligible for consideration by the full Senate; also, the official document that contains these lists and other information about the status of items of executive business.

executive communication—written statement or petition presented to Congress by the executive branch or other organization that may affect appropriations.

executive office—the administrative organization that reports directly to the president and headed by the White House chief of staff.

executive order (EO)—a rule or order issued by the president without the cooperation of Congress and having the force of law.

executive privilege—the president's constitutional right to maintain confidential communications under certain circumstances (usually related to national defense and foreign policy) within the executive branch and to resist some subpoenas and other oversight by the legislative and judicial branches.

executive report—a written committee report accompanying a matter of executive business (treaty or nomination) reported by the committee.

executive session—a period under Senate rules during which executive business is considered on the floor. (Legislation is considered only in legislative session, with its own distinct rules and practices; the Senate may go back and forth between legislative and executive session, even within the course of a day.)

F

federal depository library—libraries where congressional and other federal publications are available for free public use.

Federalist Papers—a collection of 85 articles and essays written by Alexander Hamilton, James Madison, and John Jay under the pseudonym "Publius" to promote ratification of the U.S. Constitution.

Federalist Party—early U.S. political party that advocated strong central government and held power from 1789–1801.

filibuster—the use of extreme dilatory tactics (such as making long speeches) in the Senate in an attempt to delay or prevent action.

G

germaneness—the requirement that an amendment be closely related—in terms of the precise subject purpose, for example—to the text it proposes to amend. House rules require amendments to be germane; Senate rules apply this restriction only in limited circumstances.

GOP—Grand Old Party, the nickname of the Republican Party.

GPO—Government Publishing Office, a legislative branch agency that provides publishing and dissemination services for the official an authentic government publications to Congress, federal agencies, federal depository libraries, and the American public.

grassroots—the ordinary people, as contrasted with the leadership or elite, of a political party or social organization; political activity that originates locally.

H

hearing—a formal meeting of a congressional committee (or subcommittee) to gather information from witnesses for use in its activities (that is, the development of legislation, oversight or executive agencies, investigations into matters of public policy, or Senate consideration of presidential nominations).

hearsay evidence—testimony involving statements by someone not actually in the court under oath and subject to cross examination. Data presented is not admissible as evidence.

hold—a request by a Senator to his or her party leader to delay floor action on a measure (e.g., a bill) or matter (e.g., a nomination), to be consulted on its disposition, and/or an indication that he or she would object to a unanimous consent request to consider said item of business or otherwise delay or obstruct consideration.

hopper—a wooden box on the house floor into which measures are dropped for formal introduction.

House Rules Committee—a committee in the House that, among other things, is responsible for reporting out "special rules"—simple resolutions that propose to the House tailored terms for debate and amendment of a measure on the House floor.

I

ideology—a set of ethical ideals, principles, doctrines, or myths of a social movement, institution, class or large group that attempts to explain how society should work.

impeachment—if a federal official (including a president) commits a crime or otherwise acts improperly, the House of Representatives may impeach—formally charge—that official. If the official subsequently is convicted in a Senate impeachment trial, he is removed from office. Can also disqualify the official from holding future office. Fines and potential jail time for crimes committed while in office are left to civil courts.

in camera—("in private"); sensitive matters required to be heard in private in the judge's chambers.

international agreement—legal agreements the United States enters into with other states or international organizations; they may take the form of an executive agreement entered into by the executive branch (but not submitted to the Senate for its advice and consent) or the form of a treaty.

incumbent—one who currently holds office.

J

joint resolution—a form of legislative measure used to propose changes in law, or to propose an amendment to the U.S. Constitution. Depending on the chamber of origin, they begin with a designation of either H.J.Res. or S.J.Res.

journal—the constitutionally mandated record of certain House and Senate actions, including motions offered, votes taken, and amendments agreed to. Unlike the Congressional Record, it does not contain remarks delivered in the House and Senate.

judicial branch—the system of federal courts and judges that interprets laws made by the legislative branch and rules on whether such laws are constitutional.

judicial review—review by the U.S. Supreme Court of the constitutional validity of a legislative act.

jurisdiction—a set of policy issues that fall under the purview of a specific committee (or subcommittee); full committee jurisdiction is set by chamber standing rules and precedents.

L

lame duck—an elected official or group continuing to hold political office during the period between the election and the inauguration of a successor.

landslide—an election in which one candidate defeats the other by a very large margin.

law—an act of Congress that has been signed by the president or passed over his veto by Congress.

legislative action steps—each chamber produces detailed, chamber-specific legislative action steps. Each step has a number code.

legislative branch—part of the U.S. government that creates laws; Congress.

legislative interest— a label used by committees to identify bills that were not formally referred to the committee but which the committee expresses jurisdictional or provisional interest in.

lobbying—to seek to influence public officials to support certain policies, especially members of a legislative body.

M

markup—meeting by a committee or subcommittee during which committee members offer, debate, and vote on amendments to a measure.

measure—a legislative vehicle: a bill, joint resolution, concurrent resolution, or simple resolution.

memorial—written statement or petition presented to Congress by the legislature of a state or territory that may affect the proceedings of a committee or Congress in general. Memorials may be referred by a member of the House of Representatives. The Senate does not differentiate between memorials and petitions.

motion to proceed to consider—a motion in the Senate, which, if agreed to by a majority of those present and voting, brings a measure (e.g., a bill) or matter (e.g., a nomination) before the chamber for consideration. Often referred to simply as a "motion to proceed."

motion to recommit—In the House, a motion offered by a member of the minority party at the end of floor consideration that, if adopted in its simple form, returns the measure to legislative committee. If combined with "instructions to report back forthwith," it provides one last opportunity for a minority party member to offer an amendment to the measure. In the Senate, the motion may be offered at other times during consideration of a measure, and is not prerogative of a member of the minority party; it may also be used as a means of offering an amendment.

motion to table—a non-debatable motion in the House and Senate by which a simple majority may agree to negatively and permanently dispose of a question (e.g., an amendment).

N

National Archives and Records Administration (NARA)—after the president signs a bill into law, it is delivered to NARA's Office of the Federal Register, where editors assign a public law number.

nomination—the president's formal submission of an individual's name, and the federal government position to which he or she is proposed to be appointed, for Senate consideration and potential confirmation; also, the process by which a political party chooses its official candidate for a particular office.

nominee—the candidate chosen by a political party to run for a particular office.

O

obstruction of justice—evading the legal system or procedures by not fully disclosing information of falsifying statements.

official title—a bill's sponsor designates an official title which may be amended in the course of legislative action. Bills may also have short titles. The more complex a bill becomes, the more likely the bill is to acquire additional titles.

ordered report—a committee's formal action of agreeing to report a measure of a matter to its chamber.

original bill—an introduced bill that embodies a text approved in a committee markup but not formally introduced prior to the markup. Senate committees are authorized to report original bills within their jurisdictions in addition to reporting measures that have been introduced and referred to them; some House committees also have authority to originate certain measures.

P

pardon—term used when a person found guilty is restored to not-guilty status as if he had never committed the offense.

parliamentarian—nonpartisan staff officials (one in each chamber, assisted by deputies and assistants) who provide expert advice and assistance to the presiding officer and to members on the application and interpretation of chamber rules, precedents, and practices (including referral to measures to committee).

partitioned nomination—a presidential nomination with multiple nominees may be partitioned by the Senate if the nominees follow a different confirmation path.

party caucus/conference—the official organization comprised of all members of a political party serving within a congressional chamber.

petition—written statement from any entity other than a state legislature—boards, commissions, cities, towns, individuals—that may affect the proceedings of a committee or Congress in general. The Senate does not differentiate between petitions and memorials.

point of order—a member's statement to the presiding officer that the chamber (or committee) is taking action contrary to the rules or precedents, and a demand that they be enforced.

poll—a survey to assess public opinion or to forecast an election; also refers to a place where votes are cast.

platform—a declaration of principles and policies adopted by a political party or candidate.

political machine—political group controlled by a tightly-run organization that stresses discipline and rewards its supporters, usually found in large cities and frequently accused of corruption.

political suicide—a vote or action that is likely to be so unpopular as to prevent a politician from winning election to office.

poll—a survey used to gauge public opinion concerning issues or to forecast an election.

pork barrel—the appropriation of government spending for local projects primarily as a way for politicians to gain favor with local voters.

primary—a state election in which party members vote for a candidate from within their party. The vote determines how many of the state's delegates each candidate gets.

president—the president of the United States (POTUS) is the head of state and head of government and directs the executive branch of the federal government and is the commander-in-chief of the U.S. armed forces.

president pro tempore—the senior member of the majority party in the Senate who serves as the president of the Senate when the vice president is absent.

presidential message—written statement to Congress, such as a president's budget of the State of the Union address.

previous question—non-debatable motion, available in the House and its legislative committees, which, when agreed to, cuts off further debate, prevents the offering of additional amendments, and brings the pending matter to an immediate vote.

primary election—an election held before the general election to determine the main candidates representing the various parties.

private bill—in contrast to public bills (which apply to public matters and deal with individuals only by classes), a private bill proposes to provide benefits that are restricted to one or more specific individuals (including corporations or institutions), typically when no other legal remedy is available.

privileged nomination—certain nominations entitled to expedited procedures.

pro forma session—a daily session of either chamber held chiefly to avoid the occurrence of either a recess of more than three days within the annual session or an adjournment sine die (either of which would constitutionally require the consent of the other chamber). Pro forma sessions are typically short, with no business, or very little, conducted.

proposed/offered Senate amendment— A Senate amendment is proposed or offered when a Senator has been recognized by the presiding officer, sends his/her amendment to the desk (or identifies an amendment already at the desk), and the amendment is read by the clerk. The amendment becomes pending before the Senate, and remains pending until disposed of by the Senate. Occasionally the term "called up" is used in lieu of "proposed" or "offered."

Q

quid pro quo—used in law for giving one valuable thing for another.

quorum—minimum number of members of a chamber (or committee) required for the transaction of certain types of business.

R

ranking member—the most senior (though not necessarily the longest-serving) member of the minority party on a committee (or subcommittee). The ranking member typically oversees minority committee staff and may coordinate involvement of the minority party committee members in a committee activities.

recess appointment—a temporary presidential appointment, during a recess of the Senate, of an individual to a federal government position, where such appointment usually requires the advice and consent of the Senate.

referral—assignment of a measure to a committee (or subcommittees) for potential consideration.

reserved bill number—in recent Congresses, the resolution specifying House internal rules of procedure includes reserving bill numbers for assignment by the Speaker. In the 112th Congress (2011–2012) the practice was extended to reserve additional bill numbers for assignment by the Minority Leader. In the Senate, some of the lowest bill numbers are reserved for leadership.

rider—an informal term for an amendment or provision that is not relevant to the legislation to which it is attached.

roll call vote—a vote that records the individual position of each member who voted. Such votes occurring on the House floor (by the "yeas and nays" or by "recorded vote") are taken by electronic device. The Senate has no electronic voting system; in such votes, Senators answer "yea" or "nay" as the clerk calls each name aloud.

resolution of ratification—a resolution by which the Senate, if supported by a vote of two-thirds, formally gives its advice and consent to a treaty, thereby empowering the president to proceed with ratification of the treaty.

S

sedition—the attempt to overthrow a government by force or at least interrupt its activities.

separation of powers—a doctrine of constitutional law under which three branches of government (executive, legislative, and judicial) are kept separate; also known as the system of checks and balances as each branch is given certain powers to check and balance the other branches.

silent majority—the largest part of a country's population that consists of people who are not actively involved in politics and do not express their political opinions publicly but who potentially wield significant political influence.

simple resolution—a form of legislative measure introduced and potentially acted upon by only one congressional chamber and used for the regulation of business only within the chamber of origin. Depending on the chamber of origin, they begin with a designation of either H.Res. or S.Res.

slate—a group of candidates for various offices running on a common platform.

slip law—the initial publication of a measure that has become law. Slip laws are made available online within days after enactment through the U.S. Government Publishing Office and are used until the law is published in a more permanent form. Public and private laws are then reprinted by number in the Statutes at Large, and public laws later incorporated into the U.S. Code.

special rule—a resolution reported by the Rules Committee that, if agreed to by the House, sets the terms for debating and amending a specified measure.

spin—the deliberate crafting of words and images for political effect; an attempt to shape the way the public looks at an issue or event; political advisers who spin are known as "spin doctors."

sponsor—a Representative or Senator who introduces a bill or other measure.

stump speech—a standard speech used by a politician running for office, typically given at many appearances at the local level.

subpoena—an order directed to a person to appear at a particular place and time to testify as a witness. The person may be required to bring documents and other filings to produce in evidence.

supermajority—a terms sometimes used for a vote on a matter that requires approval by more than a simple majority of those members present and voting, with a quorum being present; also referred to as extraordinary majority.

suspension of the rules— in the House, a procedure that streamlines consideration of a measure with wide support by prohibiting floor amendments, limiting debate to 40 minutes, and requiring a two-thirds majority for passage. Although rarely used, the Senate may also suspend various rules by a vote of two-thirds following one day's written notice.

Supreme Court—the highest federal court in the United States, consisting of nine justices and taking judicial precedence over all other courts in the nation.

swing vote—the undecided, usually independent, portion of the electorate that can "swing" the outcome of an election.

T

treaty—an agreement negotiated and signed by the executive that enters into force if it is approved by a two-thirds vote in the Senate, and is subsequently ratified by the president.

U

unanimous consent agreement—in the Senate, a proposal that, if agreed to, establishes the procedural guidelines for considering a measure of matter on the floor. If any member objects to such a request, it is not agreed to.

unanimous consent request—a proposal that all members (of a chamber or committee) agree to set aside one of more chamber of committee rules to take some action otherwise not in order. If any member objects to such a request, it is not agreed to.

V

veto—presidential disapproval of a bill or joint resolution presented for enactment into law. If a president vetoes a bill, it can become law only if the House and Senate separately vote (by two-thirds) to override the veto. A less common form of presidential veto—a pocket veto—occurs if Congress has adjourned without the possibility of returning and the president does not sign the measure within the required 10-day (excluding Sundays) period.

vice president—the second-highest executive officer of the U.S. government and the first person in the presidential line of succession, who will take over as president upon the death, resignation, or removal of a president. The vice president presides over the Senate, but is allowed to vote in the Senate only if necessary to break a deadlock. The vice president also presides over joint sessions of Congress.

W

whistleblower—an employee or subordinate who turns against their superiors to bring a problem out into the open.

witness tampering—intimidation or harassment of a witness before or after testimony is obstruction of justice.

whip—the party member who makes sure that all other members are present for crucial votes and that they vote in accordance with the party line.

Sources: https://www.scholastic.com/teachers/articles/teaching-content/vocabulary-political-words/; https://www.congress.gov/help/legislative-glossary/; http://bookbuilder.cast.org/view_glossary.php?book=90311&word=65976; https://courses.lumenlearning.com/atd-monroecc-americangovernment/chapter/glossary-12/; https://www.thecorsaironline.com/corsair/impeachmentglossary; https://votesmart.org/education/vocabulary#.XhY99CZKiUk; https://thelawdictionary.org/; Wikipedia; Webster's dictionary.

Historical Snapshots

1880–1881
- The plush Del Monte Hotel in Monterey, California, opened
- The country claimed 93,000 miles of railroad
- Halftone photographic illustrations appeared in newspapers for the first time
- Midwest farmers burned their corn for fuel as prices were too low to warrant shipping
- President James A. Garfield was assassinated
- The Diamond Match Company was created
- Marquette University was founded in Milwaukee
- Barnum & Bailey's Circus was created through the merger of two companies
- Chicago meatpacker Gustavus F. Swift perfected the refrigeration car
- Josephine Cockrane of Illinois invented the first mechanical dishwasher
- A U.S. Constitutional amendment to grant full suffrage to women was introduced in Congress this and every year until its passage in 1920
- Thanks to high tariffs, the U.S. Treasury had a surplus of $145 million
- The U.S. had 2,400 magazines and daily newspapers, and 7,500 weekly newspapers
- The typewriter and the telephone were both novelties at the 1876 Centennial in Philadelphia; in 1880, 50,000 telephones existed nationwide and at the turn of the century, that number tripled
- George Eastman's famous slogan "You Push the Button, We Do the Rest" helped make Kodak camera a part of many American homes

1885
- The Canadian Pacific Railroad reached the Pacific Ocean
- Baseball set players' salaries at $1,000-$2,000 for the 1885 season
- The first photograph of a meteor was taken
- Dr. William W. Grant of Davenport, Iowa, performed the first appendectomy
- Bachelor Grover Cleveland entered the White House as president
- Mark Twain's *Adventures of Huckleberry Finn* was published
- The Washington Monument was dedicated
- The U.S. Post Office began offering special delivery for first-class mail

- The Salvation Army was officially organized in the U.S.
- Texas was the last Confederate state readmitted to the Union
- Louis Pasteur successfully tested an anti-rabies vaccine on a boy bitten by an infected dog
- Leo Daft opened America's first commercially operated electric streetcar in Baltimore
- In the Wyoming Territory, 28 Chinese laborers were killed and hundreds more chased out of town by striking coal miners
- The first gasoline pump was delivered to a gasoline dealer in Ft. Wayne, Indiana

1890–1891

- Massive immigration transformed the nation, largely unaffecting rural South
- Irish women immigrants to America, in demand as servants, outnumbered men
- *Literary Digest* began publication
- Restrictive anti-black "Jim Crow" laws were enacted throughout the South
- American Express Traveler's Cheque was copyrighted
- Ceresota flour was introduced by the Northwest Consolidated Milling Company
- George A. Hormel & Co. introduced the packaged food Spam
- The International Brotherhood of Electrical Workers was organized
- Bicycle designer Charles Duryea and brother James designed a gasoline engine capable of powering a road vehicle
- Edouard Michelin obtained a patent for a "removable" bicycle tire that could be repaired quickly in the event of puncture
- Rice University and Stanford were chartered
- Bacteriologist Anna Williams obtained her M.D. from the Women's Medical College of New York and worked in the diagnostic laboratory of the city's Health Department, the first such lab in America
- Chicago's Provident Hospital became the first interracial hospital in America
- Irene Coit became the first woman admitted to Yale University
- The electric self-starter for automobiles was patented
- Important books included *Tess of the d'Urbervilles* by Thomas Hardy; *The Light That Failed* by Rudyard Kipling; *The Picture of Dorian Gray* by Oscar Wilde, and *Tales of Soldiers and Civilians* by Ambrose Bierce

1895

- Mintonette, later called volleyball, was created by William G. Morgan in Holyoke, Massachusetts
- Oscar Wilde's last play, *The Importance of Being Earnest*, was first shown at St. James's Theatre in London
- The first professional American football game was played in Latrobe, Pennsylvania, between the Latrobe YMCA and the Jeannette Athletic Club
- Rudyard Kipling published the story "Mowgli Leaves the Jungle Forever" in *Cosmopolitan* illustrated magazine
- George B. Selden was granted the first U.S. patent for an automobile
- Wilhelm Röntgen discovered a type of radiation later known as x-rays
- Oscar Hammerstein opened the Olympia Theatre, the first in New York City's Times Square district
- Alfred Nobel signed his last will and testament, setting aside his estate to establish the Nobel Prize after his death
- The Anti-Saloon League of America was formed in Washington D.C.
- The London School of Economics and Political Science was founded in England
- W. E. B. Du Bois became the first African-American to receive a Ph.D. from Harvard University

1900

- President William McKinley used the telephone to help his re-election
- Hamburgers were introduced by Louis Lassen in New Haven, Connecticut
- The cost of telephone service fell as more companies offered a 10-party line
- Cigarette smoking was popular and widely advertised
- Excavation had begun on the New York subway system
- The U.S. College Entrance Examination Board was formed to screen college applicants using a Scholastic Aptitude Test
- Puerto Rico was declared a U.S. territory
- A tidal wave in Galveston, Texas, killed 4,000 people
- The U.S. Navy bought its first submarine

1905–1906

- Industrial Workers of the World (IWW) attacked the American Federation of Labor for accepting the capitalist system
- A New York law limiting hours of work in the baking industry to 60 per week was ruled unconstitutional by the Supreme Court

- Oklahoma was admitted to the Union
- Planters Nut and Chocolate Company was created
- Samuel Hopkins Adams' *The Great American Fraud* exposed the fraudulent claims of many patent medicines
- Anti-liquor campaigners received powerful support from the Woman's Christian Temperance Union, led by Frances E. Willard
- President Grover Cleveland wrote in *The Ladies' Home Journal* that women of sense did not wish to vote: "The relative positions to be assumed by men and women in the working out of our civilizations were assigned long ago by a higher intelligence than ours."
- President Theodore Roosevelt admonished well-born white women who were using birth control for participating in willful sterilization, a practice known as racial suicide

1910–1911

- *Women's Wear Daily* began publication in New York
- 70 percent of bread was baked at home, down from 80 percent in 1890
- Father's Day and the Boy Scouts of America made their first appearances
- The concept of the "weekend" as a time of rest gained popularity
- Actress Blanche Sweet was one of D.W. Griffith's regulars in the one- and two-reelers that dominated the movie industry
- The Triangle Shirtwaist factory fire, deadly because the single exit door was locked to prevent theft, brought demands for better working conditions
- California women gained suffrage by constitutional amendment
- The use of fingerprinting in crime detection became widespread
- Marie Curie won an unprecedented second Nobel Prize, but was refused admission to the French Academy of Science
- The divorce rate climbed to one in 12 marriages, from one in 85 in 1905

1915–1916

- An attempt by Congress to exclude illiterates from immigrating, a bill promoted by the unions to protect jobs, was vetoed by President Howard Taft in 1913, reasoning that illiteracy was no test of character
- The Woman's Peace Party was founded with social worker Jane Addams, the founder of Hull House in Chicago, as its first president
- A divorce law requiring only six months of residence was passed in Nevada

- A Chicago law restricted liquor sales on Sunday
- American Tobacco Company selected salesmen by psychological tests
- Railway workers gained the right to an eight-hour day, preventing a nationwide strike
- Margaret Sanger opened the first birth control clinic in the country, distributing information in English, Italian and Yiddish
- The Mercury dime and Liberty fifty-cent piece went into circulation
- High school dropout Norman Rockwell published his first illustration in *The Saturday Evening Post*
- South Carolina raised the minimum working age of children from 12 to 14
- Stanford Terman introduced a test for measuring intelligence, coining the term "IQ" for intelligence quotient

1919–1920
- Boston police struck against pay scales of $0.21 to $0.23 per hour for 83- to 98-hour weeks.
- The dial telephone was introduced in Norfolk, Virginia
- U.S. ice cream sales reached 150 million gallons, up from 30 million in 1909
- *The New York Daily News* became the first tabloid (small picture-oriented) newspaper
- Boston Red Sox pitcher and outfielder Babe Ruth hit 29 home runs for the year and the New York Yankees purchased his contract for $125,000
- More than four million American workers struck for the right to belong to unions
- The Bureau of Labor Statistics reported that 1.4 million women had joined the American work force since 1911
- Following the 1918 strike by the Union Streetcar Conductors protesting the employment of female conductors, the War Labor Board ruled in favor of the continued employment of women
- Southern leaders of the National Association of Colored Women protested the conditions of domestic service workers, including the expectation of white male employers of the right to take sexual liberties with their servants

1925-1926
- James Buchanan "Buck" Duke donated $47 million to Trinity College at Durham, North Carolina and the college changed its name to Duke
- College football surpassed boxing as a national pastime

- With prohibition the law of the land, party-goers hid liquor in shoe heels, flasks form-fitted to women's thighs, and perfume bottles
- The Charleston, a dance that originated in Charleston, South Carolina, was carried north and incorporated into the all-black show *Shuffle Along*
- The U.S. Supreme Court declared unconstitutional an Oregon law that required all grammar school-aged children to attend school
- The Methodist Episcopal General Conference lifted its ban on theatre attendance and dancing
- Walt Disney began creating cartoons, featuring "Alice's Wonderland"
- Al Capone took control of Chicago bootlegging
- Chesterfield cigarettes were marketed to women for the first time
- The first ham in a can was introduced by Hormel
- Cars appeared in such colors as "Florentine Cream" and "Versailles Violet"
- Earl Wise's potato chips were so successful he moved his business from a remodeled garage to a concrete plant
- To fight depression in the automobile industry, Henry Ford introduced the eight-hour day and five-day work week
- With prohibition under way, the Supreme Court upheld a law limiting the medical prescription of whiskey to one pint every 10 days
- The illegal liquor trade netted $3.5 billion a year
- The movies became America's favorite entertainment, with more than 14,500 movie houses showing 400 movies a year
- *True Story Magazine* reached a circulation of two million with stories such as "The Diamond Bracelet She Thought Her Husband Didn't Know About"
- 40 percent of all first-generation immigrants owned their own homes, while 29 percent of all second-generation immigrants were homeowners
- Sinclair Lewis refused to accept the Pulitzer Prize because it "makes the writer safe, polite, obedient, and sterile"
- Martha Graham debuted in New York as choreographer and dancer in *Three Gopi Maidens*
- *The Jazz Singer*, the first talking film, made its debut
- Women's skirts, the shortest of the decade, were just below the knee with flounces, pleats, and circular gores that extended from the hip
- Ethel Lackie of the Illinois Athletic Club broke the world's record for the 40-yard freestyle swim with a time of 21.4 seconds

1930–1931

- The car boom collapsed after the Depression and one million auto workers were laid off
- Trousers became acceptable attire for women who played golf and rode horses
- Radio set sales increased to 13.5 million
- Boeing hired eight nurses to act as flight attendants
- *Fortune Magazine* was launched by Henry R. Luce at $1.00 per issue
- The University of Southern California polo team refused to play against the UCLA until its one female member was replaced by a male
- Laurette Schimmoler of Ohio became the first woman airport manager, earning a salary of $510 a year
- Alka-Seltzer was introduced by Miles Laboratories
- Clairol hair products were introduced by U.S. chemists
- For the first time, emigration exceeded immigration
- More than 75 percent of all cities banned the employment of wives
- The National Forty-Hour Work Week League formed, calling for an eight-hour workday in an effort to produce more jobs
- To generate income, Nevada legalized both gambling and the six-month divorce
- Chicago gangster Al Capone was convicted of evading $231,000 in federal taxes
- New York's Waldorf-Astoria Hotel was opened
- Silent film extra Clark Gable appeared in the movie A Free Soul, gaining instant stardom, while Universal studios recruited actress Bette Davis

1935–1936

- The Social Security Act passed Congress
- The Emergency Relief Appropriation Act gave $5 billion to create jobs
- Fort Knox became the United States Repository of gold bullion
- Nylon was developed by Du Pont
- New York State law allowed women to serve as jurors
- An eight-hour work day became law in Illinois
- A *Fortune* poll indicated that 67 percent favored birth control
- Trailer sales peaked; tourist camps for vacationing motorists gained popularity
- Ford unveiled the V-8 engine

- Recent advances in photography, like 35 mm camera and easy-to-use exposure meters, fueled a photography boom
- *Life* magazine began publication, with a claim that one in 10 Americans had a tattoo
- The National Park Service created numerous federal parks and fish and game preserves, adding a total of 600,000 additional acres to state preserves
- Mercedes-Benz created the first diesel-fueled passenger car
- A revolt against progressive education was led by Robert M. Hutchins, president of the University of Chicago
- Molly Dewson of the National Consumers' League led a fight to gain the appointment of more female postmasters

1940

- RKO released Walt Disney's second full-length animated film, Pinocchio
- *Truth or Consequences* debuted on NBC Radio
- Booker T. Washington became the first African-American to be depicted on a U.S. postage stamp
- McDonald's restaurant opened in San Bernardino, California
- President Franklin D. Roosevelt asked Congress for approximately $900 million to construct 50,000 airplanes per year
- The Auschwitz-Birkenau concentration and death camp opened in Poland
- WW I General John J. Pershing, in a nationwide radio broadcast, urged aid to Britain in order to defend America, while national hero Charles Lindbergh led an isolationist rally at Soldier Field in Chicago
- Nazi Germany rained bombs on London for 57 consecutive nights
- The Selective Training and Service Act of 1940 created the first peacetime draft in U.S. history
- The U.S. imposed a total embargo on all scrap metal shipments to Japan
- Franklin D. Roosevelt defeated Republican challenger Wendell Willkie to become the first and only third-term president
- Agatha Christie's mystery novel *And Then There Were None* was published

1945

- President Franklin Delano Roosevelt died in office and Harry Truman became president
- WW II ended

- Penicillin was introduced commercially
- Strikes idled 4.6 million workers, the worst stoppage since 1919
- The Dow Jones Industrial Average peaked at a post-1929 high of 212.50
- U.S. college enrollments reached an all-time high of more than 2 million
- Ektachrome color film was introduced by Kodak Company
- Hunt Foods established "price at time of shipment" contracts with customers
- The U.S. birth rate soared to 3.4 million, up from 2.9 million in the previous year
- New York State forbade discrimination by employers, employment agencies and labor unions on the basis of race, the first time in American history a legislative body enacted a bill outlawing discrimination based on race, creed, or color
- The Boy Scouts collected 10 million pounds of rubber and more than 370 million pounds of scrap metal during the war, while Chicago children collected 18,000 tons of newspapers in just five months

1950–1951

- The Korean War began
- Congress increased personal and corporate income taxes
- President Truman ordered the Atomic Energy Committee to develop the hydrogen bomb
- Boston Red Sox Ted Williams became baseball's highest paid player with a $125,000 contract
- Senator Joseph McCarthy announced that he had the names of 205 known Communists working in the State Department
- The FBI issued its first list of the Ten Most Wanted Criminals
- The first kidney transplant was performed on a 49-year old woman in Chicago
- Charles M. Schultz's comic strip, *Peanuts*, debuted in eight newspapers
- M&M candy was stamped with an "M" to assure customers of the real thing
- The first Xerox copy machine was introduced
- The 22nd Amendment to the Constitution, limiting the term of the president to two terms, was adopted
- Univak, the first general-purpose electronic computer, was dedicated in Philadelphia
- CBS introduced color television in a program hosted by Ed Sullivan and Arthur Godfrey

- *Jet* news magazine was launched
- Harvard Law School admitted women for the first time
- H&R Block, in Kansas City, began offering tax preparation services when the IRS stopped preparing people's taxes
- Margaret Sanger urged the development of an oral contraceptive
- For the first time in history, women outnumbered men in the U.S.
- Julius and Ethel Rosenberg were sentenced to death for espionage against the U.S.
- President Truman dispatched an air force plane when Sioux City Memorial Park in Iowa refused to bury John Rice, a Native American who had died in combat; his remains were interred in Arlington National Cemetery
- Charles F. Blair flew solo over the North Pole
- Entertainer Milton Berle signed a 30-year, million-dollar-plus contract with NBC

1954–1955

- The Supreme Court declared racial segregation in public schools illegal
- Open-heart surgery was introduced by Minneapolis physician C. Walton Lillehe
- RCA introduced the first color television set
- The $13 million, 900-room Fontainebleau Hotel opened at Miami Beach
- *Sports Illustrated Magazine* was introduced
- Dr. Jonas E. Salk, U.S. developer of anti-polio serum, started inoculating school children in Pittsburgh, Pennsylvania
- Marian Anderson, the first black soloist of the Metropolitan Opera, appeared as Ulrica in *Un Ballo* in Maschera
- Blacks in Montgomery, Alabama, boycotted segregated city bus lines, and Rosa Parks was arrested for refusing to give up her seat in the front of the bus
- *National Review* and *Village Voice* began publication
- HEW Secretary Oveta Culp Hobby opposed the free distribution of the Salk vaccine to poor children as "socialized medicine by the back door"
- Smog and poisoned air became a public concern
- Jacqueline Cochran became the first woman to fly faster than the speed of sound
- Racial segregation on interstate buses and trains was ordered to end
- The AFL and CIO merged, with George Meany as president

- The Dow Jones Industrial Average hit a high of 488, and a low of 391
- The Ford Foundation gave $500 million to colleges and universities nationwide

1960

- Four students from NC Agricultural and Technical State University in Greensboro, began a sit-in at a segregated Woolworth's lunch counter, which triggered similar nonviolent protests throughout the southern U.S.
- Joanne Woodward received the first star on the Hollywood Walk of Fame
- The U.S. announced that 3,500 American soldiers would be sent to Vietnam
- The U.S. launched the first weather satellite, TIROS-1
- *Ben Hur* won the Oscar for Best Picture
- A Soviet missile shot down an American spy plane; pilot Francis Gary Powers was captured and released 21 months later in a spy swap with the U.S.
- President Dwight D. Eisenhower signed the Civil Rights Act of 1960 into law
- The U.S. FDA approved birth control as an additional indication for the drug Searle's Enovid, making it the world's first approved oral contraceptive pill
- Harper Lee released her critically acclaimed novel *To Kill a Mockingbird*
- Presidential candidates Richard M. Nixon and John F. Kennedy participated in the first televised presidential debate
- President Eisenhower authorized the use of $1 million toward the resettlement of Cuban refugees, who were arriving in Florida at the rate of 1,000 a week
- The U.S. Supreme Court declared in *Boynton v. Virginia* that segregation on public transit was illegal

1965

- "Flower Power" was coined by Allen Ginsburg at a Berkeley antiwar rally
- The U.S. Immigration Bill abolished national origin quotas
- The Voting Rights Act, which eliminated literacy tests and provided federal oversight in elections, stimulated a dramatic increase in voting by African-Americans
- The U.S. Supreme Court struck down a Connecticut statute forbidding the use of contraceptives and eliminated state and local film censorship
- After extended hearings on cigarette smoking, Congress required package warning: "Caution: Cigarette smoking may be hazardous to your health"

1970

- Black Sabbath's debut album, regarded as the first heavy metal album, was released
- The Nuclear Non-Proliferation Treaty went into effect, after ratification by 56 nations
- Earth Day was proclaimed by San Francisco Mayor Joseph Alioto
- Paul McCartney announced the disbanding of the Beatles, as their twelfth album, *Let It Be*, was released
- Four students at Kent State University in Ohio were killed and nine wounded by Ohio National Guardsmen during a protest against the U.S. incursion into Cambodia
- The U.S. promoted its first female generals: Anna Mae Hays and Elizabeth P. Hoisington
- The Women's Strike for Equality took place down Fifth Avenue in New York City
- The first New York City Marathon took place
- Garry Trudeau's comic strip *Doonesbury* debuted in dozens of U.S. newspapers
- The North Tower of the World Trade Center was the tallest building in the world at 1,368 feet
- Alvin Toffler published his book *Future Shock*

1974–1975

- The pocket calculator was marketed
- The universal product code was designed for the supermarket industry
- 3M developed Post-it stock to stick paper to paper
- The first desktop microcomputer became available
- The Equal Opportunity Act forbade discrimination based on sex or marital status
- Minnesota became the first state to require businesses, restaurants, and institutions to establish no-smoking areas
- Top films were *Towering Inferno*, *Earthquake*, and *The Exorcist*
- McDonald's opened its first drive-through restaurants
- AT&T, the world's largest private employer, banned discrimination against homosexuals
- Harvard changed its five-to-two male to female admissions policy to equal admissions
- The Atomic Energy Commission was dissolved

- The Supreme Court ruled that the mentally ill cannot be hospitalized against their will unless they are dangerous to themselves or to others
- Chrysler, and other auto companies, offered rebates to counter record low sales
- The Rolling Stones tour grossed $13 million, and singer Stevie Wonder signed a record contract for $13 million
- A Massachusetts physician was convicted of manslaughter for aborting a fetus
- Rape laws in nine states now required less corroborative evidence necessary for conviction and restricted trial questions regarding the victim's past sex life

1980

- Yellow ribbons became a symbol of American concern for the hostages in Iran
- The divorce rate had grown from one in three marriages in 1970 to one in two
- The World Health Organization announced that smallpox had been eradicated
- A 10-year study correlated fatal heart disease to saturated-unsaturated fats
- The prime rate hit 21 percent, and gold was $880 per ounce
- Veteran's Administration study showed Vietnam vets suffered more emotional, social, educational and job-related problems than other veterans
- Top albums of the year included Pink Floyd's *The Wall*, Blondie's *Eat to the Beat, Off the Wall* by Michael Jackson and *Glass Houses* by Billy Joel
- Researchers at the University of California, San Diego, reported that "passive smoking" can lead to lung cancer
- The "Stop Handguns Before They Stop You" Committee reported: "Last year handguns killed 48 people in Japan, 8 in Great Britain, 34 in Switzerland, 52 in Canada, 58 in Israel, 21 in Sweden, 42 in West Germany, 10,720 in U.S. God Bless America"

1985

- The U.S. Army ruled that male officers were forbidden to carry umbrellas
- Highly addictive, inexpensive cocaine derivative "crack" became popular
- Parents and schools fought over AIDS-afflicted children being in public schools
- The Nobel Peace Prize went to the International Physicians for the Prevention of Nuclear War, founded by cardiologists at Harvard and in Moscow
- The Supreme Court upheld affirmative-action hiring quotas
- Rock Hudson became one of the first public figures to acknowledge his battle with AIDS, raising public awareness of the disease

1990

- The Food and Drug Administration approved a low-calorie fat substitute
- The *Hubble* space telescope was launched into orbit
- Dieting became a $33 billion industry
- John J. Audubon's book, *Birds of America*, sold for $3.96 million at auction
- Television premieres included *The Simpsons*, *Law and Order*, *Twin Peaks* and *Seinfeld*
- Women constituted 11 percent of U.S. military troops, up from three percent in 1973
- An EPA report claimed that 3,800 people died annually from second-hand smoke
- *Dances with Wolves* was named the Academy Awards' best picture; *Pretty Woman*, *Total Recall*, *Goodfellas* and *Home Alone* were also released
- The stock market hit a high of 2,999.75
- President Bush and Premier Gorbachev called for Iraqi withdrawal following its invasion of Kuwait

1995–1996

- Supreme Court ruled that only a constitutional amendment can enforce term limits on Congress
- The Dow Jones Industrial Average peaked at 5,216
- After 130 years, Mississippi lawmakers ratified the 13th Amendment abolishing slavery
- About 55 percent of women provided half or more of household income
- New York became the 38th state to reinstate capital punishment
- The 25th anniversary of Earth Day was celebrated
- The U.S. banned the manufacture of freon due to its effect on the ozone layer
- Sheik Omar Abdel-Rahman and nine followers were handed long prison sentences for plotting to blow up New York-area landmarks
- France detonated its sixth and most powerful nuclear bomb
- Congress voted to rewrite the 61-year-old Communications Act, freeing television, telephone, home computer industries to cross into each other's fields
- World chess champion Garry Kasparov beat IBM supercomputer "Deep Blue," winning a six-game match in Philadelphia

- Dr. Jack Kevorkian was acquitted of assisted suicide for helping two suffering patients kill themselves
- Liggett became the first tobacco company to acknowledge that cigarettes are addictive and cause cancer
- The first of the Nixon White House tapes concerning Watergate were released
- The Senate passed an immigration bill to tighten border controls, make it tougher for illegal immigrants to get U.S. jobs, and curtail legal immigrants' access to social services

2000

- Millennium celebrations were held throughout the world despite fears of major computer failures due to "Y2K" bug, fears that proved largely unwarranted
- President Bill Clinton proposed a $2 billion program to bring Internet access to low-income houses
- Supreme Court gave police broad authority to stop and question people who run from a police officer
- The Millennium Summit among world leaders was held at the United Nations
- President Bill Clinton created the Giant Sequoia National Monument to protect 328,000 California acres of trees from timber harvesting
- Judge Thomas Penfield Jackson ruled that Microsoft violated the Sherman Antitrust Act by tying its Internet browser to its operating system
- George W. Bush was declared the winner of the presidential race in a highly controversial election against Al Gore
- The female-oriented television cable channel Oxygen made its debut
- Carlos Santana won eight Grammy awards, including Album of the Year for *Supernatural*

2005

- George W. Bush was inaugurated in Washington, DC, for his second term as the forty-third president of the United States
- Demonstrators marched through Baghdad denouncing the U.S. occupation of Iraq, two years after the fall of Saddam Hussein, and rallied in the square where his statue had been toppled in 2003
- The Superjumbo jet aircraft Airbus A380 made its first flight from Toulouse
- The Provisional IRA issued formally ordered an end to the armed campaign it had pursued since 1969, and ordering all its units to dump their arms
- The largest UN World Summit in history was held in New York City

- Scientists announced that they had created mice with small amounts of human brain cells in an effort to make realistic models of neurological disorders

2010

- The Tea Party movement hosted its first convention in Nashville, Tennessee
- President Obama established the National Commission on Fiscal Responsibility and Reform
- The US Navy officially announced that it would end its ban on women in submarines
- The District of Columbia's same-sex marriage law went into effect
- At the 82nd Academy Awards, *The Hurt Locker* won six Oscars including the first Best Director award for a woman, Kathryn Bigelow
- President Obama signed the Patient Protection and Affordable Care Act into law aiming to insure 95 percent of Americans
- An explosion at the Deepwater Horizon oil rig killed 11 workers and sank the rig, initiating a massive offshore oil spill in the Gulf of Mexico, considered the largest environmental disaster in US history
- The Dodd-Frank Wall Street Reform and Consumer Protection Act was signed into law by President Obama
- Former US Solicitor General Elena Kagan was sworn in as Justice of the Supreme Court
- The last US combat troops left Iraq
- The San Francisco Board of Supervisors banned McDonald's Happy Meal toys, citing obesity concerns
- WikiLeaks founder Julian Assange began releasing confidential U.S. diplomatic documents
- General Motors introduced the first Chevrolet Volt plug-in hybrid electric vehicle
- President Obama signed the Don't Ask, Don't Tell repeal into law

2015

- NASA's *Messenger* spacecraft concluded its four-year orbital mission over Mercury
- Dzhokhar Tsarnaev was sentenced to death for the 2013 Boston Marathon bombing

- Cuba was officially removed from the US State Sponsors of Terrorism list
- Former Olympian Bruce Jenner became the first transgender person to appear on the cover of *Vanity Fair* magazine
- Rachel Dolezal resigned as president of the NAACP Spokane, Washington amid allegations that she claimed to be black but was actually white
- In a 6-3 decision, the Supreme Court upheld subsidies for the Patient Protection and Affordable Care Act (also known as Obamacare) nationwide
- The Supreme Court ruled that the Constitution guarantees a right to same-sex marriage
- The South Carolina State House removed the Confederate battle flag from its grounds after weeks of protest, and placed it in a museum
- *Birdman* won four Oscars including Best Picture and Best Director
- President Obama announced the Clean Power Plan which included first-ever Environmental Protection Agency standards on carbon pollution from U.S. power plants
- Kim Davis, a clerk for Rowan County, Kentucky, was found in contempt of court and jailed for five days for refusing to issue marriage licenses to same-sex couples
- President Obama ordered up to 50 U.S. special operations ground troops to be deployed in Syria to fight Islamic State militants
- Defense Secretary Ashton Carter announced that all combat roles in the military must be opened to women

2019

- SpaceIL launches the Beresheet probe, the world's first privately financed mission to the Moon
- Fifty people are killed and fifty others injured in terrorist attacks, streamed live on Facebook, on two mosques in Christchurch, New Zealand, the deadliest shooting in the country's modern history. Facebook disabled 1.5 million videos of the event
- Europe's antitrust regulators fine Google 1.49 billion euros ($1.7 billion) for freezing out online advertising rivals, bringing to nearly $10 billion the fines imposed against Google by the EU
- A four-page summary of Special Counsel Robert Mueller's report into U.S. President Donald Trump's 2016 election campaign is published by the U.S. Attorney General William Barr. It concludes that there was no collusion

with Russia—the basis of the investigation—but on the issue of obstruction of justice states: "While this report does not conclude that the president committed a crime, it also does not exonerate him."

- At the 91st Academy Awards, *Green Book* won Best Picture and Best Supporting Actor for Mahershala Ali's portrayal of Don Shirley; *Bohemian Rhapsody* led the ceremony with four awards, including Best Actor for Rami Malek's portrayal of Freddie Mercury. *Roma* and *Black Panther* also received three awards apiece, with the former winning Best Director for Alfonso Cuarón and becoming the first Mexican submission to win Best Foreign Language Film. Olivia Colman was awarded Best Actress for portraying Anne, Queen of Great Britain in *The Favourite*

- *The Overstory* by Richard Powers wins the Pulitzer Prize for fiction

- Researchers document an arctic fox's record-breaking trek of more than 2,700 miles, from Norway to Canada, as well as a speed record for her species, at one point covering about 96 miles per day

- A Texas Longhorn from Alabama sets Guinness world record with horns that are nearly 11 feet wide, longer than the Statue of Liberty's face

- Meteorologists in Southern California observe swarm of ladybugs so large it showed up on National Weather Service radar.

- Venezuela enters a constitutional crisis as Juan Guaidó and the National Assembly declare incumbent President Nicolàs Maduro "illegitimate"; Maduro severs diplomatic ties with the United States and Columbia and expels the German ambassador

- President Donald Trump confirms that the U.S. will leave the Intermediate-Range Nuclear Forces Treaty of 1987; Russia follows with suspension of its obligations to the treaty

- Catholic Pope Francis is the first pontiff to visit the Arabian Peninsula and to change the church's stance on the death penalty, arguing for its abolition

- An unmanned demonstration flight of the new crew capable version of the Space X Dragon spacecraft, intended to carry American astronauts into space, achieves successful autonomous docking with the International Space Station

- Ethiopian Airlines Flight 302, a Boeing 737 MAX 8 bound for Nairobi, crashes shortly after takeoff, killing all 157 passengers. Boeing 737 MAX 8 and MAX 9 models are subsequently grounded worldwide

- The final territory of the Islamic State of Iraq and the Levant (ISIL), located in Syria, is liberated

- Scientists from the Event Horizon Telescope project announce the first-ever image of a black hole, located in the center of the M87 galaxy
- WikiLeaks co-founder Julian Assange is arrested after seven years in Ecuador's embassy in London; he faces at least five years in prison for conspiracy to commit computer intrusion
- A major fire engulfs Notre-Dame Cathedral in Paris, resulting in the collapse of the roof and the main spire
- NepaliSat-1 is launched, Nepal's first ever research satellite to be sent into space
- A series of bomb attacks occur at eight locations in Sri Lanka, leaving at least 253 people dead and over 500 injured; this is the first major terrorist attack in the country since the Sri Lankan Civil War ended in 2009
- Comedian Volodymyr Zelensky is elected President of Ukraine in a runoff election. Zelensky portrayed a fictional Ukrainian president in the television series *Servant of the People*
- The number of deaths from the Kivu Ebola outbreak exceeds 1,000, the second deadliest Ebola outbreak in history, only surpassed by the West African Ebola virus epidemic of 2013–2016
- The Intergovernmental Science-Policy Platform on Biodiversity and Ecosystem Services warns that biodiversity loss is accelerating, with over a million species threatened with extinction
- British teenager Isabelle Holdaway is reported to be the first patient ever to receive a genetically modified phage therapy to treat a drug-resistant infection
- Taiwan's parliament becomes the first in Asia to legalize same-sex marriage; Botswana decriminalizes homosexuality; the Supreme Court of Ecuador rules in favor of same-sex marriage
- British Prime Minister Theresa May announces her resignation in the wake of Brexit failure
- South Korean newspaper Chosun Ilbo reports that North Korea executed nuclear envoy Kim Hyok-choi and four other diplomats in March after the failed Hanoi summit with the United States, and that Kim Jong-Un's top aide was sentenced to hard labor
- The 2019 FIFA Women's World Cup, held in France, is won by the United States
- Two oil tankers are attacked near the Strait of Hormuz while transiting the Gulf of Oman amid heightened tension between Iran and the United States; the United States blames Iran for the incident

- Japan resumes commercial whaling after a 30-year moratorium, following its withdrawal from the International Whaling Commission.
- The International Atomic Energy Agency confirms that Iran has breached the limit on its stockpile of enriched uranium
- The European Parliament elects Ursula von der Leyen as the new President of the European Commission, the first woman to be elected to this office in EU history
- Several U.S. states pass highly controversial fetal heartbeat bills, which ban abortions as early as six weeks, before many women are even aware that they are pregnant
- President Donald Trump declares a national state of emergency to obtain funding for his border wall; the Supreme Court declares that he can use $2.5 billion in military funding to proceed with construction
- Former Donald Trump personal attorney Michael Cohen is sentenced to three years in prison after confessing to committing to multiple crimes while working for Trump, heavily implicating Trump
- The Supreme Court rules that federal courts cannot constitutionally prevent partisan gerrymandering (redrawing district lines to benefit a political party)
- The Supreme Court blocks a citizenship question from being added to the 2020 census, which may have caused less people to respond to the census and ultimately misrepresent minority populations
- Rep. Alexandria Ocasio-Cortex releases blueprint for a new green deal to combat climate change that calls for a massive cut in carbon emissions
- The federal government is ordered to resume capital punishment with the execution of 5 federal prisoners at the direction of Attorney General William Barr
- Notable deaths in 2019 include: liberal Supreme Court Justice John Paul Stevens; African American artists Mavis Pusey and John Singleton; film director Franco Zeffirelli; boxers Pernell Whitaker and Eusebio Pedroze; fashion industry giants Gloria Vanderbilt and Karl Lagerfeld; scientist Murray Gell-Mann; and architect I.M Pei
- July 20 marked the 50th anniversary of the Apollo 11 moon landing
- Australian Kerry Robertson becomes the first person to use a new assisted dying program to end her life
- Saudi Arabia announces new rules for women, including independent travel without a male guardian's permission

- Iceland holds a funeral for the first glacier lost to climate change at the site of the Okjökull glacier
- Co-founder and CEO of Twitter Jack Dorsey's Twitter account is hacked and racist messages and bomb threats are published
- Hurricane Dorian devastates the Bahamas leaving 60 people dead and at least 70,000 homeless
- WalMart announces that it will stop selling handguns and some ammunition in the wake of the El Paso WalMart shooting
- The Joker, directed by Todd Phillips and starring Joaquin Phoenix, wins the Golden Lion at the Venice Film Festival
- Poet John Milton's annotated copy of Shakespeare's First Folio (1623) is found in a Philadelphia library in what could be the modern world's most important literary discovery
- President Donald Trump fires his third national security adviser, John Bolton
- Teen climate activist Greta Thunberg sails from Sweden to New York on an emissions-free yacht and delivers an emotional speech to the United Nations about climate change
- House Speaker Nancy Pelosi announces formal impeachment inquiry into President Donald Trump
- The World Health Organization announces that 800,000 children in DR Congo will be vaccinated as the world's largest measles epidemic claims thousands of lives
- The 2019 Nobel Peace Prize is awarded to Ethiopian Prime Minister Abiy Ahmed
- Free speech organization PEN America condemns the Nobel Committee for awarding the 2019 prize for literature to author Peter Handke, a supporter of Serbian dictator Slobodan Miloševi. Handke reportedly declared in 2014 that the Nobel Prize should be abolished because it promotes the false canonization of literature
- Houston Rockets general manager Daryl Morey deletes a tweet supporting Hong Kong democracy protesters after Chinese NBA partners severed ties with the NBA, drawing attention to the protests and sparking international controversy

Bibliography

"1912 Electoral Vote Tally, February 12, 1913." *National Archives*. 15 Aug. 2016. www. archives.gov/legislative/features/1912-election.

"1928 Presidential General Election Results." *US Election Atlas*. 2019. uselectionatlas. org/RESULTS/national.php?year=1928.

"1960 Presidential General Election Results." *U.S. Election Atlas*. 2019. uselectionatlas. org/RESULTS/national.php?year=1960.

"1964 Presidential General Election Results." *U.S. Election Atlas*. 2019. uselectionatlas. org/RESULTS/national.php?year=1964.

"1976 Presidential General Election Results." *US Election Atlas*. 2019. uselectionatlas. org/RESULTS/national.php?year=1976.

"1980 Presidential General Election Results." *U.S. Election Atlas*. uselectionatlas.org/ RESULTS/national.php?year=1980&off=0&elect=0&f=0.

"1992 Presidential General Election Results." *US Election Atlas*. uselectionatlas.org/ RESULTS/national.php?year=1992.

"2000 Presidential General Election Results." *US Election Atlas*. 2019. uselectionatlas.org/RESULTS/national.php?year=2000&off=0&elect=0&f=0.

"2008 Presidential General Election Results." *US Election Atlas*. 2019. uselectionatlas.org/RESULTS/national.php?year=2008&off=0&elect=0&f=0.

Ackerman, Kenneth D. *Dark Horse*. Viral History P, 2011.

_____. "The Garfield Assassination Altered American History, But Is Woefully Forgotten Today." *Smithsonian.com*., Smithsonian Institution. 2 Mar. 2018. www.smithsonianmag.com/history/garfield-assassination-altered-american-history-woefully-forgotten-today-180968319/.

Ackerman, S. J. "The Vote That Failed." *Smithsonian.com*. Smithsonian Institution. Nov. 1998. www.smithsonianmag.com/history/the-vote-that-failed-159427766/.

Adams, John. "Instructions Adopted by the Braintree Town Meeting." *Massachusetts Historical Society*. Papers of John Adams, vol 1. 2019. Adams Paper Digital Edition. www.masshist.org/publications/adams-papers/index.php/view/PJA01d073.

"African American Records: Freemen's Bureau." *National Archives*. 19 Sept. 2016. www.archives.gov/research/african-americans/freedmens-bureau.

"Agreement on the Cessation of Hostilities in Viet-Nam, 20 July 1954." *Mt. Holyoke*. 2019. www.mtholyoke.edu/acad/intrel/genevacc.htm.

Alexander, Michelle. *The New Jim Crow*. New York: The New P, 16 Jan. 2012.

"Alien and Sedition Acts (1798)." *Our Documents*. 2019www.ourdocuments.gov/doc. php?flash=false&doc=16&page=transcript.

Alperovitz, Gar. *The Decision to Use the Atomic Bomb*. New York: Vintage Books, 1996.

Ambar, Saladin. "Woodrow Wilson: Life Before the Presidency." *Miller Center*. University of Virginia. 2019. millercenter.org/president/wilson/life-before-the-presidency.

Ambrose, Stephen E. *The Supreme Commander: The War Years of General Dwight D. Eisenhower*. New York: Anchor Books, 1970.

Anapol, Avery. "Daughters of NY Podiatrist Allege He Helped Trump Avoid Vietnam War: New York Times." *The Hill*. 26 Dec. 2018. thehill.com/homenews/administration/422854-daughters-of-queens-podiatrist-and-fred-trump-tenant-say-father.

"Andrew Johnson, 16th Vice President (1865)." *U.S. Senate*. 2019. www.senate.gov/about/officers-staff/vice-president/VP_Andrew_Johnson.htm.

"Article 3: Life, Liberty, & Security of Person." *UDHR*. Universal Declaration of Human Rights. Columbia University. ccnmtl.columbia.edu/projects/mmt/udhr/article_3.html.

"Article X." *NPS*. National Park Service. Andrew Johnson. National Historic Site Tennessee. 14 Apr. 2015. www.nps.gov/anjo/learn/historyculture/article-x.htm.

"Articles of Confederation, 1777–1781." *U.S. Department of State*. Office of the Historian. 2016. history.state.gov/milestones/1776-1783/articles.

"Assassination of President Abraham Lincoln." *LOC*. Library of Congress. 2016. www.loc.gov/collections/abraham-lincoln-papers/articles-and-essays/assassination-of-president-abraham-lincoln/.

Bailey, Martha J., and Nicolas J. Duquette. "How Johnson Fought the War on Poverty: The Economics and Politics of Funding at the Office of Economic Opportunity." *Journal of Economic History*. vol. 74, no. 2. 2014, pp 351–88. *US National Library of Medicine*. National Institutes of Health.www.ncbi.nlm.nih.gov/pmc/articles/PMC4266933/.

Baker, Jean H. "Franklin Pierce: Impact and Legacy." *Miller Center*. U of Virginia. 2019. millercenter.org/president/pierce/impact-and-legacy.

_____. *James Buchanan,* edited by Arthur M. Schlesinger, Jr. New York: Times Books, 2004.

Banner, James M. Jr. *Presidential Misconduct: From George Washington to Today*. New York: The New P, 2019.

"Barack Obama." *YouGov*. 2019. today.yougov.com/topics/politics/explore/public_figure/Barack_Obama.

"Barbary Wars, 1801–1805 and 1815–1816." *U.S. Department of State*. Office of the Historian. Milestones. history.state.gov/milestones/1801-1829/barbary-wars.

Bauer, K. Jack. *Zachary Taylor: Soldier, Planter, Statesman of the Old Southwest*. Baton Rouge, LA: LSU P, 1993.

"Becoming America's First Lady." *Montpelier*. 2019. www.montpelier.org/learn/dolley-madison-becoming-americas-first-lady.

Bellamy, Jay. "A Stalwart of Stalwarts." *Archives*. National Archives. Prologue Magazine, vol. 48, no 3, Fall 2016. www.archives.gov/publications/prologue/2016/fall/guiteau.

Belz, Herman. "Lincoln's Construction of the Executive Power in the Secession Crisis." *Journal of the Abraham Lincoln Association*. vol. 27, no. 1, Winter 2006. pp. 13–38. *JSTOR*, www.jstor.org/stable/20149090.

Benbow, Mark E. "Birth of a Quotation: Woodrow Wilson and 'Like Writing History with Lightning.'" *The Journal of the Gilded Age and Progressive Era*. vol. 9, no. 4, Oct. 2010, pp 509–533. *JSTOR*, www.jstor.org/stable/20799409.

Benegal, Salil D. "The Spillover of Race and Racial Attitudes into Public Opinion about Climate Change." *Environmental Politics*, vol. 27, no. 4, 2018, Taylor and Francis online,www.tandfonline.com/doi/abs/10.1080/09644016.2018.1457287?journalCode=fenp20.

"Benjamin Franklin Bache." *Mount Vernon*. 2019. www.mountvernon.org/library/digitalhistory/digital-encyclopedia/article/benjamin-franklin-bache/.

Bennett, James Gordon, editor. *New York Herald*, vol. 17, no. 228, 17 August 1852. *LOC*, Library of Congress, Chronicling America, chroniclingamerica.loc.gov/lccn/sn83030313/1852–08–17/ed-1/seq-4.

Berg, A. Scott. *Wilson*. New York: G.P. Putnam's Sons, 2013.

Bergen, Anthony. "Franklin Pierce and the Consequences of Ambition." *Medium*. 23 Nov. 2015. medium.com/@Anthony_Bergen/franklin-pierce-and-the-consequences-of-ambition-577969fc81ca.

Berman, Ari. "Op-Ed: How Jimmy Carter Championed Civil Rights — and Ronald Reagan Didn't." *Los Angeles Times*. 3 Sept. 2015. www.latimes.com/opinion/op-ed/la-oe-0906-berman-carter-civil-rights-20150906-story.html.

Berman, Ari. *Give Us the Ballot: The Modern Struggle for Voting Rights in America.* New York: Farrar, Straus and Giroux, 2015.

Beschloss, Michael. *Mayday: Eisenhower, Khrushchev, and the U-2 Affair.* Open Road Media, 2016.

Bicknell, John. *America 1844*: Religious Fervor, Westward Expansion, and the Presidential Election That Transformed the Nation. Chicago, IL: Chicago Review P, 2015.

Black, Conrad. *Franklin Delano Roosevelt: Champion of Freedom.* New York: PublicAffairs P, 2003.

"Black Friday, September 24, 1869." *PBS*. American Experience. 2019. www.pbs.org/wgbh/americanexperience/features/grant-black-friday/.

Blake, Aaron. "The Extensive Effort to Bury Donald Trump's Grades." *The Washington Post*. 5 Mar. 2019. www.washingtonpost.com/politics/2019/03/05/extensive-effort-bury-donald-trumps-grades/.

Bomboy, Scott. "Lincoln and Taney's Great Writ Showdown." *National Constitution Center*. Constitution Daily. 28 May 2019. constitutioncenter.org/blog/lincoln-and-taneys-great-writ-showdown.

_____. "The Man Who Delivered California to the U.S., and Was Fired for It." *National Constitution Center*. Constitution Daily. 10 Mar. 2019. constitutioncenter.org/blog/the-man-who-delivered-california-to-the-u-s-and-was-fired-for-it.

Brands, H.W. *Reagan: The Life*. New York: Anchor Books, 2015.

Breitman, Jessica. "Francis Perkins: Honoring the Achievements of FDR's Secretary of Labor." *FDR Library*. 2016. www.fdrlibrary.org/perkins.

Brooks, Corey. "What Can the Collapse of the Whig Party Tell Us About Today's Politics"? *Smithsonian.com.* 12 Apr. 2016. www.smithsonianmag.com/history/what-can-collapse-whig-party-tell-us-about-todays-politics-180958729/.

Brown, David. "JFK's Addison's Disease." *The Washington Post*. 6 Oct. 6, 1992. www.washingtonpost.com/archive/lifestyle/wellness/1992/10/06/jfks-addisons-disease/aceb473c-a5dc-4199-9453-d3fcd3b18312/.

Brown, Everett S., and Ruth C. Silva. "Presidential Succession and Inability." *The Journal of Politics*, vol. 11, no. 1, 1949, pp. 236–56. *JSTOR*, www.jstor.org/stable/2126507.

Buchanan, James. "March 4, 1857: Inaugural Address." *Miller Center*. U of Virginia. 2019. millercenter.org/the-presidency/presidential-speeches/march-4-1857-inaugural-address.

_____. "James Buchanan. State of the Union 1860—3 December 1860."
    American History. U of Groningen. 2012. www.let.rug.nl/usa/presidents/james-
    buchanan/state-of-the-union-1860.php.

Buel, Richard Jr. *America on the Brink: How the Political Struggle Over the War of
    1812 Almost Destroyed the Young Republic*. Palgrave MacMillan, 2005.

Bunting, Josiah III. *Ulysses S. Grant*. New York: Times Books, 2004.

"Bush's Final Approval Rating: 22 Percent." *CBS News*. 16 Jan. 12009. www.cbsnews.
    com/news/bushs-final-approval-rating-22-percent/.

Butterfield, Fox. "Pentagon Papers: Eisenhower Decisions Undercut the
    Geneva Accords, Study Says." *New York Times*. 5 July 1971. www.nytimes.
    com/1971/07/05/archives/pentagon-papers-eisenhower-decisions-undercut-the-
    geneva-accords.html.

Bycoffe, Aaron, Ella Koeze, and Nathaniel Rakich. "Do Americans Support
    Impeaching Trump?" *FiveThirtyEight*. 17 Dec. 2019. projects.fivethirtyeight.
    com/impeachment-polls/.

Cain, Áine. "29 American Presidents Who Served in the Military." *Business Insider*.
    19 Feb. 2018. www.businessinsider.com/american-presidents-who-served-in-the-
    military-2016-6.

Calavita, Kitty, Henry N. Pontell, and Robert Tillman. *Big Money Crime: Fraud and
    Politics in the Savings and Loan Crisis*. U of California P. May 1999.

"Calvin Coolidge: Thirtieth President 1923–1929." *Clinton White House*.
    clintonwhitehouse4.archives.gov/WH/glimpse/presidents/html/cc30.html.

Cannon, Lou. *Governor Reagan: His Rise to Power*. New York: Public Affairs, 2003.

Caro, Robert A. *Master of the Senate: The Years of Lyndon Johnson III*. New York:
    Vintage Books, 2002.

Carson, John. *The Measure of Merit: Talents, Intelligence, and Inequality in the
    French and American Republics, 1750–1940*. Princeton, NJ: Princeton U P, 2007.

Carter, Jimmy. "Energy and the National Goals—A Crisis of Confidence."
    American Rhetoric. 2019. www.americanrhetoric.com/speeches/
    jimmycartercrisisofconfidence.htm.

Carter, Jimmy. "Nobel Lecture." *Nobel Prize*. 10 Dec. 2002. www.nobelprize.org/
    prizes/peace/2002/carter/lecture/.

Cassidy, John. "As a Businessman, Trump Was the Biggest Loser of All." *New Yorker*.
    8 May 2019. www.newyorker.com/news/our-columnists/as-a-businessman-trump-
    was-the-biggest-loser-of-all.

Celano, Daniele. "The Indian Removal Act: Jackson, Sovereignty and Executive Will." *The Purdue Historian*, vol. 8, art. 6, 2017. docs.lib.purdue.edu/cgi/viewcontent. cgi?article=1025&context=puhistorian.

Chapman, Ben. "Americans Have Forgotten the Story of Cincinnatus." *Medium*. 25 June 2018. medium.com/@Ben_Chapman/americans-have-forgotten-the-story-of-cincinnatus-b49728164ce1.

Chernow, Ron. *Grant*. New York: Penguin Books, 2017.

_____. *Washington: A Life*. New York: Penguin, 2010.

"Cherokee Nation v. Georgia." *LII*. Cornell Law School. 2019. www.law.cornell.edu/supremecourt/text/30/1#writing-USSC_CR_0030_0001_ZO.

"The Chesapeake Affair of 1807." *The Mariners Museum*. 2000. www.marinersmuseum.org/sites/micro/usnavy/08/08b.htm.

Churchill, Winston. "Prime Minister Churchill's Eulogy in Commons for the Late President Roosevelt." 17 Apr. 1945. www.ibiblio.org/pha/policy/1945/1945-04-17a.html.

"Civilian Conservation Corps." *NPS*. National Park Service. 10 Apr. 2015. www.nps.gov/thro/learn/historyculture/civilian-conservation-corps.htm.

Clay, Henry. "Clay's Resolutions January 29, 1850." *Transcript of Compromise of 1850*. *Our Documents*. www.ourdocuments.gov/doc.php?flash=false&doc=27&page=transcript.

_____. *The Speeches of Henry Clay*, edited by Calvin Colton. New York: A.S. Barnes & Co, 1857.

Cleveland, Grover. "October 1, 1888: Message Regarding Chinese Exclusion Act." *Miller Center*. University of Virginia. 2019. millercenter.org/the-presidency/presidential-speeches/october-1-1888-message-regarding-chinese-exclusion-act.

Collins, Bruce. "Clinton Impeachment: 20 Years On, Will Donald Trump Now Face the Same Fate?" *The Conversation*. 19 Dec. 2018. https://theconversation.com/clinton-impeachment-20-years-on-will-donald-trump-now-face-the-same-fate-109045.

Compton, Karl T. "If the Atomic Bomb Had Not Been Used." *The Atlantic*. Dec. 1946. www.theatlantic.com/magazine/archive/1946/12/if-the-atomic-bomb-had-not-been-used/376238/.

Cowie, Jefferson. *Stayin' Alive: The 1970s and the Last Days of the Working Class*. New York: The New P, 2010.

Cuddy, Brian. "Was It Legal for the U.S. to Bomb Cambodia?" *New York Times*. 12 Dec. 2017. www.nytimes.com/2017/12/12/opinion/america-cambodia-bomb.html.

Cull, Nicholas J. "Master of American Propaganda." *PBS*. American Experience. www.pbs.org/wgbh/americanexperience/features/the-great-war-master-of-american-propaganda/.

Cullen, James. "The History of Mass Incarceration." *Brennan Center*. 20 July 2018. www.brennancenter.org/our-work/analysis-opinion/history-mass-incarceration.

Cummings, William. "Survey of Scholars Places Trump as Third Worst President of All Time." *USA Today*. 13 Feb. 2019. www.usatoday.com/story/news/politics/onpolitics/2019/02/13/siena-presidential-ranking-survey/2857075002/.

Cummins, Joseph. "Dirty Campaigning in the Roaring Twenties: Herbert Hoover vs. Al Smith." *Mental Floss*. 17 Oct. 2008. www.mentalfloss.com/article/19897/dirty-campaigning-roaring-twenties-herbert-hoover-vs-al-smith.

Dallek, Robert. *Franklin D. Roosevelt: A Political Life*. New York: Penguin, 2018.

Daly, Christopher B. "How Woodrow Wilson's Propaganda Machine Changed American Journalism." *Smithsonian.com*. Smithsonian Institution. 28 Apr. 2017. www.smithsonianmag.com/history/how-woodrow-wilsons-propaganda-machine-changed-american-journalism-180963082/.

Dean, John W. *Warren G. Harding*. New York: Times Books, 2004.

"Declaration of Independence: A Transcription." *National Archives*. July 26, 2019. www.archives.gov/founding-docs/declaration-transcript.

Dickinson, Matthew J. *Bitter Harvest: FDR, Presidential Power and the Growth of the Presidential Branch*. New York: Cambridge U P, 1996.

Donovan, Thomas A. "'John Marshall Has Made His Decision, Now Let Him Enforce It.'—Attributed to President Andrew Jackson, 1832." *Federal Lawyer*. At Sidebar. Sept. 2012. www.fedbar.org/Resources_1/Federal-Lawyer-Magazine/2012/September/Columns/At-Sidebar.aspx?FT=.pdf.

Drehle, David Von. "Honor and Effort: What President Obama Achieved in Eight Years." *Time*. 22 Dec 2016. time.com/4616866/barack-obama-administration-look-back-history-achievements/.

Dunaway, W. F. "The Virginia Conventions of the Revolution." *Virginia Law Register*, vol. 10, no.7, Nov. 1904, p. 567–86. www.jstor.org/stable/pdf/1100650.pdf.

Dunn, Susan. *Jefferson's Second Revolution: The Election Crisis of 1800 and the Triumph of Republicanism*. New York: Houghton Mifflin Company, 2004.

Dunphy, John J. "The Lynching of Robert Prager: A World War I Hate Crime." *Medium*. 17 Nov. 2018. medium.com/@johnjdunphy/the-lynching-of-robert-prager-a-world-war-i-hate-crime-11b7a5e567a.

E.A.S. (arranger), and Charles Evarts Williams (lyricist). Lyrics to Democracy's Lament. Bangor, Maine: Chas. E. Williams, 1896. *LOC*, Library of Congress, www.loc.gov/item/ihas.200155624/.

Edwards, Sebastian. *American Default: The Untold Story of FDR, the Supreme Court, and the Battle over Gold*. Princeton, NJ: Princeton U P, 2019.

Eisenhower, Dwight. "Statement by the President Regarding U-2 Incident, May 11, 1960." *Dwightdeisenhower*. IKE Eisenhower Foundation. www.dwightdeisenhower.com/404/U-2-Spy-Plane-Incident.

_____. "Transcript of President Dwight D. Eisenhower's Farewell Address (1961)." *Our Documents*. 2019. www.ourdocuments.gov/doc.php?flash=false&doc=90&page=transcript.

Ellenbogen, Paul D. "Another Explanation for the Senate: The Anti-Federalists, John Adams, and the Natural Aristocracy." *Polity*. vol. 29, no 2, Winter 1996. pp. 247–71. jstor.org/stable/3235302?seq=1#page_scan_tab_contentsck.

"Embargo of 1807." *Monticello*. 2019. www.monticello.org/site/research-and-collections/embargo-1807.

Emerson, Bo. "When Jimmy Carter Lusted in His Heart." *AJC*. Atlanta Journal Constitution. 28 Sept. 2017. www.ajc.com/news/when-jimmy-carter-lusted-his-heart/kzdD5pLXvT3qnf5RyJlIiK/.

Eschner, Kat. "President James Buchanan Directly Influences the Outcome of the Dred Scott Decision." *Smithsonian.com*. 6 Mar. 2017. www.smithsonianmag.com/smart-news/president-james-buchanan-directly-influenced-outcome-dred-scott-decision-180962329/.

"Examining Carter's 'Malaise Speech,' 30 Years Later." *NPR*. 12 July 2009. www.npr.org/templates/story/story.php?storyId=106508243.

"Executive Secrecy." *New York Times*. 2019. www.nytimes.com/interactive/2019/us/politics/executive-secrecy-executive-power.html.

Fallows, Samuel. *Life of William McKinley, Our Martyred President*. Chicago, IL: Regan Printing House, 1901.

Farber, David R. *Taken Hostage: The Iran Hostage Crisis and America's First Encounter with Radical Islam*. Princeton U P, 2005.

Federman, Wayne. "What Reagan Did for Hollywood." *The Atlantic*. Atlantic Monthly Group. 14 Nov. 2011. www.theatlantic.com/entertainment/archive/2011/11/what-reagan-did-for-hollywood/248391/.

Feller, Daniel. "Andrew Jackson." *Miller Center*. University of Virginia. 2019. millercenter.org/president/Jackson.

Ferrell, Robert H. *Truman and Pendergast*. Columbia, MO: U of Missouri P, 1999.

Feuerherd, Peter. "The Strange History of Masons in America." *JSTOR Daily*. 3 Aug. 2017. daily.jstor.org/the-strange-history-of-masons-in-america/.

"The First Congressional Override of a Presidential Veto." *History*. U.S. House of Representatives. 2017. history.house.gov/Historical-Highlights/1800-1850/The-first-congressional-override-of-a-presidential-veto/.

"Five Items Congress Deleted from Madison's Original Bill of Rights." *Constitution Daily*. National Constitution Center. 15 Dec. 2018. constitutioncenter.org/blog/five-items-congress-deleted-from-madisons-original-bill-of-rights.

"Flight of the Madisons." *White House History*. White House Historical Association. 2019.www.whitehousehistory.org/flight-of-the-madisons.

Ford, Gerald R. "Gerald R. Ford's Remarks Upon Taking the Oath of Office as President." *Ford Library Museum*. 2019. www.fordlibrarymuseum.gov/library/speeches/740001.asp.

Fox, Justin. "Trump's 2018 Hasn't Been as Bad as Andrew Johnson's 1866." *Bloomberg*. 21 Nov. 2018. www.bloomberg.com/opinion/articles/2018-11-21/trump-s-2018-hasn-t-been-a-disaster-like-andrew-johnson-s-1866.

Frank, Jeffrey. "The Primary Experiment: Jimmy Who?" *The New Yorker*. Condé Nast. 1 May 2015. www.newyorker.com/news/daily-comment/the-primary-experiment-jimmy-who.

"Franklin Pierce's Murky Legacy as President." *Constitution Center*. Constitution Daily. 8 Oct. 2019. constitutioncenter.org/blog/franklin-pierces-murky-legacy-as-president.

Freehling, William. "John Tyler: Campaigns and Elections." *Miller Center*. U of Virginia. 2019. millercenter.org/president/tyler/campaigns-and-elections.

_____. "John Tyler: Impact and Legacy." *Miller Center*. U of Virginia. millercenter.org/president/tyler/impact-and-legacy.

Gangitano, Alex, and Miranda Green. "Collins Received More Donations from Texas Fossil Fuel Industry Than from Maine Residents." *The Hill*. 16 Apr. 2019. thehill.com/business-a-lobbying/439145-texas-fossil-fuel-industry-bests-maine-residents-for-donations-to-susan.

García, Lily Eskelsen, and Otha Thornton. "'No Child Left Behind' Has Failed." *The Washington Post*. 13 Feb. 2015. www.washingtonpost.com/opinions/no-child-has-failed/2015/02/13/8d619026-b2f8-11e4-827f-93f454140e2b_story.html.

Gardner, Michael R. *Harry Truman and Civil Rights: Moral Courage and Political Risks*. Edwardsville, IL: Southern Illinois U P, 2003.

Garrow, David. *Rising Star: The Making of Barack Obama*. New York: Harper Collins, 2017.

Geist, Christopher. "George Washington and the Evolution of the American Commander in Chief." *CW Journal*. Colonial Williamsburg. Summer 2012. www.history.org/foundation/journal/summer12/george.cfm.

"George Herbert Walker Bush." *Naval History and Heritage Command*. www.history.navy.mil/research/histories/biographies-list/bios-b/bush-george-h-w.html.

"George Washington." *White House*. 2006. www.whitehouse.gov/about-the-white-house/presidents/george-washington/.

"German U-Boat Reaches Baltimore, Having Crossed Atlantic in 16 Days; Has Letter from Kaiser to Wilson." *New York Times*. 10 July 1916.

Getchell, George H. *Our Nation's Executives and Their Administrations: The Continental and National Congress*. New York: Getchell & Fuller, 1885.

Gibson, John. "A Time for Doughfaces?" *Medium*. 21 June 2019. medium.com/@johngibsonks/a-time-for-doughfaces-16f64381f5b5.

Gillett, Rachel, and Allana Akhtar. "These Are the Top 20 US Presidents (and Why You Won't Find Trump on the List)." *Business Insider*. 4 July 2019. www.businessinsider.com/the-top-20-presidents-in-us-history-according-to-historians-2017-2.

Glass, Andrew. "Eisenhower Approves Coup in Iran, Aug. 19, 1953." *Politico*. 19 Aug. 2018. www.politico.com/story/2018/08/19/eisenhower-green-lights-coup-in-iran-aug-19-1953-788012.

_____. "LBJ Approves 'Operation Rolling Thunder,' Feb. 13, 1965." *Politico*. 13 Feb. 2019. www.politico.com/story/2019/02/13/lbj-operation-rolling-thunder-feb-13-1965-1162618.

Gompers, Samuel, John McBride, and William Green. *The American Federationist.. AFL-CIO*. American Federation of Labor and Congress of Industrial Organizations, vol. 9, 1902.

Goodwin, Doris Kearns. *Lyndon Johnson and the American Dream*. *Open Road Media*, 2015.

Gordon-Reed, Annette. *Andrew Johnson: The American Presidents Series*. New York: Times Books, 2011.

Graff, Henry F. *Grover Cleveland*. New York: Times Books, 2002.

Graham, David A. "The Strangest Thing About Trump's Approach to Presidential Power." *The Atlantic*. 7 June 2018. www.theatlantic.com/politics/archive/2018/06/the-strangest-thing-about-trumps-approach-to-presidential-power/562271/.

Grant, Ulysses. "First Inaugural Address of Ulysses S. Grant." *The Avalon Project*. Yale Law School. 2008. avalon.law.yale.edu/19th_century/grant1.asp.

_____. "Special Message—March 30, 1870." *NPS*. National Park Service. Ulysses S. Grant. 27 Feb. 2019. www.nps.gov/ulsg/learn/historyculture/grant-and-the-15th-amendment.htm.

Greenberg, Amy S. *A Wicked War*: *Polk, Clay, Lincoln, and the 1846 U.S. Invasion of Mexico*. Vintage 2013; Penguin Random House 2019.

Greenberg, David. "Rewinding the Kennedy-Nixon Debates." *Slate*. 24 Sept. 2010. slate.com/news-and-politics/2010/09/did-jfk-really-win-because-he-looked-better-on-television.html.

Greenberger, Scott S. "The Man the Presidency Changed." *Politico*. 11 Sept. 2017. www.politico.com/magazine/story/2017/09/11/chester-arthur-presidency-donald-trump-215593.

Greene, Robert II. "The Legacy of *Black Reconstruction*." *Jacobin*. www.jacobinmag.com/2018/08/web-du-bois-black-reconstruction-civil-rights.

Grossman, Jonathan. "The Coal Strike of 1902—Turning Point in U.S. Policy." *Monthly Labor Review*, vol. 98, no. 10, 1975, pp. 21-28. *JSTOR*. www.jstor.org/stable/41839484.

Grove, Lloyd. "The Man Who Was the Madison." *The Washington Post*. 7 May 1982. www.washingtonpost.com/archive/lifestyle/1982/05/07/the-man-who-was-the-madison-by-lloyd-grove/4f67af5b-a4d8-4542-aa43-9433c67d4694/.

Grunwald, Michael. "A New New Deal." *Time*. 5 Nov. 2008. //content.time.com/time/specials/packages/article/0,28804,1856381_1856380,00.html.

_____. "The Victory of 'No.'" *Politico*. 4 Dec. 2016. www.politico.com/magazine/story/2016/12/republican-party-obstructionism-victory-trump-214498.

Guardino, Peter . *The Dead March: A History of the Mexican-American War*. Cambridge, MA: Harvard U P, 2017.

Gugliotta, Guy. "New Estimate Raises Civil War Death Toll." *New York Times*. 2 Apr. 2012. www.nytimes.com/2012/04/03/science/civil-war-toll-up-by-20-percent-in-new-estimate.html.

Haggard, Robert F. "The Nicola Affair: Lewis Nicola, George Washington, and American Military Discontent during the Revolutionary War." *Proceedings of the American Philosophical Society*, vol. 146, no 2, (June 2002), pp. 139–69. *JSTOR*, www.jstor.org/stable/1558199.

Hall, Michelle. "By the Numbers: World War II's Atomic Bombs." *CNN*. 6 Aug. 2013. www.cnn.com/2013/08/06/world/asia/btn-atomic-bombs/index.html.

Hamilton, Alexander. "Letter from Alexander Hamilton, Concerning the Public Conduct and Character of John Adams, Esq. President of the United States, [24 October 1800]." *Founders Online*. National Archives. 2019. founders.archives.gov/documents/Hamilton/01-25-02-0110-0002.

Han, Lori Cox, editor. *Hatred of America's Presidents: Personal Attacks on the White House from Washington to Trump*, ABC–CLIO, LLC, 2018.

Harding, Warren. "May 14, 1920: Readjustment." *Miller Center*. University of Virginia. millercenter.org/the-presidency/presidential-speeches/may-14-1920-readjustment.

Harrison, William Henry. "Inaugural Address of William Henry Harrison." *Avalon Project*. Lillian Goldman Law Library. avalon.law.yale.edu/19th_century/harrison.asp.

Hart, Benjamin. "Concerns about Reagan's Mental Health Were Handled Very Differently Than Concerns about Trump's." *Intelligencer*. 14 Jan. 2018. nymag.com/intelligencer/2018/01/how-reagans-mental-health-concerns-were-handled.html.

Hayes, Rutherford. "April 29, 1879: Veto of Army Appropriations Bill." *Miller Center*. University of Virginia. 2019. millercenter.org/the-presidency/presidential-speeches/april-29-1879-veto-army-appropriations-bill.

Heflin, James Thomas. "Warning Against the 'Roman Catholic Party': Catholicism and the 1928 Election," *History Matters*. Congressional Record. 28 Jan. 1928. historymatters.gmu.edu/d/5073/.

Hemel, Daniel J., and Eric A. Posner. "The Logan Act and its Limits." *Lawfare*. 7 Dec. 2017. www.lawfareblog.com/logan-act-and-its-limits.

Hickey, Donald R. *The War of 1812: A Forgotten Conflict*. Chicago, IL: University of Illinois, 2012.

Himmelberg, Robert F. *The Origins of the National Recovery Administration: Business, Government, and the Trade Association, 1921–1933*. New York: Fordham U P, 1993.

"History-Essays." *Lehrman Institute*. 2018. lehrmaninstitute.org/history/Andrew-Jackson-1837.html.

Holland, Joshua. "The First Iraq War Was Also Sold to the Public Based on a Pack of Lies." *Bill Moyers*. 27 June 2014. billmoyers.com/2014/06/27/the-first-iraq-war-was-also-sold-to-the-public-based-on-a-pack-of-lies/.

Holt, Michael. "Millard Fillmore: Life Before the Presidency." *Miller Center*. U of Virginia. 2019. /millercenter.org/president/fillmore/life-before-the-presidency.

_____. "Zachary Taylor: Life Before the Presidency." *Miller Center*. University of Virginia. 2019. millercenter.org/president/taylor/life-before-the-presidency.

Hoock, Holger. *Scars of Independence: America's Violent Birth*. New York: Crown, 2017.

Hoogenboom, Ari. "Rutherford B. Hayes: Impact and Legacy." *Miller Center*. University of Virginia. 2019. millercenter.org/president/hayes/impact-and-legacy.

Hoover, Herbert. "Principles and Ideals of the United States Government." *Teaching American History*. Ashbrook Center. 2019. teachingamericanhistory.org/library/document/principles-and-ideals-of-the-united-states-government/.

_____. "Rugged Individualism." *Digital History*. 2019. www.digitalhistory.uh.edu/disp_textbook.cfm?smtID=3&psid=1334.

Horton, Emily. "The Legacy of the 2001 and 2003 'Bush' Tax Cuts." *Center on Budget and Policy Priorities*. 23 Oct. 2017. www.cbpp.org/research/federal-tax/the-legacy-of-the-2001-and-2003-bush-tax-cuts.

"How They Got There." *The St. Paul Daily Globe*. June 16, 1889. p. 12. Chroniclingamerica. LOC. Library of Congress. chroniclingamerica.loc.gov/lccn/sn90059522/1889-06-16/ed-1/seq-12/.

"How Unpopular Is Donald Trump?" *FiveThirtyEight*. 15 Dec. 2019. projects.fivethirtyeight.com/trump-approval-ratings/.

Hunter, Thomas Rogers. "The First Gerrymander? Patrick Henry, James Madison, James Monroe, and Virginia's 1788 Congressional Districting." *Early American Studies*. vol. 9, no. 3, Fall 2011, pp. 781–820. *JSTOR*, www.jstor.org/stable/23546676.

Illing, Sean. "How Meritocracy Harms Everyone—Even the Winners." *Vox*. 21 Oct. 2019. www.vox.com/identities/2019/10/21/20897021/meritocracy-economic-mobility-daniel-markovits.

"Indian Removal, 1814–1858." *PBS*. 2016. www.pbs.org/wgbh/aia/part4/4p2959.html.

Inskeep, Steve. "How Jackson Made a Killing in Real Estate." *Politico*. 4 July 2015. www.politico.com/magazine/story/2015/07/andrew-jackson-made-a-killing-in-real-estate-119727_full.html.investigatinghistory.ashp.cuny.edu/module7A.php.

Jackson, Andrew. "Andrew Jackson's Speech to Congress on Indian Removal." *National Park Service*. NPS. www.nps.gov/museum/tmc/MANZ/handouts/Andrew_Jackson_Annual_Message.pdf.

_____. "May 27, 1830: Veto Message Regarding Funding of Infrastructure Development." *Miller Center*. University of Virginia. 2019. millercenter.org/the-presidency/presidential-speeches/may-27-1830-veto-message-regarding-funding-infrastructure.

Jefferson, Thomas. "First Annual Message to Congress, 8 December 1801." *Founders Online*. National Archives. founders.archives.gov/documents/Jefferson/01-36-02-0034-0003.

_____. "From Thomas Jefferson to Yusuf Qaramanli, Pasha and Bey of Tripoli, 21 May 1801." *Founders Online*. National Archives. 2019. founders.archives.gov/documents/Jefferson/01-34-02-0122.

_____. "From Thomas Jefferson to Abigail Smith Adams, 13 June 1804." *Founders Online*. National Archives. founders.archives.gov/documents/Adams/99-03-02-1280.

_____. "From Thomas Jefferson to James Sullivan, 9 February 1797." *Founders Online*. National Archives. 2016. founders.archives.gov/documents/Jefferson/01-29-02-0231.

_____. "From Thomas Jefferson to United States Congress, 13 January 1806." *Founders Online*. National Archives, 2019. founders.archives.gov/documents/Jefferson/99-01-02-3010.

"The Jerry Rescue." *New York History Net*. New York History. www.nyhistory.com/gerritsmith/jerry.htm.

"John Adams Biography." *National Park Service*. National Historic Park Massachusetts. 31 Mar. 2012. www.nps.gov/adam/john-adams-biography.htm.

"John Jay's Treaty, 1794–95." *U.S. Department of State*. 2016. history.state.gov/milestones/1784-1800/jay-treaty.

"John F. Kennedy's Pre-Presidential Voting Record & Stands on Issues." CQ Fact Sheet on John F. Kennedy, Congressional Quarterly, Inc. , 1960. *JFK Library*. www.jfklibrary.org/learn/about-jfk/life-of-john-f-kennedy/fast-facts-john-f-kennedy/voting-record-and-stands-on-issues.

"John Wilkes Booth." *NPS*. National Park Service. 17 June 2015. www.nps.gov/people/john-wilkes-booth.htm.

Johnson, Andrew. "Speech to the Citizens of Washington." *Teachingamericanhistory*. 2018. teachingamericanhistory.org/library/document/speech-to-the-citizens-of-washington/.

_____. "State of the Union 1867—3 December 1867." *American History*. University of Groningen, 2012. www.let.rug.nl/usa/presidents/andrew-johnson/state-of-the-union-1867.php.

_____. "To James Madison from Thomas Jefferson, 20 December 1787." *Founders Online*. National Archives. 2019. founders.archives.gov/documents/Madison/01-10-02-0210.

_____. "To Thomas Jefferson from John Barnes, 31 August 1802." *Founders Online*. National Archives. 2019. founders.archives.gov/documents/Jefferson/01-38-02-0286.

_____. "Veto of the Freemen's Bureau Bill." *Teachingamericanhistory*. 2018. teachingamericanhistory.org/library/document/veto-of-the-freedmens-bureau-bill/.

Jordan, Mary. "Andrew Jackson Was a Rich Populist Who Bragged and Invited Scorn. Trump Draws New Interest in the 7th President." *The Washington Post*. 31 Jan. 2017. www.washingtonpost.com/news/post-nation/wp/2017/01/31/andrew-jackson-was-a-rich-populist-who-bragged-and-invited-scorn-trump-is-drawing-new-interest-in-the-7th-president/.

"Justice Curtis Dissenting." *American History*. University of Groningen. 2012. www.let.rug.nl/usa/documents/1826-1850/dred-scott-case/justice-curtis-dissenting.php.

Kazdin, Cole. "The Violence Central American Migrants Are Fleeing Was Stoked by the US." *Vice*. 27 June 2018. www.vice.com/en_us/article/qvnyzq/central-america-atrocities-caused-immigration-crisis.

Kelly, Martin. "Quotes from Martin Van Buren." *Thought Co*. 19 Oct. 2019. www.thoughtco.com/quotes-from-martin-van-buren-103962.

Kennedy, John F. "Address to the Greater Houston Ministerial Association." *JFK Library*. 12 Sept. 1960, www.jfklibrary.org/learn/about-jfk/historic-speeches/address-to-the-greater-houston-ministerial-association.

_____. "Civil Rights Address." *American Rhetoric*. 11 June 1963. americanrhetoric.com/speeches/jfkcivilrights.htm.

_____. "Moon Speech—Rice Stadium." *NASA*. 12 Sept. 1962. er.jsc.nasa.gov/seh/ricetalk.htm.

_____. "News Conference 10, April 21, 1961." *JFK Library*. 2019. www.jfklibrary.org/archives/other-resources/john-f-kennedy-press-conferences/news-conference-10.

Kessler, Glenn. "The Iraq War and WMDs: An Intelligence Failure or White House Spin?" *The Washington Post*. 22 Mar. 2019. www.washingtonpost.com/politics/2019/03/22/iraq-war-wmds-an-intelligence-failure-or-white-house-spin/.

Kucharsky, David. *The Man from Plains*. New York: Harper & Row, 1976.

Landis, Michael Todd. *Northern Men with Southern Loyalties: The Democratic Party and the Sectional Crisis*. Ithaca, NY: Cornell U P, 2014.

Lee, Ronald F. "Antiquities Act." *NPS*. National Parks Service. Archaeology Program. 8 Dec. 2019. www.nps.gov/archeology/pubs/Lee/index.htm.

Leuchtenburg, William E. "Franklin D. Roosevelt: Impact and Legacy." *Miller Center*. University of Virginia. 2019. millercenter.org/president/fdroosevelt/impact-and-legacy.

Lincoln, Abraham. "Emancipation Proclamation." *Our Documents*. National Archives. 2018. www.ourdocuments.gov/doc.php?flash=false&doc=34&page=transcript.

_____. "House Divided Speech, June 16, 1858" *Abraham Lincoln Online*. 2018. www.abrahamlincolnonline.org/lincoln/speeches/house.htm.

_____. "Lincoln's Response to Congress, July 4, 1861." *Gilder Lehrman*. Gilder Lehrman Institute of American History. 2012. www.gilderlehrman.org/sites/default/files/inline-pdfs/Lincoln%20Response.pdf.

_____. "Lyceum Address." *Abraham Lincoln Online*. 2018. www.abrahamlincolnonline.org/lincoln/speeches/lyceum.htm.

_____. "Message to Congress in Special Session, July 4, 1861 *Miller Center*. U of Virginia. millercenter.org/the-presidency/presidential-speeches/july-4-1861-july-4th-message-congress.

_____. "Spot Resolutions in the U.S. House of Representatives." *Teaching American History*. December 22, 1847. teachingamericanhistory.org/library/document/spot-resolutions-in-the-u-s-house-of-representatives/.

"The Louisiana Purchase." *Monticello*. 2019. www.monticello.org/thomas-jefferson/louisiana-lewis-clark/the-louisiana-purchase.

Lurie, Jonathan. *William Howard Taft: The Travails of a Progressive Conservative*. New York: Cambridge U P, 2012.

Madison, James. "Federalist No. 51." *Bill of Rights Institute*. billofrightsinstitute.org/founding-documents/primary-source-documents/the-federalist-papers/federalist-papers-no-51/.

_____. "From James Madison to Tobias Lear, 6 June 1804." *Founders Online*. National Archives. founders.archives.gov/documents/Madison/02-07-02-0300.

_____. "March 3, 1817: Veto Message on the Internal Improvements Bill." *Miller Center*. 2019. millercenter.org/the-presidency/presidential-speeches/march-3-1817-veto-message-internal-improvements-bill.

Mallon, Thomas. "Less Said." *The New Yorker*. 3 Mar. 2013. www.newyorker.com/magazine/2013/03/11/less-said.

Maraniss, David. *First in His Class: A Biography of Bill Clinton*. New York: Simon & Schuster, 1995.

"Marbury v. Madison. 5 U.S. 137 (1803)" *Justia*. 2019. supreme.justia.com/cases/federal/us/5/137/.

Marszalek, John F. *The Petticoat Affair: Manners, Mutiny, and Sex in Andrew Jackson's White House*. Baton Rouge, LA: Louisiana State U P, 1997.

Mathis-Lilley, Ben. "President Pays Gigantic Fine for Stealing from Charity." *Slate*. 11 Dec. 2019. slate.com/news-and-politics/2019/12/trump-pays-2-million-fine-for-stealing-from-charity.html.

Matthews, Christopher. *Kennedy & Nixon: The Rivalry that Shapes Postwar America*. New York: Touchstone Books, 1996.

May, Gary. *John Tyler*. New York: Times Books, 2008.

McCullough, David. *Truman*. New York: Simon & Schuster, 1992.

McDonald, Forrest. "Washington, George." *American National Biography*. Feb. 2000. www.anb.org/view/10.1093/anb/9780198606697.001.0001/anb-9780198606697-e-0200332.

McNamara, Robert. "The Christiana Riot." *ThoughtCo*. Dotdash. 17 Mar. 2017. www.thoughtco.com/the-christiana-riot-1773557.

_____. "The Era of Good Feelings." *Thought Co*. www.thoughtco.com/era-of-good-feelings-1773317.

_____. "The Spoils System: Definition and Summary." *Thought Co*. 3 July 2019. www.thoughtco.com/the-spoils-system-1773347.

McPherson, James M. *Battle Cry of Freedom: The Civil War Era*. New York: Oxford U P, 1988.

Meacham, Jon. *American Lion: Andrew Jackson in the White House*. New York: Random House, 2009.

Meacham, Jon. *Destiny and Power: The American Odyssey of George Herbert Walker Bush*. New York: Random House, 2015.

_____. *Thomas Jefferson: The Art of Power*. New York: Random House, 2012.

Medhurst, Martin J. *Before the Rhetorical Presidency*. Texas A & M University, 2008.

"Medicare and Medicaid." *LBJ Library*. 2019. www.lbjlibrary.org/press/media-kit/medicare-and-medicaid.

Meier, Michael T. "Civil War Draft Records: Exemptions and Enrollments." *Archives*. Prologue Magazine. National Archives, vol. 26, no. 4, Winter 1994. www.archives.gov/publications/prologue/1994/winter/civil-war-draft-records.html.

Meiser, Jeffrey W. *Power and Restraint: The Rise of the United States, 1898–1941*. Washington DC: Georgetown U P, 2015.

Merica, Dan. "Bill Clinton Says He Made Mass Incarceration Issue Worse." *CNN*. 15 July 2015. www.cnn.com/2015/07/15/politics/bill-clinton-1994-crime-bill/index.html.

"Military Advisors in Vietnam: 1963." *JFK Library*. 2019. www.jfklibrary.org/learn/education/teachers/curricular-resources/high-school-curricular-resources/military-advisors-in-vietnam-1963.

Miller, Char. *Gifford Pinchot and the Making of Modern Environmentalism*. Washington: Island P, 2001.

Miller, Scott. *The President and the Assassin: McKinley, Terror, and the Empire at the Dawn of the American Century*. New York: Random House, 2011; 2013.

Miscamble, Wilson D. *The Most Controversial Decision: Truman, the Atomic Bombs, and the Defeat of Japan*. New York: Cambridge U P, 2011.

Mitchell, Greg. *Tricky Dick and the Pink Lady: Richard Nixon vs Helen Gahagan Douglas-Sexual Politics and the Red Scare, 1950*. New York: Random House, 1998.

Moise, Edwin E. *Tonkin Gulf and the Escalation of the Vietnam War*. Chapel Hill, NC: The U of North Carolina P, 1996.

Moore, David W. "Americans Believe U.S. Participation in Gulf War a Decade Ago Worthwhile." *Gallup*. 26 Feb. 2001. news.gallup.com/poll/1963/americans-believe-us-participation-gulf-war-decade-ago-worthwhile.aspx.

Moore, Stephen. *Eighteen Minutes: The Battle of San Jacinto and the Texas Independence Campaign*. Dallas, TX: Republic of Texas P, 2004.

Morgan, Thomas. "The Making of a General: Ike, the Tank, and the Interwar Years." *Army History*. Army Historical Foundation. 20 Jan. 2015. armyhistory.org/the-making-of-a-general-ike-the-tank-and-the-interwar-years/.

Morris, Edmund. *The Rise of Theodore Roosevelt*. New York: The Modern Library, 2001.

Morris, Kenneth E. *Jimmy Carter, American Moralist*. Athens, GA: U of Georgia P, 1996.

Morris, Roy Jr. *Fraud of the Century: Rutherford B. Hayes, Samuel Tilden, and the Stolen Election of 1876*. New York: Simon & Schuster, 2003.

Murphy, Justin D., editor. *American Civil War: Interpreting Conflict through Primary Documents*. Santa Monica, CA: ABC–CLIO. 24 June 2019.

Naftali, Tim. "Ronald Reagan's Long-Hidden Racist Conversation with Richard Nixon." *The Atlantic*. Atlantic Monthly Group. 30 July 2019. www.theatlantic.com/ideas/archive/2019/07/ronald-reagans-racist-conversation-richard-nixon/595102/.

Nathan, James. *The Cuban Missile Crisis Revisited*. New York: Palgrave, MacMillan, 1992.

Nixon, Richard. "The Last Press Conference." *Nixon Foundation*. 2019. www.
      nixonfoundation.org/2017/11/55-years-ago-last-press-conference/.

_____. "Transcript of a Recording of a Meeting Between the President and H.R.
      Haldeman in the Oval Office on June 23, 1972, from 10:04 to 11:39 AM," *PBS*.
      www.pbs.org/newshour/extra/app/uploads/2013/11/Smoking-Gun-Transcript-v-2.
      pdf.

"National General Election VEP Turnout Rates, 1789–Present," *Elect Project*.
      University of Florida. 2018. www.electproject.org/national-1789-present.

"The National Parks: America's Best Idea." *PBS*. 2009. www.pbs.org/nationalparks/.

"National Security Act of 1947." *Office of the Historian*. Department of State. 2016.
      history.state.gov/milestones/1945-1952/national-security-act.

"Naval Chronicle Vol XXVII," USS Constitution Museum Collection.

Norman, Jim. "Solid Majority Still Opposes New Construction on Border Wall."
      Gallup. 4 Feb. 2019. news.gallup.com/poll/246455/solid-majority-opposes-new-
      construction-border-wall.aspx.

Novak, Matt. "'Speeches Must Be Short': Radio and the Birth of the Modern
      Presidential Campaign." *Pacific Standard*. 2 Oct. 2012. psmag.com/news/
      airwaves-1924-the-first-presidential-campaign-over-radio-47615.

Novkov, Julie. *The Supreme Court and the Presidency: Struggles for Supremacy*.
      Washington D.C.: Sage P, 2013.

"Oakes Ames." *PBS*. American Experience. 2019. www.pbs.org/wgbh/
      americanexperience/features/tcrr-ames/.

"Oil & Gas: Long-Term Contribution Trends." *Open Secrets*. 21 Nov. 2019. www.
      opensecrets.org/industries/totals.php?ind=E01++.

"On This Day: The First Bitter, Contested Presidential Election Takes
      Place." *National Constitution Center*. Constitutional Daily, Nov. 4, 2018.
      constitutioncenter.org/blog/on-this-day-the-first-bitter-contested-presidential-
      election-takes-place.

"On This Day, the Pullman Strike Changes Labor Law." *National Constitution
      Center*. Constitution Daily. 11 May 2019. constitutioncenter.org/blog/on-this-day-
      the-pullman-strike-changes-labor-law.

O'Sullivan, John. "Annexation." *The United States Magazine and Democratic
      Review*. vol. 17, no. 1, (July–August 1845), pp.5–10. pdcrodas.webs.ull.es/anglo/
      OSullivanAnnexation.pdf.

Onuf, Peter. "Thomas Jefferson: Life Before the Presidency." *Miller Center*. 2019.
      millercenter.org/president/jefferson/life-before-the-presidency.

"Overview of Andrew Johnson's Life." *NPS*. National Park Service. 8 Aug. 2019. www.nps.gov/anjo/learn/historyculture/overview.htm.

Pach, Chester J. Jr. "Dwight D. Eisenhower: Domestic Affairs." *Miller Center*. University of Virginia. 2019. millercenter.org/president/eisenhower/domestic-affairs.

"The Panic of 1873." *PBS*. American Experience. 2019. www.pbs.org/wgbh/americanexperience/features/grant-panic/.

Parsons, Lynn H. *The Birth of Modern Politics: Andrew Jackson, John Quincy Adams, and the Election of 1828*. New York: Oxford U P, 2009.

Payne, Phillip G. *Dead Last: The Public Memory of Warren G. Harding's Scandalous Legacy*. Athens, OH: Ohio U P, 2009.

Payson-Denney, Wade. "So, Who Really Won? What the Bush v. Gore Studies Showed." *CNN*. 31 Oct. 2015. www.cnn.com/2015/10/31/politics/bush-gore-2000-election-results-studies/index.html.

Pevar, Stephen. "The Dawes Act: How Congress Tried to Destroy Indian Reservations." *OUP Blog*. Oxford U P, 2019. blog.oup.com/2012/02/dawes-act-congress-indian-reservations/.

Pierce, Franklin. "Inaugural Address of Franklin Pierce." *Avalon Project*. Yale Law School. 2019. avalon.law.yale.edu/19th_century/pierce.asp.

Platt, Thomas Collier. *The Autobiography of Thomas Collier Platt*. New York: B.W. Dodge & Company, 1910.

Politi, Daniel. "Trump Says 'Probably Not' Prepared to Lose in 2020, Doesn't Believe He Lost Popular Vote." *Slate*. 23 June 2019. slate.com/news-and-politics/2019/06/trump-not-prepared-lose-reelection-lost-popular-vote.html.

Polk, James Knox. "Inaugural Address of James Knox Polk." March 4, 1845. *Avalon*. Yale Law School. avalon.law.yale.edu/19th_century/polk.asp.

_____. "May 11, 1846: War Message to Congress." *Miller Center*. U of Virginia. 2019. millercenter.org/the-presidency/presidential-speeches/may-11-1846-war-message-congress.

Poston, Brook. *James Monroe: A Republican Champion*. U P of Florida, 2019.

Powell, Jim. "Woodrow Wilson's Great Mistake." *Cato*. Cato Institute. 2 June 2014. www.cato.org/policy-report/mayjune-2014/woodrow-wilsons-great-mistake.

Prakash, Saikrishna Bangalore. "Stop Fighting It. America Is a Monarchy, and That's Probably for the Best." *Washington Post*. 23 June 2015. www.washingtonpost.com/posteverything/wp/2015/06/23/stop-fighting-it-america-is-a-monarchy-and-thats-probably-for-the-best/.

"Presidential Approval Ratings—Gallup Historical Statistics and Trends." *Gallup*. 2019. news.gallup.com/poll/116677/presidential-approval-ratings-gallup-historical-statistics-trends.aspx.

"Presidential Election of 1836: A Resource Guide." *LOC*. Library of Congress. 23 Oct. 2018. www.loc.gov/rr/program/bib/elections/election1836.html.

"Presidential Election of 1840: A Resource Guide." *LOC*. Library of Congress. 23 Oct. 2018. www.loc.gov/rr/program/bib/elections/election1840.html.

"Presidential Election of 1848: A Resource Guide." *LOC*. Library of Congress. 23 Oct. 2018.www.loc.gov/rr/program/bib/elections/election1848.html.

"Presidential Election of 1852: A Resource Guide." *LOC*. Library of Congress. 23 Oct. 2018. www.loc.gov/rr/program/bib/elections/election1852.html.

"Presidential Election of 1856: A Resource Guide." *LOC*. Library of Congress. 23 Oct. 2018. www.loc.gov/rr/program/bib/elections/election1856.html.

"Presidential Election of 1860: A Resource Guide." *LOC*. Library of Congress. 23 Oct. 2018. www.loc.gov/rr/program/bib/elections/election1860.html.

"Presidential Election of 1868: A Resource Guide." *LOC*. Library of Congress. 2018. www.loc.gov/rr/program/bib/elections/election1868.html.

"Presidential Election of 1872: A Resource Guide." *LOC*. Library of Congress. 2018. www.loc.gov/rr/program/bib/elections/election1872.html.

"Presidential Election of 1876: A Resource Guide." *LOC*. Library of Congress. 2018. www.loc.gov/rr/program/bib/elections/election1876.html.

"Presidential Election of 1880: A Resource Guide." *LOC*. Library of Congress. 23 Oct. 2018. www.loc.gov/rr/program/bib/elections/election1880.html.

"Presidential Election of 1884: A Resource Guide." *LOC*. Library of Congress. 23 Oct. 2018. www.loc.gov/rr/program/bib/elections/election1884.html.

"Presidential Election of 1892: A Resource Guide." *LOC*. Library of Congress. 23 Oct. 2018. www.loc.gov/rr/program/bib/elections/election1892.html.

"Presidential Election of 1896: A Resource Guide." *LOC*. Library of Congress. Oct. 23, 2018. www.loc.gov/rr/program/bib/elections/election1896.html.

"Presidential Election of 1904: A Resource Guide." *LOC*. Library of Congress. 23 Oct. 2018. www.loc.gov/rr/program/bib/elections/election1904.html.

"Presidential Election of 1912: A Resource Guide," *LOC*. 23 Oct. 2018. www.loc.gov/rr/program/bib/elections/election1912.html.

"Presidential Election of 1920: A Resource Guide." *LOC*. Library of Congress. Web Guides. 23 Oct. 2018. www.loc.gov/rr/program/bib/elections/election1920.html.

Preston, Daniel. "James Monroe: Campaigns and Elections." *Miller Center*. U of Virginia. millercenter.org/president/monroe/campaigns-and-elections.

_____. "James Monroe: Life Before the Presidency." *Miller Center*. U of Virginia. millercenter.org/president/monroe/life-before-the-presidency.

Rabe, Stephen G. *Eisenhower and Latin America: The Foreign Policy of Anticommunism*. U of North Carolina P, 1988.

Ratcliffe, Donald John. *The One-Party Presidential Contest: Adams, Jackson, and 1824's Five-Horse Race*. U P of Kansas, 2015.

Rayner, Kenneth. *Life and Times of Andrew Johnson*. New York: D. Appleton and Company, 1866, p. 117–19. babel.hathitrust.org/cgi/pt?id=loc.ark:/13960/t0zp44s4s&view=2up&seq=12&size=125.

Reiber, Beth. "It Wasn't Called Bleeding Kansas for Nothing." *Unmistakably Lawrence*. 26 July 2018. unmistakablylawrence.com/history-heritage/bleeding-kansas/.

"Remembering the Gulf War: The Key Facts & Figures." *Forces*. 7 Mar. 2017. www.forces.net/news/remembering-gulf-war-key-facts-figures#:~:targetText=According%20to%20the%20BBC%2C%20between,at%20between%20100%2C000%20and%20200%2C000.

"Residence Act." *LOC*. Library of Congress. 2016. www.loc.gov/rr/program/bib/ourdocs/residence.html.

Rice, Andrew. "Was Barack Obama Sr. 'Eased' Out of Harvard, and America, for Dating White Women?" *Politico*. 27 Apr. 2011. www.politico.com/states/new-york/albany/story/2016/05/was-barack-obama-sr-eased-out-of-harvard-and-america-for-dating-white-women-048282.

"Richard Milhouse Nixon." *Naval History and Heritage Command*. U.S. Navy. www.history.navy.mil/research/histories/biographies-list/bios-n/nixon-richard.html.

Richey, Warren. "Bush Pushed the Limits of Presidential Power." *Christian Science Monitor*. 14 Jan. 12009. www.csmonitor.com/USA/2009/0114/p11s01-usgn.html.

Richman, Sheldon L. "The Sad Legacy of Ronald Reagan." *The Free Market*. No 10. 1988. mises.org/library/sad-legacy-ronald-reagan-0.

Roberts, Chris. "The Great Eliminator: How Ronald Reagan Made Homelessness Permanent." *SF Weekly*. 29 June 2016. www.sfweekly.com/news/the-great-eliminator-how-ronald-reagan-made-homelessness-permanent/.

Robertson, James. *After the Civil War: The Heroes Villains, Soldiers, and Civilians Who Changed America*. Washington DC: National Geographic P, 2015.

"Roosevelt Pursues the Boat Thieves." *NPS*. National Park Service. 10 Apr. 2015. www.nps.gov/thro/learn/historyculture/roosevelt-pursues-boat-thieves.htm.

Roosevelt, Franklin. "Executive Order 8248—Executive Orders." *Archives*. National Archives. www.archives.gov/federal-register/codification/executive-order/08248.html.

_____. "On the Bank Crisis." 12 Mar. 1933. *FDR Library*. Marist University. docs.fdrlibrary.marist.edu/031233.html.

_____. "On the Declaration of War with Japan." 9 Dec. 1941. *FDR Library*. Marist University. docs.fdrlibrary.marist.edu/120941.html.

_____. "On Drought Conditions." 6 Sept. 1936. *FDR Library*. Marist University. docs.fdrlibrary.marist.edu/090636.html.

_____. "On the European War." 3 Sept. 1939. *FDR Library*. Marist University. docs.fdrlibrary.marist.edu/090339.html.

_____. "The Only Thing We Have to Fear Is Fear Itself": FDR's First Inaugural Address. 4 Mar. 1933. *History Matters*. historymatters.gmu.edu/d/5057/.

Roosevelt, Theodore. "Conservation as a National Duty." 13 May 1908. *Voices of Democracy*, The US Oratory Project.

_____. "December 3, 1907: Seventh Annual Message." *Miller Center*. University of Virginia. 2019. millercenter.org/the-presidency/presidential-speeches/december-3-1907-seventh-annual-message.

_____. "Roosevelt Corollary to the Monroe Doctrine." 1904. *Digital History*. 2019 www.digitalhistory.uh.edu/disp_textbook.cfm?smtID=3&psid=1259.

Rosen, Jeffrey. *William Howard Taft: The American Presidents Series: The 27th President*, edited by Arthur M. Schlesinger, Jr. and Sean Wilentz. New York: Times Books, 2018.

Rottinghaus, Brandon and Justin S. Vaught. "How Does Trump Stack Up Against the Best—and Worst—Presidents?" *The New York Times*. 19 Feb. 2018. www.nytimes.com/interactive/2018/02/19/opinion/how-does-trump-stack-up-against-the-best-and-worst-presidents.html.

Rudenstine, David. *The Day the Presses Stopped: A History of the Pentagon Papers Case*. Berkeley, CA: U of California P, 1996.

Russonello, Giovanni. "The Supreme Court May Let Trump End DACA. Here's What the Public Thinks About It." *New York Times*. 15 Nov. 2019. www.nytimes.com/2019/11/15/us/politics/daca-supreme-court-polls.html.

Salameh, Mamdouh G. "Oil Wars." *USAEE Working Paper*. No. 14–163. SSRN. 1 May 2014. papers.ssrn.com/sol3/papers.cfm?abstract_id=2430960.

Samuelson, Robert J. *The Great Inflation and Its Aftermath: The Past and Future of American Affluence.* New York: Random House, 2010.

Schroeder, John H. "Annexation or Independence: The Texas Issue in American Politics, 1836–1845." *The Southwestern Historical Quarterly.* vol. 89, no. 2, 1985, pp. 137–64, *JSTOR*, www.jstor.org/stable/30239906.

Schroeder, Richard E. *The Foundation of the CIA: Harry Truman, the Missouri Gang, and the Origins of the Cold War.* Columbia, MO: U of Missouri P, 2017.

Schweigler, Gebhard. "Carter's Dilemmas: Presidential Power and Its Limits." *The World Today*, vol. 35, no 2, 1979, pp. 46–55. *JSTOR*, www.jstor.org/stable/40395096.

Seigenthaler, John. *James K. Polk*, edited by Arthur M. Schlesinger. New York: Times Books, 2003.

"Senator, You're No Jack Kennedy." *NPR.* 23 May 2006. www.npr.org/templates/story/story.php?storyId=5425248.

Shafer, Ronald. *The Carnival Campaign.* Chicago, IL: Chicago Review P, 2016.

Shafer, Ronald G. "'He Lies Like a Dog': The First Effort to Impeach a President Was Led by his Own Party." *The Washington Post.* 23 Sept. 2019. www.washingtonpost.com/history/2019/09/23/he-lies-like-dog-first-effort-impeach-president-was-led-by-his-own-party/.

Shepard, Steven. "Poll: As Impeachment Progresses, Voter Support Remains Static." *Politico.* 11 Dec. 2019. www.politico.com/news/2019/12/11/poll-impeachment-voter-support-081122.

Sibley, Joel H. *Martin Van Buren and the Emergence of American Popular Politics.* Lanham, MD: Rowman & Littlefield Publishers, Inc. 2005.

Simpson, Brooks D. *Ulysses S. Grant: Triumph Over Adversity, 1822–1865.* Minneapolis, MN: Zenith P, 2000; 2014.

Sinkler, George. "Benjamin Harrison and the Matter of Race." *Indiana Magazine of History*, vol. 65, no. 3, 1969, pp. 197–213. *JSTOR*, www.jstor.org/stable/27789595.

Sky, Theodore. *The National Road and the Difficult Path to Sustainable National Investment.* Newark, U of Delaware P, 2011.

Smith, Jean Edward. *Bush.* New York: Simon & Schuster, 2016.

———. *Eisenhower: In War and Peace.* New York: Random House, 2012.

Stagg, J.C.A. "James Madison: Campaigns and Elections." *Miller Center.* 2019. millercenter.org/president/madison/campaigns-and-elections.

Stewart, David O. "The Surprising Raucous Home Life of the Madisons." *Smithsonian.* 10 Feb. 2015. www.smithsonianmag.com/history/surprising-raucous-home-life-madisons-180954205/.

Stockwell, Mary. "Ulysses Grant's Failed Attempt to Grant Native Americans Citizenship." *Smithsonian.com*. Smithsonian Institution. 9 Jan. 2019. www.smithsonianmag.com/history/ulysses-grants-failed-attempt-to-grant-native-americans-citizenship-180971198/.

Stokes, Bruce. "70 Years after Hiroshima, Opinions Have Shifted on Use of Atomic Bomb." Pew Research Center, 4 Aug. 2015. https://www.pewresearch.org/fact-tank/2015/08/04/70-years-after-hiroshima-opinions-have-shifted-on-use-of-atomic-bomb/.

Strauss, Robert. *Worst. President. Ever.: James Buchanan, the POTUS Rating Game and the Least of the Lesser Presidents*. Guilford, CT: LP P, 2016.

Struyk, Ryan. "George W. Bush's Favorable Rating Has Pulled a Complete 180." *CNN Politics*. 22 Jan. 2018. www.cnn.com/2018/01/22/politics/george-w-bush-favorable-poll/index.html.

"Summation of John Adams in The Soldiers Trial." *Crispus Attucks Museum*. 17 Sept. 2012. www.crispusattucksmuseum.org/summation-john-adams-boston-massacre-trials/.

Sumner, William Graham. *Andrew Jackson as a Public Man*. Cambridge, MA: The Riverside P, 1884.

"Surveying Career." *Mount Vernon*. 2019. /www.mountvernon.org/george-washington/washingtons-youth/surveying/.

Talbott, Strobe. "Reagan and Gorbachev: Shutting the Cold War Down." *Brookings*. 1 Aug. 2004. www.brookings.edu/articles/reagan-and-gorbachev-shutting-the-cold-war-down/.

Taub, Amanda. "The Republican Myth of Ronald Reagan and the Iran Hostages, Debunked." *Vox*. 25 Jan. 2016. www.vox.com/2016/1/25/10826056/reagan-iran-hostage-negotiation.

Tesler, Michael. "Racial Attitudes Remain a Powerful Predictor of Obama Vote Preference." *YouGov*. 23 Jan. 2012. today.yougov.com/topics/politics/articles-reports/2012/01/23/racial-attitudes-remain-powerful-predictor-obama-v.

_____. "The Spillover of Racialization into Evaluations of Bo Obama." *YouGov*. 10 Apr. 2012. today.yougov.com/topics/politics/articles-reports/2012/04/10/spillover-racialization-evaluations-bo-obama.

"Theodore Roosevelt and Conservation." *NPS*. National Park Service. 16 Nov. 2017. www.nps.gov/thro/learn/historyculture/theodore-roosevelt-and-conservation.htm.

Thompson, Frank Jr., and Daniel H. Pollitt. "Impeachment of Federal Judges: An Historical Overview." *North Carolina Law Review*, vol. 49, no 1, Article 9, Dec. 1, 1970. scholarship.law.unc.edu/cgi/viewcontent.cgi?article=2416&context=nclr.

Thomson-DeVeaux, Amelia. "It Took A Long Time for Republicans to Abandon Nixon." *FiveThirtyEight*. 9 Oct. 2019. fivethirtyeight.com/features/it-took-a-long-time-for-republicans-to-abandon-nixon/.

Toobin, Jeffrey. *Too Close to Call: The Thirty-Six-Day Battle to Decide the 2000 Election*. New York: Random House, 2002.

"Transcript of the De Lôme Letter (1898)." *Our Documents*. 2019. www.ourdocuments. gov/doc.php?flash=false&doc=53&page=transcript.

"Transcript of Vice President Andrew Johnson's Inaugural Address." *Ball State University*. 2019. dmr.bsu.edu/digital/collection/BrcknCivCol/id/188.

Traub, James. "The Ugly Election That Birthed Modern American Politics." *National Geographic*. Nov./Dec. 2016. www.nationalgeographic.com/history/magazine/2016/11-12/america-presidential-elections-1824-corrupt-bargain/.

Trefousse, Hans. *Rutherford B. Hayes*. New York: Times Books, 2002.

Truman, Harry. "Address Before the National Association for the Advancement of Colored People." 29 June 1947. *Voices of Democracy*. The U.S. Oratory Project. U of Maryland. voicesofdemocracy.umd.edu/harry-s-truman-naacp-speech-text/.

_____. "Transcript of Executive Order 9981: Desegregation of the Armed Forces (1948)." *Our Documents*. www.ourdocuments.gov/doc.php?flash=true&doc=84&page=transcript.

_____. "Truman Doctrine: President Harry S. Truman's Address before a Joint Session of Congress, March 12, 1947." *Avalon Project*. Yale Law School. avalon.law.yale.edu/20th_century/trudoc.asp.

_____. "Truman Statement on Hiroshima." 6 Aug. 1945. Atomic Heritage Foundation. www.atomicheritage.org/key-documents/truman-statement-hiroshima.

"Trump Investigation Guide: Impeachment, Inquiries, Lawsuits." *Bloomberg*. 22 Nov. 2019. www.bloomberg.com/graphics/trump-investigations/.

Turner, Frederick Jackson. "The Significance of the Frontier in American History." *National Humanities Center*. nationalhumanitiescenter.org/pds/gilded/empire/text1/turner.pdf.

Twain, Mark. "To the Person Sitting in Darkness." (originally published in *North American Review*, February 1901.) *Investigating History*, City University of New York.

Uenuma, Francine. "During the Mexican-American War, Irish-Americans Fought for Mexico in the 'Saint Patrick's Battalion.'" *Smithsonian*. 15 Mar. 2019. www.smithsonianmag.com/history/mexican-american-war-irish-immigrants-deserted-us-army-fight-against-america-180971713/.

Unger, Harlow Giles. *The Last Founding Father: James Monroe and a Nation's Call to Greatness*. New York: Da Capo P, 2009; 2010.

"U-2 Overflights and the Capture of Francis Gary Powers, 1960." *Office of the Historian*. U.S. Department of State. history.state.gov/milestones/1953-1960/u2-incident.

"US Economy Under Trump: Is It the Greatest in History?" *BBC*. BBC News. 27 Sept. 2019. www.bbc.com/news/world-45827430.

"U.S. Invasion and Occupation of Haiti, 1915–34." *U.S. Department of State*. Office of the Historian. history.state.gov/milestones/1914-1920/Haiti.

"Use of Weapons of Mass Destruction Should Be Included in Criminal Court's Definition of War Crimes, Say Several Conference Speakers." *UN*. United Nations. 18 June 1998. www.un.org/press/en/1998/19980618.l2882.html.

Vaughn, William Preston. *The Anti-Masonic Party in the United States: 1826–1843*. Lexington, KY: U P of Kentucky, 1983.

"Venezuela Debt Crisis." *Theodorerooseveltcenter*. Dickinson State University. 2019. www.theodorerooseveltcenter.org/Learn-About-TR/TR-Encyclopedia/Foreign-Affairs/Venezuela-Debt-Crisis.aspx.

"Vetoes by President George H.W. Bush." *United States Senate*. www.senate.gov/reference/Legislation/Vetoes/BushGHW.htm.

"Voting Rights Act." *Our Documents*. 2019. www.ourdocuments.gov/doc.php?flash=false&doc=100.

Waldman, Paul. "Is It Time to Talk about Donald Trump's Draft Dodging?" *The Washington Post*. 28 May 2019. www.washingtonpost.com/opinions/2019/05/28/is-it-time-talk-about-donald-trumps-draft-dodging/.

Walsh, Kenneth T. "The First 100 Days: Franklin Roosevelt Pioneered the 100-Day Concept." *U.S. News*. 12 Feb. 2009. www.usnews.com/news/history/articles/2009/02/12/the-first-100-days-franklin-roosevelt-pioneered-the-100-day-concept.

_____. "The Most Consequential Elections in History: Franklin Delano Roosevelt and the Election of 1932." *US News*. 10 Sept. 2008. www.usnews.com/news/articles/2008/09/10/the-most-consequential-elections-in-history-franklin-delano-roosevelt-and-the-election-of-1932.

Walters, Joanna. "Trump University: Court Upholds $25m Settlement to Give Students' Money Back." *The Guardian*. 6 Feb. 2018. www.theguardian.com/us-news/2018/feb/06/trump-university-court-upholds-25m-settlement-to-give-students-money-back.

Walther, Eric. *The Shattering of the Union*. New York: Rowman & Littlefield, 2004.

"War of 1812–1815." *U.S. Department of State*. Office of the Historian. history.state. gov/milestones/1801-1829/war-of-1812.

Washington, George. "From George Washington to Lewis Nicola," 22 May 1782, *Founders Online*. National Archives. founders.archives.gov/documents/ Washington/99-01-02-08501.

_____. "Letter of the President of the Federal Convention, Dated September 17, 1787, to the President of Congress, Transmitting the Constitution." *Avalon Project*. Yale Law School. 2008. avalon.law.yale.edu/18th_century/translet.asp.

_____. "Washington's Farewell Address 1796." *Avalon*. Yale Law School. 2008. avalon.law.yale.edu/18th_century/washing.asp.

_____. "Washington's Inaugural Address of 1789." *Archives*. National Archives and Records Administration. 2019. www.archives.gov/exhibits/american_ originals/inaugtxt.html.

_____. "To George Washington from Lewis Nicola, 22 May 1782." *Founders Online*. National Archives. founders.archives.gov/?q=nicola%2C%20 lewis&s=1111311111&sa=&r=51&sr=.

Watson, W. Marvin, and Sherwin Markman. *Chief of Staff: Lyndon Johnson and His Presidency*. New York: MacMillan, 2014.

Watt, Paul, Patrick Spedding, and Derek B. Scott. *Cheap Print and Popular Song in the Nineteenth Century*. New York: Cambridge U P, 2017.

Waxman, Olivia B. "President Trump's Approval Rating Is at a Near-Record Low. Here's What to Know About the History of Those Numbers." *Time*. 24 Jan. 2019. time.com/5511118/presidential-approval-ratings-history/.

Webster, Daniel, and Edward Everett. *The Writings and Speeches of Daniel Webster*. (National Edition, vol. 13), pp. 419–20. Boston, MA: Little, Brown & Company, 1903.

Weightman, Richard. "Monroe Doctrine Not Involved in the Santo Domingo Affair." *Chicago Daily Tribune*.18 Feb. 1905, p. 8. projects.leadr.msu.edu/ usforeignrelations/files/original/02e257b121fea966e429509a3a41d14c.pdf.

Weigley, Russell F. "Old Fuss and Feathers." *New York Times*. Books. 11 Jan. 1998. movies2.nytimes.com/books/98/01/11/reviews/980111.11weiglet.html.

Weinger, Mackenzie. "Poll: George Washington Still Tops." *Politico*. 17 Feb. 2012. www.politico.com/story/2012/02/poll-george-washington-still-tops-073032.

Weiss, Brennan. "RANKED: The Greatest US Presidents, According to Political Scientists." *Business Insider*. 16 Feb. 2019. www.businessinsider.com/greatest-us-presidents-ranked-by-political-scientists-2018-2.

Welch, Richard E. "American Atrocities in the Philippines: The Indictment and the Response." *Pacific Historical Review*, vol. 43, no. 2, May 1974, pp. 233-53, *JSTOR*, www.jstor.org/stable/3637551.

Wilentz, Sean. *Andrew Jackson: The American Presidents Series: The 7th President, 1829–1837.* New York: Times Books, 2005.

Wilker, Noelle. "Harder to Breathe: Air Quality Has Worsened Since 2016." *CMU*. Carnegie Mellon University. 25 Nov. 2019. www.cmu.edu/news/stories/archives/2019/november/air-quality-worsens.html.

Wilkie, Christina. "President Trump Is Impeached in a Historic Vote by the House, Will Face Trial in the Senate." *CNBC*. 19 Dec. 2019. www.cnbc.com/2019/12/18/trump-impeached-by-house-for-high-crimes-and-misdemeanors.html.

"William Henry Harrison." *White House*. 2019. www.whitehouse.gov/about-the-white-house/presidents/william-henry-harrison/.

Williams, Charles Richard. *The Life of Rutherford Birchard Hayes*. New York: Houghton Mifflin, 1913.

Wills, Garry. *Nixon Agonistes: The Crisis of the Self-Made Man*. Open Road Media, 2017.

Wilson, Major L. *The Presidency of Martin Van Buren*. U of Michigan P, 1984.

Wilson, Woodrow. "April 8, 1913: Message Regarding Tariff Duties." *Miller Center*. University of Virginia. 2019. millercenter.org/the-presidency/presidential-speeches/april-8-1913-message-regarding-tariff-duties.

_____. "President Woodrow Wilson's Fourteen Points." 8 Jan. 1918. *Avalon Project*. Yale Law School. 2018. avalon.law.yale.edu/20th_century/wilson14.asp.

_____. "War Message to Congress." 2 April 1917. Brigham Young University, 28 May 2009. wwi.lib.byu.edu/index.php/Wilson's_War_Message_to_Congress.

Withers, Rachel. "George H.W. Bush's 'Willie Horton' Ad Will Always Be the Reference Point for Dog-Whistle Racism." *VOX*. 1 Dec. 2018. www.vox.com/2018/12/1/18121221/george-hw-bush-willie-horton-dog-whistle-politics.

Wolfe, Thomas. *The Complete Short Stories of Thomas Wolfe*. New York: Simon and Schuster, 1989.

Woodward, Bob. *Bush at War*. New York: Simon & Schuster, 2002.

"The XYZ Affair and the Quasi-War with France, 1798–1800." *U.S. Department of State*. 2016. history.state.gov/milestones/1784-1800/xyz.

Yadon, Nicole, and Spencer Piston "Examining Whites' Anti-Black Attitudes after Obama's Presidency." *Politics, Groups, and Identities*. vol. 7, no.4, 2019, Taylor and Francis online, www.tandfonline.com/doi/abs/10.1080/21565503.2018.1438953?journalCode=rpgi20.

Yglesias, Matthew. "What Trump Has Actually Done in His First 3 Years." *Vox*. 2 Dec. 2019. www.vox.com/policy-and-politics/2019/12/2/20970521/trump-administration-achievements.

Yoo, John. "George Washington and the Executive Power." *University of St. Thomas Journal of Law and Public Policy*, vol 5, no 1, 2010–2011. scholarship.law.berkeley.edu/cgi/viewcontent.cgi?article=2272&context=facpubs.

Zarkaria, Fareed. *From Wealth to Power: The Unusual Origins of America's World Role*. Princeton, NJ: Princeton U P, 1998, p. 110.

Zimmerman, Jonathan. "Decades Later, My Fellow Democrats Should Admit Character Counts." *Wall Street Journal*. 23 Dec. 2019. www.wsj.com/articles/decades-later-my-fellow-democrats-should-admit-character-counts-11577144800.

About the Author

Micah L. Issitt is an independent scholar, historian, journalist, editor and author. He is the editor of H.W. Wilson's *Reference Shelf*, a series of contemporary issues. Recent titles include: *Alternative Facts, Post-Truth & the Information War*; *The South China Seas Conflict*; *Artificial Intelligence*; and *Immigration*. He has written *Opinions Throughout History* volumes from Grey House Publishing: *National Security vs. Civil & Privacy Rights*; *Immigration*; *Gender: Roles & Rights*; *Drug Use & Abuse*; and *The Environment*. Issitt has also written extensively for several Salem Press series, incuding *Careers In*, *Defining Documents in World History* and *Defining Documents in American History*.

His other books include *Hidden Religion* from ABC-Clio and *Hippies* from Greenwood Press, and he has written hundreds of articles for a variety of encyclopedias and reference works. Issitt lives and works in Saint Louis, Missouri.

Index